WITHDRAWN
UTSA LIBRARIES

CHRISTIANITY IN A REVOLUTIONARY AGE

A History of Christianity
in the Nineteenth and Twentieth Centuries
VOLUME I

THE NINETEENTH CENTURY IN EUROPE:

Background and the Roman Catholic Phase

CHRISTIANITY IN A REVOLUTIONARY AGE

*A History of Christianity
in the Nineteenth and Twentieth Centuries*

VOLUME I

THE NINETEENTH
CENTURY IN EUROPE

Background and the Roman Catholic Phase

KENNETH SCOTT LATOURETTE

*Sterling Professor of Missions and Oriental History, Emeritus,
and Associate Fellow of Berkeley College in Yale University*

GREENWOOD PRESS, PUBLISHERS
WESTPORT, CONNECTICUT

LIBRARY
University of Texas
At San Antonio

The Library of Congress has catalogued this publication as follows:

Library of Congress Cataloging in Publication Data

Latourette, Kenneth Scott, 1884-1968.
  The nineteenth century in Europe.

  (His Christianity in a revolutionary age, v. 1)
  Bibliography: p.
  1. Catholic Church in Europe. 2. Europe--History--
1789-1900. I. Title. II. Series.
BR475.L33 vol. 1 [BX1490]   270.8s [282'.4] 72-11976
ISBN 0-8371-5701-3

To all, both past and present,
who as his secretaries have aided the author,
these volumes are gratefully
and affectionately dedicated

Copyright © 1958 by Kenneth Scott Latourette

All rights reserved

Originally published in 1958
by Harper & Brothers, New York

Reprinted with the permission
of Harper & Row, Publishers, Inc.

First Greenwood Reprinting 1973

Library of Congress Catalogue Card Number 77-138141

ISBN 0-8371-5700-5 (Set)
ISBN 0-8371-5701-3 (Vol. I)

Printed in the United States of America

LIBRARY
University of Texas
At San Antonio

CONTENTS

PREFACE

Here is an attempt to narrate the history of Christianity in the nineteenth and twentieth centuries. The nineteenth century is regarded as beginning with the close of the Napoleonic Wars in 1815 and as ending in 1914, with the outbreak of what is usually called World War I. The twentieth century is defined as beginning with the latter year. Obviously it has not ended when, because of the inescapable date when these volumes are written, it was still in *medias res*.

Why this choice of subject and period? Important though Christianity has been and is in the history of mankind, it is being vigorously challenged. In the past two centuries such large-scale open defections from it have occurred in its erstwhile stronghold, Europe, the traditional Christendom, that some thoughtful and even friendly observers have held that beginning at least as far back as the eighteenth century the world has been progressively entering the post-Christian era. If that is true, why tell the story of a waning force and a dying faith? Why undertake it while the story is in progress and before it has reached the end of another major stage? When set against the background of all history, the century and a half which are the scope of these volumes are only a moment. But even that moment is extraordinarily complex, and the five substantial volumes which are projected for this work cannot hope to cover it fully or in great detail. To deal with it adequately would entail the labour of several lifetimes, for the surviving records are incredibly vast and are scattered over many lands, and this writing is being begun when the author is in his seventieth year, presumably with only a decade or less of working time remaining. Huge in bulk though they are, impossible of coverage by one man, the written and printed documents which must be the historian's main reliance do not permit a well-rounded account. It is part of the genius of Christianity that what, from its standpoint, are some of its most significant fruits are in humble lives which leave behind them few if any detectable records. Faced with these difficulties, the conscientious scholar might well refuse to embark on the enterprise here essayed and view with distrust the results of any such seemingly preposterous undertaking.

The reasons why the venture is being entered upon and at this time and in this form can be fairly quickly summarized. The period is one in which Christianity first became world-wide. To be sure, it was seriously threatened and that threat mounted as decade followed decade in the breath-taking speed and bewildering multiplicity of the era. Yet by forces which issued from what was once called Christendom and in which to no small degree Christianity had entered as a causative factor, all mankind was being made a neighbourhood. It was a tragically quarrelsome neighbourhood, but it was a neighbourhood. In that "one world," by the middle of the twentieth century Christianity was represented by organized churches in all but one or two of the countries which claimed political independence. In most countries outside the traditional Christendom these churches were small minorities. But they were growing minorities which were becoming rooted in indigenous leadership and self-support. Christianity had never been so widely influential as it became in the twentieth century. Although by no means dominant, its influence upon mankind as a whole was growing. As at no previous time it was being tested for its claim to universality. From the beginning it had insisted that it was for all men. Could it make good that assertion? Here was the first age in which this could be determined from experience. The seeming paradox on the one hand of threat and apparent decline in the portion of the globe which at the outset of the nineteenth century was its chief stronghold and on the other of the amazing vigour and world-wide spread of the faith would in itself make some such work as is here attempted imperative for an understanding of history and the current human scene.

Moreover, the decades saw a further apparent paradox. In the nineteenth century Christianity spread in association with the expansion of Europe. Political and economic empires were being built by European peoples. In the twentieth century Western Europe fell into a decline. Wars racked it. Internal revolutions—political, social, intellectual, and spiritual—loosed it from its historic moorings. The threat to Christianity was a phase of the revolution. In that same century most of the non-Christian world shook off the yoke of Western Europe. Yet, as revolt ended the political and economic empires of Western European nations, much which had issued from Western Europe was eagerly adopted. Natural sciences, industrial processes, mechanical appliances, forms of government, kinds of education, and ideologies which had originated in Western Europe continued to spread. Here, as in Western Europe, they worked revolution. Here, as there, they threatened the very existence of Christianity. But in the non-Occidental lands and on what had been the periphery of the Occident, the Americas, the churches, especially but not exclusively the Protestant churches, continued to grow.

In this last sentence is another reason for singling out the nineteenth and twentieth centuries for special treatment. They are preëminently the Protestant era. At the dawn of the nineteenth century Protestantism was a regional faith. By the mid-century it was world-wide and was displaying more vigour than any other branch of Christianity. To be sure, it had begun in the sixteenth century, but in 1815 it was confined to North-western Europe, to the young and thinly peopled United States, to the white populations of British and Dutch colonies, then numerically inconsiderable, and to handfuls of converts from native peoples in these colonies. A century and a half later it had spread throughout most of the globe. From it came movements which were evidence of abounding vitality. In the course of the nineteenth and twentieth centuries several of the Eastern Churches gave proof that they were far from moribund. The Roman Catholic Church, which in the sixteenth and seventeenth centuries had been planted in land after land but which in the eighteenth century had been dealt severe blows, had a resurgence of life. Yet it was from Protestantism that most of the fresh creative movements arose, including both menaces to Christianity and the new kinds of movements for overcoming those menaces and pushing forward the Christian frontiers into additional geographic and cultural areas. In the vigour and spread of Protestantism was a characteristic which set the post-1815 age apart from its predecessors.

To say glibly that the nineteenth and twentieth centuries witnessed early stages of the post-Christian era is a naïve and hasty, if understandable, generalization. It does not take sufficient account of either the past record of the faith with its ebbs and flows or the complexities and apparent contradictions of the century and a half which are the subject of these volumes. From the standpoint of history it is too soon either to affirm or to deny the accuracy of that affirmation.

While, living as we do in the midst of what is being narrated, we may not be able at this time to give definitive answers, we can at least propound questions. If these should prove to be the right ones, the very asking of them may help to shed light on the bewildering currents and counter-currents of the age which is our subject. Although living in their midst, and his lifetime has spanned slightly more than half the years with which he is dealing, it should be possible for the author to bring to bear upon them the perspective of the total previous course of the human race and of Christianity. For many years in teaching and writing the author has covered the history of the globe and of its varied cultures and especially of Christianity.

It is from this perspective that the effort is made to view the hurrying and confused fifteen decades which are our present subject. They are only a moment, but, like so many of their predecessors, they are a crucial moment. We must always bear in mind that they are the climax of centuries and in turn, so far as the historian can see, are preliminary to other climaxes, perhaps many of them.

In only five volumes we cannot hope to have a complete chronicle of all events, even of all the significant ones. The ensuing pages will contain many details. Indeed, the reader may find them so numerous as to be wearying. He may despair of seeing the woods, so many are the trees to which his attention will be called. But there may be an advantage in trying to put the entire story together. A common pattern is to be seen across both the world and the decades. Many of the same forces operated throughout the globe. We will not attempt for any country a full history of Christianity since 1815. That must be left to specialists. Rather we will endeavour to select what from the standpoint of the entire story are the more significant events, persons, and movements. We will attempt to point out the fashion in which they either are features of a comprehensive pattern or differ from that pattern.

We must try to place the story in its global setting. Since by its genius the Gospel is universal—for all men—any history of Christianity must be told against the background of all the course of mankind. This is particularly imperative in the nineteenth and twentieth centuries. The fact that then all mankind was drawn together, partly as the result, direct and indirect, of Christianity, and that for the first time Christianity became world-wide, makes it peculiarly important that we seek to view the course of Christianity in this period in its entirety and essay an estimate of its place in the inclusive human scene.

The choice of a title is deliberate. The significance of *Christianity in a Revolutionary Age* must be apparent from what has already been said: the appropriateness will become increasingly apparent as we proceed. The sub-title is *A History of Christianity in the Nineteenth and Twentieth Centuries* and not *A History of the Church in the Nineteenth and Twentieth Centuries* or *The History of Christianity in the Nineteenth and Twentieth Centuries*.

It is not a history of the Church of that period, partly because so many different and conflicting definitions of the Church are given and partly because such a title seems to focus attention on an institution or institutions. If the Church is defined as "the blessed company of all faithful people" it is obviously both more and less inclusive than the visible churches and is not always possible for the historian to discern. If institutions are meant, in the life of those institutions only part, even though a very important part, of what is embraced under the designation of Christianity is covered.

Christianity is a religion. It is compounded of many elements. Central and determinative is the Gospel of Jesus Christ, his birth, life, teachings, crucifixion, resurrection, and ascension, and what has issued from him. Wherever Christianity has gone it has taken on some of the colour of its environment, both of the cultures and of the age in which it is found. It is perpetuated chiefly through the churches, but it has stimulated the emergence of movements and organizations bearing the Christian name or a Christian symbol which are not included in the churches. That has been especially seen in the nineteenth and twentieth centuries in such bodies as the Young Men's and Young Women's Christian Associations, the World's Student Christian Federation, and the Red Cross.

It will be difficult to discern all the boundaries to our subject. We must, of course, pay much attention to the churches, to their leaders, their struggles, the movements within them, their relations with one another, their inner life of thought, instruction, hymns, and worship, and their efforts to influence the world about them. We must record their endeavour to propagate their faith. We must also say something of theological movements. We must attempt to discover a few of the lives which were transformed by the Christian faith and which are, from the standpoint of that faith, among its most significant results. We must ask the extent to which Christianity was moulded by the environment in the various countries in which it was found. We must seek to single out and record the movements in addition to the churches to which Christianity gave rise or to whose origin it contributed and the effects of Christianity on its environment. We will raise the question of how far Christianity was responsible for the political events, the currents of thought, the development of the sciences, and the mechanical inventions which made of the era an age of revolutions shaking all mankind, and to what extent if at all it contributed to the movements which threatened its existence.

Nor are we calling these volumes *The History of Christianity in the Nineteenth and Twentieth Centuries,* as though ours were the only angle of approach and these volumes the final and definitive account. Ours can be only one attempt to tell the story of Christianity in this era. It is to be hoped that it will assist others to a better achievement.

The main outline of the work can be quickly stated. First are three volumes which deal with the historic background and the nineteenth century. They begin with a brief account of the origin of Christianity. This is followed by a summary of the history to the eighteenth century. That is succeeded by a sketch, somewhat longer but still greatly condensed and dealing only with the chief events and developments in the eighteenth century and to 1815, for these did much to shape the period which is our major concern. Then comes a picture in bold strokes of the main movements of the nineteenth century. It takes all mankind in its purview but is particularly concerned with Europe. The rest of the first two volumes has Christianity in Europe as its subject, first Roman Catholic, then Protestant, and finally Orthodox. The third volume covers the nineteenth-century course of Christianity outside the traditional Christendom. The fourth and fifth volumes are devoted to the twentieth century, the decades since 1914. They are introduced by a comprehensive sketch of the world setting of the post-1914 era. Then come accounts of developments, first in Europe and next in the Americas and other parts of the world.

The materials for these volumes have been gathered over many years and from numbers of countries in Europe, Asia, Africa, and North and South America, partly through travel in all these continents, partly through conferences and correspondence with individuals, and partly, indeed chiefly, from libraries. Through most of his adult lifetime the author has known many who have been outstanding leaders in the thought and life of the churches. The majority have been Protestant but some have been Roman Catholic and a few Orthodox. He has also participated in the life of his own denomination and in the central councils of several of the movements which have crossed denominational lines, including the World's Student Christian Federation, the Young Men's Christian Association, the International Missionary Council, the World Council of Churches, the Federal Council of the Churches of Christ in America, and its successor, the National Council of the Churches of Christ in the United States of America. Through them information has been obtained and, fully as important, impressions have been gleaned of the character and spirit of the churches and organizations which bear the Christian name. For several countries the task has been made difficult by the absence of comprehensive studies or, where these exist, by their inadequacy. Much spade work has, accordingly, been necessary in monographs, biographies, and source materials, including autobiographies and collections of letters. Yet time has permitted covering only a fraction of what is related to our subject.

To mention all the men, women, universities, and libraries to whom the author is indebted would require many pages. To single out a few would be invidious. However, because of his long membership on the faculty of Yale, the author is peculiarly indebted to his colleagues in that university, especially in its Divinity School. Without the ample facilities of the Yale libraries and the ever generous coöperation of their staffs these volumes would have been impossible.

Those familiar with the author's earlier books may find themselves asking whether these volumes are not a repetition of what he has said before. The final four volumes of *A History of the Expansion of Christianity* covered all but the last few years of the period which is our present subject. Slightly more than a fourth of *A History of Christianity* was devoted to it. Obviously much that the author learned in the preparation of these works has been of advantage in the present undertaking. A few chapters are a condensation of the first, although rewritten and with a somewhat different perspective. Several chapters are an amplification of parts of the second. Yet the five volumes are essentially a new work. In preparation for them the author has done further and extensive reading and research and has gone on additional journeys to see lands of which he has written and to consult with experts on the story with which he is dealing. Some fresh insights have come, together with elaborations and modifications of earlier insights. The proportions differ from those of the earlier histories. The author thinks of the latter as a preparation for what he is here essaying and regards them and the knowledge which he acquired in writing them as background and enrichment of what, because of his age, is the last multi-volume literary project to which he will set his mind and hand.

No historian can write without bias. He may seek to be objective and to tell what actually happened. Yet if he is honest and clear-headed he knows that he is governed by presuppositions and interests which determine his selection of material and the fashion in which he sets it forth.

All this is especially the case with the topic which is ours. On it honestly held convictions differ, at times profoundly and even sharply. That is partly because, both among those who regard themselves as Christians and between Christians and the varied categories of non-Christians, debates have long raged in the field of religion and particularly over the most widely spread of the religions, Christianity.

So far as the present author is aware of characteristics which affect his research and his outlook they are as follows. He is an historian and of the school of history which prizes accuracy and objectivity. He is an American by birth and rearing. He is a Christian by profound conviction. He is a Protestant and a Baptist. Since his teens he has been committed to Christian missions and has been intimately connected with one or another phase of what is latterly known as the Ecumenical Movement. He has spent most of his life in a great university where differing views have been freely expressed. He has had extensive contacts and friendships with men and women of other faiths and of no religious faith. He has had long and intimate discussions with members of other churches than his own, both within and outside Protestantism. Originally trained in the natural and social sciences, he has never lost his interest in them. While he is able to read a dozen or more languages, several of the languages in which important material exists that is pertinent to his subject he has not acquired. At best his literary style is clear, competent in exposition, but unadorned. The author has sought to raise questions which he regards as fundamental and here and there he has ventured what appear to him to be the correct answers. From time to time he has set forth his faith, but he has not wished to obtrude it or to force it on his readers.

Before he plunges into his subject the author wishes to dedicate what follows to those who at one time or another have worked with him as secretaries. The list is long and extends over four decades. To record it is to bring back happy and grateful memories. In chronological order it is: Robert A. Abernethy, David E. Owen, Chauncey P. Williams, Rudolph Tulloch, Mrs. Charles T.

Lincoln, James Martin, Creighton B. Lacy, W. Richey Hogg, John F. Merrill, C. Edward Steele, Dorothy Ansley, Donald K. Campbell, Rudolph E. Everest, Robert C. Johnson, James M. Phillips, Hugh George Anderson, Charles E. Harvey, Paul M. Minus, Jr., and Earl R. MacCormac. The writing and most of the research back of the volumes are the author's own, but each of the above has helped in a variety of ways—a few in research, almost all with correspondence, and all in companionship. To single out any from this goodly company seems almost invidious. But the author must mention especially Mrs. Charles T. Lincoln, for her assistance has been the longest of all and to her the author is indebted for more than he or she fully realizes. For years she served as secretary. For even more years she has copied the author's books. Indeed, her skillful fingers have turned into faultless typescript most of his first drafts, often all but illegible. She has also made unfailingly useful suggestions as to literary style.

In the present volume the author is especially indebted to President Henry Pitney Van Dusen, who read the manuscript of the first five chapters and who made fruitful suggestions, and to Monsignor John Tracy Ellis, who read the remaining chapters and sent the author detailed criticisms which were of great value in the final revision.

CHAPTER I

Origins and Basic Questions

THE history of Christianity is intensely thought-provoking. That is because of the contrast between its seemingly unpromising beginning and its long-continued and increasing part in the life of mankind. It raises central questions for the historian, the philosopher, and the theologian.

The story of the beginnings of Christianity is so well known that it here needs only the barest summary, and that chiefly to point up the issues which it poses. At the outset no one who was not a member of the enthusiastic inner circle would have predicted the expanding future. To all outward appearances Christianity began as one of several Jewish sects, and by no means the most prominent of them. It found itself in an empire, that of Rome, where many religions and philosophies were competing to meet the spiritual and moral hungers of the day. Of the numerous rivals, Christianity appeared one of the weakest. Its demands were so contrary to the customs and ideals of men that it seemed preposterous to hope that it would gain a continuing footing, much less become the most widely spread and most influential of the faiths of mankind. Moreover, the Roman Empire was only one of the centres of civilization of the day. To the east lay Persia, India, and China. The last two were as highly civilized as was the Roman world and the three together covered a wider area and had a larger population than did the territory controlled by Rome. The triumph of a particular religion in the latter would by no means assure its adoption by all of either civilized or primitive mankind.

Judaism, from which Christianity issued, came out of a background far from ensuring it an influential future. It was the professed religion of the Hebrews. The Hebrews were merely one of several Semitic peoples. Politically they were never a major power but were usually a pawn between competing empires. Their architectural achievements were far less impressive than the pyramids and temples of Egypt or the temples of Babylon, Nineveh, and Greece. The religion which we call Judaism had a hard struggle for survival even among the Hebrews. The pure monotheists were long a small minority, and Jahweh, the name they gave to the One God, competed with rival deities for the allegiance of the majority. For centuries the prophets and lawgivers who shaped the faith were followed only by a "remnant" of the Hebrew people. By the time of Christ Judaism had triumphed among the Jews and the Jews were numerous and constituted communities which were widely scattered in the Roman Empire and to the east of that realm. Yet, while winning some converts, Judaism remained the faith of minorities.

Of the several sects of Judaism in the first century of the Christian era, to the casual observer that which centered around Jesus must have seemed doomed to only a transient existence. Born in humble circumstances, of a devout but inconspicuous mother, and reared in an obscure village as an artisan, Jesus appeared to have little prospect of wide or enduring influence. To be sure, he could read, he was steeped in the religious heritage and literature of his people, and he had an acute mind and a vivid and compelling personality which both won loyal friends and drew down on him determined enmity. But his public career was presumably only three years in length and possibly less, and he took none of the measures which prudence would have advised for the perpetuation of his message. He wrote no book. Our surviving records give no indication that he devoted much thought to a well-articulated organization of his followers. Of the little circle which he gathered about him one betrayed him and during the days of his flesh none of them really understood him. He talked much of the Kingdom of God. He defined it as the doing of God's will. But he believed it to be the gift of God rather than the result of the effort of men. He declared that it was at hand and, indeed, was already arriving, and that this fact constituted the Gospel, the amazing Good News. Yet he said that even to recognize it involved a reorientation of insight and purpose which was so drastic that it could best be described as a new birth or a changing of one's mind.

Membership in the Kingdom meant, as Jesus described it, qualities of character which can never be fully attained in this life by frail human beings—among them the purity of heart which includes a singleness of unselfish purpose, complete honesty and sincerity, loving one's enemies, putting first the Kingdom of God, and being perfect as God is perfect. Were these qualities to become actual among many, they would so transform existing institutions—political, economic, social, intellectual, and religious—that a basic and drastic revolution would occur. Some might long to see them triumph, but, so contrary were they to the human scene, to hope that they would do so appeared utterly fantastic.

Jesus came to his death in the humiliating form of crucifixion in company with two criminals. Ironically, it was on the charge of attempting revolt from Rome—when he had deliberately set aside political methods or objectives. At his death it looked to the spectators as though his dreams and efforts had ended in complete frustration and defeat.

Nor were the beginnings of Christianity, the religion which claimed Jesus as its central figure, much more promising. To be sure, the inner group of his followers were profoundly convinced that God had raised him from the dead, that they had seen him and talked with him, and that, while the kind of appearances they had experienced in the forty days after his resurrection had ceased, he continued to be with them. Inspired by this conviction, they proclaimed with enthusiasm and devotion the life, teachings, death, and resurrection of Jesus. But the early disciples cherished what to the outsider must have seemed as wild dreams as had their master. They insisted that Jesus had said that if he were lifted up—namely, crucified—he would draw all men to him. They declared that he had commissioned them to bring all nations to his discipleship, baptizing them into that company and teaching them to observe all that he had commanded them—and this last would include the impossible standards which he had set up for membership in the Kingdom. They believed that in Jesus the Word which was God Himself had become flesh, that only those to whom Jesus revealed Him could know God, that in Jesus the God otherwise unseen by men is seen, that no one could come to God except through Jesus, and that in Jesus God had acted supremely and once for all. They proclaimed that God is love, and that this love is unique and is revealed in Jesus, that here is God's only son, and that God so loved the world, that world which did not understand but rejected and crucified him, that God gave His only son and sent him, not to condemn the world but that the world through him might be saved. They recognized that to the Jews this story of a crucified and seemingly weak Messiah was so contrary to the fashion in which they believed God worked that they stumbled over it and were repelled by it, and that to the Greeks, trained to accept nothing which could not be justified at the bar of reason, it appeared stark foolishness. Yet they insisted that the weakness of God is stronger than men and the foolishness of God is wiser than men. They believed that in the cross with its seeming defeat God had triumphed over the dark powers of the universe, and that it is the plan of God to gather together all things in Christ, both which are in heaven and which are on earth. They recognized frankly the weaknesses and sins of many who were called disciples and who presumably had been born anew into membership in the Kingdom. They knew that none had yet fully attained to the standards set for that new life. But, undiscouraged, they prayed confidently that they might all come to a perfect man, to the measure of the stature of the fulness of Christ and be filled unto all the fulness of God. They were keenly aware of the suffering, the futility, and the bondage to decay under which not only mankind but also all creation travails in pain, like a woman in child-birth, but they cherished the confidence that in it all God who is the kind of love seen in the weakness of the incarnation and the cross is sovereign and believed that all creation would be freed and would obtain the glorious liberty of the children of God.

Here was a sweeping and comprehensive view of history and not only of history but also of the universe. It is no wonder that non-Christian philosophers of the early centuries of the new era who deigned to notice it either passed it off with urbane and amused tolerance or dismissed it with scorn as completely irrational. Nor is it strange that for the first century or so those who followed Jesus constituted only obscure groups in one of the scores of numerically minor cults which found a foothold in the cosmopolitan cities of the Græco-Roman world. And, since Jesus had not set forth clearly defined organizational and elaborate doctrinal patterns, it is not astonishing that even this minority was composed of several diverse sects, some of which bitterly denounced the others.

From the very beginning Christianity combined elements from Jesus with others which were extraneous and often obscured or contradicted them. So radically different was Jesus from what men anticipated of God that many watered him down, interpreted him in terms of a widely prevalent and pre-Christian Gnosticism, or attempted to fit him into Judaism. From the outset there were those who saw how unique Jesus was and what they believed God had done and was doing through and in him, but for a hundred years or more they may have been only a minority of those who regarded themselves as his followers.

Yet within five centuries Christianity had become numerically dominant in the Roman Empire and had begun to spread outside the borders of that realm. By the beginning of the nineteenth century it was more widely spread than ever any religion had been. In the course of the nineteenth and twentieth centuries, in spite of extensive defections and violent opposition among the peoples where it had long been strongest, Christianity was becoming rooted in more and more tribes and nations. Increasingly it was influencing the life of mankind. Since without him Christianity would not have been, Jesus, the seeming failure, has had more effect upon the history of mankind than any other of its race who has ever existed.

No thoughtful student of this record can escape questions which it provokes. Were those early Christians right whose convictions the majority bearing the Christian name eventually accepted? Did God act uniquely in Jesus? In Jesus do men look into the very heart of the universe and in him are they given, as nowhere else, authentic knowledge of ultimate reality? In him do they see what man was meant to be and can become? Has God acted in Jesus to save man from what is base and from dark powers which contest God's will? Is God self-giving love and is there evidence that this love is victorious? What if anything does history have to say about the assertion that Jesus Christ, "the lamb of God," bears or "takes away the sin [not the sins] of the world"? Is the world "saved through him"? Is God's will to be done perfectly within history? Does history give any assurance for the hope that, if not within history, beyond its course the entire creation is to be delivered from bondage "into the glorious liberty of the children of God"? If this consummation is to be reached either within or beyond history, then why in recent centuries, and especially in the nineteenth and twentieth centuries, have the major threats to Christianity issued from the nations which have long professed allegiance to it? Are these threats in part the fruit of Christianity and, if not the fruit, perversions of its fruit? If so, does Christianity contain the seeds of its own destruction? These are some of the questions on which the succeeding volumes may shed some light. In their course we will suggest answers and also raise further and related questions.

No one can hope to give the final and definitive answers to them all. But the author can hope to make suggestions which may help those who come after him to more nearly complete answers.

CHAPTER II

The Course of Christianity to the Eve of the Nineteenth Century

THE course of Christianity on this planet has thus far been brief. Its nineteen centuries are only about the latest fourth or fifth of the record of civilized mankind. They are merely a small fraction of man's sojourn before the dawn of civilization.

This may mean that if human beings and civilization continue into a prolonged future Christianity is a passing phenomenon. Indeed, many declare that this forecast is confirmed by the movements away from Christianity in the period with which these volumes deal. They are joined by those who insist that all religions as mankind has known them, including Christianity, are a stage in man's development and are to be left behind.

On the other hand, the brevity of its history up to the mid-twentieth century may mean that Christianity is still young, that Christ is to draw all men unto him, and that all nations are to become his disciples. Much in the history of Christianity seems to lend support to this hope. Yet aspects of the story modify this optimism and suggest that neither alternative is to be confirmed by the future. Even if all men were to become Christian disciples, it does not necessarily follow that they would fully attain within history to the ideal for man cherished by God and seen in Christ and his teachings. They would still be in process of "being saved"—to use Paul's apt phrase—a process to be continued after the incident of physical death.

The course of Christianity has been marked by pulsations of advance, retreat, and advance. As criteria for measuring these pulsations we may use the geographic extent of the faith, its vitality as seen in new movements to which it gives rise, and its effect on mankind as a whole. The rough outlines of the first can be easily determined. The second can also be fairly readily ascertained. The third is much more difficult fully to detect and to measure. Here the phrase "as a whole" is important. As we have seen, from the outset Christians have declared that the Gospel is for all men. If they are right, if in Christ God once for all came into history to "save the world," the history of Christianity

6

must be viewed from the standpoint of all mankind. Its perspective must be global.[1]

THE FIRST GREAT ADVANCE—TO A.D. 500

The first great advance is roughly the initial five centuries after Christ. Here, as we have suggested, is one of the most amazing stories in all history. A religion which seemed to begin as a minor sect of Judaism and to be among the least promising of all the many cults which were competing for the allegiance of the Græco-Roman world eliminated all its rivals except Judaism and became the professed faith of the overwhelming majority of what was then the most numerous section of civilized mankind. It did this in spite of the astounding claims and demands, the brevity of the public career, and the seemingly futile and frustrating death of him whom it revered as central. The achievement was in the face of prolonged and determined opposition by the government and hostile public opinion. To be sure, the final victory was won through the active endorsement of the state. However, this was not given until after almost three centuries and after the church to which the majority of Christians belonged had become, next to the government, the most widespread and powerful institution in the Roman Empire and had demonstrated its vitality as against a final determined effort by the temporal rulers to uproot it.

During these five centuries Christianity developed features which ever since have characterized it. The Catholic Church arose. After conflicts with variant forms of the faith, its membership included the large majority of those who called themselves Christians. The administrative structure of the Catholic Church was in part a reflection of that of the Roman Empire. Dioceses, the major units, took that designation from civil administration. Rome, around which the empire had grown and which for the citizens of that realm was the symbol of stable civilization, was the seat of the bishop who claimed primacy in the entire Church. With modifications, that ecclesiastical structure has been perpetuated not only in the Roman Catholic Church but also, with the exception of the place accorded the Bishop of Rome, in the several churches into which the Catholic Church later divided and which in the nineteenth and twentieth centuries enrolled the large majority of those who bore the Christian name.

In an attempt to be assured of what the Gospel was as transmitted by the original disciples, the Apostles, the books which were believed to have been written by them or by authors in their immediate entourage were assembled in

---

[1] For bibliographies for this chapter see Kenneth Scott Latourette, *A History of the Expansion of Christianity* (New York, Harper & Brothers), Vols. I, II, and III (1937–1941), and Kenneth Scott Latourette, *A History of Christianity* (New York, Harper & Brothers, 1953, pp. 1516), Chapters I–XLII.

what became known as the New Testament, a collection which Christians have since regarded as authoritative.

Inspired by the faith, first-class minds addressed themselves to the intellectual problems presented by Jesus and made contributions to theology which Christian scholars of all later centuries have studied with profound respect. Creeds were formulated, through controversies, in an attempt to express the heart of the Christian faith. Those which are called the Apostles', the Nicene, and the Chalcedonian creeds have continued to be accepted as authoritative by the majority of Christians. This intense intellectual activity was in a civilization which apart from it was saying little that was new.

The method then practised of admission to the Christian fellowship, baptism, has persisted. The major beliefs and some of the ceremonies connected with it arose which were to endure through the centuries.

Forms of worship emerged which, with modifications, have remained standard for the large majority of Christians. They centred around the Eucharist, the Holy Communion, the Holy Supper, or the Lord's Supper as it eventually came variously to be called.

What was known as the Christian year was developed. Its recurring rhythm included the Lord's Day, or Sunday, and the great festivals, chief among them the seasons centring around the advent and death and resurrection of Jesus, and the coming of the Holy Spirit. In its main features it has remained a characteristic of all but a few of the churches.

A distinction early developed between clergy and laity which has continued in most churches. The clergy became a priesthood. Ordination to the priesthood was by bishops. The bishops were regarded as successors of the original Apostles. Continuity from the Apostles through them was deemed an essential mark of the Church. This structure and these beliefs have also been perpetuated in the churches in which are still enrolled the majority of Christians.

Reverence for saints arose, often in the form of special cults. Chief among them was Mary, the mother of Jesus. To her were added the Apostles, martyrs, and many who were deemed ideal examples of the Christian faith.

Monasticism came into being. It had a rapid development and was in part a protest against the relaxation of standards for the average Christian as multitudes poured into the Church. It, too, has remained characteristic of the churches which enroll the majority of Christians.

In much of the formulation of its beliefs, worship, sacraments, holy days, ecclesiastical structure, cults of the saints, and monasticism, Christianity was influenced by its environment. Yet it was not a product of it. In it was a dynamic which subordinated its borrowings to its distinctive essence.

With one exception, in its first five centuries Christianity did not work revolutionary changes in its environment. The exception was in the realm of religion. In the Roman Empire Christianity eliminated all its rivals but Judaism and brought into being the Christian Church. That was a major achievement, especially in a civilization which was dying from lack of nerve and which was doing or saying little that was basically new. Aside from this, Christianity did not have much influence upon the manners and institutions of the Græco-Roman world. After persecutions ceased and throngs flooded the Church, the quality of Christian living deteriorated. Christianity contributed to the decline of slavery and to the termination of the gladiatorial spectacles. It made for some approximation to its standards in marriage and relations between the sexes. But it did not revolutionize Græco-Roman life and culture.

The Great Recession—a.d. 500–a.d. 950

Not far from a.d. 500 began what looked like complete disaster. The Roman Empire entered upon a long period of fatal decline. By then Christianity had come to be identified with that realm. With some exceptions, to be a Roman was to be a Christian and the vast majority of Christians were Roman citizens. At the time of the birth of Christ the Mediterranean world was sick. For two centuries or so the course of the malady was arrested by the formation of the Empire by Augustus and its continuation by the stronger among his successors. However, the basic causes were not removed. Christianity did not add to them. Yet it did not eliminate or even greatly allay them.

For about four and a half centuries blow followed blow. Enemies from abroad took advantage of the internal weakness of the Mediterranean world to pour in as conquerors. The invaders came, in the main, from two directions. From the north issued wave after wave of barbarians. Partial recovery would be effected only to be followed by another incursion and a further decline. Most of the invaders from the north were pagans, and Christianity suffered not only from the lawlessness attendant on their coming but also from the deposits of non-Christian elements in previously Christian communities. From the southeast came an even more formidable threat, a new religion, Islam, borne by the Arabs. Within two hundred years of the death of Mohammed the Moslem Arabs had overrun and mastered about half of the then Christendom. They did not exterminate the Christians in these areas. But they placed them under such disabilities that the churches dwindled and in some places eventually disappeared.

The passing of the political integration given the Mediterranean world by the Roman Empire was followed by the further break-up of the Catholic Church. That church had never found unity easy. Nor had it fully achieved it. Before it was deprived of the encompassing structure of the Roman state it had suffered from divisions and secessions. Even the intervention of the emperors from Constantine on did not prevent schisms. Each of the post-Constantinian divisions was associated with local, racial, or national particularisms—the Arians eventually with the Teutonic peoples, the Donatists with the Berbers of North Africa, the Monophysites with Syrian and Egyptian resistance to centralizing rule from abroad, the Armenians in opposition to the threat of control from Constantinople, and the Nestorians with an attempt at dissociation of the Christian name from Rome. As political unity waned, rifts which had been either latent or incomplete were widened and deepened. The Latin West and the Greek East slowly drifted apart, the one centring around Rome and its bishop and the other having its chief ecclesiastic in the Bishop of Constantinople. Perpetuating the pre-Christian role of religion in the Roman Empire, the latter tended to be subordinate to the state, for the Empire continued with its capital in Constantinople. As Roman rule became progressively weaker in the West, the Bishop of Rome had much less rivalry from the state than did his fellow bishop in Constantinople. Moreover, with the disintegration of much of civil power in the West the Church, as the champion of law and order, took over some of the functions previously performed by the state. In the West the Catholic Church became the Roman Catholic Church and continued something of the imperial temper and the spirit of political Rome.

In the West, under the continued incursion of barbarians, the quality of Christian living deteriorated. From time to time it seemed to be recovering, notably in the eighth century and the fore part of the ninth century under the great Carolingians. Then the break-up of the Carolingian empire and the Norse invasions dealt fresh blows. The Papacy reached a nadir in prestige and power, and elsewhere were marked decline and corruption.

Yet in these very years the bases of a great revival were laid. Christianity won the professed allegiance of most of the pagans who had invaded the Roman Empire from the north and here and there spread northward beyond the former borders of that realm. Some of the invaders were Christians before they effected their conquests. Others accepted the faith after they had settled in areas which had once been within the Roman lines. Long before the middle of the tenth century Ireland had become a flourishing centre of Christianity. The Germans north and east of the Rhine were won. Missionaries from the eastern remnant of the Roman Empire made converts among the Slavs, both within and outside what had once been Roman territory. Moreover, in the two centuries which immediately followed the year 500 the faith was carried eastward as far as China and was propagated up the Nile in what we now call the Sudan.

THE SECOND ADVANCE. CHRISTENDOM BECOMES EUROPE—A.D. 950–A.D. 1350

About the middle of the tenth century awakenings were taking place which were to usher in a fresh period of advance. The first great recession was ending. It had lasted for about four and a half centuries and had been the most severe which Christianity was to experience during the nearly two millenniums which now lie back of us. It had cost the faith about half the territory occupied during the first forward surge and was accompanied by a loss of morale in most of the lands which remained to it. Now a renewal began which was to plant the faith more widely than at any earlier time, was to express itself in creative movements, and was to leave a far deeper impress upon more of mankind than Chritsianity had earlier done.

The awakenings were chiefly in Western Europe. This might have seemed strange, for, except in the territories which had been lost to the Moslem Arabs, it was in Western Europe that the collapse of Roman rule had been most nearly complete. Yet that very collapse gave Christianity large opportunity. There it was not confronted with an all-powerful state as it was in the eastern continuation of the Empire. It was faced by a number of kingdoms. Most of them were little better than tribal states. The chief, that of the Franks, never controlled all in the West which had once been in the Roman Empire and for only a few reigns could be called a major power. It was not as highly civilized as was its eastern counterpart which centred around Constantinople. However, Western Europe was not as hardly pressed by Islam as was the latter and when once the Viking raids ceased, as they did in the tenth century, in contrast with Eastern Europe it was not again overrun by invaders. Here, then, the inherent creative vigour of Christianity had larger opportunity to find expression than anywhere else.

Geographically, in the four centuries which followed A.D. 950 Christianity was planted over a wider area than ever before. It was renewed in China, where it had died out before A.D. 950. Although many of them were small, Christian communities dotted Asia from the Mediterranean to the China Sea and from its centre to the south coasts of India. In spite of progressively losing ground to Islam, Christianity still existed along most of the Nile Valley, from Alexandria south into the Sudan, and was also firmly entrenched in the highlands of Ethiopia. The Scandinavians were won, both in the regions where their raids had settled them and in their homelands. The conversion of the Slavs was completed, and to this was added the conversion of the Magyars and Bulgars. From Kiev as a centre Christianity spread in Russia. No one church had a monopoly on this geographic spread: yet it was mostly from Western Europe.

Christianity continued to be vigorous in the Byzantine realms. It was a Christianity in which monasticism was prominent. In that monasticism was a strain called hesychasm. Hesychasm specialized in an individual discipline for the perfection of the Christian life and for the indwelling of the divine light through aceticism, prayer, and meditation. We will find it in Russian monasticism in the nineteenth century. Russian monasticism, and with it Russian

Christianity, stressed kenoticism, the sort of self-emptying which characterized Christ in the incarnation. It magnified humility and held up as ideals Boris and Gleb, sons of Vladimir, the first Christian ruler of Kiev, who, unresisting, were killed by a brother who wished to remove them from his path to the throne.

The wing of Christianity which had Constantinople as its chief radiating centre thought of itself as Orthodox, the guardian of the original Gospel, and more and more separated from that which centred in Rome. It did not modify as many aspects of the culture in which it was set as profoundly as did Roman Christianity the emerging culture of Western Europe. The state ·was less challenged by the Church in its control of religion and of the life of the people. This tradition was perpetuated in the lands to which Christianity was carried by representatives of the Orthodox Church. In the nineteenth and twentieth centuries we will find it, although modified, in Russia and the Balkans.

It was in Western Europe that these four centuries witnessed the greatest vitality in Christianity. The manifestations were geographic spread, new movements, and effects upon culture.

Latin Christianity was carried from Greenland on the west and north to the China Sea on the east. Much of the spread of Latin Christianity was a phase of early stages of the expansion of Western European peoples which, with an interruption in the latter part of the fourteenth and the fore part of the fifteenth century, was to be of major and mounting importance in the life of mankind. However, it did not take place automatically as a part of that expansion but arose primarily from religious conviction and devotion.

The new movements in the Christianity of Western Europe had many aspects. Numbers of them were in fresh forms of monasticism which were expressions of the urge to attain to the high standards set forth by Christ and his Apostles. Prominent among them were the Cluny houses, the Cistercians, the Carthusians, the Dominicans, and the Franciscans. The last two orders displayed a trend which was increasing in Latin monasticism. It strove to realize the ideal Christian life not in isolation, as among the hermits, or in communities removed as far as possible from contamination from the world about them, as were most of the Benedictines, but by seeking to penetrate that world, to win its members to full Christian living, and to minister to its needs. Here was a strong tendency towards what may be called activism—towards seeking to bring all the world to the Christian ideal. It was not absent in Eastern Christianity, but in Western Europe it was more marked and had a greater variety of expression. Other new movements, somewhat akin to monasticism in their efforts to fulfil completely the demands of Christ, were ones which the official church branded as heretical and sought to extirpate. Among them were the Waldensians and the Cathari or Albigenses.

Very striking were new movements in thought. Men were stimulated to address themselves to the intellectual problems presented by Christianity. To this they applied the tools inherited from the Greeks. The leaders were what were known as the school men. Among them were first-class minds, notably Anselm, Abélard, and, above all, Thomas Aquinas.

One of the most prominent features of these four centuries in Western Europe was the attempt through the Roman Catholic Church to bring all life towards the level envisioned in the New Testament. Here was a malleable society. The Roman Empire as men had once known it had collapsed and with it much of Græco-Roman culture. The traditional cultures of the barbarians who had poured into the former Roman realms had also disintegrated. The result was an approach to moral and cultural chaos. Great Christians sought to overcome the evil by working through the Church. They strove to reform the Church itself, for in the centuries of disorder its morale had suffered. Then, using the Church as an instrument, they would remake all aspects of society according to what they believed that they saw in the teachings of Christ. Eventually they captured the Papacy and through magnifying the power and developing the structure directly depending on Rome endeavoured to reach the whole body of Christians.

As a result of these and other movements the emerging culture of Western Europe was more profoundly and widely affected by Christianity than were the cultures in which Christianity was represented by the Orthodox and other Eastern churches. Society was not brought to full obedience to Christ: that is too much to expect of any culture. The scene presented stark contrasts, all the more so because of the height of the demanding ideals set forth by Christ. Yet into the life of Western Europe, with its roistering, fighting, proud, conquering barbarians, and into the remnants of the civilization which was being displaced was coming the vision of a better world ruled by a self-giving love. It entered as a potent moulding factor into every aspect of the culture which was emerging.

The effect was seen in political life. Laws were modified. Monarchs were crowned with religious ceremonies and undertook to rule as Christians. Political theories were set forth which had as a basic postulate the principle that all society, including the state, should be Christian. Attempts were made in the name of Christ to reduce the frequency and the cruelty of war. The Truce of God, advocated by church synods, sought to free certain seasons and days of the week from fighting; the Peace of God endeavoured to protect members of some occupations from the pressures of war; and chivalry was an attempt to bring the professional aristocratic warrior to conform to what were deemed Christian standards.

In the economic phases of life the Church opposed the charging of interest and enunciated principles for fixing a just price. Industry and commerce were organized by guilds, and guilds had religious ceremonies and at least in theory recognized Christian obligations for themselves and their members.

The Church concerned itself with social life. Marriage and morals were under its control. It endeavoured to regulate amusements and forbade those which it deemed inconsistent with Christian standards. Much of life revolved around the Christian calendar, with Sunday, the saints' days, and the great festivals of the Church.

The care of the poor, the sick, the orphans, the aged, widows, and strangers was enjoined by the Church. Much of this was performed by monasteries. Later a large proportion of it was taken over by voluntary lay organizations, but in the Christian name and under the blessing of the Church.

Education was due almost entirely to impulses stemming from Christianity. The abounding creative intellectual life was profoundly indebted to the faith. In the earlier years the monastic schools were important. Schools arose around cathedrals. Then came the universities. For the most part they obtained their charters from the Pope and were ecclesiastical in character. Theology was regarded as the queen of the sciences and in some universities was supreme. The mind of Western Europe was led to view the world about it as orderly, a universe, dependable, and not chaos. Plato and Aristotle were prized, but through the medium of Christian conviction. One of the achievements of the school men was to think through philosophy in terms of the Christian faith and to seek to reconcile the two.

Here was a source, perhaps the determinative source, of the scientific developments of the nineteenth and twentieth centuries and the associated creation and widespread use of machines. A great forerunner of modern science was Roger Bacon. Caught up in the zealous early days of the Franciscans, his was a first-class mind stimulated by Christian faith and devotion. Among his contemporaries, Robert Grosseteste, an earnest reformer and distinguished scholar, and the Dominican Albertus Magnus, also profoundly Christian and of a wide-ranging intellect, were greatly interested in science and contributed to its foundations. Ardent Christian faith was associated with the beginnings of the scientific achievements of the later Occident.

Thanks to the methods employed by the Church, by the year 1350 the population of much of Europe, and especially of Western Europe, was fairly familiar with the chief tenets of Christianity, professed to accept them, and in its religious beliefs and practices was moulded by them.

This does not mean that the life of Western Europe was fully Christian. Popular religion was shot through and through with superstition. In all aspects of life the contrasts between Christian ideals and practice were striking, whether in the government, in industry and commerce, in sex morals, or in the treatment of the underprivileged. Much noisome poverty existed. Stark and savage cruelty was rampant. Callous self-seeking and vaunting selfish ambition were widespread. Among the majority irreverence seems to have been frequent and perhaps general. In actual practice Western Europe was probably no more nearly Christian in the thirteenth than in the nineteenth and twentieth centuries.

However, a marked contrast existed between the two eras. In the thirteenth century, the height of what is often called "the age of faith," all but Jews and Moslems professed to be Christian and were acquainted, even if superficially, with the outstanding Christian teachings of faith and morals. The nineteenth and twentieth centuries saw an increasing departure from the faith by thousands who were of Christian ancestry. Fully as important, the routine of life in an industrialized age made difficult or impossible for thousands regular attendance at Christian instruction and public worship and in the course of two or three generations little consciousness or knowledge of anything distinctively Christian remained among them.

Because of the developments from the seventh to the fifteenth century, Europe became the heart of what may be called Christendom. The Moslem Arab conquests had overwhelmed most of the earlier centres of the faith in Western Asia and the north shores of Africa, either eliminating the churches entirely or reducing them to encysted minorities on the defensive. The survival of the faith in the lands once ruled by the Roman Empire on the north shores of the Mediterranean, the rewinning from Islam, by the year 1350, of Sicily and of most of the Iberian Peninsula, and the conversion of the peoples of Northern Europe made of that western extension of Eurasia the stronghold of Christianity.

It was in Western Europe especially that the faith was most firmly implanted and most deeply and widely moulded culture. Eastward, in the later Russia, where the heartland of Eurasia begins, many pagans were still unconverted, in the thirteenth century the Mongol conquest brought in a fresh wave of non-Christians who soon turned Moslem, and Christianity had not shaped life as profoundly as in Western Europe. It was from Western Europe that most of the geographic spread of the faith was later effected, in succeeding centuries it was there that most of the vigorous new movements arose from Christianity, and from there the forces issued which in the nineteenth and twentieth centuries revolutionized the life of both the Occident and the non-Occident.

THE SECOND RECESSION—A.D. 1350–A.D. 1500

However, in the century and a half which followed the middle of the fourteenth century it was not at all clear that Christianity would survive, either in Western Europe or elsewhere. The decades were marked by another recession in the Christian tide. It was not as prolonged as had been that which began about the close of the fifth century, nor did it result in as great loss of territory or morale. Yet it was severe.

The geographic borders of Christianity shrank more drastically than in the earlier recession, but proportionately the numerical losses were not as great as they had then been. In China the break-up of the Mongol Empire and the founding of a native Chinese dynasty were followed by the disappearance of the Christian minorities which had been planted under Mongol rule. The conversion of the main body of Mongols to Buddhism seems to have been a cause of the extinction of other Christian minorities on the northern and northwestern borders of China. The espousal of Islam by the Mongols in Central Asia and the campaigns of the zealous Moslem of Mongol descent, Timur (Tamerlane), appear to have been responsible for the demise of the Christian communities in that region. A forward surge of Islam, spear-headed by the Ottoman Turks, erased the Byzantine Empire, turned into a mosque St. Sophia, the chief cathedral of Greek Christianity, reduced the Christians in Asia Minor and Constantinople to minorities, planted the crescent in the recent solidly Christian Balkans, and carried it to the very walls of Vienna. For a time it looked as though much of Western Europe would be engulfed by this fresh Moslem wave. In its westernmost frontier, Greenland, Christianity died out as the small Scandinavian settlements vanished, presumably because of the mounting rigour of the climate. In the Sudan Islam slowly displaced Christianity. By the year 1500 in Asia, the home of its birth, Christianity was represented only by the Syrian Christians in South India, and by shrunken remnants of once great churches in the western portions of the continent. In the northern reaches of Africa the faith continued only in the mountain fastnesses of Ethiopia, in divided minorities in Egypt, and among enslaved Christian captives from Europe.

Yet, sobering as was this shrinkage of the geographic frontiers of the faith, except for the loss of the Byzantine realms the main body of Christendom was as yet intact. Indeed, it was being extended. Late in the fourteenth century the Lithuanians received baptism and throughout the period Russian monks were carrying the faith northward to the White Sea and the Arctic Ocean.

Since the heart of Christendom was now in Western Europe, the threats to the faith in that region were peculiarly ominous. They took a variety of forms.

One threat was the emergence of nation states, under monarchs who aspired to be absolute and each of whom attempted to control the Church within his borders and to make the faith ancillary to his purposes. Success would mean the denaturing of Christianity.

The efforts of the great reformers of the preceding period seemed to be issuing in a menace to the purposes for which they had laboured. They had dreamed of making the Papacy an instrument for bringing all society to the

Christian ideal. To this end they augmented the administrative and judicial machinery of the Papal curia and engaged in political manoeuvres in Italy and in much of Europe. Heavy and oppressive taxation followed, and men were attracted who saw in ecclesiastical office the opportunity to satisfy their selfish ambitions for prestige, power, and wealth. Corruption mounted. By diplomacy and war the Popes sought to enhance their position, using methods which were exactly the opposite of those of Jesus. Some Popes were openly immoral. The worst was Alexander VI (1492–1503). Handsome, able, forceful, hard-working, he lived luxuriously, had several illegitimate children, and sought to advance their interests by mixing shamelessly in Italian politics. Many of the Cardinals were little if any better. With such conditions at headquarters, elsewhere in Europe the lives of many monks and clergy were a stench in the nostrils of good men.

These years saw the first flowering of the Renaissance. The Renaissance was in part a revival of interest in the pre-Christian literature and art of the Græco-Roman world. It also was an expression of a kind of humanism, with emphasis upon the competence of man's ability and reason and a joy in man's achievements. The scholasticism of the preceding period had seemed to end in despair of human reason. Using the apparatus provided by Greek philosophy, the great school men had sought to support by reason the basic Christian convictions. However, by the year 1350 the trend had been in the direction of the denial of the ability of the human intellect to prove any of the fundamental Christian tenets: they must be accepted on faith, because they are taught by the Church and are found in the Bible. With the Renaissance came a resurgence of confidence in reason and a determination to apply it fearlessly to accepted beliefs and through it to push outward the boundaries of human knowledge, to understand and master nature, and to rejoice in beauty, whether of nature, art, or literature.

Many children of the Renaissance were devout Christians, and some of the humanists were reverent and earnest in their Christian faith and sought to purge the Church of its corruption and to set forward Christianity. Others, while outwardly conforming, were cynical and in their attitudes and lives had scant regard for Christianity.

The Renaissance was more than the re-birth by which its usual designation describes it. It was a new birth, a fresh movement. In it the Christian factor was fully as great as the pre-Christian. Its very emphasis on man was in part an expression of that dignity of the human soul which is one of the basic convictions inculcated by the Gospel. Again and again the Renaissance was perverted by man's pride, but to no small degree it was a fruit of what had been planted and nourished by Christianity in "the ages of faith." In it was an early instance of what we are to see again and again in the nineteenth and twentieth centuries. Here was a movement to which Christianity was a contributory cause, which in some of its phases was a partial perversion and enemy of Christianity, and which in other phases was a fresh surge of authentic Christian faith.

To some in the twentieth century who noted what appeared to them to be the coming of the post-Christian era, the foreshadowing was in the Renaissance. It was then, so they maintained, that the secularization of Europe had begun.

This was the more ominous for the future of Christianity because it was developing in Western Europe, the chief stronghold of Christianity, and was in part the result of movements which were deeply indebted to Christianity. The Renaissance had its roots in the preceding period in Western Europe, what we usually call the Middle Ages, the alleged "ages of faith." It was in part the outgrowth of the belief in the orderliness and dependability of the universe and in the worth and dignity of man which had been instilled by Christianity. Were forces issuing from Christianity which would eventually destroy it? Was Christianity to come to its end through the perversion of some of its best gifts? Here are questions which were to become especially clamant in succeeding centuries, never more so than in those with which these volumes are chiefly concerned.

The situation became the more grave through movements which towards the end of the fifteenth century were beginning to assume major proportions and which in the succeeding centuries were to be world-shaking. They were the geographic discoveries, explorations, and conquests by which Europeans mastered most of the world and through which European culture became dominant and the source of revolutions which shook and transformed all mankind. They began with the Portuguese explorations along the west coast of Africa and were soon followed by the discovery of America, the rounding of the Cape of Good Hope, the circumnavigation of the globe, and the building of colonial empires, at the outset chiefly by the Spaniards and the Portuguese. All were by professedly Christian peoples. With the exception of the Russians as they reached across northern Eurasia, they were by Western Europeans. Some professed a Christian motive. Indeed, it is a question whether they would have taken place had the Christian faith not emboldened and sustained several of the outstanding pioneers. Yet the voyages, explorations, and conquests were accompanied and followed by the seeking of wealth and power and the exploitation of subject peoples in ways which were in stark and tragic contradiction to the Gospel. Had Christianity been at least partly responsible for releasing forces which were a practical denial of all that it stood for and which it could not control? That question, too, will confront us even more urgently as we move on into the nineteenth and twentieth centuries.

While movements and forces were at work which seemed a prelude to the demise of the faith, individuals and movements were demonstrating that Christianity, far from being moribund, was extraordinarily vital. They, too, were chiefly in Western Europe. We think of Catherine of Siena and Jeanne d'Arc, later to be canonized by the Roman Catholic Church. We recall the German mystics and the composition of the *Theologia Germanica*. We remember the emergence of the Brethren of the Common Life and what was known as the New Devotion, out of which came the *Imitation of Christ*. We note a flowering of mysticism in England and, near the end of the period, the self-sacrificing service to the sick of the aristocratic mystic, Catherine of Genoa. We remind ourselves that a contemporary of Alexander VI was Savonarola. Out of the apparently futile scholasticism came John Wyclif, the Lollards, and John Hus. In Russia Sergius, later to be the patron saint of that country, was the outstanding figure in a new kind of monasticism which was pushing northward the borders of Christianity and was the founder of the Troitsa (Trinity) monastery, about forty miles from Moscow, the mother house of many others of its kind. In its internal life Christianity was far from sinking to as low a level as at the depths of the great recession.

Here again is a contrast which we shall find to be more and more marked as the centuries pass—between the seeming repudiation and decay of the faith and fresh and striking evidences of vitality.

RENEWAL THROUGH ABOUNDING VITALITY—A.D. 1500–A.D. 1700

When it seemed that the prospect for Christianity was peculiarly unpromising, bursts of life were seen. These ushered in a forward surge of the Christian tide through which new and potent movements arose, the faith was carried over a greater geographic extent than it or any other religion had covered, and a wider and deeper impression was made on mankind as a whole than at any earlier time.

Most of the fresh bursts of life broke out in quite unanticipated places and from unexpected quarters. They were mostly in Western Europe but a few were in Russia. Some in Western Europe gave rise to Protestantism and the movements they initiated were expelled from the Roman Catholic Church. Others were in that church.

Protestantism's earliest great figure was the Saxon Augustinian monk Martin Luther. The distinctive doctrines for which he stood and which have characterized Protestantism were salvation by faith alone and the priesthood of all believers. With these as a corollary went the right and the duty of the individual to think for himself in matters of religion. It was Luther who at the Diet of Worms declared before the emperor and the mighty of the realm that unless convinced by Scripture and sound reason he would not recant anything that he had written, for that would be to go against his conscience. He would not accept the authority of Popes and councils, for in his judgement they had contradicted one another.

Although Luther was not a child of the Renaissance, his position reflected the confidence in human reason which was one of the aspects of that movement. Here was human reason, but here was much more. Luther's affirmation came out of the prolonged and agonizing struggle through which he had reached a profound conviction of what he believed to be the heart of the Gospel. This he could not surrender without being false to what he was clear was God's word. But here was a feature of Protestantism which not only was part of the secret of its vitality but was also to cause apparently endless division.

From the outset Protestantism, true to its genius, was varied. Much of the North-west of Europe followed Luther—Northern Germany, Sweden, Norway, Denmark, Finland, and Iceland. Lutheran churches also arose in Hungary. Another wing of Protestantism was the Reformed Churches, some of which were known as Presbyterian. In them no one individual was as prominent as was Luther in those which have often been called by his name. Among their outstanding creators were Zwingli, Bucer, Farel, and, even more, Calvin, the French humanist who was long in control in Geneva and whose name is often attached to the Reformed tradition. The Reformed Churches were chiefly on the border between the Lutheran North and the Roman Catholic South and were the dominant form of Protestantism in Switzerland, much of the Rhine Valley, the Netherlands, France, and Italy. The majority of Scots accepted the Reformed faith and the Church of Scotland became Presbyterian. At the instance of Henry VIII the Church of England broke its tie with Rome: before long it adopted several features of Protestantism. Some humanists who stressed reason and applied it more drastically to the Christian faith than did the major Protestant bodies led minorities which denied the Trinity. Other minorities went further than did the majority of Protestants in following consistently the tenets peculiar to that wing of the faith: because they rejected infant baptism and insisted that true baptism was only for conscious believers they were known as Anabaptists. They were not united and were persecuted by both Roman Catholics and fellow Protestants. In England Protestants were particularly divided. Some, who would have preferred not to be known as Protestants, cherished much of the Catholic tradition and sought to hold the Church of England to it. Others, Puritans, wished to carry that church much further in the Protestant direction. Still others separated completely from the national church. Among them were the spiritual ancestors of the later Congregationalists, Baptists, and Quakers.

In part, but only in part, Protestantism was an outgrowth of the Renaissance and of the humanism associated with it. Salvation by faith alone was both like and unlike humanism. It was like it in its emphasis on the act of the individual.

It was unlike it in reliance not on human reason, for it held man to be impotent, but on the divine initiative in effecting man's salvation.

The fresh currents of life which were held within the Roman Catholic Church gave rise to what is sometimes known as the Counter-Reformation but what is more accurately designated the Catholic Reformation. They had begun before Luther, at first most markedly in Spain. They purified some of the old monastic orders and, as has been customary with revivals in the Roman Catholic Church, they also found expression in new forms of monasticism. Chief among the latter was the Society of Jesus. It had as its founder and first head a contemporary of Luther, Ignatius Loyola, a Spaniard. Among the fruits of the Catholic Reformation were the elimination of some of the worst moral and procedural corruptions in the Roman Catholic Church, the elevation of the moral tone of the Papacy and the Papal curia, a better-educated and more disciplined clergy, improved religious instruction of the laity, heightened missionary zeal, new practices of religious devotion, and augmented efforts to serve the sick, the prisoners, and the poor.

Attempts at reconciliation of Protestants and Roman Catholics broke down. Through the Council of Trent, which met intermittently from 1545 to 1563, the Roman Catholic Church not only enacted legislation to effect its own reformation but also defined its position on the issues raised by Protestants in such fashion that the latter could not acquiesce without surrendering basic principles. The breach within Western Christendom was complete.

Tragically the breach between Protestants and Roman Catholics and the divisions within Protestantism contributed to wars and were accompanied by persecutions. Wars in which the Protestant-Roman Catholic issue was an important cause long raged as civil strife in France and Germany and culminated in the Thirty Years' War (1618–1648), which laid waste much of the latter country. Partly as a result of that war the internal unity of Germany was weakened and the principle reinforced of *cuius regio eius religio*. By it each of the many princes under whose rule the realm was divided decided the religion for his territories. In England the conflicts within Protestantism were a major factor in the civil war which in the seventeenth century cost Charles I his head and ushered in the Cromwellian Commonwealth. For years persecutions were chronic—of Protestants by Roman Catholics, of Roman Catholics by Protestants, and of Protestants by Protestants. Through them Protestantism lost more ground than did Roman Catholicism. Especially in France Protestants were reduced to small minorities.

In Russia the new currents were almost entirely independent of those in Western Europe and took quite different forms. What were known as the Old Believers separated from the state church. Ostensibly this was in protest against the revision of the service books by the leaders of that body. Actually it was also in part a revolt of humble folk led by parish priests against the bishops.

Associated with the religious awakenings and divisions but only in part caused by them was the trend towards the control of the Church by the state and the emergence of national churches. This was present in all branches of the Church. In Protestantism it was seen in such national bodies as the Church of England, the Church of Scotland, the Church of Sweden, and the *Landeskirchen* of the many states, large and small, into which Germany was divided. But it was not peculiar to Protestantism. Ardently Catholic Spanish and Portuguese monarchs took measures to negate the administrative authority of the Pope within their domains, whether in Europe or the Americas. Similar measures were adopted by French kings who were intent on extirpating Protentantism within their borders: what was known as Gallicanism characterized the French church. The Pope was recognized as a symbol and tie of orthodoxy in doctrine and the various national Catholic churches were in communion with one another, but in their internal government they were more and more all but independent of Rome and were controlled by their respective monarchs. In the Rhineland the great prince-bishops who were in fact territorial lords sought a similar autonomy. In the territories which he ruled, Peter the Great augmented the already extensive control of the Orthodox Church by the crown. In Turkey the Moslem sultans insisted that no Patriarch should hold office without their consent.

In spite of the divisions brought by the awakenings and the subservience of the Church to the state, the new surges of life brought about a wider geographic expansion of Christianity than any religion had heretofore achieved. Christianity was planted firmly in the Americas both by settlers from Europe and by missions to the Indians. By the year 1750 it was nominally dominant in the West Indies, Mexico, and Central America, along the seaboard of South America, and on the eastern and southern shores of North America. It was represented by minorities along the coast of Africa south of the Sahara, and in India, Burma, Siam, the Malay Peninsula, Indochina, the East Indies, China, and Japan. The majority of the Filipinos had been won. The faith had also been carried across the northern reaches of Asia.

Most of the expansion was by Roman Catholics and in its story are some of the most heroic pages in the record of mankind. Yet Protestants were also active and the spread across the north of Asia was by the Russian Orthodox.

However, it is one of the sobering facts of history that much of the Christianity beyond the borders of Europe was anemic: this was especially true of the Roman Catholic communities. By A.D. 1700 the largest bodies of Christians outside Europe were in Latin America and were Roman Catholic. In the nineteenth and twentieth centuries they continued to constitute the main numerical strength of the Roman Catholic Church outside Europe. Yet they did not provide enough clergy to meet their spiritual needs. To make up the deficit they were dependent on Europe and, in the second quarter of the twentieth century, on the United States. In the Philippines the Roman Catholic Church did not produce enough priests to care for its adherents. The Roman Catholics in China and Africa also relied upon priests and bishops from Europe and suffered when, in the latter part of the eighteenth century, that source of supply was almost cut off. So, too, the Orthodox communities in Northern Asia were served predominantly by clergy from Europe.

Yet not all the picture was sombre. Latin American and Filipino Roman Catholicism produced some priests, even though in inadequate numbers and all too often of inferior quality. Although in numbers Roman Catholics in India dwindled in the eighteenth century, clergy were recruited among them and a few had sufficient zeal to go to Ceylon and minister to those of their faith who under Dutch rule were experiencing persecution. Some priests arose from the persecuted Chinese Roman Catholic minorities, and in Japan Roman Catholic communities, driven underground by unrelenting government action and without priests, kept the faith until, after more than two and a half centuries, toleration came.

In the centuries after 1500 the effects of Christianity were more widely felt than ever before. In Europe they were marked and were probably deepening. In theological thought the Protestant Reformation was strikingly creative. The Catholic Reformation gave rise to no theologian comparable in depth and power with those of the eleventh, twelfth, and thirteenth centuries, but from both it and Protestantism there issued new forms of education. The promise of developments in science and mathematics associated with the religious awakenings of the thirteenth century was beginning to be fulfilled. How much of it was due to the Christian faith we cannot certainly know, but Copernicus, who blazed a new trail in astronomy, was a canon of a cathedral; Kepler, who added extensively to the knowledge of astronomy, turned reluctantly from the Protestant ministry to the studies which brought him fame; Pascal, who contributed notably to mathematics, was an earnest Christian; and Isaac Newton, whose "laws" are landmarks in the history of mathematics and natural science, was devoutly religious. In government, democracy in England was clearly although not solely an outgrowth of Protestantism. The Puritan Revolution and the Commonwealth which laid the foundations for it arose largely from Christian conviction, as did democracy in the Thirteen Colonies. John Locke, who contributed mightily to political theory in both Britain and America, was a child of Protestantism. The divine right of kings, which, from another angle, was prominent in the political theory and statecraft of the period, claimed Christian sanction. International law was deeply indebted to such Christian idealists and thinkers as the Protestant Hugo Grotius and the Roman Catholic Francisco de Vitoria. Art and music gave evidence of the stimulus of the Christian faith—as, for example, in Michelangelo and Bach. In the care of the underprivileged and the poor, Christian vision and dedication continued to make marked contributions.

Outside Europe the effects of Christianity were spreading. Upon the "high" civilizations, chiefly located as they were in Asia, they were as yet very slight. Not until the nineteenth and twentieth centuries, especially the latter, were they to be marked. However, among peoples of "primitive" culture, notably in the Americas and the Philippines, and among the civilized peoples in the Americas they were striking. The indigenous religions were largely displaced. Ethical ideals and religious convictions and practices which characterized the churches in Europe were introduced and outwardly were accepted. The elements in the population of European descent were largely held to a formal allegiance to the Christian faith. Such education as existed, from the primary grades through the universities, was through the initiative of leaders in the Church and for at least ostensibly Christian purposes. The culture of Latin America was "Christian" in the sense that that of Spain and Portugal, from which it chiefly stemmed, was "Christian." In the Thirteen Colonies, especially, the ideals and the distinctive type of democracy of the new nation which was emerging were moulded to a large extent by the radical Protestantism represented by influential minorities.

From Christianity came the mitigation of the exploitation of non-European peoples by Europeans. The exploiters were nominally Christian. It was through them that Negro slavery was introduced and promoted in the New World, with the attendant colossal misery in heightening the slave trade in Africa and the raids, wars, and other barbarities which were its inevitable accompaniment. Here is one of the blackest spots in the history of mankind. Competing with it in suffering, atrocities, and horror was the initial treatment of the Indians of the Western Hemisphere. In the West Indies Indians were hunted down like wild animals. There and on the mainland they were enslaved to work the mines and plantations upon which the prosperity of the white colonists depended. Yet consciences made sensitive and wills reinforced by the Christian faith early sought to alleviate or eliminate the evils. For a generation the Jesuit Pedro Claver ministered to the Negroes at a major port of entry of the slave ships, Cartagena, and in the vicinity. Significantly, he was canonized and became the patron saint of missions to the Negroes. Even more notable is the fact that the first Christian clergyman ordained in the New World, Bartolomé de Las Casas, for most of a long lifetime took the lead in having laws placed on the statute books protecting the Indian, spear-headed efforts to enforce them, and sought by demonstration to prove that the Indian could be won to the faith apart from the protection of armed forces. In both North and South America missionaries, mostly Roman Catholic, gathered the Indians into settlements and endeavoured by peaceable methods to lead them into ordered Christian living. It was under the influence of humanitarian ideals of Christian origin that the conquest and conversion of the Philippines were accomplished and that the frontiers of Spanish control in North and South America were pushed forward.

Thought-provoking and sobering features of this era of great revivals, new movements, and unprecedented territorial spread of Christianity were the practical denials of the faith in Christendom and the emergence of movements which threatened the very existence of the Christian faith.

The denials in practice were seen in the chronic wars, many of them inspired by the craving for power of monarchs who had taken coronation oaths as Christians and who professed reverence for the Gospel. They were also in statecraft such as that associated with the name of Machiavelli and in commercial and industrial methods connected with the rise of capitalism.

In the intellectual threats to Christianity we remember the name of Descartes. Although Descartes believed that his questionings had led him to a firmer belief in the Roman Catholic faith of his childhood, his basic assumption, *cogito ergo sum,* encouraged a confidence in man's reason which might well, and repeatedly did, lead some of those who began with it to what was essentially if not patently a denial of God's act in Christ on man's behalf. Springing from both Protestantism and Roman Catholicism was Deism. It professed to arrive by reason at a belief in God as Creator, in laws, including moral laws, which He had made, and in life after death with rewards and punishments. It talked much of "natural religion" and tended to rule out God's revelation recorded in the Bible and His saving activity in the incarnation. Wearied by the religious controversies which accompanied and followed the Protestant and Catholic Reformation, many wished to by-pass them through the unemotional use of man's mind. This "age of reason" characterized much of the latter part of the seventeenth century and mounted in the eighteenth century.

In the eighteenth century the threats to Christianity multiplied rapidly and alarmingly. Christianity and the churches which were its exponents were increasingly criticized. The "age of reason" seemed to be making the faith an anachronism. The churches themselves appeared to be dying inwardly, dominated by ecclesiastics who had more interest in preserving their perquisites and position than in being worthy exemplars of the Gospel. Revolutions and wars, some of them having Christianity as one of their sources, swept across Christendom and here and there had repercussions among the rest of mankind. In one of its stages the revolution which began in France was quite openly anti-Christian. Christendom was shaken to its foundations and was never again the same. Mankind, led by what had been known as the Christian peoples, entered upon the kaleidoscopic stage in its pilgrimage whose first century and a half is the subject of these volumes. Here was an introduction to the nineteenth and twentieth centuries which augured ill for the future of Christianity.

Since this period of rationalism and of revolutions and wars was the immediate introduction to the nineteenth and twentieth centuries, we must treat it somewhat more in detail than we have the earlier course of Christianity. We turn to it in the next two chapters.

CHAPTER III

Preparation for Revolution: The Eve of the Nineteenth Century

THE eighteenth, nineteenth, and twentieth centuries were marked on the one hand by as grave threats to Christianity as that faith had known. On the other hand, in striking contrast, they were also characterized by as marked vitality as that religion had ever displayed and by a world-wide expansion and an effect upon humanity as a whole which was wider than it or any other religion had previously exerted.

THE THREATS TO CHRISTIANITY: IN GENERAL FROM WITHIN CHRISTIANITY

For Christianity threats to its continued existence were not a new experience. From the very beginning it had known them. However, the threats of the eighteenth, nineteenth, and twentieth centuries were largely of a new kind. They arose from forces which to a greater or lesser degree had their source in Christianity but which were either caricatures or perversions of the Gospel. They also came from forces within the area where the peoples were professedly Christian and which Christianity had not succeeded in fully capturing and transforming. Some forces mounted until they exploded in revolutions which either weakened Christianity or for a time seemed about to extinguish it. The early explosions were in the latter part of the eighteenth century. In the nineteenth century they recurred, but in less catastrophic fashion. In the twentieth century they reached unprecedented proportions.

The threats from within Christianity issued chiefly from Western Europe and were reinforced from areas peopled mainly from Western Europe. Thence they spread to Eastern Europe and the rest of the world. They were clearly associated with the dynamic quality of the civilization of Western Europe. But to what extent, if at all, did that dynamic quality have its source in Christianity? If Christianity was in any degree its source, why did it emerge from the Christianity of Western Europe and not from that of the East? It may well have been because in Western Europe Christianity had freer course than elsewhere. In Eastern Europe Christianity had been subjected to the control of the portion of the Roman Empire which survived in that region with its centre in Constantinople. The tradition of domination by the state persisted in areas, notably but not exclusively Russia, to which this Eastern or Orthodox form of the faith spread. Elsewhere in the East Christianity was represented by minorities which were usually on the defensive—earlier against a dominant, state-supported Zoroastrianism or Confucianism, later against an aggressive Islam or, in India, an encircling Hinduism. In Western Europe, on the other hand, the early collapse of the Roman Empire and the absence of an all-embracing, unified state strong enough to control the churches, combined with the lack of a high civilization except that inherited from the partially Christianized Rome and spread to the conquering barbarians through the agents of Christianity, gave opportunity for the inherent vigour of Christianity to have freer expression than elsewhere. Here may be at least one reason for the dynamism of Western Europe and for the threats to Christianity which came from it.

In this chapter we must speak first of the threats as they were before the coming of spectacular revolution and next note the beginnings of the awakenings in Christianity which paralleled and to some degree countered them.

Intellectual Threats: The Coming of the "Enlightenment" (*Aufklärung*)

First we must note the intellectual currents which emerged chiefly from Christianity and which preserved some of its features while denying others that were essential to it. They came from Roman Catholic, Protestant, and Jewish backgrounds.

Among the early figures who influenced both their contemporaries and later generations were the Anglican Francis Bacon (1561–1626), the nominal Anglican Thomas Hobbes (1588–1679), the devout Roman Catholic layman René Descartes (1596–1650), the Roman Catholic priest Pierre Gassendi (1592–1655), and the Jew Benedictus de Spinoza (1632–1677). They did not fully agree with one another, although Spinoza was much influenced by Descartes, but they had in common a freedom and vigour of thought which departed from the scholastic method. The fact that Descartes has been called the father of modern philosophy, although that designation may not be fully justified, is an indication of his importance. From Descartes stemmed in part the emphasis on reason which characterized much of the thought of the eighteenth century. Gassendi, mathematician and scientist, a critic of Descartes, while rejecting the Epicurean denial of God, held to much of the moral code of Epicurus and, presumably unintentionally, prepared the way for religious indifference. Spinoza believed in God, but his God was pantheistic, not Christian, and his insistence on testing the Old Testament by reason contributed to the questioning of the authority of the Scriptures.

Preparing the way for a later scepticism were writers with an amused semi-detachment which was interested in men but laughed at them rather than seeking to transform them in any Christian fashion. They belong more in *belles lettres* than in philosophy: but they were widely read. Thus François Rabelais (c. 1495–1553), a contemporary of Luther and Loyola, monk, priest, physician, in a coarse, frank humour which has given his name to its kind, caricatured life and pilloried the monasticism and education with which he was familiar. Michel de Montaigne (1533–1592), younger, but still overlapping the years of Luther and Loyola, in his *Essays* helped the French—and Europe—to view in a semi-cynical fashion both life and the religious controversies and wars which characterized his time.

More direct in its challenge to basic Christian convictions was Deism. What usually has that designation was mainly of English development but had repercussions far beyond England. Deism might also be called "natural religion." Its roots were in the distant and near past and outside England. Indeed, it has been said to have precedent in St. Paul's address on the "unknown God," and in the first chapter of his *Letter to the Romans*. It also had foreshadowings in Italian intellectual circles in the sixteenth century and in such French writers as Pierre Charron and Jean Bodin, also of that century.

He who is often said to have been the father of Deism was Lord Herbert of Cherbury (c. 1583–1648).[1] Vain, self-seeking, accommodating himself in part to the loose manners of the upper classes of his day, in his later years disappointed and embittered, he could not be called either high-minded or objective in religion or philosophy. His major treatise on religion had the significant title *De veritate prout distinguitur a revelatione, a verisimile, a possibile et a falso*. Some of the views set forth in it were further developed in *De religione laici* and *De religione gentilium*. In general he and other early Deists appear to have been seeking, in an age marked by intense strife between Roman Catholics and Protestants and between the several varieties of Protestantism, a philosophical basis for religious toleration. Religiously sceptical, in theory holding to a humanitarianism historically derived from Christianity, and wishing religious controversy removed as a factor in domestic and international conflicts, they believed that they found in universal truths discovered through reason a basis on which all intelligent men could and should unite. Lord Herbert held that these truths are that God exists, that He should be worshipped, that virtue and piety are essential to worship, that men should repent of their sins, and that there is a future life with rewards and punishments for deeds done in this life. While Deists differed greatly among themselves, many of

---

[1] A standard account of his life is *The Autobiography of Edward, Lord Herbert of Cherbury, with Introduction, Notes, Appendices, and a Continuation of the Life*, by Sidney L. Lee (New York, Scribner and Welford, 1886, pp. lxiv, 369).

them would agree on at least these convictions and held that if they were accepted the existing intolerance of differing Christian groups would disappear.

In the last quarter of the seventeenth and the first half of the eighteenth century Deism flourished and Deists tended to become increasingly scornful of orthodox Christianity and of all revealed religion. We need not here go into a lengthy account or even give a full catalogue of all the eminent representatives of Deism. A few names will suffice to show the attitude of mind which embodied it. While the classification can be debated, there is some ground for placing Hobbes on the list. Charles Blount (1654-1693), strongly influenced by Lord Herbert of Cherbury, undoubtedly belongs there and contributed to giving Deism fresh vogue.[2] John Toland (1670-1722), Irish-born, successively a Roman Catholic, Protestant, Deist, and pantheist, said to have been the first to whom the later widely used designation "free-thinker" was applied, gained early fame by his *Christianity Not Mysterious,* first published in 1696. In this he claimed to be a Christian, but while affirming that Christ had purged religion of unworthy elements, he declared that Christianity had been corrupted by various elements, including priests, who had brought into it mysteries. John Locke (1632-1704), coming out of a Puritan background, who thought of himself as a Christian, who believed in both "natural religion" and revelation, and who had deep reverence for the Bible, in his *Essay Concerning Human Understanding* set forth views which were utilized by Toland. However, although he unintentionally contributed to Deism, he was not a Deist.[3] The highly educated and sensitive Anthony Ashley Cooper, third Earl of Shaftesbury (1671-1713), said to have been a regular attendant at church and the Holy Communion, is often classed among the Deists.[4] While believing in God, he held Him to be an all-pervading and immanent force, rejected the supernatural, what he deemed God's interference with His work, and supernatural rewards and punishments, and denounced priests. Anthony Collins (1676-1729), building on Locke, became one of the leading Deists. He attacked the credibility of

[2] See excellent brief sketches of English Deism in H. R. Hutcheson, *Lord Herbert of Cherbury's De Religione Laici,* edited and translated (New Haven, Yale University Press, 1944, pp. x, 199), pp. 55 ff.; Abbey and Overton, *The English Church in the Eighteenth Century,* pp. 75–111. See also B. Willey, *The Eighteenth Century Background. Studies in the Idea of Nature in the Thought of the Period* (London, Chatto & Windus, 1940, pp. viii, 302); Roland S. Stromberg, *Religious Liberalism in Eighteenth Century England* (Oxford University Press, 1954, pp. xi, 192); G. R. Cragg, *From Puritanism to the Age of Reason. A Study of Changes in the Religious Thought within the Church of England 1660 to 1700* (Cambridge University Press, 1950, pp. vi, 247); Hazard, *European Thought in the Eighteenth Century,* pp. 395 ff.

[3] Orr, *English Deism,* pp. 83–121.

[4] Benjamin Rand, editor, *The Life, Unpublished Letters, and Philosophical Regimen of Anthony, Earl of Shaftesbury, Author of the Characteristics* (London, Swan Sonnenschein & Co., 1900, pp. xxxi, 535), *passim,* especially p. xxvii; Orr, *op. cit.,* pp. 122–129; Stephen, *History of English Thought in the Eighteenth Century,* Vol. II, pp. 15 ff.; Thomas Fowler, *Shaftesbury and Hutcheson* (London, Sampson Low, Marston, Searle & Rivington, 1882, pp. viii, 240).

the Bible and the priests who were its guardians, found in non-Christian religions parallels to the miraculous elements in the Scriptures, asserted that the prophecies in the Old Testament had not been literally fulfilled in the New Testament, and rejected as evidences of the truth of Christianity the miracles recorded in the New Testament. Matthew Tindal (1656–1733), the son of an Anglican clergyman, a fellow of All Souls College, Oxford, for a brief time in late youth a Roman Catholic, was the author of *Christianity as Old as Creation; or The Gospel a Republication of the Religion of Nature,* which so expressed the views of most Deists that it was regarded as their "Bible." He held that from the beginning and at all times God had "given mankind sufficient means of knowing what He requires of them," that no later or special revelation was needed, that the Bible contains many errors, and that the principles of "natural religion" constitute true Christianity. This "natural religion" was belief in God, worship of God, doing what makes for one's good and happiness, promoting the common happiness, and culminates in a future life.[5]

Deist views were not confined to laymen. To a greater or less degree they were held by numbers of the clergy and were found in many of the sermons preached in the English churches. They tended to exalt reason, to undercut belief in the tenets which distinguish Christianity from other religions, and to emphasize a kind of ethics which ignored the self-giving love of God in Christ. Partly through such preaching and partly through a flood of literature of which we have mentioned only a few outstanding examples, the influence of Deism was widespread in English society.[6]

In some quarters where extreme Deist convictions were not held, reason was stressed, even in the defence of Christianity against the Deists. The most famous of these defences was by Joseph Butler (1692–1752), in his later years Bishop of Durham. In *The Analogy of Religion, Natural and Revealed, to the Course and Constitution of Nature,*[7] Butler, without mentioning the Deists, sought to answer them by appealing to reason. He held that the tenets of Christianity are not contrary to reason and that revelation supplements and does not contradict reason.

During the second half of the eighteenth century Deism tended to decline in Britain. This was partly because no outstanding fresh presentation of it was made. It may also have been in part because through differing greatly among themselves Deists gave evidence that reason did not lead all men to the same conclusions and was therefore not infallible in the search for truth. To some

[5] Orr, *op. cit.,* pp. 129–144; Stephen, *op. cit.,* Vol. I, pp. 134 ff., 201 ff.

[6] Stromberg, *op. cit., passim.*

[7] This work, first published in 1736, went into many editions and for more than a century and a half was regarded as standard. An edition, edited by William E. Gladstone, appeared as late as 1896—*The Works of Joseph Butler* (Oxford, The Clarendon Press, 2 vols., 1896).

degree the decline came about because fresh and cogent thinkers cast doubt upon reason as a means to reaching truth.[8] But in doing so they also seemed further to be undermining Christianity. Thus Henry Dodwell, Jr., son of a staunch supporter of the high Anglican position, in *Christianity not Founded on Argument: and the True Principle of Gospel-Evidence Assigned,* published in 1742, argued that religion is in a sphere outside the proper scope of reason: it depends for its existence and confirmation upon inner, divine light. This both countered head-on the Deist claim that true religion could be reached through reason and cast doubt on the arguments from reason which Christians were employing in defence of their faith.[9] Widely read in his day was the polished, unprincipled, superficially learned, religiously sceptical Henry St. John, Viscount Bolingbroke (1678–1751), whose stormy and chequered political career was accompanied by much criticism, but whose highly rhetorical style appealed to many. More serious was the effect of the Scottish philosopher David Hume (1711–1776).[10] Reared in a Scottish rural parish where the Presbyterian doctrines of his day were taught, in his youth he reacted against Christianity in the form in which he had known it. Educated in the University of Edinburgh, he had years of travel and life on the Continent but spent most of his maturity in the Scottish capital. There he was a member of a brilliant circle which gave intellectual distinction to that city. He was much influenced by Locke but did not adhere to all of Locke's conclusions. He held that the Christian religion cannot be believed by any reasonable person and that mere reason cannot convince us of its truth. He dismissed the Pentateuch as unreliable and maintained that "our most holy religion is founded on faith, not on reason." He challenged the authenticity of miracles as controverting the normal uniformity of nature and therefore held them to be a fragile support for faith. So far he might be said to agree with the Deists. However, he challenged a basic conviction of Deism, causality as ground for belief in God and natural religion. He suggested that observation or experience gives us only association and sequence but affords no basis for assurance that they are necessarily connected or that there is a cause or force which produces them. This scepticism badly undercut not only much of the current philosophical support of Christianity but also the assumptions on which Deism was based. In the nineteenth century Hume had very great influence. He provided an intellectual basis for much of the thought which ran counter to Christianity. It is said that of the

[8] Orr, *op. cit.,* pp. 171–176.

[9] *Ibid.,* pp. 160–165; Stephen, *op. cit.,* Vol. I, pp. 172 ff.

[10] See a somewhat sprightly life, based upon extensive research, by J. Y. T. Greig (John Carruthers), *David Hume* (New York, Oxford University Press, Preface, 1931, pp. 436), and two of Hume's important works in David Hume, *An Enquiry Concerning Human Understanding* and *An Enquiry Concerning Principles of Morals,* reprinted from the posthumous edition of 1777, edited by L. A. Selby Biggs (Oxford, The Clarendon Press. 1894, pp. xl, 349).

eighteenth-century philosophers only Kant equalled him in his impress on succeeding generations.

Parallel with these intellectual currents in Britain and both affecting them and affected by them were others in the Western part of the neighbouring Continent which appeared to be weakening and even destroying Christianity. From Gottfried Wilhelm Leibnitz (1646–1716) came stimulating thought which led some to destructive questioning. Leibnitz regarded himself as a Christian and held firmly to the cardinal Christian convictions. Like his slightly older contemporary, John Locke, he was a Protestant and in a day of religious strife advocated religious toleration. As did Locke, he held that the Christian belief in God and Christian ethics are compatible with reason. He revered the Bible because it was authenticated by marks of supernatural intervention, but argued that the interpretation of the Bible should be controlled by reason. In Germany, divided as it was between Protestants and Roman Catholics, and where the memories of the Thirty Years' War springing out of the contesting faiths were still fresh in men's minds, Leibnitz laboured to bring about peace between Lutherans and Roman Catholics. Although he argued that faith is consistent with reason, the questions which Leibnitz raised, his failure satisfactorily to answer some of them, including his assertion that moral evil is consistent with his conviction that the universe is the best possible world, in some minds stimulated doubt.[11] While he had respect for both faith and reason, the tendency of many of those who read him was to emphasize reason at the expense af faith.

The philosophical and religious views of Leibnitz were continued in modified form by Christian Wolff (1679–1754). Wolff taught at Leipzig, Halle, and Marburg and exerted a wide influence. His emphasis upon the use, dependability, and sufficiency of reason made faith difficult for many. At Halle, a chief focal point of the Pietism of which we are to say more presently, his views aroused so much opposition that he was forced to leave, but in his later years, after a long period at Marburg, Frederick the Great reinstated him. His influence at Halle tended to reinforce the trend towards rationalism which undercut the warmth of conviction that had made that university a radiating centre of Pietism. Some of his pupils, while professing to defend the Christian faith, adopted rationalistic and mathematical approaches which for many shook confidence in the acts of God in revelation.

Leibnitz and Wolff contributed to the intellectual movement which spread

[11] Among the many editions of all or parts of Leibnitz's writings and of the voluminous books on him, see G. W. Leibnitz, *Theodicy: Essays on the Goodness of God, the Freedom of Man and the Origin of Evil*, edited with an Introduction by Austin Farrar, translated by E. M. Huggard from C. J. Gerhardt's edition of the *Collected Philosophical Works, 1875–90* (London, Routledge and Kegan Paul, 1951, pp. 448).

over much of Western Europe in the eighteenth century and which, from the enthusiastic designation given it by those committed to it, was known as the Enlightenment, or, in German, the *Aufklärung*.[12] It sought through the use of reason the emancipation of man from the shackles of the past. It was popular among the intellectuals and permeated other sections of society, especially the upper and middle classes. Much of it was Deistic, but some of it tended to thoroughgoing scepticism and atheism. In general it was contemptuous of belief in "revealed religion." It regarded scholasticism as outworn and gave an opprobrious, scornful connotation to the term "medieval." It thus weakened or destroyed the faith of many whose theology, directly or indirectly, was supported by the methods of the school men of the Middle Ages.

In Germany, one of the outstanding figures in the *Aufklärung* was the Jew Moses Mendelssohn (1729–1786). He held that no religion is absolutely true and that different religions may be best for various individuals and cultures. Another was Gotthold Ephraim Lessing (1729–1791), the son of a pastor, a friend of Mendelssohn, who, as a writer of prose, a poet, and a playwright, had a wide and profound effect. He maintained that nobility of character is found among the adherents of more than one religion and in his play *Nathan der Weise* made a Jew his hero. He held to the religion of reason and attacked miracles, prophecies, and some of the characters in the Bible.

Hermann Samuel Reimarus (1694–1768), while in England in his youth, acquired Deistic views and during a long life as professor of Hebrew and Oriental languages in Hamburg spread convictions which were contrary to much in Christianity. After his death Lessing gave his ideas further circulation by publishing fragments of his writings. Reimarus championed natural religion to the disparagement of revealed religion. He brought to the records of the life of Jesus the tests which he would apply to other ancient histories and in doing so ruled out the miraculous.

Somewhat similar were the effects of the writing and teaching of Johann Salomo Semler (1725–1791), in his mature years professor of theology and head of the theological faculty of the erstwhile Pietistic University of Halle. Although he insisted that he was an orthodox believer and attacked the views of Reimarus, he took a rationalistic approach to the faith and was a pioneer in the kind of critical study of the Bible which shook the faith of many.

A little later were Johann Gottfried von Herder (1744–1803), Johann Wolfgang von Goethe (1749–1832), Johann Christoph Friedrich von Schiller (1759–1805), and Immanuel Kant (1724–1804). Since their major works were produced either on the eve of the outbreak of revolution or during the course of revolution, we must come back to them in the next chapter. They were born and

[12] See a brief popular but competent survey in Heinrich Hoffmann-Bern, *Die Aufklärung* (Tübingen, J. C. B. Mohr, 1912, pp. 47).

largely shaped in the period before revolution became spectacular and to no small degree they were sons of the *Aufklärung,* either as its exponents or as critics of some of its trends. All three, including Herder, a court preacher, while coming from a background shaped by Christianity, troubled the orthodox by their views and to many appeared to be discrediting Christianity.

In the eighteenth century France was the scene of much vigorous thought which had striking effects not only in that country but also on much of the Occident and in later centuries on much of mankind. The general trend was to contribute to the Enlightenment and to weaken Christianity.

Among the pioneers was Pierre Bayle (1647-1706), the son of a Calvinist minister. In his youth a convert to Roman Catholicism through his Jesuit education, he abjured the Roman Catholic faith for Calvinism and held chairs in Reformed universities. A sceptic, holding reason and faith as mutually exclusive, his writings, especially his *Dictionnaire historique et critique,* were to be drawn on by later challengers of Christianity.

The most widely read of the French authors of the period were Voltaire and Rousseau. Voltaire (1694-1778), whose real name was François Marie Arouet, was a Deist. He attacked the Bible, the Church, priests, and all which seemed to him to be oppressive. Vain, irascible, making many enemies but quite unwilling to suffer martyrdom, he was not profound and owed his enormous popularity partly to the fashion in which he conformed to the intellectual temper of the times, partly to the volume of his literary output, and partly to the skill with which he handled his pen. Witty, vitriolic in his onslaughts on individuals, institutions, and ideas with which he disagreed, depending more on ridicule than on solid argument, for many he made Christianity seem 'ridiculous.'[13] He contributed mightily to the revolutionary storms which broke soon after his death.

Also contributory to these storms was Jean Jacques Rousseau (1712-1778).[14] Gifted with his pen, highly sentimental and emotional, so far as he was anything religiously he was a Deist. In contrast with Voltaire he never scoffed at the Church or at the orthodoxy of his day. Reared a Protestant, in his youth he technically became a Roman Catholic and remained such for many years. Then, also technically, and to regain his citizenship in Geneva, he returned to Prot-

[13] Of the prodigious output of and about Voltaire we may single out for mention, not because they are the best but because they are useful, the semi-popular life by Alfred Noyes, *Voltaire* (New York, Sheed and Ward, 1936, pp. 643); as a record of the influence exerted on him by British Deism Norman L. Torrey, *Voltaire and the English Deists* (New Haven, Yale University Press, 1930, pp. x, 224); John Viscount Morley, *Voltaire* (London, Macmillan & Co., 1923, pp. xiii, 365); and Hazard, *European Thought in the Eighteenth Century,* pp. 402-415.

[14] Out of the voluminous literature by Rousseau and dealing with Rousseau we may select *The Confessions of Jean Jacques Rousseau* (New York, Random House, 1945, pp. 683), and John Viscount Morley, *Rousseau and His Era* (London, Macmillan & Co., 2 vols., 1923).

estantism. In neither move was there real religious conviction. The effect of his writings was either to the neglect or to the repudiation of Christianity.

A notable group of writers, some Deists, some atheists, were associated with the *Encyclopédie,* published in seventeen volumes with supplementary volumes of plates from 1751 to 1765. More a tract for the times than a work of exact scholarship, it enlisted writers who attacked the Church, Christianity, and the existing government. Although the publishers deleted some of the more extreme passages, it aroused immense excitement and provoked strenuous opposition and criticism. Among its contributors was Paul Heinrich Dietrich Holbach (1723–1789), of German birth, whose mansion in Paris was a hospitable centre of the critical spirits of the day. Denying immortality and the existence of God, he vigorously denounced Christianity. Another was Denis Diderot (1713–1784). His was the labouring oar of editing the *Encyclopédie* and he wrote many of its articles. Educated by the Jesuits, he reacted from their teachings and eventually swung from Deism to the atheistic views of Holbach.[15] The mathematician Jean le Rond d'Alembert (1717–1763), a long-time friend of Voltaire, contributed many articles, including some on science and mathematics. Voltaire and Rousseau brought in Deistic views. The Marquis de Condorcet (1743–1794), a Jesuit-educated mathematician, violently averse to all religion, including especially Christianity, and an ardent believer in human progress, was one of the authors. Some of the other contributors, such as Montesquieu and Turgot, were not such outspoken critics of Christianity, but they represented a freedom of thought and a desire for religious tolerance which disturbed the orthodox.

The physician Julien Offray de la Mettrie (1709–1751), who died in the year in which the first issue of the *Encyclopédie* appeared, although once a student of theology under the Jansenists, became a thoroughgoing materialist, denying immortality and the existence of God and finding the end of life in the pleasures of the senses. The writings of the crudely hedonistic Claude Adrian Helvétius (1715–1771) tended in the same direction. So did those of the priest Étienne Bobbot de Condillac (1715–1780). Although he professed to hold to the faith in which he had been ordained, Condillac's psychology and theory of knowledge, influenced by Locke, could be so interpreted as to have materialistic implications.

These philosophers, as they were generally known, were intent on improving society. They rejected the conception of human nature which holds to original sin and the depravity of man. They maintained that through profiting by experience and the use of their reason men could achieve a perfect society.

---

[15] See an important study, Joseph Edmund Barker, *Diderot's Treatment of the Christian Religion in the Encyclopédie* (New York, King's Crown Press, 1941, pp. 143). See also Hazard, *op. cit.,* pp. 378 ff.

For the most part they were humanitarians, professing to desire and often actually working for the welfare of mankind. Believing in human progress, they were persuaded that essential to it was the freeing of men's minds from the shackles of ignorance and superstition.

In some respects theirs was a truncated and secularized version of the Christian hope. Educated, as most of them were, under Christian auspices, some by Jesuits and others by strict Protestants, while to a greater or less extent rejecting the faith in which they had been nourished, they inherited much from it. Utilizing what had come to them from it, they were setting in motion currents of thought and action which threatened the very existence of Christianity.[16]

The threat to Christianity seemed the more alarming when contrasts are noted between the late seventeenth and the eighteenth century on the one hand and some earlier centuries on the other. The philosophers of the seventeenth and eighteenth centuries, who with their Deistic and even atheistic rejection of historic Christianity most attracted the attention of Western Europeans, were strikingly different from the great intellectuals, chief among them Thomas Aquinas, who stood out like mountain peaks in the thirteenth century. The latter were convinced believers who devoted the energies of powerful minds to the understanding and support of the Christian faith. Voltaire enjoyed much the kind of popularity in the eighteenth century that Erasmus evoked in the sixteenth century. Each was a temperamental individualist and wielded his pen in a manner which evoked laughter and stirred thought. Yet Erasmus, while deploring much in the Christianity of his day, wished to be loyal to the faith. As one compares the *Confessions* of Rousseau with the *Confessions* of Augustine the contrast is even more striking. The latter, from the fifth century, records the spiritual pilgrimage of one who out of moral impotence had been made strong by what he believed was the work of God in him. The former, from the eighteenth century, is the record of a sordid, vain life which, touched superficially by Christianity, in spite of many good impulses never matured and ended in moral defeat and madness. That in many circles the *Confessions* of Rousseau were read instead of those of Augustine might be regarded as a symptom of the progressive de-Christianization of Christendom.

The contrast was also seen in the field of history. Augustine's *De Civitate Dei*, written in the dark days when the Roman Empire was disintegrating and setting forth a conspectus of the entire sweep of mankind's record which

[16] A very stimulating little book in which this thesis is developed is Carl L. Becker, *The Heavenly City of the Eighteenth-Century Philosophers* (New Haven, Yale University Press, 1932, pp. 168). See also a thoughtful study, Charles Frankel, *The Faith of Reason: the Idea of Progress in the French Enlightenment* (New York, King's Crown Press, 1948, pp. x, 165). On the conception of progress see J. B. Bury, *The Idea of Progress. An Inquiry into Its Origin and Growth* (London, Macmillan & Co., 1920, pp. xv, 377).

was to culminate beyond history in the eternal happiness of the City of God and of its citizens, untainted by evil,[17] had for centuries been the inspiration of thoughtful minds in Western Europe. Now there appeared, in the stately, measured prose which was in accord with the music and much of the poetry of the period, and buttressed by prodigious research, *The Decline and Fall of the Roman Empire,* by Edward Gibbon. Gibbon dealt with the story that had engaged the attention of Augustine. From his heritage, for his father had had for tutor the high Anglican William Law, famous for his *Serious Call to a Devout and Holy Life,* who profoundly influenced the Wesleys, he might have been expected to have been earnestly Christian. Indeed, in his earlier years he was a Protestant, under devout Protestant tutelage, and after a brief excursion into Roman Catholicism he returned to that faith. Yet, succumbing to the prevailing intellectual climate of opinion derived from circles which included d'Alembert and Diderot, he described the story which he had set himself to narrate as "the triumph of barbarism and religion." [18] By religion he meant Christianity. With consummate irony he attacked that faith, all the more cogently because, to avoid the legal penalties which a more forthright onslaught might have incurred, he did so in thinly veiled fashion.[19] The immediate and continued popularity of the work—its publication was begun in 1776 and was completed in 1788 and it was promptly greeted with wide acclaim—was due partly to its scholarship and literary style and partly to its being congenial to the anti-Christian temper of a large proportion of the reading public.

The fact that so much of the literature of Deism, rationalism, and scepticism was in French helped to promote its circulation. Thanks to the predominance of France in Western Europe through the Grand Monarch, French culture was widely popular and French was the language of diplomacy and of polite society. Accordingly, ideas expressed in French gained extensive currency.

DEISM AND FREEMASONRY

A development in which Deism was influential was the growth and spread of Freemasonry. Most of Freemasonry was not anti-Christian, but in some of its forms it became atheistic. As it was known in the eighteenth and subsequent centuries Freemasonry was a continuation of organizations of masons which were in the tradition of the guilds that flourished in the Middle Ages. At least as early as the seventeenth century there began to be admitted to the local organizations, or lodges, of masons in the British Isles those who did not practise the craft: to the "working" or "operative" masons were added the

[17] Augustine, *De Civitate Dei,* Book XXII, especially Chap. XXX.

[18] Edward Gibbon, *The Decline and Fall of the Roman Empire,* edited by J. B. Bury (London, Methuen & Co., 7 vols., 1899–1902), Vol. VII, p. 308.

[19] *Ibid.,* Chaps. XV and XVI in Vol. II, pp. 1–323.

"speculative" or "non-operative" masons. In time "speculative" masons became predominant. Some clergymen joined. The constitutions, rituals, and symbols were elaborated and modified. In them Deistic influences were strong. Belief in "the Great Architect of the Universe" was cherished. Here was an attempt at a "universal religion, or the religion of nature" as one of the constitutions phrased it, a common minimum religious belief which could unite all good men who had theistic convictions.

In the eighteenth century Freemasonry spread rapidly. In the British Isles its lodges multiplied, and numbers sprang up in various countries on the Continent of Europe and among those of European blood in America and India. In 1773 the Grand Orient of France was founded, exclusively national. Under the impact of the extreme wing of the Enlightenment, in 1772 a schism occurred in the Grand Orient. One wing, atheistic, rejected belief in the "Great Architect of the Universe." Its lodges became centres of anti-Christian, especially anti-clerical and anti-Roman Catholic, activity. Yet it wished, in accord with the optimism of the Enlightenment, through natural law to regenerate humanity. Although its members were small minorities of the total population, since many of them were influential its lodges became a serious threat to the churches, particularly to the Roman Catholic Church. In 1738 a Papal condemnation of Masonry was issued and in 1751 the Pope forbade to Roman Catholics any relation with Masonry on pain of excommunication.[20]

THE "ENLIGHTENMENT" AND ITS THREAT SPREAD

From the British Isles, Germany, and France, where it had its rise and chief expressions, the Enlightenment spread through most of the European portions of Christendom and to some places overseas where Christianity had been planted.

It was to be expected that the menace would be especially marked in the British Isles, Germany, and France. Here, as we have suggested, large numbers of the intelligentsia and of the upper and middle classes, while maintaining a nominal allegiance to the faith, were Deists or atheists. Even many of the clergy, both Protestant and Roman Catholic, compromised. In Germany the *Aufklärung* captured the universities, both professors and students. Opposition there was, but it seemed to be rear-guard action to defend a foredoomed cause. The new movements of which we are to speak a little later, precursors of great awakenings, as yet affected only minorities. In the strongest countries of Western Europe Christianity seemed moribund.

[20] Douglas Knoop, *The Genesis of Speculative Masonry* (printed for private circulation, 1941, pp. 31); Gaston Martin, *La Franc-Maçonnerie Française et la Préparation de la Révolution* (Paris, Les Presses Universitaires de la Révolution, 1926, pp. xviii, 306); J. S. M. Ward in *The Encyclopædia Britannica*, 14th ed., Vol. IX, pp. 732–738.

From these throbbing centres of fresh thought and hopeful dreams of a world served by enlightened men and from which the shackles of priestcraft and superstition had been stricken, the currents of the *Aufklärung* flowed outward. Their effects were mixed.

The Enlightenment made itself felt in Scandinavia. In Denmark and in Norway, the latter then governed from Denmark, it was potent.[21] In Denmark it accelerated a decline in church attendance which was already under way. In Norway it contributed to a rise of national consciousness.[22] In Sweden the Church was in poor condition to meet the new ideas. It had lost its prestige, partly through the corruption of the clergy. The populace were suffering from an epidemic of alcoholism which made the period one of moral and spiritual decay. In the middle of the century the new intellectual movements found convenient channels through Queen Louise Ulrica, a sister of the Deistic Frederick the Great, and her son, Gustavus III. Some of the higher clergy were affected by the Enlightenment, but in a mild way. The writings of Wolff were influential among the theologians and in part shaped their apologetics.[23] To the educated of Finland the Enlightenment brought, as elsewhere, indifference or hostility towards the Church. Among the clergy its early effects were more constructive than destructive. It stimulated the bringing of empirical tests to the support of religion and encouraged more emphasis upon the social and economic application of the Gospel.[24]

It was to be expected that, small countries that they were and bordered by the lands in which the Enlightenment was potent, the Netherlands and Switzerland would be affected. The atmosphere of the Netherlands was one of weariness and indifference after the intense and bitter religious controversies among Protestants during the preceding two centuries: the rationalism and religious tolerance of the Enlightenment found a welcome. For the most part the clergy of the Reformed Church, established as it was by law and under the control of the state, resisted the new currents. Societies and other organizations arose to defend the faith against the new and presumably destructive influences. The clergy were suspicious of whatever to them smacked of Descartes or Spinoza. The prevailing theology was little if at all influenced either by these two philosophers or by Leibnitz or Wolff. However, among the dissenting minorities with liberal tendencies the new currents were marked.[25] The Swiss record was also mixed, but in a somewhat different way.

[21] Koch, *Danmarks Kirke gennem Tiderne*, pp. 103–120; V. Ammundsen, in Siegmund-Schultze, *Ekklesia: Die Kirche in Dänemark*, pp. 37–40.

[22] A. Brandrud, in Siegmund-Schultze, *Ekklesia: Die Kirche von Norwegen*, p. 38.

[23] K. B. Westman, in Siegmund-Schultze, *Ekklesia: Die Kirche in Schweden*, p. 49.

[24] M. Ruuth, in Siegmund-Schultze, *Ekklesia: Die Kirche in Finnland*, pp. 46, 47.

[25] J. A. Cramer, in Siegmund-Schultze, *Ekklesia: Die Evangelischen Kirchen der Niederlande*, pp. 20, 21.

In the Protestant churches the inherited theology tended to be modified by rationalism. The writings of the Genevan Jean Alphonse Turrettini (1671–1737), with their effort to bring about the union of Protestants through by-passing the confessions which separated them, lent themselves to rationalistic interpretations. A rationalistic twist was given the historic confessions in their free "translations" by Vernet, also of Geneva.[26]

The Enlightenment had repercussions in Roman Catholic circles. Indeed, some of its most extreme exponents had been reared as Roman Catholics and educated by the Jesuits. As was to be expected, the impact of the Enlightenment upon the Roman Catholic Church was especially marked in France and Germany. It was also seen elsewhere. It differed from place to place and even from person to person. Some bishops, priests, and teachers opposed it. Others, especially among the teachers of theology, sought to adapt the faith to it. It was in the second half of the eighteenth century that the changes became most striking. In general they made for departure from the scholastic approach inherited from the Middle Ages. In some regions, notably in Germany, pilgrimages were discredited, and the life of the faithful was centred more in the parish churches. Stress was laid on the improvement of life here and now and upon achieving a better human society at the expense of preparation for life beyond the grave. More emphasis was placed upon preaching and instruction than upon the mass and the other sacraments. In Germany, where they were in close contact with each other, the distinction between the Roman Catholic and Protestant forms of the faith tended to be glossed over and some priests moved into Protestantism as more congenial to the new ideas than Roman Catholicism.[27] In Italy, Spain, and Portugal the Enlightenment was less marked than in Germany and France. Especially in Spain and Portugal the traditional adherence to scholasticism was maintained. But in them the persistence of the old forms was more an evidence of sterility than of vigour.[28]

Deism early made its way into the Thirteen Colonies which were soon to become the United States of America. So far as they had any faith, the overwhelming majority of the colonials were Protestants. Their ties were with the British Isles. Books were imported from Britain. Among them were the works of the English Deists. They influenced many, including some who were prominent in the nascent nation. Benjamin Franklin was clearly a Deist. In the mid-eighteenth century Deistic views spread widely in New England, New York, Pennsylvania, and Virginia, especially among the educated. The entrance and

---

[26] E. Staehelin, in Siegmund-Schultze, *Ekklesia: Die Evangelischen Kirchen der Schweitz*, pp. 25, 26; E. Choisy in *The New Schaff-Herzog Encyclopedia of Religious Knowledge*, Vol. XII, pp. 48, 49.

[27] On a summary of the German scene see Schnabel, *Deutsche Geschichte im neunzehnten Jahrhundert*, Vol. IV, pp. 10–13.

[28] Hocedez, *Histoire de la Théologie au XIXe Siècle*, Vol. I, pp. 13 ff., 40.

growth of Freemasonry encouraged them. As we are to see in the next chapter, during the time when the Colonies were gaining their independence and in the early days of the new nation they gained in popularity.[29]

The Enlightenment was potent in Russia. Here it became fashionable in aristocratic circles, which looked with admiration to the culture of Western Europe. During the reign of Peter the Great the shift to the West was marked. On the death of his older and half-witted brother in 1696 Peter became sole tsar. Then twenty-four years of age, endowed with an indomitable will and prodigious vigour, he conceived a curiosity for the arts and sciences of the West which led him to an extended journey in several of its countries. He introduced to Russia much of what he had seen. Western currents of thought flowed into Russia even more strongly under the highly unscrupulous and immoral but imperious German who ruled from 1762 to 1796 and who is usually called Catherine the Great. She prided herself on being "enlightened." She corresponded with Voltaire and d'Alembert and was a disciple of the Encyclopedists. Thanks in part to the impulse given by Catherine, Voltaire's writings had an enormous circulation, both in French and in Russian translations. Rousseau and the Encyclopedists, including Diderot, were popular. It became fashionable to scoff at miracles, to praise "reason" and "natural religion," and, while outwardly conforming to it, to scorn the Church and to laugh at its beliefs and the morals inculcated by it. Freemasonry entered, spread among the upper classes, and helped to give circulation to Deistic views. In it members found support for a morality partly divorced from the Church. A secularistic nationalism gained headway. Serious thinkers laid the foundations for the radicalism which sought to shatter what it deemed the injustices and irrational elements in the existing political, religious, and social structure of society. Philosophical movements influenced by Leibnitz and Wolff estranged their adherents from the Church but not always from Christianity.[30]

The Threat of State Control

Added to the threat of the undermining of the faith through intellectual currents was that of the subservience of the churches to the state and the utilization by the state of Christianity and the latter's institutions for its own purposes.

This had long been a peril. From the day when a representative of the Roman Empire delivered Christ to be crucified, tension had existed between governments and the followers of Christ. Before the Roman Empire became officially Christian the tension was expressed in persecution. Later it was seen

[29] Morais, *Deism in Eighteenth Century America*, pp. 13–28, 54–84; Koch, *Republican Religion*, *passim*.
[30] Zenkovsky, *A History of Russian Philosophy*, Vol. I, pp. 44–99.

in the efforts of the various governments which called themselves Christian to control the Church and to make it and the faith subservient to them. In the eastern continuation of the Roman Empire and in the states, such as Russia, which perpetuated its tradition, the efforts were largely successful: what was known as Cæsaropapism was the rule. One of the commonplaces of the history of Western Europe is the chronic struggle between Church and state which punctuated the Middle Ages. The state sought to dominate the Church and the Church insisted on being autonomous in the realms which its leaders believed to be its responsibility.

In the eighteenth century it looked as though the contest had been decided in favour of the state and that the Church and the faith of which it was the avowed vehicle were being made fully ancillary to the civil government. This was true whether the form of Christianity was Protestant, Roman Catholic, or that of the Eastern Churches. To be sure, in Europe except in the Moslem sections the rulers professed to be Christian and to exercise their functions as Christians. However, in their major concerns they were influenced little if any by Christian principles. Could the faith survive this subordination of the churches to governments which at best only slightly conformed to Christian standards?

From the beginning of Protestantism control by the state had characterized most of the churches through which the Reformation found expression. In country after country the secular rulers had sponsored the Reformation and had utilized it to bring the Church in their domains under their full control. Indeed, it was in Protestant circles that the term "Erastianism" was coined to describe the supremacy of the state in ecclesiastical affairs. In predominantly Lutheran countries the control was marked. Whether in Denmark, Norway, or Sweden, or in the several Lutheran states in Germany, the secular ruler was in the saddle.

In Germany the control was furthered by the principle of *cuius regio, eius religio* which had been embodied in the Peace of Augsburg (1555) and which had been weakened but not annulled by the Peace of Westphalia (1648) which ended the Thirty Years' War. In Protestant territories in Germany the prince was in theory *summus episcopus*. This meant that he controlled the administration of the Church in his domains. However, he could not ordain clergy nor could he determine doctrine. In the eighteenth century a more extensive control of the Protestant churches in Germany was advocated by the territorial system. The leading formulator and exponent was the jurist Thomasius (1655–1728). Sympathetic towards Pietism and a critic of Wolff, he lectured at the University of Leipzig and then in Halle. The territorial system held that the Church was purely a state institution, that the authority of the state was not a continuation of episcopal jurisdiction, but that it embodied the *ius circa sacra* and that in the interest of the welfare of the general good it could fully control the Church and thus could appoint pastors, regulate the liturgy, and dominate in other matters. It was opposed by the collegium system, which, while granting to the state the *ius circa sacra,* through holding that the Church had *ius in sacra* accorded the latter a nearer approach to autonomy. Because it was in accord with the temper of the times the territorial system prevailed.[31]

In England, Wales, and Ireland the established church was subject to Parliaments and the monarch. Parliaments legislated for it and the monarch appointed its higher clergy. Convocation, through which the Church of England acted as a body, did not meet, except formally, from 1717 until well along in the nineteenth century.[32] In England, moreover, many of the parish clergy were appointed by laymen.

In some places the Reformed Churches were not as tightly under the domination of the civil authorities as were the Lutheran churches and the Church of England. For example, through its General Assembly the Church of Scotland was more nearly autonomous than was the Church of England. Yet it also had ties which in some matters made it subject to the state, and in many of its parishes the minister was appointed by the lay proprietor of the lands in which the parish lay. In the Netherlands in the eighteenth century, while the Reformed Church had preserved intact the doctrines which it had formulated through synods, it was actually the servant of the state. Inwardly divided, it had no body of its own to bring it unity and was dependent on the authority of the civil government.[33]

However, in Protestantism minorities existed which did not conform to the state church. Often they maintained their independence in the face of persecution. On the Continent were Mennonites, a branch of the Anabaptists, scattered by persecution and finding haven in the Netherlands and Russia. In Germany were several small groups, outstanding among them the Moravians. In the mountain valleys of Italy the remnants of the Waldensians had taken refuge. While the Netherlands did not have full religious liberty, the Government was less intolerant than were most others, and several Protestant minorities maintained an inconspicuous existence. In England and Wales were fairly large groups of nonconformists. At the outset of the eighteenth century the most prominent were the Independents, Presbyterians, Baptists, and Quakers. They and the remnants of Roman Catholics were under legal disabilities but they were permitted. In Ireland, where the Anglicans were the established church, there were Presbyterians as well as the Roman Catholic majority. In

[31] Heussi, *Kompendium der Kirchengeschichte,* p. 342.

[32] Moorman, *A History of the Church in England,* pp. 349, 350.

[33] J. A. Cramer, in Siegmund-Schultze, *Ekklesia: Die Evangelische Kirchen der Niederlande,* pp. 21, 22.

Scotland in the eighteenth century the Episcopalians, earlier favoured by the Stuart kings, were not the state church: sturdy minorities of dissenting Presbyterians also asserted their independence as against the (Presbyterian) Church of Scotland.[34] In the Thirteen Colonies in North America, where most of the colonies had established churches—in New England, except for Rhode Island, Congregational, and in several others the Church of England—dissenters were numerous. A few colonies, notably Rhode Island and Pennsylvania, did not have a state church.

In spite of theoretical administrative control by the Pope, the Roman Catholic Church tended to be grouped by national churches. They were held together in doctrine and in communion by the tie with the Vatican, but in several of the major countries the Pope had little or no voice in the naming of the bishops and his decrees could be circulated and obeyed only with the consent of the crown. The monarch named the bishops and in other ways dominated the Church in his realms. The danger of the secularization of the official structure of the Church and of the weakening of its witness to the Gospel was fully as great in Roman Catholicism as in Protestantism. Indeed, it was even more so. The Roman Catholic Church did not have dissenting minorities which maintained their independence from the state-controlled church such as we have noted in Protestantism. The nearest approach to the dimensions attained by them was Jansenism, of which we are to say more in a moment, and even of those affected by this movement only a minority withdrew and became a distinct ecclesiastical body.

In Spain, although a rigorous orthodoxy was enforced by the Inquisition, the monarchs were jealous of their control of the Church. As far back as the fifteenth century Pope Sixtus IV granted to Ferdinand and Isabella the right to nominate bishops.[35] His successor conceded to these two monarchs the patronage of all churches and convents in lands conquered from the Moors.[36] In the first decade of the sixteenth century Popes granted to the kings of Spain the tithes in the rapidly expanding Spanish colonial territories and the *real patronato,* the right of nomination to the benefices in these territories. This gave the crown absolute authority over the Church in all these far-flung domains.[37] Moreover, the kings did not allow Papal briefs or decrees to be given publicity in their realms without their consent. When, at the outset of the eighteenth century (1700), the Bourbons acquired possession of the throne of Spain, it was to be expected that they would insist on much the same control

[34] On seventeenth-century dissent in Scotland see the excellent study by G. D. Henderson, *Religious Life in Seventeenth-Century Scotland* (Cambridge University Press, 1937, pp. 311), pp. 100–116, 158–219.
[35] McSorley, *An Outline History of the Church,* p. 495.
[36] *Ibid.,* p. 497.
[37] *Ibid.,* p. 568.

of the Church that they were exercising in France. As a result of concordats with the Holy See, the most important being that of 1753, in return for a large financial grant, the crown was entrusted with all ecclesiastical patronage.[38] In 1762 what was called a pragmatic sanction ordered that all decrees from Rome, except briefs and dispensations in matters of conscience, have the permission of the state before they were published or transmitted to their destination.[39]

The record in Portugal was very similar. There, too, was orthodoxy enforced by the Inquisition. There, also, by various stages the crown obtained a large degree of control of the Church. As in the Spanish overseas possessions, so in the Portuguese colonial empire, acquired in breath-taking fashion in the fifteenth and sixteenth centuries in Brazil, along the coasts of Africa and India, and in Malaya, the East Indies, and China, the crown was given the *padroado* of all benefices. Indeed, Portugal insisted on attempting to extend it outside its actual possessions into all India and China. Serious conflicts with the Papacy followed which were only slowly resolved and which extended into the twentieth century.[40]

What was known as Gallicanism had a long history. Its proponents asserted that the liberties it claimed went back for more than a thousand years. As eventually formulated, in the main it insisted that by divine decree the kings had powers which limited those of the Pope, that infallibility rested not with the Pope but with general councils and the bishops, and that the customs of particular churches also had rights as against the Pope. Along the way several landmarks in the assertion of Gallicanism had been established. One of the most memorable was the Pragmatic Sanction of 1438, which sought to limit the authority of the Pope in the French realms. In 1682 Louis XIV, in spite of an orthodoxy which ostensibly impelled him in his attempt to exterminate Protestantism in his domains, declared that the king had the right to receive the fees from all vacant sees and to fill vacant sees at his pleasure, that bishops could not go out of the realm without royal consent (a not too subtle way of regulating their appeals to Rome), that without royal permission no Papal legate could exercise his functions in France, that the king could legislate for the Church, and that no Papal bulls or letters could be executed without the sanction of the king. At royal initiative the declaration was endorsed by an assembly of the bishops and other clergy of France. Successive Papal protests eventually (1693) brought about a partial disavowal by Louis XIV, but Gal-

[38] Peers, *Spain, the Church and the Orders,* p. 58.
[39] Pastor, *The History of the Popes,* Vol. XXXVII, p. 25.
[40] Adelhelm Jann, *Die katholischen Missionen in Indien, China und Japan: ihre Organisation und das portugiesische Patronat vom 15 bis ins 18 Jahrhundert* (Paderborn, Ferdinand Schöningh, 1915, pp. xxviii, 540), *passim.*

licanism persisted through the eighteenth century. Gallican principles also spread to the Low Countries, and in 1786 the Council of Pistola attempted to acclimatize it in some of the Italian states.[41]

For a time Gallicanism was complicated by Jansenism. Jansenism arose in the seventeenth century through doctrinal affirmations which, claiming support in the writings of Augustine, spoke of human depravity, declared that freedom of the will was limited, and insisted that salvation was only through the irresistible grace of God. With it went moral rigourism. Jansenist views spread widely in France and the Low Countries and enlisted among others the ardent and brilliant Pascal. Prolonged controversy followed. In it the Popes, encouraged by the Jesuits, came out against Jansenism and expressed their condemnation in a succession of bulls. Some of the French bishops supported Jansenist views and appealed from the Pope to a general council. In 1718 the Pope condemned the idea of such an appeal. Many were fearful that the action of Rome in tracking down Jansenism would infringe on Gallican liberties. To some degree, therefore, Jansenism strengthened Gallicanism.[42]

Among many the Jansenist controversy created an intellectual uncertainty as to where truth lay and led them to espouse a religious toleration based upon the conviction that absolute truth had not been found and that freedom to search for it should be permitted.[43]

The trend towards national churches under the control of the civil authorities, and, in Germany, under the great prince bishops who combined civil and ecclesiastical functions, was given an impetus by what was known as Febronianism. This took its name from the pseudonym, Justinus Febronius, under which Nikolaus von Hontheim (1701–1790), Auxiliary Bishop of Trier (Treves), wrote. He seems to have received part of his inspiration from a former teacher of his at Louvain who was an exponent of views akin to Jansenism. In 1763 a book from his pen appeared, *De Statu Ecclesiae et Legitima Potestate Romani Pontificis,* which created a sensation and which, in spite of prompt Papal condemnation (1764), came out in numbers of editions, some of them revisions, and in translation in several languages. While according a priority to the Bishop of Rome, saying that in the early Church he had important functions in unifying and administering the Church, and holding that he was still necessary to the unity of the Church, it held that spurious documents had sanctioned the extension of Papal power far beyond what had been

[41] A. Degert in *The Catholic Encyclopedia,* Vol. VI, pp. 351–356; *Enciclopedia Cattolica,* Vol. V, p. 1898.

[42] *The Catholic Encyclopedia,* Vol. VIII, p. 285; E. Préclin, *Les Jansénistes du XVIIIe Siècle et la Constitution Civile du Clergé* (Paris, Librairie Universitaire J. Gamber, 1929, pp. xxxi, 578), pp. 1–273; Augustin Gazier, *Histoire Générale du Mouvement Janséniste depuis ses Origines jusqu'à Nos Jours,* Vol. I, *passim,* Vol. II, pp. 1–136.

[43] Hocedez, *Histoire de la Théologie au XIXe Siècle,* Vol. I, p. 20.

authorized by Christ or had been true in the early centuries. It maintained that the Pope was simply *primus inter pares* among the bishops and was not infallible and that the authority granted by Christ rested in the entire Church acting through ecumenial councils. It called on the temporal princes to oppose what it deemed Papal usurpations and to resist Papal decrees. It summoned Catholic princes in coöperation with the bishops and on the latter's advice to take action to curb Rome. In effect, it made for national churches 'in which the bishops would be subject to the civil power.

In spite of Papal resistance, Febronian views had wide circulation in France, Spain, Portugal, Italy, the Austrian Netherlands, and Austria. In Germany they reinforced the efforts of the prince bishops to create a national church in which the power of Rome would be greatly reduced.[44]

In the Eastern Churches the authority of the monarchs also weakened the witness to the Gospel. This could not but be true in the lands in which the rulers were Moslems. While in general they tolerated the existence of the churches, Moslem princes insisted on exercising oversight over them and saw to it that the chief ecclesiastics were subservient.

In some respects the Turkish conquest enhanced the powers of the Ecumenical Patriarch in Constantinople. The Sultans made him the responsible head of the Orthodox populations. As such he had civil as well as ecclesiastical functions. Bishops were subject to him and even the heads of the ancient patriarchates of Jerusalem, Antioch, and Alexandria, which in age outranked his see, were often filled by men who were his creatures. In theory and to a certain degree in practice he was elected by a synod of his church. Yet in fact he usually bought his office from the sultan or from Greeks who controlled the synod and retained it through sycophancy. It was customary for bishops to buy their posts. The Turkish rulers held the Patriarch and the bishops responsible for the Orthodox, almost as though they were subordinate rulers of a distinct but subject nation. That meant that the hierarchy were as much civil as ecclesiastical officials.[45]

With some exceptions in the case of outstanding Patriarchs, the Russian Orthodox Church perpetuated the Byzantine tradition of partial subordination to the civil authorities. The subordination was enhanced by Peter the Great. Masterful as he was, Peter made the Church come to heel. In 1700 on the death of the Patriarch he deliberately allowed the post to remain vacant. In 1721 he substituted for it what was customarily known as the Holy Synod. He

---

[44] F. Lauchert in *The Catholic Encyclopedia*, Vol. VI, pp. 23–26; Haag, *Les Origines du Catholicisme Libéral en Belgique*, pp. 78, 79; Hocedez, *op. cit.*, Vol. I, pp. 146, 147.

[45] Papadopoullos, *The History of the Greek Church and People under Turkish Domination*, pp. 1 ff.; Adeney, *The Greek and Eastern Churches*, pp. 311, 312.

appointed its members. In taking this step he declared it to be in fulfilment of his purpose to take upon himself "the care and regulation of the clergy and spiritual order."[46]

THE ENLIGHTENED DESPOTS EXTEND THE CONTROL OF THE STATE OVER THE CHURCH

In the latter part of the eighteenth century what were known as "enlightened despots" further extended the control of the state over the Church. They were monarchs who professed to be governed by the principles of the Enlightenment and to be seeking to improve the lot of their subjects and so of mankind by bringing to their rule the use of reason. Nearly all made at least the outward show of being Christians. Some seem to have been sincere in their profession of faith.[47] Yet they all dealt with the Church in masterful fashion. The political theory under which they operated held that the welfare of men is the purpose of the state and that this can best be attained by absolute monarchs who govern, not for their own benefit or pleasure, but for the good of the ruled. To achieve this good they will be guided by reason and seek to conform to natural law. They were to bring about Utopia. To some extent here was a semi-secularized version of the theory of Christian origin, earlier potent, that the monarch holds his authority from God, must exercise it in accordance with the laws of God as seen in the Scriptures, and must give an account to God of his use of the trust.

Outstanding among the enlightened despots was Frederick II, "the Great" (1712–1786), King of Prussia. Reared in Protestantism by a stern father, he repudiated Christianity, was enamoured of current French thought, and was the patron of such French thinkers as Voltaire and la Mettrie. Calling himself the "first servant of the state" and regarding his great power as a trust, he was an indefatigable worker and increased the efficiency of his bureaucracy. Seeking the aggrandizement of his realms, he engaged in foreign wars which imposed heavy financial burdens on his subjects. Yet, like his predecessors, he drained swamps, built canals, cleared lands, and sought to promote agriculture and industry. While exercising his mordant wit on Christianity, he stood for religious toleration. In his later years, sobered by the responsibilities and trials of his office, on the ground that it made for good morals he sought to strengthen the Church. He insisted on dominating the Church in his realms, whether it was Protestant or Roman Catholic, and reserved the right to appoint all ec-

---

[46] Frere, *Some Links in the Chain of Russian Church History*, pp. 125–130.

[47] A brief, semi-popular, competent summary is in Geoffrey Bruun, *The Enlightened Despots* (New York, Henry Holt & Co., 1929, pp. x, 105). It has an excellent selected bibliography. See also *The Cambridge Modern History*, Vol. VI (Cambridge University Press, 1909).

clesiastics in the Roman Catholic Church in his domains, from parish priests through abbots, canons, provosts, and abbesses to bishops.[48]

A younger contemporary and ardent admirer of Frederick the Great was the Holy Roman Emperor Joseph II (1741–1790). Strongly influenced by Voltaire and the Encyclopedists, and having for an instructor in political science a disciple of Wolff, he was a child of the Enlightenment. When, in 1780, the death of his mother, Maria Theresa, gave him undisputed sovereignty, he sought to rule according to reason and natural law. Like Frederick, he worked hard, but unlike the latter he was maladroit as a diplomat and was not skilled in handling men. Also unlike Frederick, he retained at least an outward respect for the Christian faith and was a communicant of the Roman Catholic Church. In the spirit of the Enlightenment he promoted religious toleration, decreed the legal equality of non-Catholics with Catholics, and sought to curb the power of the Church. He dissolved seven hundred or more monasteries, largely those of the contemplatives, limited the numbers who might be admitted to those which remained, encouraged monks to take up secular occupations, abolished some of the frequent saints' days, replaced diocesan and monastic schools with state institutions, sought to make religious ceremonies less elaborate, and expropriated some ecclesiastical possessions. He had catechisms compiled for the instruction of youth which minimized Catholic dogma and stressed morals. He wished to take from the Church all its endowments and to make its clergy dependent entirely on the state for their subsistence. He would have liked to sever all administrative connexion between the Church and Rome. He appointed bishops, replaced the diocesan seminaries with five general seminaries under the control of the state and with textbooks designed to meet his ideals, and wished to end clerical celibacy. When the Pope, alarmed, came to Vienna to dissuade the Emperor from his course, Joseph received him with every mark of respect but declined to be swerved from his purpose. In his policies Joseph was reinforced by the recently formulated Febronianism and by some of the Catholic scholars in his domains. His religious programme has usually been given the name of Josephism. It spread to some of the states of Italy where Austrian control prevailed or where Austrian influence was strong. The real author of Josephism was the chancellor, Prince Kaunitz. Committed to the Enlightenment, a reader of the *Encyclopédie,* and equipped with an indomitable will, Kaunitz persuaded Marie Theresa and Joseph II to adopt the measures associated with the latter's name.[49]

---

[48] Francis Hanus, *Church and State in Silesia under Frederick II (1740–1786)* (Washington, The Catholic University of America Press, 1944, pp. x, 432), pp. 371 ff.

[49] Ferdinand Maass, *Der Josephismus. Quellen zu seiner Geschichte in Österreich 1760–1790. Amtliche Dokumente aus dem Wiener Haus-, Hof- und Staatsarchiv* (Vienna, Herold, 2 vols., 1951, 1953), in *Österreiches Akademie der Wissenschaften in Wien. Philosophisch-historische Klasse: Fontes rerum Austriacarum: Österreichische Geschichtsquellen, Zweite Abteilung, diplomataria et*

Charles III of Spain (1759–1788) strove to reign as an elightened monarch. Although a devout Roman Catholic, he stressed the authority of the crown in ecclesiastical as in other affairs, curtailed clerical privileges, placed restrictions on the powerful Inquisition, and commanded the bishops to prevent criticism of the Government by the priesthood. Some experts in canon law argued for the independence of the Spanish church from Rome and declared that it went back to Visigothic times.[50]

In Portugal Joseph I (1750–1777), succeeding the dissolute John V (1706–1750), who had done much by his example to lower the moral tone of the nobility and the country, sought to rule in accordance with the principles of the Enlightenment. In this he was reinforced and to no small degree directed by his chief minister, Sebastian Joseph Cavalho, the Marquis of Pombal. The authority of the crown was used to work much-needed reforms in many branches of the Government. In the ecclesiastical realm the power of the Inquisition was curtailed, the authority of the monarch in patronage and the appointment of bishops was affirmed, a school for the nobles was erected under secular administration, and some of the ideas associated with the Enlightenment were introduced into the ancient university of Coimbra.[51]

Catherine II, "the Great" (1729–1796), who ruled Russia with a strong hand from 1762 until her death, was, as we have seen, committed to the Enlightenment. A woman of abounding vigour of body and mind, she read avidly in the literature of that movement. Reared a Protestant, from expediency she conformed to the Russian Orthodox Church but probably had little or no feeling for the Christian faith and was certainly without real commitment to it. She carried further the ecclesiastical policy of Peter the Great and made the Russian Orthodox Church even more a state institution. In 1768 she secularized its property. Thus she rendered the clergy fully dependent on the Government. In accordance with the *Aufklärung* she was tolerant towards forms of religion which dissented from the established church. Since through her share in the partition of Poland many Roman Catholics became her subjects, she established working relations with the Papacy. Yet she maintained the supremacy of the state over the Roman Catholic Church in her realms.

THE DECAY IN THE LIFE OF THE CHURCHES

The mounting threats to Christianity were faced by churches which were in poor condition to meet them. Not only were the large majority of Christians

---

acta, 71. Band, passim; The Cambridge Modern History, Vol. VI, pp. 635–637; Hocedez, *op. cit.,* Vol. I, pp. 147, 148; Pastor, *op. cit.,* Vol. XXXIX, pp. 421–479, Vol. XL, pp. 65–75; McSorley, *op. cit.,* pp. 703, 704, 755, 756.

[50] Hocedez, *op. cit.,* Vol. I, pp. 39, 40; Lea, *Chapters from the Religious History of Spain,* pp. 126–211.

[51] *The Cambridge Modern History,* Vol. VI, pp. 384–388; Hocedez, *op. cit.,* Vol. I, p. 39.

in churches which were increasingly controlled by unsympathetic governments, but the churches themselves largely conformed to the current climate of opinion and accommodated themselves to the less than Christian social and political structure in which they were set. That was true of the Roman Catholic Church, most of the Protestant bodies, and all the Eastern Churches. The churches did not sink to the low levels that they had reached in the dark ages after the collapse of the Roman empire or even as far as they had in the fourteenth and fifteenth centuries before the Catholic and Protestant Reformations and the fresh movements in Russia. Yet recession was marked from the vigour which they had shown in the great awakenings of the sixteenth and seventeenth centuries.

Decline in the Roman Catholic Church

The decline in the Roman Catholic Church was striking. In France the Catholic Reformation, which there had had its latest blooming, seemed to have spent its force. Outwardly the Roman Catholic Church was imposing. Its clergy were given rank before the nobility. They possessed their own central administration and their assemblies met regularly. The Roman Catholic faith was officially that of the state and the procedures associated with the revocation of the Edict of Nantes (1685) had greatly reduced the Protestant minority. While an edict of 1787 slightly eased the position of non-Catholics, public services other than those of Roman Catholics were still forbidden. The Church owned between a tenth and a sixth of the land of the kingdom, and the state could not tax it. Most education was in the hands of the Roman Catholic Church. However, monasticism was losing its appeal and the number of men and boys entering monastic houses was sharply falling off. The decline was hastened by the dissolution, through a royal commission appointed in 1768, of eight orders, the closing of 450 houses, and the prohibition of the taking of monastic vows by youths under twenty-one years of age. In some of the remaining monasteries for men luxury had crept in and morals had declined. In general the houses for women seem to have been in better condition.[52]

Among the secular clergy the situation was diverse. The higher clergy were recruited chiefly from the aristocracy, younger sons for whom provision was made in the Church, and shared the outlook of members of that class. The majority of the bishops had been educated at Saint Sulpice, an institution which by the latter part of the century had departed far from the high standards set in the preceding century by its founder, Jean-Jacques Olier. Some of the bishops were little more than nominal adherents of the faith. Among them Talleyrand (1754–1838) was outstanding. While observing the moral prop-

---

[52] Leflon, *La Crise Révolutionnaire, 1789–1846*, pp. 21–26; Pastor, *op. cit.*, Vol. XL, pp. 97–99.

erties of his position, even before his elevation to the episcopate he was known to be a "free thinker," much influenced by the writings of Voltaire and others who were critical of the Church. Others of the bishops were more at the court than in their sees and entrusted their responsibilities to young archdeacons, strangers in their dioceses. Yet in the latter half of the century several of the bishops, caught up in the humanitarian impulse of the times, were active in improving the economic life of their dioceses. They dug canals, drained marshes, distributed grain, and organized associations of the tillers of the soil. Among the bishops, too, were men who were loyal to the faith and conscientious in the observance of their duties. So, also, the cathedral chapters varied. Some were wealthy and their canons lived in luxury. Others were poor. Parish priests presented no uniform picture. Not a few were worldly and with good incomes. Others, probably the majority, poorly educated and poverty-stricken, lived close to their flocks. In general, most of the seminaries of the Sulpicians, the source of many of the parish priests, in contrast with the mother seminary, maintained their earlier zeal. Numbers of priests, non-resident, had their duties performed by vicars. The latter, appointed from year to year, were insecure. Some parish priests led scandalous lives. Others devoted themselves to their charges and diverted much of their income to the poor. In general, the parish priests, in poverty, looked with enmity upon the higher clergy. Many of the clergy to a greater or less degree subscribed to the views of the Enlightenment. Some were Jansenists and so contributed to weakening division in the Church. Freemasonry had members among the clergy, even among the bishops.[53]

The situation of the Roman Catholic Church in Germany was not much if any better than in France. The major bishops and some of the minor ones were great territorial lords. They were masters of states and their functions were fully as much secular as religious. Like the French bishops, they were recruited chiefly from the nobility. That meant that they came to their posts more from reasons of prestige and power than from a desire to nourish the Christian community. The ecclesiastical princes differed from the secular princes chiefly in that, celibates as they were, their positions were not handed down from father to son.

Moreover, Febronianism flourished in their realms. It became an excuse for growing administrative independence of the Popes. In 1786 the archbishops formally sought to restrict Papal powers in their jurisdictions, asserted their authority in marriage questions and in monasteries, schools, and hospitals, said that episcopal cases should not be referred to Rome, and cut down on the financial contributions to the Papacy.

However, in this the German church was by no means united. Fearing the

[53] Leflon, *op. cit.*, pp. 21–36; Dansette, *Histoire Religieuse de la France Contemporaine. De la Révolution à la IIIème République*, pp. 15–38; Pastor, *op. cit.*, Vol. XL, pp. 87–106.

control of the archbishops, exerted directly and from near at hand, bishops and cathedral chapters supported the authority of the more distant Rome. Moreover, a great gulf separated the parish priests from the higher clergy. The former were largely from the humbler classes while the latter, from the aristocracy, moved in quite different circles and had very different interests.

The effect of the Enlightenment on German Roman Catholicism was mixed. Among the clergy in general the *Aufklärung*, with its moral and practical emphasis, made for more emphasis on the care of souls. Among the laity it fought superstition and encouraged an increased interest in the Church, and the parish church became more a centre of community life. The *Aufklärung* promoted tolerance of the "sister churches" of Protestantism and the dream of achieving a noble and harmonious mankind. It also led many, both priests and laity, to rationalize Christian dogma, to regard the sacraments merely as symbols, and to look upon the Church primarily not as providing the means to eternal salvation but as an instrument for improving individuals and human society here and now.[54]

Italy, divided politically, was still loyal to the Roman Catholic Church. Yet in general the lay princes who ruled over the political entities which were not within the Papal States sought to augment their control of ecclesiastical affairs. In areas ruled by members of the House of Hapsburg Febronianism had its advocates. The Republic of Venice also sought to extend its power over the Church in its territories.

Few Popes of the century were outstanding for their virtues and none were notorious for their vices. The great powers, notably the French and Spanish Bourbons and the Hapsburg emperors, but also some of the others, made their weight felt in Papal elections and several of the monarchs insisted on being consulted in the appointment of Cardinals. In international affairs the Papacy was less and less an important factor. Most of the Popes were able, but they faced an adverse world. In general they laboured valiantly to deal with the issues of the time. Usually they were against the nepotism which had been the bane of many earlier reigns. All were Italians from the aristocracy. One, Benedict XIII, who wore the tiara from 1724 to 1730, was an ascetic Dominican who had sought to evade election and who continued, as Pope, to lead a life noted for its piety. Clement XII, who succeeded him at the age of seventy-eight and who reigned until 1740, was from a wealthy Florentine family and lived in splendour. Although opposed to nepotism, because of his age and infirmities one of his nephews, a Cardinal, had much influence and was severely criticized. Benedict XIV, who held the throne from 1740 to 1758, won goodwill in some quarters by his willingness to allow monarchs to have the patronage to benefices within their domains. The death of Clement XIII, who was Pope from 1758 to 1769, seems to have been hastened by the strain brought by the pressure put on him to dissolve the Society of Jesus. Clement XIV, who held the reins of power from 1769 to 1774, a Franciscan, has been accused of seeking the tiara and in doing so to have conformed to the currents of opinion which were moving against the Jesuits. Certainly it was he who, after having earlier given ground for being regarded as for them, turned against them and issued the brief which dissolved the Society. His successor, Pius VI, was confronted with the storm of the French Revolution, and of him we are to hear more in the next chapter.

We must note that, as a foreshadowing of the future, there were those in Rome, with adherents among the Cardinals, who were known as *Zelanti*. They were deeply troubled by the drift of the times towards the limitation of the powers of the Popes. They were also supporters of the Jesuits. In their stout opposition to contemporary trends they were out-voted.[55]

The Roman Catholic Church Suffers a Severe Blow Through the Suppression of the Society of Jesus

A further weakness developed in the Roman Catholic Church through the stagnation of its monastic activity. Ever since the rise of monasticism in the third century the vigour of that phase of the Church's life had been a barometer of vitality. In ages when the tides were running strong, old monastic orders flourished and new ones appeared. In the centuries when the tide was ebbing, monasteries decayed and few new orders or other forms of the monastic ideal appeared. The Catholic Reformation had had much of its expression in the revival in existing monastic orders and in the emergence of new orders and congregations. Of the new ones the most prominent was the Society of Jesus. Brought into being in the sixteenth century through the vision and organizing genius of Ignatius Loyola, it had been the chief agency in pushing back the forward surge of Protestantism. It had also been outstanding in educating Catholic youth. It had borne a large proportion of the burden of the missions which had extended the faith in the Americas, Africa, Asia, and the islands of the sea. Now, in the eighteenth century, no new order or congregation appeared which attained to anything like the proportions of the older ones, and existing orders and congregations suffered from declining numbers and zeal. To cap the climax, the Society of Jesus was first expelled from several kingdoms and then dissolved by the Pope. Here was both a body blow to the Roman Catholic Church and what seemed to be an ominous symptom of inner weakness.

[55] On the Papacy in the eighteenth century see Pastor, *op. cit.*, Vols. XXXIII–XL.

At the time of their suppression the Jesuits numbered about 23,000. The largest number were in Germany, with Italy second, France third, Spain fourth, and Poland fifth. They were in several other countries in Europe. Outside Europe they had missions in the Near East, Persia, India, China, the East Indies, several countries in Central and South America, in Mexico, and in French and British North America.[56] Widely spread as they were, with many men of ability and devotion, and thoroughly disciplined, they were more influential than their numbers indicated.

The reasons for the opposition varied. Jesuits were accused of being commercially minded, of mixing in politics, of engaging in intrigues, of justifying deceit, and of acting on the principle that the end justifies the means. With their type of organization and a form of direction through obedience to a General and with their support of Papal power, they were regarded with jaundiced eye by those who were seeking to extend the control of the crown over the Church. They were criticized for the alleged exploitation of the Indians in their missions, especially in South America. The enmity of many whites in these regions was aroused by Jesuit efforts to prevent the enslavement of the Indians and to shield them from corrupting contact with European settlers.

In 1759 the Jesuits were expelled from the Portuguese realms, both in Europe and in the overseas possessions. They were charged with being unfaithful to the rules of their Society, with instigating a war in Paraguay, and with plotting against the life of the king.[57]

Next was France. In 1764 a royal edict dissolved the Society in that kingdom, where the tide had been running against them. In the long controversy with the Jansenists, the latter had done much to discredit them. The final crisis was precipitated by the involvement of Jesuits in financial enterprises in Martinique which had brought heavy losses to French investors.[58]

It was under Charles III, who, as we have seen, sought to bring the Church more closely under the control of the crown, that Spain expelled the Jesuits. This was in 1767. Many of the regular clergy had long been jealous of them. Complications over the alleged part of the Jesuits in stirring up a revolt in Paraguay which followed the transfer from Spain to Portugal of some of the territory in which the Society had missions contributed to the hostility. For a variety of reasons much of articulate public opinion was against them. Tanucci, an influential adviser of the king, who has been held to have been the prime mover in the step, cherished views which were akin to Febronianism and seems to have been antagonized by the support which the Jesuits were giving to the

[56] Campbell, *The Jesuits,* pp. 424, 425.
[57] Pastor, *op. cit.,* Vol. XXXVI, p. 323.
[58] *Ibid.,* pp. 371–498; Campbell, *op. cit.,* pp. 478–503.

Pope. The expulsion affected not only Spain but also all the vast Spanish colonial possessions.[59]

In the year the Jesuits were expelled from Spain similar action against them was taken in Naples and Parma. The following year they were driven out of Malta.[60]

Determined and prolonged pressure was brought on two successive Popes to dissolve the Society. This came largely from the Bourbons: branches of that family were on the thrones of France, Spain, and Naples, where measures against it had already been taken. In August, 1773, Clement XIV, after several years of hesitation, ordered the suppression of the Society of Jesus.[61]

In predominantly Roman Catholic countries the Papal edict was obeyed. In most of them more lenience was shown to ex-Jesuits than in Portugal or the Bourbon domains. Indeed, in the latter the treatment meted out to them had been very harsh. In Austria, Switzerland, and most of the German states they were permitted to continue some of their functions as seculars, in places still living in community.[62]

Under two non-Catholic rulers the lot of the Jesuits was easier than under Roman Catholic princes. Frederick II of Prussia wished them to continue their educational activities among his Roman Catholic subjects. With the tacit consent of the Pope they did so. However, some Jesuits complied with the Papal decree and became seculars and several bishops refused to ordain new members of the Society.[63] Catherine the Great, scoffing free-thinker though she was, found the Jesuits useful in the education of her Roman Catholic subjects, especially those in the portions of Poland which had been seized by her in the partition of that unhappy country. She would not permit the publication in her domains of the Papal decree dissolving the Society. By a convenient legal fiction, she and the Jesuits maintained that it therefore was not in effect in her realms. The Society persisted, recruited fresh members, and elected a General. Some Jesuits in other lands were, on application, placed on the rolls of this continuing remnant. The Popes, never too happy over the suppression of the Society, are said to have given unpublicized approval. After the death of Catherine, her son and successor, Paul, was still more friendly. It was at his request that in 1801 the Pope formally reëstablished the Society in Russia, thirteen years before he authorized its restoration throughout the world.[64]

The dissolution of the Society of Jesus dealt a blow not only to the Roman

[59] Pastor, *op. cit.,* Vol. XXXVII, pp. 1–213; Auguste Crayon, *Charles III et les Jésuites de ses États d'Europe et d'Amérique en 1767. Documents Inédits* (Paris, L'Eureux, 1868, pp. lxxxviii, 442), *passim.*

[60] Pastor, *op. cit.,* Vol. XXXVII, pp. 214–257.

[61] *Ibid.,* Vol. XXXVIII, pp. 216–345.

[62] *Ibid.,* pp. 341–378.

[63] *Ibid.,* pp. 419–438.

[64] Campbell, *op. cit.,* pp. 642–664.

Catholic Church in Europe but also on the far-flung borders of its missions. Most of these missions, whether in Asia or the Americas, were continued by transferring to other orders and congregations the responsibility for them. In Paraguay, for example, they were committed to the Franciscans and in China to the Lazarists. Yet in no instance were the successors able to carry them on as effectively as had the Jesuits.[65]

DECLINE IN THE PROTESTANT CHURCHES

In Protestantism as well as Roman Catholicism the outlook seemed grim. The pulsing life which had brought about the Reformation appeared in large part to have spent its force. Fresh currents were beginning to be seen, but as yet they affected only minorities.

Because of their importance in Protestantism and in the world as a whole in the period which is our major concern, the situation in two regions, the British realms and Germany, especially demands our attention. In the British realms we must first say something of England, the country which played the largest role in the British Isles and in building the British Empire. Here the intellectual trends represented by Deism were undercutting conviction, and the close control of the dominant religious body, the Church of England, by a state which had in it much political corruption and no great zeal for the Christian faith, appeared to be rendering that body, if not moribund, at least on the way towards losing the vitality which would make it a continuing force. Indeed, several years after the appearance of his famous defence of Christianity, the *Analogy of Religion,* Joseph Butler, then Bishop of Bristol, is said to have declined the Archbishopric of Canterbury on the ground that "it was too late for him to try to support a falling church." [66] However, he was noted for his "natural melancholy." Moreover, although he had already seen something of John Wesley, he distrusted him for the "enthusiasm" which he was arousing and failed to sense the significance of what he represented.[67]

Yet much in the current state of the Church of England seemed to support Butler's pessimistic appraisal. To be sure, as in Roman Catholic France, so in Anglican England, the Church had prestige and outwardly was powerful. But, as in France, it was severely criticized and some of the accusations were justified. It was not only the general intellectual and moral climate and the control by the state which seemed to augur ill, but the character and performance of much of the clergy were discouraging.[68] As in France—and Germany—a

---

[65] Latourette, *A History of the Expansion of Christianity,* Vol. III, pp. 155, 358.

[66] Leslie Stephen, in *Dictionary of National Biography,* Vol. III, p. 521, quoting Bartlett, *Butler,* p. 96. However, this may be apocryphal.

[67] *Ibid.,* pp. 521, 522.

[68] On the Church of England in the eighteenth century see C. J. Abbey, *The English Church and Its Bishops, 1700–1800* (London, Longmans, Green & Co., 2 vols., 1887); C. J. Abbey and J. H.

great gulf existed between the higher clergy, represented by archbishops, bishops, archdeacons, and members of cathedral staffs on the one hand, and the parish clergy on the other. While in each group the incomes varied from post to post, in general those in the first category were very much larger than those in the second. As on the Continent, the higher clergy tended to live in luxury and the lower clergy to be poverty-stricken. However, while on the Continent the upper ranks, especially the bishoprics, were usually recruited from the aristocracy, in England they were filled both from the families of rank and from those of men of lowly birth. The latter found it possible to rise through ability and through cultivating the friendship of influential men. In England pluralism and absenteeism, by a tradition inherited from the pre-Reformation Church, were general. A bishop might be dean or canon or prebend of a cathedral in another see, or draw the income from a distant parish, or a priest might hold the titles and live on the revenues of several posts. This meant that the legal incumbent could not perform the duties of all his benefices. Indeed, he might never set foot in some of them. The functions either went unperformed or were assigned to poorly paid substitutes.

The bishops sat in the House of Lords and accordingly were important political figures. In the chronic strife between Whigs and Tories the leaders in the rival parties sought to fill with their creatures the sees as they became vacant. The appointments to the higher clergy were technically by the monarch. Sometimes the monarch insisted on making the choice. Queen Anne often did so, and Caroline, the consort of George II, repeatedly determined appointments. Yet prime ministers endeavoured, frequently with success, to have their men named. Among the clergy struggle for preferment and promotion was common and again and again was by unseemly methods. Since as members of the House of Lords the bishops were in London during the sessions of Parliament, which was usually about half of each year, much of the time they were absent from their dioceses. Travel was slow and difficult and they could seldom go to them while Parliament was sitting. Their positions demanded lavish hospitality and considerable pomp. All this meant that their proper episcopal functions suffered—confirmations, the examining and ordaining of clergy, and the visitation of the parishes. Even conscientious bishops, and they were by no means lacking, did not always attain the high standards in these duties that their posts properly required. In consequence, many baptized Englishmen were not confirmed and some unworthy men obtained ordination.

To be sure, among the clergy, especially the higher clergy, much learning

Overton, *The English Church in the Eighteenth Century* (London, Longmans, Green & Co., rev. ed., 1906); N. Sykes, *Church and State in England in the Eighteenth Century* (Cambridge University Press, 1934); Moorman, *A History of the Church in England*, pp. 269–314; A. R. Humphreys, *Literature and Religion in Eighteenth-Century England*, in *The Journal of Ecclesiastical History*, Vol. III, pp. 159–190; Brady, *England before and after Wesley*, pp. 19–96.

was found and the eighteenth century saw a flood of literature from their pens. A large amount of it was controversial, but some was of high grade. Yet towards the end of the century Samuel Johnson, a loyal member of the Church of England, lamented the decline of scholarship among the clergy.

Most of the lower clergy were decent men, somewhat above the average of their parishioners in education and morals. Many were woefully underpaid and supplemented their stipends by other occupations. They conducted the Sunday services, preached, and visited the sick. But usually their sermons were poor and except through them not much instruction was given children and youth. Contempt for the clergy was widespread, and many of the domestic chaplains were little better than servants.

In general, the clergy distrusted "enthusiasm," by which they meant any display of emotion in religion, but sought to inculcate ethics and a reasonable view of the faith which stressed morality and made little of the direct action of the Holy Spirit. Communion was usually only quarterly.

Among the laity departure from Christian standards of conduct was widespread. The level may not have been as low as under the Stuart Restoration in the seventeenth century. Yet heavy drinking was common in all classes, sexual irregularities were usual, and coarseness in speech and amusements, brutalizing sports, and corruption in politics were general.[69]

Among the minorities who were in dissenting bodies the eighteenth century witnessed a recession in fervour. Numerically the chief Nonconformist groups were the Congregationalists (Independents), Baptists, Presbyterians, and Quakers. As we are soon to remind ourselves, Methodism arose but it was long in separating from the Church of England into a distinct denomination. Unitarian views captured much of the Presbyterianism which had come out of Puritanism and with them came a weakening of the Christian faith. They also attracted some from other communions.

A widespread interest in religion existed, but some of it found expression in controversy, much of it barren, and on the whole neither the interest nor the controversy was as intense as in the preceding century. In the Church of England what was called latitudinarianism flourished. In general it meant religious tolerance and unwillingness to engage in the bitter debates which the seventeenth century had witnessed. For many it entailed religious indifference and more or less polite scepticism. Moreover, church fabrics were often allowed to fall into disrepair. Yet church attendance was general and in the rural districts Sunday meant a cessation from the week's occupations, greater cleanliness in person and dress, and some thought on things of the spirit.

Religiously as in other ways Scotland differed markedly from England, but

[69] Brady, *op. cit.*, pp. 99–173; Elliott-Binns, *The Early Evangelicals*, pp. 50 ff.

here, too, the prospect for the future of the faith seemed far from encouraging. To be sure, pluralism and absenteeism were rare, nor was the range of financial remuneration as wide as in the southern kingdom. After the "glorious revolution of 1668" and the departure of James VII (James II of England), the dominant religious body, as the Church of Scotland, was incontestably Presbyterian. In 1690, by the act which established it, the Westminster Confession was formally recognized and the laws were repealed which had attempted to force episcopacy upon the country. Moreover, the Treaty of Union of 1707 which brought the two kingdoms together under the Parliament at Westminster provided for the unaltered maintenance of the presbyterian form of government in the Church of Scotland: the General Assembly, which had met in 1690 for the first time in forty years, was left as the only legislative body in Scotland.[70] All this, however, did not necessarily strengthen the Church. Moreover, the right of patronage, that is, the naming of ministers to the parishes by the lay proprietors, which had been abolished in 1690, was revived by law in 1712.[71]

Episcopalianism, which James VI (James I of England), Charles I, and Charles II had tried to force on Scotland, remained. Episcopal succession was continued, and while Episcopalians were dissenters from the established church, in 1712 legislation protected them. The majority of the Episcopalians were Jacobites, supporters of the claims to the throne of James VII (James II of England) and his descendants. Most of the clergy were non-jurors—that is, they refused to take the oath of allegiance to William and Mary, Anne, and the Hanoverian kings. It was not until 1788, after the death of Charles Edward, the "Young Pretender," grandson of James VII, that the majority of the bishops and clergy began to pray for George III and his family by name.[72] The Episcopal Church drew largely from the nobility but also had many from the common people. Its strength varied in different parts of the country.

In the Church of Scotland what were known as the Moderates were predominant through much of the eighteenth century. They supported patronage, declaring that it obtained a better grade of ministers than those elected by the congregations. Among the Moderate ministers were several men of learning. In the second half of the century Scotland, previously poor, began to approach the prosperity which it was to know in the next century. In some quarters this made for education and more polished manners. In general, the temper of the Moderates meant a cooling of religious ardour. Moreover, patronage tended

---

[70] Cunningham, *The Church History of Scotland*, Vol. II, pp. 174–181, 215, 216.
[71] *Ibid.*, pp. 175, 234–236.
[72] John Parker Lawson, *History of the Scottish Episcopal Church from the Revolution to the Present Time* (Edinburgh, Gallie and Bayley, 1843, pp. xl, 588), *passim*, gives a very pro-Episcopalian, anti-Presbyterian narrative.

towards unseemly manoeuvres for preferments and a lowering of the quality of the ministers. In the latter half of the century the Moderates reflected trends which we have noted in England and on the Continent: emphasis upon reason as against revelation and antagonism towards "enthusiasm." [73]

The eighteenth century in Wales was a time of deplorable conditions in the life of the Church, in the latter part of the century partly relieved by the awakenings of which we are to hear later. The established church was slow to recover from the damage brought by the Civil War and the Commonwealth of the seventeenth century. The poverty of the country rendered the situation still more difficult. Many parish churches were in disrepair or even in ruins, numbers of the parish clergy were forced to subsist on mere pittances, a large proportion of the parsonages were unfit for human habitation, and some of the cathedrals were in need of restoration. Education was at a low ebb. Here and there good men among the clergy laboured valiantly for improvement, but only slowly did the general level rise.[74]

In the eighteenth century Ireland was recovering from the wars which had wasted it in the preceding century. Roman Catholics, under legal disabilities, were in the majority. Presbyterianism was growing, fed by immigration from Scotland. The Church of Ireland, a branch of the Anglican Communion, was established by law. Some improvement was noted as the century progressed, but in several ways the morale of the Church of Ireland suffered from evils due to the environment and to the general tenor of the times. Some of the bishops, especially the archbishops, were burdened with the responsibilities of civil government: more than once, when the lords lieutenants were non-resident, the archbishops had placed upon them much of the responsibility for the administration of the island. As in England during the period, there was a good deal of pluralism and absenteeism.[75]

At the outset and in the early decades of the eighteenth century the Protestantism of the colonies which before the close of the century were to become the United States suffered from at least three major handicaps. First, a very small proportion of the population were members of churches. Only a minority of the immigrants had come for religious reasons and outside New England the state churches were either non-existent, as in Pennsylvania, or weak. It is said that even as late as 1790, when awakenings and missionaries from Europe had considerably strengthened the churches, not more than five out of one hundred of the population were church members.[76] Second, the most widely spread of

[73] Donald Maclean, *Aspects of Scottish Church History* (Edinburgh, T. & T. Clark, 1927, pp. xi, 184), pp. 65 ff.

[74] Edwards, *Landmarks in the History of the Welsh Church*, pp. 161 ff.

[75] Phillips, *History of the Church of Ireland*, Vol. III, pp. 175 ff.

[76] Daniel Dorchester, *Christianity in the United States from the First Settlement down to the Present Time* (New York, Phillips and Hunt, 1888, pp. 793), p. 750.

the religious bodies, the Church of England, had no resident bishop. It was technically under the Bishop of London. That dignitary was represented by what were known as commissaries, but they were few in number and did not have authority to ordain clergy or to confirm the baptized. Young men who wished ordination were compelled to make the tedious and often dangerous journey to England.[77] Without confirmation the full life of the Church of England was handicapped. Moreover, the commissaries did not have the authority to remove ministers, and this made effective discipline difficult.[78] Third, the most nearly compact and the strongest of the religious bodies, the Congregational Churches of New England, seemed to be losing the zeal of earlier days: at least that was the complaint of some of their clergy. Decline had begun in the seventeenth century with the lowering of standards for church membership and it continued in the fore part of the eighteenth century.[79]

In the eighteenth century German Protestantism presented a mixed picture. On the one hand were conditions which appeared to indicate decline. On the other were currents of life which were to contribute to the remarkable vigour displayed by Protestantism in the ensuing centuries. Of the latter we are to speak a little later.

The untoward and ambiguous conditions can be briefly summarized. Since in each Protestant state the prince was, for administrative purposes, *summus episcopus,* he could control the Church in his domains. Protestant churches were, accordingly, *Landeskirchen,* territorial bodies, each coterminous with the political division of which it was a part. There was, as well, the distinction between the Lutheran and Reformed confessions. A Protestantism thus organized, divided, and state-dominated was obviously handicapped. The clergy were trained in universities where the emphasis was on intellectual orthodoxy and not on spiritual and moral discipline. Many were said to be guilty of drunkenness and adultery.

German Protestantism was also marked by two general types of movements in which the stress was placed on the intellectual formulation of the faith. This could be either a strength or a weakness.

One of the two was a kind of orthodoxy which gave importance to the historic confessions and to theological systems. It has been sometimes known as Protestant scholasticism. In the seventeenth century it had been prominent in both Lutheran and Reformed circles and in its extreme forms it was marked by acrimonious debate and spiritual sterility. Although in theory emphasizing the divine initiative and revelation, in practice it made much of reason. While

[77] Sweet, *Religion in Colonial America,* pp. 56, 57.
[78] Weigle, *American Idealism,* p. 73.
[79] Sweet, *op. cit.,* pp. 105–115; Weigle, *op. cit.,* p. 64.

weakened by the *Aufklärung* and by some forms of Pietism, it persisted into the eighteenth century and had revivals in the nineteenth.

The other type was associated with the *Aufklärung*. It too stressed reason, but after the manner of the eighteenth century. It sought to re-think Christian theology in terms of the intellectual methods and attitudes of the day. Here was the opportunity to accomplish something akin to the achievement of the school men of the high Middle Ages who wrestled with the problems presented by the new intellectual currents of that period. Now it was Protestants rather than Roman Catholics who proved fertile and creative. British Protestants were making notable contributions, but it was from German Protestantism that the most widely influential thought was to come, both in this and the following century. Many of the Germans, as of the British, were struggling with the issues. Theirs was a perilous undertaking. It might contribute to the shaping of the new age by Christianity and to the reinvigoration of the faith. On the other hand, for many it might weaken or destroy the faith. Now and in the subsequent two centuries both results followed. To them we are to recur again and again.

In our description of the *Aufklärung* we have noted some whose fruits for Christianity were more destructive than constructive. We must now name some whose effects were either ambiguous or constructive.

Johann Lorenz von Mosheim (1693-1755), best remembered as a church historian, was a pioneer in an objective, scientific approach which sought to avoid the polemic character of many of the post-Reformation studies in that field. As professor in Helmstadt and then as chancellor and professor at Göttingen, he stood for an irenic orthodoxy and had a wide influence upon many of the clergy.

We have already said something of Hermann Samuel Reimarus (1694-1768). A selection of his writings published in the 1770's after his death on the initiative of Lessing as the Wolfenbuettal Fragments precipitated vigorous controversy. The orthodox viewed them with horror. They were pioneer attempts at the historical study of the Scriptures with many defects and a strong bias towards the prevailing rationalism and natural religion. They helped to inaugurate methods of Biblical study which were widely employed in the next two centuries.[80]

We have also mentioned Johann Salomo Semler (1725-1791). Although he had in part reacted against the Pietism in which he had been reared, he taught at Halle and remained theologically conservative. In his study of the Bible he sought to get at the sources through the original languages. He held that the canon of both the Old and New Testaments had grown by degrees. In his study of the history of Christianity he stressed the natural rather than the

[80] *The New Schaff-Herzog Encyclopedia of Religious Knowledge*, Vol. XII, pp. 402, 403.

supernatural factors and endeavoured to use psychology in the understanding of history. He distinguished between theology and religion and maintained that all doctrinal formulations are human attempts to comprehend the truth which is religion. In doing so he seemed to be lessening the gap between Christianity and the non-Christian faiths.[81]

Holding to the historic confessions were Christoph Matthäus Pfaff (1686–1760), who stood for more autonomy for the Church than was allowed where the territorial system augmented the power of the state, and the church historians Johann Georg Walch (1693–1775) and Matthias Schröckh (1733–1808).[82]

The philologist Johann August Ernesti (1707–1781), a Pietist, critical of rationalism, loyal to the confessions of the Church, was a specialist in the New Testament, particularly its grammar, and maintained that the Bible must be treated as one would treat any other book. To some his orthodoxy and his scholarship seemed inconsistent.[83]

Johann David Michaelis (1717–1791), from a family of scholars, wrote prolifically and helped to give currency to the new views emerging from the scientific study of the Bible. He was a philologist and archeologist and enjoyed contemporary acclaim. Outwardly he held to the traditional orthodoxy but is said secretly to have abandoned it.[84]

Here was a ferment which had features distinctive of Germany and which was to be increasingly influential in the ensuing centuries. It was to make itself felt in most of Western Europe and much of the Americas.

CORRUPTION IN THE EASTERN CHURCHES

In part synchronizing with the decline in vigour in Roman Catholicism and Protestantism was the eighteenth-century corruption in some of the Eastern Churches. We have already seen a little of the deleterious effect of the control by the Moslem Turks on the churches within their domains. In the eighteenth century it was augmented in the Balkans by the Turkish practice of giving over the administration, both civil and ecclesiastical, in much of that region to the Phanariots. The Phanariots were Greek Orthodox Christians who lived in the Phanar district of Constantinople near to the residence of the Ecumenical Patriarch. In most of the Balkans they were aliens, had purchased their appointments from the Turks, and viewed their offices as opportunities for power and financial profit.

The corruption was in part due to the long-standing practice by which each

[81] *Ibid.*, Vol. X, pp. 354, 355. On Semler, Mosheim, Reimarus, and other historians of Christianity, see Karl Völker, *Die Kirchengeschichtschreibung der Aufklärung* (Tübingen, J. C. B. Mohr, 1921, pp. v, 92), *passim.*

[82] Heussi, *Kompendium der Kirchengeschichte*, pp. 345, 346.

[83] *The New Schaff-Herzog Encyclopedia of Religious Knowledge*, Vol. IV, p. 170.

[84] *Ibid.*, Vol. VII, p. 364.

Ecumenical Patriarch on his accession presented a gift to the sultan and to the grand vizier. In time it became a bribe. It also meant that only the wealthy could aspire to the post of Patriarch and that the incumbent was tempted to recoup his fortunes by exploiting the Christians under his charge and selling church offices.

As an example, among the Serbs, at the instance of the Greeks, in 1766 the Patriarchate of Peć, which had been a rallying point of Serbian nationalism, was abolished. Recently several of the men in the post had been Greeks, financial exactions had been heavy, and the Serbian church had fallen in arrears. The direct authority of the Ecumenical Patriarch was now extended over the Serbs. Intense and growing unrest among the Serbs against Greek control followed. The Enlightenment spread among intellectuals and the middle class and bred nationalism and anti-clericalism. Anti-clericalism was augmented by increasing factions, graft, corruption, and immorality in the leadership of the Church.[85]

Geographic Expansion Slows Down

In the eighteenth century the remarkable geographic expansion of the faith which had been in progress since the fifteenth century continued, but its pace slackened and losses were experienced. As we have seen, from the fifteenth century Christianity had displayed the widest spread that it or any other religion had achieved. It was planted in the Americas and along the shores of Africa south of the Sahara, was re-introduced to China, was carried to Japan and to many of the islands which fringed Asia, and here and there took root among pagans in Eastern Europe and by conversion and Russian migration east of the Urals. The spread had been in connexion with the geographic explorations, the commerce, the conquests, and the migrations of Europeans, mostly Western Europeans. Spain and Portugal had led the way, but latterly the French, Dutch, English, Danes, and Swedes had competed. Very early the Russians had begun moving across the northern reaches of Asia. Partly because Roman Catholic powers had the major share in the expansion and partly because of the impulse given by the Catholic Reformation, Roman Catholics had played a much larger part in the geographic extension of the faith than had Protestants or the Eastern Churches.

In the eighteenth century the rate of spread of the Roman Catholic form of the faith declined and recessions were seen. Several factors contributed. Outstanding was the waning power of Spain and Portugal. The urge which had sent them across so much of the world was slackening. A second factor was

---

[85] Adeney, *The Greek and Eastern Churches*, p. 326; W. Miller, *The Balkans* (London, T. Fisher Unwin, 2nd ed., 1908, pp. xviii, 476), pp. 73 ff.; C. Jelavich, *Some Aspects of Serbian Religious Development in the Eighteenth Century*, in *Church History*, Vol. XXIII, pp. 144–152.

the enforced exodus of the Society of Jesus from the missionary scene. The slackening of zeal in Roman Catholic circles in Europe made difficult the recruiting of enough men to care adequately for the added burdens.[86] Another factor was adverse conditions in the lands in which missions were conducted, notably in Japan and China. In Japan the prohibitions which had been enacted and enforced late in the sixteenth and in the seventeenth century were continued: Christianity had not been extinguished but it had been driven into hiding.[87] For a variety of reasons, in China the imperial government launched persecutions: Christianity did not disappear, but the numbers of Christians remained about stationary and their morale declined.[88] In India during the eighteenth century the Roman Catholics appear to have lost both in numbers and in morale.[89]

It was ominous that in Spanish and Portuguese America, as we have remarked, the area where the preceding two centuries had seen the greatest numerical triumphs in spreading the faith, indigenous clergy were slow to emerge. Some there were, the numbers were mounting, and from them the episcopate was increasingly recruited, but for missionaries the Roman Catholic Church in that area relied chiefly on Europe, and many of the bishops and parish clergy were still from the Old World. Here was an anemic Christianity which depended for its life on continued transfusions of fresh blood from abroad. In Brazil, the Portuguese area, the supply of clergy, both from abroad and indigenous, had been even less than in the Spanish colonies.[90] Moreover, in the eighteenth century the moral quality of the clergy, especially of the seculars, to whom most of the Christians were entrusted, seems to have declined.[91] Roman Catholic Christianity in Spanish and Portuguese possessions in America was ill prepared for the storms which came upon it early in the next century.

YET IN SOME AREAS GEOGRAPHIC EXPANSION CONTINUES

Grave though the situation was in Europe and on the geographic frontiers of Christianity, the prospect was not utterly bleak. Indeed, from the vantage of the twentieth century it was clear that no such recession of the Christian tide was in progress as had been witnessed from the sixth to the ninth century or from the fourteenth to the sixteenth century.

One measure of the trend was in the geographic spread of the faith. From

[86] Latourette, *A History of the Expansion of Christianity*, Vol. III, pp. 139, 152, 166, 272, 355, 356.
[87] *Ibid.*, pp. 326–335.
[88] *Ibid.*, pp. 349–359.
[89] *Ibid.*, p. 273.
[90] *Ibid.*, pp. 100, 101, 165, 167.
[91] *Ibid.*, p. 158.

the perspective of the globe as a whole, advance clearly continued. If in some areas losses occurred, in others gains were achieved. For example, in the eighteenth century, in spite of the waning energy of Spain, Franciscans enlarged the borders of Spanish rule and Roman Catholic Christianity over a wide expanse of territory through new missions among the Indians in New Mexico, Texas, and California.[92] In the Philippines the frontiers of Christianity continued to be pushed forward.[93] Protestant missions were begun in earnest on many fronts—in India, in West and South Africa, in Greenland, in Labrador, in the West Indies, and among some of the Indians in North America.[94] Russian Orthodox settlers, fur traders, and missionaries planted their form of the faith across the entire northern reaches of Asia.[95]

PERSISTENT VITALITY HAS MOUNTING EXPRESSION

The continued geographic expansion was one evidence that in spite of the adverse factors which we have been describing a persistent vitality in Christianity belied the sombre predictions they seemed to warrant. Into the adverse factors we have gone at some length. If we are to be true to the facts and really to gain some glimmering of their significance, we must not minimize them. Because of them it seemed by no means clear whether what life remained in Christianity merely betokened a belated survival, an instance of what has sometimes been termed social lag. Was not mankind moving out of the stage in which Christianity had been potent into one in which it would, perhaps slowly but no less surely, fade out of the picture? That appeared the more likely in view of the apparently strange circumstance that in part the adverse factors emerged from Christianity. To be sure, they were perversions, distorted fruits. But did not the Christian Gospel, with its initial weakness in a babe in a Bethlehem manger and its presumably hopeless frustration on a Roman cross and in a borrowed tomb, have this as its inevitable issue? Did it possess a vitality which could offset the antagonistic forces to whose emergence it had contributed?

Fully as urgent for mankind was the question whether Christianity could effectively counteract those forces which it had helped to release and which in the course of the next two centuries were to threaten the welfare and even the very existence of mankind. Could it do more than counteract them? Could it so use them as to make them a blessing and not a curse?

In the eighteenth century tides of life were present which in the next two hundred years were to swell to major proportions and which were to make

[92] *Ibid.*, pp. 125–130.
[93] *Ibid.*, pp. 315, 316.
[94] *Ibid.*, pp. 220–224, 236–239, 246, 277–282.
[95] *Ibid.*, pp. 368–370.

Christianity more potent in mankind as a whole than at any previous time. In the world of the mid-twentieth century Christianity was by no means dominant. To the objective observer, if such could be found, it would probably not be clear that it would ever be dominant. Yet the contention that when measured on a world-wide scale it was a mounting factor in the life of mankind was supported by evidence which could not be gainsaid.

The persistent vitality was in all the main branches of Christianity and in the eighteenth century was already apparent, although not as prominent as it was to become after 1815. Part of it found channels in traditional forms, especially but not exclusively in the Roman Catholic and the Eastern Churches. Some of it broke out in new ways. These were chiefly in Protestantism and helped to give that branch of the faith a larger proportional growth in numbers and influence than the other branches.

VITALITY: IN THE ROMAN CATHOLIC CHURCH

In the eighteenth century the faith as expressed through the Roman Catholic Church, while suffering from severe blows, was by no means spent. The contributions of earlier centuries were still in evidence. Ambrose of Milan, Augustine of Hippo, Benedict of Nursia, Hildebrand, Bernard of Clairvaux, Francis of Assisi, Dominic of the Order of Preachers, Thomas Aquinas, Ignatius Loyola, and Theresa of Avila, to mention only some of the more prominent of former days, were still to be reckoned with. Impulses which stemmed from them or orders which they founded continued to be potent. Even the eclipse of the Society of Jesus, serious blow though it was, came late and was to be brief. In regions where Roman Catholics predominated, the "religious," members of orders, congregations, and societies, carried on most of the schools. There, too, the large majority of the hospitals and services for the orphaned, the poor, and the indigent aged were maintained by them. The Catholic Reformation did not reach its peak in France until the seventeenth century. Some of its leaders lived into the second half of that century and others did not die until early in the eighteenth century. Thus Jean-Jacques Olier, prominent in the Oratory, lived until 1657, Vincent de Paul, founder of the Lazarists, the Sisters of Charity, and the Ladies of Charity, died in 1660, and it was not until twenty years later (1680) that the grave claimed John Eudes, the initiator of the Eudists. John Baptist de Salle, who began the Institute of the Brothers of the Christian Schools and has been called the "father of modern pedagogy," survived until 1719. Bossuet, the most famous preacher of his generation, did not die until 1704, and only in 1715 was Fénelon, Archbishop of Cambrai and the spiritual counsellor of many, gathered to his fathers. It was in the seventeenth century that in France the devotion to the Sacred Hearts of Jesus and

Mary became popular which in the nineteenth and twentieth centuries was to swell to large proportions.[96]

The currents of Christian devotion and action continued in the eighteenth century side by side with the movements which appeared to be destroying Christianity. Some in high places in the Church opposed the growing popularity of the devotion to the Sacred Heart. However, in 1765, in spite of them the feast of the Sacred Heart was given Papal approval.[97] In 1753 a. book, *Discernimento degli spiriti,* was published on judging the validity of various kinds of mysticism, by the Jesuit Roman preacher Scaramelli (1687–1752). It was to be widely used in that and the following century.[98]

Jansenism still had wide repercussions. Both in France and in other countries some of its views and practices were propagated by members of the clergy. They made for austere standards and led numbers of priests to avoid easygoing absolution and to withhold the communion from those who had not met the demands of a rigorous discipline. Here, too, was life, even though Rome, believing it to be contrary to sound doctrine, frowned upon it.[99]

Quietistic forms of mysticism which had been popular in some circles in the seventeenth century fell into disrepute. They were said to be confusing submission to the will of God with a repose which did nothing and even permitted moral laxity. They continued but were dying.[100]

Alphonsus Liguori (1696–1787) led in propagating other ways of nourishing the Christian life. Born near Naples and in his earlier years a brilliant lawyer, after a deep emotional experience he abandoned that profession and was ordained priest (1726). As a zealous preacher and missionary in Italy, in his moral instruction he took a half-way position between the rigourism of the Jansenists and the passivity of the quietists. In prayers he stressed mental short acts of love rather than prolonged meditation. He wrote extensively on ethics and the devotional life and composed many hymns. He made much of devotion to Christ and the Virgin and dwelt upon the Passion of Jesus. The influence of Liguori increased in the nineteenth century. When, in 1839, only a little over a generation after his death, he was canonized, as a moral theologian he was declared to be a doctor of the Church.[101]

During a century which seemed largely sterile in great Christian lives in the Roman Catholic Church, two others appeared in Italy who were eventually

[96] Pourrat, *La Spiritualité Chrétienne,* Vol. IV, Part 2, pp. 53–438.

[97] *Ibid.,* pp. 442–444.

[98] *Ibid.,* pp. 439–441.

[99] *Ibid.,* pp. 450, 451.

[100] *Ibid.,* pp. 427, 450.

[101] *Ibid.,* Vol. III, Part 2, pp. 449 ff.; *The Catholic Encyclopedia,* Vol. I, pp. 334–341. For the writings of Liguori, their various editions, and extensive translations, see Maur de Meulemeester, *Bibliographie Générale des Écrivains Rédemptoristes* (Louvain, Imprimerie S. Alphonse, 3 vols., 1933–1939), Vol. I, *passim.*

canonized. One, Paul Jerome Casanuova, better known by his religious name, Leonard (of Port Maurice) (1676–1751), was an indefatigable missionary in his native land. Joining a strict branch of the Franciscans, the Observant Recollets, as a preacher he made war on sin. He focussed his devotional life on the mass.[102] The other, Paul Francis Danei, better known as Paul of the Cross (1694–1775), had visions and revelations in which the Passion was prominent.[103]

From Liguori and Paul of the Cross new missionary congregations arose. As we have remarked, the rate of the emergence of such movements was a fairly dependable barometer of life in the Roman Catholic Church. The fact that few of them appeared in the eighteenth century and that a major one, the Society of Jesus, temporarily was erased was disturbing. However, a few were born, conclusive evidence of vitality. Liguori was the chief agent in the creation of the Congregation of the Most Holy Redeemer, better known as the Redemptorists. It was founded in 1732 and in 1749 its rule was given Papal approval. Having missions as its purpose, both among nominal Roman Catholics at home and among non-Christians abroad, it had an extensive growth in the eighteenth and the following centuries.[104] In its first two generations were two members who were eventually deemed worthy of canonization.[105] Closely connected with the Redemptorists was a women's congregation, the Redemptorines, founded in 1731. Liguori shared in their beginnings but did not have as large a part as in the Redemptorists.[106] They were chiefly the result of the purpose of Mary Celeste Crostarosa (1696–1755). Of an old and illustrious Neapolitan family, from an early age she gave herself to the monastic life. She was a close friend of Liguori and the initial rule of the Redemptorists is said to have come to her in a vision. Like many mystics, she not only had visions but also displayed ability as a leader and organizer. The Redemptorines did not have as wide a spread as the Redemptorists, but eventually they had houses in several countries.[107]

Paul of the Cross was the founder of the Congregation of Discalced Clerks of the Most Holy Cross and Passion of our Lord Jesus Christ, more briefly known as the Congregation of the Passion and its members as the Passionists. Its rule was framed in 1720, was given oral approval by the Pope in 1725, and obtained formal approval in 1741. As its name suggests, furthering the major concern of its originator, its purpose was to promote devotion to the Passion

---

[102] Pourrat, *op. cit.*, Vol. III, Part 2, pp. 492–496.

[103] *Ibid.*, pp. 498–503; *The Catholic Encyclopedia*, Vol. XI, p. 590.

[104] *The Catholic Encyclopedia*, Vol. XII, pp. 683–687; Heimbucher, *Die Orden und Kongregationen der katholischen Kirche*, Vol. III, pp. 313–333. For the writings of its members (aside from Liguori), see Meulemeester, *op. cit.*, Vols. II, III, *passim*.

[105] Pourrat, *op. cit.*, Vol. IV, Part 2, pp. 488, 489.

[106] *The Catholic Encyclopedia*, Vol. XII, p. 682.

[107] Favre, *A Great Mystic of the Eighteenth Century. The Venerable Sister Mary Celeste Crostarosa* (St. Louis, B. Herder Book Co., 1935, pp. 284), *passim*.

of Christ and to undertake missions and conduct retreats among Roman Catholics. It also had missions among non-Christians.[108]

In spite of the adverse spiritual climate of the eighteenth century, a few other new congregations came into being. Thus in 1722 a Breton priest, Louis Marie Grignion de Montfort, founded in France the Missionary Priests of the Society of Mary.[109] He was an ascetic, devoted to poverty and the poor, and a tireless itinerant preacher in Brittany and La Vendée. Partly through him and partly through Mary Louise of Jesus Trichet the Sisters of Wisdom came into being. They were a teaching congregation which survived into the twentieth century.[110] In 1712 Elizabeth of Surville founded, near Coutances, in Northwest France, the Sisters of the Good Saviour, to teach children and to visit the sick and the criminals.[111] The year 1752 saw the initiation in Salamanca of the Ordo Religiosus de Poenitentia, its members known as the Scallzetti or Nazareni. It was begun by Juan Varella y Losada (1724–1769), who abandoned a military career to give himself fully to his faith. It was a penitential order which for a time spread widely. However, in the stormy years at the turn of the century most of its houses disappeared and it almost died out. Later it had its mother house in Rome.[112] The Missionary Priests of St. John Baptist, better known as the Baptistini, were begun by Domenico Olivieri, a Genoese, and received Papal approval in 1755. For a time they flourished, were missionaries in Italy, and sent missionaries abroad. However, they did not survive the disorders at the end of the century. The Baptistines, the Hermit Sisters of St. John the Baptist, were founded near Genoa with the aid of Olivieri. They followed a regimen of extreme austerity.[113] In 1762 the Sisters of Divine Providence were inaugurated in Metz by Johann Martin Moye and had as their purpose spreading the faith among village youth and caring for the sick.[114] Other women's congregations begun during the century included the Sisters of the Holy Sacrament, founded in 1715, another of the same name, both in France, inaugurated in 1733, and, like the other, for teaching and the care of the sick, the Sisters of Mercy of Perigneaux, instituted in 1747, the Sisters of the Presentation of the Holy Virgin, founded in Albi in 1755, and one for the teaching of poor children, begun in Ireland in 1756.[115]

The list of new congregations is more than the catalogue which it seems at first reading. It is significant that very few were founded after the middle of

---

[108] The Catholic Encyclopedia, Vol. XI, pp. 521–525; Heimbucher, op. cit., Vol. III, pp. 309–312.

[109] Heimbucher, op. cit., Vol. III, p. 348.

[110] Ibid., p. 552; The Catholic Encyclopedia, Vol. IX, p. 384.

[111] Heimbucher, op. cit., Vol. III, p. 553.

[112] The Catholic Encyclopedia, Vol. XI, p. 637.

[113] Ibid., Vol. II, pp. 277, 278.

[114] Heimbucher, op. cit., Vol. III, p. 547.

[115] Ibid., pp. 553, 554.

the century: the forces adverse to the faith were progressively working a decay of the kind of devotion which at the high tides of religious conviction had given rise to orders and congregations. Few of the new congregations were of men. The majority were of women. No men's congregations appeared comparable in size to the Benedictines, the Cistercians, the Franciscans, the Dominicans, or the Jesuits. Moreover, all but one of the new men's congregations arose in Italy. The contrast with the great days of the Catholic Reformation was marked. In Spain these had seen vigorous reform of several existing orders and the conversion of Loyola. Now no Spanish mystics arose of the stature of Theresa of Avila or John of the Cross. It was only as recently at the seventeenth century that the Catholic Reformation had reached its height in France with new congregations of men and women: now only a few small congregations of women arose and, as we have seen, the existing men's monastic houses were having difficulty in recruiting novices. Why this sudden sharp recession we do not know. That it had occurred was obvious. In Italy the decline in fervour was not so marked. Indeed, Italy was still, as it had always been, the geographical heart of the Roman Catholic Church. Yet even there the tide was not running as strong as in some earlier centuries.

It was also significant that very few of those of the century who were adjudged worthy of canonization were in the higher ranks of the clergy. To be sure, Liguori was a bishop, but he had been given that post only late in life and against his unavailing protests. The list of recognized saints included no Pope of the period. Roman Catholics noted for their sanctity were from the rank and file, not from the official leadership.

Of importance also was the fact that the attacks of the intellectuals on Christianity were not countered by Roman Catholic apologists of the first water. No Roman Catholic of the stature of Thomas Aquinas, Albertus Magnus, or Bonaventura did for the Christianity of the eighteenth century what these giants had accomplished in so rising to the intellectual challenge of their day that for the thoughtful the Christian faith was emphatically vindicated and the threats were turned into buttresses. To be sure, scholarship there was. Although against difficulties, the Bollandists continued their massive series, the *Acta Sanctorum*. Books on theology were produced, and the Spanish Carmelites completed the *Salmanticenses* and the *Complutenses,* but they were finished before the century was well advanced. Then, too, they did not break new ground, but adhered closely to Thomistic thought and not in a fashion to meet the vocabulary of the day.[116]

Yet the Roman Catholic Church was by no means moribund. A religious body within which there could still emerge the congregations we have mentioned, which could maintain the older orders, and which could produce those

[116] *The Catholic Encyclopedia*, Vol. XIII, pp. 401, 402.

whom later generations would raise to its altars as exemplary Christians was far from dead.[117] It had seen much worse days and had not only lived through them but risen to still greater influence in the human scene.

VITALITY: ISSUING FROM PROTESTANTISM; GENERALIZATIONS

It was from Protestantism far more than from Roman Catholicism that in the eighteenth century new movements sprang. They were to contribute towards the vitality which in the next two centuries was to make it the form of Christianity most fertile in fresh expressions of the faith, in dynamic efforts to make the faith potent in fighting the entrenched ills of mankind, and in bringing Christians together in unprecedented ways. Moreover, through them Protestantism was to begin a greater proportionate expansion in numbers and territory than any other branch of the faith.

The three regions in which most of the movements originated and from which they spread were Germany, Great Britain, and what late in the century became the United States of America. We will, therefore, look at each of these regions and trace the eighteenth-century rise and course of the currents which were to swell to global dimensions. We will note, too, that currents of partly independent sources existed in other lands and were reinforced by what came from these three regions, in the eighteenth century chiefly from Germany.

As we do so we shall see that many of the movements had a family likeness and interacted on one another. In Germany they were largely what is known as Pietism, and in Great Britain and the United States they were usually grouped under the designation Evangelical. So similar were they and so interrelated that the two terms were almost interchangeable and could be and often were applied to them all. In all three regions and in the lands to which they spread they were marked by the emphasis upon personal full commitment to the Christian faith and the spiritual and moral transformation of the individual. They made much of the Bible. They affected both clergy and laity. In most of them laity had a large share and in some were dominant. They were essentially expressions of the distinctive Protestant principles of salvation by faith and the priesthood of all believers. Unlike Roman Catholic awakenings, they did not issue in fresh monastic orders and congregations. Yet they resembled them in their full dedication to God. Usually set, as were the Roman Catholic orders and congregations, in the midst of ostensibly Christian populations, where baptism was nearly universal and tended to be little more than a convention required by law or society, they sought to bring nominal Christians to a full conversion. They also were marked by missions to peoples outside

---

[117] See, for example, the record of Benedict Joseph Labre (1748–1783). Of French birth and reared by a devout uncle, a priest, he was devoted to the sick and dying and spent seven years in pilgrimage to major shrines of his faith.—*The Catholic Encyclopedia*, Vol. II, p. 442.

Christendom. They gave rise to numerous distinctive organizations, many of them of new types. Some of these, usually small communities, were not unlike monasteries in their attempt to live the full Christian life, in the world yet apart from it. But the movements in Protestantism were not concerned solely with the individual. In general they sought to influence society, and this they did by attacking social ills.

The mounting vigour in Protestantism was not confined to Pietist and Evangelical circles. It was also seen in traditional Lutheranism, in the Reformed Churches apart from Pietism, and among those in the Church of England who continued the Catholic heritage. Here and in other circles it gave rise to a flood of literature, some of it of first-class calibre, which, taking cognizance of the thought of the day, sought, sometimes by appropriating its very tools, to vindicate the Christian faith against the critics and to utilize the new intellectual approaches and insights to enrich the understanding and appreciation of the faith.

Here is not the place to attempt to cover in detail these many movements. To do so with any approach to adequacy would require several volumes. All that we can hope to do is to give the main outlines of the ones which were to have the most influence in the following centuries and to mention a few of the more prominent individuals associated with them. In the eighteenth century all of them affected directly only minorities, usually small minorities. It was not until the nineteenth and twentieth centuries that they swelled to large proportions and that their effects became world-wide.

Vitality Issuing from Protestantism in Germany

In Germany the fresh expressions of the vitality in Protestantism were largely through a variety of movements which belonged to the inclusive family of Pietism. However, other movements arose, some antagonistic to Pietism, which were also indications of renewed life.

German Pietism had a long background. It was partly a continuation of the pre-Reformation mysticism of the Rhine Valley represented by the Friends of God and the *Theologia Germanica*. It could and often did claim to be loyal to Luther and to his principles of salvation by faith and the priesthood of all believers. It had forerunners in the pastors Stephen Praetorius (1536–1603) and Philip Nicolai (1556–1608). It owed a debt to Jacob Böhme and to the Lutheran mystic Johann Arndt (1555–1621), whose *Währe Christenthum* ("True Christianity"), first published 1606–1609, had a wide circulation in German and other languages.[118] The love for Jesus and devotion to him which were prominent in much of Pietism had a long history in Lutheran Hymnody.[119]

[118] Ritschl, *Geschichte des Pietismus*, Vol. II, pp. 3–62.
[119] *Ibid.*, pp. 63–93.

German Pietism as it was known in the eighteenth century is usually said to have had as its father Philip Jakob Spener (1635–1705). Highly educated in the theology of his day, and with a doctorate from Strasbourg, Spener was a trained scholar. He had also had a deeply religious rearing and had meditated on Arndt's writings. He was familiar, directly or indirectly, with English Puritanism. Although influenced by Calvinism, he was a Lutheran and remained within that communion. While a pastor at Frankfort he began preaching that more was entailed in being a Christian than participation in the sacraments and services of the Church and abstaining from gross sins. In a sermon in 1669 he set this conviction forth in vigorous manner. He also began to make catechetical instruction more than a routine procedure. In 1670 he commenced holding in his home groups which he called *collegia pietatis* for the cultivation of the Christian life. In 1675 in a preface to a collection of Arndt's sermons which was soon published separately, as *Pia Desideria,* he pled for a reform of the Church. He wished for more gentleness and love. He argued that those training for the ministry should have an experience of conversion and that their preparation should include discipline in personal piety. He maintained that sermons should not be the dry setting forth of doctrine but should edify the congregation. He made much of the priesthood of all believers and held that the laity should participate more largely in the life and work of the Church. He stressed the study of the Bible and extempore prayer and wished a better observance of Sunday. In 1686 he went to Dresden as court preacher but aroused opposition by his strictures on the loose living of the ruler and the latter's entourage. Five years later he became pastor in Berlin. Here he had the favour of the Elector Frederick III (after 1701 King Frederick I of Prussia). In Berlin, too, through Frederick, he had a large voice in naming the members of the theological faculty of the university which the Elector was founding at Halle. Through him that faculty was made up of men who were committed to Pietism. Thus opportunity was given to see fulfilled his dream of the proper training for the ministry. Modest, irenic, paving the way for the union of the Lutherans and Reformed, somewhat dry and heavy in his literary style, and at times giving the appearance of being fearful and hesitating, Spener owed his great influence to a moral earnestness, a conscientiousness, a spiritual depth, and a courage all the more notable because of his native timidity and awakening a response in many who were hungry for that kind of leadership.[120]

Sharing with Spener in the early creative leadership of German Pietism was his younger contemporary, August Hermann Francke (1663–1727). Extremely able, Francke was already a student of the Bible and theology at Leipzig when, in his mid-twenties, he went through a period of struggle, unhappiness, and

---

[120] *Ibid.,* pp. 125–163; *The New Schaff-Herzog Encyclopedia of Religious Knowledge,* Vol. IX, pp. 53–57; Jüngst-Stettin, *Pietisten,* pp. 9–23; Schmid, *Geschichte des Pietismus.* pp. 42–148.

conviction of sin, resolved by a surge of joy and a vivid awareness of God's love and forgiveness. Persecuted in church circles, he was rescued through Spener's initiative and was brought onto the theological faculty of Halle. In Halle he was for years the dominant figure in the religious life. In addition to teaching in the university, he was pastor of a congregation, founded and maintained an orphanage, and had a school for boys in which he broadened the traditional curriculum and pioneered in new educational methods. He also had a school for upper-class girls and a school for teachers. For these institutions financial support flowed in from private donors in a way which was ascribed to answers to believing prayer.[121]

Under the influence of Spener and Francke, Halle became an outstanding centre of Pietism. In addition to those directly organized by Francke, other institutions gave expression to Pietist ideals. For example, a friend of Spener and Francke, Baron Karl Hildebrand von Canstein (1667–1719), who was converted in his twenties, founded a Bible Institute which, among other activities, published inexpensive editions of the New Testament and the entire Bible in several languages.[122] Johann Heinrich Callenberg (1694–1760) began the *Institutum Judaicum* for the education of missionaries to the Jews. It continued for more than sixty years, from 1728 to 1791. Through it many Jews were converted.[123] In 1729 King Frederick William I of Prussia required all candidates for the ministry to spend two years at Halle. Early in the century, in collaboration with others, Francke founded a *collegium orientale theologicum* for the study of the Scriptures in the original languages with the aid of other Oriental languages and to prepare commentaries on them.[124]

By the middle of the eighteenth century the Pietist influence of Halle began to wane. Spener and Francke were now dead. A decline which seems to have set in even before Francke's death was hastened by the control exercised by Frederick II, for the latter could scarcely be expected to favour Pietist practices and beliefs.[125]

Pietism was not confined to Halle, and the waning of Pietism in that centre by no means meant its death. It spread widely in Germany and as it did so it took many forms. In the state churches it made for an increase in the practice of confirmation and of the instruction which preceded it. Some of the early Reformers, Bucer among them, had favoured the continuation of that rite.

---

[121] Jüngst-Stettin, *op. cit.*, pp. 24 ff.; Ritschl, *op. cit.*, Vol. II, pp. 249–294; *The New Schaff-Herzog Encyclopedia of Religious Knowledge*, Vol. IV, pp. 367–369, Vol. IX, pp. 57 ff.; Gustav Kramer, *August Hermann Francke, Ein Lebensbild* (Halle, Buchhandlung des Waisenhauses, 1880), *passim*.
[122] *The New Schaff-Herzog Encyclopedia of Religious Knowledge*, Vol. II, p. 400.
[123] *Ibid.*, pp. 349, 350.
[124] Schmid, *op. cit.*, p. 289.
[125] Ritschl, *op. cit.*, Vol. II, pp. 545 ff.

However, it had tended to lapse. Spener, educated in Strasbourg where the Bucer tradition was strong, advocated its revival, and partly because of him it became common procedure. Some Pietists broke with the state churches. They also developed a great variety of expressions. Although Spener and Francke opposed separatist movements, even in their lifetimes these appeared, together with emotional radicalism. For instance, in Lübeck in 1692 a prophetess gathered something of a following.[126] Another, but quite different Pietist, was Gottfried Arnold (1666–1714), a mystic who had early been influenced by Arndt and who sought union with God through the love of Jesus.[127] Some Pietist groups believed the second coming of Christ to be imminent and some gathered around prophets. Other Pietists not only severed all their connexions with the state churches but also repudiated all organized religion—clergy, sacraments, church buildings, bells—and branded the Church as Babylon.[128]

Pietism gained an extensive and continuing hold in Württemberg. Here Spener came early. Here Pietism was favoured by the duke and some of the faculty of the University of Tübingen. A leader in the Tübingen faculty in furthering Pietism was Christoph Matthäus Pfaff (1686–1760). Widely travelled, a notable scholar, chancellor of the University, his support made for prestige and helped to keep the Pietist movement within the Church. In Tübingen John Albert Bengel (1687–1752) came in touch with Pietism and later was an influential teacher in a theological school. In Württemberg, too, members of the clergy espoused the movement and led the groups into which Pietists gathered. Württemberg Pietism had its chief hold in the rural population and the middle classes in the towns. In North Germany, in contrast, Pietism gained much of its following among the nobility.[129] It remained potent in Württemberg during the decades near the end of the century, when it was waning in the North.

A movement into which strong Pietist strains entered and which had a distinct organization and history and was to exert a profound and wide influence in the eighteenth and later centuries was that of the Moravians. It began with remnants of the Bohemian or Moravian Brethren who traced their spiritual origin to John Hus and others of pre-Reformation times. Expelled from their homes by the Roman Catholic Hapsburgs who had conquered their country in the Thirty Years' War, they were given asylum on the lands of Nicolas Ludwig Graf (Count) von Zinzendorf (1700–1760). Zinzendorf had Spener for a godfather, was reared in a deeply Pietist environment, and was educated

126 *Ibid.*, p. 189.

127 Jüngst-Stettin, *op. cit.*, pp. 46–57; Ritschl, *op. cit.*, Vol. II, pp. 305 ff.

128 Ritschl, *op. cit.*, Vol. II, pp. 322–382; Mallott, *Studies in Brethren History*, p. 24.

129 Ritschl, *op. cit.*, Vol. III, pp. 3–192. For an excellent summary sketch of Pietism, including that of Württemberg, see *The New Schaff-Herzog Encyclopedia of Religious Knowledge*, Vol. IX, pp. 57–67.

at Halle in the days of Francke. Ardent, able, moved by a deep personal love of Christ, he saw in the little bands of refugees a means of fulfilling his dream of carrying the Gospel to the world. They centred in a village, Herrnhut, which they erected on his estates. They maintained their distinct ecclesiastical organization, and in time Zinzendorf was consecrated as a bishop of their church. Zinzendorf sought to establish fellowship with members of other communions, including Roman Catholics, based on devotion to Christ, and longed for the unity of all Christians. He was severely criticized in several quarters: he was said to have been too lordly and domineering and at times to have held antinomian views. Yet his achievements as a leader are unquestioned. As the *Unitas Fratrum* the Moravians were found in many different parts of the world and maintained widespread missions. They sought to bring fresh life into the state churches of Europe. Beginning in 1754 annual conferences were held at Herrnhut to which both clergy and laity came to report on their labours and for encouragement and inspiration. Here was a Protestant equivalent of one of the orders or congregations of the Roman Catholic Church.[130]

A movement strongly influenced by Pietism was what is best known as the Church of the Brethren. Its chief originator was Alexander Mack, a wealthy miller from the Palatinate. He and a few others gave themselves to a study of the Scriptures. Desiring to return to primitive Christianity as they found it in the New Testament, they rejected both the state churches and the pure individualism of the extreme separatists, adopted trine (three-fold) immersion of believers, and organized a church. Missionary-minded, they multiplied but were persecuted. In 1719 some migrated to Pennsylvania, where religious tolerance offered haven. In 1729 they were followed by most of the others and their church died out in Europe. In America, although always a minority, they multiplied, shared with Quakers and Mennonites in a pacifist witness, and had an honoured history.[131]

Varied though they were, the large majority of Pietists had a common likeness. They believed in conversion, and many held that it was normally preceded by deep conviction of sin which was followed by a sudden entrance into the new life. They placed great emphasis upon the Bible and esteemed it as the standard by which to construct and test creeds, ethics, and organizations. Usually they came together in small informal groups, either inside or outside

[130] Out of the enormous literature on Zinzendorf and the history of the Moravians see J. Taylor Hamilton, *A History of the Church Known as the Moravian Church or the Unitas Fratrum or the Unity of the Brethren during the Eighteenth and Nineteenth Centuries* (Bethlehem, Pa., Times Publishing Co., 1900, pp. xi, 631); J. E. Hutton, *A History of the Moravian Church* (London, Moravian Publication Office, 2nd ed., 1909, pp. 520); William George Addison, *The Renewed Church of the United Brethren, 1722–1930* (London, Society for Promoting Christian Knowledge, 1932, pp. 228).

[131] Mallott, *op. cit.*, pp. 24–40; Otto Winger, *History of the Church of the Brethren* (Elgin, Ill., Brethren Publishing House, 1920, pp. 320), pp. 17–22.

the state churches, for fellowship, study, and prayer. They were marked by a high moral earnestness. Many of them not only condemned dishonesty and sexual offences but also looked with disfavour on the theatre, dancing, and card-playing. In this they were but holding to what had long been taught by some other communions, including the Roman Catholic Church of the Middle Ages. They were generally distrustful of an emphasis upon doctrine and sought, rather, a personal experience of Christ. Some seemed to be self-righteous and to judge unfavourably those who did not conform to their patterns. Many gave the impression of not being interested in art, science, or general culture. Their influence made for improvement in manners. For example, they raised the moral tone of much of Württemberg. They were given to philanthropy and to institutions for the care of the underprivileged. In their joyous faith and their sense of salvation and communion with God they gave birth to many hymns. Theirs was one of the streams which entered into the romantic movement. For instance, Pietism greatly influenced Friedrich Leopold, Freiherr von Hardenberg (1772–1801), better known as Novalis, poet, novelist, a pioneer in the romantic tradition, who wished to bring life, poetry, science, and religion into one whole.[132] In the course of our story we shall again and again meet German Pietism and its repercussions. In the nineteenth century it swelled to large proportions, often with direct continuity with eighteenth-century strains, and it persisted into the twentieth century.

Pietism was the occasion of much controversy. It had opponents both among the exponents of the *Aufklärung* and among the supporters of the churches. Many Lutherans believed that it was undercutting or not placing sufficient emphasis upon the orthodox formulations of doctrine which to their mind were essential to the faith.

Some of the opposition of the orthodox was from those who lamented the evils in the churches against which the Pietists protested and who sought to reduce or eliminate them, but through traditional channels. Thus Ernst Valentin Loescher (1673–1749), Lutheran pastor and superintendent at Dresden, an outstanding leader of the orthodox, opposed on the one hand Wolff as tending to philosophic indifferentism and on the other hand Pietism. But he also strove to raise the level of moral living and to deepen the spiritual life in the churches.[133]

Towards the end of the century the revival within German and German-Swiss Protestantism found fresh expression and was given an impetus through *Die deutsche Christentums Gesellschaft* ("the German Christian Fellowship"). At first known as *Die deutsche Gesellschaft zur Beförderung christlichen Wahr-*

---

[132] Johann R. Thierstein, *Novalis und der Pietismus* (Whitewater, Kan., privately printed, 1910, pp. 127. A doctoral dissertation at the University of Bern), *passim*.
[133] *The New Schaff-Herzog Encyclopedia of Religious Knowledge*, Vol. VII, pp. 11, 12.

heit und Gottseligkeit ("The German Society for the Promotion of Christian Truth and Piety"), it arose out of the efforts of Johann August Urlsperger. Believing that the friends of the Gospel should stand together, from 1777 to 1780 he wrote and travelled. From 1782 Basel was made the headquarters and became a notable centre for home and foreign missions.[134]

PIETISM SPRINGS UP AND TAKES ROOT OUTSIDE OF GERMAN LUTHERANISM

Pietism was not confined to German Lutheranism. It flourished among the Reformed Churches in the Netherlands, Germany, and Switzerland, became rooted in Lutheran Churches outside Germany, notably in Scandinavia and in the Thirteen Colonies in British America, and gave rise to missions among non-European peoples.

From its strongholds in Lutheran Germany Pietism had repercussions in the Reformed Churches in other parts of Germany and the German-speaking parts of Switzerland.

It found the ground prepared by movements among the Reformed Churches in the Netherlands which in origin were earlier than the currents issuing from German Lutheranism. Indeed, it is significant that nearly independently of each other and almost contemporaneously in the Reformed Churches of the Netherlands and in the Lutheran Churches of Germany awakenings having so many common likenesses were breaking forth. Eewood Teellinck (c. 1570–1629), a burgomaster, elder in the Reformed Church, deplored theological controversy and wrote devotional literature. His youngest brother, Willem Teellinck (1579–1629), a Reformed pastor, influenced by the English Puritans, began as a Pietist and ended as a mystic. Two of Willem's sons, Maximiliaan and Jan, were also ministers and Pietists.[135] Gijsbert Voet (1589–1676), pastor, professor in Utrecht, prodigiously learned, with an enquiring mind and a vast knowledge of theology and Oriental languages, a staunch advocate of Reformed orthodoxy and a vigorous critic of Descartes, was a warm supporter of righteous living and encouraged his students to gather in small groups for the cultivation of the devotional life. He approved similar groups in Reformed parishes.[136] Johannes Cocceius (1603–1669), a master of languages, especially Hebrew, professor in Leiden, was a chief formulator of "federal theology." He based his teaching on the Bible rather than on Reformed orthodoxy, emphasized grace and the covenant of grace, gave his theology a practical bent, and in an age of bitter theological controversy was singularly irenic. Voet was emphatic in

---

[134] Rouse and Neill, *A History of the Ecumenical Movement*, pp. 117, 118; *The New Schaff-Herzog Encyclopedia of Religious Knowledge*, Vol. III, pp. 38, 39.

[135] *The New Schaff-Herzog Encyclopedia of Religious Knowledge*, Vol. XI, pp. 287, 288.

[136] Ritschl, *op. cit.*, Vol. I, pp. 101–124; Wilhelm Goeters, *Die Vorbereitung des Pietismus in der Niederlande bis zur Labadistischen Crisis 1670* (Leipzig, J. C. Hinrichs, 1911, pp. viii, 300), *passim*.

his polemic against the federal theology and those who followed Cocceius were more disposed than their master to enter into debate. The Cocceian theology made easier the way of Pietism.[137] Both Voet and Cocceius had as a pupil Jodous van Lodensteyn (1620–1677). He moved in the direction of a mysticism which was akin to Pietism.[138] Quite different was Jean de Labadie (1610–1674). French by birth, educated by the Jesuits, for a time himself a Jesuit, he joined the Reformed Church, preached in Geneva, later was pastor in the Netherlands, and at last, refusing to subscribe to the Belgic Confession or to use the Reformed liturgy, left the Reformed Church to head a small group which dressed simply, practised community of goods, and disappeared about 1732. His writings on asceticism, meditation, and contemplation spread widely through the Reformed Churches and had an influence far beyond the circles of his immediate followers.[139] The quietist writings of the Roman Catholic Molinos and Fénelon, translated into Dutch, also made an impression on some.[140]

Many, ministers and laymen, in the Reformed Church of Holland longed to see spiritual and moral awakenings. In the 1740's, for example, the preaching of Kuypers led to conviction of sin followed by conversion and striking emotional manifestations which were similar to what was being seen not far from the same time under the preaching of Wesley and other Evangelicals in Britain and in the Great Awakening in the Thirteen Colonies in America. Conventicles arose of the converted, sometimes within the state church and sometimes separating from it.[141]

It was largely through contagion from these awakenings in the Netherlands that Pietist movements sprang up in the Reformed Churches in the portions of Germany which either bordered on Holland or were not far from its frontiers. We hear of them in the Ruhr Valley, in East Friesland, in Düsseldorf, in Wesel, and in Duisberg.[142]

In mid-Germany the Reformed Churches were so closely under the control of the state that they found it difficult or impossible adequately to discipline their members. When, therefore, the awakenings reached that region, they often led to the formation of groups outside the state churches. Only thus, it was believed, could the Christian ideals which they embodied be realized. Here,

[137] Ritschl, *op. cit.*, Vol. I, pp. 130–152; *The New Schaff-Herzog Encyclopedia of Religious Knowledge*, Vol. III, pp. 149–151.

[138] Ritschl, *op. cit.*, Vol. I, pp. 152–194.

[139] *Ibid.*, pp. 194–268; *The New Schaff-Herzog Encyclopedia of Religious Knowledge*, Vol. VI, pp. 390, 391; Heinrich Heppe, *Geschichte des Pietismus und der Mystik in der Reformirten Kirche, namentlich der Niederlande* (Leiden, E. J. Brill, 1879, pp. xvi, 503), *passim*.

[140] Ritschl, *op. cit.*, Vol. I, p. 302.

[141] *Ibid.*, pp. 283–363.

[142] *Ibid.*, pp. 367–396.

farther from the Dutch border, the influence of Lutheran Pietism was, quite understandably, stronger than that of the Netherlands.[143]

Several men stand out in the Pietism of the German Reformed Churches. A pioneer was Theodore Untereyck (1635–1693), who had been in touch with English Puritanism and Dutch Pietism. As pastor in the Ruhr and in Bremen he had a wide and profound influence. One of his converts, Joachim Neander (1650–1680), in a brief life wrote hymns which gained wide currency. Of these the most famous was "Lobe den Herrn, den mächtigen König der Ehren" ("Praise to the Lord, the Almighty, the King of creation"). Another prominent German Reformed Pietist was Friedrich Adolf Lampe (1683–1729). Born in Bremen, the son of a pastor, in his student days he was in touch with the ideas of Cocceius. As pastor and then professor at Utrecht, he belonged to the Cocceian federalist school and incorporated what he derived from it in an earnest Pietism. That Pietism also drew from Voet. He was against excessive individualism and separating from the established churches.[144] Most of the clergy who were under his influence took the same attitude.

Gerhard Tersteegen (1697–1769) in his youth gave up a mercantile career to live as a hermit, sharing his goods with the poor and subjecting a naturally weak body to physical privation. Later he softened the rigour of his asceticism and established a semi-monastic community on the divide between the Ruhr and the Wupper. The inward peace which was his great joy came through accepting the reconciling grace of Christ. He refused to conform to confessional churches, for he regarded them as sectarian, and discovered kindred spirits in biographies of great souls in many of the communions, including the Roman Catholic Church. He was an outstanding figure among the groups which can roughly be classed as Pietist and which refused to remain within the existing churches. Yet he is said never to have left the Reformed Church. He wrote extensively, conducted private devotional meetings, and was the author of numbers of hymns. Many of these found their way into the collections of the Reformed Churches.[145]

Samuel Callenbusch (1724–1803), a mystic of Barmen, who became much interested in theology and centred his writings on the conception of revelation in history seen in the Biblical story and finally accomplished on the cross, attracted a continuing following. Among other contributions, they organized a missionary society and a mission house which in the nineteenth century played a part in the extension of the faith in other lands. A Lutheran, and in touch

---

[143] *Ibid.*, pp. 397–427.

[144] *Ibid.*, pp. 428–454; *The New Schaff-Herzog Encyclopedia of Religious Knowledge*, Vol. VI, p. 405; Good, *History of the Reformed Church in Germany*, pp. 323–394.

[145] Ritschl, *op. cit.*, Vol. I, pp. 455–494; *The New Schaff-Herzog Encyclopedia of Religious Knowledge*, Vol. XI, p. 304; Good, *op. cit.*, pp. 447–470.

with the Pietism of Württemberg, Callenbusch's influence was felt in the Reformed Churches.[146]

In Switzerland, more remote from the Netherlands, German strains were more potent in Pietism than in mid-Germany. Outstanding among the Swiss Pietists was the mystic Johann Caspar Lavater (1741–1801). A native of Zürich, he spent most of his life in that city. He had a warm interest in individuals and through his insight and sympathy won the confidence of hundreds, both in Zürich and elsewhere. His correspondence with those who sought his counsel grew to large proportions. A mystic, he placed little emphasis on dogma but held to the Bible. He developed a great interest in occult psychic phenomena as manifestations of the supernatural. Although a pastor in a Reformed church, he had little use for confessional divisions but stressed the love of Christ and would have fellowship with kindred spirits in other communions.[147]

Pietism entered Denmark from Germany. In 1704 F. J. Lütkens came as court preacher to Frederick IV. He represented the Halle tradition, with a strain of Pietism which sought to remain within the state church. Early in the eighteenth century conventicles of the converted arose in Copenhagen which were very critical of the official church and denounced it as Babylon. Outstanding in their inception were two German students. The conventicles and the convictions which they expressed were, not unnaturally, met by denunciations from the pulpits of the establishment. However, Frederick IV, although far from above reproach in his private morals, was friendly to Pietism, and a great fire of 1728 which laid waste much of Copenhagen made many of the populace responsive to the Pietist preaching. Moreover, since Pietism was favoured by the king and some other members of the royal family, men of Pietist views filled some of the pulpits of the Church. In the 1730's the influence of the Moravians made itself felt: Zinzendorf himself visited Copenhagen. Under Christian VI, who came to the throne in 1730, for a time Pietism had further gains within the state church. At royal command the notable scholar, pastor, court preacher, and professor in the university Erick Pontopiddan (1698–1764) prepared a catechism and hymnal which aided the spread of Pietist teachings. The catechism was to facilitate the religious instruction compulsory for all Danes in preparation for the rite of confirmation. That rite was now enforced. Eventually Christian VI sought to eradicate all Pietist conventicles and non-conforming sects and to bring in religious uniformity. In 1741 an edict to that effect was promulgated. Yet Pietism continued. Pontopiddan, eminent as a scholar and in late middle life with a notable though stormy record as Bishop of Bergen, gave

146 Ritschl, *op. cit.*, Vol. I, pp. 565 ff.;   *The New Schaff-Herzog Encyclopedia of Religious Knowledge*, Vol. III, pp. 160, 161.
147 Ritschl, *op. cit.*, Vol. I, pp. 494–523; *The New Schaff-Herzog Encyclopedia of Religious Knowledge*, Vol. VI, pp. 423, 424.

it support in a moderate form. In the latter part of the eighteenth century the Enlightenment reinforced a secular attitude, but Pietism did not die.[148]

During this period Norway was united with Denmark under a common monarch. It was, therefore, to be expected that Pietism would have something of the course that it had in Denmark. As in Denmark, it entered and flourished in the first half of the century. Peder Hersleb (1689–1752), bishop in Christiania from 1730 to 1737, had had contact with Halle and was influenced by it. Pontopiddan as bishop in Bergen favoured integrating Pietism in the state church. The royal requirement of confirmation and the compulsory use of the catechism prepared by Pontopiddan made an impression. The edict of 1741 was adverse, and in the second half of the century the Enlightenment tended to undercut the movement. Yet, as we are to see in the next chapter, far from dying, Pietism survived and in the last decade of the century staged a notable revival under purely Norwegian leadership, that of Hauge.[149]

At the beginning of the eighteenth century the Church of Sweden was predominantly a legalistic, intellectualized, institutionalized Lutheranism. Yet the ground had been prepared for Pietism by the mysticism of Arndt: it had made its way through his writings and a hymn book. In 1677 Pietism arrived through the head of the German school in Stockholm. Spener aided it by correspondence with the queen. In the 1690's Swedish students went to the University of Halle and through them the Halle type of Pietism was reinforced. In the second decade of the eighteenth century it achieved something of a spread, but was chiefly confined to two groups in Stockholm. It was further strengthened through a Pietistic awakening among Swedish prisoners of war in Russia. In 1721 and 1726 edicts were issued against secret private gatherings and bore hard upon Pietists. The death of Francke (1727) weakened the tie with Halle and dealt a further blow. Yet in the 1730's Pietism revived and had the support of influential men among the clergy. Eric Tollstadius (died 1759), a leading pastor in Stockholm, espoused it. Eric Benzelius (1675–1743), Bishop of Linköping and in his later years Archbishop of Uppsala, was sympathetic. So was the learned Peter Murbeck (1708–1766), who was zealous for the education of youth and has sometimes been called the Francke of Sweden. Here, too, must be placed Andreas Rydelius (1671–1738), Bishop of Lund, called the first well-known independent philosopher of Sweden. Through Pietist influence, some of the bishops were more zealous in the care of souls.

More radical forms of Pietism entered, with greater emphasis upon mysti-

---

[148] Koch, *Danmarks Kirke gennem Tiderne*, pp. 93–120; *The Cambridge Modern History*, Vol. VI, p. 739. On Pontopiddan see Koch, *op. cit.*, pp. 105, 109, 110; *The New Schaff-Herzog Encyclopedia of Religious Knowledge*, Vol. IX, p. 124; Johannes Pederson in Koch and Kornerup, *Den Danske Kirkes Historie*, Vol. V, pp. 11–229.

[149] Welle, *Norges Kirkehistorie. Kirkens Historie*, Vol. III, pp. 100–146.

cism. Here Sven Rosen (died 1750) was prominent. Support came from Johann Conrad Dippel. A polemic writer, he was imprisoned in Denmark from 1719 to 1726 and on his release went to Stockholm. His doctrine of the atonement differed from that held by more conservative Pietists.[150]

Moravian Pietism also penetrated Sweden, as it did Denmark and Norway. A Swede was present at the renewal of the *Unitas Fratrum* (1727) and on his return to Sweden two years later brought a fresh and distinctive impulse to Pietist circles. In 1735 Zinzendorf made a brief visit to Sweden and found the Bishop of Lund sympathetic. Intent upon working an awakening in the established church, under the stimulus of Zinzendorf the Moravians sent some of their number to Sweden. Their missionaries were largely unlearned Swedish artisans. Since the edicts of 1721 and 1726 had not fully eliminated Pietist conventicles, in 1735, at the instance of the clergy, a still stricter order was passed in restraint of those who, like the Moravians, differed from the state church. Yet Moravian groups continued to multiply. We hear of them in Stockholm and in several other centres. Many pastors and even bishops of the state church became sympathetic. It is said that about 1750 out of approximately 3,200 pastors of the Church of Sweden not far from 100 were looking with favour on the Moravians and their type of piety. Moravian literature was widely read. The spread of the Enlightenment with its optimistic view of the world was paralleled by a spiritual hunger which led some to seek satisfaction in the Moravian message. In the last quarter of the century the Moravians continued to increase, both through immigration and by conversions through their missionaries.[151]

Lest we give a distorted picture, we must note that other new currents affected the religious life of eighteenth-century Sweden than those which issued from Pietism. The influence of Christian Wolff entered, although in a moderated form.[152] Through various channels, partly through what a preacher in the Swedish legation in London had seen in the Church of England, confirmation became much more general. Orthodoxy was less obscurantist and the quality of church life was improving. For a time in some circles Roman Catholic mysticism became popular. In the latter decades of the century, partly

[150] Hilding Pleijel, *Der Schwedische Pietismus in seinen Beziehungen zu Deutschland* (in *Lunds Univrsitets Arsskrift*, N.F. Avd. 1, Bd. 31, Nr. 4. Lund, C. W. K. Gleerup, 1935, pp. 236), *passim;* Ove Nordstrandh, *Den Aldre Svenska Pietismens Litteratur* (Stockholm, Svenska Kyrkans Diakonistyrelses Bokförlag, 1951, pp. 349), *passim;* Pleijel, *Karolinsk Kyrkofromhet, Pietism och Herrnhutism, 1680–1772,* pp. 263–369, 513–522; *The New Schaff-Herzog Encyclopedia of Religious Knowledge,* Vol. XI, p. 180.

[151] Hilding Pleijel, *Das Kirchenproblem der Brüdergemeine in Schweden: eine Kirchengeschichtliche Untersuchung* (in *Lunds Universitets Arsskrift,* N.F. Avd. 1, Bd. 33, Nr. 6. Lund, C. W. K. Gleerup, 1938, pp. 199), *passim;* Pleijel, *Karolinsk Kyrkofromhet, Pietism och Herrnhutism, 1680–1772,* pp. 377–503.

[152] Pleijel, *Karolinsk Kyrkofromhet, Pietism och Herrnhutism, 1680–1772,* pp. 522 ff.

through royal patronage, the Enlightenment made itself felt, but without such extreme effects as in some other countries.[153]

An eighteenth-century Swede whose influence spread widely and persisted into the twentieth century but who did not fit into the usual Christian patterns was Emanuel Swedenborg (1688–1772). The son of a professor of theology and bishop in the Church of Sweden, in his youth he was in a somewhat unconventional religious atmosphere, for his father was accused of making more of faith, hope, and communion with God than of dogma. Widely travelled and possessing a prodigious range of learning, especially in engineering and the natural sciences, late in life he devoted himself to religion and an intensive study of the Bible. He was convinced that through visions and dreams Christ had given him fresh revelations. He wrote voluminously and through his books influenced such first-class minds as Kant and Goethe and many men of lesser stature, both in Western Europe and in Russia. From him eventually arose the numerically small but widely spread Church of the New Jerusalem.[154]

During most of the eighteenth century Finland was attached to Sweden, both politically and culturally. Again and again it was devastated by wars between the Swedes and the Russians. The majority of the population, both Swedish and Finnish, were Lutherans. Pietism first made itself felt late in the seventeenth century, when Johannes Vigelius the elder corresponded with Spener. As in other Scandinavian countries, in the eighteenth century Pietism came in three main streams. One was the kind which was largely shaped by Spener and which remained within the Church. A second, more emotional, even ecstatic, tended to separate from the official church. A third was that of the Moravians. As in Sweden, Pietism was early given an impetus by prisoners of war returning from Russia, where they had had a deep religious experience. The pastor Abraham Achrenius (1706–1769) was outstanding as a leader. The first strongholds of Pietism were in the upper classes, but after the middle of the century, coming from the South-west, it began to take root among the masses. Its fruitage was emphasis upon a new birth issuing in a new life, warm religious poetry and hymns, more instruction before confirmation, and an increase in that rite. In the second half of the century the Enlightenment made headway. It encouraged religious tolerance and, among the clergy, more interest in improving the material and moral life of the parishioners.[155]

---

[153] *Ibid.*, pp. 543–546; *The New Schaff-Herzog Encyclopedia of Religious Knowledge*, Vol. XI, p. 181.

[154] Pleijel, *Karolinsk Kyrkofromhet, Pietism och Herrnhutism, 1680–1772*, pp. 503–513; *Swedenborg's Works* (Boston, Houghton Mifflin Co., 32 vols., no date); *The New Schaff-Herzog Encyclopedia of Religious Knowledge*, Vol. XI, pp. 183–188.

[155] Martti Ruuth in Siegmund-Schultze, *Ekklesia: Die Kirche in Finnland*, pp. 44–47; Aleski Lehtonen in *ibid.*, p. 65.

PIETISM QUICKENS THE GEOGRAPHIC SPREAD OF THE FAITH

A striking expression of the Pietist movements was missions both in Europe and in other lands. In addition to missions among the professed Christians in Europe and to the wide effects outside Pietist circles, before the outbreak of the French Revolution missions issued from Pietism to non-Christians in all five continents and many of the islands of the sea, and also to colonies of Christian ancestry in America.

Until the eighteenth century Protestants had had very few missions among non-Christians. That was partly because they were late in becoming active in commerce and colonization and because most of the non-European world was closed to them. In the seventeenth century, to be sure, Dutch Protestants had missions in South Africa, Ceylon, the East Indies, and, briefly, in Formosa, and in British North America efforts were put forth to win the Indians.[156]

In the eighteenth century Protestant missionary enterprises multiplied. Several stemmed from Halle. We have mentioned that for the Jews. In addition, personnel was provided for a mission begun by the King of Denmark and based upon a Danish trading post in Tranquebar, in South India. The two pioneers Ziegenbalg and Plütschau arrived in India in 1706. They were followed by others, most of the early ones selected by Francke. A mission board in Copenhagen had supervisory powers.[157] From that nucleus in the following two centuries several strong churches arose, some Lutheran and others Anglican. From Denmark and Norway, largely through men who had been gripped by Pietism, missions were carried on among the Lapps.[158] In Greenland a mission was inaugurated in 1721 by Hans Egede, of Norway, which continued into the following two centuries until practically all the sparse population bore the Christian name.[159] It was mostly from Halle that the men came who gathered into Lutheran congregations the German immigrants to the Thirteen Colonies. The outstanding leader was Henry Melchior Muhlenberg (1711–1787). In his youth he had come under the influence of Pietism and after his graduation from Göttingen he taught in institutions at Halle. He had hoped to serve in India, but when the door there seemed closed he accepted the invitation to go to America. That invitation was given at the suggestion of the son of A. H. Francke. Although some non-Halle ministers later joined him, it was from Halle that much of the personnel and the money came which effectively planted Lutheranism among the German-Americans.[160]

---

[156] Latourette, *A History of the Expansion of Christianity*, Vol. III, pp. 217–220, 222–224, 245, 289, 290, 303, 304, 359, 360.

[157] For a brief summary and a selected bibliography, see *ibid.*, pp. 278, 279.

[158] For a bibliography see *ibid.*, p. 65.

[159] For a bibliography see *ibid.*, p. 238.

[160] *The Journals of Henry Melchior Muhlenberg*, translated by T. G. Tappert and J. W. Dober-

Moravian missions were widespread. They had Herrnhut as their radiating centre, but in time they were also from Moravian groups elsewhere. During his lifetime Zinzendorf had much to do with stimulating them, and after his death they continued to grow. Before the outbreak of the French Revolution they were in the Danish West Indies, several of the British West Indian islands, Greenland, at least four Indian tribes in what was by then the United States, among the Negroes and Indians in the Dutch possessions in South America, among the Hottentots in South Africa, in Labrador, among the Jews in Europe, in Lapland, on the Guinea coast of Africa, in more than one place in Russia, in Ceylon, in Algiers, in Wallachia, in Persia, in Abyssinia, and in India. In most of these places the missions were transient. In several they continued into the nineteenth and even into the twentieth century.[161]

The Pietism in the Reformed Churches seems not to have played an outstanding role in the planting of the Dutch Reformed and the German Reformed Churches in the Thirteen Colonies. Yet we hear that the earliest ordained minister of the Reformed Church in Pennsylvania was a Pietist.[162]

VIGOUR IN FRENCH PROTESTANTISM

French Protestantism also displayed vigour. This was not necessarily in a Pietist fashion: it was, rather, in distinctive ways. The drastic measures taken by Louis XIV near the end of the seventeenth and the beginning of the eighteenth century to eradicate Protestantism in his realms led on the one hand to extensive migrations and on the other to a highly emotional revolt.

The migrations planted the Huguenots in many countries—among them Prussia, Holland, England, the British colonies in America, and South Africa. From their descendants came many Protestant leaders of succeeding centuries.

In Southern France a movement called the Camisards sprang up. Its adherents seem never to have numbered much more than five thousand. Its leaders and members had visions and trances and in its camps preaching, praying, and fasting were the custom. Looking for the early end of the Papacy, its members destroyed churches and killed priests. As a revolt it lasted from 1702 to 1705, when it was ruthlessly suppressed by armed force aided by a Papal bull proclaiming a crusade against it.[163] Some of its members escaped to England and there, known as the French Prophets, began a movement which flourished for

---

stein (Philadelphia, The Muhlenberg Press, 3 vols., 1942 ff.); A. R. Wentz, *The Lutheran Church in American History* (Philadelphia, The United Lutheran Publishing House, 2nd ed., 1933, pp. 465), pp. 65–86.

[161] J. E. Hutton, *A History of Moravian Missions* (London, Moravian Publication Office, 1923, pp. 550), pp. 15–166.

[162] J. H. Dubbs, *History of the Reformed Church, German* (in *The American Church History Series*, Vol. VIII, pp. 213–423, New York, the Christian Literature Society, 1895), p. 245.

[163] *The New Schaff-Herzog Encyclopedia of Religious Knowledge*, Vol. II, pp. 368, 369.

a short time. It was ecstatic, claimed to work miracles of healing, and looked for the early second coming of Christ.[164]

The Surge of Fresh Life in English Protestantism

The weaknesses which we have described in English Protestantism during the eighteenth century were but one side of the picture. In both the Church of England and the Nonconforming bodies there was life. It was seen early in the century, and in spite of the cold rationalism and moralistic preaching which characterized many of the pulpits and the pluralism of numbers of the clergy it continued to grow. It took several forms. Some of it was akin to the Catholic tradition of the Church of England. More of it had likenesses to the Pietism of the Continent and some of it was influenced by that Pietism.

An important expression was in the Religious Societies which began to appear at least as early as 1678. They were composed largely of young men and most of them seem to have been in London. Generally they had a clergyman of the Church of England as a director. They met regularly for prayer and discussion, and their members went to communion weekly or monthly and were active in philanthropic undertakings.[165] The earliest of them seem to have come into being as the result of the labours of Anthony Horneck (1641–1697), a German educated in Heidelberg, a man of saintly character whose books dealt chiefly with the devotional life and who preached with marked effect in London. About 1691 societies for the Reformation of manners began to spring up.[166] Whether or not they were due to contact with Pietism, they had a striking similarity to Pietist groups and were evidence of a temper of mind in England which was akin to Pietism. The tides of life were running strong, even if only among minorities and not in such fashion as to attract much public attention.

Two organizations founded in 1698 and 1701 respectively, the Society for Promoting Christian Knowledge and the Society for the Propagation of the Gospel in Foreign Parts, were evidence of an active missionary interest in the Church of England. They were not the first missionary organizations to arise in that church but were quite the most notable which had appeared in that communion. Both owed much to the Religious Societies, for it was from circles influenced by them that they chiefly drew their support. The immediate initiative for the formation of the Society for Promoting Christian Knowledge was from a clergyman, Thomas Bray (1656–1730).[167] The son of a farmer, trained

---

164 *Ibid.*, Vol. IV, p. 383.

165 Moorman, *A History of the Church in England*, p. 267.

166 Allen and McClure, *Two Hundred Years: The History of the Society for Promoting Christian Knowledge, 1698–1898*, pp. 7, 8; *Dictionary of National Biography*, Vol. IX, pp. 1261, 1262.

167 H. P. Thompson, *Thomas Bray* (London, Society for Promoting Christian Knowledge, 1954, pp. vii, 119), *passim*.

at Oxford, with organizing ability and a devotion which asked nothing for himself and often made costly sacrifices, he was briefly Commissary in Maryland for the Bishop of London. He wished an organization which would provide libraries for clergymen in the colonies and also in England and Wales. He enlisted the support of influential laymen and bishops.[168] Bray's dream also called for the sending of missionaries. In this phase it was given effect by the Society for the Propagation of the Gospel in Foreign Parts. For many years confined to the British Empire, the latter eventually extended its field beyond even those broad limits. In the eighteenth century it sent many missionaries to the English colonies, chiefly to those in North America.[169] Both societies continued into the twentieth century and as time passed they greatly extended their operations.

The Society for Promoting Christian Knowledge helped to provide books for the charity or circulating schools in Wales which arose early in the century from the efforts of Griffith Jones (1683–1761).[170] A priest of the established church, soon after his ordination (1709) Jones began itinerant preaching, sometimes in churches and often in the open air. He promoted schools to teach the illiterate, both youths and adults, to read the Bible in Welsh. By the time of his death over 3,000 such schools had been held, usually by travelling teachers, in which over 150,000 are said to have learned to read. The bishops were never friendly and many of the clergy opposed Jones.

From the Church of England and its sister, the Church of Ireland, in a day of intellectual attack, came outstanding defenders of the faith. We have already mentioned Joseph Butler, who, in his famous *Analogy of Religion,* turned against the enemy some of the latter's weapons. Equally notable, but with a quite different approach, was his slightly older contemporary, George Berkeley (1685–1753). Born, reared, and educated in Ireland and in later years Bishop of Cloyne on that island, Berkeley was largely a product of the Irish branch of the Anglican communion. In his philosophy and theology he supported Christianity against "free-thinkers" in a fresh manner which in the nineteenth and twentieth centuries made him an important figure in thought both in and outside the Church. Rejecting the methods of medieval scholasticism, he did not adopt the extreme rationalism which in his day seemed to undercut much of

168 Allen and McClure, *op. cit.,* pp. 13 ff.

169 H. P. Thompson, *Into All Lands: The History of the Society for the Propagation of the Gospel in Foreign Parts, 1701–1950* (London, S.P.C.K., 1951, pp. xiii, 760), *passim,* especially pp. 6–91; C. F. Pascoe, *Two Hundred Years of the S.P.G., An Historical Account of the Society for the Propagation of the Gospel in Foreign Parts, 1701–1900* (London, at the Society's Office, 1901, pp. xli, 1429); C. F. Pascoe, *Classified Digest of the Records of the Society for the Propagation of the Gospel in Foreign Parts, 1701–1892* (London, at the Society's Office, 1893, pp. xvi, 980).

170 *Dictionary of National Biography,* Vol. X, pp. 991, 992.

belief in revelation, but developed his own form of idealism and held that it reinforced the faith.[171]

From the Church of England issued notable devotional writings, buttressed by efforts at consistent Christian living. Outstanding was William Law (1686–1761). A Tory, long a supporter of the exiled Stuarts, he was the author of polemic writings. But he exerted the widest influence and was best remembered for two books, *A Treatise on Christian Perfection* (1726) and *A Serious Call to a Holy and Devout Life* (1728). Here he owed a debt to the pre-Pietist German mystic Jakob Böhme. He endeavoured to practise what he preached and for a time a small group gathered about him who sought to live simply in Christian community and to give themselves to the needy.[172]

From early in the eighteenth century the Nonconformist churches also showed vigour, looming larger than did groups on the Continent which dissented from the state churches. As we have suggested, the strongest Nonconforming groups were the Independents (Congregationalists), the Presbyterians, the Baptists, and the Quakers.

After the intense activity of the preceding century a degree of lethargy had come upon the dissenters. They still were subject to legal and social disabilities. For instance, they were taxed to support the Church of England and could not take degrees in the universities. Yet the Toleration Act of 1689 removed some of the more galling restrictions.

In the Nonconforming churches fresh evidences of vitality began to appear. One of these was in hymns. Isaac Watts (1674–1748) was a pioneer; the first collection of his hymns was published in 1707. Until he wrote, in the English churches, both of the establishment and those outside it, the singing in public worship was mostly psalms. Hymns were few and generally of inferior quality. Watts, an Independent (Congregational) minister, wrote hymns which put that form of poetry safely in English public worship. Some were based upon psalms: others were entirely fresh creations. Several were in common use throughout the period covered by our volumes. Among them were "Joy to the world, the Lord has come," "O God our help in ages past," "When I survey the wondrous cross on which the Prince of Glory died," and "Jesus shall reign where'er the sun doth his successive journeys run."[173] Philip Doddridge (1702–1751), a younger contemporary of Watts, was consciously inspired by the latter and took him as a model. Among his hymns which continued to be

---

[171] *The Works of George Berkeley, Bishop of Cloyne,* edited by A. A. Luce and T. E. Jessop (London and Edinburgh, Thomas Nelson and Sons, 6 vols., 1949–1953).

[172] *The Works of the Reverend William Law, M.A.* (London, 1762, reprinted by G. Moreton, 9 vols., 1892, 1893). See a brief biographical sketch in *Dictionary of National Biography,* Vol. XI, pp. 677–681.

[173] Manning, *The Hymns of Wesley and Watts,* pp. 78–105; Thomas Wright, *Isaac Watts and Contemporary Hymn-Writers* (London, C. J. Farncombe & Sons, 1914, pp. xii, 280), *passim.*

sung in the nineteenth and twentieth centuries were "Awake my soul, stretch every nerve and press with vigour on," "How gentle God's commands," and "O God of Bethel by whose hand thy people still are led." In addition, prompted by Watts, he wrote *The Rise and Progress of Religion in the Soul,* which had a prolonged and wide circulation.[174]

Another of the contributions of the Nonconformists to eighteenth-century England was in education. Since they were excluded from the universities, the Nonconformists organized their own institutions of learning and called them academies. Some of the academies had a greater flexibility in curriculum and were more alive intellectually than were the Oxford and Cambridge of that day.

The most potent of the new religious movements in England in the eighteenth century was what is usually given the name of Evangelical. Its lineage can be traced to the Puritan tradition, construed in its broadest sense. That tradition had been potent since the sixteenth century. In large degree it was shaped by the Reformed faith and had close kinship with it. Like the Pietists it stressed conscious conversion following a deep sense of sin and issuing in disciplined living. A literary expression which had a wide and prolonged circulation was John Bunyan's *The Pilgrim's Progress* (1678). The Evangelical movement was indebted to the slightly older Pietism on the Continent and both influenced and was influenced by the Great Awakening in the Thirteen Colonies. It began within what in the opinion of some was the moribund Church of England. Much of it remained within that communion and in the nineteenth and twentieth centuries continued as an important stream in its life. It affected the Nonconformist bodies, some profoundly, and by the end of the eighteenth century it had given rise to Methodism. In the nineteenth and twentieth centuries the Methodist churches were to become world-wide and in numbers and influence were to be one of the major families of Protestantism. They were a characteristically Protestant expression of such fresh bursts of life as in the Roman Catholic Church gave birth to monastic orders and congregations. It is thought-provoking that the eighteenth century, nearly sterile in new monastic movements in the Roman Catholic Church, saw the emergence of this outstanding major branch of Protestantism.

As with the story of Pietism to which it was closely akin, we must confine our notice of the Evangelical movement to the barest and most essential summary. Its outstanding early figures were John Wesley (1703–1791), his brother Charles Wesley (1707–1788), and George Whitefield (1714–1770). The Wesleys were sons of Samuel and Susanna Wesley, each of whom had a Nonconforming clergyman as father. Samuel Wesley, a priest of the Church of England, was in charge of the rural parish of Epworth. He organized one of the Re-

---

[174] *The Works of the Rev. P. Doddridge, D.D.* (Edward Baines, 10 vols., 1802–1805); *Dictionary of National Biography,* Vol. V, pp. 1063–1069.

ligious Societies which were then multiplying. The quite remarkable Susanna Wesley bore him nineteen children and reared her brood by carefully organized discipline. John, studious and throughout his life a diligent reader, graduated from Oxford, became a fellow of Lincoln College of that university, and from time to time returned to Epworth to assist his father. Charles, like John, went to Christ Church, Oxford, and while there formed, with two others, a group for cultivating the Christian life by reading, stimulating one another in their studies, and frequent communion. Returning from a period in Epworth in November, 1729, John became their leader. In retrospect he regarded this group as the first rise of Methodism. Methodism was a term in use in the seventeenth century and was given to the group, also known as the Holy Club, as a nickname, descriptive of its disciplined way of life. John Wesley tended to emphasize practices inherited from the Catholic tradition of the Church of England. He fasted twice a week, went often to communion, and sought to help the prisoners in the local jail. At the outset he was profoundly influenced by Law. The latter's *Serious Call* was published in 1729, the year of the founding of the Holy Club, and John Wesley sought him out. Yet he eventually reacted against some of Law's views. In 1735 he preached a sermon which he later declared to have contained the essence of all that he was to proclaim later. In 1735 too the group was joined by George Whitefield, who, after his ordination a year later, began the amazing preaching career which contributed to the awakening on both sides of the Atlantic. It was also in 1735 that John and Charles Wesley went to Georgia, the recently founded colony which had arisen from Christian philanthropy, as missionaries of the Society for the Propagation of the Gospel in Foreign Parts. It was while on the outward voyage and in Georgia that they were brought in touch with the Moravians and came to feel that the latter had a quiet inward peace and an assurance of salvation through Christ to which the brothers were as yet strangers. Charles, ill, soon returned to England and was followed a few months later by John. Although leaving with a sense of frustration, John looked upon the little group of earnest spirits whom he had gathered as the second important step in the rise of Methodism.

Back in London, transforming light came. The brothers asked counsel of a Moravian. He impressed on them the necessity of self-surrender and the possibility of instantaneous conversion and joy in conscious salvation. On May 21, 1738, that joy came to Charles. Three days later it found John. The place was a meeting of a Religious Society on Aldersgate, not far from St. Paul's Cathedral. The occasion was the reading of the preface to Luther's *Commentary on Romans*. As Wesley said in his journal: "About a quarter before nine, while he [Luther] was describing the change which God works in the heart through faith in Christ, I felt my heart strangely warmed. I felt I did trust in Christ,

Christ alone, for salvation; and an assurance was given me that he had taken away my sins, even mine, and saved me from the law of sin and death."

Inspired by this fresh experience the brothers became radiating centres of religious contagion. Both lived to an advanced age and had a half-century in which to convey to others what had found them. Charles preached extensively but was best remembered for his hymns.[175] In them he set forth with the magic of poetry the theological convictions which were integral to his hardly won but firmly held faith. Set to music they sang themselves into the lives of thousands. Among the more famous were "Jesus, lover of my soul," "Love divine, all loves excelling," "O for a thousand tongues to sing my great Redeemer's praise," "Rejoice, the Lord is king," and "Ye servants of God, your master proclaim."

John also wrote hymns but expressed himself chiefly in sermons, books, and pamphlets, and in organization. After the illuminating hour on Aldersgate, with characteristic initiative, he went to the headquarters of the Moravians, in Herrnhut. Although frankly critical of what he found, he adopted and adapted some of the Moravian methods. In the course of the years he also put into English verse German hymns which expressed convictions that he shared with their authors. They were among the channels through which the tides of life in German Protestantism made themselves felt in the English-speaking world.

Once more in England, John preached widely. The burden of his message was repentance, faith, conscious acceptance by God, the wonder and joy of forgiveness, and daily growth towards the perfection set forth in the teachings and life of Christ. To him, as to Charles, Christ "breaks the power of cancelled sin" and Christ's "blood can make the foulest clean." At first he spoke only in Societies and churches. Soon, however, urged by Whitefield, who, preaching in the open air to miners, had seen the tears coursing down their coal-begrimed faces, he also began preaching outdoors. His message aroused much criticism. In the churches the congregations and their clergy, wedded to the rationalistic approach of the day, objected to his "enthusiasm," taking that word in its original meaning of direct inspiration or possession by God. They were also offended by his conviction that they were sinners who stood in need of salvation and that the road to it was not church attendance and conformity to the sacraments, but conviction of sin, repentance, and faith. Again and again in his journal John records that, having spoken in a particular church, he is not to be allowed to preach there again. Often, in his meetings outdoors and indoors, individuals and mobs attempted to do him physical violence. Yet he persisted

[175] *The Poetical Works of John and Charles Wesley . . . collected and arranged* by G. Osborn (London, Wesleyan-Methodist Conference Office, 13 vols., 1868–1872); Manning, *The Hymns of Wesley and Watts*, pp. 7–77; R. Newton Flew, *The Hymns of Charles Wesley: A Study of Their Structure* (London, The Epworth Press, 1953, pp. 79), *passim.*

and in spite of the inconvenient forms of transportation and the difficult roads of the day travelled thousands of miles yearly "to spread Scriptural holiness over the land." When charged with intruding by his preaching on the parish of a fellow clergyman of the Church of England, he declared: "the world is my parish." In a somewhat different sense this became a watchword of his followers and successors.

In spite of intense opposition, many were won. Wesley organized his converts into "societies" and these in turn into "groups" and "classes" under the direction of expert leaders for the cultivation of fellowship and the moral and spiritual life. Laymen began preaching. At first he was perturbed and would have forbidden them. But his mother warned him that to do so might thwart the Holy Spirit. He yielded and lay preachers became characteristic of Methodism.

The societies multiplied. In 1790 they were said to have 71,668 members in Great Britain. In earlier years Wesley attempted to visit them all, but as they and preachers increased in numbers he grouped them by circuits to be supervised by "superintendents" appointed by himself. He brought his preachers together in "annual conferences." Over them all he exercised an autocratic control. An activist, he promoted the circulation of cheap editions of good books and assisted deserving poor and aspiring business men.

In his later years John Wesley, to the grief of his brother Charles, took a step which eventually led his followers out of the Church of England into a distinct denomination. At first his societies, although not subject to the control of its bishops, remained within that church. Their members availed themselves of its sacraments. As time passed, in the Thirteen Colonies, then become independent of the mother country, Anglican clergymen were too few to give the communion to the rapidly growing numbers of Methodists. Wesley believed that as a presbyter of the Church of England he had as much authority to ordain presbyters as any bishop. Accordingly, he and a fellow presbyter ordained two for the United States and later he ordained others for Scotland. To the end of his days he thought of himself as a faithful son of the Church of England. Doctrinally he did not separate from it. Yet in time Methodism broke away.[176]

The Evangelical awakening was by no means entirely contained within Methodism. And, while it was deeply indebted to the Wesleys, it was not fully dependent on them. Within the lifetime of the Wesleys other aspects of the

[176] Of the enormous bibliography by and about John Wesley the following will prove useful: *The Journal of the Rev. John Wesley, A.M.*, edited by N. Curnock (London, The Epworth Press, 8 vols., 1938); F. J. McConnell, *John Wesley* (New York, Abingdon-Cokesbury Press, 1939, pp. 355); and *The Letters of the Rev. John Wesley, A.M.*, edited by J. Telford (London, The Epworth Press, 8 vols., 1931). On the effects of Wesley and on the early history of Methodism, see J. W. Bready, *England: Before and After Wesley: The Evangelical Revival and Social Reform* (London, Hodder & Stoughton, 1938, pp. 463); L. F. Church, *The Early Methodist People* (London, the Epworth Press, 1948, pp. viii, 286).

movement were seen. Thus Whitefield, originally closely associated with them, broke with them on a question of theology. They were Arminians, believing that Christ had died for all men and that every man had sufficient free will to accept the salvation so freely offered. Whitefield came to believe in predestination. At first the separation was heated. Later personal reconciliation was effected, but the difference in doctrine persisted. Whitefield was not an organizer, but his preaching contributed to the Welsh Calvinistic Methodists.[177] Whitefield was also given support by Selina, Countess of Huntingdon (1707–1791). For a time a member of one of Wesley's societies, she believed in predestination and built up what was known as the Countess of Huntingdon's Connexion, later the Calvinistic Methodists, which eventually moved out of the Church of England.[178]

The Welsh Calvinist Methodists arose primarily from the preaching of Howel Harris (1714–1773) [179] and Daniel Rowlands (1713–1790).[180] Both were members of the established church and Rowlands was in priest's orders. Rowlands is said to have been converted through the preaching of Griffith Jones. In 1735, three years before their transforming experience came to the Wesleys, both Harris and Rowlands began the preaching, quite independently of each other, from which a religious awakening spread like wildfire through Wales. John Wesley eventually heard of them and was friendly. Rowlands organized his followers into societies which in 1743 began holding a central assembly, and Whitefield came to know him and assisted him. His bishop eventually suspended Rowlands from his clerical functions. Harris was aided by the Countess of Huntingdon. He and Rowlands later parted company and most of the movement adhered to the latter.

Older Nonconforming bodies felt the fresh surge of life. This was especially true of the Independents. In the last third of the century their churches grew in number, their meeting houses were crowded, and new ones were built. Preachers were trained and lay preachers multiplied.[181] The Baptists also increased in the last decade of the century and were to have the pioneer, William Carey, of the overseas missions of the Evangelical forces.[182]

A growing number who were in hearty accord with much in the Evangelical awakening and were known as Evangelicals remained within the Church of England. While many of them were indebted to Methodism and its leaders, others had come to their distinctive experience and convictions quite apart

177 A. D. Belden, *George Whitefield—the Awakener. A Modern Study of the Evangelical Revival* (New York, Abingdon-Cokesbury Press, 1930, pp. xvii, 302), warmly sympathetic.
178 *Dictionary of National Biography*, Vol. IX, pp. 133, 134; Elliott-Binns, *The Early Evangelicals*, pp. 134–142.
179 *Dictionary of National Biography*, Vol. IX, pp. 133, 134.
180 *Ibid.*, Vol. XVII, pp. 350, 351.
181 Dale, *History of English Congregationalism*, pp. 580–593.
182 Whitley, *A History of British Baptists*, pp. 195 ff.

from the Methodists.[183] Some, too, had personal friendships with Watts and Doddridge.[184] Before the middle of the century Evangelicals among the clergy were relatively few and widely scattered. About the middle of the century they began to increase. Not far from the same time English Deism reached its peak and began to decline.[185]

We can take the space only for brief mention of a few of the early leaders. We must certainly name William Grimshaw (1708–1763).[186] In his student days at Cambridge he had led a dissolute life and during his early years as curate in a parish he was but little better. Then a series of events sobered him; he became faithful in his parish duties and was visited by a sudden profound experience similar to that of the Methodists. In 1742 placed in charge of a chapel in Yorkshire, he soon wrought a transformation of morals and an improvement in Christian faith in a community which had lapsed into near-paganism. He travelled extensively in the North, preaching, and attracted great audiences. He became a close friend of John Wesley.

John Newton (1725–1807) had a striking spiritual pilgrimage.[187] For years he was a sailor and led a wild and adventurous life, denying God and indulging in coarse dissipation. Change came slowly, and even after a conversion of an Evangelical kind he remained for a time the master of a ship engaged in the African slave trade. Then, remedying his defects in education by extensive reading, he was ordained and became curate at Olney. There he and the poet Cowper (1731–1800), who was also an Evangelical, wrote the hymns which were collected under the name of Olney. Among those of Newton which had enduring use were "Glorious things of thee are spoken" and "How sweet the name of Jesus sounds in a believer's ear." Among those by Cowper were "O for a closer walk with God" and "There is a fountain filled with blood." In 1780 Newton became vicar of a London parish. He had great skill as a director of souls.

Rowland Hill (1744–1833)[188] was from a very different background. A younger son of a baronet, from boyhood he was deeply religious. During his student days at Cambridge he gathered around him a group not unlike the Holy Club of Oxford. Partly through the influence of an older contemporary, also a Cambridge graduate, John Berridge (1716–1793),[189] who had had a dis-

183 Elliott-Binns, *op. cit.*, pp. 120–143.

184 *Ibid.*, p. 146.

185 *Ibid.*, pp. 234 ff.; G. C. B. Davies, *The Early Cornish Evangelicals, 1735–60. A Study of Walker of Truro and Others* (London, S.P.C.K., 1951, pp. 229), *passim*.

186 Loane, *Cambridge and the Evangelical Succession*, pp. 15–64; Elliott-Binns, *op. cit.*, pp. 148–153.

187 Elliott-Binns, *op. cit.*, pp. 256–262; *The Works of the Rev. John Newton* (New Haven, Nathan Whitney, 4 vols., 1826).

188 Edwin Sidney, *The Life of the Rev. Rowland Hill A.M.* (New York, Robert Carter, 1848, pp. 412).

189 Loane, *op. cit.*, pp. 65–116.

tinguished record as a scholar and as vicar at Everton, near Cambridge, had stirred up a revival and had become an inveterate itinerant evangelist, Hill also devoted much of his time to itineracy. For that reason he had difficulty in being ordained and never was allowed to proceed beyond the diaconate. Eventually he preached in a chapel erected for him in London. Here the liturgy of the Church of England was used, but the pulpit was open to men of all denominations.

Henry Venn (1724-1797) [190] came from a long line of high church clergy. Also a graduate of Cambridge, he was curate at Clapham, on the outskirts of London, soon to be noted as a centre of outstanding lay Evangelicals, then for twelve years was in a parish in Yorkshire where through his ministry a moral and spiritual transformation was wrought, and in later years had a parish not far from Cambridge and from that coign of vantage exerted a continuing influence in the university. It was partly through him that Charles Simeon (1759-1836) [191] was led to give his life to a ministry in that academic community which was to have its chief fruitage in a later period.

The Swiss Jean Guillaume de la Fléchère (1729-1785), better known as John William Fletcher, came to England in his young manhood, was caught up in the Methodist movement, and was a close friend of John Wesley. Ordained in the Church of England, he was given the parish of Medeley, in the Severn Valley, and there spent most of the rest of his working life.[192]

Many Evangelicals were active in philanthropy. Two of their most prominent laymen, John Thornton (1720-1790) and his son Henry Thornton (1760-1815), were wealthy and gave generously to aid the underprivileged, to circulate the Bible and other Christian literature, and to purchase advowsons—the right of presentation to a benefice—to ensure that parishes as they fell vacant were filled by Evangelicals.[193]

Later, as we are to see in the next chapters and subsequent volumes, the Evangelical awakening gave rise to extensive missions at home and abroad.

Before 1789 three important developments, Sunday Schools, the founding of Georgia, and prison reform, issued from the awakening.

The Sunday School movement is usually said to have sprung from the imagination and initiative of Robert Raikes (1735-1811).[194] Strictly speaking, Sunday Schools did not begin with him: as early as the seventeenth century Sunday, free from secular occupations, had here and there been utilized for schools for the underprivileged to teach illiterates to read as a means of religious

---

[190] *Ibid.*, pp. 117–171.

[191] *Ibid.*, pp. 175–220.

[192] Elliott-Binns, *op. cit.*, pp. 296–298.

[193] *Ibid.*, pp. 449, 450.

[194] Thomas Walters, *Robert Raikes, Founder of Sunday Schools* (London, The Epworth Press, 1930, pp. 128), *passim*.

instruction. However, it was from Raikes that the impetus came which started what in the nineteenth and twentieth centuries assumed world-wide proportions as one of the most prominent aspects of Protestantism. Raikes inherited from his father a newspaper in Gloucester. He used it to advocate the reform of prisons and the better treatment of criminals. Grieved by the fashion in which boys and girls were running riot on Sunday, in 1780 he began a school on that day. At first it was only for boys. It taught them to read the Bible. It worked improvement in those who came and in their neighbourhood. Through his journal he gave publicity to the enterprise. Many were impressed and similar schools were started in other places. Laymen became enthusiastic supporters. Among them were Henry Thornton and a London merchant, William Fox. To promote and guide the movement, the latter founded the Sunday School Society which later became the Sunday School Union.

A project for bettering the lot of paupers and criminals was the inception of the colony of Georgia. It did not spring directly from the Evangelical or the Pietist movement, but it had close connexions with both. Georgia was begun by James Edward Oglethorpe (1696–1785) as a way of affording opportunity for debtors and other victims of the laws of England and as a refuge for persecuted Protestant minorities. It was also for the protection of the other colonies against Spain. The first settlement was made in 1733. It was Oglethorpe who induced the Wesleys to go to Georgia: indeed, Charles was his secretary. Oglethorpe was responsible for bringing Whitefield to the colony. To Georgia also came Moravians.[195]

He who is counted as the outstanding pioneer in the reform of English prisons was John Henry Howard (1726?–1790).[196] A Nonconformist of Evangelical convictions, from his inherited wealth Howard early began to erect model cottages and to provide elementary education for children. Then he became acquainted with the frightful conditions in the jails and prisons of the country and in 1773 set about ameliorating them. Because of his initiative, in 1774 Parliament passed laws designed to remedy some of the worst features. Howard travelled extensively in Britain and on the Continent to study prisons and hospitals and in an appeal to the humanitarian sentiment of the day gave publicity to his findings.

THE SURGE OF LIFE IN SCOTTISH PROTESTANTISM

The eighteenth-century awakenings in Scotland were largely independent of

---

[195] Robert Wright, *A Memoir of General James Oglethorpe* (London, Chapman and Hall, 1867, pp. xvi, 414)—see, especially on the Wesleys, pp. 90–92, 136–138, 170 ff.; Leslie F. Church, *Oglethorpe: A 'Study of Philanthropy in England and Georgia* (London, The Epworth Press, 1932, pp. xviii, 335)—on the S.P.C.K. and prison reform see p. 9; Amos Aschbach Ettinger, *James Edward Oglethorpe, Imperial Idealist* (Oxford, The Clarendon Press, 1936, pp. xi, 348)—see especially pp. 153–206.

[196] *Dictionary of National Biography*, Vol. X, pp. 44–48.

those in England. Some connexion there was. For instance, John Wesley was in Scotland again and again, and Methodist societies sprang up.[197] Whitefield also preached in Scotland.[198] Moreover, the Great Awakening in America was known in Scotland, was viewed sympathetically by many, and helped to stimulate a deepened religious interest.[199] However, the quickening of life in Scottish Christianity was largely indigenous. In 1709 a Society for the Propagation of Christian Knowledge was organized in Edinburgh. Although suggested by the example of the Anglican society with a similar name and receiving some help from England, it was clearly Scottish. It assisted in the improvement of education and the religious life in the Highlands. In the first half of the eighteenth century the General Assembly and others in the Church of Scotland engaged in extensive efforts to encourage in that area a presbyterian structure in place of the episcopalianism that had been imposed under the later Stuarts and to improve the religious and moral life.[200] Missionaries and catechists were appointed to reach the scattered population.[201] From time to time in the 1730's and 1740's revivals were seen in some of the Highland parishes, and here and there was marked improvement in morals.[202] As in the United States in the frontier revivals early in the next century, those in the Highlands more than once broke out from the preaching preparatory to the communion. Revivals also occurred in the Lowlands. However, in spite of occasional local awakenings in the 1760's, 1770's, and 1780's, after the middle of the century the Highlands suffered from a decline in religious fervour—in part associated with the renewed right of patronage of the lay lords.[203]

Much of the vigour of Scottish religious life was displayed in theological debates and controversies and in secessions from the Church of Scotland. In the second half of the century Moderate views, often strongly smacking of indifference, spread widely among clergy and laity, but they evoked protests. The prevailing theology was that of the Reformed faith as expressed in the Westminster Confession. In it was the doctrine of predestination and election. Salvation was held to come only by the grace of God, a grace which no one deserved or could earn. From time to time differing views entered. Now and then Arminianism showed its head, with a softening of the rigours of predestination and election. Some were accused of Socinianism, with its stress upon the

[197] Wesley, *Journal*, Vol. III, p. 522, Vol. IV, pp. 61, 216–220, 315, Vol. V, pp. 111, 224, 255, 362, 453, Vol. VI, pp. 19, 105, 235, 498, Vol. VII, pp. 162, 387.
[198] Cunningham, *The Church History of Scotland*, Vol. II, pp. 312–318.
[199] Miller, *Jonathan Edwards*, pp. 169, 196, 225, 309.
[200] Macinnes, *The Evangelical Movement in the Highlands of Scotland*, pp. 61 ff.; Mackay, *The Church in the Highlands*, pp. 196 ff.
[201] Macinnes, *op. cit.*, pp. 198 ff.
[202] *Ibid.*, pp. 154 ff.; Mackay, *op. cit.*, pp. 186 ff.; Hetherington, *History of the Church of Scotland*, pp. 356, 357.
[203] Macinnes, *op. cit.*, pp. 108, 113, 161; Mackay, *op. cit.*, pp. 210 ff.

humanity of Christ and its challenge to the doctrine of the Trinity. We read of what was called neonomianism, which taught that the New Testament laid down a new law and that through obedience to it salvation could be at least partly earned. We also hear of the "Marrow Men," holding to the core of the Christian faith as set forth first in a seventeenth-century English book by Edward Fisher, *The Marrow of Modern Divinity*. It had in it a warm Christian faith with much of the Puritan heritage, but it modified Calvinism and there were those who were quick to bring its exponents before the ecclesiastical courts.[204]

The Moderates were reinforced by two philosophers, Thomas Reid (1710–1796) and Dugald Stewart (1753–1828). Stewart largely followed the views of Reid. Reid, from a long line of ministers, was also ordained and for some years was in charge of a parish. Later he was professor of philosophy in Aberdeen and then the successor of Adam Smith as professor of moral philosophy at Glasgow. He sought to refute the scepticism of Hume. After having followed Berkeley he dissented from the latter's idealism. His was a "common sense" approach, which appealed to the testimony of experience and to beliefs common to rational beings. He held that presuppositions exist which may be challenged but which cannot be disproved and must be accepted. Among them are the existence of the material world and the reality of the soul. His philosophy seemed to many to provide a sound intellectual basis for belief in Christianity. For two or more generations it was widely accepted in Scottish theological circles. It was to be very influential in Protestant thought in the United States and, for a time early in the nineteenth century, in French Roman Catholic theology. In Germany Reid was early supplanted by Kant, but Schopenhauer had a high respect for him.[205]

Most withdrawals from the Church of Scotland were not so much on theological issues general to other branches of the Church as over questions peculiar to Scotland. There were the Cameronians, so called from one of their prominent ministers, Richard Cameron. During the reign of Charles II they had risen against what they held to be a violation of the Covenant taken in the reign of his father in protest against the attempt to force episcopacy on the country. They had not been willing to recognize William in 1688, for that monarch, while of the Reformed faith, had accepted the Church of England and its bishops. In the eighteenth century and later they held out, a small and diminishing group, in theory not participating in a government which seemed to them to be

---

[204] Macinnes, *op. cit.*, pp. 169 ff.; Cunningham, *op. cit.*, pp. 249–256, 396–400; Hetherington, *op. cit.*, pp. 342, 344; Mackay, *op. cit.*, pp. 70, 71.

[205] *The Works of Thomas Reid, D.D., Now Fully Collected with Selections from His Unpublished Letters, Preface Notes, and Supplementary Dissertations by Sir William Hamilton, Bart.* (Edinburgh, Maclachlan and Stewart, 2 vols., 1863); *The Works of Dugald Stewart* (Cambridge, Hilliard and Brown, 7 vols., 1829).

apostate.[206] In 1733 Ebenezer Erskine led in forming what was generally known as the Secession. It sprang from his opposition to the appointment of ministers by patrons without the free choice of the congregations.[207] The Seceders organized themselves into the Associate Synod, independent of the established church. In 1747 it split into the Burghers and the Anti-burghers. The issue was whether the members should take the oath required of a burgess "that he professed and allowed within his heart the true religion presently professed within the realm and authorized by the laws thereof." Ebenezer Erskine and his brother, Ralph, supported the "Marrow Men": both were notable preachers and helped prepare the way for the revivals in the latter part of the century and the nineteenth century. In 1761 the Presbytery of Relief was constituted by three ministers who withdrew from the Church of Scotland in criticism of patronage and as a refuge for all who sought relief against the evils of patronage and the disregard of the wishes of the congregations.[208] What were sometimes called the Glassites, followers of John Glas (1695-1773), who had been a minister of the Church of Scotland but had been expelled because of his theological views, organized separate congregations. Glas's son-in-law, Robert Sandeman (1718-1771), extended the movement to London and New England.[209] The Old Scots Independents arose in the 1760's.[210]

In 1766 it was said that in addition to the Episcopalians and Roman Catholics 120 meeting houses of dissenters from the established church were attended by about 100,000. In 1773 the Burgher Associate Synod was reported to have 59 congregations served by 43 ministers, the Anti-burgher Associate Synod 97 congregations and 77 ministers, the Relief Synod 19 congregations and 14 ministers, the Cameronians 9 congregations and 7 ministers, and the Independents 6 congregations. The figures seem to indicate a substantial growth.[211]

Mysticism, which was found almost irrespective of the ecclesiastical affiliations of those influenced by it, was also present, though it is impossible to give statistics. Much of it eludes observation. Yet late in the seventeenth and early in the eighteenth century there were enough in Aberdeenshire who corresponded with the French mystics, Fénelon, Madame Guyon, and Antoinette Bourignon, to bring down on the trend, called Bourignonism, the condemnation of the General Assembly.[212]

In spite of much which seemed cold and dead in Scottish Protestantism in the eighteenth century, much of vitality existed. It was shown in the growth of

[206] Cunningham, *op. cit.*, Vol. II, pp. 122, 164, 165, 179, 180.
[207] *Ibid.*, pp. 287 ff.
[208] *Ibid.*, pp. 329, 330, 357–359; McNeill, *Modern Christian Movements*, pp. 77–79.
[209] *Dictionary of National Biography*, Vol. VII, pp. 1296, 1297; *Dictionary of American Biography*, Vol. XVII, pp. 744, 745.
[210] Ross, *A History of Congregational Independency in Scotland*, pp. 33–40.
[211] Macinnes, *op. cit.*, p. 83; Cunningham, *op. cit.*, Vol. II, p. 414.
[212] Macinnes, *op. cit.*, p. 168.

dissent from the established church; but also within the established church many held to the conviction that conscious conversion was prerequisite to assurance of being among those whom God had elected to salvation. The evidence of conversion was not only the experience of conviction of sin followed by the joyous knowledge of God's forgiveness but also chastity, temperance, the sparing use of temporal things, giving to every man his own, and avoidance of the defilements of the world.[213] Much was made of the communion. Tests were applied to those who wished to receive it and tokens were issued to those adjudged to be qualified to come to the Lord's table. We learn of weekly informal assemblies for prayer and mutual encouragement in Christian living. Moral conditions were far from perfect. Drunkenness was common, sexual irregularities were frequent, Sunday was not always observed, and gambling was prevalent. Yet earnest attempts were made to ban the theatre as demoralizing and in other ways the Church attempted to enforce discipline.[214] Here was much in common with Continental Pietism and with the Evangelicalism of England and Wales. Here, too, was preparation for the great awakenings of the nineteenth century.

THE GREAT AWAKENING IN THE THIRTEEN COLONIES

Parallel with the Pietist movements on the Continent of Europe and with the Evangelical movement in England were revivals in the Protestantism of the Thirteen Colonies. Now and again they were a feature of seventeenth-century New England. In the fore part of the eighteenth century they broke out in what was known as the Great Awakening. The Great Awakening swept through most of the Thirteen Colonies and profoundly affected a large proportion of the population. It revitalized many congregations but in some of the churches led to sharp division. A precursor of the revivalism which was to characterize much of the Protestantism of the United States of the nineteenth and twentieth centuries, it was one of the means by which was achieved the prodigious growth in the percentage of the population having a church membership that was one of the most striking features of the record of Christianity in that country.

The Great Awakening had no one origin or leader. It arose in several centres in the 1720's and the 1730's. Thus it was slightly later than the first flowering of Pietism in Germany under Spener and at Halle under Francke, was roughly contemporary with the peak of Zinzendorf's activities, and in its beginning antedated the transforming experiences of the Wesleys and Whitefield. The way for it was prepared by favouring factors in several sections and groups.

[213] *Ibid.*, pp. 180–190.
[214] Cunningham, *op. cit.*, Vol. II, pp. 352–356; Maclean, *Aspects of Scottish Church History*, pp. 80, 81.

Much of the religious heritage of those of Anglo-Saxon stock both in New England and in the other colonies was what in the broadest use of that term was Puritan. This, as we have seen, was an earlier expression of what recurred in the Evangelical movement in England and in the revivals in Scotland. In New England Cotton Mather was in correspondence with the Halle Pietists. Pietism had made itself felt among some of the German immigrants in Pennsylvania and Georgia. The Scotch-Irish who in the eighteenth century were seeking to better their economic lot by coming to America and who were finding homes on the frontier in Pennsylvania, the Great Valley of Virginia, and the piedmont region of the South, were Presbyterians by background and thus were predisposed to the kind of preaching which was the instrument of the Awakening.[215] In many places a spiritual destitution with an inherited background of Christianity made for a religious hunger among the unchurched majority.[216]

The Great Awakening is usually said to have begun in the Raritan Valley under the preaching of Frelinghuysen.[217] Theodorus Jacobus Frelinghuysen (1691–c.1748) was a German, the son of a Reformed pastor, and was reared and educated under strong Pietist influences. Because he had ministered to the Dutch, he knew that language. Moved by a sense of mission he accepted an invitation to a Dutch Reformed church in the Raritan Valley in New Jersey and arrived in 1719. From the outset he denounced complacent formalism and self-righteousness and proclaimed the necessity of conviction of sin and repentance as preliminary to conversion and as the only door to eternal life. Fearless, forceful, and extremely able, through his preaching he brought conviction to many. Several of the Dutch clergy supported him. In 1726 the revival reached a high point and spread to other Dutch communities.[218]

Another source of the Great Awakening was the teaching of William Tennent (1673–1746). A native of Ireland and reared and ordained in the (Anglican) established Church of Ireland, he became a Presbyterian. Before or after coming to America he was in touch with the Erskine who was later to be the chief figure in the formation of the Associate Synod. He arrived in America in 1716 or 1718 and in 1726 became pastor of a Presbyterian church at Neshaming in Bucks County. There he began a school for the training of ministers. Until that time, Presbyterians from the Middle Colonies wishing to enter the ministry had to attend either Harvard or Yale or one of the universities on the other

[215] Otho T. Beall, Jr., and R. H. Shryock, *Cotton Mather* (Baltimore, Johns Hopkins University Press, 1954, pp. ix, 241), pp. 3, 93; P. H. B. Frelinghuysen, *Theodorus Jacobus Frelinghuysen* (Princeton, 1938, pp. vii, 89), p. 18; Gewehr, *The Great Awakening in Virginia*, pp. 3, 4, 26–36.

[216] Gewehr, *op. cit.*, pp. 26–36.

[217] The best account of Frelinghuysen is in Frelinghuysen, *op. cit.* See also *Dictionary of American Biography*, Vol. VII, pp. 17, 18.

[218] Sweet, *Religion in Colonial America*, pp. 274, 275.

side of the Atlantic. Tennent wished them to be given opportunity for education nearer home. He did most of the teaching. He sympathized with the Great Awakening which was then beginning and welcomed Whitefield. Critics of the revival looked with scorn upon his school and held that it was lowering the educational standards of the ministry. In derision they called it the Log College. The name stuck. However, it was a precursor of the College of New Jersey, later Princeton University.[219]

Students and graduates of the Log College became preachers of the revival. They were pastors of churches and several of them were also itinerants. Among them were four sons of William Tennent, the most notable being Gilbert (1703–1764). At Whitefield's suggestion he travelled through New England and for several weeks preached in Boston.[220]

The most famous American-born leader of the Great Awakening was Jonathan Edwards (1703–1758).[221] Reared in the Connecticut Valley, he graduated from the infant Yale, after brief pastorates taught there for a time, and then succeeded his father-in-law as pastor of the church in Northampton, Massachusetts. His was a first-class mind, one of the greatest that America has produced. He read and was influenced by Locke, Newton, and the Cambridge Platonists—a seventeenth-century group who stressed the love of God and emphasized Plotinus rather than Plato. Edwards was nourished in the Reformed tradition with its strongly Calvinistic content. He was also a mystic. These several elements he combined in a lambent Christian faith. He wrote extensively, largely on theological subjects, and became a leading figure in what was later known as New England theology.

At Northampton striking developments occurred. Edwards' father-in-law had baptized the children of the unconverted and had admitted the unconverted to the Lord's Supper. Edwards preached the heinousness of sin, portrayed in lurid colours the fate of the unsaved, and dwelt upon the necessity of conversion. As a result, in 1734–1735 a wave of conviction swept over the village. The emotional accompaniments, to some appearing bizarre, were not unlike those which soon were to be concomitants of the preaching of Whitefield, John Wesley, and others of the Evangelicals. Later, in a reaction, Edwards was forced to leave Northampton, but the repercussions of his ministry were felt not only in New England and elsewhere in the Thirteen Colonies but also, largely through his

---

[219] Alexander, *Biographical Sketches of the Founder, and Principal Alumni of the Log College,* pp. 18–32; G. H. Ingram in *Journal of the Presbyterian Historical Society,* Vol. XIV, pp. 1–27; *Dictionary of American Biography,* Vol. XVIIII, pp. 369, 370.

[220] Alexander, *op. cit.,* pp. 33 ff.; *Dictionary of American Biography,* Vol. XVIII, pp. 366–370.

[221] The bibliography on Edwards is prodigious. No complete edition of his works has been published, although one is in progress (1958). Several incomplete editions have been issued. One of them is *The Works of Jonathan Edwards* (New York, G. & C. & H. Carvell, 10 vols., 1830). Among the many biographies, one is Perry Miller, *Jonathan Edwards* (New York, William Sloane Associates, 1949, pp. xv, 348).

writings, in Scotland and parts of England. He died soon after becoming president of the College of New Jersey.

Whitefield made six trips to America and at one time and another preached from Georgia to Boston. He thus helped not only to spread but also to give a degree of unity to the Great Awakening.[222]

Other men aided in the Awakening. Among them was Muhlenberg. With his Pietist background he naturally sympathized with it. In Virginia Samuel Davies did much to follow up what had been given an impetus by the visit of Whitefield and the preaching of men from the North. In New England and the Middle Colonies the Great Awakening came to a peak about 1740 and 1741.[223]

However, revivals did not cease. They continued, especially through the Baptists and the entrance and multiplication of Methodism. In 1759 in Virginia the Baptists were almost non-existent. In 1790 they are said to have numbered about twenty thousand. Drawn largely from those of low incomes and of slight or no education, they were usually recruited by preachers of their own background and through meetings marked by emotional excitement with physical contortions, trembling, rolling, and falling on the ground. They met with persecution from members of the Church of England who, with the aid of legal measures, sought to restrain what they believed to be dangerous fanaticism. Their growth was associated with the rise of democratic sentiment in politics and society.[224] Fed by the Great Awakening, the Baptists increased in others of the Thirteen Colonies. By 1790 legal toleration had been achieved.[225]

Methodism also flourished. Although the Wesleys had been in Georgia in the 1730's, it was not until some years later that Methodism entered the Thirteen Colonies. It came first through a few immigrants. Then, in 1769, missionaries sent by John Wesley arrived in Philadelphia. Others followed. True to Methodist principles, they travelled, preached, and organized societies. In 1784 Methodist societies were said to have about fifteen thousand members, eighty-three formally recognized preachers "in connexion," and hundreds of local preachers and exhorters. Growth was particularly marked in Virginia, where the way had been prepared by the preaching of Devereux Jarratt, a clergyman of the established church. In spite of Wesley's pronounced criticism of the movement for the independence of the Thirteen Colonies, growth continued during the war which ended in the attainment of that goal.[226]

---

[222] Sweet, *op. cit.*, pp. 276–278; L. E. Brynestad in *Journal of the Presbyterian Historical Society*, Vol. XIV, pp. 112–127.

[223] Brynestad, in *op. cit.*, Vol. XIV, p. 136; Gewehr, *op. cit.*, pp. 40 ff.

[224] Gewehr, *op. cit.*, pp. 106–137; Sweet, *Religion in Colonial America*, pp. 301–306.

[225] Torbet, *A History of the Baptists*, pp. 239 ff.

[226] Gewehr, *op. cit.*, pp. 138–166; Hicks, *Early American Methodism*, Vol. I, pp. 1–72; Sweet, *op. cit.*, pp. 306–311.

As was true of the awakenings on the Continent of Europe and in the British Isles, one of the results of the revivals in the Thirteen Colonies was missions to traditionally non-Christian peoples. Among the most accessible were the Indians and the Negroes. Missions to the Indians were not new. They had been begun in the seventeenth century and in several places. Now, however, fresh ones were undertaken. Some were by men from across the Atlantic. The Moravians had them. In several of the colonies emissaries of the Society for the Propagation of the Gospel in Foreign Parts laboured among the Indians. The (Scottish) Society for the Propagation of Christian Knowledge supported David Brainerd (1718–1747), a sensitive product of the Great Awakening in New England, as a missionary to the Indians. Out of the Great Awakening new missions were inaugurated for Indians in New England and New York.[227] Efforts were also made to win the Negroes who had been imported as slaves. Some were by missionaries of the Society for the Propagation of the Gospel in Foreign Parts. Others were by the Moravians. The Great Awakening spread to the Negroes, but by 1789 the conversions among them through Baptists and Methodists, later to be notable, had only barely begun.[228]

Another result of the revivals in the Thirteen Colonies was the initiation of schools and colleges.[229] We have noted that the College of New Jersey, later Prineton University, was begun in part as a continuation of the Log College. At the outset Dartmouth College was a mission school for the Indians. So was Hamilton College. The charity school opened in Philadelphia through the preaching of Whitefield was the foundation on which was built the University of Pennsylvania. The beginnings of Queen's College, later Rutgers University, and the College of Rhode Island, eventually Brown University, can also be traced to the revivals.[230]

As on the other side of the Atlantic, the revivals led to controversy, some of it vigorous and even bitter, and to fresh divisions. This was true in more than one denomination. The advocates of the revivals were often known as the "new lights" and the "new side," and their opponents as the "old lights" or the "old side."[231]

Several currents of life in the Protestantism of the Thirteen Colonies were not indebted to the Great Awakening. Among them were those stimulated by the missionaries of the Society for the Propagation of the Gospel in Foreign Parts. They were also seen among the Quakers. Outstanding among the latter was John Woolman (1720–1772). A native of New Jersey, he had an extremely sensitive conscience, lived simply, gave much of his time to travelling and

[227] Latourette, *A History of the Expansion of Christianity*, Vol. III, pp. 220–224.

[228] *Ibid.*, p. 225.

[229] Gewehr, *op. cit.*, pp. 219 ff.

[230] Sweet, *op. cit.*, pp. 314–317; Weigle, *American Idealism*, p. 316.

[231] Sweet, *op. cit.*, pp. 288–291; Weigle, *op. cit.*, p. 116.

preaching among Quakers in the colonies, and bore sturdy witness against Negro slavery. He died while on a mission to England. His *Journal* is among the great devotional classics.[232]

The Awakenings Lead to Efforts for Christian Unity

As had been true across the centuries of other fresh bursts of life in Christianity, the awakenings of the eighteenth century gave rise to new divisions in the Christian ranks. Like those of previous periods, some were contained within existing ecclesiastical structures and others broke away and formed independent groups. By its nature Protestantism was especially productive of such divisions. Yet it was not their exclusive source.

In contrast, also among the features of the eighteenth-century Protestant awakenings were efforts at Christian unity. They were facilitated by what those committed to the awakenings had in common. Through what in the broad sense is termed Pietism and Evangelicalism ran a characteristic pattern. The Scriptures were revered as authoritative. It was maintained that the new, eternal life envisioned in the Gospel is entered by a conscious conversion which issues from repentance and faith and that it is possible because of the act of God for man's redemption through the incarnation, the cross, the resurrection, and the Holy Spirit. In general the trend was to make much of the priesthood of all believers, of a growth in Christian character through a discipline which opened channels for the Holy Spirit, and of humanitarian measures which sought to relieve suffering and to fight entrenched evils. Much was in accord with the universal Christian tradition. Yet the emphasis was distinctly Protestant. It made for coöperation among the awakened.

The efforts at unity were by no means confined to Pietists and Evangelicals. Several arose from other backgrounds. Some were from the humanitarianism and toleration which characterized much of the Enlightenment and which were given a Christian direction. Others had in them such political considerations as the desire of a monarch for religious unity in his realms. In several a mixture of motives entered.

Here we can merely name a few of the eighteenth-century efforts at unity. In the course of our narrative we shall have occasion to describe further developments as one of the striking characteristics of the next two centuries.[233] Heinrich Rudolf travelled extensively among the Eastern Churches, seeking to discover what all Christians had in common and to help to bring about on the

[232] *The Journal and Essays of John Woolman, Edited from the Original Manuscripts with a Biographical Introduction* by Amelia Mott Gummere (New York, The Macmillan Co., 1922, pp. xxii, 643).

[233] See a comprehensive survey in the standard work, Ruth Rouse and Stephen Charles Neill, editors, *A History of the Ecumenical Movement 1517–1948* (London, S.P.C.K., 1954, pp. xxiv, 822). On the stage covered in this chapter see Martin Schmidt in *ibid.*, pp. 99–122.

basis of apostolic simplicity a fellowship of all awakened souls of all communions. Zinzendorf sought for union in Europe and America to be realized on Moravian fundamentals. In a hymn book, in a book of liturgies, and in another of litanies he drew on many sources, Protestant, Roman Catholic, and Eastern. The (Anglican) Society for Promoting Christian Knowledge assisted the (Lutheran) Danish-Halle mission in India. We hear of a set of projects from German Pietist sources for bringing together Protestants and Roman Catholics and associated with it a plan to unite Reformed and Lutherans. This latter had the endorsement of the King of Prussia, eager as he was for religious unity in his realms. Several small groups in Germany and England dreamed of a unity of select souls from many communions having a common experience.

A movement for Christian unity which did not spring primarily from Pietism centred around Alphonse Terrettini (1671–1737), professor of church history in Geneva. In 1708 he led a group seeking to bring about a unity which would be consistent with variety. He enlisted the support of Frederick I of Prussia. Queen Anne of England was sympathetic. But the death of the two monarchs, in 1713 and 1714 respectively, gave a blow to his hopes. Yet he persevered.[234]

Complex interrelated efforts at Christian unity were associated with Daniel Ernst Jablonski (1660–1741), the philosopher Gottfried Wilhelm von Leibnitz (1646–1716), William Wake (1657–1737, Archbishop of Canterbury 1716–1737), the French Roman Catholic preacher, Jacques Benigne Bossuet (1627–1722), Christoph Royas de Spinola (1626–1695), General of the Franciscans and later Bishop of Wiener-Neustadt, and the Lutheran Gerhard Walter Molanus (1633–1722).

Jablonski[235] was of Polish stock, German rearing, Bohemian Brethren ancestry, and Reformed faith. As a young man he had been secretary to John Dury, who in the seventeenth century was an indefatigable promoter of Christian unity. In his youth he had been a student in Oxford and there had become a close friend of William Wake and had obtained a favourable impression of the Church of England. In 1693 he began a residence of almost fifty years in Berlin and became an intimate friend of Spener but did not succeed in winning him to his project. Although a careful student of doctrine, he believed the basis of union to be in the Christian way of life and in worship. He wished to bring Continental Protestantism to accept the episcopate after the Anglican pattern, for he regarded the Biblical orthodoxy of the Moravians and the episcopacy as enduring and valuable legacies of the early Church. It was characteristic of his

[234] Schmidt in Rouse and Neill, *op. cit.*, pp. 107–109; *The New Schaff-Herzog Encyclopedia of Religious Knowledge*, Vol. XII, pp. 42–44.

[235] Schmidt in Rouse and Neill, *op. cit.*, pp. 109 ff.; *The New Schaff-Herzog Encyclopedia of Religious Knowledge*, Vol. VI, p. 72.

earnestness and versatility that he sought to introduce in Brandenburg ethical societies on the pattern of those which he had seen in England and that he was chiefly responsible for the organization of the Berlin Academy of Sciences. He was hopeful of bringing the church in the domains of the King of Prussia into accord with the Church of England by having the king adopt for his realms episcopacy and liturgy after the Anglican pattern. This, however, came to nought. Wars and the deaths of the monarchs of Prussia and England presented insurmountable obstacles.[236]

Molanus [237] was prominent in the church in Hanover. He sought the union of the Reformed and Lutherans but, in contrast with Jablonski, he believed that it must be on the basis of doctrine. For political purposes the Duke of Hanover wished the religious unity of his subjects. This meant not only Reformed and Lutheran but also Roman Catholics. At the command of the King of Prussia, in 1703 a theological conference was held in Berlin. Here Molanus urged his doctrinal programme. However, the premature publication of a secret plan presented to the King of Prussia by the Pietist Winckler in which the latter urged compulsory union at royal command provoked such controversy that the conference came to nought. Spinola had extended conferences in Hanover with Molanus and other Protestant theologians (1683) in the hope of having a great assembly convened to promote the unity of the Church, but this proved impracticable. A few years later correspondence of Molanus with Bossuet broke down over the issues of the Papacy and the infallibility of the Church.[238]

Leibnitz cherished a grandiose dream of the unity of mankind under the leadership of a Christian Europe united through a single Church and an imperial state. He would have Germany take the central role. Eventually he worked out a theory of a Philadelphia Society embracing all the earth and bringing mankind to perfection. The society would be a unit embracing Church and state and for the promotion of culture. As an instrument he wished ecumenical councils. He carried on an extensive correspondence with Bossuet, hoping to win him and through him the Roman Catholic Church to the support of his programme. Bossuet was courteous and irenic but made it quite clear that his church could not accede to the proposal.[239]

As a young man William Wake had been in Paris as chaplain to the British Embassy. There he had come in touch with theologians in the Sorbonne who supported Gallicanism. He thought that he saw a possibility of a union of the Church of England and the Church of France. He was encouraged by a reply

---

[236] Sykes in Rouse and Neill, *op. cit.*, pp. 152–154.

[237] Schmidt in Rouse and Neill, *op. cit.*, p. 111; *The New Schaff-Herzog Encyclopedia of Religious Knowledge*, Vol. VII, pp. 444, 445.

[238] Schmidt in Rouse and Neill, *op. cit.*, p. 116.

[239] *Ibid.*, pp. 112–117.

of some in the Sorbonne in which they agreed that differences in forms of worship need not constitute an insuperable barrier, that the invocation of the saints was not essential to prayer but that each Christian might have direct access to God, that the use of images was not indispensable in worship, that elevation of the host might be omitted in the Eucharist, that in the communion the laity might partake of both the bread and the wine, and that the authority of the bishops proceeded from God alone. Wake wished the Gallican church to declare its independence of the Pope as his own church had done. He also corresponded with Reformed and Lutherans on the Continent, hoping to bring them into the union. However, Gallicanism had not gone far enough to sever its ties with Rome and in Germany the rivalries of Hanover and Brandenburg proved an obstacle.[240]

NEW LIFE IN RUSSIAN CHRISTIANITY

What was happening in the Eastern Churches? What if any indications were there, old or new, of vitality to meet the threats of the age?

For several of the Eastern Churches the main evidence of vitality was that they survived. Some, as in Persia and in the realms of the Ottoman Turks, were in lands where Islam had for centuries been politically dominant. Conversions to Islam could and did take place. Conversions from Islam were all but impossible: both Moslem law and custom forbade them. If converts were made they either were killed or had to conceal their identity. In Ethiopia (Abyssinia) the government was ostensibly Christian, but the Ethiopian Church was a kind of mountainous island surrounded by a sea of aggressive Islam and persistent paganism. Except for an abortive attempt by the Jesuits in the sixteenth and seventeenth centuries to win it to allegiance to Rome, an attempt which weakened rather than strengthened it, the Ethiopian Church had almost its only contacts with other Christians through the Coptic Church. The latter body, defending itself against Islam, could do little but help it exist. The Syrian Church in South India was in effect a distinct caste in a predominantly Hindu environment. It made few if any converts and lost few of its constituency. These churches suffered from being encysted minorities. Being on the defensive, to prevent it from becoming lost or corrupted they endeavoured to preserve unchanged what had come from their ancestors in creed, organization, and liturgy. They were, therefore, resistant to innovations. Fresh movements would be viewed with alarm as weakening solidarity. Yet in the eighteenth century the attrition which had been marked seems either to have slowed down or to have ceased. Moreover, all the Eastern Churches preserved monastic institutions. While some, perhaps most of them, had become stagnant, at least a few

---

[240] Norman Sykes, *William, Wake. Archbishop of Canterbury 1657–1737* (Cambridge University Press, 2 Vols., 1957), Vol. I, pp. 252–314, Vol. II, pp. 1–88.

monks attempted the radical Christian living which had been the original purpose of monasticism.

The Russian Orthodox Church presented a somewhat different picture. Here the state, powerful and expanding its territories, was ostensibly Christian. Conservation there was. Much of the inherited temper persisted. Monasticism was perpetuated. In contrast with the activism of the Christianity, Roman Catholic and Protestant, of the West, kenoticism was strong. By kenoticism was meant the "emptying" of self which had characterized the incarnation. It held as ideal humility, not seeking one's own, withdrawal from the world, the discipline of self-renunciation, recognition of one's sin, the plea for divine forgiveness, and prayer. It was no accident that then and in the following century the "Jesus prayer," "Lord Jesus Christ, Son of the living God, have mercy on me a sinner," or some equivalent of it, appealed to many in devout circles and that hesychasm, with its form of spiritual discipline, had a revival.[241] The revival was aided by the translation into Slavonic, late in the eighteenth century, of the *Philokalia,* a collection of meditations and directions for cultivating the life of prayer by monks of earlier centuries.[242] Leading Russian Christians regarded Moscow as the "third Rome." They believed that the first Rome had succumbed to the heresy of the Latins with its over-organization and worldly imperialism, that the second Rome, Constantinople, had fallen victim to the Turks, and that the centre of true Christianity was now Moscow.

In the late seventeenth and the first part of the eighteenth century the Russian Orthodox Church presented the contrast on the one hand of the emergence of movements, notably the Old Believers, which were an indication of vigour in their dissent from the establishment, and on the other hand of the enhanced control by the state which was inaugurated by Peter the Great.

That contrast continued and was heightened. We have seen the accentuation of state control by Catherine the Great. Yet dissident minorities increased and in the state church were fresh stirrings of life. The Old Believers (Raskolniks, "Schismatics") persisted. Some had so far renounced the old church that they would not accept priests ordained in it. Since they had no bishops, they were without priests. They broke up into several sects. Other Old Believers were so far willing to regard the state church as Christian as to accept the services of priests who had been ordained in it and even to do so without re-baptizing them. Some also received without re-baptism converts from the state church.[243] The Khlysty, a radical mystical sect, claimed that their founder lived in the

---

[241] Scupoli, edited by Nicodemus of the Holy Mountain, revised by Theophan the recluse, translated by E. Kadloubovsky and G. E. H. Palmer, *Unseen Warfare* (London, Faber & Faber, 1952, pp. 280), pp. 1–28.

[242] *Writings from the Philokalia, on Prayer of the Heart,* translated from the Russian text by E. Kadloubovsky and G. E. H. Palmer (London, Faber & Faber, 1951, pp. 420), *passim.*

[243] Bolshakoff, *Russian Nonconformity,* pp. 46–82.

seventeenth century. They increased in the eighteenth century and split into more than one branch. Persecuted, they went underground.[244] The influence of Protestantism seems to have been in part responsible for the emergence of the Dukhobors, or Wrestlers with the Spirit. They first appeared in the eighteenth century in the Ukraine. They were mystics who held a variety of views, some departing widely from historic Christianity. Many lived in groups which held their property in common.[245] The Molokans, "Milk-drinkers," so called in derision because they did not observe the fasts of the Orthodox Church and drank milk during Lent, seem to have begun in the eighteenth century as an offshoot of the Dukhobors. They, too, tended to live in communistic groups. They made much of the morality of the Old Testament.[246]

In the first half of the eighteenth century Freemasonry was introduced from England and spread among the aristocracy. In the latter part of the century mystical tendencies entered from German Freemasons. That type of Masonry was promoted by a German, Johann Schwartz, a Rosicrucian and pantheist. He died in 1784 and the movement was then led by Nicholas Novikov (1744–1818), an educator and philanthropist who did much for Russian schools and for friendly societies.[247]

In the eighteenth century Protestantism began to be represented by immigrants, some of them of groups persecuted in Western Europe. Desiring their industry and thrift as a help to Russian economy, Catherine the Great encouraged numbers of them to settle in her domains and as inducements promised special privileges and toleration.[248]

In the eighteenth century the Roman Catholic Church was in Russia. Jesuits were active and, as we have seen, were allowed by Catherine the Great to continue after the society had been dissolved by the Pope. However, they won only a few converts, and then mostly among the aristocracy.[249]

Influences came into the Russian Orthodox Church from both Roman Catholics and Protestants. In most seminaries for the training of clergy the teaching was in Latin and textbooks were adaptations of ones written by Roman Catholic and Protestant theologians. The thought of Augustine now made its way into Russia. Pietist writings were circulated.[250]

Increased control by the state, though a handicap to the inner vitality of the Russian Orthodox Church, by no means entirely crushed it. Indeed, in some ways it strengthened it. Retreating from politics and the political structure,

[244] *Ibid.*, pp. 82–95.
[245] *Ibid.*, pp. 97–105.
[246] *Ibid.*, pp. 105–109.
[247] *Ibid.*, pp. 99, 100; Zenkovsky, *A History of Russian Philosophy*, Vol. I, pp. 82, 83, 93–98.
[248] Bolshakoff, *op. cit.*, p. 113.
[249] *Ibid.*, pp. 143–145.
[250] Fedotov, *A Treasury of Russian Spirituality*, pp. 182, 183.

pursuing the traditional kenoticism, many Russian Orthodox Christians emphasized the way of the mystic and the life of the spirit. Outstanding in this trend was Tikhon Zadonsky, or Timofey Sokolov as he was first called (1724–1783).[251] A scion of a poor family, as a scholar in a theological seminary he early made his mark. Monk, then bishop, he was inclined towards the contemplative solitary life. In a sense he wished to live outside of history. He desired not so much to sanctify life as to transfigure it. To him reason without divine enlightenment is blind, but in the light of Christ it sees. As bishop he was an excellent administrator and pastor. He preached, trained and disciplined clergy, improved the quality of the monasteries, and organized a seminary. Yet after four years he resigned and retired to a monastery. He showed the impact of Western religious life. Among the books of which he was author was an adaptation of one in Latin by a seventeenth-century Bishop of Norwich. His lectures on systematic theology centred around redemption, were devotional in nature, and breathed something of the spirit of Western Pietism and Evangelicalism. Yet he was essentially Russian. As monk his counsel was sought by many. He found ways of relieving the physical wants of the poor. He knew the temptations of the flesh and while not going to an extreme was an ascetic.

Païsius Velichkovski (1722–1794) gave marked impetus to a revival of monasticism.[252] A student in Kiev, he left the academy there before completing his course, visited hermitages in Moldavia, and spent much time on Mt. Athos, steeping himself in its particular forms of mysticism. A patient scholar, he was familiar with Greek patristic literature and planned revisions of the old Slavonic translations of the Fathers to make them of more use in Russian monasteries. He was known as a *starets*, or elder, an early representative of the *startzi* who were to be important in nineteenth century Russian religious life. As such his guidance in things of the spirit was sought by many. It was through some of his disciples that towards the end of the eighteenth century the monastery Optina Pustyn was revived and became a centre from which in the following century were to come many *startzi* and currents which would help shape the Orthodox Church.

Gregory Savvich Skovoroda (1722–1794)[253] was educated in the Kiev Academy, where Western influences had been strong, travelled extensively in Western Europe, knew several of its universities, and became acquainted with much of its thought. Returning to Russia, he was never ordained but for some years taught intermittently in theological seminaries. He then severed formal connexions with the ecclesiastical structure and became a wanderer. He felt

[251] Nadejda Gorodetzky, *Saint Tikhon Zadonsky, Inspirer of Dostoevsky* (London, S.P.C.K., 1951, pp. xii, 249), *passim*; Fedotov, *op. cit.*, pp. 182–241; Zenkovsky, *op. cit.*, Vol. I, pp. 50–52.
[252] Zenkovsky, *op. cit.*, Vol. I, pp. 52, 53.
[253] *Ibid.*, pp. 53 ff.

himself always to be a member of the Church, but he was insistent on preserving untrammelled his freedom of thought. Reverencing the Scriptures and rooted in them, he developed his own philosophy, a philosophy which was to bear fruit in the next century.

A SUMMARY LOOK

As we cast our eyes back over the portion of the eighteenth century which preceded the outbreak of the French Revolution, how shall we appraise it?

Our story has had to do primarily with Europe and especially with Western ·Europe. Here was the region in which Christianity had plowed most deeply. Here, chiefly in the western peninsular extension of the Eurasian land mass, the overwhelming majority of the population were professedly adherents of that faith. Here, partly because it had been given opportunity centuries earlier by the disintegration of civilization following the break-up of the Roman Empire and the invasion of barbarians and partly because it was without the effective competition of another high religion, its inherent vigour had done much to shape the culture which arose.

At the outset of the eighteenth century every aspect of the civilization of Western Europe bore the impress of the Christian faith. The degree of that impress varied.

In the religion which was called Christianity many elements inconsistent with the Gospel were all too palpably present. Superstitions persisted, some of them of long standing and others of recent entrance. In their relations with one another the churches were far from being exemplars of the love which prompted the incarnation. Within the individual churches jealousies and quarrels were denials of that love. The "fruit of the Spirit," "love, joy, peace, long-suffering, gentleness, goodness, faith, meekness, temperance," was nowhere perfectly embodied. Yet the churches continued to set forth the ideal. Practice was far in arrears. Measured by reverence for God in speech and in act, by regard for other individuals, by honesty in deed and word, by purity in sex relations, by restraint in the use of food and drink, especially in the consumption of alcohol, and in other ways, it seemed at times as though conditions had never been worse. Yet in the care of the sick, the maimed, the aged, the orphans, and the poor the existence of thousands of institutions was evidence that the love for neighbour enjoined by Christ was potent.

The Christian faith had stimulated Western Europeans to regard the universe as a universe, orderly, dependable, the creation and under the control of One who in Christ had revealed Himself, to take advantage of what the Greeks had accomplished before them, and to venture forth confidently in new ways to an understanding of the world about them and to utilize its resources for the benefit of men. Precisely to what extent Christianity was responsible for the beginnings of science cannot be ascertained. That in them it played an important part is certain.

In much of literature and art Christianity clearly had marked effects. In such men as Dante and in more recent men of literature, such as Shakespeare and Milton, its impress was obvious. Without it the work of such artists as Michelangelo and of such musicians as Palestrina either would not have been or would have had a quite different character.

In economics, standards of honesty and fair dealing as well as thrift were recognized, but the degree of approximation to them was not easily measured and they were not dominant.

Even though they departed from them, often widely, government, law, and politics ostensibly honoured Christian principles. Monarchs in theory ruled by divine right: they were crowned by Christian rites and were supposed to conform to Christian standards. Chiefly in England, partly although not chiefly from Christian motives, attempts had been made to bring the monarchs to obedience to a law which was above them and which they did not enact and thus to safeguard the rights and dignity of subjects. Wars were chronic, but under the impulse of the Christian faith efforts had been put forth to bring them under the control of law, as by Francis of Vitoria and Hugo Grotius, and even entirely to eliminate them, as in plans formulated in the seventeenth century. Earnestly Christian minorities, some of them Anabaptists, Mennonites, and Quakers, for conscience' sake abjured all participation in war.

In the expansion of Europe which began on a large scale in the latter part of the fifteenth century, sincere Christians, stirred to fresh sensitivity and courage by the Catholic Reformation, had sought to curb the heartless exploitation of the non-Europeans upon whom Europeans were impinging. Through Europeans, Christianity was displaying the world-wide expansion which in the nineteenth and twentieth centuries was to mount to breath-taking proportions.

The dynamic forces issuing from Christianity were most potent in Western Europe. In general at the beginning of the eighteenth century Eastern Christians were minorities, usually small minorities, on the defensive; if in any region, as in the Balkans and in parts of Armenia, they were majorities, they were either subject to non-Christian rulers or were chronically in fear of being brought under their control. In the one major exception, Russia, large non-Christian enclaves existed and only a few generations had elapsed since the rule of the Moslem Mongols had been shaken off.

In the brief span of time covered by this chapter the movements to which Christianity gave rise or contributed still issued chiefly from Western Europe. They displayed sharp contrasts. Several of them, although indebted to Christianity and preserving features which they drew from it, so far distorted the inner genius of the faith that they threatened its existence. This was true of Deism and of some of the trends in philosophy. While holding in part to conceptions of God and human nature historically derived from Christianity, they denied the validity of the heart of the Christian faith—the self-revelation of God in the Scriptures and in the incarnation, cross, resurrection, and the coming of the Holy Spirit. Western European reliance upon reason came largely out of Christianity's nurturing of a belief in the orderliness and dependability of the universe, the dignity of man, and man's ability to grow in his understanding of the universe. Yet by divorcing their use of reason from humble and conscious dependence on God, many who trusted in it were in fact, either consciously or unconsciously, denying its source and falling victims to the hubris which is one of the gravest perils of mankind. Much of the optimism, belief in progress, and humanitarian interest of the Enlightenment issued from Christianity. So, too, did much of the "free-thinking" of the period. Yet many who displayed these attitudes and convictions were rejecting Christianity. Whether more or less negation of the faith existed than in earlier centuries cannot be determined in any statistical fashion. Even at the height of the Middle Ages, in the so-called "age of faith," much scorn for Christianity was found and quite open denial of it in morals. Yet now, from movements and attitudes to which it had contributed, threats were developing as serious as any that Christianity had faced.

The churches seemed ill prepared to meet the threats. Except for minority groups, they were bound hand and foot to governments which were making them subordinate to political purposes. Morally the leaders of the churches had not sunk to such depths as had been seen in earlier major ebbs in the tide of faith. But that leadership seemed to have little prospect of effectively meeting the threat.

However, the situation was far from hopeless. Here and there were movements in which the faith was breaking forth in renewed vigour. It was impelling some to use the scholarly tools of the age to a better understanding of the Scriptures. Numbers were examining the faith afresh and were endeavouring to present it in convincing fashion, using the vocabulary of the day. None was as outstanding as Origen, Augustine, Aquinas, Luther, and Calvin had been in their respective generations. But several attempts were notable.

The evidences of vitality were found in all the major wings of the faith—the Orthodox, the Roman Catholic, and the Protestant. All three were enlarging the geographic frontiers of the faith. In each new movements were emerging. However, it was in Protestantism that most of the fresh currents were seen, and especially through Pietism and Evangelicalism.

Christianity continued to make itself felt in all aspects of the civilization of Christendom. Among thousands, even though minorities, it was bringing religion towards an approximation to the standards set forth by and in Christ.

From it came the vision and the dynamic not only for the traditional means of allaying suffering but also for fresh attacks on chronic ills. It inspired new efforts and approaches in education. It stimulated creative intellectual activity. From it issued great music, such as came from Johann Sebastian Bach (1685–1750) and George Frederick Handel (1685–1759). From it sprang fresh attempts to bring Christians together in the unity of love. Here and there were beginnings of new efforts to offer the Gospel to all mankind, efforts which later assumed major proportions.

Now, near the close of the eighteenth century, came a storm of revolution and wars which for the time appeared to doom Christianity in much of Christendom. That storm had many sources and causes, economic, political, and ideological. It sprang partly from the hopes aroused by Christianity and from ideologies which were in some degree its fruit, although sadly distorted fruit. It arose also from the failure of the churches to meet the hopes and desires to which Christianity had contributed. Christianity was by no means the only cause of the storm. It may not even have been the chief source. Yet it contributed to forces which for a time appeared to be destroying it. But from it in the midst of storm issued movements of mounting strength. They were not spectacular. Back of them, as in earlier periods, were humble, inconspicuous lives. It is to the course of this storm and to these movements that we must now turn. Through them the curtain rises on the drama which is our major concern—the drama of the nineteenth and twentieth centuries.

CHAPTER IV

The Storm of Revolution

IN THE year 1789 a storm broke in France which was to rack Western Europe for a little more than a quarter of a century and to shake much of the rest of the world. Significantly, it had its origin in the western part of Christendom, where Christianity had been more potent than in any other major division of mankind, and in France, which in the eighteenth century had been the leading power in Western Christendom. From there it spread to Russia, had revolutionary repercussions in most of the areas in other continents controlled by the peoples of Western Christendom, impinged upon the non-Europeans in these areas, and was felt, although only slightly, among nations which were as yet outside the orbit of Europe.

The French Revolution and the wars emerging out of it represented the explosive release of pressures which had long been mounting and of forces which were to continue in the nineteenth and twentieth centuries. To them other forces were to be added, also from Western Christendom. In both centuries they worked revolutions. Not always were the revolutions as spectacular as from 1789 to 1815. Indeed, in striking contrast with what had preceded it and what came after it, the century from 1815 to 1914 saw no general war in Christendom. Yet the revolutions continued. They were political, intellectual, religious, economic, and social. Now and again, as in 1830, 1848, and 1870, they broke out in explosions, but, for protracted violence, compared with that of 1789–1815, they were minor. However, we must not permit the relative absence of wars to obscure the fact that major revolutions were in progress. The Western Christendom of 1914 was very different from the Western Christendom of 1815. Moreover, the forces operating in it were spreading to the rest of mankind. There, too, they were effecting changes: beginning with 1914 the changes mounted with bewildering and breath-taking rapidity.

We have used the term Western Christendom deliberately. As we have said more than once, it was in this region, where Christianity had long had a nearer approach to free course than anywhere else on the globe, that the revolutions originated. It was from there that they billowed forth over the rest of the human race. We shall need repeatedly to ask how far if at all Christianity was responsible for them. We will also note, as a recurrent theme, the threat and the challenge they brought to Christianity and the fashion in which from Christianity issued movements which sought to meet the one and to use the other as an occasion for fresh advances and achievements.

In the sayings of Jesus as remembered by his intimates are the cryptic words: "I am come to send fire on the earth. . . . Suppose ye that I am come to give peace on earth? I tell you nay, but rather division." It may not be distorting Jesus' meaning to see in these words a prophecy which from at least the eighteenth century was in process of fulfilment. What was released by him and through him was like fire, a force of immeasurable potential. Like fire, it could be used for either man's woe or man's weal. Misdirected it could give rise to explosions which might shatter civilization and even destroy mankind. Harnessed in the fashion in which he who sent it intended, it could bring man to undreamed-of heights of well-being and noble living. In the hands of some, perhaps of many, because their purposes were mixed, the fire would have ambiguous results, partly destructive and partly constructive. Its coming would heighten the conflicts inherent in human nature.

Whether or not this is what Jesus meant, as a matter of history it is what happened from the eighteenth century onward. What came through Jesus and entered into Christianity as its creative dynamism, on the one hand contributed to forces which shook all mankind; issuing from a tragic distortion of what came through him, they threatened Christianity and in time the very existence of mankind. On the other hand, movements issued from Christianity which, utilizing what came through Jesus in partial or full accord with his purpose and will and spreading throughout the earth, enabled millions of individuals to live triumphantly in the midst of revolution and, inspired and empowered by him, to devise and use means to offset destruction and to make the revolutions contribute to the welfare of great segments of mankind and, indeed, of all the human race.

In the quarter-century of storm between 1789 and 1815 both these contrasts were present. On the one hand, and spectacularly, were the uses of the fire which threatened destruction. On the other, and little observed at the time except by small minorities, or, if observed, not appraised at their full significance, were the uses which were to be constructive and which, continuing in the following centuries, were to attain major proportions.

Whether man's misuse of what came through Jesus would prevail against its right use and whether civilization and Christianity itself would perish from the earth, at the middle of the twentieth century the historian as historian could not wisely undertake to say. He noted that even Christians gave quite different answers. They appeared in the discussion of Christian hope which in the 1950's engaged many Christians.[1]

EARLY MUTTERINGS OF THE STORM

As from the vantage of the mid-twentieth century the historian looked back over the course of the storm, he could see that its outbreak in 1789, sudden though it seemed, had given forewarnings of its approach. Some were in ideological movements which we sketched in the last chapter. Others were in the economic situation. Some were in the blindness and ineptitude of the ruling classes in Europe and especially in France.

Two of the mutterings of the on-coming storm were in revolutions among Anglo-Saxon peoples: in the British Isles in the seventeenth century and in the Thirteen Colonies in North America early in the third quarter of the eighteenth century. In both, impulses had come from Christianity. Foreshadowing what was to happen in the nineteenth and twentieth centuries, they were from Protestant Christianity and mainly from Puritanism and its associated movements.

Religion was only one of several factors in the civil war in the British Isles in the seventeenth century. However, the role played by religion, particularly by the Puritan phase of Protestantism, was both large and significant. Prominent were the fear that the king would favour the Roman Catholics, the conscientious insistence by the king on what he conceived to be his divinely commissioned responsibility to be supreme in the state, the attempt to force episcopacy on Scotland and the resistance of the Scottish Presbyterians, the Puritan element in England which wished a further movement towards Protestantism and especially towards Presbyterianism in the church of that country, and the demands of the Independents and the even more radical Protestant groups. Without them the struggle might not have occurred. Certainly they largely determined its complexion.

For slightly over a decade (1649–1660), in the Commonwealth and the Protectorate, Protestantism of a fairly extreme kind was dominant. Cromwell and the Independents were in the saddle. Cromwell laboured to bring to realization a Christian state of a Protestant kind and to make domestic and foreign policies conform with Christian principles as he understood them.

With the death of Cromwell (1658) the experiment was doomed. For the moment the restoration of the Stuarts (1660) seemed to erase what had been achieved. Yet after the flight of James II and the accession, in 1688, of William and Mary, something of what had been jeopardized was salvaged. The Declaration of Rights of 1689 was framed and espoused by earnest Christians. The

---

[1] See the many papers and books issued in connexion with the preparation for the meeting of the World Council of Churches in 1954 and the papers which came out of that meeting.

Protestant element in the Church of England persisted, Presbyterianism was restored in Scotland, and in England the dissenting Protestant groups survived. By gradual steps, chiefly in the nineteenth century, democracy as Anglo-Saxons understood it was achieved in the government of the United Kingdom.[2]

Out of Puritanism and as an aftermath of the English revolution came John Locke. His *Treatises on Government* had a large part in inspiring and shaping the democracy of Britain and the United States and also had repercussions on the Continent. It was from Puritanism in the broad sense—including not only those who wished to "purify" the national church but also Independents and Baptists—that the Anglo-Saxon form of democracy was chiefly sprung.[3]

In the revolution out of which issued the independence of the United States the Protestant Christian element was present but was less prominent than in the British revolution of the preceding century. The ideals of the new country were partly derived from the radically Protestant groups which were prominent in the early settlements. The Puritans largely shaped New England. The Quakers initiated Pennsylvania and for some years were outstanding in that colony. They shared in inaugurating one of the sections which united in New Jersey. Other religious refugees, among them Huguenots, Moravians, and Germans of more than one confession added to the Protestant strain in the new nation. The Christian ideals and the sense of a fresh adventure in building a society which would conform to Christian principles were vividly displayed in the Great Seal of the United States. There a pyramid as yet only well begun is underneath the eye of God, with the caption *annuit coeptis,* which may be translated "He approves the beginnings," and is supported by the words *novus ordo seculorum,* "the new order of the ages." But the large majority of the colonists did not come to America from religious motives. Most of them were impelled by the desire to improve their economic or social status, and some had been transported as undesirables. Partly influenced by Locke, many of the clergy, especially in New England, had been preaching the doctrines of popular sovereignty.[4] Yet in the struggle for political independence the desire to create a country which would be worthy of the designation "Christian" was not as outstanding among those who led as it had been in Oliver Cromwell. Moreover, some of the leaders, notably Thomas Jefferson and Benjamin Franklin, were more Deist than Christian.[5] However, back of them was Christian ancestry and their ideals gave evidence of that heritage.

[2] In the prodigious amount of literature on this revolution a useful summary, with bibliographies, is in *The Cambridge Modern History,* Vol. IV, Chaps. 8, 9, 10, 11, 12, 15, 16, 19 (Cambridge University Press, 1906).

[3] Nichols, *Democracy and the Churches,* pp. 29–38; Stumpf, *A Democratic Manifesto,* pp. 131–137.

[4] Alice M. Baldwin, *The New England Clergy and the American Revolution* (Durham, N.C., Duke University Press, 1928, pp. xiii, 222), *passim.*

[5] Nichols, *op. cit.,* pp. 39, 40.

THE MAIN STORM: A PRELIMINARY OUTLINE

Here is not the place for an extended account of the storm which had its origin and its centre in France. However, it so profoundly affected the nineteenth and twentieth centuries that apart from it they cannot be understood. We must, then, briefly summarize the main oulines of the tempest which broke upon the world in 1789. We will first trace the general course of the storm before the man on horseback became its central figure. We will then note developments after Napoleon took charge. Next we will sketch the other revolutionary forces which were emerging in Western Europe. At the time they did not attract as much attention as the political and military aspects but in the ensuing century and a half they were to swell to major proportions.

Then we will describe the effects on Christianity and the response of that faith to the revolution and to the challenge of the new world which was beginning to emerge from the revolution. Here, as in the preceding chapter and in subsequent chapters, we will begin with the Roman Catholic Church, go on to Protestantism, and conclude with the Eastern Churches.

THE STORM BREAKS: THE PRE-NAPOLEONIC COURSE

That the storm first broke in France and there was most violent and had its chief radiating centre is highly significant. In the eighteenth century France was the most powerful state in Western Europe. Its prestige under Louis XIV, whose long reign covered the second half of the seventeenth and the opening years of the eighteenth century, made for the spread of the French language and literature and of French manners and opened the way for French ideas. What happened in France could not but affect profoundly the rest of Western Christendom and would have repercussions in Eastern Christendom.

That the storm had its inception in France was, in the main, for two reasons.[6] One, as we have suggested, was the failure of the French monarchy to grapple intelligently and successfully with the problems of French society and government. The France of the eighteenth century had many features which to the men of the Enlightenment were irrational and cried aloud for change. The administrative divisions were inherited from a long past and were clearly anachronistic. The lower classes bore the weight of the heavy financial burdens imposed by the chronic wars and the maintenance of the court, the nobility, and the Church, and the upper classes, although far more able to support them, were largely exempt. The peasants laboured under exactions and duties which had come down from feudalism, yet the reasons which under

---

[6] No one bibliography or survey is sufficient to cover the vast literature evoked by the French Revolution. A good survey and a selected bibliography incorporating the results of research to the beginning of the twentieth century is in *The Cambridge Modern History*, Vol. III (Cambridge University Press, 1904, pp. xxviii, 875), Chaps. IV–IX, XII–XVI. Highly selected later bibliographies are in Hayes, *Modern Europe to 1870*, pp. 805–807.

feudalism may have given them some justification had ceased to exist. "Enlightened despotism" had palpably failed. Conditions were no worse than in other parts of the Continent and were not as bad as in some other countries, but the monarchy had proved itself incapable of dealing with them. In an effort to satisfy his ambition, Louis XIV had plunged the nation into a series of costly wars. His successor, Louis XV, often under the sway of shallow-brained mistresses, was even less competent. Louis XVI, virtuous in his private life and well-meaning, lacked the ability which his position demanded. A second reason why the storm broke in France was the power of the Enlightenment. Voltaire, Rousseau, the Encyclopedists, and others of the *philosophes* had a wide following among the *bourgeoisie* and the intellectuals and had won some of the clergy and nobility.

When the storm broke, those profoundly committed to the Christian faith had little or no part in shaping it. As we have suggested, in some respects the Enlightenment was a fruit of Christianity and was a secularized and therefore a distorted and emasculated version of that faith. But in contrast with the English and American revolutions, the positive Christian element was lacking. The leadership of the French Revolution was Deist or atheist.

The immediate occasion of the outbreak of the storm was the financial embarrassment of the crown. To help meet it the Estates General was summoned. It was composed of three Estates, the clergy, the nobility, and the commoners. When, in May, 1789, the Estates General convened at Versailles, the Third Estate, which earlier had had but little voice but was now representative of the growing power of the *bourgeoisie,* demanded that the Three Estates, instead of voting separately by houses, constitute themselves a National Assembly in which each member would have one vote and that it address itself, in accord with the ideals of the Enlightenment, to a thoroughgoing reorganization of France. In opposition to the royal command but later with the king's reluctant assent this was done. Conflict between the National Assembly and the king led to the intervention of the Paris populace. On July 14, 1789, as a protest against royal despotism, a Paris mob attacked and destroyed the Bastille, a fortress and prison which symbolized the autocratic power of the monarch. Citizens of Paris set up their own government, the *Commune,* with a national guard representing the rank and file. This the king was constrained to recognize. In October, 1789, a throng from Paris made its way to Versailles clamouring for bread, and on its demand Louis XVI, his Queen, Marie Antoinette, and their children accompanied it to Paris.

From then onward the pace of the Revolution quickened. Throughout the country the machinery of royal government broke down. Towns and cities set up communes staffed by elected officers and supported by national guards. In many places in the countryside peasants stormed the *châteaux* and made away with the documents which were legal evidence of feudal institutions. The National Assembly set itself to construct a new government and a fresh order of society. Reinforced by a dramatic scene in which nobles and clergy renounced their special privileges, so far as legislation was able it abolished the feudal system with its rigid class distinctions. In 1791, with the unwilling approval of the king, it promulgated a constitution which it had framed. This opened with a Declaration of the Rights of Man which included "liberty, property, security, and resistance to oppression," equality in rights, the right of each citizen to participate, through his representatives, in the formation of law, liberty of the press, freedom of speech, religious toleration, and the inviolability of property. In place of the old, which had arisen in a variety of ways across the centuries and which was anything but logical, a uniform administrative system was devised for the nation. The king was retained, but his powers were greatly curtailed. A Legislative Assembly with a single chamber was set up.

These events and actions were accompanied by a rapid growth of nationalism. It and popular sovereignty were closely allied. Steps were taken to provide a national system of education and national military service. In 1791, as a result of the action of the citizenry, Avignon, long Papal territory, was annexed to France.

The government set up under the constitution of 1791 had before it a task which it proved incapable of meeting. In addition to operating a structure with which the French people had had little or no previous experience, it faced foreign war. Many of those who stood to lose by the new regime, mostly nobles and clergy, fled the realm and as *émigrés* sought to enlist foreign aid to restore the old order. Through much of Western Europe the privileged classes, seeing their positions threatened, were thoroughly alarmed. In August, 1791, the King of Prussia and the Hapsburg Holy Roman Emperor formally declared that the restoration of order in France was the common interest of all the sovereigns of Europe. The response in France was a declaration of war (April, 1792). In the early stages of the war the French suffered defeats and the commander of the Austrian and Prussian troops seemed about to march on Paris. For some weeks anarchy threatened. The Legislative Assembly was panic-stricken and helpless. A revolutionary radical commune in Paris took over. The Legislative Assembly voted to suspend the king from office and called for the election of a National Convention to draw up a new constitution. In a spasm of fear, in September, 1792, the extremists set about massacres in which hundreds in Paris and the provinces were executed as aristocrats and royalists and thus a menace to the Revolution and France.

The National Convention began operations on September 20, 1792, and governed the country until 1795. It abolished the monarchy and constituted France a republic. Louis XVI was tried, condemned, and executed (January

21, 1793). Foreign invasion was repelled and the National Convention, now confident, proposed to carry the Revolution beyond the borders of the country and not to be content until in the territories held by its troops the principles of equality had been adopted and "free and democratic governments" had been set up. Thus the National Convention declared war on the standing order in all Europe. In defense the existing governments in Prussia, Austria, Great Britain, Holland, Spain, and Sardinia formed a coalition to overthrow the French Republic and to restore the monarchy. Pro-royalist revolt broke out in La Vendée. To combat the internal menace, from the summer of 1793 to the summer of 1794 the Committee of Public Safety carried through the "Reign of Terror." Thousands in Paris and the provinces who were regarded as threats to the Republic were slaughtered. Eventually, by the conservative Thermidorian Reaction, some of the extremists were sent to the guillotine and the Terror ended.

To defend the nation and to spread the Revolution abroad, the then novel procedure of compulsory military service for all able-bodied young men was adopted and a "nation in arms" was substituted for the professional troops which had been traditional in Europe. French armies occupied the Austrian Netherlands, the later Belgium, and the territories on the left bank of the Rhine. In Holland the Batavian Republic supplanted the House of Orange. Triumphant militarism captured France. In its domestic regime the National Convention began preparing a single code of laws for the nation, forbade primogeniture, protected women in holding property, made the French language the sole medium of instruction in the country (thus furthering linguistic unity in a land of several dialects), adopted the metric system as a means of achieving uniformity in weights and measures, broke up large landed estates, and for a time fixed wages and prices of commodities.

In 1795 a constitution was adopted which placed the Government under a Directory of five. The Directory continued until 1799. In internal administration the Directors proved incompetent. During their tenure, however, French arms were carried victoriously into other parts of Europe. This was primarily the work of Napoleon Bonaparte.

THE STORM: THE NAPOLEONIC PHASE

It was in 1793 that the young Corsican began to come to the fore. In that year he expelled the British from Toulon. In 1795 he protected the National Convention against the Paris populace. In 1796 he acquired for France Savoy and Nice. In 1797 he compelled Austria to cede to France the Austrian Netherlands and the Ionian Islands. In 1798 he invaded Egypt. Although the British navy cut off his army from France, he managed to make his way back to Paris, a popular hero. Thanks in part to what he had accomplished, in 1799

France had on its northern and eastern borders and in Italy satellite republics in which the principles of the Revolution were being applied. They were the Batavian Republic in Holland, the Helvetian Republic in Switzerland, and in Italy the Ligurian, Cisalpine, Etrurian, Roman, and Parthenopean republics. But in 1799 France's enemies so far turned back the tide that the armies of the Directory were driven out of Italy and most of the puppet republics collapsed.

On his return from Egypt Bonaparte was hailed as he who could save France from her foes. He quickly obtained his appointment to supreme military command and the promulgation of another constitution, under which he became First Consul. He was now dominant in France.[7] He was utterly selfish, overweeningly ambitious, colossally egotistical, and completely unscrupulous. Yet he claimed to be the champion of the Revolution. He was a military genius of the first order. He was also a great administrator. He had extraordinary energy. During the early years of the Consulate he led France to victory over her Continental enemies. England was undefeated but in 1802 a treaty was negotiated even with her.

In the brief interval of peace between 1802 and 1804 Bonaparte devoted himself primarily to internal problems. He gave France the centralized, vigorous, efficient government which it needed after the turmoil of the revolutionary years. While curbing liberty he preserved equality. He improved the finances of the country and promoted its economic prosperity. He completed the codification of the laws which had been begun by the National Convention. He constructed a system of public education. He promoted a vast programme of public works. He crushed internal resistance.

An autocrat in fact, Bonaparte made himself one in name. In 1802 he was declared Consul for life. Late in 1804 in the presence of the Pope he crowned himself Napoleon I, Emperor of the French. Under the new title he declared that, as formerly, he was conserving and promoting the Revolution. Yet the puppet republics were transformed into kingdoms and over them were placed members of his family.

Napoleon's reign was marked by foreign wars. Even before his coronation Great Britain, alarmed by Bonaparte's colonial projects and the threat to her trade, had renewed the struggle. To break her, his greatest enemy, Napoleon planned the invasion of England. From that he was deflected by the English skill in forming and financing a coalition against him. Turning on his Continental foes, Napoleon defeated in succession Austria, Prussia, and Russia. The King of Sweden was induced to name as his successor Bernadotte, one of Napoleon's generals. Under pressure from Napoleon a drastic reorganization of Germany was carried out. The number of its states was greatly reduced.

[7] On Napoleon and the Napoleonic era see *The Cambridge Modern History*, Vol. IX (The Cambridge University Press, 1906, pp. xxviii, 946) and its appended bibliographies. For a selection of more recent works see the bibliographies in Hayes, *op. cit.*, pp. 807, 808.

The Holy Roman Empire at last came to an inglorious end and the Austrian Hapsburgs renounced their empty headship for the title of Emperor of Austria. Prussia, at the mercy of the conqueror, was shorn of much of its territory.

At the apogee of his power, Napoleon overreached himself. To crush his mortal enemy, Great Britain, now scarcely disputed mistress of the seas and dependent on foreign trade, he formulated his "Continental System" to close to her the markets of the Continent and thus to force her to her knees. It was partly to bring them to compliance with this programme that he undertook to overrun Spain and Portugal. Late in 1807 and in the fore part of 1808 Napoleon's armies invaded the Iberian Peninsula. Lisbon was occupied. The Bourbons were forced to resign and in their place Napoleon's brother Joseph was put on the Spanish throne. The reforms of the French Revolution were imposed on the land. But, declaring herself the ally of any nation in Europe which sought to throw off the Napoleonic yoke, Britain came to the aid of the resistance. Spanish nationalism embarrassed the French armies by guerrilla tactics. Austria adopted the French system of compulsory military service and, while defeated and forced to give a princess, Marie Louise, to displace Josephine as Napoleon's empress, was allowed to retain its position as a major power. In Prussia a surge of nationalism led to reforms in part on the French pattern, with the abolition of serfdom and the institution of compulsory military service. A break with Russia, finally precipitated by the tsar's unwillingness or inability to conform with the "Continental System," led to an ill-starred invasion of that country (1812) and to a disastrous retreat from Moscow which broke the might of Napoleon's military power. Much of Europe now revolted. The tsar proclaimed his purpose to liberate the European peoples and supported it with an army. Led by Prussia, much of Germany rose against the oppressor. Austria joined the coalition. Britain aided with financial subventions. In October, 1813, at the "Battle of the Nations" at Leipzig, Napoleon was decisively defeated. Most of the puppet regimes which he had erected on the French borders and in Italy and Spain collapsed. The Allies invaded France and captured Paris (March 31, 1814). Napoleon was forced to abdicate and was relegated to the island of Elba. The Bourbons were restored to the thrones of France and Spain.

Napoleon made a dramatic but unsuccessful attempt to regain power. In February, 1815, he reappeared in France. The nation rallied to him. But the Allies were determined to crush him. At Waterloo, on June 18, 1815, Wellington for the English and Blücher for the Prussians dealt his armies the final blow. Abdicating a second time and throwing himself on the mercy of the English, Napoleon was sent, a prisoner, to remote St. Helena. On May 5, 1821, death removed him from the scene.

The battle of Waterloo ushered in the ninety-nine years of relative peace which were the nineteenth century.

THE LESS SPECTACULAR REVOLUTIONS

While the American Revolution was attracting the attention of the Western world and while the French Revolution and Napoleon were shaking political and social Europe to its foundations, other forces were operating which were to contribute quite as potently to the continuing revolution of the nineteenth and twentieth centuries. They were varied but each posed a challenge to Christianity which at times became a threat. Both the challenge and the threat were fully as great as those presented by the more spectacular and violent political aspects of the revolution. In the ensuing decades they were to mount to ever more staggering proportions.

One of these forces was the Industrial Revolution. It was introduced by the application of water and steam power to machinery. It led to the development of new machines, to the rise of factories, to the growth of cities, and to new social and economic institutions, and contributed to fresh theories for the organization of society. In 1815 it was only in its infancy. Its full onslaught was to come later.

The Industrial Revolution began slowly in the first half of the eighteenth century. It mounted in the second half of the century and during the period of the American and French revolutions and the wars of Napoleon.[8] It had its earliest marked development in Great Britain. Indeed, until after 1815 most of it was here. At the outset it was most striking in the manufacture of cotton goods. Britain had long been expert in the making of woolens but for fine cottons had been chiefly dependent on Asia. Now a combination of assets led it extensively into the fabrication of cotton goods. One of these was inventive genius which devised machinery for the production of yarn and cloth in quantities. Outstanding among the inventions were the flying shuttle (1733), which speeded up weaving, the spinning jenny (patented 1770), which enabled one worker to turn out more thread, the roller spinning frame (patented by Arkwright in 1769 and 1775, an improvement over a process devised about thirty years earlier), and the mule (1779), which, combining features of both the frame and the jenny, produced a thread which successfully competed with that of India. At first these devices were operated by hand or by water-power. In 1785 Watt's steam engine, devised in 1769 and successfully completed in 1776, an improvement over the steam engines which for several decades had been used to pump water out of coal mines, was harnessed to the machines for the

---

[8] Of the large bibliography the following surveys provide excellent introductions: J. L. and Barbara Hammond, *The Rise of Modern Industry* (London, Methuen & Co., 1925, pp. xi, 280); L. C. A. Knowles, *The Industrial and Commercial Revolutions in Great Britain during the Nineteenth Century* (London, George Routledge & Sons, 1921, pp. xii, 412), especially pp. 1–109; A. P. Usher, *An Introduction to the Industrial History of England* (Boston, Houghton Mifflin Co., 1920, pp. xxii, 529, xxxiv); L. W. White, *Industrial and Social Revolution, 1750–1937* (London, Longmans, Green, & Co., 1938, pp. vii, 308).

manufacture of cottons. The power loom was invented in 1785 by a clergyman, Cartwright, and through improvements in 1787 and 1803 quickly achieved wide use. In 1793 the invention of the cotton gin in the United States by Whitney facilitated the cleaning of the raw cotton and soon made the young republic the main source of cotton fibre.

The rapid increase in the use of the new machinery was made possible by improvements in the production of iron and steel. They first emerged on a large scale in Great Britain, where they were favoured by the proximity of deposits of coal and iron and the nearness of both to water which facilitated their transportation and utilization. Some of the first improvements were made early in the eighteenth century by Quakers who for conscience' sake did not patent them but permitted them to be generally available for the public good. In the second half of the century, notably in the 1780's, further improvements increased the production of pig iron, bar iron, and steel. Devices which substituted coal for charcoal from the dwindling forests were of assistance.

Simultaneously with the burgeoning manufacture of cotton and the production of iron and steel went advances in other industries.

The coming of the machines made for the passing of cottage industries and the rise and growth of factories. Through the factories the owners, increasingly a capitalist class, brought the machines together, directed their operations, and marketed the products. The machines were served by employed labourers. Numbers of the latter were women and children. In many factories and factory towns and in the mines from which the coal essential to them was obtained, the hours and conditions of labour were destructive of health and morals. Labour conditions may have been not much if any worse than under earlier forms of industry, but they were incredibly bad.

The growth of manufacturing and mining rendered better transportation imperative. Roads had been all but impassable for heavy freight, and footpads had rendered travel perilous. Now good roads were constructed, many of them turnpikes, financed by tolls. In the second half of the eighteenth century hundreds of miles of canals were dug.

The movement for better roads and for canals was reinforced by a revolution in agriculture. By what was known as enclosure, lands which had been traditionally open to the common use of villagers became private property and the kind of strip farming through which much cultivation had been accomplished was ended. This made for larger estates and for advances in methods and crops. To bring their products to the growing towns and cities and to ports for export improved means of transport were required.

The Industrial Revolution was not confined to Great Britain. It began to be seen on the Continent. For example, in France Joseph Marie Jacquard (1752–1834) developed a loom for weaving silk which, improved partly through what he learned of an earlier loom by Jacques de Vaucanson (1709–1782), by 1806 had become so useful that it was declared to be public property.

The multiplication of factories, the rise and growth of manufacturing towns and cities, and the agricultural revolution brought changes in the social structure which, like other features of the revolution, were both a threat and a challenge to Christianity. The village life, largely self-sufficient and with the parish church as integral and even central, began to break up.[9] Women appeared as labourers in factories and mines and on the new agricultural estates. The machines threw out of employment many who had formerly earned their livelihood by spinning at home.[10] Under the new conditions could the churches retain and increase their influence on the population? Could Christianity provide the impetus to reform whatever evils came out of the transition? The challenge and the threat were first apparent on a large scale in Great Britain. In the course of the following centuries they spread to all Christendom—and to all the world.

A revolution was also occurring in economic theory. The coincidence, in 1776, of the American Declaration of Independence and the publication of Adam Smith's *An Inquiry into the Nature and Causes of the Wealth of Nations* has often been remarked. The book's advocacy of *laissez faire* and what was later glorified as "free enterprise" was a landmark. In the next two centuries the principles it propounded, including free trade and the revolt from mercantilism, were to have a wide though vigorously contested vogue. They were to confront Christians with serious problems.

In the realm of the sciences man's horizons were being pushed outward in a fashion which in the nineteenth century increasingly proved disconcerting to the Christian faith of many. On the basis of what he believed that he found in the Scriptures Archbishop Usher (1581–1656) of the (Anglican) Church of Ireland had compiled a chronology which placed the creation of the world at 4004 B.C. Now geologists were pointing out that even this planet had a history which dwarfed that brief span.[11] Thus in the second half of the eighteenth century the Frenchman G. L. L. Buffon (1707–1788) drew up a tentative time scheme for the earth (published in 1778) based on the theory, early put forward by Descartes and Leibnitz, of the prolonged progressive cooling of an incandescent mass. In 1795 the British physician James Hutton (1726–1797) came out with two volumes setting forth the theory, in 1802 presented in more readable form by John Playfair (1748–1829), that the processes at work in the present are those which in the past shaped the geologic history of the planet. Lamarck (1744–1829), the French paleontologist, partly anticipated the theory

---

[9] J. L. and Barbara Hammond, *The Village Labourer 1760–1832*, pp. 1–206.
[10] Pinchbeck, *Women Workers and the Industrial Revolution 1750–1850*, pp. 55–66, 111 ff.
[11] Geikie, *The Founders of Geology, passim.*

of evolution which, formulated a generation or so later by Darwin, troubled many of those who accepted the Biblical story of creation.

In astronomy man's horizons were also lifted. Astronomical instruments were being improved, the stars were being mapped, Uranus and two of its satellites were discovered, the moon was being carefully studied, the general direction of the sun's movement through space was determined, and the existence of binary stars was established. The aberration of light was proved. The hypothesis was advanced that the Milky Way is made up of innumerable clusters of stars and that other systems resembling it exist.[12]

Chemistry was an area in which important advances were achieved. For instance, the Nonconformist clergyman Joseph Priestley (1733-1804) made important discoveries in gases, among them the isolation of oxygen. Probably slightly earlier, although not published until later, Scheele, of Sweden, was responsible for a similar discovery. Lavoisier gave oxygen its name. Before 1815 Dalton had postulated the existence of atoms and had worked out tables by which the weight of elements and their compounds were measured with the hydrogen atom as the base. In this he was followed by Berzelius (1770-1848), whose major work was done shortly after 1815.

Before 1815, largely in the eighteenth century, important discoveries concerning electricity were precursors to effects in man's life which were to be revolutionary.

It was during the period spanned by the French Revolution that Immanuel Kant (1724-1804) began to exert the profound influence on European thought which was to persist through the nineteenth and into the twentieth century.[13] Born and reared in the strong Pietist centre Königsberg, Kant was familiar with that strain of Protestantism. His range of intellectual interests was extensive and he read prodigiously. He was untravelled, never married, and, physically misshapen, short of stature, and frail, by rigid discipline made his body serve him until an advanced age. He was late in maturing. Not until 1781 did *Kritik der reinen Vernunft* ("The Critique of Pure Reason"), his first book to attract wide attention, appear. It was in 1787 that its second and enlarged edition was published.[14] On the one hand, it seemed to be an effective answer to the philosophical scepticism of Hume. On the other hand, it limited human knowledge to the data given us by our senses and organized by the patterns of the mind. In organizing what comes to us, so Kant said, we employ space, time, and the categories or forms of thought: we cannot know things in

[12] Abetti, *The History of Astronomy*, pp. 153-182.

[13] *Kant's Werke* (Berlin, Georg Reimer, 15 vols., 1902-1913). A good account in English is by E. Caird, *The Critical Philosophy of Immanuel Kant* (Glasgow, James Maclehose and Sons, 2nd ed., 2 vols., 1909).

[14] *Immanuel Kant's Critique of Pure Reason*, translated by F. M. Müller (New York, The Macmillan Co., 2nd ed., 1907, pp. lxxix, 808).

themselves. Thus he limited the scope of reason and weakened confidence in the rational processes so highly esteemed in the eighteenth century. He argued that the grounds on which the Deists and Wolff had sought to establish the existence and character of God were indefensible. The traditional arguments for the being of God, Kant held, are also untenable. It is not surprising that the Prussian government commanded him not to write or lecture on religion. Its distrust was not lessened by his *Kritik der practischen Vernunft* ("Critique of Practical Reason"), published in 1788.[15] To be sure, in that work Kant argued that God must exist. He held that man is confronted by the "categorical imperative," an unconditional and unqualified moral obligation, that obedience to it is never complete in this life and so demands immortality for its fulfilment, that conformity to it brings happiness, and that since only God can make happiness the outcome of virtue, we must believe that He is. In his *Die Religion innerhalb der Grenzen der blossen Vernunft* ("Religion within the Limits of Unaided Reason") Kant went further. He declared that any one who conforms to the categorical imperative is a son of God and is pleasing to God. He held that Jesus Christ was the highest example of that conformity and therefore of that sonship.

Here was a philosophy which for penetration could not but command respect. It was a landmark in Western thought. It was in the stream of German Idealism which may be said to have begun with Leibnitz. Christian theologians, whether Protestant or Roman Catholic, henceforward had to take it into account. Kant has been called "the philosopher of Protestantism." Obviously he came out of a Protestant background and preserved much of what he derived from it. Yet he was also in the tradition of "natural religion." In him religious belief was based upon morality and "practical reason": eighteenth-century rationalism, though attacked, was still potent.

Even before the storm of the French Revolution and the wars of Napoleon had passed, intellectually Western Europe was moving away from the climate of opinion in which they had arisen. As Kant and others were challenging the rationalism and Deism which had contributed to them, so in literature the romantic movement was beginning to supplant the measured rationalism of eighteenth-century authors. Rousseau had aided it. He who is said to have been the greatest poet of Germany, Johann Wolfgang von Goethe (1749–1832), although not to be confined to any one school, was hailed by the romanticists as one of them. While his greatest work, *Faust,* with its philosophy of life, could not have been written by one who had not been immersed in the Christian tradition, it is not the product of one who himself was a convinced Christian. In his long life he had responded to various influences, among them

[15] Immanuel Kant, *Critique of Practical Reason and Other Writings on Moral Philosophy,* translated by L. W. Beck (The University of Chicago Press, 1949, pp. xv, 370).

Pietism. He was deeply religious, but not in a Christian sense. Goethe's younger friend, Johann Christoph Friedrich von Schiller (1759–1805), poet, philosopher, and dramatist, did most of his significant writing while the French Revolution was in progress. Reared a Protestant, in his youth he planned to be a theologian. A moral idealist, influenced by Kant and impressed with the tragedy of life, at times he spoke for the nationalism which was one of the prominent currents of the time.[16]

It was during the period of the French Revolution that Johann Gottfried von Herder (1744–1803), poet and philosopher, completed his life. Slightly older than Goethe, he helped to shape the latter's youthful years and for long was his friend. A clergyman and for almost a generation court preacher and general superintendent in Weimar, he was officially and presumably sincerely a Christian. He has been called, in somewhat hyperbolic appraisal, the shaper of a new epoch and the spiritual father of the Germany of the nineteenth century. He sought to nationalize German poetry, encouraged an interest in German art, helped to lay the foundations of comparative philology and religion, and endeavoured to establish a philosophical basis for his religious convictions.

The creative years of Johann Gottlieb Fichte (1762–1814) fell entirely in the quarter-century after 1789. A philosopher, early influenced by Kant, he believed profoundly in God and the moral order of the universe. But he was not an orthodox Christian.[17]

During these years Georg Wilhelm Friedrich Hegel (1770–1831) was working out his philosophy, but it was not until after 1815 that he attained the enormous influence which was to place his stamp on much of the thought of the nineteenth and twentieth centuries.

In the literary world still other currents were seen. *Sturm und Drang* took its name from a drama of 1776 by Klinger. Classicism was evident. Some of the expressions of these currents represented the struggle of the human spirit with the eternal questions of man's existence and the nature of the universe, but seldom did they come out with a clearly Christian answer.

The tradition of rationalism persisted, and the dream of the dignity of man and the worth of the individual and of achieving a society in which these would be given full recognition was still cherished. Again and again in the next century and a half it was to give rise to fresh ideologies, to reinforce existing ones, and to contribute to revolutions.

We need also to remember that the stormy years of wars and political revolutions heard for the first time the compositions of Haydn (1732–1809), Mozart (1756–1791), and Beethoven (1770–1827), music which helped to form the taste of later generations.

[16] Shuster, *Das Werden der Kirche*, pp. 388 ff.
[17] For an important essay on Fichte, see Emanuel Hirsch, *Die idealistische Philosophie und das Christentum* (Gütersloh, C. Bertelsmann, 1926, pp. x, 326), pp. 140–190.

THE STORM AND THE CHRISTIAN RESPONSE: GENERALIZATIONS

Meanwhile, how was Christianity faring? Here was a storm sweeping across Europe which arose partly from Christian sources. The preliminary mutterings in the British Isles in the seventeenth century had Christianity as a large element. In those in America in the third quarter of the nineteenth century Christianity was a contributing factor but probably not as largely so as in its English predecessor. The French Revolution was brewed from a number of ingredients. Some were of Christian provenance, but for the most part they were distortions of that source. The Revolution was captured by a man who saw in it a means of his own aggrandizement and in whom the lust for power was dominant. Economic forces were being released which were partly from man's desire for achievement and also were utilized by many as a means to power over their fellows. Impelled by his curiosity, and with a daring which was characteristic of him, Western European man, having explored much of the globe, was peering into the universe outside his planet and was seeking to penetrate the mysteries of his physical environment. Through philosophy and literature he was essaying to comprehend himself and the nature and validity of his knowledge. His soul was expressing itself in great music. In the midst of these storms and varied movements how would Christianity respond? Could it in any way offset or correct the perversions of its gifts? Could it so operate that the perversions would afford opportunities which it would utilize for man's good?

During the storm of revolution evidences of the vitality within Christianity mounted. Except among minorities they attracted little attention. They appeared to be dwarfed by the political and social upheavals of the times. But in the nineteenth and twentieth centuries their dimensions and their effects increased.

Of the major branches of Christianity, the Roman ·Catholic Church was dealt the most severe blows. As we have more than once reminded ourselves, the storm had its rise and main centre in France, which by profession was predominantly Roman Catholic. Some of the most violent repercussions of the storm were in the Roman Catholic portions of Germany, in Italy, where that church had its capital, and in Spain and Portugal, which from the fifteenth century had been the main sources of the geographic extension of that church. Much of the violence of the storm was directed by deliberate design against the Roman Catholic Church. As we are to see, although this did not become fully obvious until well along in the nineteenth century, the net result was drastic changes in the Roman Catholic Church.

During the storm the movements continued which were to make Protestantism world-wide and give it the leading place in Christian thought. To a large extent its main strength was in regions which were less subject to the full force of the storm than were those where the Roman Catholic Church was the prevailing form of the faith. As we are to see, it proved more adaptable than the latter to some of the aspects of the continuing revolution. From it, in response to the new situations, more novel movements emerged than from any other branch of the faith. Most of these came after 1815, but some of them made their initial appearance during the height of the storm.

The storm affected the Eastern Churches less immediately than it did the Roman Catholic Church and Protestantism. During its course, however, influences, chiefly from Protestantism, made themselves felt in the Russian Orthodox Church which gave rise to some modifications. The most important repercussions came after 1815.

The Storm and the Roman Catholic Church: in France

It was to be expected that the impact of the French Revolution and Napoleon upon the Roman Catholic Church would be the most disorganizing in France. Action after action of the state brought a succession of drastic changes, made for weakening internal divisions, at one stage became a frontal attack, and eventually subordinated the Church to the state more effectively than ever it had been under the old regime.

The actions which altered the place of the Roman Catholic Church began early. The step by which the Estates General became the National Assembly meant a diminution of the influence of the clergy. The clergy no longer sat as a separate body with distinct powers: they were now simply members of the Assembly. Here, whether as Jansenists, free-thinkers, or Protestants, the majority were hostile.[18] Yet it was the support of the lower clergy which helped to make this possible. In the memorable scene on the night of August 4, 1789, when the nobility renounced their special privileges and feudal rights were abolished, the clergy, both priests and bishops, vied with the lay lords in the enthusiasm of the hour.[19] The question was early raised about the continuation of the tithe, one of the main sources of ecclesiastical revenue. In the ensuing controversy the Archbishop of Paris on behalf of the clergy placed the proceeds of the tithes "in the hands of a just and generous nation," trusting the National Assembly to provide the means to maintain divine worship "with decency and dignity," to see that the churches were served with "virtuous and zealous clergy," and that "the poor were succoured." The Assembly legalized the step.[20]

In November, 1789, the National Assembly decreed that the property of the Church should be at the disposal of the nation for the maintenance of worship

---

[18] *The Cambridge Modern History*, Vol. VIII, p. 194; Phillips, *The Church in France, 1789–1848*, p. 8.

[19] Leflon, *La Crise Révolutionnaire*, pp. 46, 47; Phillips, *op. cit.*, p. 8.

[20] Leflon, *op. cit.*, p. 47, citing *Moniteur*, Vol. I, p. 132; Phillips, *op. cit.*, p. 8.

and the clergy and the relief of the poor. By this, in principle, the clergy became servants of the state. The decree also ordered that no *curé* should have a stipend of less than 1,200 livres a year.[21] Hard pressed for money, for the financial distress which had precipitated the Revolution had been aggravated rather than assuaged, the National Assembly ordered the sale of ecclesiastical lands. Part of the proceeds were assigned to give stability to the *assignats,* the paper money issued by the Government.[22]

The dissolution of many of the monasteries and congregations of the religious soon followed. Here the National Assembly was but utilizing powers which had been previously exercised by the crown: in 1768 a royal commission had closed more than a thousand such communities. In February, 1790, the National Assembly decreed that monastic vows were no longer binding, that the religious who wished to leave their houses should be pensioned, that those who so desired might live in community and should be grouped in designated houses, that nuns should not be disturbed, and that for the present congregations engaged in public education and in works of charity should be allowed to continue.[23] The responses of the monks varied. Some elected to pursue their accustomed way of life: many welcomed release from their vows. Of the nuns the large majority seem to have chosen to hold to their rule and to remain in their convents.[24]

Steps were taken towards negating the privileged place of the Roman Catholic Church. In April, 1790, the National Assembly, while declaring its loyalty to the Roman Catholic faith and its purpose to maintain the observance of its worship, held that it had no power over conscience or religious convictions and declined to consider a motion which would have made Roman Catholicism the religion of the state.[25] To some Roman Catholics the Declaration of the Rights of Man which headed the constitution of 1791 was disturbing—all the more so since in December, 1789, the National Assembly put Protestants on a legal equality with Roman Catholics and in 1790 accorded that status to the Jews of Bordeaux and in 1791 to the Jews of Alsace. The Assembly also stood for the freedom of the press.[26]

More drastic was the Civil Constitution of the Clergy. It grew out of the work of the Ecclesiastical Committee of the National Assembly. On that committee were men with Jansenist sympathies who, hoping for the reform of the Church, helped to give to the proposal its radical nature. Associated with what was usually called Jansenism but having an independent and earlier origin

[21] Leflon, *op. cit.,* p. 47, citing *Moniteur,* Vol. II, p. 126.
[22] Leflon, *op. cit.,* pp. 49–51.
[23] *Ibid.,* pp. 51, 52.
[24] *Ibid.,* pp. 54–56.
[25] *Ibid.,* p. 54, citing *Moniteur,* Vol. IV, p. 110.
[26] Leflon, *op. cit.,* pp. 53, 54; Aulard, *Christianity and the French Revolution,* pp. 49–57.

were convictions formulated by Edmond Richer (1560–1631). Richer, a canonist of the Sorbonne, wished the Church to return to what he called its primitive practices. He held that the power of the keys rested with the great body of Christians. Each parish should have a voice in choosing its pastor and the pastor should exercise that power on its behalf. Richer wished the authority of the bishops reduced, including that of the Pope, and more to be given to the parish priests and their flocks. For several years Jansenism and Richerism were potent in the ecclesiastical life which arose from the Civil Constitution of the Clergy.

On July 12, 1790, the Civil Constitution of the Clergy, with amendments, was enacted by the National Assembly. It sought, in an extreme Gallican fashion, to reorganize the Catholic Church in France so as to erase some of the anachronisms, to make the Church more responsive to the will of the populace, and to separate it administratively from Rome. The 135 dioceses of quite unequal dimensions were reduced to 85, each of which corresponded to a civil department. The 18 archbishops were replaced by 10 metropolitans. The parishes were made to correspond with the size of the population. Some kinds of ecclesiastical offices were abolished. The voters of the department were to elect the bishop, and the electoral body of the district was to choose its pastor. No one was to be disqualified from voting on the ground that he was not a Catholic. The bishops and pastors might choose their vicars. The pastor was to receive from his bishop his canonical institution and the bishop his canonical powers from his metropolitan. But the metropolitan was forbidden to apply to the Pope for his confirmation. Yet to preserve the witness to the unity of the faith and of communion the metropolitan was to notify the Holy See of his election. The Constitution also fixed the salaries of the different grades of the clergy. To meet the chronic ill of absenteeism, it provided that the clergy must reside in their respective charges.[27]

The Civil Constitution of the Clergy was a compromise. To the enemies of the Church it did not go far enough. Nor, for men with Jansenist sympathies, did it sufficiently reform the Church.[28] To some degree it freed the parish clergy from control by their bishops. Presumably it rendered both bishops and parish clergy more responsive to the wishes of their constituencies. Yet it effected no separation of Church and state. Nor was it intended to cause a schism in the Roman Catholic Church. The Pope, while shorn of his administrative powers in France, was still regarded as the head of the Church and the centre and symbol of unity. Catholic dogma was not touched.[29]

---

[27] Leflon, *op. cit.,* pp. 57, 58; *The Cambridge Modern History,* Vol. VIII, pp. 195–197; F. Préclin, *Les Jansenistes du XVIIIe Siècle et la Constitution Civile du Clergé. La Développement du Richérisme, la Propagation dans la Bas Clergé 1713–1791* (Paris, Librairie Universitaire, J. Gamber, 1929, pp. xxxi, 578), *passim;* Aulard, *op. cit.,* pp. 57–64; Ledré, *l'Église de France sous la Révolution,* pp. 66 ff.

[28] La Gorce, *Histoire Religieuse de la Révolution Française,* Vol. I, pp. 254–261.

[29] Leflon, *op. cit.,* pp. 58–61; Phillips, *op. cit.,* pp. 12, 13.

The Civil Constitution of the Clergy precipitated division within the Roman Catholic Church in France and evoked the opposition of Rome. The Pope, Pius VI, early expressed to Louis XVI and to two French archbishops his deep concern over the situation and warned them of the danger of schism.[30] Yet the king yielded to pressure and gave his formal approval to the document. On August 24, 1790, it was promulgated.[31] The large majority of the bishops believed that they must protest and on October 30, 1790, issued an *Exposition des Principes sur la Constitution Civile du Clergé* in which they declared that the Constitution changed the structure of religion without the consent of the Church and so contradicted the principles which should govern the relations of Church and state.[32] The National Assembly could not back down without jeopardizing its authority. On November 27, 1790, it decreed that all bishops, clergy, and other ecclesiastical functionaries must swear to support the Constitution. To this, on December 26, 1790, the king had reluctantly to give his sanction.[33] Only a small minority of bishops and clergy took the required oath. Out of 160 bishops only 7 complied, and of them only 4 were in charge of dioceses. The lower clergy were not as nearly unanimous in their rejection: the proportion varied from place to place. Some attempted to take the oath with reservations. So far as statistics are available, it seems probable that slightly more than half refused.[34]

The Pope was slow to make a definitive pronouncement. His situation was far from enviable. Himself conservative, presumably he believed that if he were to place himself flatly against the trend in France he might render more difficult the efforts of the moderates who were seeking to prevent the kind of drastic action which would precipitate a breach. To be sure, in several letters he made clear his opposition to the direction in which the National Assembly was moving. He wrote his approval to clergy who stood out against the Assembly[35] and expostulated with a Cardinal who had given his assent to the Civil Constitution of the Clergy.[36] However, not until March 10, 1791, did he issue the lengthy brief *Quod aliquantum*, which expressly condemned that document. In April and May he followed this with other letters of similar tenor.[37] To carry through the programme prescribed by the Civil Constitution of the Clergy would mean a breach with Rome. Rather than submit to the

[30] Letters of Pius VI to Louis and the Archbishops of Bordeaux and Vienne, July 10, 1790, in Theiner, *Documents Inédits relatifs aux Affaires Religieuses de la France, 1790 à 1800*, Vol. I, pp. 5, 7, 9.

[31] La Gorge, *op. cit.*, Vol. I, pp. 295, 296.

[32] Leflon, *op. cit.*, p. 65; Latreille, *l'Église Catholique et la Révolution Française*, Vol. I, pp. 91, 92; La Gorge, *op. cit.*, Vol. I, p. 306.

[33] Leflon, *op. cit.*, pp. 66, 67.

[34] *Ibid.*, pp. 67–73.

[35] Theiner, *op. cit.*, Vol. I, pp. 22–26.

[36] *Ibid.*, pp. 28–32.

[37] *Ibid.*, pp. 32 ff.; Aulard, *op. cit.*, pp. 68 ff.

National Assembly, numbers of the bishops and many of the lower clergy fled the country.[38]

Undeterred by the Papal thunders, the National Assembly adhered to its purpose. In the fore part of 1791 elections were conducted to fill eighty of the eighty-five sees into which the Civil Constitution of the Clergy had divided the country. The other sees were held by bishops who had taken the prescribed oath. In the consecration of the new prelates the attempt was made to conserve the apostolic succession. The only bishop who would consent to act was Talleyrand. From the beginning he had gone along with the Revolution, although usually seeking moderation.[39] Resting on what they claimed as their Gallican rights, the bishops attempted to prevent the publication in France of the Papal briefs and held that Rome had no legal right to condemn them.[40] However, Papal briefs commending the loyal bishops and threatening with excommunication the clergy who conformed to the Constitution were smuggled in, surreptitiously printed, and given a wide circulation.[41] In the meantime, in spite of some local opposition, parish priests had been elected.[42]

Thus two ecclesiastical structures came into being. One adhered to Rome and the other to the National Assembly and the Civil Constitution of the Clergy. Bishop was set against bishop and priest against priest. They contested for the control of the church fabrics, the bells, the sacraments, and the funerals. Scenes of violence followed.[43] In its closing days the National Assembly attempted to make peace and to enact a general amnesty. But the Legislative Assembly which convened under the constitution of 1791 was more intransigent and sought to suppress the non-jurors.[44]

For the Roman Catholic Church worse was to follow. In the massacres provoked by the fear of foreign invasion many clergy and monks were killed. Anti-clerical and anti-Christian sentiment mounted. The Legislative Assembly more and more curtailed the church which had been set up under the Civil Constitution of the Clergy.[45] When, in September, 1792, the Legislative Assembly was succeeded by the National Convention, it was a question whether even that church would survive. To be sure, the Convention formally declared that it did not intend to deprive the populace of the services of the Catholic clergy.[46] Some of the revolts against the Republic coincided with reverses in the foreign war and, since they were ostensibly in part in defence of throne

---

38 Leflon, *op. cit.*, p. 69.
39 La Gorge, *op. cit.*, Vol. I, pp. 399 ff.; Phillips, *The Church in France, 1789–1848*, p. 18.
40 Pastor, *History of the Popes*, Vol. XL, pp. 182 ff.
41 *Ibid.*, pp. 194 ff.
42 Leflon, *op. cit.*, pp. 76, 77.
43 *Ibid.*, pp. 77–86; La Gorge, *op. cit.*, Vol. I, pp. 415 ff.
44 Leflon, *op. cit.*, pp. 87 ff.
45 Latreille, *op. cit.*, Vol. I, pp. 137, 138.
46 *Ibid.*, p. 136.

and altar, augmented the anti-Christian sentiment of those in control. Radicals, powerful in the Convention, were frankly anti-Christian. The Gregorian calendar, with its Christian associations, was abolished (October, 1793) and for it was substituted a purely secular one counting time from the inauguration of the Republic rather than from the birth of Christ. In Paris the bishop and several of his clergy were forced to resign and (November, 1793) in the cathedral of Notre Dame a young woman was enthroned as the Goddess of Reason. It is said that in the spring of 1794 in only 150 parishes in France was mass still celebrated.[47] Encouraged by a decree of the Convention of November, 1793, which exempted from deportation married priests, numbers of the clergy entered into matrimony. Of the 85 bishops under the Constitution, 24 abdicated or renounced their functions, 23 apostatized, and of the latter 9 married.[48] In an attempt to offset the atheistic cult of reason, Robespierre, a Deist, exerted his influence to have officially inaugurated (June, 1794) a religion of the Supreme Being with a belief in the immortality of the soul.[49] This, it will be noted, was during the Reign of Terror. In that revolutionary orgy many of the clergy were executed.[50]

During the reaction which terminated the Terror and under the Directory which followed the National Convention the anti-Christian measures in France were not so severe. The Catholic Church again raised its head. However, its course was by no means smooth. Early in 1795, partly to bring peace in the rebellious districts in the west, the National Convention conceded a degree of religious liberty.[51] But the Constitutional Church, if we may so designate that which had come into being under the Civil Constitution of the Clergy, suffered from a diminished number of priests and bishops, and the non-juring clergy were also few and had small chance of recruiting to their ranks and obtaining support. Since Church and state were now separated, both groups were in difficulty. Church buildings were national property. In May, 1795, a decree made possible the occupation of some of them by the Catholics, but only with the provision that those who worshipped in them should formally agree to submit to the laws of the Republic. This created fresh divisions, for numbers of the previous non-jurors accepted the new conditions.[52] For a time the Directory maintained the anti-Christian policy of the National Convention. In it were men who were frankly anti-Christian. Public education was secular and the non-Christian state cult was maintained. Yet the Constitutional Church revived. Moreover, the non-jurors were reinforced by priests who returned from

[47] *Ibid.,* pp. 154–158, 166; Phillips, *op. cit.,* pp. 28, 29; Aulard, *op. cit.,* pp. 100–123.
[48] Leflon, *op. cit.,* pp. 125, 126; Aulard, *op. cit.,* pp. 100 ff.
[49] La Gorge, *op. cit.,* Vol. III, pp. 477 ff.; Ledré, *op. cit.,* pp. 175 ff.
[50] Aimé Guillon, *Les Martyrs de la Foi pendant la Révolution Française* (Paris, Germaïn Mathiot, 4 vols., 1821).
[51] Leflon, *op. cit.,* pp. 131, 132.
[52] *Ibid.,* pp. 131–138.

exile, and some of them were quite uncompromising in their loyalty to Rome. In several areas the latter regained the parishes, rang their bells, and raised their crosses. In 1796 services were held in more than 32,000 parishes.[53] In 1797 persecution was renewed, but not in as severe a form as earlier. In that year, moreover, the Constitutional Church held a national synod in Paris in which it sought to place itself on a better footing. It declared that since Paul had said that the powers that be are of God, every French Catholic should obey the laws of the Republic and that the Gallican Church would not admit to the body of its pastors any who were not loyal to the Republic or who refused to give the assurance prescribed by the law. In the later days of the Directory an attempt was made to launch a new official cult, that of Theophilanthropy, which was clearly anti-Christian.[54]

The coming to power of Bonaparte brought the Church a less unfavourable regime. Yet Napoleon was insistent on making the Church serve his purposes. Although a nominal Roman Catholic, he could not be said to understand the Christian faith. To him the Church was an institution potent in human affairs and to be made to further his ambitions. He therefore sought peace with it, but on his own terms. Late in 1799 he was responsible for several measures which lightened the restrictions on it.[55] Before many months he entered into negotiations with Pius VII for a concordat. Many obstacles were to be overcome. Anti-clerical, anti-Christian forces in France remained strong. Such questions as relations with the Constitutional Church and the non-juring clergy and the place of the married clergy were not to be disregarded. Rome was under the necessity of asking the attitude of the refugee Bourbon king, Louis XVIII.[56] Yet in July, 1801, agreement was reached and a concordat was signed.

As was inevitable, the concordat was a compromise. In general, in contrast with the conditions of the preceding decade, it was a victory for Rome. The Republic formally conceded that the Roman Catholic faith was the religion of the large majority of the French. Nothing was said about the Civil Constitution of the Clergy, but the terms of the concordat in effect nullified it. In collaboration with the Government Rome was to make a fresh arrangement of the dioceses and the bishops of the parishes. The existing bishops were to resign. If any refused, the Pope was empowered to dismiss them. The First Consul, i.e., Bonaparte, was to name the bishops, and the Pope was to give them their canonical authority. The bishops, in conjunction with the Government, were to appoint the parish priests. Bishops and priests were to take the oath of alle-

[53] Latreille, *op. cit.*, Vol. I, pp. 209 ff.; Phillips, *op. cit.*, p. 39; Jervis, *The Gallican Church and the Revolution*, pp. 283 ff.

[54] Leflon, *op. cit.*, pp. 145–155.

[55] *Ibid.*, pp. 168, 169; Jervis, *op. cit.*, pp. 326 ff.

[56] Leflon, *op. cit.*, pp. 172–190; La Gorce, *op. cit.*, Vol. V, pp. 48–139, 199–227; Jervis, *op. cit.*, pp. 335 ff.

giance to the Government. The state was to pay the salaries of the clergy. The Government was to place in the hands of the bishops all church buildings not yet alienated which were necessary for public worship, but the Pope was not to trouble owners of former ecclesiastical property. Catholics could create pious foundations. The Pope was to grant to the First Consul all the rights enjoyed by the former monarchs. The Catholic Church was to have freedom of public worship, but subject to regulations which the Government judged necessary for peace and order. While the Pope had made important concessions, so far as a document could effect it, the schism of the Gallican Church from Rome was at an end.[57]

Yet under the provision of the concordat that the Government might regulate the Church in such fashion as it deemed essential to domestic peace and order, the state, through "Organic Articles," ordered that no acts, bulls, or decrees of the Holy See or acts of General Councils be circulated in France without its permission and declared that the consent of the Government was prerequisite to the holding of provincial councils and synods, that without the permission of the state no Papal official could exercise authority on French soil, that the state had supervision of discipline and even of doctrine, that no bishop could found a chapter or a seminary without permission from the Government, that the rules of the seminaries must be approved by the First Consul, that a single catechism and liturgy should be adopted for all France, and that except Sundays no feast days should be set.[58] The Pope did not like the Organic Articles and delivered an allocution against them.

The concordat had unanticipated results. Eventually it served to knit the French Roman Catholic Church more closely together under the bishops and the Pope. Since the bishops now had full control of the parish priests, the clergy, earlier divided, could present a solid front. By failing to restore to the bishops their former lands, the concordat made them more dependent on the Pope and facilitated the growth of the ultramontanism which in the next century was to be marked.[59]

As First Consul, in the brief years of peace between 1802 and 1804, Bonaparte, as part of his programme for the internal ordering of France, had the Roman Catholic Church in the Republic reorganized in accordance with his will and the concordat. At his request a Papal legate was appointed to represent Rome, but Bonaparte insisted that he must not act independently of the will of the First Consul. The dioceses and parishes were again delimited.

---

[57] Leflon, *op. cit.*, pp. 191–193; Latreille, *op. cit.*, Vol. II, pp. 32–37; Phillips, *op. cit.*, pp. 55–74. See a translation of the text in Poulet, *A History of the Catholic Church*, Vol. II, pp. 369–371; Ledré, *op. cit.*, p. 298 ff.

[58] Leflon, *op. cit.*, pp. 194, 195. Extracts from the text, translated, are in Poulet, *op. cit.*, Vol. II, p. 371.

[59] *The Cambridge Modern History*, Vol. IX, pp. 187–189.

Ostensibly for purposes of economy, as against pre-Revolutionary days their number was much reduced. The new body of bishops was made up partly of those drawn from the Constitutional Church, partly of those of the old regime, and partly of new men. The parish clergy were recruited from both the Constitutional Church and the non-jurors.

All this was not done without difficulty. Some of the bishops of the Constitutional Church gave trouble. Opposition came from bishops and clergy who had fled the country: several of the bishops refused to resign their sees and formed a non-juring body, the *petite église,* which continued until 1893. The Roman Catholic Church was not happy over the religious liberty accorded Protestants and over civil marriage. During the Revolution few priests had been ordained and a shortage developed: in 1809, out of a total of 31,870, a third were over sixty and by 1815 the number had declined to 24,874.[60]

When, in 1804, Bonaparte became Napoleon I, Emperor of the French, his coronation, as we have said, was in the presence of the Pope. Bonaparte insisted that the Pope come to Paris for the occasion. The Cardinals raised many objections, but the Pope overrode them. In Paris he received the submission of the bishops of the Constitutional Church who until then had held aloof: that particular schism was ended. The Pope also obtained the ecclesiastical marriage of Napoleon and his wife Josephine, a tie previously sealed only by a civil ceremony. At the coronation he anointed the emperor and empress, blessed the imperial insignia, and after the coronation gave the imperial couple his blessing. Yet Napoleon placed the crown on his own head and on the head of Josephine: the Pope was not allowed to do it.[61] While emulating Charlemagne, Napoleon was not responsible to the Pope for the imperial crown, as Charlemagne and his successors in the Holy Roman Empire had been. But the sanction of the Pope was obtained for Napoleon's throne, thus making easier the loyalty of Catholics, and the subordination of the Pope to the emperor was advertised. The progress of de-Christianization was seen in the contrast between Charlemagne and Napoleon. Whatever his faults, the former was, from his standpoint, sincerely Christian. The latter's faith was at best nominal.

While much of the anti-Christian temper of the Revolution persisted and Bonaparte had had some opposition from it in carrying through the ratification of the concordat by the Government, the tide of faith was beginning to return. This was seen in the resumption of the charitable work of some of the orders and congregations. It was also evidenced in the acclaim which greeted the publication, in 1802, the year after the concordat, of *Génie du Christianisme, ou Beautés de la Religion Chrétienne* by René Francis Augustus, Viscount de

---

[60] Leflon, *op. cit.,* pp. 198 ff.; Latreille, *op. cit.,* Vol. II, pp. 47 ff.; *The Cambridge Modern History,* Vol. IX, p. 186; Jervis, *op. cit.,* pp. 359 ff.

[61] Nielsen, *The History of the Papacy in the XIXth Century,* Vol. I, pp. 260 ff.

Chateaubriand (1768-1848). A nobleman of the old regime who had fled from the Revolution, for a time Chateaubriand shared the scepticism of many of his class. But moved by the dying prayer of a deeply religious mother and the execution of a loved and religious sister, he returned to the faith in which he had been reared. Skilled with his pen, through this book, a rhapsodic apologetic for the faith, he profoundly touched thousands, including many of the younger generation.[62]

However, the relations between Pope and emperor became more strained. As we are to see in a moment, this was partly because of Napoleon's Italian policies. It was also because of the emperor's divorce of Josephine and his marriage to Marie Louise. In addition, Napoleon sought complete control over the French church and over the Cardinals. The Pope, resistant, was kept a virtual prisoner, first in Avignon, then Savona, then Fontainebleau. An Ecclesiastical Council, headed by Cardinal Fesch, Napoleon's uncle, and formed in January, 1811, by order of the Emperor, attempted to manage the affairs of the French church, had stormy sessions, and did not always accord with the imperial wishes. In 1813 the Concordat of Fontainebleau was signed. It was a compromise, but the Pope was not satisfied with it and abrogated it. On the defeat of Napoleon, in 1814, the Pope was freed and returned to Rome.[63]

THE STORM AND THE ROMAN CATHOLIC CHURCH: IN ITALY AND ROME

As the Revolution dealt severe blows to the Roman Catholic Church in France, the most powerful nation in Western Europe, so it also brought grave problems to that church in Italy, including Rome, the administrative centre and main stronghold of that branch of the faith. Secularization did not go as far as in France. By the time French arms had been carried effectively into Italy the most acute stage of the belligerently anti-Christian phase of the Revolution had passed. Yet the old order was badly shaken, the Popes were dealt with cavalierly, and the Papal States were curtailed and for a time abolished.

The triumphs of French arms in Italy in 1796 and 1797 made possible by the genius of Bonaparte brought embarrassment to the Roman Catholic Church and the Pope. Badly governed and suffering from economic distress, the Papal States were in no position to offer effective opposition. In 1796 Bonaparte's armies moved into them. In June, 1796, an armistice negotiated through the good graces of the Spanish envoy to the Vatican, while humiliating to the Pope, left the Pontiff in partial control of his realms. However, the French

---

[62] Viscount de Chateaubriand, *The Genius of Christianity; or the Spirit and Beauty of the Christian Religion,* translated by C. I. White (Baltimore, John Murphy & Co., 15th rev. ed., 1856, pp. 763); Phillips, *op. cit.,* pp. 42–54.

[63] *The Cambridge Modern History,* Vol. IX, pp. 193–201; Leflon, *op. cit.,* pp. 250–273; Phillips, *op. cit.,* pp. 122 ff.

demands for the proposed treaty which should follow the armistice were so drastic that the Pope refused to accede to them. War again broke out. Again resistance was hopeless. This time a treaty was negotiated, but with more humiliating terms than the one which the Pope had rejected. Late in 1797 an incident gave the French an excuse for marching on Rome. In February, 1798, a French army occupied the city, the Pope was deposed as temporal monarch, and a republic was proclaimed.[64] The Pope's person was declared inviolable and he was to be permitted to exercise his spiritual functions. However, eighty years of age and ill, he was sent into exile to Siena. The Cardinals who remained in Rome were treated with indignity. Rome and the Papal States were despoiled of art treasures and manuscripts to enrich Paris. Churches and palaces in Rome were plundered. After a few months in Siena, Pius VI found refuge in a Carthusian monastery near Florence. The political situation made necessary the removal of the mortally ill Pontiff to Parma and then to Briançon, Grenoble, and Valence. He was declared to be a prisoner of the French Republic. It was at Valence, on the Rhone, that he died (August 29, 1799).[65]

The history of Pius VI seemed to bode ill for the church which he headed and the office which he bore. Although he was said to favour the Society of Jesus, before his accession the Papacy had, under pressure, surrendered that support of the Roman Catholic Church. He had had to face Josephism in Italy and Austria, with its challenge to Papal authority. The French Revolution had annulled such power in France as Gallicanism had left to the Holy See, had disestablished the Church, and had made official a non-Christian cult. The Papal States had been taken from the Pope and he had died a prisoner of the government which had led in the anti-Christian measures. A man of worthy character, Pius VI had not disgraced his office by vice, as had some of his predecessors of the fifteenth and sixteenth centuries, or by a combination of vice and weakness, as had some of those who had occupied the throne of Peter in the latter part of the ninth and in the tenth century. Nor was he confronted with rival Popes, as had been many of those who had gone before him. Yet not since the advances of Islam in the seventh and eighth centuries had there been in the West such extensive defections from the faith. To be sure, the Protestant Reformation had torn away from the Papacy more millions, but that had been ostensibly from loyalty to the Gospel. Now the losses were through a denial of the Gospel. The kind of piety produced by the Roman Catholic Church, for Pius VI was above the average of that of his century, seemed impotent against the new revolutionary forces.

In the several republics in Italy which at the end of the century owed their existence to French arms, ecclesiastical property was used to fill war chests,

[64] Pastor, *History of the Popes*, Vol. XL, pp. 289–334.
[65] *Ibid.*, pp. 335–389.

monasteries were forbidden to accept additional novices, and their inmates were granted freedom to reënter the world. The clergy were required to take the oath of obedience to the laws of the state.[66]

Nor was the gloom relieved during the early years of the next Pontiff, Barnaba Chiaramonti (1740–1823), Pius VII. A scion of the Italian nobility, as a youth Chiaramonti had entered the Benedictine order and had taught in its schools. Pius VI, a friend of his family, had made him Bishop of Tivoli and then of Imola and had raised him to the Cardinalate. As Bishop of Imola he had remained by his post during the French invasion and had instructed his flock to submit to the French-founded Cisalpine Republic: he held that a democratic form of government was not incompatible with the Gospel.[67] He was elected at a conclave held in Venice, which was then under Austria, but was not the candidate of the Austrians. They had sought to put in a man favourable to them. He owed his election partly to Ercole Consalvi (1757–1824), who was to prove one of the most skilful diplomats ever to serve the Holy See. Pius VII soon elevated him to the Cardinalate, made him Secretary of State, and leaned upon him heavily in administration, in the negotiations for the Concordat of 1801 with Bonaparte, and in later important matters. The Papal coronation was not in Rome but in Venice. Since, with the French reverses, temporary as they proved, the Roman Republic had collapsed, Pius VII found it possible to take up his residence in the Eternal City. This he did amid the welcoming acclaims of the populace. Consalvi was especially interested and gifted in politics. He was also conservative and adamant against the Revolution. He was seldom dismayed by reverses. Pius VII was deeply religious, amiable, conscientious, inclined to be sympathetic with the Revolution, and fluctuated between optimism in favouring circumstances and deep depression and even terror when the tide was adverse. His interests and training were those of a monk and theologian. He was entirely devoid of self-seeking, lived simply, and was careful to avoid nepotism. At times he yielded to pressure: yet he had undoubted courage and on occasion was adamant in holding to his decisions. He sought to save the Roman Catholic Church from its current distress, not by political means, but by a revival of its spiritual life. Through a strengthening of its inner vigour he would have it reconquer the soul of society.[68]

For a time in Italy as in France an outward show of friendly relations with Napoleon was maintained. Anti-clerical, anti-Christian sentiment was not nearly as marked south of the Alps as in France. It behooved Napoleon, there-

[66] Hermelink, *Das Christentum in der Menschheitsgeschichte von der französischen Revolution bis zur Gegenwart*, Vol. I, p. 89.

[67] Nielsen, *The History of the Papacy in the XIXth Century*, Vol. I, pp. 207–209.

[68] *Ibid.*, pp. 213–218; Pouthas, *l'Église Catholique de l'Avènement de Pie VII à l'Avènement de Pie IX*, pp. 63–67.

fore, to win, so far as possible, the friendship of the Roman Catholic Church. The incorporation of Piedmont (September, 1802) into the French Republic brought with it the extension of the French ecclesiastical programme to that area. After negotiations extending over six months Pius VII, at first unwilling, consented to the new delimitation of the dioceses which was entailed.[69] In December, 1802, the constitution of the French puppet, the Cisalpine Republic, had at its head an article recognizing the "apostolic and Roman Catholic religion as the religion of the state." In January, 1802, the Organic Law of the Republic of Italy for the Clergy had already been enacted which provided for the nomination of the bishops by the Government and their canonical institution by the Pope, the appointment of the parish priests by the bishops with the consent of the Government, the exemption of the clergy from military service, the return of ecclesiastical property not yet alienated, the endowment of cathedral chapters and seminaries, and the recognition of the right to refuse to bless marriages against which canonical obstacles stood. In September, 1803, a concordat was reached which was more favourable to the Church than was that with France in 1801.[70]

However, with renewed French victories and the life-and-death struggle between Napoleon and Great Britain, Pius VII was brought almost as low as had been Pius VI. The coronation of Napoleon as King of Italy was followed, in June, 1805, without previous agreement with the Holy See, by a decree which governed ecclesiastical affairs and introduced the French civil code, including the law of divorce. Pius VII aroused the wrath of Napoleon by refusing to nullify the marriage of the latter's brother, Jerome. In 1806 Napoleon sought to force Pius VII to side with him, as "Roman Emperor," against his enemies and to break off relations with them. The Pope was to join the "Continental System." This the Pope refused to do, but, partly to appease the emperor, he dismissed Consalvi, whom Napoleon regarded as a major obstacle. However, he declined to yield to the emperor's demands about certain sees in Neapolitan territory. In February, 1808, French troops occupied Rome and in May, 1809, Napoleon decreed the Papal States annexed to his empire. Pius VII ordered his troops not to resist but countered with a bull excommunicating those guilty of the step. In retaliation Napoleon had the Pope taken captive to Avignon and thence to Savona, near Genoa, and had his Secretary of State imprisoned. Pius VII, seemingly impotent so far as the force of arms was concerned, had a powerful weapon at his command. He declined to perform any pontifical functions. The news of the bull of excommunication and of the Papal imprisonment was secretly circulated in France. The Pope would not nullify the marriage of Napoleon to Josephine or countenance his marriage to Marie

---

[69] Pouthas, *op. cit.*, pp. 119, 120.
[70] Leflon, *La Crise Révolutionnaire*, pp. 195–197; Pouthas, *op. cit.*, pp. 121–124.

Louise. In Italy bishops and priests who refused to assent to a decree (February, 1810) which extended to all the empire the Gallican status of the Church were transported to Corsica. Action was taken against Cardinals, including Consalvi, who did not bow to the imperial wishes. They were placed in various provincial towns and deprived of their property and insignia. Napoleon had difficulty in filling episcopal sees as they became vacant. The Pope refused to give canonical institution to bishops. For a time he appeared to yield, but in a manner inacceptable to Napoleon. He demanded his liberty: Napoleon ·demanded his resignation. In 1812, to prevent the English from carrying off the Pope, Napoleon had him brought, as we have said, to Fontainebleau, near Paris.[71]

When the tide turned against Napoleon, it turned in favour of Pius VII. After the Allies, on their triumphant advance towards Paris, crossed the Rhine, Napoleon offered the Pope a treaty which would restore the Papal States. This the Pope refused, on the ground that the restoration, being an act of simple justice, was not subject to a treaty. Early in 1814, on Napoleon's order, the Pope was again taken to Savona. This at least was on the road back to Rome. Napoleon's abdication was soon followed by Pius VII's return to Rome. On the way he appointed Consalvi to be Secretary of State and directed him to go to Paris to negotiate with the victors. The Treaty of Paris, with its provisional settlement, had been framed before Consalvi could reach that city. It did not accord to the Pope all his territories. For instance, Avignon and the adjoining Comtat-Venaissin were left with France and some of the Italian possessions were given to Austria, but, undiscouraged, Consalvi laboured at Vienna, where the negotiations for the general settlement were held, for the full reëstablishment of the Pope in his former possessions.

During the "Hundred Days" of Napoleon's dramatic bid for his old power, Pius VII again became a refugee, this time in Genoa. Yet·he refused to place Napoleon under excommunication. After Waterloo he once more returned to the Eternal City.[72]

THE STORM AND THE ROMAN CATHOLIC CHURCH:
IN THE AUSTRIAN NETHERLANDS

The Revolution and Napoleon worked momentous changes in the Roman Catholic Church in the Austrian Netherlands, the future Belgium. In June, 1794, the armies of Revolutionary France overran the Austrian Netherlands, the ecclesiastical principality of Liège, the monastic county of Stavelot-Malmedy,

71 Nielsen, op. cit., Vol. I, pp. 283 ff.; Leflon, op. cit., pp. 241 ff.; Latreille, l'Église Catholique et la Révolution Française, Vol. II, pp. 143 ff.; Allies, The Life of Pope Pius the Seventh, pp. 128 ff.; The Cambridge Modern History, Vol. IX, pp. 192 ff.; Pouthas, op. cit., pp. 138 ff.
72 The Cambridge Modern History, Vol. IX, p. 201; Nielsen, op. cit., Vol. I, pp. 338–340; Leflon, op. cit., pp. 279 ff.

and the duchy of Bouillon. The region was loyally Roman Catholic. Jansenism, Febronianism, and Josephism had not made significant inroads. The University of Louvain was incontestably orthodox. In Liège some anti-clericalism existed, but for the most part the people of the area did not welcome religious innovations. On October 1, 1795, the region was formally annexed to the French Republic. This meant the extension to it of the ecclesiastical policies of the Republic. The clergy were required to obey the laws of the new regime and were forbidden to wear their customary garb. Except for those devoted to the conduct of schools and the care of the sick, all religious houses were suppressed. Communes were enjoined not to contribute to the support of public worship. Popular opinion was resistant and the clergy asked that the enforcement of the laws be suspended until Rome had been heard from. The non-juring priests continued to function. The renewal of religious persecution in France in 1797 was extended to the Netherlands. Sunday was abolished, all religious orders were suppressed, and the University of Louvain was closed. Non-juring priests were ordered banished. However, from their refuges in forests and private homes, many of them continued to serve their flocks. In 1798 the application of the French laws of conscription to the region provoked revolt. Thousands of priests were ordered deported, but in fact all but a few hundred escaped arrest. From London some of the bishops continued to direct resistance.

In 1799 Bonaparte introduced milder measures, but many of the clergy still refused to take the oath of fidelity to the Republic. The Concordat of 1801 further eased the religious situation. The episcopal sees were rearranged, but no bishops of the Constitutional Church were placed over them. In 1802 Catholic worship was renewed.

Yet opposition continued. A minority maintained that the concordat had been forced on the Pope and held out as part of *la petite église* which we have met in France. A priest, Corneille Stevens (1747–1828), from his hiding place vigorously attacked several of the imperial measures, including the official catechism and the new festivals. The clergy resented the compulsory teaching of Gallicanism in the seminaries and refused to advocate from their pulpits the laws of military conscription. When Napoleon took over the Papal States, the Belgians regarded the step as persecution. Some of the youth were attempting to think through the ideology of the Revolution in terms of the Catholic faith, a trend which was to bear fruit in the nineteenth century, but as a whole the populace welcomed the overthrow of the Corsican.[73]

THE STORM AND THE ROMAN CATHOLIC CHURCH: IN GERMANY

The French Revolution and Napoleon profoundly altered the map of Ger-

[73] *The Catholic Encyclopedia*, Vol. II, pp. 395 ff.; *The Cambridge Modern History*, Vol. IX, pp. 415, 416; Haag, *Les Origines du Catholicisme Libéral en Belgique (1789–1839)*, pp. 43 ff.

many and in doing so wrought what was little short of a revolution in the structure and temper of the Roman Catholic Church in that land. The great ecclesiastical states with their prince bishops and many a smaller ecclesiastical state either disappeared or were badly weakened. The ecclesiastical princes who through the Febronian doctrines had sought administrative independence of Rome so largely lost their territories and their power that eventually they were constrained to seek support from the Pope rather than freedom from him.

The main outlines of the story are as follows. In the winter of 1792–1793 the French armies took Speyer, Worms, and Mainz, on the left bank of the Rhine. The Archbishop of Mainz fled incontinently. The French sought to propagate revolutionary ideas, but soon their plundering activities turned the populace against them. They were forced to retire, yet only temporarily. Before many months they were even more powerful in the Rhine Valley, and in 1795 the King of Prussia, to free his hands to obtain a slice of Poland in the third partition which erased that unhappy land from the map for more than a hundred years, agreed not to interfere with the French seizure of the entire left bank of the Rhine. In 1797, as a result of Napoleon's victorious campaign in Italy, the Holy Roman Emperor was compelled also to give France a free hand on the left bank of that river. The German princes whom that step deprived of possessions were to be compensated by territory on the right bank of the Rhine. This was the task of a congress which had begun its labours when war again broke out. The new war resulted in additional French victories. By the ensuing Peace of Lunéville (February 9, 1801) the cession to France of the left bank of the Rhine was confirmed. To compensate the princes who had lost land, Napoleon, Prussia, and Russia led in a division among them of the ecclesiastical states and most of the imperial cities (1803). Bavaria, Baden, Württemberg, Hesse, and Prussia especially profited. Napoleon thought by enriching the South German states to tie them to his cause. Over a hundred units were apportioned. Among them were some small secular ones, but also among them were many ecclesiastical properties. Mitre after mitre "tumbled into the Rhine." In 1803 the Imperial Diet decreed that the suzerainty of the ecclesiastical princes of the Holy Roman Empire was ended and that the lands of the Church were to be handed to the secular princes. In 1806 Napoleon drew together several German states into the Confederation of the Rhine, distributing among its members the territories of a number of counts and knights of the Holy Roman Empire. That year the Holy Roman Empire ceased to exist.

In the meantime, what were now French territories on the left bank of the Rhine had been subjected to the general ecclesiastical policy of the Republic. The French entered Cologne in 1794. In 1796 all ecclesiastical property in the part held by the French was seized by the civil authorities. Under the arrangements made possible by the Concordat of 1801 Cologne was incorporated into the new see of Aachen. In 1802 all religious orders in the French portion of the former archdiocese were suppressed and their properties were confiscated. This, with the secularization in 1803 of the portion of its territory on the right bank of the Rhine, brought that ancient princely ecclesiastical state to an end. Similarly, in 1797 Mainz was ceded to France. The Archbishopric of Trier, whose incumbent, like those of Cologne and Mainz, was one of the seven Electors of the Holy Roman Empire, shared the fate of its two sisters. In 1797 Trier and its territories on the left bank of the Rhine passed to France and its university was suppressed. In 1801 it was made a suffragan see of Mechlin. In 1803 its properties on the right bank of the Rhine were secularized.[74] The left bank of the Rhine was divided into four departments. The clergy were required to take an oath "against kingdom and anarchy." The decrees against such public expressions of the faith as religious processions and the ringing of bells were not rigorously enforced. Nor was it easy to exact from the clergy compliance with the law that the civil marriage ceremony must precede the religious one.[75]

In the German territories outside those annexed to France the acquisition of ecclesiastical possessions by the several states was followed by great changes. The clergy were given their support by the state. Most of the Catholic universities were discontinued: only three, Freiburg, Münster, and Würzburg, remained. The state took over education. Theological faculties were founded in the state universities, their appointment and salaries coming from the government. Not only had the ancient archiepiscopal states of Cologne, Mainz, and Trier disappeared, but a fourth, Salzburg, was also erased. Of the more than twenty dioceses in Germany, in the first decade of the nineteenth century more than half were without incumbents and were administered by vicars. Each large state set about a fresh delimitation of dioceses. The Roman Catholic Church lost its independent hierarchical organization and its clergy were in effect reduced to a civil bureaucracy. As early as 1800 Bavaria, although a Catholic monarchy, had begun a general reorganization of the Church on Josephist principles. A council composed of three Protestants and two Roman Catholics was appointed to supervise religious affairs, but the Pope remonstrated and the council was discontinued. Some other German states, including Württemberg, Baden, and Prussia, put the administration of the churches under a single minister. Monasteries and abbeys were dissolved and their inmates were pensioned. A large proportion of German Roman Catholics were now ruled by Protestant princes.

Politically Roman Catholicism lost as against Protestantism, and its adherents were deprived of many of their accustomed facilities for church life. In 1811

[74] *The Catholic Encyclopedia*, Vol. IV, p. 119, Vol. IX, p. 552. Vol. XV, p. 44.
[75] Hermelink, *op. cit.*, Vol. I, p. 89.

Prussia formulated a plan for putting her Roman Catholic subjects under a Prussian Patriarch. While that was not carried through, the King of Prussia insisted upon bringing the Roman Catholic Church in his realms, including his portion of Poland, under his full control. As a Protestant he recognized the Pope only as a secular prince, and he was determined that all his Catholic subjects honour him, the king, as the head of the Catholic Church in his domains. Monasteries were required to renounce the authority of foreign heads of their orders and preparation was made for their secularization. Bishops were placed under royal control and their *imprimatur* on Catholic writings was not accorded recognition. The king refused to concede the divine right of the Catholic Church and restricted the communication of bishops and clergy with Rome.[76]

Karl Theodor Anton Maria von Dalberg (1744–1817), from an ancient noble German family, became important. In 1802 he was appointed Archbishop of Mainz. With the abolition and reshuffling of sees, he was transferred, still with the title of Elector of the Holy Roman Empire, to Ratisbon (Regensburg). This was permitted to retain its position as an ecclesiastical state. Failing in his attempt as Elector and Arch-Chancellor of the Holy Roman Empire to preserve that hoary but moribund institution, he sought and won the support of Napoleon and worked for a concordat for all Germany and for the position for himself of Patriarch for Germany. In 1806 Napoleon appointed him Prince Primate of the Confederation of the Rhine. The Pope and his entourage were greatly alarmed by this development. They feared that it would mean a realization of a Josephist dream, with a German church largely independent of Rome. That fear was by no means groundless. For example, he who in 1802 became Dalberg's vicar-general for the Diocese of Constance was Ignaz Heinrich von Wessenberg (1774–1860). We are to meet Wessenberg again, for most of his activity was after 1815. Yet already he was cherishing a combination of Josephist and Febronian aspirations. He was to be an advocate of a German national church, loosely connected with Rome but supported by the state. He wished to liberalize that church in a number of ways and to have the state protect it against Papal interference. To prevent the attainment of that goal the Pope sought concordats with individual German states rather than with the Confederation. In this he was supported by the opposition of the states to Dalberg's designs, for in them they rightly saw a menace to their power. Napoleon urged on the Pope a concordat with the Confederation, but in December, 1808, Pius VII broke off negotiations. In 1814 he ordered Dalberg to depose Wessenberg.[77]

The defeat of Napoleon profoundly altered but did not completely change

[76] *The Cambridge Modern History*, Vol. IX, pp. 201–203; Hermelink, *op. cit.*, Vol. I, pp. 140–146, 166, 167; Schnabel, *Deutsche Geschichte im neunzehnten Jahrhundert*, Vol. I, pp. 5–7.

[77] *The Cambridge Modern History*, Vol. IX, pp. 202, 203; *The Catholic Encyclopedia*, Vol. XV, pp. 590, 591; Hermelink, *op. cit.*, Vol. I, pp. 138–167.

the course of events. The Roman Catholic Church in Germany was never restored to the position which it had held before the irruption of the French Revolution. Gone were the ecclesiastical principalities with their mixture of religious and secular functions. As we have seen, their heads had long been scions of aristocratic houses and had been chosen not for their sanctity but as a means of providing for younger sons. Hereafter, the episcopate and the cathedral chapters were more and more recruited from the ranks of the parish clergy. The way to revival and reform was open. By the innovations the Roman Catholic Church in Germany was freer than it would otherwise have been to face the problems brought by the nineteenth century. As we are to see, that century and its successor brought grave problems of many kinds. Yet the inner vitality of the Church, relieved of some of the encumbrances of the old order, was more able than it would otherwise have been to rise to the challenge of the new day.[78]

THE STORM AND THE ROMAN CATHOLIC CHURCH: IN SPAIN AND PORTUGAL

In Spain the immediate official reaction to the outbreak of the French Revolution was to put forth every effort to prevent its ideas from seeping into the country. In December, 1789, the Inquisition commanded the surrender of all papers coming from France or having revolutionary implications. It declared heretical all works of modern philosophy. Attempts were made to seize every print depicting events in France. In August, 1792, a further endeavour was made to suppress all news from France. The following year a prohibition was issued against any allusion, favourable or unfavourable, to French affairs. The repetition of these orders is evidence that they were not fully effective. In 1802 the admission was made that in spite of all that had been done to shut them out books offensive to the Inquisition were being circulated.[79]

In one way and another the revolutionary forces spread and had effects upon the Church. In 1798, although probably more from the pre-Revolutionary trend of control of the Church by the crown than from repercussions from republican France, King Charles IV authorized the confiscation and sale of religious houses and foundations under lay patronage, with the provision that the owners should be compensated in government bonds. In 1805 he obtained Papal permission to appropriate a substantial amount of Church property. Soon after his invasion of Spain Napoleon ordered the reduction of religious houses by two-thirds. In 1809 his brother Joseph, now put on the throne of Spain by the invader, extended that order to all monasteries. So far as French troops could do it, the programme was carried out. It was often accompanied by the killing of

[78] Schnabel, *op. cit.*, Vol. IV, pp. 18–20.
[79] Lea, *Chapters from the Religious History of Spain Connected with the Inquisition*, pp. 162–165, 168–171.

monks and secular priests, because many of them shared in the national uprising against the hated foreigner. Resistance to the French was partly on the ground that they were infidels. In 1812 a Cortes springing from a national movement and with liberal tendencies framed what was known as the Constitution of Cadiz. That document declared that the national religion "is and will be for ever the Catholic, apostolic, and Roman religion which alone is true." The Cortes made Teresa of Avila co-patron of Spain, putting her alongside the Apostle James. However, the Cortes suppressed many religious houses, prohibited appeals for money for the rebuilding of religious houses which had suffered from the invasion, and confirmed the expropriation by the state of the property of such houses as had been suppressed by the invaders. The Papal Nuncio, protesting these actions, was expelled from the country and bishops who objected were suspended or exiled. Moreover, the Cortes suspended elections to sees and other ecclesiastical dignities, diverted to the state the incomes of these offices and the property of the military orders, confiscated Church treasures which were not being used in public worship, seized the funds of various charitable bodies, and channeled some Church dues to reducing or supporting the public debt. In 1813 the Inquisition was ordered suppressed.[80]

In Portugal the destruction wrought by the French invaders and the measures taken to expel them could not but affect Church life and ecclesiastical properties.

The Storm and the Roman Catholic Church: Added Blows to Geographic Expansion

The storm of the French Revolution and Napoleon dealt additional blows to the geographic expansion of the Roman Catholic Church. As we have seen, from the fifteenth century onward that expansion had been spectacular and had planted the faith firmly in large parts of the Americas, in great sections of Asia and its fringing islands, and along the coast of Africa. Most of that spread had been under the aegis of Spain and Portugal. As we have also seen, in the eighteenth century expansion had slowed down and here and there had turned into retreat.

The new blows were grave. Fewer missionaries could be sent. To be sure, some were appointed. For instance, between 1791 and 1815 the Lazarists were able to put at least sixteen recruits in China.[81] The *Société des Missions-Étrangères* of Paris, which had extensive enterprises in the Far East, was severely crippled. In 1792 its directors scattered. Some went abroad, but efforts

---

[80] Peers, *Spain, the Church, and the Orders,* pp. 60–62; F. Mayrick, *The Church in Spain* (London, Wells Gardner, Darton & Co., 1892, pp. xiv, 450), pp. 437, 438); *The Cambridge Modern History,* Vol. IX, p. 206.

[81] *Catalogue des Prêtres, Clercs et Frères de la Congrégation de la Mission qui ont travaillé en Chine depuis 1697* (Peking, 1911).

to reëstablish the seminary of the society outside of France failed. In 1805, in an attempt to make French missions serve his purposes, Napoleon permitted the seminary to be reopened in France, but when, in 1809, he broke with the Pope, he dissolved it. For a time only one director, and he in England, could continue the European headquarters of the society.[82] In 1798 the Congregation for the Propagation of the Faith, the central agency through which the Roman Catholic Church supervised its missions, was driven out of Rome. From 1810 to 1814 Napoleon sought to manipulate it in such fashion as to make it a tool of his ambitions.[83] Obviously the invasion of Spain and Portugal and the attendant wars, guerrilla resistance, and the harsh treatment of religious houses cut down the numbers of reinforcements which could be dispatched to the missions in the Americas and Asia. The setting up of the provisional governments in Spanish America which acted in the name of the Bourbon sovereign and the suspension of the traditional direction of missions from the mother country were handicaps.

THE STORM AND THE ROMAN CATHOLIC CHURCH: THE BEGINNINGS OF REVIVAL

After the severe blows dealt it in the geographic centres of its historic strength, the Roman Catholic Church might have been adjudged to be moribund. Handicapped as it was by the weaknesses of which we spoke in the last chapter, when the storm of revolution broke it seemed in no position to weather it. Or if it came through it would presumably be so weakened that it would not be able to cope successfully with the forces which wrought the revolutions in the traditional Christendom that followed the Napoleonic Wars. Even if, in revulsion against the destruction of the storm, something of the old order should be restored and along with it the once familiar structure of the Roman Catholic Church, the clock could not be completely turned back.

However, as we are to see in later chapters, the Roman Catholic Church experienced a remarkable revival which mounted as the nineteenth and twentieth centuries proceeded.

Even before the final defeat of Napoleon in 1815 evidence was seen of continuing vitality and of a rising tide of faith. Again and again it became clear that among large numbers, probably a majority of the populations of the Latin lands and the adjacent sections of Germany, the Low Countries, and Switzerland—the historic stronghold of the Roman Catholic Church—the faith had been too deeply rooted to be quickly killed. The weeping, praying throngs which flocked to Pius VI and Pius VII on their exiled journeys were unmis-

[82] A. Launay, *Histoire Générale de la Société des Missions-Étrangères* (Paris, 3 vols., 1894), Vol. II, pp. 258–277, 297–302, 343–347, 424–430.

[83] J. Schmidlin, *Die Propaganda während der napoleonischen Invasion,* in *Zeitschrift für Missionswissenschaft,* Vol. XII, pp. 112–115.

takable proof of a vast if unorganized loyalty which might at the time be impotent but which must be reckoned with for the future. In Chateaubriand's *Génie du Christianisme* numbers who had been opposed to the Revolution found support for their convictions. Others who had once favoured the Revolution but had been disillusioned by its excesses welcomed it as an apology for a faith in which they would like to believe.

The Society of Jesus was revived. In 1801 Papal approval was given to its existence in Russia. In 1804 it was restored in the Kingdom of the Two Sicilies, and in 1814 Pius VII authorized its full reconstitution throughout the world.[84] As we have seen, the Society had never completely disbanded, but in various guises and in more than one country it had maintained its existence, and had done so with the knowledge and tacit approval of Rome.[85] Now that permission was openly given for its rehabilitation, it rapidly regained its former prominence.

In spite of the storm and partly because of it, new congregations came into being. In 1800 Madeleine Sophie Barat (1779–1865) founded the Society of the Sacred Heart. During the height of the Revolution, with its anti-Christian drive, she had been trained in the religious life in Paris itself, by her brother, who was associated with a group which was keeping alive, under another name, the Society of Jesus. The first convent of the new society was opened in 1801 in Amiens. The members gave themselves to teaching and thus to an attempt to revive the faith by addressing themselves to the young.[86] Not far from the same time the Congregation of the Sacred Heart of Jesus and Mary came into being. Its creator was Coudrin, who was ordained priest in Paris in the tempestuous revolutionary year of 1792. In 1800 he took vows as a religious. On a street called Picpus he found quarters (about 1805) from which his congregation derived its popular designation, the Picpus Fathers. The congregation was activist, had missions at home and outside the Occident, and maintained a perpetual adoration of the Blessed Sacrament.[87] In 1802, almost contemporary with these two movements, and without collusion with them, Edmund Ignatius Rice (1762–1844) founded in Waterford the Christian Brothers of Ireland. From a devout family, he had thought of going to the Continent and taking monastic vows. He was dissuaded and instead for a time was a merchant. Appalled by the destitute state of the urchins of Waterford who, while nominal Roman Catholics, shared in the desperate poverty of most of the population of Ireland, he founded a school for them. The movement spread to other towns

[84] Campbell, *The Jesuits, 1534–1921*, pp. 680, 684 ff.
[85] Nielsen, *The History of the Papacy in the XIXth Century*, Vol. I, pp. 343–345.
[86] *The Catholic Encyclopedia*, Vol. II, p. 283.
[87] *Ibid.*, Vol. XIII, pp. 308, 309.

and cities. In 1820 the Pope constituted it a religious institute and eventually it was widely extended.[88]

During the stormy years Germany witnessed vigorous movements in Roman Catholic circles. Around the Princess Amalie Gallitzin (1748–1806) with its centre in Münster and not under clerical control a mystic-pietist Catholicism arose. One of its leaders, Franz von Fürstenberg, had friendly relations with Protestants and with Goethe. A colleague of Fürstenberg, Bernhard Overberg, trained a generation of priests and teachers and so helped to extend the influence of the circle. Largely through contact with the circle Count Leopold Stolberg, who had been reared a Protestant, became, in 1800, with his family, a Roman Catholic. He reached the conviction that Protestantism gave rise to Deism, atheism, and rationalism, he had no use either for Kant or the *Aufklärung,* and he believed that the hope of certainty and order lay in the Roman Catholic Church.[89] In 1805 a Catholic Bible Society, paralleling a similar contemporary one by Protestants in Great Britain, was founded in Regensburg by Michael Wittmann and issued a translation of the New Testament and Psalms. However, in 1817 it fell under Papal prohibition. Leander von Ess served as an agent of the British and Foreign Bible Society and circulated a translation of the Bible. This, too, was eventually forbidden by Rome.[90] The patriotic movement of 1809 expressed itself in part in religious revivals in private circles. They had as a leader and spiritual director Clemens Maria Hofbauer, the first German Redemptorist. A man of great sanctity, he ministered to all classes— the lowly, the bourgeoisie, and the nobility. Friedrich von Schlegel (1772–1829), poet, critic, scholar, romanticist, who at one time sought a syncretism of various religions, with his wife, a Jewess by ancestry, a daughter of Moses Mendelssohn, in 1808 became a Roman Catholic. He proved to be a vigorous apologist for his newly acquired faith.[91] Powerful also in the German Roman Catholic awakening was Johann Michael Sailer (1751–1832). He attempted to get back to the early Church and stressed not so much dogma as the inner life and the care of souls. He had marked influence upon the rising generation of clergy and laity. His contemporaries called him the German Fénelon.[92]

In the young United States the years compassed by the French Revolution and Napoleon saw the beginnings of that growth of the Roman Catholic Church which in the nineteenth and twentieth centuries was to reach notable

---

[88] *Ibid.,* Vol. III, p. 170, Vol. XIII, pp. 40, 41.

[89] Schnabel, *Deutsche Geschichte im neunzehnten Jahrhundert,* Vol. IV, pp. 47, 48; Hermelink, *Das Christentum in der Menschheitsgeschichte von der französischen Revolution bis zur Gegenwart,* Vol. I, pp. 239–242; *The New Schaff-Herzog Encyclopedia of Religious Knowledge,* Vol. XI, pp. 102, 103; Goyau, *l'Allemagne Religieuse, Le Catholicisme,* Vol. I, pp. 274 ff.

[90] Hermelink, *op. cit.,* Vol. I, p. 308.

[91] Schnabel, *op. cit.,* Vol. IV, pp. 48, 49; Jean-Jacques Anstett, *La Pensée religieuse de Friedrich Schlegel* (Paris, Société d'Édition des Belles Lettres, 1941, pp. 491), *passim.*

[92] Schnabel, *op. cit.,* Vol. IV, pp. 50 ff.; Goyau, *op. cit.,* Vol. I, pp. 291 ff.

proportions. In 1784 John Carroll, a former Jesuit, of an old and prominent Roman Catholic family in Maryland, was appointed Prefect Apostolic for the new nation. The United States was thus taken out of the jurisdiction of the Prefect Apostolic of London. In 1789 his fellow clergy elected Carroll bishop and the following year, with authorization from Rome, he was consecrated (in England) Bishop of Baltimore. He laboured indefatigably and travelled extensively through the infant republic. In 1804 he was made Archbishop with continued jurisdiction over the entire country. For the training of clergy and laity he founded Georgetown College (1789) on the outskirts of the nation's capital. He was aided by refugees from Europe, largely from France. Augustinians, Dominicans, Franciscans, and Trappists entered. In 1812 the Sisters of Loretto at the Foot of the Cross and the Sisters of Charity of Nazareth were inaugurated, both in Kentucky. Carroll also had a valiant co-labourer in a convert, Elizabeth Ann Seton, who founded the first American congregation, the Daughters of Charity, pioneers in Roman Catholic elementary education in the United States.[93]

In Canada as a result of the cession to Great Britain (1763) the Roman Catholic Church gained rather than lost. To be sure, the new regime was officially Protestant. However, to keep the Canadians from siding with the revolting Thirteen Colonies, the British Government made concessions. The Quebec Act of 1774 and the Constitutional Act of 1791 confirmed the religious toleration promised at the annexation. At first forbidden, eventually communication was permitted between the Bishop of Quebec and Rome.[94] Since it became the symbol and tie of French Canadian particularism, the Roman Catholic Church won the deepened loyalty of that element in the population.

THE STORM AND PROTESTANTISM: IN GENERAL

As we move from the Roman Catholic Church to Protestantism, we do well to remind ourselves of some general considerations at which we have already hinted.

1. For the most part Protestantism was less directly hit by the storm than was Roman Catholicism. In France, where the storm centred, Protestants were only a small minority. They were a still smaller minority in Italy, the country, next to France, which was the most seriously disrupted. Germany, including Austria, was profoundly altered, but the main force of the storm impinged upon the sections nearest to France, and these were where German Roman Ca-

[93] Peter Guilday, *The Life and Times of John Carroll, Archbishop of Baltimore 1735–1815* (New York, The Encyclopedia Press, 2 vols., 1922), Vol. I, pp. 202, 343, 447, 496 ff., Vol. II, pp. 502, 506 ff., 567; Annabelle M. Melville, *John Carroll of Baltimore: Founder of the American Hierarchy* (New York, Charles Scribner's Sons, 1955, pp. ix, 338), *passim*.

[94] E. H. Oliver, *The Winning of the Frontier* (Toronto, The United Church Publishing Co., 1930), pp. 79, 81–94, 104.

tholicism had its chief strongholds. The purely Protestant parts of Germany were less affected. Switzerland was deeply involved, but there the two forms of the faith were about equally represented. The Low Countries were early overwhelmed, but here also the territory was shared by the two Western wings of the faith: the later Belgium was Roman Catholic and the Netherlands predominantly Protestant. Scandinavia, solidly Protestant, did not escape the storm but being farther from its focus was less altered. The British Isles and the United States, both, with the exception of Ireland, prevailingly Protestant, were drawn into the storm, but the one chiefly in an attempt to curb it and the other in the effort to keep aloof from it.

2. Partly because Protestantism was less in the main path of the storm than was the Roman Catholic Church, the movements which characterized it before the storm broke in its full fury more nearly continued than did some outstanding features of Roman Catholicism as they existed on the eve of the storm. The Roman Catholic Church in France was so severely shaken that it could not as effectively assert Gallicanism. The ecclesiastical structure in Germany which had made Febronianism possible was all but swept out. Josephism still had advocates but lacked the kind of support from Catholic temporal rulers which had once made it formidable. The Papal States were restored, but in a little over half a century the nationalism evoked by the storm was to extinguish them. In contrast, except in Germany, the Netherlands, and Switzerland the organizational framework of Protestantism came through unaltered, and in these three lands it was not as nearly revolutionized as was that of the Roman Catholic Church in France, Germany, and parts of Italy. The Pietism and Evangelicalism which had been growing before the storm broke continued to mount. Most of the revolutionary forces other than the French Revolution which we met at the outset of this chapter had not yet attained sufficient dimensions seriously to affect Protestantism.

3. The one notable exception to the generalization in the last sentence was that the intellectual currents which partly arose from Protestantism, and some of which challenged and even threatened it, also continued, although in modified form. In the quarter-century of the acute stage of the storm they were most marked in Germany.

4. The geographic spread of Protestantism which had begun before the French Revolution continued and grew. Indeed, several of the most significant beginnings of new phases of that spread were seen during the most tempestuous years of the storm. This was in contrast with the Roman Catholic Church.

From these generalizations we turn to particular countries and regions.

THE STORM AND PROTESTANTISM: IN FRANCE

Protestants in France were so small a minority that we must not take the space to say much about them. They shared with Roman Catholics some of the vicissitudes of the Revolution. However, eventually they derived one benefit from it, toleration.

One French Protestant of these years was so outstanding that he must be mentioned. That was John Frederic Oberlin (1740–1826). As a pastor in the Vosges Mountains, building upon what had been accomplished by a predecessor, he worked a transformation in a poverty-stricken rural district which brought him deserved renown. He began his pastorate before the Revolution, in 1767, and had already accomplished much through schools, preaching, pastoral care, and economic measures when the tempest reached his remote villages. It made for added hardships, but he survived them and lived to be acclaimed by both Napoleon and the restored Bourbons.[95]

THE STORM AND PROTESTANTISM: IN GERMANY

In Germany Protestants gained in the new order. In predominantly Catholic states Protestantism was tolerated. In general parents could choose the form of the faith in which their children were to be reared. In Bavaria in 1801 a Protestant was given the rights of a citizen.[96]

It was to be expected that the surge of life in German Protestantism which expressed itself in Pietism would continue. Old forms persisted, including the closely related Moravians, and new ones came into being. By its very genius Pietism tended to proliferate, with numerous leaders with distinctive convictions and many groups. Württemberg was still a Pietist stronghold. The great patriarch of Württemberg Pietism, Johann Albrecht Bengel (1687–1752), had been gone for a generation when the French Revolution began to make itself felt, but his influence remained strong. Some of those affected by him developed at Tübingen a kind of study of the Bible which saw the Revelation of John as a key to the "last times" and also stressed Biblical theology. Most of the working years of an outstanding lay leader of Württemberg Pietism, Johann Michael Hahn (1758–1819), were in the quarter-century which spanned the French Revolution and Napoleon. In the 1790's he organized his followers in a fashion which meant congregations independent of the state church. He was much influenced by Böhme, was strongly ascetic, and gave expression to his convictions in a prodigious outpouring of letters, songs, and other writings.[97] One who worked for a time with Hahn and who after 1785 remained aloof from the Church was George Rapp. In 1803 a rescript directed against him led to his migration with a few hundred of his followers to the United States. Another Württemberg Pietist group believed that the Christian, when he had

---

[95] Beard, The Story of John Frederic Oberlin, passim.
[96] Hermelink, Das Christentum in der Menschheitsgeschichte von der französischen Revolution bis zur Gegenwart, Vol. I, pp. 146–148.
[97] Ibid., pp. 221, 222.

been really found by the faith, could no longer sin.[98] Contact was made between the Pietism of Tübingen and that which we have already noted in the lower part of the Rhine Valley. Here, where the influence of Tersteegen persisted, the physician Samuel Callenbusch (1724–1803) was a leader whom we met in the previous chapter. Influenced by both Böhme and Leibnitz, he worked out a theology which was to be potent in a particular school of thought in Erlangen. His most distinguished pupil was the Reformed pastor Gottfried Menken (1768–1831).[99] Another Reformed pastor, Gottfried Daniel Krummacher (1774–1837), through his preaching first at Wulfrath and then in the neighbouring and larger Elberfeld, gave rise to awakenings.[100] Johann Heinrich Jung-Stilling (1740–1817), born near Göttingen, a writer of devotional works, a physician, for a time a friend of Goethe, in later years an intimate of the Grand-duke of Baden, found that Kant freed him from determinism, but, convinced by Kant that reason could not show him God, held that God is known by special revelation. Shocked by the French Revolution and the repudiation of Christianity by many, he believed that the end of the world was at hand. He regarded the Moravians as the nucleus and rallying point of the true Church. Through his writings he helped many, bewildered by the events and movements of the day, to a warm and satisfying Christian faith.[101] Johannes Jänicke (1748–1827) as preacher in the Bohemian Bethlehem Church in Berlin was the centre of the Moravian movement in that capital. In 1800 he opened a school in Berlin which was associated with the Pietist centre in Basel and was for the training of missionaries.[102] These examples by no means exhaust the Pietist leaders and movements of the period. However, they may serve as evidence of the vigour and variety of the life of which they were expressions.

In several aspects of German life Pietism had a wide-reaching and profound influence. It furthered education, especially for the masses. It stressed the dignity of the common man. It encouraged the use of German rather than Latin in scholarship, in teaching, and in general literature. It was one of the forces making for German nationalism in the revolt against Napoleon.[103]

Another expression of German Protestantism in the years of storm was an attempt to relieve some of the suffering brought by the wars. Johannes Daniel Falk (1768–1826), a literary man who was trained in theology at Halle, became

[98] *Ibid.*, pp. 222–224.

[99] *Ibid.*, pp. 229, 230; *The New Schaff-Herzog Encyclopedia of Religious Knowledge*, Vol. III, pp. 160, 161.

[100] Good, *History of the Reformed Church in Germany*, pp. 486–494.

[101] Hermelink, *op. cit.*, Vol. I, pp. 232–236; *The New Schaff-Herzog Encyclopedia of Religious Knowledge*, Vol. XI, p. 97.

[102] *Johann Jänicke . . . nach seinen Leben und Werken dargestelt von Karl Friedrich Ledderhose . . . herausgegeben von G. Knak* (Berlin, G. Knak, 1863, pp. xii, 246), pp. 19–30, 40, 41, 72, 73, 96 ff.

[103] Koppel S. Pinson, *Pietism as a Factor in the Rise of German Nationalism* (New York, Columbia University Press, 1934, pp. 227), *passim*.

associated with that Weimar circle which had Goethe as its most distinguished figure. He was stirred by the tragic lot of the children left parentless through the vicissitudes of the day. In 1813 he founded the Society of Friends in Need to care for the orphans. In their education he used methods somewhat akin to those of his contemporary, Pestalozzi, of whom we are to hear more in a moment. He employed his literary talents to write songs which had in them a note of joy. He made confidence in God the centre and aim of all action. Falk was only the most prominent of several who devoted themselves to children made destitute by the wars.[104]

As part of the movement for the circulation of the Bible which had prominent and pioneer expression in the British and Foreign Bible Society, in 1814 Bible societies were begun in Berlin and Elberfeld. They were in part thank-offerings for the liberation from Napoleon.[105]

Currents in theology and in Biblical subjects were evidence of a vitality which in the nineteenth and twentieth centuries was to make Germany a leading centre of creative Protestant thought. As we have seen, they had begun before the French Revolution. During that storm they continued and fresh ones emerged. We have already noted Immanuel Kant. By 1815 Georg Wilhelm Friedrich Hegel (1770–1831) had largely formulated the philosophy which in the next two centuries was to give him an outstanding influence in a wide range of human life. A Protestant by rearing, in 1788 he entered Tübingen as a student of theology and in 1793 received a certificate in that subject. This training was obvious in his later work. However, his major interests were elsewhere. It was during the years of storm that Karl Daub (1765–1836) came to the fore. In 1795 he was appointed to the Heidelberg faculty. There he aroused both vigorous polemic opposition and enthusiastic acclaim as "the greatest of living university teachers." He sought to reconcile theology and philosophy. He was impressed in turn by Kant, by the romantic movement and Schelling, and in his later years by Hegel. He rejected both supernaturalism and rationalism.[106] Friedrich Heinrich Jacobi (1743–1819) was a somewhat contradictory mixture of materialism and Pietism. In his emotions he was a Christian and his faith was grounded upon a revelation of God in the heart. In his intellect he was a pagan.[107]

He who was to be the most widely influential Protestant theologian of the fore part of the nineteenth century and whose effect, although waning, persisted into the twentieth century was Friedrich Daniel Ernst Schleiermacher (1768–1839). Since his major writing was not completed until after 1815 and

[104] *The New Schaff-Herzog Encyclopedia of Religious Knowledge,* Vol. IV, pp. 270, 271.
[105] Hermelink, *op. cit.,* Vol. I, p. 308.
[106] *The New Schaff-Herzog Encyclopedia of Religious Knowledge,* Vol. III, p. 359.
[107] *Ibid.,* Vol. VI, pp. 80, 81.

his chief repercussions were subsequent to that year, we must reserve to the next volume more extended mention. However, his formative years were chiefly in the era of the French Revolution and Napoleon and before the latter's downfall he was commanding attention in Germany. Schleiermacher had for father a military chaplain and for mother a woman of deep religious faith, the daughter of a Reformed pastor. His father had had a transforming experience through the Moravians and entrusted his son to one of their schools. To the end of his life Schleiermacher was deeply indebted to the Moravians and in his later years declared himself to be still one of them. Indeed, his theology was based upon *Gefühl,* which may be paraphrased as "religious experience." But, in contradiction to that early environment, his critical faculty was strong and he failed to have the type of religious experience which the Moravians prized. In the Moravian school where he was enrolled Kant's writings were proscribed. But Schleiermacher managed to obtain a copy, read it secretly, and was captivated. Although maintaining friendly relations with the Moravians, he went to Halle, where Kant was being studied. There he became acquainted with the philosophy and theology of the *Aufklärung.* In 1794 he was ordained. From 1796 to 1802 he was chaplain of a hospital in Berlin. Here he became intimate with a circle of intellectuals which included some of the brilliant and religiously sceptical minds of the romantic school, among them the as yet unconverted Friedrich von Schlegel.

It was under the stimulus of this contact that Schleiermacher wrote his first important book, *Über die Religion. Reden an die Gebildeten unter ihren Verächtern* ("Discourses on Religion to the Educated among Those Who Scorn It").[108] It was a revolt against the cold rationalism of the *Aufklärung* and, an expression of the author's warm personal faith, to numbers of the younger generation it put religion in terms which seemed to make it intellectually respectable. Some of the older men were polite but unconvinced. For example, Goethe thought it "too Christian." On the other hand, many of the orthodox viewed it with alarm and even anger. Several regarded it as pantheism of the school of Spinoza. The next year, in 1800, his *Monologen* ("Monologues") appeared. In them, influenced by Fichte's subjective idealism, he set forth his moral philosophy.

From 1802 to 1804 Schleiermacher was pastor in Pomerania, much occupied in teaching the young and in preaching. There he wrote a critical work on theories of ethics in which he dealt especially with Plato. As pastor he became interested in reforming the Church. He advocated freedom of belief and wished to bring together the Lutherans and the Reformed.

In 1804 he went to Halle as professor of theology and philosophy. The

---

[108] First published in Berlin, 1799, by Johann Friedrich Unger. See the centenary edition edited with a new introduction by Rudolf Otto (Göttingen, Vanderhoek & Ruprecht, 1906, pp. xlv, 191).

exigencies of war led to the suspension of the university and, a refugee, he came in contact with the suffering brought by the conflict. His reaction against the Napoleonic invasion quickened his patriotism, but he was not uncritical of the policies pursued by Prussia and he was sympathetic with democracy.

In 1807 Schleiermacher took up his residence in Berlin. He shared in the founding of the university and in 1810 became the first dean of its theological faculty. As preacher in Trinity Church he helped to inspire his hearers to take their part in the liberation of the country from Napoleon. He also strove to stem the reaction towards conservatism. It was in Berlin that he spent the rest of his life.[109]

THE STORM AND PROTESTANTISM: IN SWITZERLAND

It was in 1797 that the storm of the French Revolution broke upon Switzerland. In 1798 the French organized the country into the Helvetic Republic. At first numbers of pastors adjusted themselves to it, even welcomed it, and the Moravians favoured it. However, the attitude of many was soon altered by the violence of the "liberators" and the new order imposed on the land. For instance, Johann Caspar Lavater (1741–1801), the distinguished minister in Zürich, noted for his dislike of religious strife, his preaching, and his extensive and warm pastoral care, at the outset greeted the change but soon became critical, and died of a wound inflicted by a lawless French soldier.[110] Under the new regime, in accordance with the general French policy, religious toleration was introduced, confessional schools were impossible, civil marriage was the law, and the clergy were required to assume more duties as state officials. Tithes and compulsory baptism were abolished. When, in 1803, a federal form of organization was adopted and each canton was permitted to regulate its ecclesiastical affairs, something of the pre-Revolutionary position of religion was restored. In several cantons both Catholics and Protestants were given official status. In some, pastors were elected by the vote of the parishioners; in others they were chosen, as before the Revolution, by the ruling councils. Here and there Pietist movements were forerunners of awakenings in the nineteenth century.[111]

One of the important developments in Switzerland during these years was the work of Johann Heinrich Pestalozzi (1746–1827). The grandson of a pastor,

---

[109] Of the enormous literature on Schleiermacher the following will prove useful: Wilhelm Dilthey, editor, *Aus Schleiermacher's Leben. In Briefen* (Berlin, Georg Reimer, 4 vols., 1860–1863); Wilhelm Dilthey, *Leben Schleiermachers* (second edition, enlarged but still incomplete, by Herman Mulert, Berlin, Walter de Gruyter & Co., Vol. I, 1922, pp. xxxii, 879); W. B. Selbie, *Schleiermacher: A Critical and Historical Study* (New York, E. P. Dutton & Co., 1913, pp. ix, 272).

[110] *The New Schaff-Herzog Encyclopedia of Religious Knowledge*, Vol. VI, pp. 423, 424.

[111] Hermelink, *Das Christentum in der Menschheitsgeschichte von der französischen Revolution bis zur Gegenwart*, Vol. I, pp. 167–171; Leonhard von Muralt, in Siegmund-Schultze, *Ekklesia. Die evangelischen Kirchen der Schweiz*, pp. 37–39; W. Hadorn, *Geschichte des Pietismus in den Schweizerischen Reformierten Kirchen* (Constance, Carl Hirsch, 1902, pp. xxii, 521), pp. 385 ff.

he had his education in Zürich and there came under the influence of Lavater. His thoughts were early turned to reform. Although deeply religious, to carry out his purpose he turned from theology to law. In the 1770's he was already giving himself to the education of underprivileged children and formulating the principles of education which made him famous. He disliked catechisms and dogmatic forms, for they seemed to him sterile, but, reacting against an earlier enthusiasm for Rousseau, he stressed the Bible and the Christian virtues. In the new order which followed the French invasion, in one institution after another he further developed an educational programme which won wide acclaim and was influential in many countries. While many of the orthodox looked at him askance, he thought of himself as Christian and sought to follow what seemed to him to be the ethical teachings of Christ and the New Testament.[112]

THE STORM AND PROTESTANTISM: IN THE NETHERLANDS

On the eve of the French "liberation" of the Netherlands the dominant religious body in that country was the Reformed Church. The French invasion was in January, 1795. In 1798 the Batavian Republic arose, a creation of the French. With it came the separation of Church and state. The constitution of 1798 decreed that each congregation must care for its own interests and had various provisions which if enforced might have led to the extinction of the Reformed Church. The constitutions of 1801 and 1805 gave more freedom. The Church suffered from the incorporation of the Netherlands into the Napoleonic empire. In 1808 and 1809 financial support from the state was not forthcoming. In 1812 Napoleon proposed to unite at least some of the several churches into which the Protestantism of the country was divided and have the structure placed under the direction of the state. His downfall prevented the plan from being carried out.

However, during the years of revolution and French domination, varied developments were seen. At least some were indications of vigour. The doctrinal controversies which had long absorbed much of the energy of the Netherlands Reformed Church lessened because the churches were too much involved in maintaining their existence to engage in them as actively as before. No effective church censorship of books was possible, and university professors were able to pursue theological and Biblical studies with more freedom than earlier. The trend among professors and most of the clergy was towards liberalism and rationalism and away from the orthodoxy of the Synod of Dortrecht. The latter persisted chiefly among the rank and file of such of the laity as were deeply concerned for the faith. The Evangelical movement in Britain was beginning

---

[112] Roger de Guimps, *Pestalozzi: His Life and Work,* translated from the second French edition by J. Russell (New York, D. Appleton and Co., 1890, pp. xix, 438), *passim;* Otto Eberhard, *Pestalozzi, ein Klassiker der Seelenführung* (Gütersloh, C. Bertelsmann, 1926, pp. 96), *passim.*

to have repercussions. From the minority affected by it, and patterned in part upon the London Missionary Society (organized in 1795), the Netherlands Missionary Society was founded (1797). A new hymnal published in 1807 attracted much attention. In 1796 an effort was made by the Remonstrants, a theologically Arminian liberal group, to unite all Protestants, but almost all the other churches refused to join. Several societies were formed to achieve unity among Protestants. The most promising was *Christo Sacrum,* begun in 1797. It did something to draw together members of the several churches, but those who adhered to it were ejected as heretics from the Netherlands Reformed Church and found it necessary to form themselves into a distinct religious body. An attempt was made to inaugurate a national structure for the various Mennonite congregations.[113]

THE STORM AND PROTESTANTISM: IN SCANDINAVIA

While the Scandinavian countries were affected by the French Revolution, they were more nearly on its periphery than were Germany, Switzerland, and the Netherlands and were late in being drawn into it. Not until after 1800 did the storm reach them. Then they were caught in the life and death combat of the Titans. In 1807 a British expedition bombarded Copenhagen and seized what was left of the Danish navy. The Danes thereupon sided with Napoleon. They soon prepared to attack Sweden. In 1808 a Russian army invaded Finland and in 1809 Sweden ceded it and the Åland islands to Russia. Sweden was also compelled to give up most of Pomerania and to exclude British goods. King Charles XIII of Sweden, old, childless, and infirm, designated as his successor Bernadotte, one of Napoleon's marshals, and that country was thus given a new ruling line which retained the throne throughout the rest of the period covered by our volumes. For a time Norway profited, as a neutral, by a growth in commerce from the wars of the French Revolution and Napoleon. Her population continued the increase which had marked it in the eighteenth century. Nationalism was rising and so produced restlessness against the tie with Denmark. The restlessness was augmented when, after the British bombardment of Copenhagen, Norway was compelled by Denmark to side with Napoleon and, cut off from the profitable English market, her commerce was ruined and her food supply failed. Early in 1814 Denmark was penalized and Sweden compensated for her loss of Finland by the placing of Norway under the Swedish royal house.

In Denmark varied religious currents were present. Kant was being read.

[113] Siegmund-Schultze, *Ekklesia. Die evangelischen Kirchen der Niederlande,* pp. 22, 23, 75, 82; Brandreth in Rouse and Neill, *A History of the Ecumenical Movement,* p. 290; N. Van der Zijpp, *Geschiedenis der Doopsgezinden in Nederland* (Arnheim, Van Loghum Slaterus, 1952, pp. 263), pp. 189–193.

Rationalism was strong. One of its representatives, Bastholm, from 1783 to 1800 chaplain to the king, tended to regard Christ chiefly as an ancient philosopher. Although Balle, from 1783 to 1808 Bishop of Zealand and as such the leading churchman, was critical of the scepticism which entered from the French Revolution, he and Bastholm collaborated in a handbook of religion (1791) which emphasized the intellectual and moral elements in the faith. A new hymnal in which Balle was one of the editors and which was authorized in 1798 had rationalistic overtones. Church attendance fell off and in the new century it did not immediately recover. For a time even theological students seemed without deep convictions. Yet Pietism continued in several forms, including the Moravians. In 1793 Lavater was in Copenhagen. Moreover, not far from the turn of the century indications were seen of a change in the religious climate and of fresh vitality. Largely through the labours of a Scot who had come to Copenhagen en route as a missionary to India, the Danish Bible Society was organized, with the Bishop of Zealand as its head. Still more significantly, it was during these years that the character and faith were being formed of two who were to have a profound effect on Danish Christianity in the nineteenth and twentieth centuries. These were J. P. Mynster (1775–1854) and N. F. S. Grundtvig (1783–1872). Grundtvig especially was to be a continuing influence. We are to hear more of both men in a later period.[114]

In Iceland, tied as it was to Denmark, some of the currents from that land made themselves felt. This was especially true of the *Aufklärung*. Even before 1789 it had begun to enter through men who had been shaped by it in their student days in Copenhagen. While the masses were only slowly affected, a hymnal issued in 1800 under its influence did much to spread it.[115]

The latter part of the eighteenth and the fore part of the nineteenth century witnessed a nationalistic movement in Norway. Out of it came, in 1811, a university, so that it was no longer necessary for theological students to go to Copenhagen for their preparation. Rationalism was still present among the higher clergy: it is said that in 1814 four of the five Norwegian bishops were in that category.

A movement began in Norway which was associated with nationalism and with stirrings of class consciousness among the farmers, but which was primarily a variety of Pietism. No other religious awakening which arose in Scandinavia in this period was so widely and persistently potent. It was led by Hans Nielsen Hauge (1771–1824). Hauge was from the farmers. In Norway in contrast with Denmark the peasants were free and not serfs. It was to

---

[114] Koch, *Danmarks Kirke gennem Tiderne*, pp. 131 ff.; Ammundsen in Siegmund-Schultze, *Ekklesia. Die Kirche in Dänemark*, pp. 38 ff.; Koch, in Koch and Kornerup, *Den Danske Kirkes Historie*, Vol. VI, pp. 11–139.

[115] Helgason in Siegmund-Schultze, *Ekklesia. Die Kirke in Island*, p. 22.

this level of society, independent, inclined to be critical of the upper classes with which the pastors tended to mingle, that Hauge chiefly appealed. He was reared in a home noted for its solid, serious character and its earnest religious life. A sober youth, he was brought up on Luther's catechism, Pontopiddan, and such writers as Arndt. On April 5, 1796, after a long inner struggle, he had a transforming experience similar to the one which earlier in the century had come to John Wesley in the Aldersgate meeting. It started him on a career of preaching. The following eight years were for him ones of almost ceaseless activity. He traversed much of Norway, preaching, and from his pen flowed a stream of letters, tracts, and books. His preaching was incisive and emotional. He denounced the sterile orthodoxy and inconsistent lives of the pastors. He stimulated others to lay preaching and fostered the emergence of a chain of small brotherhoods, closely interlocked, each under the supervision of a house father. He encouraged trade and industry and thus improved the economic standing of his followers. Although Hauge advised his supporters to remain in the state church, many of the clergy, smarting under his criticisms and fearing that he might start a popular revolt, stoutly opposed him. From 1804 to 1811 he was imprisoned for violating the conventicle law of 1741. Indeed, he had already been arrested ten times on that charge. In 1809 he was released for a few months to promote the manufacture of salt. In 1814 he was convicted of violating the act against conventicles and was sentenced to two years of hard labour. Through the intervention of friends the sentence was commuted, but the suffering through which he had gone left him physically a broken man and he could never again go at the pace of his eight active years. However, he continued to write and the movement which he had begun did not die. If anything, it grew. Lay preachers carried it on. Like Hauge, they stressed conversion. They contributed to a warm Pietism which remained within the official church and persisted into the twentieth century.[116]

The picture in Sweden was far from uniform. A decline in spiritual fervour and church life seemed general. Drunkenness was widely prevalent and many of the clergy became its victims. Sceptical thought associated with the French Revolution made inroads. The *Aufklärung* had a following, even among the higher clergy. Pietism continued in several forms, including that of the Moravians. But the leaning towards Moravianism of the unfortunate King Gustavus IV, whose incompetence led in 1809 to his dethronement, in some quarters brought that movement into disrepute. In the South the later years of the period saw a stagnation in Moravian circles. Seminaries for the practical train-

---

[116] A. Chr. Bang, *Hans Nielsen Hauge og hans Samtid* (Christiania, Jacob Dybwad, 2nd ed., 1875, pp. 551), *passim;* V. H. Günther, *Hans Nielsen Hauge, Norwegens Erwecker* (Neumünster, Christophorus-Verlag, 1928, pp. 288), *passim;* Einar Molland, *Fra Hans Nielsen Hauge til Eivind Berggrav* (Oslo, Gyldendal Norsk Vorlag, 1951, pp. 110), pp. 11–32; *The New Schaff-Herzog Encyclopedia of Religious Knowledge,* Vol. V, p. 170.

ing of clergy in connexion with universities were begun in Uppsala in 1806 and in Lund in 1809. The years of disaster, 1808–1809, with the loss of Finland and territories in Germany, stirred the souls of many and stimulated a national awakening. The influx of Idealism and romanticism from Germany brought fresh impulses to literature and religion. In 1819 a new hymnal which had been in preparation for a number of years was given official authorization. In it a great preacher and poet, J. O. Wallin, later to be the Primate of the Church of Sweden, had a moulding part and to it contributed many hymns. Indeed, the hymnal in use in the Church of Sweden in the mid-twentieth century contained more selections by him than by any other author. In the South and West Henry Schartau, outstanding preacher and spiritual counsellor in Lund, embodied much of a kind of Pietism which rejected Moravianism as too emotional. Through him many of the clergy took the lead in furthering the spiritual life rather than leaving it to conventicles. Under the example of England in 1808 a society was organized in Stockholm for the circulation of tracts, and in 1815 the Swedish Bible Society was formed. In the North, under Moravian influence, lay preachers and conventicles were multiplying and some of the clergy reflected Moravian convictions: they prepared the way for revivals in the nineteenth century. The influence of Swedenborg spread. Missions continued in the far North among the Lapps.[117]

Because of the political tie, until 1808–1809 the course of religious life in Finland was not unlike that in Sweden. Here, too, the *Aufklärung* had exponents among the clergy: in the 1790's it reached the apex of its influence. It is said not to have been as potent as in Sweden, but it was strongly represented on the theological faculty where many of the pastors were trained. Swedenborg had followers. As in Sweden, Pietism was represented, in the tradition both of Francke and Halle on the one hand and of the Moravians on the other. Also as in Sweden, much of the Pietism remained within the official church.

Here too the years 1808–1809 marked a transition, particularly because of the severing of the political tie with Sweden and the forcible alignment with Russia. The *Aufklärung* waned and romanticism increased. Attempts at reform begun in the early years of the century by the Bishop of Abo (Turku) in an improved training of the clergy and teachers were maintained. Swedish influence persisted. Wallin's hymnal was introduced, as were a catechism and a handbook. The Pietist awakening was reinforced by impulses from Stockholm and

[117] K. B. Westman in Siegmund-Schultze, *Ekklesia. Die Kirche in Schweden*, pp. 49, 50; Emil Liedgren, *Svenska Kyrkans Historia*, Vol. VI (Stockholm, Svenska Kyrkans Diakonistyrelses Bokförlag, 1946, pp. 382), pp. 11–210; H. Pleijel, *Herrnhutismen i Sydsverige* (Stockholm, Svenska Kyrkans Diakonistyrelses Bokförlag, 1925, pp. xxvii, 302), pp. 140 ff.; Holmquist, *Handbok i Svensk Kyrkohistoria*, Vol. II, pp. 243 ff., Vol. III, pp. 7 ff.; Brilioth, *Svensk Kyrkokunskap*, pp. 151, 152.

England and had Paavo Ruotsalainen (1777–1852) as an outstanding leader. However, modifications were made in the Swedish heritage.[118]

THE STORM AND PROTESTANTISM: IN ENGLAND

The French Revolution worked no striking changes in the Protestantism of England. The presence of French refugee priests helped to soften the traditional prejudice against the Roman Catholic Church, but very few conversions to that branch of the faith were made. The main currents which were ,present on the eve of the storm continued, and some of them were strengthened. The Evangelical awakening, for example, while still deeply affecting only minorities, grew. From it emerged additional movements, organizations, and notable figures. Unlike German Protestantism, the English Protestantism of the period gave birth to no strikingly fresh formulations of Christian theology: no one appeared who could compare in wide influence with Schleiermacher. The currents of outstanding strength were, rather, akin to Pietism. More than on the Continent they were the sources of new organizations for missionary outreach at home and abroad and of movements for social, moral, and educational reform and advance. In them activism rather than reflexion was strong.

The Methodist movement which had begun with the Wesleys moved further towards separation from the Church of England and grew in numbers. The Wesleys regarded themselves as remaining within the Church of England. However, as we have seen, before 1789 John Wesley had taken on himself the functions of a bishop, or, as he preferred to translate the Greek word, a superintendent, and had ordained ministers for the United States and Scotland, where the Anglican communion was numerically weak and did not have enough priests sympathetic with Methodism to give the communion to the growing numbers of its adherents. In 1789 he ordained men for work in England. After Wesley's death (1791) Methodists continued to multiply. In 1815 they were three times as numerous in Great Britain and Ireland as they were in 1791. In 1784, in anticipation of the time when he would not be living to continue the direction which he had given the Methodist societies, Wesley by a Deed of Declaration named a "Conference" of one hundred of his preachers to guide the movement. In 1791, shortly after his death, the preachers met in Conference and thereafter continued to do so year by year. Only gradually, however, did they provide for the observance of the Lord's Supper in their own chapels and outside the parish churches of the establishment. This and ordination were the crucial points on which the connexion with the Church of England depended.[119]

[118] Wolfgang Schmidt, *Finlands Genom Tiderna* (Stockholm, Svenska Kyrkans Diakonistyrelses Bokförlag, 1940, pp. 331), pp. 194–225; Brilioth, *op. cit.*, pp. 151, 152; Siegmund-Schulze, *Ekklesia. Die Kirche in Finnland*, pp. 47, 48, 65 ff.

[119] A. W. Harrison, *The Separation of Methodism from the Church of England* (London, The

Methodism early experienced division. In 1797, led by Alexander Kilham (1762–1798), a preacher who had been expelled from the Conference because of his advocacy of procedures which would give more of local control to Methodism, the Methodist New Connexion was founded. In 1815 and early in 1816 the followers of William O'Bryan, an ardent itinerant evangelist who refused to be bound in his preaching journeys by the rules of the Conference, constituted themselves the Bible Christian Methodists. The two dissident groups had much in common and might haye united, but they were separated geographically: the Methodist New Connexion was strongest in the North and the Bible Christians were in the South-west, in Devon and Cornwall.[120]

Within the Church of England the Evangelicals continued to grow. In Cambridge, where, as we have seen, there was a succession of strong Evangelicals, Charles Simeon (1759–1836) exerted a profound influence.[121] In Oxford for several decades after the Wesleys had ceased to have it as their residence the Evangelical witness was weak or absent. No one kept it as prominently before the university as did Simeon at Cambridge. During much of the period of the French Revolution, under Evangelical leadership St. Edmund Hall was a radiating centre of the movement. However, it was regarded as the weakest of the colleges and among most undergraduates and dons Evangelicals were viewed with amusement or scorn. Daniel Wilson (1778–1858), forthright and vigorous, who in later years was Bishop of Calcutta, was a tower of strength. After 1806 conditions began to improve, but Oxford did not compare with its sister university as a nurturing mother of Evangelicals.[122]

At its outset the historic Nonconformist bodies looked upon the Methodist movement with suspicion and even antagonism, partly because John Wesley was distrustful of dissent, partly because most Independents and Baptists were Calvinists and Wesley was an Arminian.[123] Eventually, however, Methodism had its effect. Before the end of the eighteenth century Congregationalists and General Baptists were caught up in the revival and were adding to their num-

---

Epworth Press, 1945, pp. 66), *passim;* Townsend, Workman, and Eayrs, *A New History of Methodism,* Vol. I, pp. 383–388.

[120] Townsend, Workman, and Eayrs, *op. cit.,* Vol. I, pp. 488 ff.; Edwards, *After Wesley,* pp. 46–52.

[121] *The Entire Works of the Rev. Charles Simeon, M.A.,* Prepared by Thomas Hartwell Horne (London, Henry G. Bohn, 21 vols., 8th ed., 1845); Charles Hugh Egerton Smyth, *Simeon & Church Order, a Study of the Origins of the Evangelical Revival in Cambridge in the Eighteenth Century* (Cambridge University Press, 1940, pp. xx, 315), *passim;* J. C. Pollock, *A Cambridge Movement* (London, John Murray, 1953, pp. xv, 288), pp. 2–7; Leonard Elliott-Binns, *The Evangelical Movement in the English Church* (London, Methuen & Co., 1928, pp. xv, 171), pp. 37–39.

[122] J. S. Reynolds, *The Evangelicals at Oxford, 1735–1871* (Oxford, Basil Blackwell, 1953, pp. xi, 212), pp. 58 ff.; M. L. Loane, *Oxford and the Evangelical Succession* (London, Lutterworth Press, 1950, pp. 295), pp. 135 ff.

[123] Duncan Coomer, *English Dissent under the Early Hanoverians* (London, The Epworth Press, 1946, pp. viii, 136), pp. 108 ff.

bers. Many touched by Methodism allied themselves with the Congregational Churches and some with the Baptists. Moreover, a general quickening of life was experienced, not all of it through Methodist channels.[124]

From English Protestantism came movements for reform and the improvement of society. The contrast with the storm that was sweeping across much of the neighbouring Continent may be significant. That storm was violent, characterized by a mixture of humanitarian idealism and anti-Christian passion and captured by a selfish drive for power. While to its origin and some of its features impulses contributed which had their rise in predominantly Protestant countries, its outbreak and centre were in a people overwhelmingly Roman Catholic by profession, and the destruction it wrought was mainly in regions which were prevailingly of that faith. In England, on the other hand, at the same time reforms were in progress which were as yet less drastic, which were accomplished with little or no violence and with much less of hatred and passion, and in which selfish aspirations for power were by no means so prominent. The initiative and leadership were largely, although not entirely, from those who had been deeply stirred by the Evangelical awakening. The contrast persisted into the nineteenth and twentieth centuries. In the violent revolutions of those years several of the contributing systems of thought, notably Marxist Communism, were formulated in theoretically Protestant lands, but their leadership was mainly from those who had been reared in either a Roman Catholic or an Orthodox environment.

The contrast may point to basic differences among the major branches of Christianity. Protestantism, with its emphasis upon the freedom of the individual in thought and action, stimulated the emergence of proposals for the improvement of mankind. Since Protestantism was less inflexible than the other two major wings of Christianity, in the structure of its institutions, whether political or ecclesiastical, changes were accomplished less explosively. To a great extent they were begun and carried through by men and women who had been stirred by the religious revivals which characterized Protestantism. Roman Catholicism and Orthodoxy were less flexible and more resistant to alterations, whether in their own structures or in society as a whole, and far more explosively anti-Christian movements were led by those who were from *milieux* in which the Roman Catholic Church or an Orthodox Church was the prevailing form of religion.

During the quarter-century of the French Revolution and Napoleon the contrast was marked. Before that day changes had been wrought in the British Isles and the British colonies. Some, notably in the seventeenth century in the British Isles and in America just before the French Revolution, had been

[124] Henry W. Clark, *History of English Nonconformity* (London, Chapman & Hall, 2 vols., 1911, 1913), Vol. II, pp. 246–286.

marked by violence. Yet the destruction was less extensive than in the storm which exploded in France. Moreover, in the eighteenth century non-violent change was beginning to come out of the awakenings in British Protestantism. This was seen in improvements in education, in efforts to better the conditions in prisons, and, as exemplified in the journals of John Woolman, in the early stirrings of conscience over Negro slavery. Now efforts for reform mounted. They seem not to have been stimulated by what was taking place on the Continent. In some quarters those who promoted them were at times resisted on the ground that they smacked of what the large majority in England abhorred in the French Revolution. The British reforms were indigenous. They were effected by the efforts of small minorities in a time of foreign wars in which Britain was fighting for her existence and in the face of opposition which in its own interest was utilizing the fear of the spread of the storm to England to curtail the traditional hard-won liberties of the nation.

That fear was not entirely without foundation. Some in Britain sympathized with the French Revolution. Influential in stimulating and helping to shape their views was the pamphleteer and agitator Thomas Paine (1737-1809). Born in Norfolk of a Quaker father and Church of England mother, in his childhood he had attended the meetings of the Friends and to the end of his colourful life bore something of their impress. In early manhood he went to America. There in the pamphlet *Common Sense* (1776), shortly before the Declaration of Independence, he came out in advocacy of that step and with condemnation of monarchy as a form of government. In 1791 and 1792 he had published in London in two successive parts a book, *The Rights of Man,* which was an ardent defense of the French Revolution with invidious comparisons with English institutions. In *The Age of Reason,* similarly written in two parts, in the mid-1790's Paine came out vigorously as a Deist, with sharp criticisms of the Bible and of Christianity. A controversialist, master of a vivid and uncompromising style, he had a wide reading and attempts were made in England to suppress his writings.[125] It was in this heated atmosphere that the Evangelical reformers laboured.

The prince of these reformers was William Wilberforce (1759-1833).[126] Son of a wealthy merchant of Hull, he inherited a large fortune. Precocious and always of delicate health, at Cambridge his charm, wit, engaging conversation, and hospitable love of company won him hosts of friends. Except in gambling he did not fall victim to any of the prevalent vices of the wealthy of the day,

---

125 Of the voluminous literature by and about Paine see especially *The Complete Writings of Thomas Paine,* collected and edited by Philip S. Foner (New York, The Citadel Press, 2 vols., 1945); Moncure Daniel Conway, *The Life of Thomas Paine* (New York, G. P. Putnam's Sons, 2 vols., 1908).

126 Robert Isaac Wilberforce and Samuel Wilberforce, *The Life of William Wilberforce* (London, John Murray, 5 vols., 1838); R. Coupland, *Wilberforce, A Narrative* (Oxford, The Clarendon Press, 1923, pp. 528).

but he had no serious interest in religion. He was already in Parliament and a friend of the younger Pitt when, in the 1780's, in two journeys on the Continent, he was converted. This came about through his travelling companion, Isaac Milner (1750–1820).[127] Milner, a clergyman and brilliant mathematician, eventually President of Queen's College and Vice-Chancellor of Cambridge University, was a younger brother of Joseph Milner (1744–1797),[128] an ardent Evangelical. Isaac also had Evangelical views, and the reading which he and Wilberforce did on their trip—in Doddridge's *Rise and Progress of Religion in the Soul* and the New Testament—deepened his faith as well as brought conviction to Wilberforce. Wilberforce sought John Newton as his spiritual counsellor. The change led to a radical alteration in his way of life. Some years later, in 1797, he came out with a small book which gave his mature reflexions. This, *A Practical View of the Prevailing Religious System of Professed Christians, in the Higher and Middle Classes, Contrasted with Real Christianity,* went into many editions and was translated into several languages.[129] He deplored what seemed to him to be the steady decline of Christianity in England, with the growth of prosperity, the multiplication of great cities, and the prevalence of the commercial spirit, so that Christianity "now seldom occupies the attention of the bulk of nominal Christians" and "the time is fast approaching when . . . to believe in it will be deemed the indication of a feeble mind." He outlined and defended what were to him the characteristics and beliefs of true Christianity and the fashion in which it had promoted the general welfare of the political community.

Wilberforce continued to serve in Parliament and there took the leadership in a campaign against Negro slavery. He was not the pioneer. Others had been before him. They included some Quakers and Thomas Clarkson (1760–1846), the son of a clergyman. After many seeming failures, in 1807 Wilberforce obtained an act of Parliament abolishing the slave trade within the British Empire. In some countries a little earlier, in others later, action was also taken to end the trade. Not always was it, as in England, engineered by men from profoundly Christian motives. Only after 1815 was Negro slavery itself generally abolished.

In his anti-slavery campaign Wilberforce was aided by a circle of friends, Evangelicals of the Church of England, most of them wealthy and laymen. They constituted what were sometimes called the "Saints" and sometimes the "Clapham Sect." [130] The latter designation was from a village then on the out-

---

[127] *Dictionary of National Biography,* Vol. XIII, pp. 456–459.

[128] *Ibid.,* pp. 464, 465.

[129] See an American edition, "from a late London edition" (New York, American Tract Society, no date, pp. 375).

[130] Ernest Marshall Howse, *Saints in Politics. The "Clapham Sect" and the Growth of Freedom* (University of Toronto Press, 1952, pp. xv, 215), *passim.*

skirts of London where for some years Wilberforce and several men of like mind made their homes and where Evangelical clergymen Henry Venn and later his son, John, were in charge of the local parish. Among the group were Zachary Macaulay, father of the historian, John Shore, later Lord Teignmouth, Charles Grant, John Thornton, uncle of Wilberforce, and Thornton's three sons, Samuel, Robert, and Henry. It was in Henry Thornton's house that they usually assembled.

The group was concerned not only with Negro slavery. It addressed itself to other evils. One or more of its members fought for reform in elections to Parliament and in penal and game laws, for the abolition of the press gang, for the relief of the boys who swept the chimneys, and for labour and factory legislation. They were generous in their private philanthropies. They promoted the founding and growth of the Church Missionary Society, the British and Foreign Bible Society, the Sunday School Society, the Society for Bettering the Condition and Improving the Comforts of the Poor, and other similar organizations. They were active in the inauguration of Sierra Leone as a refuge for freed slaves and a centre for the evangelization of Africa.[131]

Arising partly from the Evangelical movement and partly from Christian impulses through other channels, advances in education were achieved. In a broad way they remind one of what was being accomplished through Pestalozzi. We have already noted the Sunday Schools. Beginning on the eve of the French Revolution they continued to multiply during the years of storm, and that in spite of criticism in some church circles.

A close friend of Wilberforce and, like him, with an Evangelical conversion, was Hannah More (1745–1833).[132] She early acquired literary fame and in London mixed in the upper intellectual and social circles. Only gradually did she move into Evangelicalism. Like Wilberforce, she had Newton as a spiritual counsellor. In time she became a member of the Clapham circle. After her espousal of Evangelical doctrines she wrote tracts and books for moral and religious improvement which had a wide circulation. Seeking seclusion and rest, she and her sisters established a summer home some miles south of Bristol, the city where they had long conducted a school for girls. In the neighbourhood, in the Mendip Hills and adjoining regions, at first through the initiative of Wilberforce, they discovered among miners and farm labourers appalling conditions of poverty, ignorance, vice, and lack of religious instruction. Without attacking the economic and social structure which to no small degree contributed to these conditions, they sought to alleviate them by schools. In the

---

[131] On the Clapham group and others who were associated with Wilberforce, see John Campbell Colquhoun, *William Wilberforce: His Friends and His Times* (London, Longmans, Green, Reader, and Dyer, 1867, pp. vii, 459), *passim*.

[132] M. G. Jones, *Hannah More* (Cambridge University Press, 1952, pp. xi, 284), *passim*.

face of no little indifference and opposition, in the years which immediately followed 1789 they began and multiplied them.

Two movements for schools for the poor were inaugurated by Joseph Lancaster and Andrew Bell. Joseph Lancaster (1778–1838),[133] deeply religious and intended by his parents for the Nonconformist ministry, had wished to go as a missionary to the Negroes of Jamaica. In his teens he joined the Society of Friends. In his youthful enthusiasm he began to gather children to teach them to read. Lack of funds stimulated him to devise a method by which older pupils taught younger ones. He had the gift of promotion and organization and in the period of the French Revolution and Napoleon, with financial aid from Quakers and the endorsement of the royal family, he multiplied schools which utilized his method. A society was organized to further the programme and "Lancastrian schools" became numerous. Unstable emotionally, visionary, and chronically in debt, Lancaster died a disappointed man. An older contemporary, Andrew Bell (1753–1832),[134] developed a somewhat similar system. A clergyman of the Church of England, for some years after 1787 Bell was a chaplain of the East India Company. In the fashion of the company's employees of the day, in that service he accumulated a comfortable fortune. Yet he was by no means entirely mercenary. In 1789 he became superintendent of the Madras Male Orphan Asylum, an institution for the children, usually half-Indian, of military men employed by the company. There, quite independently of Lancaster and earlier than he, he used older pupils to instruct the younger ones. Returning to England, he founded schools on a similar pattern. In his lifetime about twelve thousand were begun. Controversy developed between the supporters of Lancaster and of Bell. Lancaster intended his schools, while distinctly Christian, to be non-sectarian. Bell was aided by those who wished the schools to be under the direction of the Church of England.

In the period of the French Revolution and the Napoleonic Wars some reinforcement for reform came from the ranks of Methodism, but not as much as from the Evangelicals within the Church of England. Although John Wesley was wide-ranging in his activities and did much through his inexpensive editions of good literature to further popular education, in politics he was a Tory. In the generation after his death the majority of Methodists were politically conservative. Their preachers strove to spread what they called Scriptural holiness and they were against dancing, the theatre, the use of tobacco, and the prevailing drunkenness. But as yet they made no effort to promote legislation to remedy the lot of those who were suffering from the enclosure of the common lands or from the initial stages of the Industrial Revolution. From Methodists came strong support for the campaign against the slave trade. They early or-

[133] *Dictionary of National Biography*, Vol. XI, pp. 480–483.
[134] *Ibid.*, Vol. II, pp. 149–152.

ganized and multiplied Sunday Schools, and the curriculum included reading and writing as well as the study of the Bible. They were active in various forms of private philanthropy. They were predominantly of the middle class, supported the Government in its wars against Napoleon, and were against the kind of republicanism associated with the French Revolution. Yet Methodism had a democratic strain. Some of it found expression in the Methodist New Connexion and the Bible Christians. Moreover, the training in class-meetings, in reading-circles, and as lay preachers helped prepare leaders for the liberal democracy of the nineteenth and twentieth centuries.[135]

In this period the impulse for political reform and democracy was not so much from Evangelicals. Nor did it come from most of the other Nonconformists. Congregationalists and Baptists, like the others, were concerned mainly with the transformation of individual character and with the antislavery movement and the efforts for prison reform and to curb smuggling and the use of alcoholic beverages.[136] Political reform had advocates, rather, among the extreme religious liberals, including Unitarians, such as Joseph Priestley (1733–1804) and Richard Price (1723–1791).[137]

Beyond the reforms which it was achieving and the philanthropies in which it was fertile,[138] through the alterations, some of them profound, in individual lives which it was accomplishing, the Evangelical awakening was making for moral and social changes in ever-widening circles. By the transformation of individuals it combatted the low state of morals characteristic of much of eighteenth-century England and accentuated by the conduct of the Prince of Wales and Prince Regent, the future George IV. It promoted the individual discipline, personal responsibility, thrift, improved economic status, and education of those who were caught up in it. The form of government in most of the Nonconforming congregations gave training to many in the management of affairs which is important for a democracy.[139] It seems probable, moreover, that the concern for the welfare of subject peoples which in contrast with the scienceless exploitation of the eighteenth century characterized British colonial administration in the nineteenth century was given a marked impetus by the Clapham Evangelicals who concerned themselves actively with the affairs of India. Less conspicuous and more difficult to trace was the possible contribution

[135] Edwards, *After Wesley, passim;* E. R. Taylor, *Methodism & Politics, 1791–1851* (Cambridge University Press, 1935, pp. xi, 227), pp. 54 ff.; H. F. Mathews, *Methodism and the Education of the People, 1791–1851* (London, The Epworth Press, 1949, pp. 215), pp. 9–70.

[136] Bebb, *Nonconformity and Social and Economic Life 1660–1800,* pp. 163 ff.

[137] Stromberg, *Religious Liberalism in Eighteenth-Century England,* p. 161. On Price see *Dictionary of National Biography,* Vol. XVI, pp. 334–337.

[138] As in Eric McCoy North, *Early Methodist Philanthropy* (New York, The Methodist Book Concern, 1914, pp. viii, 181), *passim.*

[139] Bebb, *op. cit.,* pp. 167 ff.

to the romantic movement in British letters late in the eighteenth and in the fore part of the nineteenth century.[140]

One of the most important fruits of the Evangelical awakening was the impetus to the world-wide spread of Christianity. Not until 1813 did the Methodists form societies for that purpose and it was only in 1817–1818 that an inclusive one, the Wesleyan Methodist Missionary Society, was constituted. However, long before that time they had been active in reaching outside the British Isles. The outstanding pioneer was Thomas Coke (1747–1814). Of Welsh birth and rearing, the heir to an ample fortune, short of stature, handsome, charming, Coke had graduated from Oxford and was a clergyman of the Church of England and a curate when he threw in his lot with John Wesley. Fervid, restless, with a wide vision, on extensive journeyings he aided the spread of Methodism in the United States and the West Indies and died on his way to Ceylon with a party of missionaries to plant Methodism in that island newly taken from the Dutch.[141] It was to carry on and enlarge what he and others had begun that auxiliary societies and eventually a general society were organized.[142]

Earlier than the Wesleyan Methodist Missionary Society was the Baptist Missionary Society, begun in 1792. Chiefly responsible for it was William Carey (1761–1834). The son and grandson of parish clerks and teachers in a village school in the Midlands, as a young apprentice Carey joined the Baptists and became a pastor of one of their churches. To support his growing family he preached, taught school, and made and mended shoes. With a wide-ranging and enquiring mind but little formal education, he acquired several languages, read books of travel, and had plants as a hobby. It was on his repeated prodding that several of his communion founded the Baptist Missionary Society. In 1793 he and another were sent to India by the young organization. There, after initial incredible hardships, eventually operating from the Danish post at Serampore near the larger Calcutta, he had a notable career with repercussions not only in India but also in Burma, the East Indies, and China.[143]

Partly at the impulse given by Carey, in 1795 the London Missionary Society was organized. The new body was intended to be one in which Christians of many denominations could join—Nonconformists, Methodists, and members of the Church of England. Later it drew its support chiefly from Congrega-

[140] Frederick C. Gill, *The Romantic Movement and Methodism. A Study of English Romanticism and the Evangelical Revival* (London, The Epworth Press, 1937, pp. 189), *passim*.

[141] Samuel Drew, *The Life of Thomas Coke* (London, Thomas Cordeux, 1817, pp. xix, 391); Warren A. Candler, *Life of Thomas Coke* (Nashville, Publishing House of the M.E. Church, South, 1923, pp. 408).

[142] G. G. Findlay and W. W. Holdsworth, *The History of the Wesleyan Methodist Missionary Society* (London, The Epworth Press, 5 vols., 1921–1924), Vol. I, pp. 36–72.

[143] S. Pearce Carey, *William Carey D.D., Fellow of the Linnæan Society* (New York, George H. Doran Co., Preface 1923, pp. xvi, 428), *passim*.

tionalists. Its first mission was to islands in the Pacific recently disclosed to the English-speaking world. By 1815 it had begun missions in West and South Africa, China, India, and the East Indies.[144]

In 1899 Evangelicals in the Church of England, among them some of the Clapham circle, wishing to send missionaries under a distinctly Anglican organization and yet viewing the Society for Promoting Christian Knowledge and the Society for the Propagation of the Gospel as too "high churchly," founded what was eventually called the Church Missionary Society. In its inception and its early days Charles Simeon was very influential. By the year 1815 the Church Missionary Society had representatives in Sierra Leone, India, New Zealand, and the West Indies and was about to send men to help quicken the ancient churches of the East.[145] The year 1799 saw the formation of the Religious Tract Society. Members of the Clapham group were also active in the founding of the British and Foreign Bible Society, in 1804. That organization enlisted support from communicants of various denominations. Before the end of the Napoleonic Wars it had issued the Bible in Welsh, Gaelic, Irish, Syriac, and various languages of the Continent of Europe.[146]

In other ways the Evangelicals within the Church of England furthered the spread of Christianity. In 1793, when the charter of the East India Company came before Parliament for renewal, with Wilberforce as their chief spokesman they obtained better provision for chaplains for the company's employees. Through it several Evangelical clergymen, graduates of Cambridge where they had been under the influence of Simeon, went to India. Indeed, Simeon thought of India almost as his "diocese," and later, when it was given a bishop, as his "province." A few of the chaplains began missionary efforts for Hindus as well as for professed Christians.[147] The most famous was Henry Martyn (1781-1812). After a distinguished scholarly record at Cambridge he went to India, there in a few brief years became outstanding, especially in translations of the New Testament, and died on his way back to England.[148] In 1813, when the

[144] Richard Lovett, *The History of the London Missionary Society, 1795-1895* (London, Henry Froude, 2 vols., 1899), Vol. I, pp. 3 ff., 117 ff.

[145] Stock, *The History of the Church Missionary Society*, Vol. I, *passim*.

[146] William Canton, *A History of the British and Foreign Bible Society* (London, John Murray, 5 vols., 1904-1910), Vol. I, *passim*.

[147] Eyre Chatterton, *A History of the Church of England in India since the Early Days of the East India Company* (London, Society for Promoting Christian Knowledge, 1924, pp. xxiv, 823), pp. 108 ff.; Charles Hole, *The Early History of the Church Missionary Society for Africa and the East to the end of A.D. 1814* (London, Church Missionary Society, 1896, pp. xxxviii, 677), pp. 19, 20; *Memorial Sketches of the Rev. David Brown with a Selection of his Sermons, Preached at Calcutta* (London, for T. Cadell and W. Davies, 1816, pp. xviii, 495), *passim;* Hugh Pearson, *Memoirs of the Life and Writings of the Rev. Claudius Buchanan, D.D.* (Boston, Samuel T. Armstrong, 1818, pp. 444), *passim*.

[148] Of the large bibliography on Martyn, see especially *Journals and Letters of the Rev. Henry Martyn, B.D.*, edited by S. Wilberforce (London, R. B. Seeley and W. Burnside, 2 vols., 1837), and George Smith, *Henry Martyn* (London, The Religious Tract Society, 1892, pp. xii, 580).

East India Company's charter again came up for renewal, Wilberforce and others put in it provision for an ecclesiastical establishment of a bishop and three archdeacons for the company's territories and what was tantamount to permission for missionaries in its possessions.[149] Evangelicals were also active in seeing that spiritual care was given in the colonies which in the next few generations were to give rise to the Commonwealth of Australia. At the outset the white settlers were largely convicts. With the first contingent, sent in 1787, was a chaplain, an Evangelical.[150] Samuel Marsden, also an Evangelical, arrived in 1793; energetic, with a broad vision, he did much to further Christianity not only in Australia but also in New Zealand and other islands in the South Seas.[151]

Here was a movement for the spread of Christianity which, with similar ones in other parts of the British Isles, the Continent of Europe, and the United States, was to give so great an impulse to the geographic expansion of Protestantism that it is often said to have begun a new stage in the history of Christian missions. As yet it was supported only by small minorities, but the minorities were growing. It contributed mightily to the world-wide extension of that form of the faith which was one of the most striking features of the history of the nineteenth and twentieth centuries.

THE STORM AND PROTESTANTISM: IN WALES

We have seen that before 1789 the Evangelical awakening had reached Wales. Here the Welsh Calvinistic Methodists had arisen, largely through the preaching of Howel Harris and Daniel Rowlands. Harris died in 1773 and Rowlands in 1790. Yet their demise did not halt the growth of Methodism. For years most Methodists remained in the established church. However, by 1815 the separation had occurred. This was partly under the leadership of Charles of Bala, a priest of the Church of England who as curate in a Welsh mountain parish had preached the revival and then had become an itinerant. The break was made when, in 1811, eight lay preachers were ordained by the Methodist Association, followed, in 1812, by the ordination of eleven more. By 1815 Independents and Baptists, who long had been stationary in numbers, began a rapid growth which was to continue in the nineteenth century.[152]

THE STORM AND PROTESTANTISM: IN SCOTLAND

During the quarter-century when revolution and war were sweeping the

149 Stock, *op. cit.*, Vol. I, pp. 100–104; Wilberforce and Wilberforce, *The Life of William Wilberforce*, Vol. IV, pp. 118 ff.

150 James Bonwick, *Australia's First Preacher, the Rev. Richard Johnson. First Chaplain of New South Wales* (London, Sampson Low, Marston & Co., pp. vii, 264), *passim*.

151 J. B. Marsden, editor, *Memoirs of the Life and Labours of the Rev. Samuel Marsden of Paramatta, Senior Chaplain of New South Wales, and of His Early Connexion with the Missions to New Zealand and Tahiti* (London, The Religious Tract Society, c. 1858, pp. viii, 326), *passim*.

152 Edwards, *Landmarks in the History of the Welsh Church*, pp. 187, 202–209.

neighbouring Continent, marked changes were taking place in Scotland in both general and religious life. The Industrial Revolution was beginning to make itself felt. Population was increasing. Cities were growing. Roads and communication were improving. Foreign commerce was mounting. The country was still poor, but standards of living and wages were rising, both on the farms and in the towns, whiskey was replacing the less expensive beer and ale, the drinking of tea was becoming general, and here and there better houses and even mansions were being built. The quality of teaching and scholarship in the universities was improving. Cultured circles which had become notable in the second half of the century continued and were reinforced. The first volume of the poetry of Robert Burns was published in 1786, and in 1796 his brief, meteoric career was ended by death.[153]

The religious life of Scotland had two main developments. One was the decline of what had been known as Moderatism. The other was the continued growth of Evangelicalism with the awakenings and various new movements which were associated with it.

One factor in the decline of Moderatism was the reaction against the French Revolution and the consequent distrust of liberal views. Another appears to have been a lack of competent leadership.[154]

The Evangelical revivals in Scotland came in part from contacts with the Evangelical awakening in England. As we have seen, John Wesley and White-field both preached in Scotland. Rowland Hill and Charles Simeon were there.[155]

Of the many sons of Scotland who contributed to the growth and vigour of the revivals during this period, none were more notable than two brothers, Robert (1764–1842) and James Alexander (1768–1851) Haldane.[156] Of aristo-cratic stock and inheriting wealth, the Haldanes were given a good education. In their youth both saw service at sea, Robert with the royal navy and James with the East India Company. Both early left the sea. Both were bold, ardent, with a reputation for fearlessness. Both were converted at about the same time, in 1794. In neither was the change sudden. In his boyhood Robert had had some intention of entering the ministry. In their sea-going days the brothers had been under the intermittent influence of David Bogue (1750–1825), a Scot, pastor of an Independent church in Gosport, near Portsmouth and Southampton. He was an Evangelical and one of the founders of the London Missionary Society, the

[153] James Mackinnon, *The Social and Industrial History of Scotland from the Union to the Present Time* (London, Longmans, Green & Co., 1921, pp. viii, 298), pp. 1–44.
[154] Mathieson, *Church and Reform in Scotland*, pp. 100 ff.
[155] *Ibid.*, pp. 67, 68; Macinnes, *The Evangelical Movement in the Highlands of Scotland 1688–1800*, p. 143; Haldane, *Memoirs of the Lives of Robert Haldane of Airthrey, and of His Brother, James Alexander Haldane*, pp. 128–135, 183, 184.
[156] Haldane, *op. cit., passim.*

British and Foreign Bible Society, and the Religious Tract Society.[157] In 1796 Robert, stirred by the reports of Carey's enterprise in India and by the founding of the London Missionary Society, formulated a project for a mission in that country in which the personnel would include himself and Bogue. Since the East India Company refused its permission, the plan was abandoned. In 1796 James Haldane accompanied Charles Simeon on a preaching tour in the Highlands. He himself soon began preaching, largely as an itinerant. Robert sold part of his property and used some of the proceeds to erect "tabernacles" for preaching in several towns and cities. In connexion with the tabernacles, Congregational churches were organized. James was ordained to be the pastor of the one in Edinburgh. Robert undertook to found a seminary for the education of preachers. In consultation with Macaulay of the Clapham group, he brought children from Africa to be reared as Christians. The brothers were active in furthering Sunday Schools. Robert had thousands of tracts printed and circulated. Before long he, too, began preaching. Trouble and division soon came to the infant Congregational churches, partly because the brothers rejected infant baptism and adopted Baptist views and because Robert withdrew his support from churches which did not share them. However, the churches continued and in 1812 drew together in the Congregational Union of Scotland for mutual support and to give financial aid to the weaker churches.[158]

The effects of the Evangelical awakening were not confined to those who broke away from Presbyterianism into Congregational, Baptist, and Methodist bodies. For the time being, the large majority of those who were committed to the awakening remained within the Church of Scotland. Their numbers mounted. In the General Assembly the Evangelical clergy were in a minority, but it was a growing one. They protested against patronage, by which was meant, as we have seen, control by the lay proprietors of appointments to parishes. Against the sentiment of the Moderate majority, they promoted Sunday Schools. In a society where, as in contemporary Scandinavia and England, drunkenness, even among the clergy, was condoned, they preached against intemperance. They fulminated against the rack-renting of the poor. They encouraged education and the distribution of religious literature.[159] In 1810 and early in 1811 Thomas Chalmers (1780–1847), who had been licensed to preach in his twentieth year and was already being recognized as one of the most promising scholars and preachers in the Church of Scotland, after a long inner struggle induced by deaths in his family and a discouraging illness, was led through the reading of Wilberforce's Practical View to a full Evangelical

[157] Dictionary of National Biography, Vol. II, pp. 764, 765.
[158] Ross, A History of Congregational Independency in Scotland, pp. 76–99.
[159] Donald Maclean, Aspects of Scottish Church History (Edinburgh, T. & T. Clark, 1927, pp. xi, 184), pp. 90, 91.

experience.[160] Chalmers is particularly important for his place in Scottish religious history after 1815.

The growth of Evangelicalism in Scotland was seen both in the emergence of missionary societies and in resistance to them. In 1796 the Glasgow Missionary Society and the Scottish Missionary Society were organized.[161] In 1797 the Haldanes, who had aided in the formation of the latter society, assisted in the founding in Edinburgh of a Sunday School society.[162] In 1798 they joined in the inauguration in Edinburgh of the Society for Propagating the Gospel at Home: it helped to further the improvement of religious conditions in the Highlands.[163] In 1811 the Edinburgh Gaelic School Society was founded. The following year the Glasgow Gaelic School Society was begun. The purpose of each is sufficiently indicated by the name, but the latter did not confine itself to teaching in Gaelic.[164] Before 1800 the Northern Missionary Society came into being.[165]

The resistance to the missionary movement was made vivid in a famous debate in the General Assembly of 1796. Two presbyteries had suggested that the Church should "contribute to the diffusion of the Gospel over the world." Hill, the leader of the Moderates, opposed the adoption of the measure. In spite of the dramatic appeal of one of the advocates: "Rax me that Bible," followed by his reading the Great Commission at the end of Matthew's Gospel, the proposal was defeated through a motion which gave guarded endorsement to praying for missions but disapproved of collections for that purpose. Yet the fact that this was by a vote of fifty-eight to forty-four was evidence of a substantial minority who favoured immediate action for missions abroad.[166]

Both the similarities and the contrasts between England and Scotland were striking. In each country the rationalism of the eighteenth century, while still strong, was waning and, as with the closely similar Pietism in some of the Protestant lands on the Continent, the tide of the Evangelical awakening was mounting. In each it was still potent only among minorities. In both it was giving rise to societies for the spread of the faith at home and abroad and to efforts for some kinds of reform and for a general improvement in morals. However, in Scotland less effort was being put forth for Parliamentary action.

More prominent were the differences between the two countries in the character of the state church and of dissent. In England the establishment was

---

[160] William Hanna, *Memoirs of the Life and Writings of Thomas Chalmers* (New York, Harper & Brothers, 4 vols., 1851, 1852), Vol. I, pp. 148–193.

[161] D. Mackickan, *The Missionary Ideal of the Scottish Churches* (London, Hodder & Stoughton, 1927, pp. 238), p. 74.

[162] Mathieson, *op. cit.*, p. 83.

[163] Mackay, *The Church in the Highlands*, p. 227.

[164] *Ibid.*, p. 232.

[165] *Ibid.*, p. 226.

[166] Hetherington, *History of the Church of Scotland*, pp. 379, 380.

Anglican, with a prevailingly Arminian theology but with Calvinism influential among some of the Evangelicals. In Scotland the establishment was Presbyterian, with professed adherence to a Calvinistic theology but, in Moderatism, now declining, a relaxing of some of the tenets associated with that system. In England what was to become the largest of the Nonconforming bodies, the Methodists, the product of the Evangelical awakening, was drawing away from the established church, and the Evangelicals who remained within that church were probably a minority of those committed to the awakening. In Scotland the largest Nonconforming body was the Episcopalians. By 1815 most of them had given up their endorsement of the Stuarts, for in 1788 the "Young Pretender," Charles Edward Stuart, had died, and, although he insisted on his claims, his brother, a Cardinal, was not a feasible aspirant for the throne. Most of their clergy now began praying for the Hanoverian monarch. In 1792 the disabilities earlier placed on the Scottish Episcopalians because of their association with the attempts to re-seat the Stuarts were repealed.[167] There were some Roman Catholics, mostly in the Highlands. The Presbyterians who had withdrawn from the Church of Scotland were small although growing minorities and the Congregationalists, Baptists, and Methodists were not only in numbers but also proportionately much less considerable than in England. Not until 1843 did a great body of Evangelicals withdraw from the established church. They then, as we are to see in the next volume, remained Presbyterians, were a much larger percentage of the Presbyterians of Scotland than were all the Nonconformist Protestants of the population of England, and were without exact parallel in any movement south of the border.

THE STORM AND PROTESTANTISM: IN IRELAND

In Ireland, it will be recalled, Roman Catholics were in the majority, but the established church was Anglican, the Church of Ireland. There was also, chiefly in the North, a substantial minority of Presbyterians, of Scottish origin. Like the Roman Catholics, they were under legal disabilities. They were a yeoman peasantry and a commercial middle class, rising in wealth and numbers. In 1774, 1778, and 1782 some of the restrictions on Roman Catholics had been lightened. In 1793 Roman Catholics were granted the franchise and were freed from some other handicaps. In 1780 and 1782 several of the legal disabilities of the Presbyterians had been removed. Methodism was gaining a footing.

In general, during the quarter of a century before 1815 the Church of Ireland registered an improvement in the quality of its life. To be sure, many of the

---

[167] Thomas Stephen, *The History of the Church of Scotland from the Reformation to the Present Time* (London, John Lendrum, 4 vols., 1845), Vol. IV, pp. 395–434; John Parker Lawson, *History of the Scottish Episcopal Church from the Revolution to the Present Time* (Edinburgh, Gallie & Bayley, 1843, pp. lx, 588), pp. 335 ff.

clergy were non-resident. However, more bishops were appointed who took their duties seriously. Some of them insisted, not without success, that their clergy reside in their parishes. The revival of the office of rural dean made for better administration. New churches were erected and old ones repaired. Although conditions were far from ideal, better provision was made for schools. In 1792 the Association for Discountenancing Vice and Promoting the Knowledge and Practice of the Christian Religion was founded. It prospered and within a few years it improved catechetical instruction, helped to circulate New Testaments, organized many Sunday Schools, and opened schools which were available to adherents of all creeds but conducted on Anglican principles.[168]

The act which in 1800 effected the union of Great Britain and Ireland had as one of its provisions the union of the Churches of England and Ireland "as now by law established" into "one Protestant Episcopal Church, to be called 'The United Church of England and Ireland.' "[169]

But the experiment of a "Protestant Irish nation" entered upon generations earlier had palpably failed. It was only a question of time when the Church of Ireland, enrolling as it did only a sixth or seventh of the population and only slightly more than half of the Protestant minority, would be disestablished.

THE STORM AND PROTESTANTISM: IN THE UNITED STATES

For the United States the quarter-century which followed 1789 was momentous. The year 1789 saw the inauguration of the Federal Government under the Constitution through which the country was to operate throughout the next centuries. The period witnessed the rapid westward extension of the population. After determined efforts to preserve neutrality, in 1812 the young nation was drawn into the European struggle in the form of a second war with Great Britain.

So far as the people of the United States had a church affiliation, it was overwhelmingly Protestant. Religiously the quarter-century was marked by eight movements. They were the popularity and the beginning of the decline of Deism, the growing separation of Church and state, the achievement by some of the churches of a national organization, a rising tide of revivals with a consequent growth in church membership, the inception of a few new denominations, alterations in theology, initiation of enterprises for carrying the faith beyond the borders of the United States, and the beginnings of movements for social and moral reform.

In the 1790's Deism was gaining in the United States. Numbers were sympathetic with the French Revolution, partly because it seemed to be extending some of the principles espoused by the American Revolution. Since Deism was

[168] Walter Allison Phillips, editor, *History of the Church of Ireland from the Earliest Times to the Present Day* (Oxford University Press, 3 vols., 1933), Vol. III, pp. 242–293.
[169] *Ibid.*, pp. 287, 288.

influential in the French Revolution, many were enamoured of it. Paine's *The Age of Reason* had a wide reading and helped to bring to the rank and file views which had heretofore been held chiefly among some educated liberals. Before 1815 the Deistic wave had begun to recede, but it left continuing deposits in the religious views of many.[170]

The loosening of the ties between Church and state proceeded rapidly. In several of the Thirteen Colonies they had been either non-existent or less close than in Western Europe. The first amendment to the Constitution of the United States, which came in force in 1791, declared that "Congress shall make no law respecting an establishment of religion or prohibiting the free exercise thereof." This was not binding on the states. However, before 1789 in several states the struggle for full religious freedom, with disestablishment, had been won. Others now moved in that direction. In 1798 Georgia reached the goal. Connecticut approached it in 1791 but did not fully attain it until 1818. Complete disestablishment in Massachusetts was not realized until 1833. Disestablishment did not mean disavowal of Christianity:[171] the Congress and the armed forces of the Federal Government had chaplains, and the President took the oath of office on the Bible. Yet no one church was established by law, and religious liberty was the rule.

Several of the denominations achieved national organizations. In 1789 the first General Convention of the Protestant Episcopal Church brought into one body those formerly connected with the Church of England. At a convention held in Connecticut a priest, Samuel Seabury (1729-1796), had been chosen bishop and sent to Britain for consecration. The English bishops felt themselves unauthorized to administer it, but he obtained it (1784) from the non-juring bishops of the Episcopal Church in Scotland. However, it was not Seabury, but William White, rector of Christ Church in Philadelphia, who brought about the organization of the Protestant Episcopal Church. A constitutional convention was held in Philadelphia (1785) with representatives from seven states, but without Connecticut. Bishops were chosen, an act of Parliament was obtained permitting their consecration by bishops of the Church of England, and two, one of them White, received the rite in London in 1787 and a third in 1790. Here was the first of the many branches of the Anglican communion which arose outside the British Empire.[172] In 1820 numbers of the Lutheran congregations came together in a General Synod.[173] In 1788 the majority of Presbyterians formed a national structure, the Presbyterian Church in the

---

[170] G. Adolf Koch, *Republican Religion: the American Revolution and the Cult of Reason* (New York, Henry Holt & Co., 1933, pp. xvi, 334), *passim*; Morais, *Deism in Eighteenth Century America*, pp. 120 ff.

[171] Stokes, *Church and State in the United States*, Vol. I, pp. 358 ff.

[172] S. D. McConnell, *History of the American Episcopal Church 1600-1915* (Milwaukee, Morehouse Publishing Co., 11th ed., 1916, pp. xx, 468), pp. 215 ff.

[173] Weigle, *American Idealism*, p. 157.

United States of America, with presbyteries and synods capped by the General Assembly. For a time the Congregational churches of New England sent delegates to the General Assembly. Many of the Presbyterian clergy were trained in Congregational Yale. Beginning with a Plan of Union adopted in 1801 by the General Assembly and the General Association of the Congregational churches of Connecticut, for nearly a generation Presbyterians and New England Congregationalists coöperated in establishing churches on the Western frontier.[174] A large proportion of the Baptists joined in the General Missionary Convention of the Baptist Denomination in the United States of America, inaugurated in Philadelphia in 1814. Because it met every three years it soon became known as the Triennial Convention.[175]

In spite of the surge of Deism, the quarter-century was also characterized by mounting revivals and with them gains in the conversion of a partially de-Christianized population and of the non-Christian Negroes and Indians.

As we have hinted, in colonial days only a small percentage of the population were members of churches. On coming to the New World the large majority did not renew the connexion with churches which had been obligatory in the Old World but which here was either not demanded or not rigorously enforced. Exact statistics are not obtainable, but in 1789 there are said to have been about 3,000 religious organizations and congregations. Of these the largest number, 658, were Congregationalists and the next largest, 543, the closely related Presbyterians. Third were Baptists, with 498, fourth Episcopalians, with 480, and, with much lesser numbers, in descending order, Quakers, German and Dutch Reformed, Lutherans, and Roman Catholics. This was for a population of about 3,000,000.[176] It seems to mean that at the most not more than one in ten of the population was a communicant. Another set of figures declares that in 1800, out of a population of 5,305,925, there were 3,030 churches, 2,651 ministers, and 364,872 communicants. This would indicate that slightly less than seven out of a hundred were communicants. The same estimate counts at most less than one out of four as Christian.[177] Here was a challenge to the churches.

In the 1790's and in the first decade of the new century the tide of revivals rose higher than in the fore part of the eighteenth century under the Great Awakening. It had never fully subsided, but during the War of Independence it had receded. Now it was seen in several sections of the country. Yale was one

---

[174] Robert Ellis Thompson, *A History of the Presbyterian Churches in the United States* (New York, The Christian Literature Co., 1895, pp. xxxi, 424), pp. 63–67, 342–356; Leonard J. Trinterud, *The Forming of an American Tradition. A Re-examination of Colonial Presbyterianism* (Philadelphia, The Westminster Press, 1949, pp. 352), pp. 279 ff.

[175] Torbet, *A History of the Baptists,* pp. 267, 268.

[176] Stokes, *op. cit.,* Vol. I, p. 273.

[177] Daniel Dorchester, *Christianity in the United States from the First Settlement down to the Present Time* (New York, Phillips & Hunt, 1888, pp. 795), p. 750.

of its centres. There in 1795 Timothy Dwight (1752-1817), a grandson of Jonathan Edwards, became president. In the little more than twenty years of his leadership revival after revival swept its campus and young men went from it to further revivals in various parts of the country. The revivals also radiated from other centres in New England.[178] In Virginia even the preoccupation with the struggle for independence did not fully quench the revivals. In the 1780's they broke out afresh, finding channels through several denominations— Baptists, Presbyterians, and Methodists. They were associated with the growth of democracy, for they stirred the masses, gave them leadership, and in the fight for religious freedom helped to make them articulate. As in the Great Awakening and as in Great Britain and on the Continent, the revivals stimulated education.[179]

Through much of the country, and particularly in rural districts and large sections of the frontier in the West and South Methodism was an agency for winning the lukewarm and the non-Christians, for nurturing them in the faith, and for inspiring and training them to win others. In Francis Asbury (1745-1816) it had able leadership.[180] Asbury was born in England of humble parents and had little formal education. Reared in a deeply religious home and serious from his boyhood, in his teens he was brought in touch with the Methodists and became a local preacher. Then, in his early twenties, he began to give full time to itinerant preaching. In 1771 he responded to an appeal of John Wesley for men for America. He never married but gave himself unstintedly to his mission. When his fellow Methodist preachers from England left because of the War of Independence, Asbury remained. In spite of Wesley's open criticism of the revolting colonists, during the war Methodists continued to multiply. Asbury did much to keep their growing societies together. In 1784, the war being over and the independence of the United States having been recognized by the mother country, Wesley sent Thomas Coke to America as superintendent and appointed Asbury to be superintendent with Coke. At Asbury's insistence a Conference of the Methodist preachers was called. In 1784 they met in Baltimore and organized the Methodist Episcopal Church in the United States of America. Asbury refused to act as superintendent unless chosen by the Conference. The Conference elected both him and Coke, and Coke and two elders ordained by Wesley ordained him successively as deacon, elder, and superintendent. The designation of bishop became more general than that of superintendent.

[178] Keller, *The Second Great Awakening in Connecticut, passim.*
[179] Gewehr, *The Great Awakening in Virginia,* pp. 167 ff.
[180] Of the extensive writings by and about Asbury, see *The Journal of the Rev. Francis Asbury, Bishop of the Methodist Episcopal Church from August 7, 1771 to December 7, 1815* (New York, The Methodist Episcopal Church, 3 vols., 1821), and Ezra Squier Tipple, *Francis Asbury, the Prophet of the Long Road* (Cincinnati, The Methodist Book Concern, 1916, pp. 333).

Since Coke was seldom in the United States, it was upon Asbury that the administration of the new church fell. He had no home but travelled almost incessantly, often over rough roads and trails, across swamps, and over rivers where was neither ferry nor bridge. During no little of the time he was ill. Like Wesley, he read extensively and in a variety of literature. Also like Wesley he was preacher, organizer, and administrator. Success was made possible by scores of devoted preachers. Many of them, like himself, were unmarried and itinerant. The plan of assigning them circuits was admirably adapted to the new country with its scattered population. The circuit riders preached wherever they could find opportunity—in taverns, schoolhouses, private homes, or outdoors. Groups and classes with lay leaders carried on in the intervals between visits.

Typical of many circuit riders and outstanding among them was Peter Cartwright (1785–1872). Born in a rough section of the Kentucky frontier, in his middle teens he was converted and began to preach. Although having almost no formal education and disdaining preachers with it, he was courageous and muscular and had a shrewd knowledge of human nature, a keen sense of humour, and, above all, profound conviction. Congregations sprang up, with resident ministers. Most of those reached were white, but a substantial minority were Negroes.[181]

A distinctive form of the revivals was the camp-meeting. The camp-meeting arose from gatherings held in preparation for a celebration of the Lord's Supper. Begun by Presbyterians, they were soon utilized by Methodists and Baptists. Although the revival had commenced in 1797, the first of what came to be typical camp-meetings seems to have been held in Kentucky in 1800. In the following years they multiplied. They were often marked by intense emotion which took bizarre forms, but these had accompanied the preaching of Wesley and the Great Awakening as well as other earlier mass religious movements.[182]

The revivals placed a distinctive stamp on the Protestantism of the United States. They became a normal method of reaching out to the de-Christianized and the non-Christians and of quickening the faith of the Christians. They and the conception of the Gospel and of the Christian life taught in them were

---

[181] On American Methodism in these years see also J. M. Buckley, *A History of Methodists in the United States* (New York, The Christian Literature Co., 1896, pp. xix, 714), pp. 225–345; Wade Crawford Barclay, *History of Methodist Missions*, Vol. I (New York, The Board of Missions and Church Extension of The Methodist Church, 1949, pp. xli, 449), pp. 92–165. On Peter Cartwright see *Autobiography of Peter Cartwright, The Backwoods Preacher*, edited by W. P. Strickland (New York, Hunt & Eaton, 1856, pp. 525), *passim.*

[182] C. C. Cleveland, *The Great Revival in the West, 1797–1805* (The University of Chicago Press, 1916, pp. xii, 215), *passim;* Sweet, *Religion in the Development of American Culture,* pp. 148–153; Weigle, *op. cit.,* pp. 151–153.

characteristic of the churches of which the large majority of American Protestants were members.

This meant that the Protestantism of the United States belonged predominantly to what in the broad sense of these terms was known on the other side of the Atlantic earlier as Puritanism and later as Pietism and Evangelicalism. The churches in which most American Protestants were enrolled were akin to what we have found as Pietism on the Continent and Evangelicalism in the British Isles. On the Continent and the British Isles Pietists and Evangelicals were and remained minorities of those who called themselves Protestants. That in the United States they were a growing majority was highly important for the Christianity of the nineteenth and especially the twentieth century. The Protestantism of the United States became increasingly influential in worldwide Christianity, both in the planting and nourishing of the faith outside the Occident and in the traditional Christendom: the tradition which developed in the United States loomed ever larger in the world scene.

It was mainly but not entirely from the revivals that by 1815 new denominations were emerging in the United States. Two were closely akin to Methodism, the United Brethren in Christ and the Evangelical Association. The United Brethren arose chiefly around Philip William Otterbein (1726–1813).[183] Otterbein was born in Dillensburg, in Nassau, the son of a Reformed pastor and teacher. He was educated in a school where Pietist influence was strong and where Doddridge's *The Rise and Progress of Religion in the Soul* was recommended reading. In 1752 he went to America as one of a band of young men who were recruited as missionaries to the German Reformed by Michael Schlatter, the pioneer agent of the Dutch Reformed Church to that group. While pastor in Lancaster, Pennsylvania, he had a profound experience of the Pietist kind. In 1774 he became pastor of an independent Evangelical German Reformed Church in Baltimore. He did much itinerant preaching and found other Reformed ministers who were in accord with his convictions and who looked to him as their leader. He and Asbury entered into a fast friendship. In 1789 the ministers who collaborated with Otterbein met in the latter's parsonage in the first formal conference of what became the United Brethren Church. It adopted a confession of faith and a body of rules for the new organization. In 1800 at another conference Otterbein and Boehm (a former Mennonite whose preaching had led to awakenings) were elected bishops and the name "United Brethren in Christ" was adopted. The church grew rapidly, chiefly among the German-speaking population.

[183] A. W. Drury, *The Life of Rev. Philip William Otterbein, Founder of the Church of the United Brethren in Christ* (Dayton, United Brethren Publishing House, 1884, pp. 384), *passim;* D. Berger, *History of the Church of the United Brethren in Christ,* in *The American Church History Series,* Vol. XII (New York, The Christian Literature Co., 1894), pp. 309–382.

The Evangelical Association began among the Germans in Pennsylvania through Jacob Albright (1759–1808).[184] Albright was of German Pietist parentage and was reared a Lutheran. After service in the War of Independence he married, bought a farm, cultivated it, and made tiles. Through the shock of the loss of several of his children, his own narrow escapes from death, and the guidance of two of the Otterbein circle, in early middle life he came to a profound experience of salvation. He united with a Methodist church and in 1796 began itinerant preaching. Conversions multiplied, primarily among the Germans. In 1800 his followers took the first steps towards coming together into an organized fellowship and in 1803 ordained him. He had friendly contacts with Asbury, but the latter was emphatic that there was no room in the Methodist Church for those preaching only in German. In 1807 Albright's followers held their first official annual conference. The group adopted "The Newly-Formed Methodist Conference" as their name, an episcopal government, and elected Albright bishop. The movement continued to grow and in 1816 took the name Evangelical Association. Conferences on possible union with the United Brethren were held, for both bodies were warmly evangelistic and had the German population as their common field. However, it was not until the twentieth century that they finally merged.

From the revivals, largely west of the Alleghenies on the relatively fluid frontier, movements sprang up which, seeking to avoid sectarianism, took the name of Christian or Disciples of Christ. They had their chief pioneers in Barton W. Stone (1772–1844) and Alexander Campbell (1788–1866).

Barton W. Stone [185] was born in Maryland, was educated in a school in North Carolina taught by a Presbyterian minister, was converted, and, in spite of some reservations on accepting the Westminister Confession, was ordained by the Presbyterians. He preached in Kentucky at the time of the beginnings of the camp-meetings. He and a few other preachers who were active in the revivals could not accept the unconditional election to salvation which they found in the Confession but held that all sinners were capable of believing. Dissenting from their synod, they constituted themselves the independent Springfield Presbytery and gathered their followers into societies. Weary of denominational differences, they soon (1803) voluntarily dissolved their presbytery and sought to bring about a union of believers under the simple designation of Christian and having the Bible as their only creed. Their followers increased and were organ-

---

[184] Raymond W. Albright, *A History of the Evangelical Church* (Harrisburg, Pa., The Evangelical Press, 1945, pp. xix, 501); Samuel P. Spring, *History of the Evangelical Association* in *The American Church History Series*, Vol. XII, pp. 383–439.

[185] Charles Crossfield Ware, *Barton Warren Stone, Pathfinder of Christian Union. A Story of His Life and Times* (St. Louis, The Bethany Press, 1932, pp. xiv, 357), *passim;* William Garrett West, *Barton Warren Stone, Early American Advocate of Christian Unity* (Nashville, Disciples of Christ Historical Society, 1954, pp. xvi, 245), *passim.*

ized into churches, with Stone as their acknowledged leader. He was an ardent evangelist and carried his preaching into Ohio and Indiana.

Almost simultaneously but quite independently, out of revivals groups calling themselves Christian emerged in New England and in Virginia and North Carolina.[186]

Not far from the same time Alexander Campbell was becoming the leader of a similar movement.[187] Thomas Campbell, father of Alexander, was a Presbyterian minister, born in Ireland of Scottish ancestry, and had been in contact with Rowland Hill and James Haldane. In 1807 he came to the United States in search of health and wider opportunities and made his centre at Washington, Pennsylvania. In 1809, without expressly withdrawing from the Presbyterians, he and some of his hearers formed the Christian Association of Washington with the maxim: "Where the Scriptures speak, we speak. Where the Scriptures are silent, we are silent." Before joining his father in America, Alexander Campbell had several months in the University of Glasgow. While there he came in touch with the Haldane movement and with the ideas of Glas and Sandeman. He also read *The Marrow of Modern Divinity*. In 1809, when twenty-one years of age, he joined his father in Pennsylvania. He had an eager mind, read widely, possessed gifts of leadership, and soon was participating in what his father had begun. He sought to share in what he called a new Reformation. The Campbells organized a church distinct from the Presbyterians and in it Alexander was ordained. He and his father became convinced that infant baptism was un-Scriptural and they and their wives were immersed by a Baptist preacher. For a time they coöperated with the Baptists but after 1815 broke with them. Eventually Alexander Campbell's followers took the name Disciples of Christ. In a later volume we will see the fashion in which they and Stone's movement coalesced.

Another denomination coming out of the revivals was the Cumberland Presbyterians.[188] Its first presbytery was organized in 1810 in the Cumberland country in Kentucky and Tennessee. The separation from the mother body came partly because of the unwillingness of the latter to waive certain educational requirements for ordination of young men who had come up through the revivals and who had not had as much formal training as was customarily required. It came also because of the rejection of the doctrine of predestination, for in the revivals the clergy of the new body in urging their hearers to repent were assuming that all had the ability to do so.

186 Ware, *op. cit.*, pp. 154–156.

187 Benjamin Lyon Smith, *Alexander Campbell* (St. Louis, The Bethany Press, 1930, pp. 399), *passim;* Winfred Ernest Garrison, *Religion Follows the Frontier: A History of the Disciples of Christ* (New York, Harper & Brothers, 1931, pp. xiv, 317), pp. 1–128.

188 Robert V. Foster, *A Sketch of the History of the Cumberland Presbyterian Church* in *The American Church History Series*, Vol. XI, pp. 257–309.

Two of the new denominations did not emerge from the revivals. They were the Universalists and the Unitarians.

In 1790 an association of Universalist churches was formed in Philadelphia and in 1793 a convention for the New England churches was held. In 1803 a convention adopted a statement of beliefs. The most eminent early leader was Hosea Ballou (1771–1852), a New Englander.[189] The movement was strongest in New England but was never more than a small minority.

Although also never more than a minority, the Unitarians were much more prominent and among their members counted many eminent in various walks of life.[190] The movement arose out of the Congregational churches in and around Boston. It was influenced by similar currents in England and was partly a protest against the Great Awakening and had tendencies toward Arminianism and Socinianism. Early representatives of the trend were Charles Chauncy (1705–1787), eminent pastor of the First Church of Boston, and Jonathan Mayhew (1720–1766), scion of a long line of missionaries to the Indians and pastor in Boston. In 1775 the oldest congregation of the Church of England in New England, King's Chapel, Boston, formally disavowed belief in the Trinity. In 1805 a man of pronounced anti-Trinitarian views was appointed to the professorship of divinity in Harvard. The outstanding spokesman was the saintly William Ellery Channing (1780–1842), a pastor in Boston.[191] It was he who in 1815 accepted the name Unitarian for the movement.

The most striking developments in theology in the United States before 1815 were in New England. Here was what was then the largest and most nearly compact religious body in the new nation, the Congregationalists. It had a tradition of learning and most of its ministers were educated in Harvard or Yale, the oldest and the third oldest college in the country. The theological background was what is usually called Calvinistic: the Westminster Confession was standard. The quarter-century from 1789 to 1815 saw an important stage in the development of what was usually termed New England theology.[192] The distinctive features are generally said to have begun with Jonathan Edwards. His preaching and writing and his share in the Great Awakening were a profound stimulus to thought. On the one hand were some who were sharply critical of Edwards, among them Charles Chauncy and the movement which

[189] Richard Eddy, *History of Universalism* in *The American Church History Series*, Vol. X, pp. 251–293.

[190] Joseph Henry Allen, *A History of the Unitarians . . . in the United States* in *The American Church History Series*, Vol. X, pp. 1–246; George Willis Cooke, *Unitarianism in America* (Boston, American Unitarian Association, 1902, pp. xi, 463), pp. 1–123; Conrad White, *The Beginnings of Unitarianism in America* (Boston, The Beacon Press, 1955).

[191] John White Chadwick, *William Ellery Channing* (Boston, Houghton Mifflin Co., 1903), pp. xiv, 463), *passim*.

[192] George Nye Boardman, *A History of New England Theology* (New York, A. D. F. Randolph Co., 1899, pp. 314), pp. 1–220; F. H. Foster, *A Genetic History of New England Theology* (The University of Chicago Press, 1907, pp. xv, 568).

developed into Unitarianism. On the other hand were those who either carried further some aspects of Edwards' teaching or were stimulated by it to fresh creativity. Among them was Samuel Hopkins (1721–1803), a younger friend of Edwards and like him a graduate of Yale. His writings gave rise to a school of thought known as Hopkinsianism.[193] Another was Timothy Dwight, a grandson of Edwards. As president of Yale he exerted a wide influence.[194] Still another was Nathanael Emmons (1745–1840), also a Yale graduate and for more than fifty years pastor in Franklin, Massachusetts. He developed one phase of Hopkinsianism and in connexion with his parish trained several scores of ministers.[195] These three, together with those who revered them, were committed to the revivals.

In 1808 Andover Theological Seminary was founded in protest against the Unitarianism of Harvard. In it joined the Hopkinsians and those who held more nearly to the historic Calvinism. It and the Yale Divinity School, begun in 1822, were centres in further developments in the New England theology of which we are to hear in a later volume.

Both in New England and elsewhere among an increasing proportion of Christians in the United States the movement of thought was away from the Augustinian-Calvinistic theology that had prevailed in most of the churches. It was seen in Universalist and Unitarian circles, but they remained small minorities. For the majority it was an outgrowth of the revivals. Whether it was by Hopkins, Dwight, or Emmons, or by such former Presbyterians as Stone and Campbell, or by Otterbein with his Reformed background, the traditional doctrine of predestination was being modified or repudiated to make room for the appeal to all men to repent and believe. Some still clung to the inherited theology and defended it, but the drift was away from them. In this the Methodists and many of the Baptists joined.

As on the Continent of Europe and on the British Isles from the Pietist and Evangelical awakenings, so in the United States from the revivals springing from these traditions issued efforts not only to extend the faith in the domestic scene but also to plant it in other lands. They began slightly later than in Great Britain. In 1810 there came into being the American Board of Commissioners for Foreign Missions.[196] The stimulus which brought it to birth was from a group led by Samuel J. Mills, Jr., who had come out of a Hopkinsian parsonage, who in his undergraduate days at Williams College had been the

193 *The Works of Samuel Hopkins* (Boston, Doctrinal Tract and Book Society, 3 vols., 1854).

194 Timothy Dwight, *Theology, Explained and Defended* (Middletown, Conn., Clark & Lyman, 5 vols., 1818–1819); Charles E. Cunningham, *Timothy Dwight* (New York, The Macmillan Co., 1942, pp. viii, 403).

195 *The Works of Nathanael Emmons* (Boston, Congregational Board of Publication, 6 vols., 1860–1863).

196 Joseph Tracy, *History of the American Board of Commissioners for Foreign Missions* (New York, M. W. Dodd, 2nd ed., 1842, pp. viii, 452), pp. 25 ff.

nucleus of a society called the Brethren which was pledged "to effect in the persons of its members a mission or missions to the heathen," and who with his fellows had come as students to Andover Theological Seminary.[197] In Andover the Brethren were joined by Adoniram Judson.[198] Judson was in the first party of missionaries sent by the new organization. Before it had reached India, its destination, Judson and another, Luther Rice, had become Baptists. Judson went as a pioneer to Burma, and Rice returned to the United States to organize the Baptists to support him. From this arose, as we have seen, in 1814 the General Missionary Convention of the Baptist Denomination in the United States of America for Foreign Missions.[199] In 1816 the American Bible Society was founded. In its inception Mills had a share. It had been preceded by local and state Bible societies.[200] Not long after 1815 a number of other missionary societies sprang up, organized on a national scale.

As with missionary societies on a national scale, so in reform movements, the revivals in the United States were a little later in stimulating concerted action than were those in the British Isles. It was not until after 1815 that the antislavery movement was well under way. Yet in the 1770's Samuel Hopkins and many Quakers came out against slavery, and in the 1790's Methodist preachers were almost unanimously opposed to it. Some Presbyterians who were active in the awakenings and a number of Baptists freed their slaves, as did Barton W. Stone. Several leading Unitarians, among them William E. Channing, were outspoken in their opposition to slavery.[201] Before 1815 the temperance movement was in its early stages and in 1814 and 1815 peace societies were organized.[202]

Protestantism and especially the revivals had an important share in stimulating the growth of democracy in the United States. While in the Thirteen Colonies strong trends towards democracy had existed, largely the fruit of Puritanism and other forms of radical Protestantism, in 1789 remnants of the aristocratic structure of society survived. Stressing as they did the salvation of the common man and in most churches the participation of the rank and file of the laity in the government of the local congregations and the central structures, the revivals furthered democratic ideals and helped to train many in democratic procedures. As a result, in contrast with what was taking place on

[197] Gardiner Spring, *Memoirs of the Rev. Samuel J. Mills* (New York, The New York Evangelical Missionary Society, 1820, pp. 247), *passim*.
[198] Stacy R. Warburton, *Eastward: The Story of Adoniram Judson* (New York, Round Table Press, 1937, pp. xi, 240), *passim*.
[199] William Gammell, *A History of American Baptist Missions in Asia, Africa, Europe, and North America* (Boston, Gould, Kendall and Lincoln, 1849, pp. xii, 359), pp. 17 ff.
[200] Henry Otis Dwight, *The Centennial History of the American Bible Society* (New York, The Macmillan Co., 2 vols., 1916), Vol. I, pp. 15 ff.
[201] For detailed references see Latourette, *A History of the Expansion of Christianity*, Vol. IV, pp. 346–348.
[202] For detailed references see *ibid.*, Vol. I, pp. 393, 394, 397, 398.

the Continent of Europe, the progress towards democracy, as, for example, in the national election of 1800, was achieved with little or no violence.

THE STORM AND PROTESTANTISM: IN CANADA

As a result of the American Revolution the Protestant population was growing in what in the next century was to become the Dominion of Canada. Even before that event there had been Protestants in Nova Scotia. They were largely from New England and were mostly Congregationalists and Baptists. With the Revolution many of those loyal to Britain took refuge in Nova Scotia. For lack of clergy Congregationalism had declined, but in 1776 a revival sprang up through the preaching of Henry Alline, who had been born in Rhode Island and as a boy had been brought to Nova Scotia by his parents. After his death the movement continued. It encouraged the growth of Baptist churches.[203] The spread of the Church of England in Nova Scotia was furthered by missionaries of the Society for the Propagation of the Gospel, by the establishment of that church by the first colonial assembly (1758), and by the coming of many Loyalists. In 1787 a bishop was consecrated for Nova Scotia with jurisdiction as well over Bermuda, Newfoundland, New Brunswick, Prince Edward Island, and what were then known as Upper and Lower Canada, the later provinces of Ontario and Quebec. In New Brunswick the first extensive settlements were by Loyalists, chiefly Anglicans.[204] Both the Society for the Propagation of the Gospel in Foreign Parts and the Society for Promoting Christian Knowledge helped to nourish the Church of England in Canada.[205] The Presbytery of Nova Scotia was formed in 1817, chiefly by ministers of the Secession Churches of Scotland. The following year the Presbytery of Canada was constituted for Upper and Lower Canada. Ministers, largely from churches dissenting from the Church of Scotland, came from Scotland and the United States. The Dutch Reformed Church of the United States sent missionaries into Upper Canada. The Government gave grants of land for the support of "Protestant clergy" in Upper Canada, and to these both Anglicans and Presbyterians laid claim.[206] Methodism was planted in Canada at the outset chiefly by preachers from the United States. They laboured in Nova Scotia and in Upper and Lower Canada. During the war between the United States and Great Britain which broke out in 1812, preachers from the United States were not allowed in Canada. Preachers arrived from Britain. Friction developed,

---

[203] Maurice W. Armstrong, *The Great Awakening in Nova Scotia, 1776–1809* (Hartford, American Society of Church History, 1948, pp. x, 141), *passim*.

[204] Arthur Wentworth Eaton, *The Church of England in Nova Scotia and the Tory Clergy of the Revolution* (New York, Thomas Whittaker, 1891, pp. xiv, 320), *passim*.

[205] For pertinent literature see the footnotes in Latourette, *op. cit.*, Vol. V, pp. 16, 17.

[206] William Gregg, *History of the Presbyterian Church in the Dominion of Canada* (Toronto, Presbyterian Printing and Publishing Co., 1885, pp. 646), pp. 17, 136, 143 ff.; Latourette, *op. cit.*, Vol. V, p. 18.

mainly after the war, between the representatives of the two kinds of Methodism. Not until later was it resolved.[207]

THE STORM AND PROTESTANTISM:
PROGRESS TOWARDS CHRISTIAN UNITY IN ACTION

The years of storm witnessed efforts to bring to realization the dreams of Christian unity. Most of them were from the awakenings of the period and were more for unity in common action than for the organic union of churches. As yet they engaged only small minorities of Protestants, but they were precursors of more extensive movements. One aspect was the employment by the Society for Promoting Christian Knowledge and the Church Missionary Society, both of them British by nationality and Anglican in their constituencies, of Lutheran missionaries trained on the Continent in Pietist schools.[208] Another was in the various organizations in England and the United States in which Evangelicals of more than one denomination coöperated. Such were the London Missionary Society, the American Board of Commissioners for Foreign Missions (in which for several years Congregationalists, Presbyterians, Dutch Reformed, and some Lutherans collaborated), the British and Foreign Bible Society, and the American Bible Society. The Plan of Union, begun in 1801, by which Congregationalists and Presbyterians joined forces in meeting the challenge of the frontier, issued in churches which for a time had features of both denominations. The frontier movements calling themselves Christians and Disciples of Christ were, as we have seen, fresh approaches to unity.[209] In its first decade (1804–1814) the British and Foreign Bible Society through its agents established affiliated societies in several European countries among Lutherans, Reformed, Russian and Greek Orthodox, and had friendly relations with ecclesiastics and Patriarchs of some of the Eastern Churches. In 1805 William Carey proposed that a conference "of Christians of all denominations" be convened in Capetown in 1810 to consider common problems and that similar conferences be held every ten years. He thus anticipated what was to be achieved late in the nineteenth and in the fore part of the twentieth century.[210]

THE STORM AND PROTESTANTISM: PROGRESS IN GEOGRAPHIC EXPANSION

While in the years of storm the geographic expansion of the Roman Catholic Church, so striking since the fifteenth century, was marking time and here and there receding, Protestantism was planted in new areas and was advancing in some where it was already present. It was thus continuing an expansion which

---

[207] Barclay, *History of Methodist Missions,* Vol. I, pp. 166–190; J. E. Sanderson, *The First Century of Methodism in Canada* (Toronto, William Briggs, 2 vols., 1908), Vol. I, pp. 27–38, 57, 58, 89, 96, 97.

[208] Sykes in Rouse and Neill, *A History of the Ecumenical Movement,* p. 161.

[209] Yoder in Rouse and Neill, *op. cit.,* pp. 233, 235.

[210] Rouse in Rouse and Neill, *op. cit.,* pp. 311, 312.

in the nineteenth and twentieth centuries was to become phenomenal and was to make it world-wide. That expansion was partly by the migration of Protestant peoples and the missions which held them to the faith and partly through missions among non-Christian peoples. Then as later it was chiefly but by no means entirely from the British Isles and the United States. Through the moving frontier and the revivals Protestantism was stretching westward in the United States. Through immigration, partly of Loyalists from the young United States, it was being planted in Canada. By chaplains among the unpromising convict material it was taking root in Australia. Missions among non-Christians were introducing it for the first time or were increasing it among the Negroes and Indians of the United States and the Negroes of the West Indies, here and there along the West coast of Africa and in South Africa, in parts of India, and in Burma, China, and some of the islands of the Pacific. In Asia, Africa, and the islands of the Pacific Protestants were still infinitesimal minorities, but that they appeared at all while the traditional Christendom was being so badly shaken was striking evidence of vitality.

THE STORM AND THE EASTERN CHURCHES

Except for Russia and Egypt, the Eastern Churches were in lands so much on the periphery of the storm that at the time they were affected little if at all. Only later, when the revolutionary forces operating in Western Christendom spread outward, did they feel the full effects. In spite of the Napoleonic invasion, there seems to be no evidence that the Coptic Church was seriously disturbed. The Orthodox Churches in Greece and the Balkans continued to suffer from evils brought by the Turkish rule, chiefly the ones of which we have already spoken, namely, the corruption of the higher. clergy through what amounted to the purchase of their offices and the rule of the Phanariots. Moreover, the metropolitans tended to spend their time in Constantinople rather than in their dioceses. However, by 1815 some improvement was observed.[211]

In Russia the period of the storm was marked by important developments. Some were indigenous and others came from Western Europe. In the second and third partition of Poland Russia recovered most of the territory there which had once been hers. It contained many former Orthodox who under a shift to Polish rule a little over two centuries earlier had become Roman Catholic Uniates. In 1794 permission was given them to return to the Orthodox fold and about two million of them did so.[212] Platon, a very able Metropolitan of Moscow, worked out a compromise which enabled Old Believers to become communicants of the established church while adhering to the rites which had been

[211] Papadopoullos, *Studies and Documents Relating to the History of the Greek Church and People under Turkish Domination*, pp. 59, 131, 147, 157.
[212] Frere, *Links in the Chain of Russian Church History*, p. 162.

the ostensible reason for their dissent.[213] In the anti-French reaction which followed the invasion by Napoleon many Russians repudiated the atheism and materialism which were associated with the Revolution. In doing so some renewed their loyalty to Orthodoxy as part of the Russian tradition.[214] Others turned to the Pietism of the West. Arndt's *True Christianity* had a wide circulation.[215] Prince Golytsyn, Procurator of the Holy Synod, converted through Pietist influences, encouraged the founding of the Russian Bible Society (1813) and became its first president. Philaret Drozdov (1783–1867), a kind of successor to Platon, furthered the translation of the Bible into the vernacular.[216] He read Swedenborg and was much impressed by him. Writings of Jung-Stilling which forecast the early end of the world were put into Russian and were popular in some circles.[217] The colonies of Protestants from Western Europe, encouraged for economic reasons, continued their quiet way and exerted an unspectacular influence.

To the quickening of religious life Tsar Alexander I (1777–1825) gave a great impetus. Reared in the court of Catherine II, he had imbibed much of the religious scepticism of that circle and also some of the ideals which went into the French Revolution. Well-meaning, egotistic, he came to the throne in 1801 with all the ardour of youth and sought to be the benefactor of his people and of mankind. In his entourage were deeply religious men who had been impressed by Protestant mystics of the West. Through them in 1812 Alexander had a kind of conversion and aided projects for furthering Christianity. In 1815 he met Madame de Krüdener, of the Baltic nobility. After a varied life, much of it unhappy, in literary and aristocratic circles in many places in Europe, through contact with the Moravians in her home city, Riga, she had experienced a sudden conversion. Later she had friendships with several of the Pietists and mystics of her day, among them Jung-Stilling. She is said, although on doubtful authority, to have been the immediate inspiration of the Holy Alliance in which, at the instance of Alexander, he and the rulers of Prussia and Austria agreed (September, 1815), to "take as their sole guide the precepts of that Holy Religion, namely the precepts of justice, Christian charity, and peace." [218]

Added to the fresh surge of life in the Christianity of Russia was the monastic revival stimulated by Païsius Velichkovski. It was aided by a Slavonic translation, in 1793, of the *Philokalia,* an anthology designed to further the "Jesus

[213] *Ibid.,* p. 170.
[214] *Ibid.,* p. 171.
[215] Zenkovsky, *A History of Russian Philosophy,* Vol. I, p. 104.
[216] Frere, *op. cit.,* pp. 170, 171.
[217] Ernst Benz, editor, *Die Ostkirche und die russische Christenheit* (Tübingen, Fursche-Verlag, 1949, pp. 175), pp. 129, 130.
[218] Ernest John Knapton, *The Lady of the Holy Alliance* (Columbia University Press, 1939, pp. ix, 262), *passim,* especially pp. 88, 89, 147 ff.

prayer" as embodied in hesychasm. One form of the "Jesus prayer" was "Lord Jesus Christ, have mercy upon me"; another was "Lord Jesus Christ, Son of the living God, have mercy on me, a sinner." Ideally it was to be repeated unceasingly. In the hesychast discipline it was to be timed with breathing or the beating of the heart.[219]

The eastward spread of the Russian Orthodox Church across northern Asia continued. Begun centuries earlier, by 1789 it had reached the Pacific and Kamchatka. Now it was carried across Bering Strait into North America. In 1794 what seems to have been the first mission to Alaska arrived on Kodiak Island.[220]

BY WAY OF SUMMARY

Can we trace any main trends through the crowded and stormy years which we have attempted to cover in this chapter? To essay it may lead to oversimplification. Even what we have given is at best a summary, and a summary which has, perforce, left out many significant details and even some important phases. Yet it may be of assistance to endeavour to suggest characteristics and trends that have a bearing on the story which these volumes are seeking to unfold.

The distinguishing feature of the years was revolution. That the revolution had its centre and its chief immediate effects among the peoples of Western Christendom is of high importance not only for these years but also for the nineteenth and twentieth centuries. Such questions emerge as to what extent if at all Christianity was responsible for it, why, if Christianity is either one cause or a major cause, it operated in this fashion here rather than in Eastern Christendom, and the still deeper question of how the Gospel functions in individual lives and in civilization. From what we have recorded in the preceding pages it seems clear that Christianity was at least one source of the revolution. It is also a defensible hypothesis that the revolution developed in Western rather than Eastern Christendom because in the former, for reasons growing out of history, Christianity was less obstructed by political and religious factors than in the latter.

The revolution really dated from the Renaissance and the Protestant Reformation. Possibly it had begun earlier. In the forms which were dominant from 1789 to 1815 it had its foreshadowings in the Puritan Revolution in the British Isles in the seventeenth century and its immediate preliminaries in the American Revolution of the fourth quarter of the eighteenth century. But the years 1789–1815 saw only one stage.

[219] Fedetov, *A Treasury of Russian Spirituality*, p. 281; *Writings from the Philokalia on Prayer of the Heart*, translated by E. Kadloubovsky and G. E. H. Palmer (London, Faber & Faber, 1951, pp. 420), *passim*.

[220] Hubert Howe Bancroft, *History of Alaska, 1730–1885* (San Francisco, A. L. Bancroft Co., 1886, pp. xxxviii, 775), pp. 303, 304, 352, 699.

The revolution had many facets and eventually affected all aspects of civilization. They were in the realms of ideas, politics, religion, industry, transportation, agriculture, and economic theory, and in the accompanying changes in social structure. They included the widening of men's horizons on the age of the earth, on the structure of matter, and on the dimensions of the universe in which man finds himself. They led to a progressive emancipation of man's mind and included a humanitarian concern for the welfare of man and hope for improvements in that welfare. In these particular years the forms which the revolution assumed were chiefly political and into them entered philosophical and political theories.

In the quarter century which is the theme of this chapter the revolution became stormy. The storm had its chief centre in France, in the eighteenth century the most powerful of the states of Western Europe. From there it spread, in its latter phases through the ambition and genius of Napoleon. As was to be expected, its most profound effects were in France and her immediate neighbours. Yet it had repercussions in most of Christendom, including the New World.

Although the revolution had Christianity as one of its sources, some of its manifestations were militantly anti-Christian: they were a violent continuation of some of the more peaceful trends of the Enlightenment and its associated Deism and rationalism.

The years brought early steps towards what was a new phenomenon in history, the secular state. In the countries most affected a partial separation of Church and state followed. Attempts were made to have the state take over such functions as marriage and education and to divorce them from religion. Here was a movement which in the next two centuries was to become world-wide.

Of the major forms of Christianity from 1789 to 1815 the Roman Catholic Church suffered the most acutely from the revolution. At first the results appeared to be purely destructive. In France non-Christian cults were officially set up. In France and in several other countries the Church was placed under a stricter control by the state than had hitherto been true, even during the height of Church-state conflicts of the Middle Ages—although not much if any more than had been the case after the Reformation in some of the predominantly Protestant lands. The ecclesiastical states of Germany were destroyed. Two successive Popes were kept in confinement and for a time the Papal States were abolished. Many monasteries were dissolved.

Yet the effects were not wholly adverse. Indeed, the Roman Catholic Church was freed from some age-long encumbrances. Except for a brief renewal after 1815, the tradition had been extinguished which filled the episcopal sees in France with the younger sons of the nobility, placed a gulf between the bishops and the parish priests, and in the higher echelons of the clergy made for luxury, absenteeism, and corruption. The dissolution of the monasteries was not a total loss: in some of them monastic ideals had been honoured more in the breach than by observance. Gallicanism, Febronianism, and Josephism had been either destroyed or weakened. The changes paved the way for an augmented exercise of Papal powers in the entire Roman Catholic Church and gave opportunity for the Papacy to be more a religious and less a political institution. The termination of Papal temporal power in the loss of the Papal States, at the time temporary but ultimately reducing them to a symbolic few acres, provided opportunity for the enhancement of the Pope's spiritual and moral functions. Gone were the days which made possible an Alexander VI. Although not by its own choice, the Roman Catholic Church was being emancipated from that dependence on a form of power which was contrary to the Gospel but which the collapse of the Roman Empire more than a thousand years earlier had seemed to make necessary. It must now rely more on what the apostle had called the weakness of God which had been seen in the cross.

In the Roman Catholic Church before 1815 evidences of continuing and even enhanced vigour were beginning to be seen. The Society of Jesus was revived. New congregations, ever an indication of vitality and devotion, were appearing. Significantly, they were chiefly for the conduct of schools. Here was promise of rearing the oncoming generations in the faith and, through action, of meeting the spirit of the new day, with its emphasis on this-worldly service. Conversions were recorded from the ranks of those who were either lukewarm or had given up the faith. The popularity of Chateaubriand's *Génie du Christianisme*, the dimensions of which would discourage the casual reader and which was the work of one who, reared in the faith, had all but abandoned it for the current Enlightenment and then had come back to it, was an indication of a reaction towards the Roman Catholic Church. Less spectacular but probably more significant was the loyalty of millions of humble folk. Their adherence in years of storm was evidence that although for many, perhaps the majority, the Christianity of Europe was superficial, for at least a minority the faith was cherished from deep conviction.

During the years covered by this chapter Protestantism suffered far less than did Roman Catholicism. Because of the geographic location of its chief centres it was spared the full impact of the revolution. Yet it was far from escaping. Here and there, as in France, the Netherlands, Switzerland, and much of Germany, it was deeply affected. The indirect attack of Deism and the more pronounced onslaughts of such popularizers as Thomas Paine alienated some from the faith and stimulated others to more active support.

Within Protestantism the tide of awakenings which had begun in the seventeenth century and which, indeed, in one form or another had been continuous since the Reformation, was mounting. The awakenings took various forms, but in general they had a family likeness and might be covered by the inclusive term of Pietism or Evangelicalism. They stressed personal repentance and commitment, conscious conversion, and a life showing the fruit of the Spirit. As yet they moulded only minorities, but the minorities were growing.

Either as the major or as a minor factor the Pietist and Evangelical awakenings contributed to several movements. They entered into the chief formulations of philosophy and theology which arose in this period. While Kant was not primarily their product, he was born and reared and spent his life in Königsberg. Königsberg was a strong Pietist centre and in his youth he was under marked Pietist influences. How far Hegel and Schelling were affected by the Pietism of their native Württemberg, which still lingered in Tübingen during their student days, would be difficult to determine. It may have been more by reaction against it than from any positive sympathy for it. Yet Hegel especially maintained a strong interest in Jesus and Christianity and, far from repudiating either, believed that he had attained to a better appreciation of both and to a more intelligent loyalty to them than prevailed in Pietist or orthodox circles. Schleiermacher, who before 1815 had begun the formulation of Christian faith and experience which was to make him the most widely influential Christian theologian emerging in this period from any branch of the Church, was in many respects a child of Pietism. In so many countries Pietism and Evangelicalism promoted schools that advances in education can be said to have been a characteristic fruit. In general the schools were for the underprivileged. Experiments in education were stimulated. The circulation of the Bible and the creation and distribution of other Christian literature were common to all forms of the awakenings. In Pietism and Evangelicalism what in the broadest sense of the term could be called moral and social reform was almost universal. It had varied manifestations. In some circles it was in small, tightly knit communities which attempted to govern all aspects of their life by Christian principles. In many the awakenings made for sobriety, industry, thrift, and generous giving. Here and there were beginnings of the campaigns for temperance in the use of alcoholic beverages which in the nineteenth century were to assume major proportions. In Britain and the United States, where the slave trade and Negro slavery were large problems, Evangelicals and kindred groups, notably the Quakers, were active in efforts against them. In several countries the awakenings either directly or indirectly furthered democracy. Almost all the awakenings gave rise to efforts to spread the Christian faith at home, and out of several of them sprang movements to take the faith to other countries. Always they led to a deepened devotional life. From them were born new hymns: as was true of many other awakenings in other centuries, especially but not exclusively in Protestantism, they found expression in song.

The awakenings profoundly modified Protestantism. They were true to the genius of that branch of the faith: more than the state churches they carried to its logical application the central emphasis of Protestantism. They stressed justification by faith, with the experience of the conscious new birth which follows from faith. Usually they had in them a strong lay element, presumably an application of a corollary of justification by faith, the priesthood of all believers. While on the Continent and in the British Isles those whom they won continued to be minorities, in the United States eventually, at least in theory, the majority of church members acceded to the principles which they embodied: in the broad sense of that term the majority of Protestants in the United States were in the Puritan, Pietist, or Evangelical tradition. Moreover, most of the Protestant enterprises which sought to hold to the faith the populations of the new sections in the United States and of the other new nations which in the nineteenth and twentieth centuries arose from the migrations of European stock were staffed and supported by those of that tradition. This also was true of most of the missions which planted the Protestant faith throughout the world outside the Occident. As a result, increasingly Protestantism took on the complexion of its Pietist-Evangelical strain. Mainly through that strain came the beginnings and the leadership of the Ecumenical Movement which in the nineteenth and twentieth centuries swelled so greatly.

Of the Eastern Churches, by 1815 only that in Russia had begun seriously to feel the impact of the revolution, which, as we have repeatedly seen, stemmed from Western and not from Eastern Christendom. The Russian Orthodox Church was tied hand and foot to the state. Dissenting indigenous groups had appeared before 1789. By 1815 the Pietist-Evangelical movements were beginning to have some repercussions, but mainly in the upper levels of society.

CHAPTER V

Revolution Mounts and Proliferates:
The Nineteenth-Century Setting

THE passing of the storm of the French Revolution and the wars of Napoleon did not mean the end of revolution. In the century which followed 1815 revolution mounted and became more complex. Not until 1914 did it again break out as tempestuously as it had in the French Revolution and the Napoleonic era. Then and in the following decades it was to be more widely and profoundly shattering than it had been even in the quarter-century after 1789. Politically the nineteenth century—if we give as boundaries for that period the years 1815 and 1914—was less marked by violence than its predecessors and successors. No war engulfed all Europe. Wars there were, but they were localized and for the most part brief. Yet the revolution became more varied and the several aspects which it had begun to display before 1815 were enlarged and intensified. The threat and the challenge to Christianity were, accordingly, heightened.

WESTERN CHRISTIANITY THE POSSIBLE DETERMINATIVE
SOURCE OF REVOLUTION

As in its earlier stages, the revolution developed in Western Christendom and among the peoples of Western Europe, whether they were in Western Europe itself or in the new nations arising out of the migrations from that part of the world. It was in Western Christendom that it had its most pronounced immediate effects. From Western Christendom it began that spread to Eastern Christendom and the rest of the world which by 1914 was to have startling effects and after that year was to involve and engulf all mankind. In the second half of the twentieth century its global manifestations seemed only to have begun.

As earlier, we must ask what if any causal connexion existed between the rise and development of the revolution among Western Europeans and the fact that Western Europeans constituted Western Christendom. Was Christianity the determinative cause? If so, why at the outset did the revolution appear only in Western Christendom and not as well and simultaneously in Eastern Christendom? Moreover, is it significant that most of the ideas and processes issuing in the revolution had their inception among peoples and individuals which were under strong Protestant rather than Roman Catholic influence and that their most explosive although not always their most permeating effects were in nations where the Roman Catholic Church and the Eastern Churches or one or another of the non-Christian faiths were the dominant expressions of religion?

That Christianity was an exciting factor in the revolution seems probable. To be sure, Western Europe was an heir of pre-Christian Græco-Roman civilization as well as of Christianity. But it was by no means the sole heir. In the seventh and eighth centuries, through the Arab conquests which it had inspired, Islam had become the master in about half of what had once been the Roman Empire and so was also heir of Greece and Rome. In the early centuries of their mastery the Moslem Arabs developed a high civilization. But they did that in regions where Christians were still large minorities. In time Arab culture produced less and less that was new and became sterile. It seems to be more than a coincidence that the progress of sterility went hand in hand with the decline in numbers of the Christians in Arab lands and the retreat of the Christians into encysted communities which sought by tenacious opposition to change to preserve their faith. It may well be that in the combination of the Greek and Roman heritage with Christianity lies the secret of the revolutionary character of Western European civilization and that the latter rather than the former was the determinative factor.

Here, as we have suggested, may be the reasons why the revolution arose in Western rather than Eastern Christendom. From the seventh century on, most of the Eastern Churches were on the defensive against Islam and in that defense sought first of all to conserve the deposit which they inherited from the past. Moreover, the strongest of them was in the Byzantine realms. There the tradition persisted from pre-Christian days of the domination by the state of religion and the institutions of religion. Consequently Christianity had less freedom than in the West, where the Roman Empire early disintegrated and was not immediately followed by strong civil governments. In the Eastern Churches, especially those looking to Constantinople as their centre, the more earnest Christians tended to retreat from activism into monasteries, to contemplation, and to interior prayer: in the Russian Orthodox Church the socially passive kenotic temper had more vitality than did efforts to mould society. In Western Europe, in contrast, in the ages of disorder which followed the collapse of the Roman Empire, the Church, led by men who were inspired by its faith, attempted to bring order in an anarchic society. Through the Church, efforts, partly but far from entirely successful, were persistently made to shape all aspects of civilization—religious, political, economic, intellectual, and artistic.

Perhaps here is the chief source of the revolutionary dynamism in Western civilization.

PROTESTANTISM ESPECIALLY A SOURCE OF REVOLUTION

Here, too, may be a reason why the revolution stemmed more from the Protestant than the Roman Catholic form of Christianity. In endeavouring to permeate all of the life of Western Europe with the Christian faith the Roman Catholic Church sought to control it. In doing so it gradually erected a great structure and continued much of the imperial spirit of *Romanitas*. This made the Roman Catholic Church resistant to change. To be sure, it contained a vitality which before the mid-twentieth century had enabled it to stage an amazing recovery from the blows dealt it in the storm of the French Revolution and Napoleon. Yet it had less flexibility and freedom than Protestantism and from it came less stimulus to strikingly fresh ideas. When fresh ideas emerged, the revolutions to which they gave rise met more resistance than in Protestantism and hence tended to be more explosive. The greater flexibility of Protestantism permitted freer course to the dynamic inherent in the Gospel than did any other major form of the faith.[1]

Moreover, the contributions to the revolution were more from the Puritan-Pietist-Evangelical strains of Protestantism than from the Protestantism which was not moulded by them. That may have been because they were more vigorous and put less emphasis upon unchanging dogma. It may also have been because in them was more of the individualism arising from the response of each believer in faith to the Gospel.

Here was a grave danger. With its dynamism, individualism, and weakness of institutionalized control, Protestantism, and especially Protestantism of the Puritan-Pietist-Evangelical traditions, was a source of some movements which so denied or distorted the Gospel or so mixed it with elements contrary to the Gospel that they became a threat to Christianity and a secularizing menace not only to Christianity but also to all religion.

Yet the Protestant could reply that this was the risk God took in the seeming weakness of the incarnation and in the fashion in which He permitted men to nail His Son to a Roman cross. Seeking to create sons and not robots, He gave men a degree of free will. In sending His Son in what to men looked like weakness He respected that freedom, even though Christ came to what appeared to be defeat in a futile death. Yet with a great burst of inspired insight the Apostle

---

[1] See an essay, Ernst Troeltsch, *Protestantism and Progress. A Historical Study of the Relation of Protestantism to the Modern World*, translated by W. Montgomery (London, Williams & Norgate, 1912, pp. xi, 210). For the thesis that Protestantism, especially in its Reformed tradition, had a much larger share than Roman Catholicism in the observational and experimental sciences, see R. Hooykaas, *Science and Reformation*, in *Cahiers d'Histoire Mondiale* (Neuchatel, Éditions de la Baconnière), Vol. III (1956), pp. 109–141.

declared that in this the foolishness of God was wiser than men and the weakness of God was stronger than men. Has Protestantism, then, been more nearly true to the genius of the Gospel than have the other two great wings of Christianity?

Here are basic questions of history. Has the event proved the accuracy of the Apostle's affirmation? With all of its departures from the Gospel has Protestantism been more loyal than have the Roman Catholic Church and the Eastern Churches? Upon these questions the story to which we have set ourselves may shed some light.

As we suggested in the last chapter, the revolution of which Christianity appears to have been at least one of the sources and in the midst of which Christianity lived its life in the nineteenth and twentieth centuries was very complex. It took many forms. It was in part political; it was in part social; to no small degree it was intellectual; its economic phases were conspicuous; it had striking religious and moral aspects. As time passed the revolution proliferated and developed more and more phases. As we seek to describe it, in attempting to simplify the complex we will list and briefly describe the main aspects one by one. This is in spite of the fact that they interacted and in reality were inseparable. The order chosen is somewhat arbitrary: in it is no attempt to find a sequence inherent in the events.

The Revolution: The Political Phases

Perhaps it is just as well to begin with the political phases. Before 1815 they were the most spectacular. From time to time in the nineteenth century they again became prominent. Yet they were not accompanied by as much violence or by such extensive and prolonged wars as in the seventeenth and eighteenth centuries.

Into the political aspects of the revolution at least two factors entered. One was the continuation of the urge for democracy which had been potent in the major political revolutions of the preceding three centuries. Another was the closely related nationalism. Usually but not always the achievement of political unity through nationalism was accompanied and even aided by the adoption and development of democratic political institutions. In general nationalism was characterized by the ambition to expand, either at the expense of neighbours or in the building of a colonial empire overseas, and to grow in wealth and material power and prestige. As such it gave rise to wars.

In the political revolutions the role of Christianity was ambiguous. On the one hand it was less conspicuous than in the two and a half centuries which followed the Reformation: in no political upheaval was Christianity as obviously an inciting cause as in those in England in the seventeenth and America in the eighteenth century. Moreover, the trend of the revolutions was towards a secular state. More and more the Church was disestablished and the state took over functions, such as education and the control of marriage and the family, which had previously been under the Church. Much was made of the slogan "A free church in a free state." Each was ideally emancipated from the control of the other. In several countries the ideal was approximated. In the process Christianity appeared to be relegated to a progressively declining position and in some countries to be about to be bowed out. On the other hand the role of Christianity was still important. From it, as we have repeatedly said, came ideals and impulses which contributed to the rise and growth of democracy. The fact that they were less conspicuous does not necessarily mean that they were less potent. From men in whom Christian motives were prominent came at least some of the leaders in the march of democracy in Britain. From a sadly twisted misapprehension of Christianity arose the T'ai P'ing movement of the 1850's and 1860's, the first foreshadowing of the revolution which was to sweep across China late in the nineteenth and in the twentieth century. From Christianity, too, issued the anti-slavery movement which was prominent as a cause of the American Civil War (1861–1865).

The list of political revolutions which punctuated the nineteenth century is long. Here we can take the space merely to call attention to the more prominent which must figure in our story. Among them a place must certainly be given to those through which the Latin American peoples achieved their independence and embarked upon their experiments with democracy. They began in Haiti during the French Revolution and the Napoleonic Wars and continued intermittently until, in 1898, the last of the Latin American colonies, Cuba, was given its independence. The internal struggle for democracy persisted long after that date. On the Continent of Europe the first spectacular year was 1830, when the restored Bourbons were forced to give way to a more nearly democratic government under Louis Philippe as "King of the French." In 1830, too, Belgium achieved its independence. Liberal movements soon followed in Portugal and Spain and were accompanied by civil wars. In 1832 a notable Reform Act was enacted in Great Britain which was a step towards making Parliament more responsive to the will of the people. The year 1848 witnessed a striking set of explosions on the Continent of Europe. In France the "July monarchy" of Louis Philippe was followed by the Second Republic. In most of the rest of Western Europe that event was quickly succeeded either by violent revolts against the established order or by more peaceful steps towards governments representative of the majority. In England in 1848 the Chartist movement which demanded more of democracy in government reached a dramatic climax, but further legislation to broaden the franchise did not come until 1867. For a time after 1848 in several countries the tide of revolution ebbed. For example, in 1852 the Second Republic in France gave way to the Second Empire, with Louis Napoleon, nephew of Napoleon Bonaparte, as emperor. But the ebb was only a pause.

In the third quarter of the century nationalism was outstanding in the revolutionary tide. It saw the unification of Italy under a liberal monarchy. Chiefly through the efforts of Bismarck, Germany, with the exclusion of Austria, was united, with Prussia and its ruling house, the Hohenzollerns, as the controlling nucleus. The climax came in 1871, after a successful war with France, in the proclamation, in the Hall of Mirrors at Versailles, of the German Empire.

The defeat of France in 1870 precipitated the fall of Louis Napoleon and the Second Empire and brought about the inauguration in that country of the Third Republic.

Nationalism was growing elsewhere in Europe. In the course of the century it led to the independence of Greece and the emergence of other Balkan peoples from domination by the Ottoman Turks. By 1914 Rumania, Serbia, and Bulgaria had obtained their independence. In the process wars took place, among them that bearing the name of Crimea, in 1853–1856, the nearest approach in the century to a general European conflict.

The engagement of Russia in war with Japan in 1904–1905 led to what proved to be an abortive revolution in the tsar's realms.[2]

In general the political trend was towards a secular state in which the middle class was increasingly powerful but in which those in the social and economic scale below the middle class were beginning to have more voice. Particularly in lands where Roman Catholics were in the majority the movement towards a secular state led to conflict with the Church. Again and again monastic property was confiscated and attempts were made to reduce the role of the orders and congregations in the instruction of youth. The Jesuits especially were looked upon as enemies. In Protestant lands the conflict was generally not so acute, but the tendency to a secular state was no less strong. Everywhere in the former Christendom the trend was towards civil marriage and taking education out of the hands of the Church. To a greater or less extent instruction in religion was continued in the schools, but increasingly the latter were financed and directed by the government.

In political life the prevailing temper was one of optimism. The belief in progress, marked in the eighteenth century in the Enlightenment, persisted and mounted. Here and there were those who viewed the course of events with

[2] *The Cambridge Modern History*, Vols. X, XI, XII, is useful for the political history. Briefer and including only Europe is Hayes, *Modern Europe to 1870*, pp. 583 ff., and Hayes, *Contemporary Europe since 1870*, pp. 1–356.

fear, dislike, and profound distrust.[3] Yet the general atmosphere in the Western world was one of trust in man's ability to achieve an ideal society.

The Revolution: The Economic Phases

The trend towards secularism and optimism was reinforced by economic developments—a continuation, proliferation, and rapid enhancement of what began in the eighteenth century. One phase was the Industrial Revolution. Yet the Industrial Revolution did not comprise the whole: here was the growing mastery by man of wide ranges of his physical environment.

As before 1815, so during the fore part of the nineteenth century Great Britain led in the new processes: during several decades she had almost a monopoly. They and her part in the defeat of Napoleon had assured her the mastery of the seas. Her navy was supreme. Her merchant marine carried her flag and her commerce to every port. A rapid increase in population and immigration from Ireland provided her with the needed labour. As her capital accumulated through the profits of the new processes London became the financial capital of the globe.

Before the close of the century other countries were becoming industrialized. The rapid growth of the United States both aided and was aided by the development of industries. On the Continent British capital and technicians stimulated the early industrialization of Belgium. Of the major countries on the Continent, although in the eighteenth century she had made a promising start, France lagged behind Britain. After the completion of her political unification, Germany, now that internal trade barriers were lowered or eliminated, quickly forged ahead and by 1914 was a formidable rival.

The differing rates of industrialization had significance for Christianity. They meant that the problems posed for Christianity first became acute on a large scale in Great Britain. Since Great Britain was predominantly Protestant, it was that branch of the faith which they first seriously challenged. Within a few decades, but not in a major way until the latter half of the century, they became acute in the United States, Belgium, France, Germany, and North Italy. Here may be a reason why British and especially English Protestants wrestled with the problems earlier than did those of the United States. The social gospel, so marked in the United States in the last quarter of the century, arrived in force much later than did Christian Socialism in England and the agitation in that country by Evangelicals for legislation to protect labour. Here may also be the clue to the relatively late attempts of Roman Catholic prelates to deal with the issues created by industrialization: until past the middle of the century the Popes were more concerned with the problems raised by the emergence of

---

[3] For one of many examples of this, see T. P. Neill, *Juan Cortes: History and Prophecy* in *The Catholic Historical Review*, Vol. XL, pp. 385–410.

liberalism in politics. That was seen in the emphases in the Papal *Syllabus of Errors,* published in 1864, and in the fact that the encyclical *Rerum novarum,* hailed by Roman Catholics as a major pronouncement of the "workingman's Pope," Leo XIII, and addressed to the questions raised by industrialization, was not given to the world until 1891. Since the industrialization of the lands of the Eastern Churches came even later, these bodies were still more tardy in formulating attitudes towards it.

In the leadership of Britain in the Industrial Revolution, soon followed by the United States, is clearly one reason for the rapid growth of Protestantism in the nineteenth century. So far as they had a religious allegiance, the peoples of both countries were predominantly of that wing of the faith. As we have said, and will again and again note, in the nineteenth century proportionately Protestantism spread much more rapidly than did either of the other major forms of Christianity. From it, too, sprang more novel movements in method and in thought than from the other two. For them industrialization was not the only source: some currents in theology and philosophy showed its influence —as with Maurice in England, the social gospel in America, and possibly Ritschlianism in Germany—but others were quite unaffected by it. Yet such developments as the Young Men's and Young Women's Christian Associations and the Salvation Army would not have come into being had it not been for the social conditions which arose from the Industrial Revolution. Moreover, the enormous territorial spread of Protestantism was chiefly in connexion with the emergence of the new nations of Canada, Australia, New Zealand, and South Africa from emigration from the British Isles, with the growth of British colonies, commerce, and imperial possessions (as in Africa, India, and Burma), and with the westward expansion of the United States. But for its remarkable inner vitality, Protestantism would not have risen to the challenge. Yet the challenge and the opportunity came from the economic phase of the revolution.

How far if at all were the Industrial Revolution and its associated movements due to Christianity and especially to Protestant Christianity? They seem to be part of that dynamism of Western Europe to which we have more than once called attention. Can more than coincidence be found in the fact that Western Europe was also Western Christendom? Did a causal connexion exist between the emergence of the Industrial Revolution and its coming in an England where Protestantism predominated, where the Puritan heritage was still strong, and at a time when the Evangelical awakening was beginning? Can more than chance association be established between the mounting industrialization of Britain and the rising tide of revivals in British Protestantism? If the answer to any of these questions is yes, was Christianity and especially Protestant Christianity a determining or even a contributing cause to the Industrial Revolution, was the economic factor a major source of the Evangelical awakening, or must responsibility for each be assigned to quite disparate causes? We do not know. But it may well be that the clue is at least in part to be found in the confidence and daring engendered by Christianity through its conviction that men live in an orderly universe controlled by One who is self-giving love, and especially in Protestantism and the Protestantism of the Evangelical tradition with its emphasis upon individual initiative.

The chief steps and phases of the progress towards man's mastery of his physical environment are so familiar that for our purposes they require only the briefest summary. At first the power-driven machinery and factories were mainly in textiles, particularly cotton textiles. Soon they extended to shoe-making, brewing, flour-making, and the manufacture of furniture and others of the accompaniments of man's physical life. The inexpensive production of glass jars and tin receptacles encouraged the mass preservation of foods. Ways of condensing and drying milk were devised. Machinery, notably the reaper, was applied to agriculture. Chemical fertilizers were manufactured and enriched the soil. Facilitated by the proximity of deposits of coal and iron ore, the production of iron and steel mounted and helped to supply the demand for machines. Means for easy and less expensive transportation multiplied. The steamboat came and, in spite of the fact that the sailing-ship was improved, by the 1880's in tonnage it had surpassed the latter in trans-oceanic traffic. Screw propellers began to displace the paddle wheel. The steam turbine was invented. Steam was applied to the railway, and a network of railroads soon spanned the industrialized countries and reached into undeveloped areas. By the end of the century electric street-cars were supplanting horse-drawn cars and electric inter-urban lines were built. The bicycle was invented and, supplied with pneumatic rubber tires, multiplied. Before 1914 the internal-combustion engine was being developed and automobiles were appearing. By that year the first heavier-than-air machines had begun their flights. In the latter part of the century petroleum and its products came into increasing use. The inexpensive production of cement aided the construction of roads and buildings. Methods of communication were rapidly and vastly improved. The electric telegraph spanned land and sea. The telephone was invented. By the year 1914 wireless telegraphy had been devised. The typewriter, wood-pulp paper, and new methods of printing facilitated correspondence and the production of books, newspapers, and magazines. At first as a by-product of the production of coke in the iron and steel industry gas was being utilized for lighting and heating. Electricity was being harnessed to lighting. Before the middle of the century means of vulcanizing rubber had been found. Also before the mid-century the first photographs had been made and by the end of the century photography had been accepted as a normal accessory of life. Moving pictures came in the 1890's and the first cinemas or moving picture theatres in the decade after 1900. Central heating, bathrooms, lavatories, refrigeration, linoleum, and sewing machines made the home more comfortable and sanitary and lightened the task of the housewife.

The Revolution: Other Forms of Man's Mastery of His Physical Environment

In connexion with the mastery of man's physical environment we must remind ourselves of the advances in medicine and surgery. Nursing was very old, but the modern nursing profession developed in the latter part of the nineteenth century. It was also in the second half of the century that anesthesia and antiseptics took some of the terrors from surgery and reduced the death rate. The development of bacteriology and the work of such men as Louis Pasteur, Rudolf Virchow, and Robert Koch brought striking advances in preventive medicine.

The Revolution: The Challenge of Man's Mastery of His Physical Environment

The revolution in man's mastery of his physical environment confronted Christianity with major challenges. Men tended to rely on the new processes to fulfil their desires, to be absorbed in them, and to view religion, including Christianity, as either irrelevant or a pleasant but dispensable adjunct to a happy life. New learned professions developed to aid man in utilizing his physical environment. Engineering in its many ramifications arose. Men were trained in agriculture, forestry, and business administration. Theology, once "the queen of the sciences," was relegated to a secondary role. In intellectual circles it was often looked upon with puzzled or amused contempt. The clergy were no longer regarded as the leading learned profession. Except in communities where the old order lingered the parson was no longer *the* person. Labourers tended to drift away from the Church. Vast shifts of population swelled the industrial and commercial centres. In the latter, patterns of life differed from those of an older age. The very successes of the Church in an earlier day now became a handicap. The Church had adjusted itself to a society which was prevailingly rural and in which, compared with those of the nineteenth century, cities were small. Now the Church was faced with the necessity of erecting many new structures and of making its way in a society where, except in some sections where the changes had disturbed the inherited customs little if at all, the community and its interests no longer revolved around the parish and its church.

The economic revolution also accentuated grave social evils. In the industrial and commercial towns and cities a large proportion of the population, poverty-stricken, lived in festering slums. In emerging factories and mines safeguards against accident and disease were lacking, hours of labour were long, women and children were employed under conditions which were a threat to decency and health, and until the public conscience became active, remedial legislation was non-existent. *Laissez faire,* reinforced by the theories associated with the name of Adam Smith, made for a minimum of government control and a maximum of individual initiative under free competition. While, ideally, enlightened selfishness should have promoted the welfare of all, in practice the selfishness was usually far from enlightened. Would Christian faith and ethical standards be sufficient to cope with the clamant ills? [4]

The new processes made possible a more fully integrated nation-state and augmented the destructiveness of war. Through the new media of transportation and communication it became possible to weld together an entire people more closely than ever before. A government could now indoctrinate its citizens and in a time of emergency could quickly mobilize the resources of a nation. The universal military service introduced during the French Revolution spread. Through the machine and other inventions the weapons of destruction became more effective. Until 1914 these possibilities were not widely put into practice: beginning with that year, as we are to see, they were developed with revolutionary results. During the nineteenth century efforts arising from Christian faith were being made to abolish or at least to reduce the frequency of war and to mitigate its horrors. However, after 1914, although expanded, they proved insufficient. Here, too, was a major challenge to Christianity.

The Revolution: Man's Expanding Knowledge of His Physical Environment; The Era of Science

In some ways the increased knowledge by man of his physical environment was even more a threat and a challenge to Christianity than was the greater mastery of his physical environment. It so rapidly broadened man's horizons that many had difficulty in reconciling the new perspectives with their understanding of the Christian faith. As we saw in the last chapter, this increase of knowledge had begun well before 1815. However, it was confined to relatively small circles. In the course of the nineteenth century the range and amount of knowledge not only rapidly grew; much of it also became the common property of the educated and in more or less garbled form was familiar to the majority of the population.

Again, as with the gains in man's mastery of his physical environment, the

---

[4] The literature of the mastery of man over his physical environment, the rise of modern industry, and the associated social changes is prodigious. Here we must take the space to mention only a few books, to which we have already called attention. They have to do chiefly with England. They are White, *Industrial and Social Revolution 1750–1937;* Usher, *An Introduction to the Industrial History of England,* pp. 287 ff.; Dietz, *An Economic History of England,* pp. 392–534; Hammond and Hammond, *The Village Labourer 1760–1832,* pp. 166 ff.; and Pinchbeck, *Women Workers and the Industrial Revolution, 1750–1850, passim.*

story is so familiar that we need only outline it and seek to point out its significance for Christianity.[5]

In the eighteenth century through geology the study of the history of the planet had made progress. In the nineteenth century it registered amazing advances. In England the early discoveries were assembled and interpreted by Charles Lyell (1797–1875) in his *Principles of Geology*, first published in 1830 and issued in successively revised editions to 1872. On the Continent as well as in Britain Western European man was studying the past history of the 'earth and scientist after scientist was adding to the fund of knowledge.[6]

A major event was the publication in 1859 of Charles Robert Darwin's (1809–1882) *On the Origin of Species by Means of Natural Selection, or the Preservation of Favored Races in the Struggle for Life*. This was followed, in 1871, by his *The Descent of Man and Selection in Relation to Sex*. In the hypothesis it was set forth that species come into being through "natural selection" by which in the incessant struggle for existence those individuals survive which possess variations from their fellows that are of advantage in their particular environment. They assumed that individuals develop "acquired characteristics" and by heredity pass them on to their descendants. Darwin was not entirely original. He took over from Lamarck the transmission of acquired characteristics. He was familiar with Lyell's *Principles of Geology*. He had been much impressed by the *Essay on Population* (1798) by Thomas Robert Malthus (1766–1834), a clergyman of the Church of England, in which the thesis was put forward that population, always pressing on the means of subsistence, is kept within bounds only by war, pestilence, famine, misery, and vice: he applied this to all organic life. Almost simultaneously Alfred Russel Wallace (1823–1913) had arrived, quite independently, also with a stimulus from Malthus, at a similar hypothesis.

What was called "Darwinism" quickly became controversial and appeared to be a major threat to Christianity. Many scientists adopted it with enthusiasm. In England Thomas Henry Huxley (1825–1895), master of a readable literary style, helped to popularize it. He it was who coined the term "agnostic" to describe the position of one who believed the evidence insufficient to affirm or deny religious convictions. In Germany Ernst Heinrich Haeckel (1834–1919), a biologist of note, was convinced of the truth of Darwinism and gave it wide currency. He used it to support a purely materialistic view of life. By professing

---

[5] Useful summaries are to be found in Hayes, *Contemporary Europe Since 1870*, pp. 187–220, 519–528; F. Sherwood Taylor, *A Short History of Science and Scientific Thought, with Readings from the Great Scientists from the Babylonians to Einstein* (New York, W. W. Norton & Co., 1949, pp. 368), pp. 145 ff.; Dampier, *A History of Science*, pp. 217 ff.; and L. L. Woodruff, editor, *The Development of the Sciences* (New Haven, Yale University Press, 1923, pp. xiv, 327), *passim*.

[6] Geikie, *The Founders of Geology*, pp. 333 ff., stresses especially the role of English geologists.

to trace the descent of man from lower forms of life Darwinism seemed not only to render untenable the Biblical account of the creation of all life and of man in particular but also to deprive man of a soul and of immortality. Earnest Christians rose to the defence of the faith, sometimes with heat and little intelligence. Others endeavoured to show that whatever of fact was disclosed by "evolutionists" was not incompatible with Christian faith but, rather, enriched it. Yet it was significant and typical of what happened to many that Darwin himself, who during part of his student years was preparing for the ministry of the Church of England, did not pursue that profession. He was not an atheist. Indeed, he once called himself a theist. But, after much pain, he had felt himself forced, in all honesty, to give up the orthodoxy of his youth and to describe himself as an agnostic.[7]

Scientific achievement was by no means invariably associated with a surrender of the Christian faith. For example, Johann Gregor Mendel (1822–1884), whose experiments attached his name to a theory of organic inheritance, was abbot of an Augustinian monastery and carried on his investigations in the monastic garden. He was not the only instance. Man after man, eminent among them Louis Pasteur (1822–1895), whose attainments in science won the respect of their fellows, remained devoutly Christian. Indeed, in the greatest scientists there were usually an intellectual integrity, a willingness and even an eagerness to ascertain truth, a humility before facts, and a teachableness which had kinship with Christian ideals and may have been indebted, consciously or unconsciously, to the milieu of Western Europe, in which Christianity had so long been a moulding factor.

Breath-taking discoveries were made in chemistry and physics and thus in the constitution of matter. The existence of molecules was postulated. Molecules were found to contain atoms. In the 1890's atoms, in turn, were declared to consist of electrons. About the middle of the century the wave theory of light was propounded. Knowledge of electricity was advanced and the theory of electromagnetism was put forward, with the conviction that light-waves are akin to electromagnetic oscillations. In the 1890's X-rays were discovered and radium was isolated from pitchblende. In 1901 Max Planck published the quantum theory and on the eve of 1914 Albert Einstein was beginning to formulate a theory of relativity which soon was to revolutionize conceptions of the universe and of matter.

Mathematics was expanded. Its new developments helped to make possible forward strides in physics, chemistry, and astronomy.

In astronomy enormous advances were being achieved. Improvements in

[7] *The Life and Letters of Charles Darwin, Including an Autobiographical Chapter,* edited by his son, Francis Darwin (London, John Murray, 3 vols., 1887), Vol. I, pp. 45, 304–317.

telescopes and the utilization of photography, reinforced by discoveries in chemistry and physics and the use of the spectroscope, expanded man's knowledge of the stellar universe and revealed it as far more extensive than the most daring had dreamed.

All these ramifications of what were called the natural sciences bred a confidence in scientific procedures and won for them great prestige.

REVOLUTION: IN THE STUDY OF RELIGION

Many sought to apply scientific methods to the study of religion in general and of Christianity in particular. As they did so, would faith in Christianity be weakened or even dissolved? As time-distances shrank and as he came more and more into contact with other cultures, Western European man compared religions, including Christianity, with one another and developed histories of religion. In his study of man he created a branch of science which he called anthropology and related it closely with what he described as the science of society, or sociology. He found religion to be an integral phase of these sciences. As scholars applied to Christianity the principles and tests which they employed with other religions and religion in general, to many of them and those who read their findings it seemed to lose its distinctiveness as expressing the unique and final revelation of God. Its development and the Bible, as a collection of documents associated with it, were subjected to the methods of study that were used with other religions and with writings esteemed sacred by their adherents. All religions came to be regarded by many as man's search for meaning and for the unknown. Beginning on a primitive level with early man, religion was seen, in the course of its history, to take many forms. In spite of differences, they had common patterns, some of which were shared by Christianity. Writings in the field multiplied. Outstanding, partly because of the numerous volumes which during his long life came from his pen, was James George Frazer (1854–1941). *The Golden Bough,* first published in 1890, brought him fame and was preceded and followed by other studies.[8] But he was only one of the more prominent specialists. Not all of Christian background who approached the study of religion from the historical and comparative standpoint abandoned the Christian faith. However, large numbers, both of the experts and especially of the thousands who had a smattering of the findings of the experts, either gave up their faith in the Gospel as God's unique initiative for man's salvation or felt it weakened. Here was a major challenge, especially as Christian missionaries and their supporters attempted to spread their faith among adherents of other religions.

[8] For selections from Frazer's writings see *Man, God, and Immortality. Thoughts on Human Progress. Passages Chosen from the Writings of Sir James George Frazer and Edited by the Author* (New York, The Macmillan Co., 1927, pp. xvi, 437).

REVOLUTION: IN THE KNOWLEDGE OF MAN AND HIS MIND

The application of science to the study of man's mental processes revolutionized the understanding of man. To some it made for mechanistic determinism as the key to man's mind. For many it supplanted the Church and Christianity with the psychologist and the psychiatrist.

Psychology and its ramifications attracted increasing attention. Within it many theories and schools of thought developed.[9] In some the functioning of the mind was viewed as completely controlled by the physical. Since, partly under the influence of Darwinism, the psychological processes of men and other animals were believed to be similar, experiments were carried on with various kinds of life to gain information about human psychology. For example, Wilhelm Max Wundt (1832–1920), trained in medicine and professor of philosophy at Leipzig, who established the first experimental laboratory and did much to develop psychology as a separate science, used as subjects animals as well as men. In the 1890's the Russian Pavlov conducted experiments with dogs which led him to put forward the theory of "conditioned reflex," namely, that movements of bodily members are in response to stimuli from without. In the United States in the latter part of the century various forms of what was called functional psychology were developed. In them mental life was described as a biological function of adjustment between impressions upon the body and the reaction of the body upon the world. Out of this, on the eve of 1914, John B. Watson formulated behaviouristic psychology. In it response was declared to be fully dependent on stimulus: it was, therefore, a kind of determinism which ruled out God.

Fairly early in the century attempts were made to apply science to the treatment of mental diseases. Mental diseases were classified. Late in the century Sigmund Freud developed what he called psychoanalysis, a term which within his lifetime gained wide currency.[10] In treating disease he sought to penetrate to the subconscious and emphasized childhood experiences and the role of sex. Shortly before 1914 one of his pupils, C. G. Jung, departed from him in saying that in addition to sex such drives as fear and shame may give rise to inner conflicts and issue in abnormalities.

By no means all psychologists ruled out God or postulated such complete

[9] Among the sketches of developments in psychology and its related sciences the following will prove useful: Wilbur S. Hulin, *A Short History of Psychology* (New York, Henry Holt & Co., pp. vi, 189); Edna Heidbreder, *Seven Psychologies* (New York, The Century Co., 1933, pp. viii, 450); J. C. Flugel, *A Hundred Years of Psychology 1833–1933: with an Additional Part on Developments 1933–1947* (London, Gerald Duckworth & Co., 2nd ed., 1951, pp. 424); George Sidney Brett, *Brett's History of Psychology,* edited and abridged by R. S. Peters (London, George Allen & Unwin, 1953, pp. 742); and Gardner Murphy, *An Historical Introduction to Modern Psychology* (New York, Harcourt, Brace & Co., 1930, pp. xvii, 470).

[10] *The Basic Writings of Sigmund Freud,* translated and edited, with an introduction, by H. A. Brill (New York, The Modern Library, 1938, pp. vi, 1001).

identity between consciousness and the nervous system as would invalidate confidence in the survival of the individual after the death of the body. As time went on, many of the clergy called in psychologists and psychiatrists to assist in caring for those whom they were counselling.

However, here, too, was a challenge to Christianity. Could Christianity be demonstrated to be compatible with whatever of verifiable fact was ascertained by psychology and its related sciences? Could psychology yield insights ,which would enrich the understanding of the Christian faith and enable Christians to enter more fully into the abundant life that was a fruit of their faith and to assist others to do so?

REVOLUTION: THE CHALLENGE OF PHILOSOPHERS AND MEN AND WOMEN OF LETTERS AND MUSIC

In the Western world during the nineteenth century philosophy had a rich and varied development. Some of the first-class philosophical minds of the century were convinced Christians and made their chief contribution through theology. To them we will recur in later chapters and volumes. Others were friendly and thought of themselves as within the Christian tradition, but their effect was ambiguous. Still others implicitly or explicitly repudiated Christianity.

Of those whose effect was ambiguous the most prominent was Georg Wilhelm Friedrich Hegel (1770–1831). We have already met him, but it was not until after 1815 that his system was formulated in a fashion to be given to the world.[11] His was a comprehensive mind. He sought to bring into one inclusive system all the universe. He held that there is an Absolute Mind or Spirit which is timeless, eternal, and all-embracing. By the logical method which he formulated and which he called *dialectic,* Hegel endeavoured to show the connexion between everything and everything else. Each individual, he maintained, is conditioned by human society, human society is inter-related with the earth, and the earth is an organic part of the universe. In man the Absolute has become conscious of itself. Whether he regarded the Absolute as conscious of itself apart from men was debated by Hegel's followers. Some interpreted him as holding that the Absolute is eternally perfect Mind or Spirit which is not dependent on men for knowledge of its own existence. Hegel was an Idealist. Although he rejected the term as applied to himself, he was in fact also a

---

[11] Of the enormous literature by and about Hegel the following are useful for our purpose: Georg Wilhelm Friedrich Hegel, *Lectures on the Philosophy of Religion together with a Work on the Proofs of the Existence of God,* translated from the second German edition by E. B. Speirs and J. B. Sanderson (London, Kegan Paul, Trench, Trubner & Co., 3 vols., 1895); Edward Caird, *Hegel* (Edinburgh, Wm. Blackwood and Sons, 1883, pp. viii, 224); R. Mackintosh, *Hegel and Hegelianism* (Edinburgh, T. & T. Clark, 1903, pp. viii, 301).

pantheist, for he regarded the Absolute not as the creator of the world but as the world in its organic unity. To him the Absolute Idea is all reality or the universe. This Absolute Idea operates through a dialectic of many triads. Each triad consists of thesis, antithesis, and synthesis. The synthesis becomes the thesis of another triad, which in turn has its thesis, antithesis, and synthesis. So each triad is succeeded by another triad. Hegel believed that in Christianity was the most adequate expression of truth that is possible for religion. "It is the Christian religion which is the perfect religion," he said. He saw in the Trinity the representation of the truth that the Absolute is three in one. He found a place for the incarnation and for the union, through worship, of the believer with God. He believed that the truth of Christianity is independent of the historicity of the events recorded in the New Testament—that historicity was for the experts to determine. He employed traditional Christian terms in such fashion that he seemed to endorse them, and gave to them a significance which fitted in with his philosophy. Many Christians, therefore, held that they could accept the Hegelian philosophy and continue to be loyal to their faith.

A younger contemporary of Hegel, Auguste Comte (1798–1857), repudiated Christianity. He had for father a devout Roman Catholic. He formulated a new religion, that of humanity, which he believed conserved the values of Roman Catholicism without being cumbered by its dogmas. This religion was Positivism. In it he put forward as a substitute for God the Great Being, namely, all who have in the past laboured for the improvement of mankind. He gave to Positivism forms of worship. Comte sought to realize an ideal society in which industry would be triumphant, all would have opportunity for mental development and for work, and wars and internal revolutions would cease.[12] For a time Positivism enjoyed something of a vogue, particularly among intellectuals. It had followers especially in Russia, Latin Europe, and Latin America.

Also younger than Hegel and contemporary with him was Arthur Schopenhauer (1788–1860). Influenced by Kant and Herder, a friend of Goethe, holding with Kant to Idealism, he contended that the "will" and the "thing-in-itself," so important in Kant, are the same. By "will" Schopenhauer meant striving, impulse, desire, emotion, and instinct. In our striving, he maintained, we are unable to divorce ourselves entirely from intuition and so do not fully arrive at reality. Yet, he held, the "will to live" is radically opposed to intelligence. A thoroughgoing pessimist, egotistical, loving no one but perhaps his dogs, he held that evil is inescapable, good secondary, and happiness an illusion. He

[12] *The Positive Philosophy of Auguste Comte,* translated by Harriet Martineau (New York, William Gowans, 1868, pp. 838); John Stuart Mill, *The Positive Philosophy of Auguste Comte* (New York, Henry Holt & Co., 1875, pp. 182).

denied personal immortality and held that in the universe men are the only intelligent beings.[13]

Ludwig Feuerbach (1804-1872), the son of a jurist, studied under Hegel. As a philosopher he wrote extensively. He early denied personal immortality. He regarded religion as "identical with self-consciousness—with the consciousness which man has of his nature." To him God is not objective reality but is a projection of what man conceives to be his own needs.[14]

Belonging to the second half of the century was Friedrich Wilhelm Nietzsche (1844-1900). Through both his father and his mother he was descended from Protestant clergymen but rebelled against family pressure to enter their profession. He rejected Christianity. He held that God does not exist and that belief in Him was already nearly extinct, and that what was taught by Jesus and Paul, with its emphasis on love, pity, and sympathy was counter to the Greek values and so was bad. He felt that Christianity fostered a slave mentality and that in furthering democracy, the emancipation of slaves, equal rights for women and workingmen it was preserving inferior stocks and making for the mental and physical decline of modern Europeans.[15]

Schopenhauer, Feuerbach, and Nietzsche all had an extensive reading, not only in Germany but also in other countries, and in this seemed symptomatic of an extensive rejection of Christianity. Here and in Comte was a continuation and possibly an accentuation of what we found in the eighteenth century, a more open repudiation of Christianity than had been seen since the conversion of Western Europe.

Less widely read was Franz Kafka (1883-1924). A native of Prague, a Jew, a deep pessimist, he rejected both his ancestral religion and Christianity.[16]

With the intellectuals may also be placed the musician Wilhelm Richard Wagner (1813-1883). Egotistical, believing Christianity to have effected a Jewish corruption of the German spirit, he sought through musical drama to exalt pre-Christian German paganism. His operas won for themselves a wide hearing and were long in vogue.

A similar trend was seen in Great Britain. There the denial of Christianity was not always as emphatic as on the Continent, but in some it was as pronounced and it may be that the effect of those who did not denounce it as strongly was wider and more penetrating than was that of the more vituperative dissidents. Thus a contemporary of Schopenhauer, Feuerbach, and

---

[13] Arthur Schopenhauer, The World as Will and Idea, translated by R. B. Haldane and J. Kemp (London, Kegan Paul, Trench, Trubner & Co., 3 vols., 8th ed., no date).

[14] Ludwig Feuerbach, The Essence of Christianity, translated by Marian Evans (George Eliot) (Boston, Houghton Mifflin Co., 2nd ed., 1881, pp. xx, 339).

[15] H. A. Reyburn, Nietzsche (London, Macmillan & Co., 1948, pp. viii, 500); Hubben, Four Prophets of Our Destiny, pp. 83 ff.

[16] Hubben, op. cit., pp. 129 ff.

Nietzsche, Thomas Carlyle (1795-1881), while holding to a belief in God and, as recorded in *Sartor Resartus*, after a profound struggle arriving at positive convictions, as a young man gave up his purpose of preparing for the ministry of the Church of Scotland and abandoned the Christian faith. The Utilitarians had as their founder Jeremy Bentham (1748-1832). He proposed as a guiding principle for legislation "the greatest happiness of the greatest number." He did not attack Christianity as such, but he was anti-clerical and sought to discredit dogmatic Christianity.[17] James Mill (1773-1836), long the chief companion of Bentham, because of changing convictions early found it impossible to go on with the ministry of the Church of Scotland in which he had been licensed and believed that some of the basic Christian doctrines were against sound morals.[18] His son, more famous, John Stuart Mill (1806-1873), educated according to Bentham's counsel, had been given very little religious instruction.[19] Yet while disavowing supernatural sanctions for ethics, he held that Utilitarianism was in agreement with the moral teachings of Jesus and of Christianity. While he believed in God, he did not think of Him as omnipotent, omniscient, or completely benevolent, but as limited by matter and force.[20] The Utilitarians made a great impression on the thought of the nineteenth century, especially in Britain.

Herbert Spencer (1820-1903) in his extensive writings dealt with evolution in a comprehensive fashion. He it was who coined the phrase "survival of the fittest." He traced evolution in the universe, in geology, in biology, and in human society. He was an optimist, believed in progress, and looked forward to an era of universal peace when every duty would become a pleasure. In his youth he had been under strong religious influences. His father and mother were Methodists, but his father later attended a Quaker meeting, and he himself attended both the Methodist chapel and the Friends meeting. The uncle who helped in his education was one of the Evangelical clergy of the Church of England. Gradually the religious beliefs in which Spencer had been nurtured faded. He came to believe that religion had its origin in the fear of the spirits of the ancestors. He rejected atheism and pantheism but could not accept theism. He continued as an agnostic, but, while holding that the mystery surrounding religion is insoluble, as he grew older he became more tolerant of religious creeds.[21] For a generation or more his writings had a wide circulation.

Numbers of Britain's intellectuals who could not be classed as philosophers

---

[17] Robertson, *A History of Freethought in the Nineteenth Century*, pp. 87, 88.

[18] *Ibid.*, p. 200; *Autobiography of John Stuart Mill*, pp. 27–29.

[19] *Autobiography of John Stuart Mill*, p. 30. On John Stuart Mill see also Michael St. John Packe, *The Life of John Stuart Mill* (New York, The Macmillan Co., 1954, pp. xvi, 567), *passim*.

[20] Wright, *A History of Modern Philosophy*, pp. 452, 453.

[21] Herbert Spencer, *Autobiography* (London, Williams & Norgate, 2 vols., 1904), Vol. I, pp. 83, 150–152, 346, Vol. II, pp. 466–471.

also gave up the Christian faith. Through their writings they contributed to the widespread doubt. Thus Leslie Stephen (1832–1904), a priest of the Church of England, publicist and man of letters, read Kant and Mill and felt that he could no longer call himself a Christian.[22] Matthew Arnold (1822–1888), poet and critic, son of the distinguished clergyman and educator Thomas Arnold, for whose memory he had great reverence, sadly recognized—as recorded in *Dover Beach* [23]—the loss of his boyhood faith. The novelist Mary Ann (Marian) Evans, later Mrs. J. W. Cross (1819–1880), who was best known by her pen name, George Eliot, was reared in a devout Evangelical home, rebelled against the views in which she had been nurtured, but always kept a sympathetic understanding of deeply religious Evangelicals. Thomas Hardy (1840–1928), novelist and poet, in his later years hailed as the outstanding man of letters in the English-speaking world, in his early life was a believing Christian but by the time he had reached manhood had relinquished his Christian convictions. To his mind, as seen in *The Dynasts* and elsewhere, men's lives are governed by blind, unconscious, purposeless cosmic forces.[24]

Tennyson and Browning presented the Christian faith in a constructive manner but bore witness to the struggle through which sensitive souls passed to positive affirmations of Christian belief. While undersanding orthodox Christianity, Browning rejected it and on at least one occasion vehemently declared that he was not a Christian.[25]

Some in Britain vigorously denounced Christianity. They did so in spite of laws which sought to protect the Christian faith. Such was Charles Bradlaugh (1833–1891). As a lad he was a Sunday School teacher, but had been alienated by the intolerance of his pastor, an Anglican clergyman, who denounced as "atheistical" his adolescent questions about the Gospels and the Thirty-nine Articles. Largely self-educated, he became a Deist and then a militant atheist. George Jacob Holyoake, who adopted the term "secularist" to describe himself and others who held similar views, organized the National Secular Society. Of this in time Bradlaugh became the president. He and others of his convictions won thousands of converts. In the ferment which characterized much of nineteenth-century England, societies for "free thought" burgeoned and took many forms. All agreed in denouncing orthodox Christianity.[26]

Somewhat similar trends were seen in the United States. Thus Ralph Waldo Emerson (1803–1882) in his earlier manhood was pastor of a Unitarian church

[22] *Dictionary of National Biography, Second Supplement*, pp. 398–405.
[23] *Dictionary of National Biography, Supplement*, pp. 70–75; Shafer, *Christianity and Naturalism*, pp. 158–161.
[24] Shafer, *op. cit.*, pp. 235, 256. See also Thomas Hardy, *The Dynasts*, Preface, and such passages as the *Fore Scene* and the *After Scene*.
[25] Robertson, *op. cit.*, p. 289.
[26] *Ibid.*, pp. 295 ff.

and preached sermons which to some later Unitarians would have seemed conservative and near to historic orthodoxy.[27] However, he gave up the pastorate and found himself in sympathy with Carlyle. Emerson's nobility of character and his persuasive eloquence won a wide hearing. In the latter part of the century an outstanding figure was William Graham Sumner (1840–1910) of Yale. An Episcopal clergyman, in early manhood he had been pastor of a parish. Later as economist and sociologist and an ardent student of Herbert Spencer, he found his Christian convictions evaporating.[28] John Dewey (1859–1952) formulated a philosophy of instrumentalism which because of his connexion with educational theory and methods had a wide vogue. While he declared that he was not an atheist, his conception of God was far from that of Christianity.[29] In the militant camp was Robert G. Ingersoll (1833–1899). The son of a clergyman who had served Congregational and Presbyterian parishes, he was prominent as a lawyer, an orator, and a politician. A man of high moral character, he called himself an agnostic, welcomed *The Origin of Species,* and from the lecture platform pointed out what in the Bible and Christianity seemed to him to be untenable.[30]

Late in the century Henri Louis Bergson of France (1859–1941) formulated a philosophy which became popular. While not openly anti-Christian and used by some Christians to enrich their insights, it seemed to make Christianity unnecessary and outmoded.[31]

On the Continent many of the nineteenth-century writers of fiction, poetry, and drama challenged Christianity and especially the conventional Christianity which they saw about them. That was true of Bjornstjerne Björnson (1832–1910), son of a Norwegian pastor, and of Henrik Johan Ibsen (1826–1906), also of Norway, who, widely read in theology, was intensely critical of contemporary Christianity. In Denmark the Jew Georg Morris Cohen Brandes (1842–1927), literary critic and historian, was out of line with the Christian tradition. The egotistic Victor Hugo (1802–1885), the greatest literary influence in nineteenth-century France, while appreciative of Christian character, was not a help to the Christian cause. In his youth a Voltairean sceptic, for a time he became a Roman Catholic but later gave up that faith.[32]

[27] *Young Emerson Speaks. Unpublished Discourses on Many Subjects by Ralph Waldo Emerson* edited by Arthur Cushman McGiffert, Jr. (Boston, Houghton Mifflin Co., 1938, pp. xxxix, 276), *passim.*

[28] Harris Starr, *William Graham Sumner* (New York, Henry Holt & Co., 1925, pp. vi, 557), p. 543.

[29] John Dewey, *A Common Faith* (New Haven, Yale University Press, 1934, pp. 87), *passim.*

[30] *Dictionary of American Biography,* Vol. IX, pp. 469, 470.

[31] A. D. Lindsay, *The Philosophy of Bergson* (London, J. M. Dent & Sons, 1911, pp. viii, 247); D. B. Kitchin, *Bergson for Beginners. A Summary of his Philosophy* (New York, The Macmillan Co., 1913, pp. vii, 252).

[32] Vidler, *Prophecy and Papacy,* pp. 149, 150.

REVOLUTION: IN THE STUDY OF THE BIBLE

Inevitably the critical methods of dealing with historical records developed by scholars of the eighteenth and especially of the nineteenth century were applied to the Bible. This was partly to obtain a text as near to the original as possible and partly to seek to ascertain the authorship and the accuracy of the narratives. Much was done reverently and led to an enlargement of an understanding of the Jewish background and the origins of Christianity and to a deepened appreciation of the faith. For many, however, its impact was so revolutionary that it weakened or destroyed confidence in the inspiration of the Scriptures and in Christ and the Gospel. It gave rise to controversy, some of it bitter, which continued, often intensified, into the twentieth century.

Two books which stirred debate and had wide repercussions were the *Leben Jesu* ("Life of Jesus") by David Friedrich Strauss (1808–1874), the first volume of which appeared in 1835, and *Vie de Jésus* ("Life of Jesus") by Joseph Ernest Renan (1823–1892), which was published in 1863.[33]

Strauss was a serious student who in Tübingen and Berlin had acquired a foundation in theology and philosophy. He wrote his *Leben Jesu* in one year while teaching at Tübingen and when still in his twenties. He insisted that the Gospel narratives must be studied like any other book. He did not believe that the authors of the Gospels were deliberate fabricators, but into the Gospels, so he held, had come the element of "myth" as that term was used by Hegel. He declared that "the supernatural birth of Christ, his miracles, his resurrection, and ascension, remain eternal truths, whatever doubts may be cast on their reality as historical facts" and that "the dogmatic significance of the life of Jesus remains inviolate." Yet he pointed out what seemed to him to be contradictions in the narratives, came out against the virgin birth of Jesus, and cast doubt on the accuracy of the records of the sayings and deeds of Jesus. The book was brilliantly written and created an immense sensation. Bitter criticism was directed against Strauss by those holding to the traditional beliefs. It hounded him through life, especially as in later writings he became more polemical. In his *Christliche Glaubens Lehre*, published in 1841 and 1842, he traced the history of Christian doctrines in such a way as to cast doubt on their validity. Eventually he gave up belief in a personal God and in immortality.

The *Vie de Jésus* was not as substantial a work of scholarship as was the *Leben Jesu*.[34] Renan had been reared in a devout Breton home, had begun preparing for the Roman Catholic priesthood, but before coming to ordination, through reading, including much of German Protestant theology, had arrived

---

[33] *The Life of Jesus Critically Examined*, by David Friedrich Strauss, translated from the fourth German edition by Marian Evans (George Eliot) (New York, Calvin Blanchard, 2 vols., 1860). On Strauss see *The New Schaff-Herzog Encyclopedia of Religious Knowledge*, Vol. XI, pp. 110–112.

[34] Ernest Renan, *Vie de Jésus* (Paris, Calmann-Lévy, no date, pp. cv, 552).

at the conviction that to remain loyal to truth he must leave the church of his youth. In spite of opposition by the orthodox he eventually held a chair in the Collège de France. The *Vie de Jésus* was written from a Maronite seminary on Mt. Lebanon. In it Jesus emerged as a gentle Galilean, proclaiming the Kingdom of God. He was born in Nazareth the son of Joseph and Mary. He is made an attractive but unpractical and rather futile figure. The resurrection did not really occur, but belief in it arose from the hallucination of the women who cared for the body of the crucified. The book was very readable and had a wide circulation. Renan ended as a sceptic who looked upon the universe as a bad joke.[35]

REVOLUTION: THE CHALLENGE OF SOCIALISM

The nineteenth-century revolution threatened Christianity from still another angle—from programmes advanced for the reorganization of society. The atmosphere of political revolution combined with the changing structure of society brought by the Industrial Revolution to evoke proposals for a much more radical remaking of the collective life of mankind than was envisioned by the political liberalism gaining headway. The century was one in which capitalism, private enterprise, open competition, and the minimum of control by the state were the prevailing pattern in the Western world. However, as the evils which were the concomitant of that pattern became apparent, many, believing in the perfectibility of man and of society, rebelled against the prevailing *laissez faire*. Numbers of the rebels were known as Socialists.

Socialists and Socialism presented great variations. In general they sought to bring into all realms of life, including especially the economic, the egalitarianism which liberals envisioned in the political structure of society. Some Socialists were Christians. More were frankly non-Christian and even anti-Christian.[36] Henri de Saint-Simon (1760–1825), sometimes called the father of French Socialism, who at one time had Comte as his secretary and whose ideas helped to shape Positivism, holding that the masses needed some kind of religion, for a time advocated Deism and then what he called "New Christianity." He maintained that God had founded the Church, but that the only true Christian principle, the duty of all men to regard one another as brothers, had been perverted. He declared that this principle, restored to the place which it had in the primitive Church, would aid society in its chief purpose, the most rapid improvement in the lot of the poor. However, the followers of Saint-Simon did not think of themselves as Christians.[37] The view of the universe put forward by Charles

[35] *The New Schaff-Herzog Encyclopedia of Religious Knowledge*, Vol. IX, pp. 483 ff.
[36] G. D. St. Cole, *A History of Socialist Thought* (New York, St. Martin's Press, 2 vols., 1953–1954), is a good survey.
[37] Laidler, *Social-Economic Movements*, pp. 49 ff.

Fourier (1772–1837) could scarcely be called Christian, and the communities which sprang up in an attempt to put his theories into practice, including the Brook Farm in Massachusetts, while they probably would not have come into being in a society which had not been permeated by Christianity, were not Christian.[38] Pierre-Joseph Proudhon (1809–1865), in his private morals strict and upright, held that "property is theft," advocated Anarchism, namely, a form of society devoid of all government, and, while at one time he said that Christianity should not be rejected but be more deeply interpreted, within a few years he attacked all religion and especially Christianity.[39] The Russian aristocrat Bakunin (1814–1876) advocated violence in the achievement of Anarchism, with the slogan "Neither God nor master." [40]

He who through his influence must be called the outstanding formulator of Socialism and of Communism was Karl Marx (1818–1883).[41] His grandfather was a Jewish rabbi. When Karl was a child his father had become a Christian for the prudential reason which led many Jews of that day to accept baptism, namely, conformation to the dominant religion of the culture in which they were set. He was, therefore, reared a Christian. An ardent student, he was first impressed with Kant and Fichte but when still in his teens abandoned them for Hegel. He did not follow Hegel completely. At twenty-three he took his doctorate in philosophy at Jena. In his mid-twenties he became a Socialist. In his late twenties he formed a friendship with Friedrich Engels (1820–1895), son of a wealthy manufacturer. The two collaborated and Engels helped Marx financially as well as in his literary labours. They were chiefly responsible for the *Communist Manifesto,* issued in the revolutionary year of 1848. Nearly ignored at the time, it became a landmark in the development of Socialism. It ended with the climactic challenge: "The proletarians have nothing to lose but their chains. They have the world to gain. Workingmen of all countries, unite." Much of his working life Marx spent in London, part of the time in dire poverty. It was in London that he produced *Das Kapital* ("Capital"). There, too, he had a share in the founding of the International Working Men's Association—the First International—and wrote its declaration of principles. In 1867 came the first German edition of the initial volume of *Das Kapital.* In it Marx disclosed what he believed to be the course of history. History, so he held, is

---

[38] *Ibid.,* pp. 56–60.

[39] *Ibid.,* pp. 64–69; Robertson, *op. cit.,* p. 39.

[40] Robertson, *op. cit.,* p. 347.

[41] Of the enormous body of literature by Marx and especially about him the following may be selected: Karl Marx, *Capital. A Critique of Political Economy,* translated from the third German edition by S. Moore and E. Aveling, edited by Frederick Engels, revised and amplified according to the fourth German edition by E. Untermann (New York, The Modern Library, 1906, pp. 869); and Franz Mehring, *Karl Marx: The Story of His Life,* translated by E. Fitzgerald, edited by Ruth and Heinz Norder (New York, Covici Friede, 1935, pp. 608).

determined by economic factors. Capitalism was digging its own grave. The capitalists were growing richer and the labourers poorer with more of ignorance, brutality, and mental degradation. Eventually the latter would revolt and take over the land and the means of production. Here was the inevitable evolution of society: but the evolution could be hastened by human action. Engels completed *Das Kapital,* left unfinished by Marx's death. According to its materialistic interpretation of history Christianity, like other religions, is but a reflection of economic and social stages in evolution and will disappear.

Revolution Begins Impinging on Non-Western Cultures

By the year 1914 the revolution which had begun in Western Christendom was spreading to the rest of mankind. That spread was only in its initial stages. After 1914 it was to be rapidly and vastly augmented. It came chiefly through the impact of Western Christendom.

The expansion was partly by migrations of peoples of Western European stock and culture; as settlements of Western Europeans mounted they and their culture impinged upon the peoples of the Americas and Australasia and led to the rapid disintegration of the indigenous cultures.

The expansion was also partly through the extension of the political control of Western peoples over non-Western peoples. The building of colonial empires which had commenced in the latter part of the fifteenth century was now renewed and accelerated. The leader was Great Britain. By 1914 its empire included Australia, New Zealand, much of Asia and Africa, large sections in the Americas, and many islands in the several oceans. The French empire was chiefly in Africa. The United States extended its possessions across North America and by the end of the century had through island-hopping in Samoa, Hawaii, and the Philippines jumped the Pacific. The Dutch had rounded out their territories in the East Indies. Germany had staked out possessions in Africa and the Pacific. Belgium had acquired a vast estate in the Congo Valley.

An even wider expansion was through commerce and the investment of capital. Scarcely the remotest segment of mankind was untouched. With the awakenings in Christianity which, as we are to see, in spite of the threats were one of the most striking features of the life of Western European peoples, that faith was carried to almost every land and people. This was partly through holding the migrants to their ancestral religion and partly through missions among non-Occidentals. In proportion to their numerical strength and geographic extent at the outset of the century Christianity was spread more by Protestants than by Roman Catholics, but both wings of the faith greatly extended their borders. Except by migrations the Eastern Churches had very little share.

Through these several channels Western culture was being carried into all parts of the world. Even had it not been changing, its impact would have proved revolutionary. Since it was itself undergoing revolution its effect on non-Occidental peoples was doubly revolutionary. Before it primitive cultures rapidly yielded. By the end of the century numbers of them were disintegrating. Advanced cultures were more resistant, but before World War I ushered in a new century all of them were giving evidence of change. Everywhere in the twentieth century that change was to swell.

Summary: Threat and Challenge

Seldom if ever had the very existence of Christianity been as seriously menaced as it was by the revolution of the nineteenth century. Its course had never been easy. Peril had accompanied it since the Jewish religious authorities delivered Jesus to the representative of Rome and that representative had him nailed to a cross.

Now, however, in ways without exact precedent the menace came on many fronts. In so far as the revolution was the fruit of Christianity, although the distorted and perverted fruit, that religion appeared to be digging its own grave. Political revolution with the growth of the liberal democracy which was deeply indebted to ideals derived from Christianity was issuing in a kind of state which was moving towards secularism. Man's growing mastery and knowledge of his physical environment—to at least some degree the outcome of confidence in the orderliness and dependability of the universe drilled into the Western European mind and spirit by the Christian faith—on the one hand was creating a new kind of social structure to which the churches had difficulty in adjusting their programmes, was bringing colossal ills in the exploitation of labour, and was seeming to make religion unnecessary. On the other hand it was appearing to make Christianity untenable for honest minds. The age was committed to science, and to many science and religion seemed incompatible. The application to the Bible of the scholarly methods which were being used with other historical records appeared to throw doubt on the reliability of the book which Christians revered as divinely inspired and infallible. But to many the regard for truth inculcated by Christianity seemed to leave no alternative to such studies. Numerous formulators of methods of improving society, including Marx, the leading creator of Socialism, had abandoned Christianity and were denouncing it. Yet in some respects their programmes were secularized versions of Christian apocalypticism and eschatology. It is doubtful whether ever before any religion had so seemed to be bringing on its own demise by forces which it had released.

Moreover, Christianity appeared ill prepared to meet the threat. It did not present a united front. It was represented by a wide variety of churches, each of which claimed to be the custodian of the faith in its purity and either looked askance at the others or openly condemned them as having departed from the truth. In addition to denouncing one another, all the main forms of the faith— the Eastern Churches, the Roman Catholic Church, and Protestantism—suffered from internal divisions. Moreover, through earlier successes, they had come to be identified with political, economic, and social orders and with forms of thought which the revolution was destroying.

The revolution was bringing to Christianity both a challenge and an opportunity. If Christianity was sufficiently vital it could rise to the threats and become more potent in the affairs of man than it had ever been. The very openness of the threats could be an advantage. It could make more patent the contrast between the world and the Gospel than had been usual when all yielded the latter lip service. Because revolution was in progress, Western civilization was fluid and could be moulded by a religion with vigour adequate to the task. As the revolution spread outside the Western world Christianity, if its adherents seized the opportunity to plant it among all peoples, could shape all mankind as never before.

As we proceed with our attempt to unfold the story we shall see that to a far greater extent than most observers expected Christianity met the threats and rose to the challenge and the opportunity. In many ways the nineteenth century was the greatest that Christianity had thus far known. In the number of fresh movements to which it gave rise and in its impact upon the human race as a whole—not merely on one segment of it—it had never before been as influential. At the close of the century it was far from being dominant. It was still a minority movement, and far from measuring up to the high standard set by and in Christ. Yet from the global standpoint it was more of a factor than it had ever been. After 1914, in spite of the acceleration of the revolution both in extent and in intensity, the world-wide effect of Christianity continued to mount.

CHAPTER VI

The Roman Catholic Church and the Nineteenth-Century Stage of the Revolution: A General Outline of Its Response in Europe

IT WAS in Europe that the revolution presented the Roman Catholic Church with its most crucial challenges. In Europe was the geographic heart of Christendom, whether Roman Catholic, Protestant, or Eastern. In Latin Europe the Roman Catholic Church had its headquarters. Here was its capital, Rome. Here had originated all its major monastic movements. Here had been written almost all its outstanding works on theology. The most striking seeming exception to this last generalization was Augustine, but while of African birth Augustine was Latin by culture, had been converted in Italy, and wrote in Latin. Presumably the fashion in which the Roman Catholic Church met the challenge in Europe would determine its course elsewhere.

As we survey the response of the Roman Catholic Church in Europe to the challenge we will turn first of all to the Papacy. In the nineteenth and twentieth centuries the Papacy exercised a more effective control over the Roman Catholic Church than it had at any previous time. Not even the great Popes of the thirteenth century, powerful though they were, had been able to exert as much actual authority over that church or to obtain such full acquiescence within it to their claims as did the occupants of the throne of Peter in the latter half of the nineteenth century. Any account of the history of the Roman Catholic Church in this period, therefore, should begin with a narrative of the developments which centred in the Popes.

We will then summarize the course of the orders, congregations, societies, and similar movements in the Roman Catholic Church. In no previous hundred years had as many new ones emerged as in the nineteenth century. The Society of Jesus was revived and grew. Several of the older orders were strengthened. Numerous societies and congregations were born which took the customary vows of chastity, poverty, and obedience. In one form or another each had the aspects of a monastic community. Other societies arose for specific purposes whose members did not assume the vows of those who gave themselves fully to the religious life. Some were for the undergirding of missions through gifts and prayer. Others were for fellowship and service. Taken together they enlisted in the support of the Roman Catholic Church a large body of loyal and devoted clergy and laity. For many of those baptized in the Roman Catholic Church their faith was little more than conventional. Yet a substantial core existed, largely in the orders, congregations, and societies of various kinds, of those who were committed to the faith and who in practice were more under the direction of the Papacy than had ever previously been true. Through them the Roman Catholic Church had at its heart a more closely knit constituency than either of the other two major wings of Christianity or any of the non-Christian religions, which enrolled a large and widely scattered body of adherents.

We will follow the account of the orders, congregations, and societies with one of the devotional life of Roman Catholics. This will include the traditional forms of worship and devotional practices inherited from earlier centuries, new forms, and outstanding individuals and movements. That here was a marked revival in the Roman Catholic faith will become clear. It was on several levels, some of them popular, some for the experts in the devotional life, and some among the intellectuals.

We must sketch developments in theology, dogma, and other features of the Roman Catholic faith which fall within the realm of the intellect. Here we must ask how far and in what ways the Roman Catholic Church responded to the main currents of thought of the revolution in the midst of which it was set.

Thus far we will have dealt with those aspects of the history of the Roman Catholic Church in nineteenth-century Europe which transcended national boundaries and which in degrees that varied from country to country had repercussions throughout its entire constituency, whether in Europe or outside Europe. We must go on to trace the course of the Roman Catholic Church in each of the major countries of Europe. Here we will begin with France, for that was the land in which the revolution on the Continent had first centred and from which it spread. We will next pass to Italy, for here was the geographic heart of the Roman Catholic Church. It would seem natural from there to move to the other Latin countries, Spain and Portugal, and from them to Belgium, Holland, Germany, Switzerland, the Austro-Hungarian Empire of the Hapsburgs, in that order, and finally to Poland, Scandinavia, and the British Isles.

We must also note how from the loyal core of Roman Catholics the geographic spread of their branch of the faith was renewed. The Roman Catholic Church was now planted more widely than ever before—and almost entirely by emigrants and missionaries from Europe. This was the more remarkable in view of the fashion in which because of various phases of the revolution a great many professed Roman Catholics were drifting away from the Church. It is still more thought-provoking that more of the initiative and of the missionary staff came from France than from any other country, in spite of the fact that, unless it may have been in Latin America, de-Christianization appeared to have proceeded further in that land than anywhere else.

As we proceed we shall see that the Roman Catholic Church, the largest of the Christian bodies, presented a striking contrast. On the one hand it professed to be the divinely commissioned custodian of the most important gift of God to man, the way to an eternal life of blessedness, and in its ecclesiastical structure was the most widely spread organization which man had ever seen, headed up in a court which in the twentieth century displayed more pomp than any other on earth. On the other hand it regarded itself as persecuted and not only rejoiced in its long roster of martyrs but also stressed its present martyr role.

CHAPTER VII

The Roman Catholic Church and the Nineteenth-Century Stage of the Revolution: The Attitudes and Growth in Power of the Papacy

WHEN, in 1815, Waterloo and the deportation of Napoleon to the distant St. Helena brought to an end the stage of the revolution which had broken out in France in 1789 and which, captured by the Corsican, had ultimately involved most of Europe and the Americas, the outlook for the Papacy did not seem promising. To be sure, the Pope had returned to Rome. What was called the age of Metternich had set in. So far as that Austrian aristocrat and the monarchs who had joined in repressing Napoleon could accomplish it, the old order was being restored. The principle of "legitimacy" for which France's representative at the Congress of Vienna, the versatile Talleyrand, had sought recognition was adopted.

The territorial *status quo* was not fully reëstablished. For instance, Austria was accorded large territories in Italy, Prussia was given extensive additional portions of Germany, and to Russia went the major part of Poland. But the Bourbons were put back on the thrones of France, Spain, and the Two Sicilies. In France the close association of throne and altar was to some degree revived. All the major monarchs of Europe except the King of England, the Sultan of Turkey, and the Pope subscribed formally to the Holy Alliance, with its affirmation of the Christian faith. Yet Europe could not soon forget the fashion in which revolutionary France had divorced the Church in that land from administrative connexion with the Papacy and in which Napoleon had humiliated two Popes. Moreover, the basic revolution had not been checked. For a few years politically the clock seemed to have been turned back, but the liberal and radical ideas which had found outlet in the French Revolution did not die. The movements within the Roman Catholic Church which sought to limit the administrative authority of the Pope had only been scotched: they had not been killed. Gallicanism, although weakened, survived. So did something of the traditional near-autonomy of the Roman Catholic Church in Spain. In Germany and Austria ideas akin to Febronianism and Josephism had powerful advocates.

FORCES MAKING FOR THE REVIVAL AND STRENGTHENING OF THE PAPACY

Yet conditions existed which favoured the Papacy. As we have remarked, large numbers, mainly humble folk, in spite of the storm of revolution and scepticism were loyal to the Roman Catholic Church and to the Pope as its head. In addition, as we have also pointed out, a revival of faith was beginning. This was seen partly in Chateaubriand's *Génie du Christianisme* and the acclaim with which it was greeted. Many were disillusioned or repelled by what they saw of the revolution and its fruits and sought haven in a church which to them appeared to offer security in a world whose foundations were crumbling. The currents which made for secularization and de-Christianization were still potent, but the counter-currents were rising and were stronger than they had been since the seventeenth century. They would not necessarily augment the power of the Papacy, but the presumption would be that in a church which in principle centred in that institution they would do so.

Two authors who were products of the counter-currents and contributed to them were Joseph Marie Comte de Maistre (1783–1821) and Félicité Robert de Lamennais (1782–1854). Each gave a marked impulse to the resurgence of the power of the Papacy.

Joseph Marie Comte de Maistre was of the aristocracy of Savoy. He was ardently French and believed that country to have a divine mission. Educated by the Jesuits, he had early conceived a hearty detestation for eighteenth-century philosophical rationalism. He looked upon the Reign of Terror as a means by which God was purging France the better to prepare her to fulfil His purpose for her. He served his prince, the King of Sardinia, and his country in a number of official capacities. In his brief life he wrote extensively. His most influential work, *Du Pape*, published in 1819, was widely acclaimed and its enormous circulation was evidence of the existence of thousands who shared its convictions. It also contributed to the strengthening and spread of those convictions. While not unfavourable to constitutional monarchy and representative institutions, Maistre held that they were the outgrowth of Christianity. He condemned the Jacobin conception of liberty, the idea of popular sovereignty, and the theory of social contract, and argued that true liberty comes out of age-long struggles and entails stern moral self-discipline and obedience to conscience. He maintained that each nation should be guarded against the abuse of the power to which it is subject and that this could be accomplished only by a sovereignty superior to all others. That sovereignty he found in the Papacy. He said that a republican Christian Church was impossible, that councils were not sufficient, since they met only intermittently, that the authority of the Pope was essential to a General Council, and that the supremacy of the Pope had always been recognized in the Church. He declared that the Papacy had saved European civilization from the barbarians. He insisted that in the Church the Pope is sovereign, that as sovereign his decisions are not subject to appeal, and that since in his teaching he exercises sovereignty, in that teaching he must be infallible. He averred that no Pope had ever made a mistake in a matter of faith. It was his belief that schismatic Christians who did not acknowledge the authority of the Pope would fall into Protestantism and that the inevitable end of Protestantism was philosophical indifference.[1]

Lamennais was born of middle-class merchant stock, of a father who was Catholic because he believed religion to be a bulwark of morality. Emotional, self-willed, craving affection, and subject to fits of melancholy, the young Lamennais was encouraged to read widely.[2] His brother Jean, serene, given to good works, a priest eager for the renewal of the Church, had a marked influence on him. Through Jean, in his early twenties he was converted and read in preparation for the priesthood. He and Jean hoped for the renaissance of the Church and of the Catholic faith. In 1809 he came out with *Réflexions* condemning the eighteenth-century philosophers and outlining a programme for the reorganization of the Roman Catholic Church in France. Appalled by the subservience of the French Cardinals and bishops to Napoleon and thrilled by the steadfastness of the Pope against the pressures from that autocrat, he and his brother made a prolonged study of the history of the episcopate and the Papacy which issued in a three-volume work, *Tradition* (published in 1814), in which Lamennais believed that he had fully vindicated the ultramontane position and had shown Gallicanism to be untenable. In 1816 Lamennais was ordained deacon and then priest, steps which he took after much hesitation and depression, but with a clear sense of vocation. In 1817 he came out with the first volume in *Essai sur l'Indifférence en Matière de Religion* ("Essay on the Indifference in the Subject of Religion"), which was to be followed by the second volume in 1820 and the third and fourth volumes in 1823. In them he worked out a fresh apologetic for the Christian faith as against eighteenth-century rationalism. Their general purpose was not unlike that of Schleiermacher in his *Über die Religion. Reden am die Gebildeten unter ihren Verächtern,* published in 1799. The approach was quite different, but both books

[1] Le Comte J. de Maistre, *Du Pape* (Lyon, J. B. Pelagaud et Cie, 8th ed., 1845, pp. xl, 508); Elio Gianturco, *Joseph de Maistre and Giambattista Vico (Italian Roots of de Maistre's Political Culture)* (Washington, Murray & Heister, 1937, pp. ix, 240), *passim; The Catholic Encyclopedia,* Vol. IX, pp. 554, 555.

[2] See an excellent study of Lamennais in Vidler, *Prophecy and Papacy, A Study of the Church and the Revolution* (New York, Charles Scribner's Sons, 1954, pp. 300). His works are in *Oeuvres Complètes de La Mennais* (Paris, various publishers, 18 vols., 1836–1856). A standard work by a Roman Catholic priest is Charles Boutard, *Lamennais, Sa Vie et ses Doctrines* (Paris, Perrin et Cie, 3 vols., 1913).

were frontal attacks on attitudes associated with the intellectual denials of the Christian faith. They were evidence that a defence of Christianity could be from novel and not previously utilized angles and that Christianity was still displaying creative vigour. What concerns us for the moment in the *Essai* is partly the acclaim with which it was greeted and partly the anti-Gallican, ultramontane temper of the book. Later we shall see the subsequent history of Lamennais, his rejection of the union of Church and state, his espousal of political liberalism, his wide and profound influence in France and in some other parts of Europe, his conflict with the hierarchy, and his eventual break with the Roman Catholic Church and the Papacy.

In addition to the rising tide of faith and the writings of men such as Maistre and Lamennais, other factors contributed to the revival and strengthening of the power of the Papacy. The great ecclesiastical states of Germany were never fully restored. The sees remained, but to a large extent they were in territories which were now controlled by the staunchly Protestant Kings of Prussia: their heads deemed it wise to have the support of Rome and Febronianism was weakened. Through much of Europe those who feared a fresh outbreak of political revolution as a prelude to chaos regarded the Papacy as a symbol of order and authority. The romantic movement glorified the Middle Ages and with them the Papacy. In France the fashion in which the state had dealt with the Church, first under the National Assembly, then under the Republic and the Empire, had led the clergy who had suffered under the persecution to value the Papacy as their best support. In France, too, the lower clergy had seen in Rome their chief protection against the arbitrary power accorded the bishops under the Organic Articles enacted during the Consulate. In Germany the exigencies of the time left many episcopal sees vacant, sometimes for years. Therefore those wishing dispensations which bishops had generally reserved to themselves turned for them to Rome and revitalized in practice the doctrine that the Pope is the "universal bishop." In Germany, moreover, in some states under the administration of Protestant princes, Roman Catholics were a minority and not unnaturally looked to the Pope for assistance against their governments. These governments, on their side, regarded with disfavour the possibility of having to face a strong united Germany-wide Roman Catholic Church and preferred to enter into separate agreements with Rome for the regulation of ecclesiastical affairs. The revived Society of Jesus constituted a bulwark of Papal authority.[3] In the Austrian Netherlands, the later Belgium, even before the French occupation, resistance to Hapsburg power had made Josephism unpopular and had nurtured ultramontane convictions and reliance on Rome as a counter to imperial claims.[4]

[3] Aubert, *Le pontificat de Pie IX*, pp. 262, 263.
[4] Vidler, *op. cit.*, p. 120.

In the years immediately after 1815 the combination of the character of the reigning Pontiff and the abilities and the measures of his Secretary of State gave an initial impetus to the prestige of the Papacy. By his patience and courage under the pressures and imprisonment by Napoleon, his lack of vindictiveness towards that monarch and his family, and his sincere piety Pius VII won from millions respect and veneration which accrued not alone to him but also to his office. His Secretary of State, Consalvi, by diplomacy enhanced the position of Rome.

Ultramontanism was not quickly triumphant. The restoration of the Bourbon monarchy in France brought with it the return of clergy who had been committed to Gallicanism. Movements in Germany which we have noticed and of which we are to hear more were hostile. Yet gradually, by steps which we will record in the appropriate places, ultramontanism won.

In general, and notably during the first two-thirds of the century between 1815 and 1914, the Popes set themselves against many aspects of the revolution, particularly those which were political. While in the latter third of the period a more conciliatory attitude was adopted, the Pope who reigned in the later decades was firm in his opposition to some important trends. As we have hinted and as we are to see again and again, under Papal leadership the Roman Catholic Church tended to become an ever more tightly knit minority resistant to much of the revolution. But it was not content to be on the defensive. It sought to capture the world. Assisted by a hierarchy more and more under the direction of the Pope and a growing body of men and women completely devoted to it through the vows of poverty, chastity, and obedience, and with a large body of laity organized in one way and another under the control of the hierarchy and so of the Pope, the Roman Catholic Church was endeavouring to fulfil what it believed to be its divine commission to bring all mankind to discipleship. Even when they were in opposition to the attitudes associated with the revolution, doctrines which had heretofore been latent or debated by the Church's theologians were set forth in language which was meant to be unequivocal and final. The gulf between the Roman Catholic Church and other branches of Christianity was broadened and deepened. Yet the Roman Catholic Church spread. In much of Europe multitudes who as a matter of historic social convention were baptized into its fold tended to drift away from it. But, as we have suggested and are to see further, migrations and missions planted it around the world. More and more it took root in many lands and peoples.

The part which the Papacy had in this process is best sketched chronologically. We will attempt reign by reign to summarize Papal policies and achievements.

It is interesting and possibly significant that the increase in the effective centralized control of the Roman Catholic Church under the Papacy was paralleled by the growth in Protestantism of what was eventually called the Ecumenical Movement. We have noted the efforts among Protestants from the sixteenth century onward to bring about unity in their ranks and among all Christians. They had a few immediate effects. In the nineteenth century, as we are to see, both the efforts and the effects mounted. Because of the divisive nature of Protestantism and the lack of precedent for the kind of unity possible to Protestants, in the nineteenth century in their outward manifestations the Protestant efforts at unity were less successful than was the Papacy in the Roman Catholic Church. In the twentieth century they made rapid strides.

Pius VII (1800–1823), from 1815 to the End of the Pontificate

We have already seen something of Pius VII, for his pontificate began in 1800 and nearly two-thirds of it fell in the years before the final exile of Napoleon. As we have said, he was deeply religious, a Benedictine, and a theologian. He lived simply, avoided nepotism, and hoped that a renewal of its inner life would enable the Church to recapture society.

The settlement which followed Waterloo restored much that had been taken from the Papacy during the preceding years. Consalvi represented Rome at the Congress of Vienna and by long-standing tradition as the Pope's representative was accorded formal precedence over the other diplomats. His astuteness won for the Holy See more than but for him would probably have been awarded it. He obtained the restoration to the Pope of most of the territories in Italy which had been included in the States of the Church.[5]

The restoration of the Papal States posed a problem which could not be easily or quickly solved. In a day when nationalism and political liberalism were mounting in close association with each other, could the Papal States survive? The demand for Italian unity on the basis of democracy had been stimulated by the French Revolution and the Napoleonic era. It was to grow. How would the Papacy meet it? Would it refuse to compromise with it? Would it make concessions without fully yielding? Would it yield fully? If so, would it do so willingly, or would it do so reluctantly and only under compulsion? Here were major questions which were not to be answered completely until the twentieth century. They were more than local; in them were issues which were world-wide. The response of the Papacy to them would be part and parcel of the Papal reply to the global political and social movements of the era. It would therefore provide a way for gauging that reply.

Ercole (Hercules) Consalvi (1757–1824) was not only the ablest Papal diplo-

[5] Hermelink, Geschichte das Christentum in der Menschheitsgeschichte von der französischen Revolution bis zur Gegenwart, Vol. I, pp. 349, 350; Leflon, La Crise Révolutionnaire, pp. 301–303; Nielsen, The History of the Papacy in the Nineteenth Century, Vol. I, pp. 350–358; Schmidlin, Papstgeschichte der neuesten Zeit, Vol. I, pp. 134–144; Pistolesi, Vita del Sommo Pontefice Pio VII, Vol. IV, pp. 133 ff.

mat of the period. He was also the outstanding administrator and statesman in the service of the Holy See during the first quarter of the nineteenth century.[6] While he did not always have his full way, no other single person so shaped the Papal policies under Pius VII subsequent to the fall of Napoleon. Even after his death their main outlines were largely followed by the next Pope, Leo XII.

Consalvi was of noble Italian ancestry. He had part of his early education in a school in Frascati and there became acquainted with some of the outstanding families of Rome. He completed his studies in the Ecclesiastical Academy in Rome which had been founded by Pius VI. He specialized in civil and canon law and was taken into the service of Pius VI. As secretary of the conclave in Venice which chose a successor to Pius VI he had an influential share in the election of Chiaramonti as Pius VII. Pius VII quickly appointed him Pro-Secretary of State and before long made him Cardinal and Secretary of State. In Rome Consalvi instituted reforms in the administration of the city and put the currency on a sounder basis. He was the Papal agent in the negotiations with Napoleon of the French concordat of 1801. Through his support of Pius VII in the latter's break with Napoleon Consalvi brought down on his head the wrath of the emperor. As we have seen, to appease Napoleon he was dismissed from the Secretaryship of State. Like his master, he refused to sanction Napoleon's divorce of Josephine and marriage to Marie Louise. In high dudgeon the emperor sought to depose him. For a time he was banished to Reims and kept under close surveillance. On Napoleon's fall he was reappointed Secretary of State. As we have said, he was the chief negotiator for the Pope of the diplomatic settlements which followed.

Those negotiations concluded, Consalvi took charge of the administration of the States of the Church whose return to the Pope he had obtained. French rule had brought the abolition of many of the traditional practices which now seemed anachronisms. At the instance of Consalvi, in July, 1816, Pius VII issued the *motu proprio* which became a kind of constitution for the Papal States. By it the cities and nobles lost accustomed privileges and monopolies and exemptions were abolished. The French provisions for taxes and customs were continued. After the French manner, for administrative purposes the States were divided into seventeen delegations. Over each a prelate was appointed as delegate, an office which corresponded to the French prefect. Members of the laity were placed in subordinate but still important offices. Steps were taken towards reforms in the administration of justice, a uniform legal code, and a

[6] *Mémoires du Cardinal Consalvi Secrétaire d'État du Pape Pie VII avec une introduction et des notes par J. Crétineau-Joly* (Paris, Henri Plon, 2 vols., 1864); Engelbert Lorenz Fischer, *Cardinal Consalvi. Lebens- und Charakterbild des grossen Ministers Papst Pius VII* (Mainz, Franz Kirchheim, 1899, pp. xv, 350).

system of education. The methods of taxation were changed.[7] Measures were inaugurated to improve agriculture, industry, and transportation, to reduce brigandage, and to better the police system.[8]

The changes were made in the face of strong opposition. To many they seemed to smack of the hated French innovations. Several of the Cardinals and numbers of subordinate clergy were critical. Others who were dispossessed of inherited privileges were unhappy.[9]

The authority of the Pope was enhanced by concordats or agreements with several states, both Roman Catholic and Protestant. By taking the initiative in regulating ecclesiastical affairs in the new Europe, the Papacy was strengthening the precedent for its control of the entire Roman Catholic Church. This was especially significant in Germany. Here the Holy Roman Empire had ceased to exist and only a vague shadow of it was created by the Congress of Vienna in the form of a loose German Confederation. Some, including Dalberg and especially Wessenberg, wished a united German Catholic Church and desired a concordat for all Germany. A German church recognized by a comprehensive concordat would have weakened the administrative power of the Papacy. By entering into separate arrangements with several of the German princes Rome blocked the realization of that dream. With Spain the concordat of 1753 was revived. In 1817 Sardinia restored ten dioceses which had been abolished by the French. Difficulties developed in connexion with a concordat with France. In 1817 one was negotiated which annulled that of 1801 and reaffirmed that of 1516, but the French parliament refused to ratify it, the Government proposed a law to govern ecclesiastical affairs which proved unsatisfactory to Rome, and in 1819 a compromise was reached by which it was agreed that for the time being the concordat of 1801 would hold. In 1817 a concordat with Bavaria was negotiated, but it met with opposition from a government which wished to exert the same control that it had over Protestant bodies and it was not fully implemented. Consalvi obtained with Naples (1818) the concordat which he desired, and, after a break between Rome and Naples in 1820, in 1821 the concordat again came into force. Through long negotiations, in 1827, in the next pontificate, a concordat was reached with the King of the Netherlands which arranged ecclesiastical affairs in Belgium. In 1821 Prussia concluded an arrangement, promulgated in the form of a bull, which was somewhat favourable to the Papacy. Because of the persistence of the Josephist tradition a new

---

[7] Leflon, *op. cit.*, pp. 312, 313; Nielsen, *op. cit.*, Vol. I, pp. 360, 361; Ranke, *Die römischen Päpste in den letzen vier Jahrhunderten*, pp. 420 ff.; Fischer, *op. cit.*, pp. 303–306; Schmidlin, *op. cit.*, Vol. I, pp. 145 ff.

[8] Ranke, *op. cit.*, pp. 439–445; Schmidlin, *op. cit.*, Vol. I, pp. 157–159; Leflon, *op. cit.*, pp. 314, 315.

[9] Ranke, *op. cit.*, pp. 447–455.

concordat with Austria proved impracticable, but as an indication of loyalty to the Holy See, in 1819 the Austrian emperor paid a state visit to Rome.[10]

In a number of other countries the Papacy took measures other than formal concordats to make its authority effective in ecclesiastical affairs. This was accomplished in several Italian states.[11] A reorganization of the Swiss dioceses was achieved.[12] Difficulties arose with some of the German states on the Upper Rhine. Baden, Württemberg, Hesse-Darmstadt, Electoral Hesse, and Hesse-Nassau sought to regulate their ecclesiastical affairs by legislation. They wished to restrict the Papal powers to consenting to the delimitation of diocesan boundaries by the states. To this Pius VII would not agree. The situation was complicated by the fact that the governments were Protestant. The princes were eager to exercise the same powers over the Catholic Church within their borders that they possessed over the Protestant churches. Here was a source of conflict with Rome which continued for many years. In the face of the long-standing fear of the Roman Catholic Church, in England Consalvi obtained a lessening of prejudice.[13]

In 1814 Pius VII created a Congregation of Extraordinary Ecclesiastical Affairs, in succession to one which had been set up in 1804 to deal with conditions in France, but with more extended territorial coverage. It had under its purview both states with Roman Catholic and states with non-Roman Catholic governments. Sometimes Pius VII was tempted to believe that the former gave him more trouble than the latter. The Congregation was a symbol as well as an instrument of insistence by Rome of Papal authority over the entire Roman Catholic Church.[14]

Another step towards augmenting the power of the Papacy in the Roman Catholic Church was the restoration of the Society of Jesus. It will be remembered that under various guises the Society had persisted in several countries, that in 1801 Papal recognition had been accorded it in Russia, and that in 1804, at the instance of King Ferdinand of the Two Sicilies, it had been revived in his realms. Requests for the full reconstitution of the Society mounted. The powerful Cardinal Pacca urged that the step be taken. Consalvi was dubious but was too occupied in Vienna to be an active opponent. Some of the other Cardinals questioned whether it was proper for the Pope to reverse the action

[10] Schmidlin, *op. cit.*, Vol. I, pp. 178 ff.; Nielsen, *op. cit.*, Vol. I, pp. 368–371; Fischer, *op. cit.*, pp. 309 ff.; Leflon, *op. cit.*, pp. 322. For some of the documents see Pistolesi, *op. cit.*, Vol. IV, pp. 177 ff.

[11] Leflon, *op. cit.*, pp. 324, 325.

[12] *Ibid.*, pp. 336, 337.

[13] Schnabel, *Deutsche Geschichte im neunzehnten Jahrhundert*, Vol. IV, pp. 35–41; Leflon, *op. cit.*, pp. 347–349; Hermelink, *op. cit.*, pp. 349, 350; John Tracy Ellis, *Cardinal Consalvi and Anglo-Papal Relations, 1814–1824* (Washington, The Catholic University of America Press, 1942, pp. xi, 202), *passim*.

[14] Leflon, *op. cit.*, p. 322.

of a recent predecessor. Yet on August 7, 1814, Pius VII entered the Jesuit church in Rome and, after celebrating mass at the altar of Ignatius, had the bull publicly read which renewed the Society. Protests against the action came from Portugal and Brazil; in France the Society faced difficulties; and feeling against it so rose in Russia that in 1815 the Jesuits were expelled from Moscow and St. Petersburg and in 1820 from all Russia and the Russian portion of Poland. But Ferdinand VII of Spain welcomed them back in his domains, they were favoured in Piedmont, and they quickly established footholds in Vienna and elsewhere.[15]

Pius VII and Consalvi were intent upon strengthening the Papacy in still another fashion. They sought to make Rome the chief centre of European culture. Under the direction of Consalvi many of the works of art and of the books and manuscripts which had been taken from Rome, chiefly by the French, were returned.[16] During the French occupation and the absence of the Pope the population of the city had dwindled, clergy had declined in numbers, and the historic churches had fallen into disrepair. In spite of the severe distress of the Papal treasury, Pius VII had many of the churches repaired, furthered the excavations of ancient Rome, renovated and enriched the museums and the Vatican library, sought to clean up the poorer sections of the city, and reorganized universities in Rome and other centres in the Papal States. The measures were so far successful that Rome attracted many artists, architects, and students of antiquity.[17] However, as Pius VII and Consalvi conceived it Rome was to become much the kind of cultural centre that the Renaissance Popes had made it. They did not attempt to capture or direct the new intellectual and scientific forces that were prominent in the revolution which was moulding the new century.

Rome gained in a kind of prestige which was of doubtful value in a revolutionary world by being the residence of several princes who had been ousted from their thrones by the political changes of the era. It was also visited by reigning princes, both Roman Catholic and Protestant.[18]

In additional ways under Pius VII the Papacy was reviving and augmenting its position. They included the renewal of monasteries, orders, and congregations of religious and the resumption of the geographic expansion of the faith. By a single edict 1,824 men's and 622 women's houses were ordered restored.[19]

Under Pius VII the Papacy took measures which set it against some of the

[15] Nielsen, *op. cit.*, Vol. I, pp. 345–349; Schmidlin, *op. cit.*, Vol. I, pp. 357–359.

[16] Fischer, *op. cit.*, pp. 297–300.

[17] Leflon, *op. cit.*, pp. 315, 316; Nielsen, *op. cit.*, Vol. I, p. 372; Schmidlin, *op. cit.*, Vol. I, pp. 163–178.

[18] Nielsen, *op. cit.*, Vol. I, pp. 371, 372.

[19] Nippold, *Geschichte des Katholozismus seit der Restauration des Papstthums* (Vol. II of *Handbuch der neuesten Kirchengeschichte*), p. 28.

trends of the day. Through them it aroused antagonism among many of its nominal children and also contributed to what we have noted and will have occasion again and again to remark: the character of the Roman Catholic Church as an ever more closely knit body set against many of the currents in the world about it but seeking to win the allegiance of all men. Pius VII declined to subscribe to the Holy Alliance. That is not strange, for had he consented he would have been joining in a declaration framed by a member of the Russian Orthodox Church (which he deemed schismatic) and agreed to not only by Roman Catholic monarchs but also by Protestant princes. Then, too, he would have tacitly admitted that secular monarchs were on an equality with him. Moreover, the Holy Alliance seemed to the Pope to embody a vague religiosity, to subordinate God to Caesar, and to make the Pope a companion to rulers who were pursuing policies which he was condemning.[20] The congregations which supervised the Index and the Inquisition were revived. The latter found that 724 accusations of heresy awaited its attention.[21] In 1814 in a letter to two archbishops Bible societies were condemned. Owing partly to the stimulus of the example and the efforts of the agents of the British and Foreign Bible Society, Bible societies had sprung up in several places on the Continent. They had as their purpose the circulation of the Scriptures in the vernaculars and without comment. Rome had not been averse to the reading of the Bible by the laity. Indeed, from time to time Popes had encouraged it. However, since, when not supervised by the hierarchy and interpreted in the sense which the Roman Catholic Church regarded as correct, the study of the Scriptures by the laity had across the centuries contributed to numbers of movements which that church labeled as heresies, the wide distribution of Bibles in unauthorized editions could not but be looked upon as highly dangerous.[22]

These several actions of Pius VII or with his concurrence did not command unanimous support in his entourage. We have already noted the opposition to some of Consalvi's measures. The College of Cardinals contained some gifted men with positive opinions who were by no means always in agreement with them. One of the ablest was Bartolommeo Pacca (1756–1844).[23] A group, not tightly organized, the *Zelanti,* advocated the strengthening of the Papacy as against the regional and national attempts to limit it such as Gallicanism, Febronianism, and Josephism. They also set their faces against the liberal movements of the day, in both politics and religion.[24]

In Rome and the Papal States and elsewhere in Italy the *Carbonari* laboured

[20] Leflon, *op. cit.,* pp. 303, 304.
[21] Nippold, *op. cit.,* p. 28.
[22] *Ibid.*
[23] Ranke, *op. cit.,* Vol. II, pp. 446–455; Leflon, *op. cit.,* pp. 317, 318.
[24] Leflon, *op. cit.,* pp. 317–320; Pouthas, *l'Église Catholique de l'avènement de Pie VII à l'avènement de Pie IX,* pp. 262, 263.

and plotted for a politically united liberal Italy. Their motto was "Despotism annihilated." They regarded the Catholic Church as a major enemy. Working with them from time to time were the *Guelfs,* originally a society opposed to French domination. Another group, the *Sanfedists,* also known as *Centurions,* founded in the Kingdom of Naples in the time of French rule, coöperated with the *Zelanti* against the *Carbonari* and the *Guelfs.* In 1820 revolts, partly fomented and led by the *Carbonari,* broke out in Naples against the king and in 1821 in the North against the Austrians.[25] By a bull issued in 1821 Pius VII condemned the *Carbonari.*[26] The revolts were put down.

Death came to Pius VII on August 20, 1823. He was then eighty-one years of age. His mental powers had not failed and in his daily walks through the streets of Rome he was a benign figure who gave his blessing to chance passers-by.[27] A fall which resulted in a broken hip proved fatal.[28]

It is interesting and perhaps significant that Pius VII outlived Napoleon by a little over two years. The Pope had been grieved by the emperor's loneliness and sufferings on St. Helena and, forgiving the anguish which that monarch had caused him, recalled gratefully what he chose to regard as the Corsican's reëstablishment of the Christian faith in France.[29] The one represented the Roman Catholic Church, the other the revolution. Both the Roman Catholic Church and the revolution owed their strength not primarily to physical force, although both had utilized it—the Roman Catholic Church more in earlier days than now. Their power was in the realm of the spirit and in ideals which moved the souls and minds of men. Both were indebted to the Christian Gospel, the Roman Catholic Church consciously, the revolution less consciously. In both the Gospel had been compromised by its environment. Would either ultimately triumph? If so, which would it be? Or would both continue indefinitely side by side, each expanding its territorial coverage and in chronic reciprocal antagonism? At the time of the death of Pius VII the outcome was ambiguous.

Leo XII, 1823–1829

With the death of Pius VII the smouldering enmity against his great minister, Consalvi, came to a head. Metternich believed that Consalvi had not been sufficiently firm in resisting liberal movements. He held the Cardinal responsible for Rome's refusal to join fully in the armed measures to suppress the liberal revolts of 1820 and 1821 in Spain and Italy, and Austria made it clear that it

---

25 Hales, *Pio Nino,* pp. 23, 28; Leflon, *op. cit.,* pp. 318–320; Nielsen, *op. cit.,* Vol. I, pp. 372, 373; Ranke, *op. cit.,* Vol. II, pp. 457 ff.
26 Nielsen, *op. cit.,* Vol. I, p. 374.
27 Wiseman, *Recollections of the Last Four Popes and of Rome in Their Times,* p. 34.
28 Leflon, *op. cit.,* p. 375; Schmidlin, *op. cit.,* Vol. II, pp. 362, 363.
29 Nielsen, *op. cit.,* Vol. I, pp. 374, 375.

would oppose the choice of Consalvi as successor to Pius.[30] The *Zelanti* among the Cardinals distrusted Consalvi as too liberal. The reforms which he had instituted in the Papal States had alienated those whose privileges had been annulled. To many of the Cardinals he had seemed dictatorial; they considered that he had gathered too much power in his own hands. They also believed that in the concordats and other agreements which he had negotiated with the various governments he had not been sufficiently firm in upholding the rights of the Roman Catholic Church.[31]

Consalvi did not long survive Pius VII. In spite of the fact that some years earlier the two had had a severe quarrel, he gave to the successor of Pius VII counsel in which, with customary prescience, among other recommendations he stressed the importance of paying special attention to South America and Russia. He advised the holding of a jubilee year as a way of promoting the prestige of the Papacy. He urged the continuation of the policy of working for the emancipation of the English Catholics. The new Pope honoured him, appointed him Prefect of the Congregation for the Propagation of the Faith, and followed some of the main lines of the policies which he had devised. Consalvi made provision for a suitable monument to Pius VII. On January 24, 1824, less than six months after his great patron, he breathed his last. His final words were: *"Io sono tranquillo"* ("I am at peace"). They were a fitting close to a life spent unstintedly in the midst of the storm of revolution.[32]

In the conclave which elected the successor to Pius VII several influences contended. The *Zelanti* were prominent. The Roman Catholic monarchs were actively interested, for the attitude of the Pontiff could go far towards shaping the political future in several lands, especially in Italy. Against one candidate who was supported by the *Zelanti* the Austrian Government opposed its veto and thus blocked what otherwise seemed to be his certain choice. The *Zelanti* thereupon concentrated their votes on Annibale Francesco Clemente Melchior Girolamo della Genga (1760–1829). It was rumoured that France would object, but when two French Cardinals endorsed him, enough others of the Sacred College swung to him to determine the outcome.[33]

Genga, who took the title of Leo and is known as Leo XII, was a scion of the Italian nobility. He had had part of his education in Rome and there, as a youth, had attracted the attention of Pius VI. He became a favourite of that Pope, was much in his company, and was rapidly promoted. He had spent a

[30] *Ibid.*, p. 374; Joseph N. Brady, *Rome and the Neopolitan Revolt of 1820–1821. A Study in Papal Neutrality* (New York, Columbia University Press, 1937, pp. 201), *passim*.

[31] Leflon, *op. cit.*, pp. 379, 380.

[32] Fischer, *Cardinal Consalvi*, pp. 333–357.

[33] Nielsen, *The History of the Papacy in the Nineteenth Century*, Vol. II, pp. 1–5; Leflon, *La Crise Révolutionnaire*, pp. 379–384; Schmidlin, *Papstgeschichte der neuesten Zeit*, Vol. I, pp. 368–374.

large part of his life as Papal Nuncio, first in Lucerne and then in Germany. The reports of him from Germany were mixed: some represented him as exemplary; others, presumably out of malice, hinted at scandal.[34] For a time when Pius VII was being mistreated by Napoleon Genga retired to the monastery of which he was the titular head and gave himself to hunting birds, to beautifying the chapel, and to teaching the peasants to sing the music of the Church. After Pius VII returned to Rome he called Genga again into his service and sent him to Paris to congratulate Louis XVIII on the latter's restoration. There occurred the sharp clash between Consalvi and Genga and the latter returned to his monastery. But Pius VII would not permit him to withdraw and appointed him Cardinal and in 1820 summoned him to Rome to an administrative post.[35] At the time of his election Leo XII was a sick man. To one who saw him as the Cardinals assembled he appeared tall, emaciated, pale, and feeble.[36] It is said that when, as ritual required, he was asked after the decisive vote whether he would accept, he protested that the Cardinals were electing a corpse.[37]

Frail though he was and often handicapped by sickness, Leo XII surprised his physicians by his tenacity on life and the diligence with which he performed his duties. The six years of his reign witnessed several achievements. He was frugal in his personal expenses, sought to bring the Papal finances into order, and reduced taxation. In his initial encyclical, issued in May, 1824, he gave an indication of his policy. He urged the bishops to be examples of sound morals and doctrine, to be diligent in pastoral visitation, to pay attention to the seminaries, and to be discreet in their ordinations and choose with care the men who were to be pastors. He condemned tendencies to toleration and indifference whether in matters civil or religious. He reaffirmed his predecessor's opposition to Bible societies. Throughout his reign he set himself against Gallicanism and Josephism and sought to rally the bishops to the support of the Papacy. Following the advice of Consalvi, he proclaimed a jubilee year, a step which his predecessor had contemplated but because of the tempestuous years of most of his reign had not ventured to take. Leo sought to put the churches of Rome in better physical condition and to revive the spiritual life of the city. He reorganized education and placed it under a special congregation. He pronounced against the freedom of the press and books which seemed to him evil, and encouraged the Congregation of the Index to be more strict in its supervision of literature. He took vigorous action against the *Carbonari*—had some of them executed, others imprisoned, and still others exiled.[38] All these measures tended

[34] Nippold, *op. cit.*, Vol. II, p. 75; Leflon, *op. cit.*, p. 384.
[35] Schmidlin, *op. cit.*, Vol. I, pp. 367, 368.
[36] Wiseman, *op. cit.*, p. 135.
[37] Schmidlin, *op. cit.*, Vol. I, p. 374.
[38] Leflon, *op. cit.*, pp. 388, 392; Schmidlin, *op. cit.*, Vol. I, pp. 447–454, 467–469.

to renew the Roman Catholic Church and to move in the direction of making it a more compact body set against the revolutionary tide.

As was to be expected from one in sympathy with the *Zelanti*, in his administration of the Papal States Leo XII annulled some of the measures of Consalvi: he gave the clergy a larger share in the Government and restored several of the former privileges of the nobility.[39]

Leo XII endeavoured to improve the morals of the populace and of the clergy. By his economies and his insistence that officials attend to their duties and by his unwavering opposition to nepotism on the part of any of his subordinates[40] he made himself unpopular with many among both his official family and the masses.

Leo XII took an active interest in the Church in its several national settings. He moved towards regaining what had been lost in revolutionary Latin America.[41] In Europe he was not content with what survived of trends towards administrative independence but sought, with some success, to assert the authority of his see, whether it was in France, Germany, Switzerland, the Netherlands, Italy, Spain, Portugal, Russia, or the British Isles.[42] In France Lamennais was still in his anti-Gallican ultramontane stage and was only beginning to move towards the political liberalism which was to lead to his conflict with the Church. Leo welcomed him in Rome and showed him distinct favour, although he may not, as is sometimes thought, have intended to raise him to the Cardinalate.[43] The struggle to make the Papal weight felt in the various German states continued with varying successes and failures. The conversions to Roman Catholicism from the German intellectuals and nobility which were associated with the romantic movement reached their peak.[44] In the Austrian possessions in North Italy the Pope still faced the traditional Josephism.[45] In the stormy political scene in Spain and Portugal Rome had a complex problem. It was confronted by the anti-clericalism of the liberals and in its efforts to maintain the Roman Catholic faith at times seemed to side with the conservatives. On the other hand, by its appointment of bishops in revolting Spanish America it appeared to countenance the independence of the colonies and therefore aroused the ire of the Spanish crown.[46] Moreover, by sending representatives to Spanish America without the approval of the crown Leo was setting aside

[39] Leflon, *op. cit.*, pp. 390, 391.

[40] Nielsen, *op. cit.*, Vol. II, pp. 24, 25.

[41] Schmidlin, *op. cit.*, Vol. I, pp. 437–445; Thornton, *The Church and Freemasonry in Brazil, 1872–1875*, pp. 65 ff.

[42] Schmidlin, *op. cit.*, Vol. I, pp. 395 ff.

[43] Vidler, *Prophecy and Papacy*, pp. 94–97; Wiseman, *Recollections of the Last Four Popes*, pp. 209–211.

[44] Schmidlin, *op. cit.*, Vol. I, pp. 405–413.

[45] *Ibid.*, p. 435.

[46] *Ibid.*, pp. 427–429.

a long-standing precedent which accorded to the monarch ecclesiastical patronage in the overseas possessions. In the British Isles the situation was rendered peculiarly difficult by the struggle for equal political rights for Roman Catholics, especially in Ireland, and by the historic antagonism of the ruling Protestant minority of Ireland and of the Protestant majority in Great Britain. Leo XII sought to foster the Roman Catholic minority in England, as had his predecessor. Among other measures, he was friendly to the English College in Rome which Pius VII had reëstablished.[47] It was in the year of his death that the emancipation of Roman Catholics in the United Kingdom was accomplished.[48]

In spite of his chronic ill health, Leo XII maintained a daily schedule which would have exhausted many men with much larger physical reserves. His hours of sleep were few. He ate sparingly, gave unhurried time to his personal devotions, spent long hours in his audiences and at his desk, and officiated at public functions and at public masses on high days of the ecclesiastical year to a greater extent than had any other Pope of recent times.[49]

It was on February 10, 1829, when he was in his sixty-ninth year, that his frail body refused longer to bear the burdens to which Leo had subjected it. In his epitaph, which he composed, he described himself as the least of the heirs of the name of the first Leo, "the Great."[50] He had not fully satisfied either the *Zelanti* or those who favoured Consalvi's policies, but he had laboured hard and conscientiously. Yet in Rome the majority heaved a sigh of relief when death brought his career to an end.[51]

Pius VIII, 1829–1830

In the conclave which followed the death of Leo XII several factions struggled for control. The *Zelanti* were in the majority but could not unite on a candidate. The governments of both France and Austria let it be known that they wished the election of a moderate. After meeting for five weeks the Cardinals chose Francesco Saviero Castiglioni (1761–1830). Castiglioni was of a noble Italian family and was learned in canon law, Biblical literature, and numismatics. He had had administrative experience in several posts, including bishoprics and posts in Rome. He had suffered imprisonment because of his opposition to Napoleon. After his release Pius VII had rewarded him with the Cardinal's hat and is said to have wished him for his successor. Out of gratitude Castiglioni took the title of Pius. He was mild in temper and was not likely to go to extremes or to have a particularly vigorous pontificate.[52] Sixty-seven

---

[47] Wiseman, *op. cit.*, pp. 92, 197–203.
[48] Schmidlin, *op. cit.*, Vol. I, pp. 429–431.
[49] Wiseman, *op. cit.*, p. 201.
[50] *Ibid.*, pp. 220–222.
[51] Leflon, *op. cit.*, p. 410.
[52] *Ibid.*, pp. 410–413; Nielsen, *op. cit.*, Vol. II, pp. 31–39; Schmidlin, *op. cit.*, Vol. I, pp. 474–480; Wiseman, *op. cit.*, pp. 225–233.

years of age at the time of his election and reported to be unwell, he could not expect many years in his high office. He was considered to be friendly to France. He named as his Secretary of State Giuseppe Albani (1750–1834), then in his late seventies. Albani was from a noble family which had provided Rome with one Pope and at least two Cardinals. He was Austrian in his sympathies. Wealthy and worldly, he owed his appointment partly to his share in obtaining the election of Castiglioni.[53] Yet the latter warned the members of his own family to keep away from Rome, for he wished to avoid even the suspicion of nepotism.

Pius VIII had too brief a reign to permit of major achievements. Elected late in March, 1829, he died on November 30, 1830. He thus had only a few days over twenty months on the throne. In general both he and Albani were inclined to follow the main lines of the policy laid down by Consalvi. Pius VIII fulfilled the hope of France and Austria in being a moderate. For example, he abolished the system of espionage set up by Leo XII. But that did not mean that he compromised with revolutionary trends and forces. In his opening encyclical he denounced those who declared that entrance to salvation could be by all religions, condemned Bible societies and secret societies, upheld the sanctity of the laws of marriage, and urged the bishops to give care to the education of the young. By laying claim to authority over all Christians and their bishops he gave offense to some of the Gallicanly minded of the episcopate.[54]

Even during his brief reign Pius VIII had to face a fresh upheaval of political revolution. The year 1830 witnessed the first major explosion of nationalism and political liberalism since the Congress of Vienna. As in 1789, the storm first broke in France, led by Paris. There it forced Charles X off the throne. Charles X was less compromising with liberal views than his predecessor, Louis XVIII. He was also ardently Roman Catholic: the revolt, therefore, had anticlerical aspects. Moderates won. Supported by the liberal bourgeoisie they seated on the throne the "citizen king" Louis Philippe, of a branch of the house of Bourbon. The quick success of the revolution in France encouraged political liberals elsewhere in Europe. The Belgians, overwhelmingly Roman Catholic, rebelled against the rule of the Dutch king, a Protestant. They obtained their independence under a liberal constitutional monarchy, with results for the Roman Catholic Church to which we are to recur in a later chapter. Civil strife between liberals and conservatives broke out in Spain and Portugal. In several German states liberals rioted and won temporary concessions. Central Italy saw outbreaks against the Hapsburg rulers, and it was only through Austrian troops despatched by Metternich that they were suppressed. As we shall see in a mo-

[53] Nielsen, *op. cit.*, Vol. II, pp. 42, 43; Leflon, *op. cit.*, p. 414.
[54] Leflon, *op. cit.*, p. 415; Nielsen, *op. cit.*, Vol. II, pp. 43, 44.

ment, uprisings troubled the Papal States. Poles fought, unsuccessfully, to throw off the Russian yoke.

In general, Pius VIII and Albani opposed the liberal movements. They attempted to make the best of the situation in France. Counter to the wishes of some of the Cardinals Pius recognized Louis Philippe and conferred on that religiously lukewarm monarch the title which had been given his predecessor, "his most Christian Majesty," and thus believed that he was supporting legitimacy.[55] However, in Belgium Rome frowned on the close association of liberals and Catholics.[56] In the main, as was to be expected, particularly from the Austrian sympathies of Albani, Rome stood by the princes against the liberals.[57]

In matters of doctrine Pius VIII was conciliatory towards Lamennais and a German writer, Günther, who were moving away from orthodoxy.[58] Nor was he as outspoken as some of the *Zelanti* would have wished in opposing measures in Germany which were compromising the claims of the Roman Catholic Church.[59]

What course Pius VIII would have pursued had his life been prolonged into the critical years which followed 1830 we do not know. As it was, death intervened.

GREGORY XVI, 1831–1846

The conclave which was to choose a successor to Pius VIII met late in December, 1830, under difficult circumstances. The tide of revolution was mounting. The Catholic powers were deeply concerned and their wishes would help to shape the outcome. Austria's veto blocked one candidate. The opposition of Spain made impossible the choice of another. The impatient Roman populace threatened the conclave with the creation of a republic if the Cardinals did not arrive at a decision by February 12, 1831. Several of the *Zelanti* united on Cappellari. Albani opposed him in the name of Vienna, but a courier brought the word that Metternich would be happy if Cappellari were chosen and Albani yielded. Cappellari pled with his colleagues not to place upon him the burden of the office. However, he was a monk and the general of his order and his confessor commanded him to accept. Since obedience was one of his monastic vows, he complied.[60]

Bartolomeo Alberto Cappellari (1765–1846) was from lesser nobility whose

[55] Leflon, *op. cit.*, p. 421.
[56] *Ibid.*, p. 423.
[57] Pouthas, *l'Église Catholique de l'avènement de Pie VII à l'avènement de Pie IX*, p. 275.
[58] *Ibid.*, p. 274.
[59] Leflon, *op. cit.*, pp. 415–417.
[60] *Ibid.*, pp. 428, 429; Schmidlin, *op. cit.*, Vol. I, pp. 511–516; Friedrich Engel De Janosi, *Zwei Studien zur Geschichte de österreichischen Vetorechts. I. Das Konklave vom 1846*, in *Festschrift zum 200jährigen Bestand des Haus-, Hof- und Staatsarchivs*, II (Vienna, 1951), pp. 283–293.

members on both sides of his house had been in the service of the state. He had early shown an inclination to the religious life and in his teens against the wishes of his parents he had joined the Camaldolese. The Camaldolese had arisen in the tenth and eleventh centuries as one of the most strictly ascetic of the new bodies of an era when the tide of monastic devotion was running strong. Cappellari was a diligent and able student who specialized in philosophy and theology. He showed the direction of his mind by coming out in his late youth (1799) with a book, *Il Trionfo della Santa Sede* ("The Triumph of the Holy See"), in which, in the midst of the current attack on the Papacy and the Church, he expressed his faith in the ultimate victory of both. Here was an augury of the direction which his reign would take. Eventually he moved to Rome, where in time he became abbot of the monastery of which Gregory the Great had been the head before he became Pope, and which had been transferred from the Benedictines to the Camaldolese. He had the confidence of Pius VII and Leo XII. In 1826 he was created Cardinal and appointed Prefect of the Congregation for the Propagation of the Faith. In that post he had experience in diplomacy and became intimately acquainted with the Roman Catholic Church on its geographic frontiers. He took the title of Gregory in memory of Gregory XV, the founder of the Propaganda.[61]

The new Gregory came to the Papal throne in a time of both severe challenge and high opportunity. Throughout Western Europe the flood of revolution was mounting. Some within the Roman Catholic Church, among them Lamennais and the circle which he was gathering about him and many who were influential in Belgium, believed that the Christian faith was compatible with political liberalism and were convinced that the Church should make its peace with it. What attitude would Gregory XVI take? Some liberal Italian nationalists were insisting that the Papal States, at least as they then existed, were an anachronism. Could the Pontiff find ways of preserving them? Spanish America, now mostly independent politically, required wise and courageous statesmanship in Rome if the Catholic Church within its borders was to recover from the shocks dealt it in the stress of the struggle for emancipation from the Spanish crown. Life within the Roman Catholic Church was reviving. So far the recovery was apparent only among minorities, but the minorities were growing. It was making itself manifest in conversions, in popular forms of devotion, in the renewal of old orders and congregations and the emergence of new ones, and in fresh efforts to reinforce the geographic spread of the faith, such as the Society for the Propagation of the Faith, the Leopoldinen-Stiftung, and the Ludwig-Missionsverein. Could Rome so encourage and utilize

[61] Leflon, *op. cit.*, pp. 429, 430; A. Giabanni, *l'Ambiente Monastico di Don Mauro Cappellari*, in *Gregorio XVI, Miscellanea Commemorativa*, Part I, pp. 185–200; Schmidlin, *op. cit.*, pp. 518, 519; Wiseman, *op. cit.*, pp. 263–269; *The Catholic Encyclopedia*, Vol. VII, p. 7.

them that they would strengthen both the Church and the Papacy? Missionaries were being sent in increasing numbers and the Church was being revitalized in some non-Occidental lands where it had been declining and was being planted among peoples who had not heretofore known it. Could Rome assist missions and in such fashion that control by the Papacy over Catholics on the territorial frontiers would be enhanced? Through emigration from Europe Roman Catholics were multiplying in the United States and in Australia. With Catholic emancipation in the British Isles and Irish migration to the growing industrial and commercial centres in England and Scotland the Roman Catholic Church in those two countries, especially England, was increasing in numbers and emerging from its long-standing disabilities. If the Supreme Pontiff acted wisely he could lead the Roman Catholic Church to unprecedented advances and could greatly augment the actual power of his office and make it more nearly approximate to what had long been the Papal claims. Moreover, although coming to his post in his mid-sixties, Gregory XVI was in superb health and had the prospect of many years of vigour in which to pursue a consistent policy and to swell the ranks of the College of Cardinals with able men of his own choosing.

The prospects of success were ambiguous. By his monastic rearing in one of the strictest of the orders of medieval origin and by his unhappy experiences under the radicalism of the French Revolution and Napoleon, Gregory XVI was ill prepared either to understand or to sympathize with the new movements. The convictions which he had set forth in *Il Trionfo della Santa Sede* were evidence that in principle he had not relinquished the claims of the Papacy to control society and to bring it to Christian standards.[62] His association with the *Zelanti* was unpromising. His second Secretary of State had the same general attitude. The first had been Bernetti. Clever, worldly, Bernetti had refused ordination, apparently regarded revolutions as inevitable, and was pessimistic about the possibility of preserving the Papal States. But he was opposed to the liberal tendencies of the age.[63] Dismissed because he had angered Metternich, he was followed by Lambruschini, who had been General of the Barnabites and archbishop. He was strongly anti-liberal, for legitimacy, for the domination of society by the hierarchy and the Pope, and he worked hand in glove with the Jesuits. Gregory was eventually dominated by him.[64] At first sight the Cappellari Pope was not prepossessing in appearance or manners. He spoke only Latin and Italian and so had to resort to an interpreter with many of those from abroad with whom he had to deal. Yet he had abounding physical energy,

[62] P. Dalla Torre in *Gregorio XVI*, Vol. II, p. 112; Leflon, *op. cit.*, pp. 430, 431; Schmidlin, *op. cit.*, Vol. I, pp. 519, 520.

[63] Nielsen, *op. cit.*, Vol. II, pp. 29, 61, 72–74; Schmidlin, *op. cit.*, Vol. I, pp. 528–535.

[64] Nielsen, *op. cit.*, Vol. II, pp. 74, 75; Schmidlin, *op. cit.*, Vol. I, p. 535.

was a prodigious and tireless worker, lived abstemiously, maintained an even more rigid discipline with long hours at his various duties and few hours of sleep than we have remarked in Leo XII, and was noted for independence of judgment and courage in decisions. One who knew him well spoke of his personal kindness and his charities in relief of distress.[65]

The world had not long to wait to see how Gregory XVI would act. Revolt in his own immediate domains, the Papal States, broke out in the first few weeks of his reign. Since he did not have at his disposal a large body of well-disciplined troops, it looked as though the insurgents would take over the Papal domains. Liberal nationalists, they adopted as their banner a tri-colour which later was to become the flag of the united Italy. Gregory promised reforms, but this did not satisfy the rebels. He therefore asked the assistance of Austria. That power was not at all unwilling. It had interests in North Italy which were threatened by the movement and it was also glad of the opportunity to augment its influence. The Austrian troops quickly suppressed the uprising. However, France was unhappy over the increase of Austrian power in a region where she also had ambitions, and Louis Philippe came out for a constitutional regime in the Papal territories. He appealed to London, and Austria to Berlin and St. Petersburg. Accordingly, the five powers, Austria, France, the United Kingdom, Prussia, and Russia, following the precedent of concerted effort to keep the peace and preserve legitimacy in Europe, through their plenipotentiaries held a conference in Rome, but without Papal participation. They outlined a programme for thorough-going reforms and reorganization of the government of the Papal States which included municipal and provincial elective councils with lay representation and more laymen in other official posts. Gregory took the position that he was an independent prince, that he had already promised reforms, and that he would consult his own best judgement as to what these should be. The reorganization which he enacted incorporated some of the features of the powers' programme, but it gave less place to lay and more to ecclesiastical participation. However, it was comprehensive and embraced administration, the judiciary, finances, and such other measures as the promotion of steam navigation, a decimal money, subventions to insurance against damage by storm, fire, and accidents, a central bank in Rome, a savings bank, a chamber of commerce, and the reorganization of the customs to ease transactions with other countries.[66]

The jealousies between Austria and France and the unsatisfied aspirations of the Italian liberals brought further complications. In July, 1831, on French in-

[65] Wiseman, *op. cit.*, pp. 318–329.

[66] Pio Ciprotti, *Cenni sulla legislazione di Gregorio XVI*, in *Gregorio XVI*, Vol. I, pp. 113 ff.; P. Dalla Torre, *L'opera riformatrice ed amministrativa di Gregorio XVI*, in *ibid.*, Vol. II, pp. 29–121; Leflon, *op. cit.*, pp. 432–437; Schmidlin, *op. cit.*, Vol. I, pp. 520–539.

sistence the Austrian troops were withdrawn. Revolt soon revived. Albani, who had been appointed to head a commission for part of the States, without consulting Gregory recalled the Austrians. The Austrians responded with alacrity and the insurrection was again crushed. France, fearful of Austrian intentions, sent in troops which occupied Ancona, in the Papal territories. In 1838 both powers withdrew their forces.[67] However, the Papal States continued to be a problem and were criticized for administrative ineptitude and corruption.[68]

The entire movement for Italian unity, the *risorgimento*, with its associated liberalism, constituted an increasing problem for the Papacy. In it were several strains. "Young Italy," organized by Mazzini, who began his revolutionary career by joining the *Carbonari*, wished all Italy to be a republic with Rome as its capital. For obvious reasons it tended to be anti-clerical and to regard the Pope as a major enemy. Its chief recruit was the colourful Garibaldi. Another group, led by Gioberti, a priest, and Count Cesare Balbo, advocated a liberal federated Italy with the Pope as its head and the conciliator of its diversified interests. Another worked for a united Italy under a constitutional, liberal monarchy headed by the King of Sardinia of the House of Savoy.

As his years in office lengthened, Gregory XVI became increasingly intransigent and the pressures mounted. Lambruschini especially was opposed to all innovations. He regarded even congresses of scholars as possible centres of infection. In the Papal States repressive measures became more and more severe and those desiring change, driven underground into secret societies, became potentially more violent. As Gregory's life approached its end the pressures were mounting. Paralleled by unrest in much of the rest of Western Europe, they were fairly certain to explode with spectacular results.[69]

The policy of Gregory XVI towards liberal movements elsewhere in Europe was no less hostile. In France Lamennais was leading, partly through a periodical, *Avenir*, and through an organization, the *Agence générale*, in an attempt to bring together Catholicism and democratic ideals in government. Numbers were being attracted but opposition was developing. Late in 1831 he and his friends, Montalembert and Lacordaire, went to Rome hoping to obtain Papal approval. In March, 1832, Gregory received them affably but was non-committal. However, in the first encyclical of his reign, *Mirari vos* (August 15, 1832), implicitly but not explicitly by naming it, he censured *Avenir*. Accordingly *Avenir*, which had been provisionally suspended by its editors, was, by their act, permanently discontinued, and the *Agence générale* was dissolved. Lamennais was willing to conform in the religious sphere but believed himself free

[67] Leflon, *op. cit.*, pp. 433–435.

[68] Schmidlin, *op. cit.*, Vol. I, p. 538.

[69] Leflon, *op. cit.*, pp. 437–440; Schmidlin, *op. cit.*, Vol. I, pp. 549–556; A. M. Ghisalberti, *Gregorio XVI e il Risorgimento*, in Gregory XVI, Vol. II, pp. 123–134.

to think and act in the political sphere.[70] Prophet-like, he continued to dream and believed that the Church was just about to enter upon one of its greatest days. In *Paroles d'un Croyant*, published April 30, 1834, while attempting to avoid speaking of the Church or intruding in ecclesiastical matters, he described what he held to be the early impending transformation of society by the act of God in casting down the oppressors of the poor and the dawn of a new age of justice, peace, and love. In the meantime, in December, 1833, he had submitted to the doctrine set forth in *Mirari vos*. *Paroles d'un Croyant* created an immense sensation, quickly passed through many editions, and was translated into other languages. In June, 1834, by the encyclical *Singulari nos*, Gregory condemned the book. Lamennais was never formally excommunicated, but it was clear that Rome had spoken against the political and social views which he championed.[71] The movement of which Lamennais was the centre seemed to be broken, but it was at the price of a clear-cut stand of the Papacy against the kind of political and social liberalism which he believed to be Christian.

A similar crisis developed in Belgium. There Lamennais and *Avenir* had a large following among Roman Catholics. By condemning explicitly freedom of conscience, freedom of the press, and the separation of Church and state, *Mirari vos* came out against what was entailed in one of the ideals of Lamennais, "a free Church in a free state." Lamennais had reinforced a movement which was already strong towards a union of Catholics and political liberals. The Belgian constitution of 1831 gave reciprocal independence to the Church and state but did not completely separate the two.[72] It granted freedom of religion in membership in religious bodies, in the naming of bishops by the Holy See, in the appointment and dismissal of pastors by the bishops, in the erection of schools, in the recognition of religious orders, in the supremacy of the Pope over the episcopate, and in correspondence with Rome without the permission of the state. Much of this was in the direction in which Rome would like to move. Obviously it strengthened ultramontanism. But Gregory XVI was not entirely content with the constitution and its approach to the separation of Church and state. Numbers of the Belgian conservatives enthusiastically hailed *Mirari vos*. Some of the liberal Catholics held that it did not apply to Belgium: several retired from public life; others sought by interpretation to soften the Papal pronouncement. Many of the liberals became vigorously opposed to ultramontanism.[73]

[70] Vidler, *Prophecy and Papacy*, pp. 184 ff.; J. A. Ryan in *The Catholic Historical Review*, Vol. XXIII, pp. 31–37.
[71] Vidler, *op. cit.*, pp. 227–257; Leflon, *op. cit.*, pp. 442–449.
[72] See text in Ehler and Morrall, *Church and State through the Centuries*, p. 272.
[73] Leflon, *op. cit.*, pp. 454, 455; A. Simon in *Gregorio XVI*, Vol. II, pp. 399 ff.; Haag, *Les origines du Catholicisme libéral en Belgique (1789–1839)*, pp. 156 ff.; Schmidlin, *op. cit.*, Vol. I, pp. 595 ff.

The situation in Poland was even more confused. There the revolt against Russian rule was incited by leaders who were indifferent or hostile to the Roman Catholic Church. However, they sought to enlist the support of the Roman Catholic clergy, for the Poles were overwhelmingly of that faith and Catholic support would be essential to victory. The uprising, therefore, was both nationalistic and religious. Soon after its onset and his accession Gregory (February 9, 1831) addressed a letter to the Polish bishops urging them to heed the counsel of Paul to obey the civil power as ordained of God. That meant obedience to the tsar. He followed this (June 9, 1832) with a brief, *Superiori anno,* in which he declared that submission to the power instituted by God was an unalterable principle, said that some artisans under the guise of religion were rebelling against the legitimate authority of the princes, and called upon the bishops to employ all their vigilance against the agitators. *Superiori anno* was given wide publicity by the Russian Government and fell like a clap of thunder on the Poles who were struggling for their freedom. The then tsar, Nicholas I, was completely out of sympathy with the liberalism of his predecessor, Alexander I, and abrogated the constitution which the latter had granted the Poles. Gregory XVI was not happy over the tsar's attempts to bring the hierarchy to heel. He was greatly distressed when the tsar, partly in his effort to crush Polish particularism and partly in pursuance of his Pan-Slavic policy, compelled thousands of Uniates to return to the Russian Orthodox fold. The Uniates were descendants of Orthodox who late in the sixteenth century through the activity of the Jesuits and political pressures from their Roman Catholic Polish and Lithuanian overlords had submitted to Rome but had been permitted to retain their liturgy and some of their ecclesiastical customs. Now, in 1839, many of the Uniates were constrained to renew the connexion with the church of their fathers. Gregory protested the Russian action. Long negotiations followed. In 1845 Nicholas I visited Rome and saw the Pope. In time, but not until the reign of Gregory's successor, a concordat was signed which partly relieved the strain.[74]

In Germany under Gregory XVI the Papacy made its weight felt—in ways different from those used in Poland, but, as in Poland, through conflict. In Austria friction over Josephism still prevented the completion of a concordat, but the situation was easing.[75] Acute difficulties arose in the lower Rhine in the territories which had been awarded to Prussia by the Congress of Vienna. The immediate issues were two. One centred about the theology of Hermes. Georg Hermes (1775-1831) from doubt had struggled through to Christian faith, had been ordained priest, and had worked out a way to the acceptance of Roman

[74] Leflon, *op. cit.,* pp. 456–460; R. Lefevre, *S. Sede e Russia e i colloqui dello Czar Nicolo I nei documenti vaticani (1843–1846)* in *Gregorio XVI,* Vol. II, pp. 159–293; Schmidlin, *op. cit.,* Vol. I, pp. 627–639.
[75] Leflon, *op. cit.,* p. 465; Schmidlin, *op. cit.,* Vol. I, pp. 585–587.

Catholic theology which he presented persuasively first at Münster and then while on the faculty of the University of Bonn. His writings and his lectures were widely popular. Although rejecting much in Kant and Fichte, he was strongly influenced by them. His approach was from the basis of doubt resolved by reason and appealed to many who, while in general accepting the confidence of the *Aufklärung* in reason, wished to remain Catholics. For some years those who followed Hermes filled several of the chairs of theology and philosophy in the Catholic faculties of the German universities. The Archbishop of Cologne, Spiegel, supported him. Yet to many conservative Roman Catholics the Hermesian system seemed to be by-passing or undercutting the authority of the Church.[76] The other issue was that of mixed marriages between Protestants and Roman Catholics and whether all the children of such unions should be reared in the Roman Catholic faith.

These questions, especially the second, had troubled Pius VIII, for the Prussian monarch had decreed that the offspring of mixed religious parentage should be reared in the church of the father, and the Roman Catholic Church held that mixed marriages should be permitted only if the bride and groom promised to bring them up in the Catholic faith. Pius VIII reiterated that position but Spiegel had consented to a working compromise with the Prussian king.

Although Hermes was now dead, his views were still popular, and by a brief (September, 1835) and a decree (January, 1836) Gregory XVI condemned the approach of Hermes. He was also firm on the question of the children of mixed marriages. The Prussian Government wished the Roman Catholic bishops, by silence, to disregard the Papal decisions. When, although on the nomination of the King of Prussia, he succeeded Spiegel in the archiepiscopal see of Cologne, Droste-Vischering stood by Rome on both issues. He had long been opposed to Hermes. He insisted that students and clergy accept without reservation the Papal condemnation of the Hermesian views. He repudiated the compromise of Spiegel on mixed marriages. In November, 1837, the King of Prussia had Droste-Vischering arrested and imprisoned and also threw into prison Dunin, Archbishop of Poznan, for threatening with suspension priests who blessed mixed marriages without any promise of the Catholic rearing of their offspring.

[76] Brück, *Geschichte der katholischen Kirche in Deutschland im neunzehnten Jahrhundert*, Vol. II, pp. 466 ff.; *The Catholic Encyclopedia*, Vol. VII, pp. 276–279; *The New Schaff-Herzog Encyclopedia of Religious Knowledge*, Vol. V, p. 242; *Dictionnaire de Théologie Catholique*, Vol. VI, pp. 2287–2303; *Lexikon für Theologie und Kirche*, Vol. IV, p. 991; Hocedez, *Histoire de la Théologie au XIXe Siècle*, Vol. I, pp. 177 ff.; Georg Hermes, *Einleitung in die christkatholische Theologie* (Münster, in der Coppenrathschen Buch- und Kunsthandlung, 2nd ed., 2 vols., 1831); Georg Hermes, *Studir-Plan der Theologie: Ein Anhang der Philosophischen Einleitung* (Münster, in der Coppenrathschen Buch- und Kunsthandlung, 1819, pp. 32); Wilhelm Esser, *Denkschrift auf Georg Hermes* (Cologne, Du Mont-Schauberg, 1832, pp. 198); Chr. Guil. Niedner, *Philosophiae Hermesii Bonnensis Novarum Rerum in Theologia Exordii Explicatio et Existimatio* (Leipzig, Sumptibus I. C. Hinrichsii, 1839, pp. viii, 71).

These actions aroused a storm of protest. In 1840 under a new king, Frederick William IV, the two prelates were released. Rome had prevailed.[77]

During the pontificate of Gregory XVI religious strife developed in Switzerland. Among other facets of the struggle were the efforts of liberals to loosen the tie between the Roman Catholic Church and the Pope. The issue was not yet resolved when death called Gregory from the scene.[78]

In another volume we will have more to say about developments in the New World. Here we must note that as Prefect of the Propaganda Cappellari had been active in extending Papal initiative in the highly delicate situation in Spanish America. In an explosive domestic scene in which the Roman Catholic Church was deeply involved care had to be taken to give as little offense as possible to the sensitive government of the mother country. Yet the new regimes in Spanish America which had clearly established their independence must not be antagonized. In their territories the Roman Catholic Church, badly weakened during the prolonged struggle for independence, must, if possible, be strengthened by adequate episcopal supervision. This had been one of the concerns of Cappellari while head of the Propaganda. It continued to be a deep interest of his after he became Gregory XVI. Conditions in Brazil and Haiti also engaged his attention. In general, he augmented Papal authority in Latin America and made for the recovery of the Roman Catholic Church in that vast area.[79]

During the pontificate of Gregory XVI the Roman Catholic Church in the United States was growing rapidly: Papal authority in that church was unchallenged and was vigorously exercised. The growth was predominantly by immigration. The country was under the Propaganda and it was mainly through that congregation that Rome exerted its supervision. The decisions of the successive provincial synods of the hierarchy were sent to Rome for approval. Largely but not entirely on the recommendation of these synods additional bishoprics were created for the supervision of the faithful. Although suggestions for personnel to fill vacant sees came from the United States, the appointments were from Rome. Rome supported the bishops in their prolonged struggle with "trusteeism," the effort of the laity to control the property and the choice of clergy of the parishes: it consistently took the stand that it had in Europe against some of the democratic trends of the day.[80]

---

[77] Leflon, *op. cit.*, pp. 465–470; Schnabel, *Deutsche Geschichte im neunzehnten Jahrhundert*, Vol. IV, pp. 133 ff.; Hocedez, *op. cit.*, Vol. I, pp. 195–201; Brück, *op. cit.*, Vol. II, pp. 268 ff.

[78] Schmidlin, *op. cit.*, Vol. I, pp. 589–595; Leflon, *op. cit.*, pp. 464, 465.

[79] W. J. Coleman, *The First Apostolic Delegation in Rio de Janeiro and Its Influence in Spanish America. A Study in Papal Policy 1830–1840* (Washington, The Catholic University of America Press, 1950, pp. xii, 468), *passim;* Thornton, *The Church and Freemasonry in Brazil, 1872–1875*, pp. 68 ff.; Pedro de Laturia, *Gregorio XVI y la Emancipacion de la America Española* in *Gregorio XVI*, Vol. II, pp. 295–352.

[80] Schmidlin, *op. cit.*, Vol. I, pp. 645–648; Thomas O'Gorman, *A History of the Roman Catholic*

In Canada Gregory increased the number of dioceses for the growing population. He also provided added episcopal supervision for the rapidly mounting body of Roman Catholics, chiefly Irish, in Australia and Tasmania.[81]

In England the Oxford movement with its resulting conversions of Anglicans, some of them outstanding, to the Roman Catholic Church and the immigration from Ireland made imperative additional episcopal care. This was provided by an increase in vicariates apostolic. While in charge of the Propaganda Cappellari had been much interested in England. His friendship with Wiseman, rector of the English College in Rome and later head of the English hierarchy and Cardinal, augmented that concern. Not until 1908, however, was England removed from the supervision of the Propaganda and given a hierarchy on the same footing with that of countries which were not thought of primarily as mission fields.[82]

Gregory also interested himself in troubled Ireland and made his weight felt in strengthening the Roman Catholic Church in that island, especially in educational matters related to the controversial question of the Queen's Colleges established by Parliament.[83]

As former Prefect of the Propaganda Gregory had especially at heart the spread of the faith outside the Occident: in an allocution to the Cardinals in 1838 he declared that after his elevation to the Papacy he had made the planting and enlargement of missions his chief care.[84] As we have said and as we shall see later, his reign coincided with a remarkable forward surge in Roman Catholic missions. This was not primarily from either his initiative or his aid but came out of the renewal of life in the Roman Catholic Church. Yet he gave it his support and thus not only assisted it but also affirmed the control of the Papacy over the Roman Catholic Church on its expanding geographic frontiers. He endorsed several institutions and societies in Europe which had missions as their purpose. He made appointments to the hierarchy in Western Asia and Egypt. He welcomed the opportunity to restore the Church in the regions of North Africa which were being brought under French rule and where for centuries it had been all but extinct. On the recommendation of the Propaganda he appointed numerous vicars apostolic in Burma, Siam, Malaya, and Indochina. He also appointed them in China, where the first Anglo-Chinese War (1839–1842) made possible the renewal of the missions which had long been under the pressure of chronic persecution. Vicars apostolic were named for

---

Church in the United States (New York, The Christian Literature Co., 1895, pp. xviii, 515), pp. 340 ff.

[81] Schmidlin, *op. cit.*, Vol. I, p. 648.

[82] H. E. G. Rope, *Gregory and England* in *Gregorio XVI*, Vol. II, pp. 373 ff.; Wiseman, *Recollections of the Last Four Popes*, pp. 299–302, 329–332; Schmidlin, *op. cit.*, Vol. I, pp. 608–612.

[83] Wiseman, *op. cit.*, pp. 329–331; Schmidlin, *op. cit.*, Vol. I, pp. 612, 613.

[84] Schmidlin, *op. cit.*, Vol. I, p. 663.

Korea, the Ryu Kyu Islands, the East Indies, and several of the island groups of the Pacific.[85] A vicar apostolic was a bishop who exercised his authority not in his own name but in that of the Pope and so represented direct Papal control more than did bishops who ruled in their own name.

Gregory gave Portugal the alternative of fulfilling her obligations under her *padroado,* or right of patronage, granted centuries earlier, and supporting and staffing missions in all India, or relinquishing her claim. Since Portugal would do neither, Gregory appointed vicars apostolic to various areas in India, to be independent of the Portuguese bishops, and in 1838 abolished the *padroado.* The Portuguese refused to recognize the legality of these acts, and the Archbishop of Goa excommunicated some of the vicars apostolic. Thus came the "Goanese schism." But Gregory stood firm, maintaining the authority of his see, and not until the next pontificate was a compromise reached.[86] Gregory also strongly advocated the creation of clergy in mission lands and the promotion of indigenous priests to the episcopate.[87]

Gregory conformed to a dream of his immediate predecessors in attempting to make Rome the cultural centre of Europe. He established a museum for Etruscan antiquities, another for Egyptian antiquities, and still another in the Lateran Palace for the art and sculpture of the ancient past.[88] He encouraged the study of the archeology of Christian Rome.[89] He made repairs in the Vatican and enlarged the Vatican museum and the Vatican library. He added art objects to the Quirinal. He furthered the academies, higher schools, and the university in Rome. He restored the walls and some of the ancient structures of the city and promoted the excavation of the forums.[90] He encouraged painters and sculptors and facilitated Gaetano Moroni in his *Dizionario di erudizione storica ecclesiastica da S. Pietro fino a nostri Giorni,* a compilation of 120 volumes, a mine of information concerning the Pontifical court, the organization of the curia, and the Church.[91]

As with earlier Popes of the nineteenth century, these cultural efforts took traditional forms. They were a preservation and glorification of the past. They were not promoting the new science and learning. They were in line with the general temper of the ecclesiastical and political policies of the reign. Like them, they did not seek to adjust the Papal programme to the revolution which in its many phases was engulfing Europe. Rather they sought to resist or ignore it. They were in accord with the ideal of an unalterable faith supported by a

85 Schmidlin, *op. cit.,* Vol. I, pp. 663–674; C. Costantini, *Gregorio XVI e le Missioni* in *Gregorio XVI,* Vol. II, pp. 1–28.
86 Schmidlin, *op. cit.,* Vol. I, p. 669.
87 Costantini, *op. cit.,* pp. 14–16.
88 *Gregorio XVI,* Vol. I, pp. 201–287, 365–403.
89 Romano Fausti in *ibid.,* pp. 405 ff.
90 Schmidlin, *op. cit.,* Vol. I, pp. 339 ff.
91 *Gregorio XVI,* Vol. I, pp. 135 ff.; Nielsen, *op. cit.,* Vol. II, pp. 81, 82.

changeless church in a rapidly changing world. The Papacy was slow to adopt even the mechanical appliances of the new day. It was late in introducing the steamboat to the Papal States and even tardier in permitting the building of railways. Here was a stability which appealed to many who were seeking security in a revolutionary age.

Gregory XVI gave the support of his office to fresh expressions of the historic Roman Catholic piety. He welcomed devotion to the Virgin Mary. He endorsed the validity of a vision of the Virgin which had led to the conversion of Ratisbonne, a Jew, and which issued in the inauguration by the latter of the congregation of *Notre Dame de Sion* which had as its object the winning of Jewish women to the faith.[92] He promised plenary indulgence to wearers of medals in honour of the immaculate conception of the Virgin. To more than one church and to the Dominicans he gave permission to add the word *immaculata* to the preface of the Mass of the Blessed Virgin. Some urged him to proclaim the immaculate conception as dogma, but he hesitated to do so, not because he doubted it or his own infallibility but presumably because he questioned whether a Pope should take such a step without the backing of an ecumenical council.[93] Under him numbers of beatifications and canonizations maintained a long-standing prerogative of the Papacy.[94] He made much of relics and at the time of a cholera epidemic in Rome as a protection against the disease led through the streets a procession which carried a picture of the Madonna attributed to Luke.[95]

Gregory XVI encouraged the revival and reform of existing monastic orders and the emergence of new congregations of religious.[96] In doing so he aided in the increase of bodies of celibates who devoted themselves fully to the service of the Church under the direction of the Pope.

Somewhat similarly Gregory sought to keep clergy and laity from compromising what he believed to be the Catholic faith. This he did by reminding the priests of their religious mission, by warning them against taking part in political activities with liberals, and by his stand on mixed marriages.[97]

He also promoted the bringing of worship, including public services, the cult of saints, and music, into accord with Roman practices.[98]

In summary, in Gregory XVI the Papacy was filled by a monk who viewed with distrust and hostility almost all phases of the revolution. He sought to maintain unchanged the Roman Catholic faith as it had been handed down

[92] Nielsen, *The History of the Papacy in the Nineteenth Century*, Vol. II, pp. 76, 77.
[93] *Ibid.*
[94] Schmidlin, *op. cit.*, Vol. I, pp. 654, 655.
[95] Nielsen, *op. cit.*, Vol. II, pp. 79, 80.
[96] Schmidlin, *op. cit.*, Vol. I, pp. 658–661.
[97] *Ibid.*, p. 657.
[98] *Ibid.*

from the past, and so asserted the authority with which he believed that his office had been divinely commissioned. He repeatedly employed it against those who would accommodate Roman Catholicism to the political and intellectual currents associated with the revolution. He made the Papacy more effective in the Roman Catholic Church than it had been for many years, whether within Europe or in the Americas, Asia, and Africa. In doing so he sharpened the antagonism of many who were committed to the revolution. Backed by the loyal among the laity, by the conservatives among the clergy, and by the religious both of the revived older orders and of the new congregations, he furthered the process by which the Roman Catholic Church was becoming an ever more tightly knit organization under Papal leadership holding against the hostile world of the revolution to what it believed the Christian faith to be.

Because of the length of his pontificate Gregory XVI appointed the majority of the Cardinals and most of the other high officials in the Papal curia who were in office at the time of his death. As was to be expected from his character and convictions they were largely conservative and in the tradition of the *Zelanti*.[99] Many of them were saintly and in general they seem not to have been susceptible to bribery.[100] Presumably the majority would seek to choose as the successor to Gregory one who would carry on the tradition which he had maintained.

PIUS IX (1846–1878) : THE ELECTION AND THE LIBERAL PHASE, 1846–1848

The expectation of the choice of a conservative as Pope did not at first seem to be fulfilled. In the electoral conclave the *Zelanti* were powerful. They had as their leading candidate Lambruschini. However, many in Rome had been restive under the repressive measures of Gregory and Lambruschini and among the Cardinals were those who sympathized with them. Their leader was Bernetti, whom Lambruschini had displaced as Secretary of State. In the first ballot the latter had more votes than any other. It is said that his opponents pressed for an early decision before the arrival of one or more distant Cardinals who would be expected to support him and perhaps bring with them an Austrian veto to the name of a liberal. However, Metternich seems to have thought the election of any but a conservative so unlikely that he had not planned a veto. As it was, Lambruschini failed to win the number necessary to election and the choice fell on Cardinal Mastai, who was believed to be a liberal.[101] Out of gratitude to his early benefactor, Pius VII, Mastai took the title of Pius.

The new Pope, Giovanni Maria Mastai-Ferretti (1792–1878), was from the lesser nobility. In his youth he had served for a time as a soldier in the Papal

99 *Ibid.*, pp. 649 ff.
100 Hales, *Pio Nino*, pp. 31, 32.
101 Aubert, *Le pontificat de Pie IX (1846–1878)*, pp. 12, 13; Hales, *op. cit.*, pp. 17–19; Trollope, *The Story of the Life of Pius the Ninth*, Vol. I, pp. 113 ff.; Nielsen, *op. cit.*, Vol. II, pp. 102–110.

troops but chronic epilepsy blocked his way to promotion. He thereupon sought a career in the Church and lenient Papal dispensations removed the canonical obstacles presented by the malady. He appears to have outgrown that disability.[102] Certainly it did not prevent him from having a longer tenure of the Papal throne than any of his predecessors. In 1823–1824 he went to South America as secretary and chaplain to a Papal legate. From 1827 to 1834 he was Archbishop of Spoleto in the Papal States. There in a poverty-stricken mountainous diocese he made a good record. Under him the religious and moral life of the see improved. During the uprising of 1831 he fled. Returning, he was welcomed by the populace and was lenient with those who had shared in the insurrection. From Spoleto Mastai was moved to the Bishopric of Imola, in the Romagna, also in the Papal States. This was a promotion, for the post was considered to be a step towards the Cardinalate. Imola was in a notoriously turbulent area and was distraught by the troubles of the 1830's. By his many good works in schools and charitable institutions and improving the discipline of both clergy and laity and by his clemency in dealing with the insurgents Mastai won favour with the liberals. Mastai was deeply devout. He was devoted to the Virgin Mary and would take no important step without imploring her assistance and protection. He was later often called "the Pope of prayer."[103]

In the first months of his rule Pius IX seemed to confirm the hopes of those who wished a liberal Pope. In July, 1846, he proclaimed an amnesty to political offenders. Liberals acclaimed the step and Metternich deplored it.[104] Pius made striking changes in the Papal States. He took steps towards building railways and lighting the streets of Rome with gas. He projected an institute to improve agricultural methods and rural education. He granted a degree of freedom to the press. He himself visited jails as part of a programme for prison reform. He set about the liberalizing of the criminal code. He simplified customs procedures. He excused Jews from the customary required attendance at Christian sermons. He created a *Consulta* of laymen chosen by indirect vote and presided over by a Cardinal.[105]

For a time Pius IX was the idol of many of the nationalists who longed for Italian unity. He himself was attracted by the dream cherished by some of a federated Italy headed by the Pope.[106] To Italian patriots this hope seemed to be confirmed by the resistance of Pius to an Austrian move in the summer of

---

[102] Trollope, *op. cit.*, Vol. I, pp. 1–24; Schmidlin, *Papstgeschichte der neuesten Zeit*, Vol. II, pp. 6 ff.

[103] Schmidlin, *op. cit.*, Vol. II, pp. 9–11; Trollope, *op. cit.*, Vol. I, pp. 79 ff.; Hales, *op. cit.*, pp. 32–36.

[104] Hales, *op. cit.*, p. 57; Nielsen, *op. cit.*, Vol. II, pp. 119–121; Schmidlin, *op. cit.*, Vol. II, pp. 24, 25. See also F. Engel-Janosi, *French and Austrian Political Advice to Pius IX, 1846–1848,* in *The Catholic Historical Review*, Vol. XXXVIII, pp. 1 ff.

[105] Hales, *op. cit.*, pp. 58–64; Schmidlin, *op. cit.*, Vol. II, pp. 25–31.

[106] Hales, *op. cit.*, pp. 37, 38, 63.

1847. In July, 1847, when crowds were celebrating the anniversary of the amnesty of the preceding year, the Austrian commander in Lombardy attempted to forestall outbreaks in Italy by reinforcing the garrison which under the Vienna settlement was maintained in Ferrara, in the Papal States. Popular resistance led to sending in more Austrian troops. When full occupation by Austrian forces followed, the Papal Secretary of State threatened to break off diplomatic relations with Austria and to excommunicate the offenders. In December, 1847, the Austrian forces withdrew to the citadel where they clearly had a treaty right to be. This and other Papal actions made Pius IX extremely popular with many who were zealous for a liberal, united Italy.[107]

However, Pius IX began to see that the expectations cherished by the liberals would involve him in inconsistencies. He could scarcely be the head of a united Italy and fulfil his functions as the head of a religious body which transcended national boundaries. His granting of representative liberal political institutions to his subjects in the Papal States was counter to the genius of a church which was moving away from limitations on the authority of the Pope towards acceptance of Papal absolutism. His first encyclical on doctrinal matters, *Qui pluribus*, issued November 9, 1846, was largely the work of the conservative Lambruschini and upheld the positions of Gregory XVI. It condemned the basic principles of religious liberalism.[108]

Moreover, Pius IX began to be alarmed by the direction which events had taken and to which his anti-Austrian stand had contributed. Italian patriots were intent on clearing Italy of all foreign rule. That meant driving out the Austrians. This the Pope had no intention of doing.[109] The liberal tide was rising, was becoming radical, and here and there was assuming aspects which disturbed him. In 1847, for example, civil war broke out in Switzerland and the *Sonderbund*, an alliance of Catholic cantons, was defeated. The victors ordered the expulsion of all members of religious orders. Soon a new constitution inaugurated a federal state with freedom of religion throughout its territory.[110]

Pius IX: The Revolutionary Year 1848 Forces Him into the Ranks of the Conservatives

Events which came to a climax in 1848 cured Pius IX of his liberal leanings, made him an arch conservative and the continuator of Papal opposition to the revolution, and moved him further towards the affirmation of doctrines which

---

[107] Hales, *op. cit.*, pp. 62–67. For a study of the early years of the pontificate see Raffaele Ballerini, *Le Prime Pagine del Pontificato di Papa Pio IX* (Roma . . . Civilta Cattolica, 1909, pp. vii, 232), by a Jesuit, employing useful sources.

[108] Aubert, *op. cit.*, pp. 19, 20.

[109] Hales, *op. cit.*, p. 67.

[110] Aubert, *op. cit.*, pp. 23, 24.

had long been implicit in the faith and organization of the Roman Catholic Church and which set it against prevailing trends in the revolutionary Occident. The year 1848 witnessed the collapse of much of the barrier which the diplomats of 1815 had attempted to build against the tide of revolution. As in 1789 and 1830 the first major breach in the wall was in France. The "July monarchy" of Louis Philippe was overthrown and the Second Republic was set up. Louis Napoleon was elected president and before many years was to inaugurate the Second Empire. In Austria Metternich resigned and fled in disguise to England. Soon the emperor granted a constitution for Austria. In Hungary liberals took command and abolished some of the inherited feudal institutions. Bohemian liberals obtained the Hapsburg emperor's promise of autonomy for their country. Italian nationalists drove out the Austrians. King Ferdinand of the Two Sicilies was forced to accept a liberal constitution. In Germany liberals wrung concessions from several of the princes and took steps towards the unification of the country. While reaction soon set in and some of the gains won by the liberals were lost, the pre-1848 structure of Western Europe was never fully restored.

At first Pius IX seemed to bow to the storm. On March 18, 1848, he granted a constitution to the Papal States. It set up a High Council and a Council of Deputies. But these bodies had strictly limited powers and the Pope retained the veto over their measures.[111] The previous month, in a *motu proprio* (February 10, 1848), Pius appeared to some to give his endorsement to a united Italy, and his words "O Lord God, bless Italy" were so interpreted by ardent patriots.[112] In March it looked as though an Italian League would be formed with Rome as a member, the precursor of an Italian federal state, presumably with the Pope as its head.[113]

Then the Pope's attitude changed. He shocked those working for the unification of Italy when he refused to join in the war to drive the Austrians out of their holdings in the country.[114] In a decisive allocution on April 29, 1848, he repudiated any share in the scheme to make Italy into a united republic under his presidency and urged Italians to remain loyal to their sovereigns.[115]

Politically the march of events went sharply against Pius. The defeat of Piedmont, which had led in the effort to oust the Austrians from Italy, and the restoration of Austrian rule were followed by a swing to the extremists, those with Mazzini as their hero, who wished a republic. Four men in quick succession as prime minister attempted to govern in Rome under Pius. The fourth,

[111] Hales, *Pio Nino*, p. 71.
[112] *Ibid.*, p. 70; Berkeley, *Italy in the Making, January 1st 1848 to November 16 1848*, pp. 70, 71.
[113] Berkeley, *op. cit.*, pp. 130–136.
[114] Hales, *op. cit.*, pp. 73–77; Berkeley, *op. cit.*, pp. 153 ff.
[115] Berkeley, *op. cit.*, p. 180.

Rossi, was assassinated by extremists (November, 1848). A few days later the Pope, disguised, secretly fled from Rome and took refuge in Gaeta, some distance south of Rome, in the territories of the King of Naples. The revolutionaries set up the Republic of Rome and declared the temporal power of the Pope ended (February, 1849).[116] To Rome came the leading revolutionaries, Mazzini and Garibaldi. Pius denounced the republic, forbade Catholics to coöperate with it, and called upon France, Austria, Spain, and Naples to restore Papal rule. To forestall action by Austria and Naples and to prevent the augmentation of Austrian power in Italy, France responded and sent troops. They took possession of Rome, the republic collapsed, and Pius IX returned to the city. Quite disillusioned with political liberalism, he was resolved to govern both the Papal States and the Church as absolute monarch.[117]

Pius IX: The Tottering of Papal Authority in the States of the Church is Paralleled by the Extension of Papal Authority in the Roman Catholic Church

While, under the impact of the revolutionary forces, Italian nationalism and democratic ideas were undermining his political power in the Papal States, Pius IX was expanding the authority of his office in the Roman Catholic Church. This he did in at least two ways. One was by extending his administrative control of the ecclesiastical structure and enhancing that structure where it had previously been weak. The other was by proclaiming by his own act the immaculate conception as dogma to be believed by all the faithful.

The extension of Papal administrative control and initiative was seen in several lands and areas. In Germany not far from 1848, in spite of contrary convictions which we shall have occasion to note a little later, ultramontanism was represented by strong individuals and become almost a distinct party in the Roman Catholic Church.[118] In France in the 1840's and 1850's the swing to ultramontanism was pronounced. In his textbooks on theology, which were widely read, Gousset, Archbishop of the important see of Reims from 1840 to 1846, came out strongly against Gallicanism. The custom grew of referring questions of discipline and forms of worship to Rome, priests were encouraged to appeal to Rome against the decisions of their bishops, precedent for the request for Papal sanction for the holding of provincial councils was reinforced, in 1849 the proposal to hold a national council was successfully blocked, and some works favourable to Gallicanism were placed on the Index.[119] In the very year of his flight from Rome Pius IX had all but decided on the restoration of

---

[116] Hales, *op. cit.*, pp. 91–98; Aubert, *Le Pontificat de Pie IX*, pp. 33–35.

[117] Hales, *op. cit.*, pp. 101–133; Aubert, *op. cit.*, pp. 35–38.

[118] Aubert, *op. cit.*, pp. 268–270; Schnabel, *Deutsche Geschichte im neunzehnten Jahrhundert*, Vol. IV, pp. 267–269.

[119] Aubert, *op. cit.*, pp. 270–276.

the hierarchy in England. In 1850 the formal step was taken: it was by Papal act and the bishops were Papal appointees.[120] A little later, in 1853, after a petition in 1847 and following long negotiations with the Dutch Government, the hierarchy was renewed in the Netherlands.[121] Several of the Latin American countries were still disturbed by internal conflicts which followed political independence, and in them anti-clericalism was often prominent. In the 1850's, 1860's, and 1870's Pius IX repeatedly acted to strengthen the Roman Catholic Church in Latin America, appointed bishops, and created new dioceses. In 1865 he authorized the establishment in Rome of the Collegio Pio Latino Americano for the preparation of clergy for that region. Those trained in it would presumably be especially loyal to Rome and the Pope.[122] The growth of the Roman Catholic Church in the United States and Australia, chiefly through immigration, and in Canada also enhanced the effective authority of the Papacy, for here no serious challenge was given to the control by Rome of the ecclesiastical structure. Similarly the rapid expansion of missions outside the Occident was under the direction of the Propaganda and so of the Pope.[123] Pius IX made his weight felt in the complicated religious picture in Russia and in the portions of Poland under Russian control.[124] The progress towards religious liberty in Scandinavian countries enabled him to encourage steps for the nourishing and increase of the small Roman Catholic contingents in those overwhelmingly Protestant lands.[125]

It was on December 8, 1854, that Pius IX solemnly proclaimed, on his sole authority, in the bull *Ineffabilis Deus* the immaculate conception of the Virgin Mary as a doctrine revealed by God and to be believed firmly and constantly by all the faithful. As the bull defined it, the doctrine held "the Blessed Virgin Mary to have been, from the first instant of her conception, by a singular grace and privilege of Almighty God, in view of the merits of Christ Jesus the Saviour of mankind, preserved free from stain of original sin." Not all theologians had agreed that the conception had been immaculate in the sense defined by the bull. The Dominicans especially had dissenters. But with the Roman Catholic revival, the doctrine was widely and increasingly cherished and pressure was brought on the Pope to give it his official endorsement. Pius IX was by no means unwilling, for, as we have said, his devotion to her whom the faithful venerated as the mother of God was sincere and deep.[126] In 1848, when the crisis over the Papal States was already acute, he appointed a commission to

[120] Hales, *op. cit.*, pp. 139–142; Aubert, *op. cit.*, pp. 67–71.
[121] Hales, *op. cit.*, pp. 144, 145; Aubert, *op. cit.*, pp. 63–66.
[122] Schmidlin, *Papstgeschichte der neuesten Zeit*, Vol. II, pp. 150–161; Thornton, *The Church and Freemasonry in Brazil, 1872–1875*, pp. 95, 96, 102 ff.
[123] Schmidlin, *op. cit.*, Vol. II, pp. 207–213, 230 ff.
[124] *Ibid.*, pp. 213–223.
[125] *Ibid.*, pp. 224, 225.
[126] Aubert, *op. cit.*, p. 291.

go into the question. While in exile in Gaeta, he asked the bishops for their prayers and advice. The large majority of the several hundred replies were enthusiastic in their endorsement. When the Papal pronouncement was finally made, it could, therefore, be assured of the overwhelming support of articulate Roman Catholics. The fact that at a time when the threat to the autonomy of the Papal States was mounting a Pontiff could win general acceptance in his church for a statement of such importance on a matter of faith was evidence of the growing acquiescence of the central loyal core of Roman Catholics in the assertion of Papal authority. The act was severely criticized by Christians in other churches and tended to widen the gulf between them and the Roman Catholic Church.[127]

Pius IX: The Loss of the Papal States

In the continuing sweep of the political phases of the revolution the Papal States were lost. For our purposes a brief summary will suffice.

Pius IX returned to Rome under the protection of the troops of Louis Napoleon without compromising himself with pledges to his benefactor, and he did not adopt the programme which Napoleon desired. However, he carried through some changes in the administration of the Papal States. Among them was an increasing proportion of laymen in the government.[128]

In the administration of his territories and in his diplomatic dealings with other governments, Pius IX had the able assistance of his Secretary of State, Cardinal Antonelli. Although thoroughly secular in his attitude, avaricious, and seeking to promote the interests of the members of his family and of his illegitimate children, Antonelli was loyal to the Pope, courageous, able, and shrewd.[129]

Neither Pius IX nor Antonelli was a match for the mounting sentiment for the unification of Italy and the skill with which Cavour, as prime minister of the Kingdom of Sardinia, a realm with its main strength in Piedmont in the North-west and often referred to by that name, was preparing the way for the integration of Italy as a constitutional monarchy under the rule of the House of Savoy. By bringing Sardinia into the Crimean War on the side of France and Great Britain, Cavour curried the friendship of those powers. In 1859, through his diplomacy, France joined Sardinia in a war on Austria which issued in the acquisition of Lombardy by Sardinia. As repercussions from the war, some sections of Central Italy, including the Romagna, a part of the Papal States, acceded to Piedmont. Against the annexation of the Romagna Pius and

[127] Dictionnaire de Théologie Catholique, Vol. VII, columns 845–1218; The Catholic Encyclopedia, Vol. VII, pp. 674–680. The text and translation of the bull are in Schaff, The Creeds of Christendom, Vol. II, pp. 211, 212. A translation is also in Doheny and Kelly, Papal Documents on Mary, pp. 9 ff.
[128] Hales, op. cit., pp. 152–166.
[129] Ibid., pp. 151, 152; Aubert, op. cit., pp. 85, 86.

Antonelli protested in vain, especially since Napoleon, bribed by the grant of Savoy and Nice by Sardinia, viewed it complacently. In 1860 revolt against the Bourbon King of the Two Sicilies broke out in Sicily. Aided by the nationalist adventurer Garibaldi, it quickly succeeded, spread from Sicily to the mainland, and eliminated the Bourbons. To obtain the union of Italy Sardinia intervened. Sardinian forces invaded the Papal States, defeated the Papal troops, and marched on Naples. Garibaldi agreed to the annexation of the Bourbon domains by Sardinia. Over the protests of Pius the Papal States except Rome and the territory immediately around it were also annexed by Sardinia. In March, 1861, Victor Emmanuel exchanged the title of King of Sardinia for that of King of Italy. Italian nationalists wished Rome as the capital of the country, but Napoleon, while not opposing the annexation of the rest of the Papal territories, would not consent and kept French troops in the city. This he did to placate Catholic sentiment in Europe, especially in France, and to continue French influence in Italy. In 1870, engaged in his disastrous war with Prussia, Napoleon, in dire need of all his troops, recalled the French garrison. Thereupon Victor Emmanuel, on the pretext of maintaining order in what was left of the Papal States, against Papal protests sent troops to occupy Rome. The Pope had a small army of his own, but to prevent bloodshed in what could be only a futile defence he ordered it to make merely enough resistance to show that it and he were yielding under protest. In September, 1870, Victor Emmanuel's troops took possession. By a strange irony, of which we shall have more to say, this was slightly over two months after Papal infallibility had been formally proclaimed.

Pius refused to consent to the elimination of his temporal rule, but he was impotent. Through much of the Roman Catholic world vigorous protests were made. However, they were ineffective in stimulating effective intervention by foreign governments.[130]

Since the Pope would not enter into a treaty regularizing the new order, the Italian Government took unilateral action. This it did in November, 1870, by enacting the Law of Guarantees—which served as a *modus vivendi* until the Lateran Treaty of 1929 in which the Papacy at last came to terms with the civil regime. The Law of Guarantees assured the Pope of the rights and status of a purely spiritual sovereign, immunity from arrest, and protection against treason. He was to be free to have diplomatic relations with governments, to have his own personal guard, his own postal and telegraphic services, and the use, although not the ownership, of the Vatican, the Lateran, and Castel Gandolfo. In compensation for his lost territories and their revenues, he was to be

130 Hales, *op. cit.*, pp. 184–252, 313–317; Aubert, *op. cit.*, pp. 79–106, 359, 360; Schmidlin, *op. cit.*, Vol. II, pp. 66–93; Nielsen, *The History of the Papacy in the Nineteenth Century*, Vol. II, pp. 375 ff.; Wallace, *The Papacy and European Diplomacy*, pp. 116 ff.

given a substantial annual monetary grant. The state surrendered its claim to name bishops and to try spiritual cases in its courts. Except in the allocation of benefices to the clergy, the state was not to employ the *exequatur*, namely, its permission before a bishop could exercise his functions or a Papal bull be published, or the *placet*, its formal consent before an ecclesiastical document could be circulated in its territory.[131]

Pius would not assent to the Law of Guarantees or to the loss of his domains. He refused the annual indemnity and regarded himself as a prisoner in the Vatican.[132] The faithful were also forbidden either to vote or to stand for office under the government which had deprived him of his territories.[133]

The effect of the Pope's attitude was to sharpen the distinction in Italy between practising and nominal Roman Catholics. Those who gave primary allegiance to the Church obeyed. Those who were more Italian and patriotic than Catholic, while maintaining a formal connexion with the Church, regarded the Pope's injunction as hostile to the nationalism which they prized.[134]

During the controversy over the relations of the Papacy with the civil power, Pius and Victor Emmanuel remained on friendly personal terms. In their extensive correspondence Pius treated the king as a son of the Church for whom he cherished a pastoral and affectionate concern, and the king addressed the Pope with dutiful deference. On political policies they differed, but they did not become enemies.[135]

PIUS IX: THE HARDENING ATTITUDE TOWARDS THE REVOLUTION

As the years passed, Pius IX was strengthened in the conviction that many features of the revolution through which the Occident was passing were a threat to the Christian faith. He believed that, as the head on earth of the Church, he must stand against them. Particularly had his conflicts with Mazzini, Garibaldi, and Piedmont, and in France with Napoleon III, deepened his concern and his belief that acquiescence or compromise would be a violation of the obligations of his high office. But they were not the only occasions or the sole causes. He was acutely aware of trends in other lands which were highlighted by his experience with Italy and France. Moreover, he had been deeply involved in the consideration of the intellectual formulations by which some of the Church's sons were attempting to reconcile the Christian faith with the current climate of opinion. Some of these efforts he or his immediate predecessors had con-

---

[131] Hales, *op. cit.*, pp. 317, 318; Aubert, *op. cit.*, p. 368; Halperin, *Italy and the Vatican at War*, pp. 104–135.

[132] Aubert, *op. cit.*, pp. 368–370.

[133] *Ibid.*, p. 370.

[134] *Ibid.*, pp. 370, 371; Halperin, *op. cit.*, pp. 374 ff.

[135] See the extensive correspondence in Pirri, *Pio IX e Vittorio Emanuele II del loro carteggio privato*, *passim*.

demned. Social theories existed which challenged the Church and its faith. Again and again he spoke out.

Even before the climax brought by the loss of Rome, Pius IX issued a sweeping indictment of what seemed to him evil in contemporary attitudes and governmental policies. This was on December 8, 1864, the tenth anniversary of the proclamation of the immaculate conception. It took the form of an encyclical, *Quanta cura,* which announced a jubilee year for 1865, and an accompanying document, *Syllabus errorum,* or Syllabus of Errors. The latter was particularly formidable. It was directed to the bishops and was a brief digest of allocutions, encyclicals, and apostolic letters of Pius IX. Although it did not bear the signature of the Pope and he may have been neither its originator nor its compiler, the responsibility for its publication was clearly his.[136]

The Syllabus covered a wide range. It was mainly negative, stating emphatically what the Pope disapproved. By implication the positive affirmations of the Papacy were clear. In eighty succinct paragraphs the position of Rome on issues then much in controversy was set forth.[137]

At the outset pantheism, naturalism, and absolute rationalism were denounced, with their positions that God is none other than nature; that human reason is the sole arbiter of truth and falsehood and good and evil; that all the truths of religion are derived from human reason; that Christian faith contradicts human reason and that divine revelation not only does not promote but even hinders the perfection of man; that the miracles recorded in the Scriptures are poetic fiction; and that Christ himself is a myth.

Then followed the listing as error of what was denominated moderate rationalism, with its assumptions that theology must be treated in the same manner as philosophy; that all dogmas of the Christian religion are to be dealt with by scientific methods and that human reason is able to arrive at the truth of even the most recondite dogmas; that the Church should never pass judgement on philosophy, but should tolerate the errors of philosophy and leave their correction to philosophy; that the decrees of the Apostolic See and the Roman congregations impede the free progress of knowledge; that the methods and principles which the school men applied to theology are not congruous with the progress of the sciences; and that philosophy must be treated without reference to supernatural revelation.

The Syllabus next turned its attention to what it labelled indifferentism and latitudinarianism. In this it included as errors the teaching that every man is free to embrace and profess the religion which, guided by the light of reason,

[136] Hales, *op. cit.,* pp. 256, 257; Aubert, *op. cit.,* pp. 253–255.

[137] The Latin text and the English translation are in Schaff, *op. cit.,* Vol. II, pp. 213–233. For a preface and a running commentary, critical of the Syllabus, see Bury, *History of the Papacy in the 19th Century,* pp. 1–46.

he believes to be true; that men through any religion can find the way to eternal salvation; that we may cherish at least a well-founded hope for the eternal salvation of all who are not in the true Church of Christ; and that Protestantism is another form of the Christian religion in which it is as possible to be pleasing to God as in the Catholic Church.

The Syllabus lumped together Socialism, Communism, secret societies, Bible societies, and clerico-liberal societies and called attention to the various encyclicals and allocutions in which "pests of this kind" had been excoriated.

Then the Syllabus turned to what it deemed errors concerning the Church and its rights. Among them it named the assertions that the Church does not enjoy peculiar and enduring rights conferred on her by her divine Founder, but that the civil power can determine the rights and limits within which she may exercise authority; that the ecclesiastical power should not wield its authority without the permission of the civil government; that the Catholic Church does not have the power to define dogmatically that the religion of the Catholic Church is the only true religion; that the obligation by which all Catholic teachers and writers are bound applies only to those matters which by the judgement of the infallible Church are set forth as dogmas to be believed by all; that Roman Pontiffs and ecumenical councils have exceeded the limits of their power, have usurped the rights of princes, and have even erred in defining matters of faith and morals; that the Church does not have the power to invoke force and does not have direct or indirect temporal power; that the Church does not have the innate right of acquisition and possession; that the ministers of the Church and the Roman Pontiff should be completely excluded from all charge and dominion over temporal affairs; that bishops do not have the right to publish their apostolic letters without the permission of the state; that dispensations granted by the Roman Pontiff must be considered as null unless they have been requested by the civil government; that the immunity of the Church and of ecclesiastics has its origin in civil law; that exemption of the clergy from military service may be abolished without violating natural law and equity; that the teaching of theological subjects is not exclusively under the jurisdiction of the Church; that there would be nothing to forbid a general council or an act of all peoples from transferring the supreme pontificate from the Bishop and city of Rome to another state; that the decision of a national council does not admit of further discussion and that the civil power can accept it as final; that national churches can be instituted by separation from the authority of the Roman Pontiff; and that arbitrary acts of the Roman Pontiffs have contributed to the division of the Church into East and West.

Next were taken up what were regarded as errors about the civil society, both in itself and in its relations with the Church. Among them were that the civil state is the origin and source of all rights; that the teaching of the Catholic

Church is opposed to the well-being and interests of human society; that in a conflict of laws between the two powers the civil law should prevail; that the civil authority may intervene in matters of religion, morals, and spiritual government and hence can pass judgement on instructions issued by pastors for the guidance of consciences; that the entire direction of public schools in which the youth of Christian states are educated, except to a certain extent episcopal seminaries, must appertain to the civil power; that in clerical seminaries the method of study is subject to the civil power; that a system separating instruction from the Catholic faith and the power of the Church may be approved by Catholics; that the civil power has the right to prevent ministers of religion and the faithful from communicating freely with one another and the Roman Pontiff; that the secular power possesses the right to present bishops and to require them to take possession of their dioceses before having received canonical institution from the Holy See; that the secular authority has the right to depose bishops; that the state has the right to alter the age prescribed by the Church for the religious profession by men and women and may forbid religious establishments to admit any to solemn vows without its permission; that the civil government may assist all who wish to quit the religious life and may suppress religious orders, collegiate churches, and simple benefices and appropriate their goods and revenues; that kings and princes are not only exempt from the jurisdiction of the Church but are also superior to it in litigated questions of jurisdiction; and that the Church should be separated from the state and the state from the Church.

What were regarded as errors concerning natural and Christian ethics were described as follows: that moral laws do not need divine sanction; that philosophy and morals and also civil laws may and must depart from divine and ecclesiastical authority; that no other forces are to be recognized than those which reside in matter, and all moral teaching and excellence should consist in the increase of riches by every possible means and in the enjoyment of pleasure; that all human duties are but vain words; that authority is nothing but the sum of numerical superiority and material force; that the principle of non-intervention by the Church should be proclaimed and observed; that it is permissible to refuse obedience to legitimate princes and to rebel against them; and that the violation of a solemn oath and every wicked action repugnant to the eternal law are worthy of the highest praise if done for the love of country.

A group of what were labeled as errors was concerned with Christian marriage. Among them were the denial that Christ had raised marriage to the dignity of a sacrament; that the sacrament of marriage is only an adjunct to a contract, is separable from it, and consists merely in the nuptial benediction; that in many cases divorce may be pronounced by the civil authority; that the Church does not have the authority to lay down the impediments to marriage, but that the civil power possesses it and can annul them; and that a civil contract may among Christians constitute true marriage.

The civil power of the Pope inevitably was a matter of concern. Two assertions were described as errors, namely, that Catholics differed among themselves on the compatibility of the temporal with the spiritual power and that the abolition of the civil power possessed by the Apostolic See would contribute to the liberty and prosperity of the Church.

A concluding blast was directed against what were adjudged errors of modern liberalism. These were that it was no longer expedient that the Catholic religion should be the only religion of the state to the exclusion of other forms of worship; that in some countries called Catholic, immigrants should be permitted the public exercise of their own religion; and that religious liberty does not corrupt the morals of the people.

The final paragraph in this section and in the Syllabus is so significant and created such a stir that it should be quoted in full. It was declared to be an error that *"Romanus Pontifex potest ac debet cum progressu, cum liberalismo at cum recenti civilitate sese reconciliare at componere."* ("the Roman Pontiff can and should reconcile himself to and agree with progress, liberalism, and modern civilization").

We have given so much of the Syllabus of Errors because it summarized as does no other single document the attitude of Pius IX towards the revolution sweeping across Christendom. Some of the issues with which it dealt had been chronic for centuries: to those familiar with the earlier course of Christian history they have a familiar ring. Most of the issues arose out of the revolution in which the Roman Catholic Church was set.

The Syllabus aroused a storm of criticism in the secular and Protestant press. It produced something like consternation among many who wished to remain within the Roman Catholic Church but were seeking ways of reconciling the Christian faith with the currents of thought and the political theories and movements which were a part of the revolution.[138] In denouncing the ideal of a "free church in a free state" Pius IX was slapping down those who wished by that device to make secure a place for the Roman Catholic Church in the revolutionary world. In condemning the demand that as head of the Roman Catholic Church the Pope take the lead in adjusting the Christian faith to the revolution Pius seemed to many to be piloting the bark of Peter towards shipwreck.

Yet in contrast with the criticism and the sorrowful protests with which it was greeted, the Syllabus had its staunch defenders. They welcomed it as a courageous attempt to stem the tide towards unbelief.

138 For a summary of the reaction see Aubert, *Le Pontificat de Pie IX*, pp. 255–261.

The net effect of the Syllabus of Errors was to widen and deepen the gulf between the Roman Catholic Church and the revolution and to rally the faithful to the defense and support of the Christian faith as interpreted by that church. In the main Pius IX was keeping the bark of Peter to the course which it had held across the centuries. He was applying to current conditions principles and claims which earlier Popes had been asserting as of the essence of the Christian faith. To him and to the Roman Catholic Church there gathered a following, numbering millions, increasingly knit together under the direction of himself and his successors, aware of the enmity of the world about them, even glorying in it and the attendant conflicts and martyrdoms, and, far from being solely on the defensive, seeking to win that world to the faith.

The next Pope, as we shall see, sought to find points of contact with that world and to influence it in ways consistent with the faith of the Roman Catholic Church, but the positions taken so frankly by Pius IX were never explicitly repudiated. The document was not an *ex cathedra* utterance and so was not officially infallible. But coming from the Pope it could not be disregarded.

PIUS IX: PAPAL CONTROL OF THE ROMAN CATHOLIC CHURCH AND THE ROLE OF THE POPE AS THE INFALLIBLE SPOKESMAN FOR THE CHURCH ARE EMPHATICALLY AFFIRMED; THE VATICAN COUNCIL

In the pontificate of Pius IX a further important step was taken towards knitting the Roman Catholic Church more firmly together under the Pope. That was through the Vatican Council of 1869–1870. This gathering, denominated by the Roman Catholic Church the twentieth ecumenical council in direct succession to the one held in Nicea in 325, formulated in forthright fashion what were regarded by the majority as implicit from the beginning of the Church—the administrative supremacy of the Pope within the Church and the infallibility of *ex cathedra* pronouncements of the Pope on matters of faith and morals.

As we have repeatedly noted, since 1815 ultramontanism, namely, the enhancement of the position of the Papacy in the Roman Catholic Church, had been mounting. Pius IX strongly encouraged it.[139] He added to the trend by summoning bishops for *ad limina*—official—visits to Rome more frequently than had his predecessors (visits facilitated by the improved means of transportation which were a phase of the revolution), by promoting the spread of Roman rites, liturgy, and clerical costume, by distributing Roman titles, and by intervening in disputes between bishops and their clergy. He created a number of non-Italians Cardinals, thus broadening the geographic base of that body as a symbol of the universality of the Roman Catholic Church.[140] The pronounce-

[139] *Ibid.*, pp. 262–277.
[140] Hales, *Pio Nino*, p. 280.

ment on the immaculate conception was a striking move in the direction of ultramontanism. The reverence in which Pius himself was held in some circles was a contributory factor.[141]

The reverence for Pius IX was a feature of what has been called the new ultramontanism. The new ultramontanism saw in the Roman Catholic Church headed by the Papacy the one hope for the reconstruction of society on the ruins left by the demise of the old. The old society inherited from the Middle Ages had been sick unto death. The final *coup de grâce* had been dealt by the revolution of which the years after 1789 had been the culmination. The new order must be built by the Church. The Church must be headed by the Pope. The Pope must act authoritatively and speak infallibly. So ran the argument.[142] The Jesuits threw their weight on the side of the neo-ultramontanism. The Roman periodical, *Civilta Cattolica,* which supported it, was begun by one of them and became more and more an inspired organ of the Vatican.[143]

The Vatican Council was not called primarily to formulate Papal infallibility. Two days before the publication of *Quanta cura* and the Syllabus, Pius IX told the Cardinals that he had long had in mind the convening of an ecumenical council and asked their opinion. Although a minority dissented, the majority favoured the proposal as affording opportunity in the ferment of the times for a clear statement of Catholic doctrine and a condemnation of current errors. To them the crisis seemed graver than any which had confronted the Roman Catholic Church since the last council regarded by that church as ecumenical, the one bearing the name of Trent and held in the sixteenth century to effect the reformation made imperative by the rise of Protestantism. Indeed, a much longer time had elapsed since such a council than between any of the earlier ones.[144]

A commission of five Cardinals was set up to make the preparations. Under the injunction of strict secrecy a letter was sent to a selected number of bishops asking for subjects to be taken up by the council. Many of the replies proposed as topics the chief errors of the times and the affirmation of the Christian dogmas, including the nature of the Church and the Roman primacy and prerogatives.[145]

Although the issue of Papal infallibility had not loomed large in the original purpose of the council, as the date for the assembly neared it became clear that here would be a central issue. Numbers of Catholics, especially among the intel-

---

141 Butler, *The Vatican Council,* Vol. I, pp. 76, 77; Aubert, *op. cit.,* p. 289.

142 Ward, *William George Ward and the Catholic Revival,* pp. 82 ff.; Butler, *op. cit.,* Vol. I, pp. 57 ff.

143 Hales, *op. cit.,* pp. 283, 284.

144 Butler, *op. cit.,* Vol. I, pp. 81, 82; Granderath, *Geschichte des vatikanischen Konzils,* Vol. I, pp. 27–45.

145 Granderath, *op. cit.,* Vol. I, pp. 46–56; Butler, *op. cit.,* Vol. I, pp. 82, 83.

lectuals and those known as liberals, broke into print in criticism of the proposed dogma.[146]

The council convened on December 8, 1869, on the Feast of the Immaculate Conception, an even fifteen years after the proclamation of the dogma. It continued until the autumn of 1870. By that time the Franco-Prussian War had broken out, the French troops had been withdrawn from Rome, and the city had been occupied by the forces of the Kingdom of Italy. On October 20, 1870, the Pope formally suspended the sittings. The council had not completed all the programme that had been mapped out. A number of projects which had been prepared for its consideration had not come up for vote and some had not even been distributed among the members. Yet what had been accomplished was of major importance. Decrees had been drafted, debated, modified, and adopted, and were later promulgated by the Pope.[147]

First a positive statement of the Catholic faith was adopted and errors were described and anathematized.

Next came a section on the constitution of the Church. It was called the "Constitutio Dogmatica Prima de Ecclesia Christi." It asserted the primacy of Peter as ordained by Christ and of the Bishops of Rome as his successors. It held that all the faithful must agree with the Roman Church and that the Roman Church headed by its Pontiff has power over all other churches. It declared that the Roman Pontiff has "full and supreme power of jurisdiction over the universal Church, not only in things which belong to faith and morals, but also in those which relate to the discipline and government of the Church spread throughout the world." It declared that this power of the Pope did not prejudice the power of the bishops, but, rather, that the episcopal authority was strengthened and protected by "the supreme and universal pastor." It also maintained that the "see of holy Peter remains ever free from all blemish of error" and "that it is a truth divinely revealed that the Roman Pontiff, when he speaks *ex cathedra,* that is, when in discharge of the office of pastor and doctor of all Christians, by virtue of his supreme apostolic authority, he defines a doctrine regarding faith and morals to be held by the universal Church, by the divine assistance promised to him in blessed Peter, is possessed of that infallibility with which the divine Redeemer willed that his Church should be possessed for defining doctrine regarding faith or morals; and that therefore such definitions of the Roman Pontiff are irreformable of themselves, and not from the consent of the Church." [148] By carefully limiting Papal infallibility to *ex cathedra* utter-

---

[146] Hales, *op. cit.,* pp. 285–290; Wallace, *The Papacy and European Diplomacy,* pp. 56 ff.; Acton, *Essays on Freedom and Power,* pp. 301, 302; Butler, *op. cit.,* Vol. I, pp. 106–129; Granderath, *op. cit.,* Vol. I, pp. 150–302; Simpson, *Roman Catholic Opposition to Papal Infallibility,* pp. 106–216.

[147] Butler, *op. cit.,* Vol. II, pp. 166, 167; Aubert, *op. cit.,* p. 360.

[148] The Latin text with a German translation is in Granderath, *op. cit.,* Vol. III, pp. 503–615,

ances as the pastor and doctor of all Christians on doctrine regarding faith and morals, the decree made it clear that not all Papal pronouncements were in that category. Precisely when these conditions had been met was not stated, nor did experts on canon law fully agree as to exactly when they had been fulfilled. That remained a subject of debate.[149] The decree did not go as far as some protagonists of infallibility had wished.

Several leading statesmen viewed with hostile eye canons which were proposed to accompany the decrees and which dealt with the relations of Church and state: some talked of intervention by their governments.[150] In contrast with the Council of Trent, no government was represented. Although they were not invited, it was made clear that the Catholic powers could have participated. The fact that none did so was evidence of the growing breach between the civil governments and the Roman Catholic Church and of the position of the latter as set against many of the currents of the times.[151]

Within the council the chief differences were over the issue of Papal infallibility. The council was large. It was composed chiefly of bishops, and at the sessions six hundred or more were normally present. The total enrollment began with 719 and in January swelled to 744. For several weeks the question of Papal infallibility was not formally brought up. It had been deemed best to withhold it until the request came from the bishops. The bishops were divided on the wisdom of putting the question to the council. The opposition was chiefly from French and Germans. Some of the French were ardent supporters of ultramontanism, but others were critical. Most of the German bishops believed it inexpedient to have infallibility considered.[152]

Outside the council the discussion waxed warm. In France Montalembert, a liberal Catholic, long known for his opposition to Gallicanism, in the last utterance before his death came out against the new ultramontanism. In Germany, Döllinger, a prominent Catholic scholar whom we are to meet again, was vigorous in his denunciation of infallibility.[153]

On the preliminary vote of the question of approval of the declaration of infallibility 451, or three-fourths, were in favour; 88, between a sixth and a seventh, were flatly opposed; and 62, slightly more than a tenth, approved with reservations. Ninety-one bishops abstained from voting. Before the final vote 60 of the dissenters sent a letter to the Pope saying they could not alter their votes,

---

and the Latin text and an English translation are in Schaff, *The Creeds of Christendom*, Vol. II, pp. 234–271.

[149] For some of these different views see Butler, *op. cit.*, Vol. II, pp. 209 ff.

[150] *Ibid.*, pp. 3 ff.

[151] *Ibid.*, Vol. I, pp. 104, 105.

[152] *Ibid.*, pp. 204–206; Simpson, *op. cit.*, pp. 237–267.

[153] Bury, *History of the Papacy in the 19th Century*, pp. 109–116; Nielsen, *The History of the Papacy in the Nineteenth Century*, Vol. II, pp. 320 ff.; Simpson, *op. cit.*, pp. 233–237,

but would absent themselves: of those voting only two, an American and an Italian, were in the negative.[154]

It was indicative of the growing power of the Papacy in the Church that, in contrast with all the former councils, the Pope claimed the exclusive right to initiate proposals to come before the council. It was also significant that the decrees of the council were introduced by the words: "Pius, bishop, servant of the servants of God, with the approval of the sacred council." This was in contrast with the corresponding formula of the preceding council, that of Trent: "The sacred synod, lawfully assembled under the Holy Ghost, under the presidency of the legates of the Apostolic See, ordains." Obviously the emphasis had been changed from the council to the Pope as the authoritative organ of the Church.[155]

Similarly symptomatic of the growing power of the Papacy was the fact that all the bishops submitted to the decrees of the Vatican Council. Even those who had expressed themselves as against the declaration of Papal infallibility accepted the decision.[156] Whatever their private judgement may have been, now that the Church had spoken through its recognized organ they regarded its pronouncements as having the authority of God.

That Pius IX welcomed the decisions of the council was clear. Although he professed to leave the council to the guidance of the Holy Spirit, it was obvious that before the council assembled and during the sessions his convictions in the main were in accord with what was eventually decided and that he favoured the ultramontane elements. That in doing so he was gratifying a personal desire for power is by no means so certain. He was a man of deep and genuine piety who had a quiet confidence in God, who scrupulously observed his daily meditations, who delighted in saying his breviary on his knees, and who spent much time in prayer before the Blessed Sacrament. As one sympathetic observer said, he was not a saint: he had his weaknesses, among them a quick temper. But that he sought to fulfil conscientiously what he conceived to be the duties of his high office appears to be undebatable.[157]

It must be said, moreover, that the decisions of the Vatican Council, especially those which stressed the administrative authority and the infallibility of the Pope, represented the convictions of the large majority of those Roman Catholics who were sincerely committed to the faith. Like the majority of the

---

[154] Bury, *op. cit.*, pp. 126–128; Simpson, *op. cit.*, pp. 267–271. See from one of the opposition: *Letters from Bishop McQuaid from the Vatican Council*, in *The Catholic Historical Review*, Vol. XLI, pp. 408–441. See also Raymond J. Clancy, *American Prelates in the Vatican Council*, in *Historical Records and Studies*, Vol. XXVIII, pp. 7–135.

[155] Bury, *op. cit.*, p. 79.

[156] Hales, *op. cit.*, p. 310; Aubert, *op. cit.*, pp. 361, 362; Butler, *op. cit.*, Vol. II, pp. 168 ff.; Moss, *The Old Catholic Movement*, pp. 215 ff.

[157] Aubert, *op. cit.*, p. 291.

council, they believed that here was nothing new, but only what had always been implicit in the deposit of the faith entrusted to the Church. They welcomed the formulations as required by the revolutionary times in which they found themselves. Through the council's decrees, so they held, the Church was ordering its forces to meet a hostile world and, confident in the promise given to Peter and the Church, the better to lay siege to the city in which their enemies were entrenched.

The submission of the bishops, the sincerity of the Pope in his purpose to serve the faith, and the concurrence of the majority of the faithful did not estop criticism of the Vatican Council. Few serious protests came from any Latin country. They were not even widespread in France, where liberal Catholicism had been strong. To be sure, a Carmelite, Charles (Père Hyacinthe) Loyson (1827–1912), a scholar and preacher who attracted large audiences, denounced the Syllabus and the decrees of the Vatican Council,[158] but he had little following among the clergy. In France the lower clergy seem to have been solidly behind the decrees and against those of their bishops who had voiced opposition.[159] Criticism was vocal in England. Lord Acton, noted Roman Catholic scholar, had been in Rome during the council. Hating all absolutism, whether civil or ecclesiastical, he regarded the declaration of infallibility as both false and wicked and did what he could to prevent its enactment. Although he expected excommunication, he was spared what to him would have been a grievous deprivation, for he regarded himself as a good Catholic and held the Church to be holier than its officials.[160] Gladstone, Prime Minister in the United Kingdom at the time of the Vatican Council, a close friend of Acton, came out with a vigorous pamphlet in which he excoriated the decrees as constituting a basic change in the policies of the Roman Catholic Church and, together with the Syllabus, evidence of a prior allegiance of British Roman Catholics to the Pope and therefore a threat to the loyalty which Englishmen owed to their queen and her government.[161] Yet Cardinal Manning, the head of the English hierarchy, had been one of the most active proponents of Papal infallibility and insisted that it was not a new doctrine but was of the essence of the faith and had been

---

[158] His spiritual pilgrimage took him out of the Roman Catholic Church. Of the extensive literature by him and about him see, as examples, Father Hyacinthe, *Catholic Reform: Letters, Fragments, Discourses,* translated by Madame Hyacinthe Loyson (London, Macmillan and Co., 1874, pp. xlv, 233); Albert Houtin, *Le Père Hyacinthe dans l'Église Romaine, 1827–1869* (Paris, Émile Nourry, 1920, pp. 395); Albert Houtin, *Le Père Hyacinthe Réformateur Catholique, 1867–1893* (Paris, Émile Nourry, 1922, pp. 362); Albert Houtin, *La Père Hyacinthe, Prêtre Solitaire, 1893–1912* (Paris, Émile Nourry, 1924, pp. 430); Theodorus [Mullinger], *The New Reformation,* pp. 100–104; *Enciclopedia Cattolica,* Vol. VII, p. 158.

[159] Butler, *op. cit.,* Vol. II, pp. 169–171; Granderath, *op. cit.,* Vol. III, pp. 664 ff.

[160] Acton, *Essays on Freedom and Power,* pp. 299 ff.; Simpson, *op. cit.,* pp. 326–333; *Dictionary of National Biography, Second Supplement,* pp. 8–12.

[161] W. E. Gladstone, *The Vatican Decrees in Their Bearing on Civil Allegiance: A Political Expostulation* (New York, Harper & Brothers, 1875, pp. 168), *passim.*

long maintained by English Catholics.[162] In the United States the secular press following the proceedings of the council had varied attitudes. A few newspapers and periodicals were friendly or neutral, but the majority were critical or frankly hostile.[163]

Pius IX: Criticism of the Vatican Council Gives Rise to an Old Catholic Movement and the Loss by Rome of Minorities

In Germany, Switzerland, and Austria criticism led to open schism. Some of the German bishops who had been opposed to the pronouncement of the dogma of Papal infallibility were slow in submitting. The last was Karl Josef von Hefele (1809–1893), distinguished as a church historian, but in April, 1871, he published the decrees in his diocese. Persistent opposition came from professors in the universities. Of these the most conspicuous was Johann Josef Ignaz von Döllinger (1799–1890),[164] a noted church historian. In 1869 under the pseudonym of Janus he had come out with *The Pope and the Council*,[165] a trenchant attack on infallibility. When on returning from the council his Archbishop gave his report and declared that there was but one Church, neither new nor old, Döllinger is reported to have replied: "But they have made a new one." [166] When the Archbishop called upon him to submit, Döllinger asked for time. After several weeks he said: "As a Christian, as a theologian, as a historian, and as a citizen, I cannot accept this doctrine." He was supported by most of the professors in his university, that of Munich. A few days later the Archbishop excommunicated him and one of his associates.[167] Elsewhere parish priests and professors who refused to submit were deprived of their posts and forbidden to perform any ecclesiastical function. Under pressure, some conformed.[168]

Feelings ran high. Pius IX is reported to have declared the opposition to be more formidable than the French Revolution and more to be dreaded than the Communists. In a pastoral letter the German bishops insisted that Papal infallibility was essential as a safeguard against the current critical methods of scholars and the independence of modern thought.[169] In the excited atmosphere of the time the apprehensions of the Pope seemed to be confirmed by the appearance of resistance not only in Germany but also in German Switzerland: individuals

---

[162] [Manning, Henry Edward, Cardinal] Henry Edward, Archbishop of Westminster, *Petri Privilegium: Three Pastoral Letters to the Clergy of the Diocese* (London, Longmans, Green, & Co., 1871, pp. viii, 236), pp. 140, 151, 236; *The Vatican Council and Its Definitions*, Chap. V.

[163] J. R. Beiser, *The Vatican Council and the American Secular Newspapers, 1869–70* (Washington, The Catholic University of America Press, 1941, pp. 327), *passim*.

[164] *The New Schaff-Herzog Encyclopedia of Religious Knowledge*, Vol. III, pp. 466–468.

[165] Janus, *The Pope and the Council*, authorized translation from the German (London, Rivingtons, 1869, pp. xxix, 425).

[166] Moss, *The Old Catholic Movement*, p. 226; Simpson, *op. cit.*, pp. 316–325.

[167] Moss, *op. cit.*, pp. 231, 232.

[168] *Ibid.*, pp. 230, 231; Theodorus [Mullinger], *op. cit.*, pp. 97, 98.

[169] Moss, *op. cit.*, pp. 232, 233; Theodorus [Mullinger], *op. cit.*, p. 116.

in Austria, Ireland, Spain, and Bohemia as well as Hyacinthe Loyson of France were vocal.

The dissenters assembled in a congress in Munich in September, 1871. To it came not only dissident Roman Catholics but also Anglicans, Greek Orthodox, a few Protestants, and priests from the church with headquarters at Utrecht which had broken with Rome in the eighteenth century. Out of the Munich gathering arose an organization, the Old Catholic Church, a protest against what it deemed the innovations of the Vatican Council. Adhering to what it believed to be the historic or old Catholic position, it repudiated the dogmas put forward by that council, held to the Creed of Pope Pius IV which had been formulated by the Council of Trent, demanded the expulsion of the Jesuits, a share of the laity in ecclesiastical affairs, and reforms in the Church, and expressed the hope of union with the Eastern Orthodox and for understanding with Anglicans and Protestants.[170]

In the course of the next few months congregations were formed in a number of places, chiefly but not exclusively in Germany and Switzerland. The Old Catholic Archbishop of Utrecht travelled through them administering confirmation. Other congresses were held. More congregations were formed. A bishop was elected, and episcopal consecration was obtained through him who was then (August, 1873) the only surviving bishop of the Old Catholic Church in Holland. Sympathy with the Old Catholic Church was expressed by the governments of Prussia, Baden, and Hesse.[171] In 1873 the German Government officially recognized the Old Catholic bishop. The first synod of the Old Catholic Church was convened in 1874 and came out for voluntary confession, the use of the vernacular in church services, and abolishing fees for masses.[172] Before many years three Old Catholic Churches had arisen, each in full communion with the others—in Germany, Switzerland, and Austria. In each the laity had a larger share in the administration than in the Roman Catholic Church, the compulsory celibacy of the clergy was annulled, and the priests were not under obligation to recite the breviary.[173]

Closely associated with the Old Catholics were conferences which sought to promote the unity of the churches. Assembled at the invitation of Old Catholic leaders, they were not officially representative of the churches but were private meetings of theologians. In them were Old Catholics, Anglicans, members of some of the Eastern Churches, and Protestants. The first convened in Bonn in

---

[170] John Friedrich von Schulte, *Der Altkatholicismus: Geschichte seiner Entwicklung, inneren Gestaltung und rechtlichen Stellung in Deutschland* (Giessen, Emil Roth, 1887, pp. xv, 683), *passim;* Theodorus [Mullinger], *op. cit.,* pp. 122 ff.; Moss, *op. cit.,* pp. 234 ff.

[171] Theodorus [Mullinger], *op. cit.,* pp. 128 ff.; Moss, *op. cit.,* pp. 237 ff.

[172] Moss, *op. cit.,* pp. 258, 259.

[173] *Ibid.,* pp. 271 ff.

1874. Döllinger was in the chair. A second in Bonn in 1875 also had him as chairman.[174]

The Old Catholic movement, although always of small minorities in Europe, continued and grew. Congregations arose in France and Italy. Beginning in 1889 biennial International Old Catholic Congresses were held. In the 1890's in the United States, some Polish Catholics, restless under the control of Roman Catholic bishops who were largely Irish, formed an independent organization which became the National Polish Church in the United States, obtained episcopal consecration through Old Catholic bishops in Europe, and were in communion with the Old Catholics. Several other groups, most of them small, sprang up in England and on the Continent. In the 1890's a movement began in Poland which made headway among the peasants, but it was condemned by Rome (1906). Its adherents, known as the Mariaviten Union, persisted, and one of its leaders was consecrated bishop (1909) by Old Catholic bishops. At one time it was said to have 200,000 members. Later it dwindled.[175]

PIUS IX: THE SIGNIFICANCE OF STRENGTHENING THE POWER OF HIS OFFICE AND OF THE REACTION TO IT

What was the total effect of the ultramontane movement under Pius IX? That the majority of the bishops and of articulate Roman Catholic opinion welcomed the strengthening of the effective authority of the Pope is clear. Great Popes in earlier centuries, notably Gregory I, Gregory VII, and Innocent III, had been more potent in the political sphere than had Pius IX, and more than one Pope had put forth sweeping claims for his office, but not in recent centuries if ever had a Pope made the authority of his office so felt within the Roman Catholic Church as a whole.

In the triumph of ultramontanism several facts seem significant as throwing light on the temper of the times and on the course of the revolution which was sweeping across the Occident. One, which we have repeatedly noted, was the acceptance by practising Roman Catholics, in many quarters with enthusiasm, of the increase in the effective power of the Pope within their church. They could now present a more nearly unified front in facing and attempting to win a world whose indifference and hostility had been augmented by the revolution. Second, with a few exceptions the opposition was not from the thoroughly Latin lands—Italy, Spain, and Portugal. Like the Protestant Reformation it was chiefly from North-western Europe. Yet, third, in contrast with the sixteenth century, no such extensive secession from the Roman Catholic Church was seen as that brought by the initial Protestant movements. Only small minorities withdrew, and they attempted to preserve their catholic character. Although

[174] *Ibid.,* pp. 260–270.
[175] *Ibid.,* pp. 278 ff.

exercising to some extent the judgement of the individual as against the majority, they did not incorporate the most distinctive Protestant tenet, justification by faith alone, or its corollary, the priesthood of all believers. Was there here an indication that the tide of religious fervour was not running as strong as in the sixteenth century? The defection from Christian moral standards within the Church was not nearly as great as had been that which provoked the Reformation, both Catholic and Protestant, of the sixteenth century, but indifference and the tacit or open rejection of the faith was now much more widespread than had been true in the generations immediately before the Reformation. Secularism, or the departure from religion, was now more overt, both in Latin and in Northern European lands, than it had been in the Europe in which the Reformation arose. Does this mean that Christianity was dying among Western European and especially traditionally Roman Catholic peoples? In later chapters we shall have occasion again and again to recur to this question.

Pius IX: His Last Years Are Troubled by German Nationalism and the *Kulturkampf*

The growing power of the Papacy in the Roman Catholic Church under Pius IX was paralleled by conflicts with the rising tide of nationalism which was one of the striking phases of the revolution. We have already met it in Italy and have seen that in the very year of the triumph of Papal authority in the Roman Catholic Church registered by the Vatican Council it deprived the Pope of the last remnant of the Papal States. Shortly after the dispersal of the council another contest arose with nationalism, this time in the guise of the newly formed German Empire.

The German Empire, the culmination of the movement for German unity which sprang from German nationalism, was proclaimed on January 18, 1871. The chief creator was Bismarck. A Protestant, he had achieved the realization of the nationalist dream by uniting Germany under the leadership of Prussia.

To Bismarck, intent upon welding together a nation which had long been a loose conglomeration of fragments, the Roman Catholic Church, with its allegiance to the Pope, a foreigner, seemed a serious threat. To reduce the threat he took vigorous action. He was confronted by determined Roman Catholic opposition, led by the Pope. Since Austria was not in the German Empire, Protestants constituted a majority in the latter realm and Roman Catholics were a minority. Yet, in spite of the reverse recently suffered by the Pope in the annexation of his territories by the Kingdom of Italy, Bismarck was defeated. That defeat was not completed during the reign of Pius IX, but before the death of Pius Bismarck's retreat had begun. In administering defeat the Papacy took an important but not a leading role. Success was due, rather, to the Roman Catholics of Germany.

To the attitude of Bismarck a number of factors contributed. He was annoyed by the pressure of German Catholics and Polish Catholics under German rule for intervention against the extinction of the temporal power of the Pope. He held the priests responsible for obstacles placed in the way of his attempted assimilation of the Poles, predominantly Roman Catholic, who were under Prussian jurisdiction. He was irritated that the Catholics were drawing together in a distinct political bloc, soon to be called the Centre Party. The Syllabus of Errors aroused his apprehension, apprehension heightened by the dogmas enunciated by the Vatican Council and by the measures taken by Roman Catholic bishops against Germans who dissented from those dogmas. He and many other Germans feared that the promulgation of Papal infallibility foreshadowed the interference of the Pope, a foreign potentate, in Germany's domestic affairs. He was concerned lest through the action of the clergy the Catholic allegiance of the South German states only recently incorporated into the empire would weaken the tie to the newly formed Reich. He was friendly to the Italian Government and wished its support against Austria and France: he would resist pressures to restore the Papal States.[176]

The *Kulturkampf*, "battle for civilization," a designation given by one of the supporters of the anti-Roman Catholic measures, broke out in 1871. In June of that year the government commanded the Roman Catholic bishops not to bar Old Catholic professors from continuing in their duties. In July the Catholic department in the Ministry of Religion in Prussia was abolished on the ground that it was meddling in Polish affairs. In December a law was enacted which under penalty of two years' imprisonment forbade any clergyman to discuss matters of state. In February, 1872, Falk, the newly appointed minister of religion in Prussia, inaugurated a programme for bringing the educational system of that kingdom directly under state control instead of operating, as heretofore, through the Evangelical Church and the Roman Catholic Church. For ambassador to the Holy See Bismarck proposed a German Cardinal, Prince von Hohenlohe, who during the Vatican Council had been a thorn in the side of the Pope and friendly to the views of Döllinger. Pius refused to receive him and Bismarck broke off diplomatic relations. Bismarck declared that the German Empire would never repeat the humiliation of the Emperor Henry IV in his conflict with Pope Gregory VII and go to Canossa. In July, 1872, legislation expelled the Jesuits from Germany and with them as "affiliated" bodies the Religious of the Sacred Heart, the Redemptorists, and the Lazarists.[177] A speech by Pius IX saying that the Church was prepared to suffer persecution

[176] Wallace, *The Papacy and European Diplomacy*, pp. 187–194, 254–256; Aubert, *Le Pontificat de Pie IX*, pp. 385, 386. For a good bibliography on the entire struggle and a summary of one aspect, see R. W. Lougee in *Church History*, Vol. XXXIII, pp. 219–235.

[177] Aubert, *op. cit.*, pp. 387, 388; Wallace, *op. cit.*, pp. 194–201; Ruhenstroth-Bauer, *Bismarck und Falk im Kulturkampf*, pp. 9 ff.; Béhaine, *Léon XIII et le Prince de Bismarck*, pp. 31 ff.

at the hands of Bismarck aroused the latter's displeasure.[178] The Pope also denounced those Germans who made it a crime to put the laws of God and the Church above those of the empire.[179] In April, 1873, the Prussian constitution was amended to assure the state control over the preparatory education, appointment, and dismissal of the clergy and to declare that the churches, both Roman Catholic and Protestant, were subject to the laws of the state and to the supervision of the state as defined by law.[180] To this, obviously, the Pope could not consent and be consistent with views which he had more than once emphatically expressed.

From the Roman Catholic viewpoint worse was to follow. The following month what were called the Falk or May Laws were enacted. Among the provisions to which the Pope and the hierarchy objected were the implementation of the amendments of the constitution for the control by the state of the education of the clergy, the examination of the candidates by the state at the end of their course, the right of veto by the state of any or all clerical appointments, the final voice of the civil courts in appeals to them from ecclesiastical courts, and, as a measure directed towards the assimilation of the Poles, the requirement that all religious instruction be in German.[181]

For resisting the laws several Roman Catholic bishops and hundreds of priests and chaplains were imprisoned, seminaries closed, newspapers suspended, and fines imposed. Some of the bishops and clergy sought asylum abroad.[182]

The conflict was heightened by attacks of some of the French bishops and the French Catholic press on Bismarck's measures. Bismarck, alarmed by the rapid recovery of France from the defeat of the Franco-Prussian War and the possibility that the French might seek revenge, smarted under the assaults and brought pressure on the French Government to have them suppressed.[183]

More fuel was added to the flames. In May, 1874, further legislation intensified the pressure on the Roman Catholics and widened the rift between Bismarck and the Centre Party. Attempts by fanatics on the life of Bismarck embittered the Iron Chancellor and his supporters. Bismarck proposed to suppress entirely the German embassy to the Holy See.[184] Most of the episcopal sees were vacant. The bishops obtained power from the Pope to appoint as substitutes priests designated only by their initials, or as refugees in Holland, Belgium, Austria, and Rome secretly directed their dioceses.[185] In the main the

[178] Wallace, *op. cit.*, pp. 200, 201.

[179] Aubert, *op. cit.*, p. 388.

[180] Wallace, *op. cit.*, p. 209.

[181] *Ibid.*, p. 210; Aubert, *op. cit.*, p. 389; Foerster, *Adalbert Falk*, pp. 210 ff.; Ruhenstroth-Bauer, *op. cit.*, pp. 38 ff.

[182] Schmidlin, *Papstgeschichte der neuesten Zeit*, Vol. II, pp. 184, 185.

[183] Wallace, *op. cit.*, pp. 212–233.

[184] *Ibid.*, pp. 236 ff.; Ruhenstroth-Bauer, *op. cit.*, pp. 55 ff.; Foerster, *op. cit.*, pp. 237 ff.

[185] Aubert, *op. cit.*, p. 291.

German Catholics rallied to their clergy and were knit together as a resistant bloc. Early in 1875 through an encyclical Pius IX threatened excommunication to all who obeyed the objectionable Prussian laws, urged the faithful to stand firm, and extolled the imprisoned bishops as martyrs.[186] The Belgian Government became involved. A possible *rapprochement* between Austria and Italy and talk of reconciliation between the latter and the Pope seemed to the sensitive Bismarck to threaten Germany with a hostile alliance of France and those two powers.[187] Bismarck declared that the Roman Catholic Church was the Pope, that before the Vatican Council the bishops had had the right to think for themselves, but that now they were mere Papal prefects.[188] In April, 1875, the financial assistance granted to the Roman Catholic clergy by the state was discontinued. In May, 1875, all orders and congregations except those which nursed the sick were excluded from Prussia. The following month saw the abolition of the three paragraphs in the Prussian constitution which had been the foundation of the Catholic church in that realm.[189]

The *Kulturkampf* was not pressed with equal vigour in all the German states. Prussia was the chief storm centre. The stress was severe in Bavaria, predominantly Catholic though that kingdom was. It was intense in Baden, Hesse-Darmstadt, and Saxony. It was marked in the newly annexed Alsace-Lorraine. Württemberg and Oldenburg were but slightly affected.[190]

Before the death of Pius IX Bismarck was beginning to retreat. The attitude of Pius was such that no compromise with him was possible, and in 1877 it was clear that Bismarck was wearying of the struggle. The alliance between himself and the liberals in waging the battle was unnatural for one as conservative as he. He needed the support of the Centre Party in some of his legislation. Elections in France which brought those in favour of a republic into power and were a defeat for the ultramontane Catholic elements removed the fear of the intervention of that country. Bismarck's attention was being diverted to issues in Central and Eastern Europe. Not until the next pontificate were the obnoxious measures either rescinded or relaxed, but before Pius IX passed from the scene it was becoming clear that the Roman Catholic Church was winning. Bismarck did not go to Canossa, but he found ways of withdrawing from the battle.[191]

The net results of the *Kulturkampf* are not easily appraised. A major object of Bismarck, German unity, was both furthered and hindered. In supporting Bavaria in its resistance to Rome Bismarck helped to knit into the new German

[186] Wallace, *op. cit.*, p. 241; Ruhenstroth-Bauer, *op. cit.*, p. 65.
[187] Wallace, *op. cit.*, pp. 245, 247.
[188] *Ibid.*, p. 247.
[189] *Ibid.*, p. 251; Ruhenstroth-Bauer, *op. cit.*, pp. 65 ff.
[190] Schmidlin, *op. cit.*, Vol. II, pp. 187, 188.
[191] Wallace, *op. cit.*, pp. 251–254.

Empire a state which had been an obstacle to unity. On the other hand, in its opposition to Bismarck's measures the Centre Party was consolidated and drew into its ranks non-German elements, among them Poles and Alsatians, mostly Catholic, who were opposed to Bismarck's programme of centralization: the effort to defeat Bismarck drew German Roman Catholics together and strengthened their loyalty to the Pope and their church. The *Kulturkampf* had something of the same effect elsewhere in Europe, notably in France and Belgium. Confronted in Germany by persecution, many Roman Catholics who had been hesitant about accepting whole-heartedly the decrees which issued from the Vatican Council rallied to the support of the Pope.[192]

Pius IX: The Closing Years

His last years brought Pius IX many burdens. At the end of the Vatican Council he was in his seventy-ninth year. His triumph in that gathering had been overshadowed by the loss of his temporal domains. The Old Catholic schism and the *Kulturkampf* quickly followed and gave him no respite from burdens which would have crushed many younger men. In Austria in the early 1870's the Government adopted measures which, while less drastic than those of Bismarck, favoured the Old Catholics, were hostile to the Jesuits, modified the exclusively Catholic character of the universities, and restricted the control by Rome of the Church.[193] The Swiss Federal Government took the part of the liberals against the Vatican decrees. Charles [Hyacinthe] Loyson was given a parish in Geneva. A revision of the Swiss constitution in 1874 augmented the measures against the Jesuits, forbade the formation of new monasteries and religious orders, and confirmed the prohibition of new bishoprics without the consent of the central government.[194] In Spain and Portugal anti-clericalism was strong. In the former country a revolution which lasted from 1868 to 1876 brought in a constitutional monarchy, then, from 1873 to 1875, a republic, in 1875 the restoration of a liberal Bourbon monarchy, and measures hostile to the Roman Catholic Church.[195] In Italy itself Pius had the pain of seeing many monasteries dissolved, their properties confiscated, several churches in Rome suppressed, seminaries for the training of priests placed under the oversight of the state, civil marriage made obligatory, and other measures taken by the Government against which he was powerless.[196]

Yet Pius lived long enough to discern the foreshadowing of victory in the *Kulturkampf*. Negotiations were under way which led to the reëstablishment

192 *Ibid.*, pp. 255–260.
193 Aubert, *op. cit.*, pp. 393, 394.
194 *Ibid.*, p. 396.
195 *Ibid.*, pp. 400–402.
196 Schmidlin, *op. cit.*, Vol. II, p. 119.

of the hierarchy in Scotland.[197] The fact that he had reigned longer than any other Pope brought him great reverence from the faithful. The "year of jubilee" in 1875 drew large crowds to Rome. In 1877 the celebration of the half-century of his being raised to the episcopate was the occasion of the outpouring of devotion from all the Roman Catholic world. While he was never reconciled to the loss of the Papal States nor outwardly resumed friendly relations with the head of the realm which had annexed them, in his later months Pius IX was in secret correspondence with Victor Emmanuel. When, a few days before his own death, the king was *in extremis,* Pius sent a priest to lift the censures of the Church, enabled the monarch to receive the last sacraments, and permitted Christian rites at the funeral.[198] But Pius was clearly aging. His death, February 7, 1878, marked the end of an epoch.[199]

LEO XIII (1878–1903): ELECTION, EARLY HISTORY, AND CHARACTER

The election of the successor to Pius IX was quickly accomplished. On the third ballot the choice fell on Gioacchino Vincenzo Raffaele Luigi Pecci (1810–1903). Pecci was born in the mountain town of Carpineto in Central Italy and on both sides of his house was of aristocratic descent. His mother, very devout, was a member of the Third Order of St. Francis. An older brother became a Jesuit. He himself was educated by the Jesuits and as a student had a notable scholarly record. He earned a doctorate in theology and, at first headed for diplomacy, had advanced work in canon and civil law. He laid the foundations for remarkable skill in the Latin language and a knowledge of scholastic philosophy and theology.[200] In 1837, after some hesitation on his part, he was ordained to the priesthood but, unlike his brother, did not join an order. He entered the service of Gregory XVI and among other posts was successively Papal delegate to Benevento and Perugia. In both assignments he displayed marked administrative gifts, achieved law enforcement against banditry, and promoted economic and other reforms. In his early thirties he was appointed Nuncio to Belgium and sought to mediate between sharply contending forces in that country. The fact that he did not succeed and was recalled did not cost him the confidence of Pius IX. In 1846 at the request of the populace Pecci was appointed Bishop of Perugia. There he improved the preparation and morals of the clergy, embellished the churches and built new ones, encouraged preaching, promoted frequent retreats and missions, furthered the faith of the

---

[197] Aubert, *op. cit.*, p. 397.

[198] Hales, *Pio Nino,* p. 328.

[199] Aubert, *op. cit.*, pp. 497–499.

[200] Boyer d'Agen, *La Jeunesse de Léon XIII d'après sa Correspondence Inédite* (Tours, Alfred Mame et Fils, 1896, pp. 703), *passim;* Hayward, *Léon XIII,* pp. 45 ff. On the election see Friedrich Engel De Janosi, *Austria and the Conclave of 1878,* in *The Catholic Historical Review,* Vol. XXXIX, pp. 142–166.

laity through better instruction in the catechism and through confraternities and brotherhoods, and founded a missionary institute. He stood against the elimination of the Papal States, civil marriage, the suppression of religious orders, the secularization of the possessions of the Church, and the enforced military service of the clergy. Yet in pastoral letters he declared that the Christian religion was basically compatible with modern advances and that far from being an enemy of civilization and progress the Church promoted all aspects of human knowledge and was the mother of all true culture. In 1853 Pecci was created Cardinal and in 1877 was called to Rome to the important post of Camerlengo.[201]

Pecci was slightly less than sixty-seven years of age when, with this record behind him, he became Pope Leo XIII. He held that post for a few weeks more than twenty-five years and died at the advanced age of ninety-three. Abstemious almost to asceticism in his private life, he celebrated public functions with dignity and gave large sums to charity. Less free in granting individual and group audiences than his predecessor, and in contrast with the latter's wit and humour grave and serious in manner and at times imperious, more than Pius IX he sought to bring together the divergent elements in the Church and, so far as he could do so without compromising what he deemed the essential character of the Church and the Christian faith, to adjust the methods of the Roman Catholic Church to meet the changing times. He did not disavow any of the positions taken by Pius IX in the Syllabus of Errors. Indeed, from the beginning to the end of his reign he stood as emphatically as had Pius for the authority of the Church, sought the restoration of the Papal States, and forbade the faithful to take office or vote under the Kingdom of Italy which had appropriated those states. On one or another occasion he attacked Socialism and Freemasonry, warned against what in the next pontificate was condemned as "Modernism," and as clearly resisted some of the trends of the revolution as had Gregory XVI and Pius IX. But he displayed great interest in science and literature, promoted the study of astronomy by equipping the Vatican observatory with modern instruments and a large staff, endorsed the founding of pontifical universities, including ones in Beirut, Toulouse, Lyons, Ottawa, and Washington, sought friendly relations with Protestant rulers and non-Christian monarchs, and in other ways endeavoured to meet constructively the situations and problems brought by the revolutionary age. A skilful diplomat and a statesman of the first rank, he markedly enhanced the prestige of the Papacy. To be sure, Leo XIII had the advantage of reigning in a time of peace and prosperity. No major European war troubled the quarter of a century in which

[201] Schmidlin, *Papstgeschichte der neuesten Zeit*, Vol. II, pp. 334–337; Soderini, *Il Pontificato di Leone XIII*, Vol. I, pp. 81 ff.; Hayward, *op. cit.*, pp. 55–67.

he sat on the throne of Peter. No political revolution comparable to those of the preceding nine decades disturbed any European state and in Western Christendom as a whole wealth was mounting and optimism and confidence in progress were general. Yet in that time of relative calm the currents of the revolution, if not so obviously destructive, were running strong, and it was a tribute to his skill and his character that Leo XIII won the respect not only of his own church but of much of the world outside that church.

In his diplomacy Leo XIII had an able assistant in Mariano del Tindaro Rampolla (1843–1913). Born in Sicily of aristocratic lineage, Rampolla had had experience in Spain as Papal Nuncio. In 1887 Leo created him Cardinal and appointed him Secretary of State. Yet it was Leo who was responsible for the main outlines and many of the details of the relations with governments.[202]

Though able as administrator and diplomat, Leo XIII is not to be classed with the worldly Popes of earlier centuries. He did much to reinforce the rising tide of the inner life of the Roman Catholic Church. He encouraged the orders and congregations which were reviving and multiplying. He preached the benefits of the rosary and set the example by his own practice, favoured devotion to the Sacred Heart, instituted the feast of the Holy Family, and incited Roman Catholics to the study of the Scriptures. During his reign 248 episcopal and archiepiscopal sees and 48 vicariates or prefectures apostolic were created.

Leo XIII: Early Acts

At the outset of his reign Leo XIII displayed his firm adherence to the historic positions of the Roman Catholic Church. In his opening encyclical he bewailed the evils which beset mankind and the ignoring or denial of the chief truths on which society was based. He declared that the main underlying cause of the distresses of society were the disregard of the authority of the Church and the Pope, the war against God and the Church, the restrictions on the functions of bishops and priests in their care of souls, the annexation of the Papal States, the suppression of the religious orders, and the confiscation of church property. He called attention to the historic services of the Church in abolishing slavery and in promoting education, learning, and the arts, and held it to be the duty of the Papacy to save, unite, and enlighten society, especially in Italy. He outlined a programme for the episcopate to offset the errors of the time by improving the instruction in the schools, preserving the sanctity of marriage, and improving morals.[203]

[202] *Enciclopedia Cattolica*, Vol. X, pp. 517, 518; Crispolto Crispoti e Guido Aureli, *La Politica di Leone XIII da Luigi Galimberti a Mariano Rampolla su Documenti Inediti* (Rome, Bontempelli e Invernizzi, 1912, pp. 584), *passim.*
[203] Schmidlin, *op. cit.*, Vol. II, pp. 349, 350.

LEO XIII: VICTORY IN THE *Kulturkampf*

Although his initial encyclical seemed to be a reiteration of the policies of Pius IX, Leo XIII early took steps to ease some of the tensions which he inherited. He was prompt to seek an end of the *Kulturkampf*. As we have suggested, he found Bismarck by no means unwilling to explore a way out of an embarrassing situation if that could be accomplished without too grave a loss of face.[204]

In 1878 negotiations were begun which eventually brought victory in the *Kulturkampf*. Leo was not the sole or even the chief negotiator. He took an active part, but the chief pressures were from the German Roman Catholics operating through the Centre Party. In 1880 some relaxation was made in the administration of the laws to which the Roman Catholics objected. In 1882 and 1883 other modifications were enacted. By 1884 diplomatic relations with the Vatican were reëstablished. In 1885 the consent of the Kaiser to the choice of the Pope as mediator in a dispute between Spain and Germany over the Caroline Islands not only raised the prestige of Leo but also proved gratifying as a step towards full reconciliation. In 1887 most of the remaining adverse legislation was removed and Bismarck declared the *Kulturkampf* ended. Of the acts which had raised the storm there remained those against the Jesuits and for the oversight of schools by the state, and it was not until later that the measures which had banished many of the clergy were allowed completely to lapse. But for several years exiled bishops had been returning and appointments had been made to some of the vacant sees.[205]

The Roman Catholic Church had won. The Iron Chancellor, the most powerful statesman on the Continent of Europe in the second half of the nineteenth century, had been forced to retreat. Here was striking evidence that the Roman Catholic Church was a factor, both political and religious, which could not be disregarded and that since the days of the French Revolution and Napoleon I it had achieved an amazing recovery.

LEO XIII: RELATIONS WITH THE KINGDOM OF ITALY

We have already hinted that towards the Kingdom of Italy Leo continued in the main the policies of Pius IX. He seems to have believed that Antonelli had been too intransigent and he encouraged Catholics to see that their names were included on the registers for both the municipal and parliamentary elections, but he still held that for at least the time being it was unwise for them either to vote or to hold office in the national government. On his election he

---

[204] Ruhenstroth-Bauer, *Bismarck und Falk im Kulturkampf*, pp. 88, 89.

[205] Schmidlin, *op. cit.*, Vol. II, pp. 455 ff. French translations of the pertinent documents are in Béhaine, *Léon XIII et le Prince Bismarck*, pp. 225 ff. The volume also includes valuable first-hand observations of the author. See also Hayward, *Léon XIII*, pp. 159 ff.

did not give the blessing customary from a new Pope publicly, for this would have implied acquiescence in the annexation of the Papal States, but from an interior *loggia*.

In their attitude towards the Roman Catholic Church Italians were divided. Many were loyal. Many regarded the Church as an enemy. The Government confiscated numerous ecclesiastical properties and, contrary to the Law of Guarantees, demanded that no bishop take office without its permission. In numbers of instances it delayed that permission and in at least one notable case offered so much opposition that the bishop resigned.

Leo acted vigorously. He took measures to ensure the careful screening of names for vacant dioceses so that his appointments would be men of worthy character. He denounced attacks by the press, Protestant propaganda, and the ostracism of the catechism from the municipal schools. He encouraged the multiplication of Catholic schools in Rome and personally subsidized some of them. He spoke out against the Government's insistence on the *exequatur*.[206] He set himself against a bill which would have given precedence to civil over religious marriage and the bill failed of passage.[207] He sought to induce other governments to bring pressure on the Italian Government to ensure his safety and freedom of action.[208]

The conflict between loyal Catholics and the anti-clericals continued. Although Leo encouraged Catholics to vote in local elections, on the national scale, as we have said, he held to the principle of "neither electors nor elected."[209] With the encouragement of the Pope, Catholics held congresses and organized themselves into study circles, welfare clubs, and workers' associations and formed rural banks, day and evening schools, and other institutions.[210] On the other hand, partly in response to these activities, anti-clerical clubs were formed. The Government became even more vigorous in its dissolution of religious orders. Against the protests of Leo tithes were abolished. With the consent of the Government, in 1886 numbers of congresses were held in which the Church and the Pope were denounced.[211] The Freemasons were strongly anti-clerical and in 1884 and 1892 Leo emphatically condemned them.[212]

Leo sought to raise the quality of Catholic life by insisting that to meet the revolutionary world the clergy be prepared not only in dogma but also in philosophy, physics, and history and urged the faithful to be generous in the support of seminaries.[213]

[206] Soderini, *Leo XIII, Italy and France*, pp. 4–17.
[207] *Ibid.*, pp. 20, 21.
[208] *Ibid.*, pp. 30, 31.
[209] *Ibid.*, pp. 35, 87.
[210] *Ibid.*, pp. 41, 114.
[211] *Ibid.*, pp. 42, 57, 73.
[212] *Ibid.*, p. 102.
[213] *Ibid.*, p. 40.

What was known as the Roman question was a chronic source of tension. Leo XIII continued to insist that the independence of the Pope could be assured only if he had territory in which he was the ruler. He held that the territory did not need to be as extensive as the former Papal States but that it must be adequate.[214] To him this was made doubly apparent when on at least one occasion an Italian court claimed jurisdiction in a dispute which involved only the members of the Papal household and issues solely in that household. To some this was tantamount to summoning the Pope himself to appear before the court.[215] Disorders in Rome, among them one directed against the body of Pius IX when it was being carried to a new resting-place and one against French pilgrims who were expressing their enthusiasm for Leo XIII, seemed to prove that the Italian Government was either unwilling or unable to afford protection to the Pope.[216]

The Roman question became international. While deploring any thought of armed intervention by other governments, the Pope went so far as to ask Spain and Austria what their attitudes would be in case he were forced to leave Rome.[217] The Italian Government strongly opposed an invitation to the Pope to send representatives to the Hague Peace Conference in 1899, for that would imply recognition of his status as an independent sovereign. The Italian delegates at the gathering also stood against his inclusion in the membership of the Permanent International Court of Arbitration.[218]

While the Italian Government did not take quite as drastic measures against the Roman Catholic Church as did the Prussian Government at the height of the *Kulturkampf*, it did not retreat to the same degree as did Bismarck.[219]

Leo XIII: Relations with the Government of France

In France Leo XIII had slightly if any better success than in Italy. During his pontificate, as we are to see more at length in a later chapter, France was governed by the Third Republic. At the outset it was not clear whether the Monarchy, the Bonapartist Empire, or the Republic would prevail. As time passed the Republic was more firmly seated. This meant, in the main, that the revolutionary forces which had created the First and Second Republics were in control. On the whole they were anti-clerical and in general the strongly Roman Catholic elements rallied to the royalist cause. Roman Catholics were badly divided and did not form a distinct bloc as did the Centre Party in Germany. Liberal Catholics were inclined to side with the Republic. The radical

---

[214] *Ibid.*, pp. 60 ff.
[215] *Ibid.*, pp. 43–45.
[216] *Ibid.*, pp. 24–26; Schmidlin, *Papstgeschichte der neuesten Zeit*, Vol. II, pp. 413, 420.
[217] Soderini, *op. cit.*, pp. 95, 96.
[218] *Ibid.*, p. 113.
[219] Schmidlin, *op. cit.*, Vol. II, p. 409.

democrats tended to identify the Roman Catholic Church with the Monarchy and were, accordingly, even more vehemently anti-clerical than they would otherwise have been. Leo's sole concern was to protect and strengthen the Church and the Christian faith.

Leo's task as upholder of the Church was never easy. In May, 1877, shortly before the outset of his reign, Gambetta, outstanding leader of the republican forces, had campaigned on the slogan: *Le cléricalisme, voilà l'ennemi.* While after a brief term as prime minister, in 1882 Gambetta was removed by death, the attitude which he voiced persisted. In 1880 what were known as the Ferry Laws curtailed Church schools.[220] That same year decrees ordered all Jesuit houses and educational establishments closed and required all unauthorized religious congregations to apply for authorization. Against them the episcopate, the clergy, and the Pope protested.[221] A compromise was quietly reached with the French premier, but when it became public, a storm arose which shut some of the houses.[222] Financial measures adverse to the Church (1884) brought protests from the Holy See.[223] In an encyclical, *Nobilissima Gallorum gens,* in February, 1884, Leo voiced his regret that "the eldest daughter of the Church" had departed from its traditions, and exhorted the bishops to exercise vigilance in the education of the young and the maintenance of the principles of the Christian life, the priests to obey their superiors, and the faithful to pray that the country might be spared the curse of irreligion.[224] In 1885 an encyclical, *Immortale Dei,* attempted to define the degree to which the Church could accept the liberties on which modern society rested. It held that "the greater or less participation of the people in the government has nothing blameable in itself."[225] In a governmental crisis of 1888–1889, when some French Roman Catholics gave vigorous support to Boulanger, who aspired to a dictatorship, the Pope instructed the Nuncio not to take sides but to preserve a passive attitude.[226] Successive administrations sometimes seemed to respond to pressure from Rome but pled counter-pressures on them from radical anti-clericals. In the main, their policies made for the progressive de-Christianization of France.[227] The Government moved fairly steadily in the direction of the separation of Church and state. Although Leo tolerated this in countries such as the United States, Great Britain, and Scandinavia, where the governments were in the hands of Protestants, he was profoundly opposed to it in traditionally Roman

[220] Soderini, *op. cit.,* p. 137; Schmidlin, *op. cit.,* Vol. II, p. 436.
[221] Soderini, *op. cit.,* pp. 152–160; Schmidlin, *op. cit.,* Vol. II. p. 437.
[222] Soderini, *op. cit.,* p. 163.
[223] *Ibid.,* pp. 181, 182.
[224] *Ibid.,* p. 183.
[225] Phillips, *The Church in France, 1848–1907,* pp. 215, 216. See a translation of the text in Leo XIII and Husslein, *Social Wellsprings,* pp. 65–90.
[226] Soderini, *op. cit.,* pp. 196–198.
[227] *Ibid.,* pp. 175, 195, 199, 203.

Catholic lands for he believed it tantamount to an official declaration of atheism.[228]

As it became clear that the Republic was to continue and that both the royalist and the Bonapartist groups were losing, Leo was increasingly of the conviction that in France the course for Roman Catholics was participation in government. Thus they could protect the Church. Yet he believed that he ought not to intervene directly and instruct the faithful to support the Republic: that would be denounced by anti-clericals as an attempt at dictation in French domestic politics. Therefore he wished the initiative to come from French Catholics. On January 10, 1890, in the encyclical Sapientiae Christianae, Leo repeated what he had already said, that the Church was not opposed to any form of government so long as religion and moral discipline were untouched and declared again that the Church would not side with any party. Numbers of French Catholics welcomed the pronouncement. After long talks with the Pope, Cardinal Lavigerie, Archbishop of Carthage, in the recently French-acquired North Africa, came out emphatically for Roman Catholic support of the Republic. This aroused a storm of criticism from both the extreme Right and Left. But the French bishops, following the lead of the French Cardinals, while protesting the measures against the Church, recommended the support of the Republic. On February 16, 1892, in an encyclical, Inter innumeras sollicitudines, published in French, Leo declared it obligatory to accept the Republic and urged Catholics by measures on the electoral and political plane to obtain the correction of the legislation which had been hostile to religion.[229] Since this utterance, like the act of Lavigerie, angered both the monarchists and the ultra-radicals, in May, 1892, Leo, in a public letter to the French Cardinals, reiterated in other words what he had set forth in the encyclical. Still not all Catholics complied. In June, 1892, Leo again spoke and asked not only Catholics but also non-Catholics to coöperate in promoting the religious life of France and in stemming the tide towards the religious and moral ruin of the country.[230]

The Papal policy rallied many Roman Catholics to the Republic, but it did not halt the anti-clerical trend or allay the controversies between the ardent advocates and the enemies of the faith. In the 1890's the celebrated Dreyfus case heightened the bitterness. The Pope insisted that race should not enter into the issue (Dreyfus was a Jew), and that the rights of the accused should be respected. But the majority of Roman Catholics lined up against Dreyfus, and the eventual clear proof that his condemnation had been a miscarriage of jus-

[228] Ibid., p. 201.

[229] Ibid., pp. 203–222; Phillips, op. cit., pp. 230, 232, 233. See a translation of the text in Leo XIII and Husslein, op. cit., pp. 142–163. For the text of Lavigerie, see Jarry, l'Église contemporaine, Vol. II, pp. 210, 211.

[230] Soderini, op. cit., pp. 226–230.

tice further discredited the Catholic cause.[231] Action was taken against religious congregations which had not been formally authorized by the Government. Attempts of Leo to allay the storm by advising some of the accused were taken as proof of the truth of what opponents had said, that the congregations were under the control of an alien. In 1901 the Associations Act was passed which augmented the difficulty of obtaining authorization. Its enforcement led to the expulsion of hundreds of religious from the country and the closing of about nine thousand schools which they had been conducting. Monks and nuns were scattered.[232] Even in his last months the aged Leo was troubled by a dispute with the French Government over the nomination of bishops.[233]

When Leo XIII breathed his last, it looked as though his efforts on behalf of the Roman Catholic Church in France had failed: yet, as we shall see in a later chapter, although a minority and divided, practising French Roman Catholics were the source of many vital movements, missionary, theological, social, and devotional. In France the Roman Catholic Church, sore bested, was far from dead. Although it had not won as it had in Germany in the *Kulturkampf* and Leo had not accomplished what he had hoped, at least he had from time to time moderated the storm against the Church, for a while had narrowed the gulf between the Republic and Roman Catholics, and had contributed to lessening the divisions among the faithful.

LEO XIII: RELATIONS WITH THE GOVERNMENTS OF AUSTRIA-HUNGARY, BELGIUM, SPAIN, PORTUGAL, AND LATIN AMERICA

From the relations of Leo XIII with the governments of Italy and France we pass naturally to those with the governments of other traditionally Roman Catholic countries.

With the Hapsburg Dual Monarchy, Austria-Hungary, relations were much less strained than with Germany, Italy, or France. To be sure, although Josephism was all but dead, the influence of Jews and Freemasons in the government was said to be strong and the Catholic nobility and the clergy were reported to be far from zealous in the faith. At times pressure was brought on Vienna by the Vatican to intervene in behalf of the Papal sovereignty, but the inclusion of Italy (1882) in the German-Austrian alliance made Austria reluctant to take steps which would provoke her new ally.[234] In the complex ethnic tensions which troubled the Hapsburg empire, Leo approved the Slavic rite, thus in part taking the side of the Slavs against the Germans, but he advised the Poles

---

[231] Phillips, *op. cit.*, pp. 250–258; Soderini, *op. cit.*, p. 251.
[232] Soderini, *op. cit.*, pp. 250 ff.; Schmidlin, *op. cit.*, Vol. II, pp. 430–435; Phillips, *op. cit.*, pp. 263–271.
[233] Phillips, *op. cit.*, p. 271.
[234] Schmidlin, *op. cit.*, Vol. II, pp. 474–476.

and the Hungarians to obey the Hapsburgs and placed the Roman Catholic Church in the internationally debatable Bosnia-Herzegovina under the protection of Austria.[235] Leo sought to arouse the episcopate and the nobility to correct what seemed to him the religious indifference and godlessness of the Austrian schools and to break the monopoly of the press by elements unfriendly to the Church. He endeavoured to rouse Austrian Catholicism to new life and to stimulate reform in the monasteries.[236] In Hungary he opposed mixed marriages and making marriage a purely civil affair.[237]

In Belgium as in other predominantly Roman Catholic lands Leo XIII was faced with strife between the anti-clericals and the elements which clung strongly to the Church. Liberal governments which sought to curtail the power of the Church in education and to place the instruction in state schools under lay control which would be religiously neutral alternated with governments which supported the Church. The conflict was severe. Three times anti-clerical forces cut off diplomatic relations with the Vatican. Leo protested against both the withdrawal of the Belgian representative and the legislation which made for religiously neutral schools. He also praised the Belgian episcopate and the faithful for their stand against these measures. With elections which brought a Catholic majority into power in Parliament, diplomatic relations were resumed and the school laws were altered in favour of the Church. By the close of his reign Leo was privileged to see the Roman Catholic Church in Belgium pulsing with a life which found expression in schools, newspapers, extensive benevolence, flourishing religious orders and congregations, and foreign missions.[238]

During the pontificate of Leo XIII Spain was relatively peaceful. The turmoil of the previous decades had been followed by the restoration of the Bourbons (1875). No such severe struggle in which religious issues were involved distracted the country as in the preceding decades. Nor during these years did Spain experience such bitter controversies between anti-clericals and the supporters of the Church as we have seen in Germany, Italy, and France. Alphonso XII, who came to the throne in 1875, maintained friendly relations with the Holy See. In the early 1880's a proposal was encouraged by strongly proclerical Carlist elements to undertake a mass pilgrimage to Rome to protest the loss of the Papal States and the "imprisonment" of the Pope. But it contributed to dissensions in Spain, and by an encyclical (December 8, 1882) Leo cautioned Spanish Catholics not to identify the interests of the Church with a particular

[235] *Ibid.*, p. 476.
[236] *Ibid.*, pp. 477, 478.
[237] *Ibid.*, pp. 479–481.
[238] *Ibid.*, pp. 435–441.

political party. When the early death of Alphonso (1885) threatened a renewal of civil strife, Leo gave his support to the royal widow, Maria Christina, who served as regent for Alphonso XIII: the Papal Nuncio, Rampolla, soon to become Leo's Secretary of State, baptized the posthumous infant. Leo thus helped to allay the danger of an internal convulsion. Later more than once he admonished Spanish Catholics to bury their internal differences and party strife and to give themselves unitedly to promoting the interests of the Church and the nation. Towards the end of Leo's life the religious issue became acute, with the threat of measures akin to those which were being taken in France against the congregations and orders. Both Rampolla and Leo encouraged the religious communities to abide by the law.[239]

Like Spain, during Leo's pontificate Portugal was comparatively peaceful. But with the misrule of King Charles I, who had the throne from 1880 to his assassination in 1908, unrest mounted. Early in his reign Leo succeeded in negotiating a settlement of the controversial question of the Portuguese right of patronage in India: Portugal surrendered its claim to control the appointment of most of the bishops in India outside its possessions and the Papacy confirmed Portugal's power to name the bishops in its territories and in four other sees.[240] As in Spain, in Leo's later years anti-clericalism led to attempts to restrict religious orders.[241]

As we are to see in a later volume, in Latin America the course of the Roman Catholic Church was chequered. It varied from country to country and in each country from decade to decade. In every country, as in European lands where the Roman Catholic faith was the traditional religion of the majority, the contest between anti-clericals and the supporters of the Church was chronic. In Spanish America the wars of independence had been accompanied by the conflicting attempts of Spain and the new governments to control the Church. From them the latter emerged badly weakened. With the gradual restoration of order ecclesiastical conditions improved, but the indigenous clergy were insufficient to fill the need for pastoral care and clergy still came from Europe. In 1899 a South American council was held to deal comprehensively with the problems of the Church on that continent. Because jealousies between the various countries would have proved a handicap had the gathering met in any Latin American land, the council convened in Rome, thus emphasizing the role of the Holy See. During his reign Leo had the pleasure of authorizing the creation of a number of episcopal sees in several of the countries.[242]

[239] *Ibid.*, pp. 441–446.
[240] Latourette, *A History of the Expansion of Christianity*, Vol. VI, pp. 75, 76, and accompanying footnote references to authorities.
[241] Schmidlin, *op. cit.*, Vol. II, pp. 445–448.
[242] *Ibid.*, pp. 448–454.

LEO XIII: RELATIONS WITH GOVERNMENTS AND PEOPLES OUTSIDE
TRADITIONALLY ROMAN CATHOLIC LANDS

In most lands outside the traditionally Roman Catholic portions of the globe Leo XIII made his office more and more felt and contributed to the growth of his church.

He sought to encourage the Roman Catholic Church in England. Conversions from the Church of England and immigration from Ireland were giving it marked impetus. In an encyclical of April 15, 1895, Leo praised the English for many of their qualities and for their eagerness for reunion with the See of Peter. However, he made the achievement of that goal more difficult by a decision published in September, 1896, after careful study by a commission which he had appointed, that Anglican orders were not valid. This was a damper on a movement to heal the breach between Rome and the Church of England, a movement led by Lord Halifax, president of the English Church Union.[243]

Relations between Leo XIII and England were complicated by conditions in Ireland and the attitude of Cardinal Manning, head of the English hierarchy. In 1886, after the defeat of Gladstone in his effort to give home rule to that distraught land, Irish bishops and priests supported the Home Rule League in its "Plan of Campaign" with its use of intimidation and boycotting. Leo sent (1887) a Papal delegate to Ireland to enquire into the situation. A decree of the Inquisition followed (1888) which condemned the boycott. This, Manning felt, would inflame the Irish as smacking of Papal intervention in their domestic affairs. Manning also opposed the suggestion of establishing diplomatic relations between the Court of St. James and the Holy See—partly on the ground that it would intensify anti-Catholic feeling in England and partly because it would be interpreted by the Irish as a channel through which the English Government would seek to influence the Vatican in Irish affairs and obtain the appointment as bishops of men who would coöperate with it. Continuing diplomatic relations were not opened, but Manning was unhappy because Leo sent a special envoy to congratulate Queen Victoria on her jubilee (1887).[244]

We have noted that one of the first acts of Leo as Pope was to complete what had been initiated by Pius IX and restore the hierarchy in Scotland.[245]

In Switzerland Leo XIII inherited a difficult situation. Because of an anti-clerical movement at least two bishops were in exile. Leo exerted himself to bring peace and had the satisfaction of seeing advances in Catholic schools, publications, and charitable activities.[246]

---

[243] *Ibid.*, pp. 489, 490; *The Catholic Encyclopedia*, Vol. I, pp. 491–498.

[244] Purcell, *Life of Cardinal Manning*, Vol. II, pp. 622–632, 732–743; Schmidlin, *op. cit.*, Vol. II, pp. 488, 492–494.

[245] Schmidlin, *op. cit.*, Vol. II, p. 491.

[246] *Ibid.*, pp. 482–485.

The Netherlands caused Leo XIII much less anxiety than did some other countries. Roman Catholics, while a minority, were a growing minority. Freedom was enjoyed, as by other religious bodies, to conduct schools. A priest organized a Roman Catholic political party which was able to gain some concessions.[247]

Leo XIII sought to better the lot of Roman Catholics in the Russian Empire. One of his earliest official acts was a friendly letter to Tsar Alexander II, assuring him of the loyalty of his Roman Catholic subjects. Most of these subjects, it will be recalled, were in the portion of Poland under Russian rule, and in the preceding pontificate differences over the Russian policy towards the Roman Catholics, especially the Uniates, had led to a break in diplomatic relations between Moscow and the Holy See. Leo attempted to obtain more freedom for his church. Early in his reign his encyclical (December 28, 1878) against Socialism and Nihilism had a favourable reception in Moscow and with official permission was published in Warsaw. When, in 1881, Alexander II perished through a Nihilist bomb, Leo was prompt to express his sympathy. The new tsar, Alexander III, sent a friendly reply and Leo followed it with wishes for a prosperous reign and for closer coöperation. Lessening of restraints on the Roman Catholic Church ensued which were in the nature of a compromise. However, complaints continued to reach Rome of measures which had as their purpose the continued re-incorporation of the Uniates into the Orthodox fold. Leo won more of the goodwill of the tsar by opposing Italian participation in the renewal of the Triple Alliance of Germany, Austria-Hungary, and Italy (1887), a menace to Russia, and by assisting in the formation of the Franco-Russian Alliance. In 1894 Russia instituted an embassy to the Vatican. With the accession of Nicholas II relations were still more improved.[248]

During the pontificate of Leo XIII the legal obstacles to the spread of the Roman Catholic faith in overwhelmingly Lutheran Scandinavia were lowered. This was because of the liberalism that made for a religious indifferentism and toleration which in some other contexts Leo and his predecessors bewailed. When Pecci was elected Pope, only in Sweden had Roman Catholics been organized under a vicariate apostolic. In Denmark and Norway they were under prefects apostolic. During Leo's reign sufficient progress was made in the latter two countries to erect vicariates apostolic. In all three countries in 1903 Catholics were still small minorities, but some converts had been won and advances had been achieved in schools and congregations of religious.[249]

In the Balkans and the Turkish Empire Leo XIII reinforced the efforts of his predecessors to win religious freedom for Roman Catholics and to bring

[247] *Ibid.*, pp. 485–487.
[248] *Ibid.*, pp. 508–514.
[249] *Ibid.*, pp. 506–508.

members of the dissident Eastern Churches into communion with Rome. Rather than insisting on the adoption of the Latin rite, he especially encouraged the growth of Uniate bodies. He stressed the creation of an indigenous clergy: he strengthened existing seminaries in Rome for the education of Uniate priests and furthered the founding of others—in 1878 for the Melchites, in 1880 for the Copts, in 1882 for the Syrochaldeans, in 1883 for the Armenians, in 1886 for the Bulgars, in 1895 for the Greeks, and in 1896 for the Ruthenians.[250]

Through immigration the Roman Catholic Church in the United States continued the phenomenal growth of which we are to say more in a later volume. In it Leo XIII took a deep interest and assisted in many ways.[251]

Leo XIII also actively concerned himself with Canada. In the 1890's the Canadian bishops raised their voices against a law in Manitoba which provided for public schools that were religiously neutral. Leo sent his private chamberlain, Merry del Val, then early in his notable career in the Vatican, to investigate. He followed Merry del Val's report with a letter supporting the bishops. Modifications in the law restored the peace. Leo also increased the metropolitan and suffragan sees in the country, raised an Archbishop of Quebec to the Cardinalate, and created an Apostolic Delegation to represent him in Ottawa, the capital.[252]

In Australia the Roman Catholic Church was strong, chiefly through Irish immigration. Leo encouraged it by adding new dioceses and by giving official approval to the findings of provincial councils. He also erected a province for the smaller Roman Catholic community in New Zealand.[253]

Leo XIII supported the missions on the geographic frontiers of the Roman Catholic Church in Africa, South and East Asia, and the islands of the Pacific: he has been sometimes called the missionary Pope. His reign coincided with a rapid extension of Occidental penetration and control of the non-Occidental portions of the globe. It saw the partition of Africa south of the Sahara, the threatened partition of China, a phenomenal growth in European commerce, and striking developments in the disintegration of non-Occidental cultures under the impact of the Occident. A statesman with a world outlook, Leo was keenly aware of the opportunity which these movements gave for the planting and nourishing of Christian communities outside the historic Christendom. Through encyclicals he sought to quicken the interest of Catholics in the world mission and to move them to its support through prayer, giving, and personnel. He encouraged organizations which were raising funds for missions. He sought to establish friendly contacts with non-Christian rulers in Asia and Africa.[254]

[250] Ibid., pp. 514–522.
[251] Ibid., pp. 494–499.
[252] Ibid., pp. 499, 500.
[253] Ibid., p. 500.
[254] Ibid., pp. 500–506.

In India he inaugurated (1886) an Apostolic Delegation to represent him and give cohesion to his church in that land. After the settlement of the question of the Portuguese right of patronage, he quickly (September, 1886) created a hierarchy for India. To train an indigenous clergy, in 1890 he saw to the founding in Kandy, Ceylon, of a seminary to train secular priests for that island and India. He wished it to have standards as high as those of any seminary in Europe.[255] To meet the new situation brought by the annexation of the Philippines by the United States, Leo inaugurated an Apostolic Delegation for the islands and took other measures to help the Roman Catholic Church adjust to the new order.[256] The sensitivity of France over any possible infringement on the protectorate which she claimed over Catholic missions in China was an obstacle to as much direct action by Rome as Leo took in India. But he concerned himself with the missions in China and on at least one occasion addressed a letter to the emperor. In 1891 he created a hierarchy for Japan.[257]

LEO XIII: PRONOUNCEMENTS ON POLITICAL PRINCIPLES

In his dealings with governments Leo XIII displayed a firmness which was unafraid to state what he believed to be the Christian position, even when it was frankly counter to the trends of current movements. In general he did not depart from the affirmations of Gregory XVI and Pius IX. At the same time, more than his immediate predecessors, wherever he felt that he could consistently do so, he sought common ground with the forces of the new age and attempted to conciliate rather than antagonize. His was a clear and logical mind. With his marked facility in the Latin language, again and again he set forth his convictions in cogent and unmistakable terms. A look at some of his encyclicals may shed light on the policies and acts which we have summarized in the preceding pages.

Early in his reign, in *Quod apostolici muneris* (December 28, 1878) Leo came out as vigorously as had Pius IX against Socialism.[258] On February 10, 1880, in *Arcanum*, he was emphatic that the state could not dissolve Christian marriage.[259] The next year (June 29, 1881) in *Diuturnum illud* he averred that any form of government was permissible if it promoted justice and that the people might choose the form under which they would live: but he insisted that all right to rule is from God, and that from the Christian standpoint civil power is not from the consent of men.[260] A little over four years later (November 1,

---

[255] Latourette, *op. cit.*, Vol. VI, pp. 76, 94, 99; Schmidlin, *op. cit.*, Vol. II, pp. 523, 524.
[256] Schmidlin, *op. cit.*, Vol. II, p. 526.
[257] *Ibid.*, pp. 526–529.
[258] Leo XIII and Husslein, *Social Wellsprings*, pp. 14–23; Hughes, *The Pope's New Order*, pp. 36–40.
[259] Leo XIII and Husslein, *op. cit.*, pp. 25–46.
[260] *Ibid.*, pp. 49–62; Hughes, *op. cit.*, pp. 54–59.

1885) in *Immortale Dei* he defined what he conceived to be the Christian constitution of the state. He said that both Church and state have their authority from God, that each has its divinely appointed functions, that there can be only one true Church, and that the Church has power and judgement over all that relates to the salvation of souls and the worship of God. He denounced what he regarded as the rage for innovations. Among the innovations he listed the failure of the state to recognize the authority of God, the effort of the state to control the Church, and the doctrine that sovereignty resides in the multitude with no reference to God. He labelled freedom of thinking and publishing whatever the individual wished without let or hindrance as "the fountain head of many evils." He insisted that it is "not lawful for the state . . . to hold in equal favour different kinds of religion" and that to exclude the Church, founded by God, "from the business of life, from the power of making laws, from the training of youth, and from domestic society is a grave and fatal error." He was stoutly against the separation of Church and state. Yet he held that the people might share in the government, and that no one should be "forced to embrace the Catholic faith against his will."[261] On June 20, 1888, in *Libertas praestantissimum* Leo defined what he believed to be Christian liberty. To him any liberty excluding a subjection of man to God was to be condemned: as he saw it, Christian liberty is not freedom to worship or not to worship God as the individual chooses.[262] Nearly two years later, on January 10, 1890, Leo followed *Libertas praestantissimum* with *Sapientiae Christianae*. As we have seen, this, although couched in terminology which had general application, was primarily directed to the situation in France. It declared that the Church refused to ally itself with any party and had "no care what form of government exists in a state."[263] When his pontificate was drawing to a close, in *Graves de communi* (January 18, 1901) Leo defined Christian popular action. This he did not identify with Christian democracy, although he approved what he believed Christian democracy should mean. He returned to his earlier denunciation of Socialism and held that Christians should not be lured into compliance with that school of political and economic thought.[264]

From this brief survey of his utterances on political issues it must be clear that Leo XIII was not afraid to stand against currents which were running strong in the political world and to state what seemed to him to be unchanging Christian principles and to apply them to the time. Yet he sought to be constructive rather than merely negative. Wherever he could do so without compromising what he believed to be basic truths he endeavoured to conciliate.

261 Leo XIII and Husslein, *op. cit.*, pp. 65–90; Hughes, *op. cit.*, pp. 59–69.
262 Leo XIII and Husslein, *op. cit.*, pp. 115–139; Hughes, *op. cit.*, pp. 76–85.
263 Leo XIII and Husslein, *op. cit.*, pp. 143–163; Hughes, *op. cit.*, pp. 85–94.
264 Leo XIII and Husslein, *op. cit.*, pp. 229–241.

Leo XIII: Attempts to Shape the Economic and Social Revolution

Much more than his predecessors Leo XIII sought to bring to accord with Christian standards the economic and social patterns which were emerging from the revolution. So far as can be judged from their official pronouncements, his predecessors seem scarcely to have been aware of the Industrial Revolution and of the basic changes which it was working in society. Leo was keenly appreciative of the problems to which the Popes earlier in the century had addressed themselves. He was also awake to the issues posed by the Industrial Revolution. With the rapid advance of industrialization they had become more acute. He faced them frankly, and, while he rejected the Socialist solutions, he attempted a constructive approach to them and outlined positive principles for meeting them.

Leo's most notable document in this area was the encyclical *Rerum novarum,* dated May 15, 1891.[265] The wide and continuing acclaim given it in Roman Catholic circles was evidence of its significance. It began by pointing out that the revolution, long felt in political life, had spread to social and economic life and was marked by great disparity between the enormous fortunes of a few individuals and the utter poverty of the masses and by moral degeneracy. The encyclical therefore addressed itself to the condition of the labouring classes. Looking back to the Middle Ages, Leo saw the beginning of modern troubles in the disappearance of the old workingmen's guilds. He also found a source of contemporary ills in the disregard of the Church's historic condemnation of usury. Leo excoriated Socialism as a solution to the problem brought by the Industrial Revolution. He came out plump for the right of private property. He declared that to hold out the dream of a classless society free from suffering was to ignore human nature: he held up as the ideal coöperation between classes. Workers, he said, were "to carry out honestly and fairly all equitable agreements entered into" and were never to resort to violence in defending their cause. The owner and employer, he maintained, were under obligation to respect the worker's dignity as a man, not to treat workmen as bondsmen or chattels, to give employees time for their religious duties, to guard them against occasions for sin, never to tax them beyond their strength or employ them in work unsuited to their age or sex, to "give every one what is just," and to refrain "from cutting down wages whether by force, by fraud, or by usurious dealing." The rich, so Leo insisted, while having the right to the possession of money, do not have the right to use it as they wish but must give to the

---

[265] Of the extensive bibliography on the encyclical see Soderini, *Il Pontificato di Leone XIII,* Vol. I, pp. 395–421; Leo XIII and Husslein, *op. cit.,* pp. 167–204; Hughes, *op. cit.,* pp. 146–158; J. Husslein, *The Christian Social Manifesto, An Interpretative Study of the Encyclicals Rerum Novarum and Quadragesimo Anno of Pope Leo XIII and Pope Pius XI* (Milwaukee, The Bruce Publishing Co., 1931, pp. xxiv, 329).

needy what remains over from meeting their own needs and maintaining their standing and must employ their temporal prosperity "for the perfecting of their own nature" and as stewards "of God's providence for the benefit of others."

Leo affirmed that there was no disgrace in poverty or in having to earn one's living by work, that it was the desire of the Church that "the poor should rise above poverty and wretchedness and better their condition in life," and that "Christian morality, when adequately and completely practised, leads of itself to temporal prosperity." In solving the social problem, Leo declared, the Church and all human agencies must collaborate. The state must take care that its laws and institutions bring about public well-being and private prosperity. The latter are dependent on well-regulated family life, respect for religion and justice, moderate and fair taxation, progress in the arts and trade, and the abundant yield of the soil. These the state can and should promote. The distinctive purpose of the state is "to see to the provision of those material and external helps, the use of which is necessary to virtuous action." The state has the duty "to safeguard private property by legal enactment and protection," to do its utmost to forestall strikes, to protect the workman's spiritual interests, and so to regulate the conditions of labour, such as the hours and places where work is done, the employment of women and children, and the ensuring of provision for rest, that the labourer is justly dealt with.

Leo took up the complicated question of wages. He came out against a current economic theory associated with *laissez faire* that they are the outcome purely of the free consent of employer and employee and that the state should do no more than see that a wage contract was enforced. To be just, wages should, so Leo maintained, be sufficient to support in comfort a "frugal and well-behaved wage-earner," his wife, and children, and enable him to save and to become an owner of property. Thus property would become more equitably distributed. For the settlement of disputes over wages Leo recommended boards of arbitration. He favoured private organizations such as trade unions and opposed the attempts of the state to suppress them. In Catholic trade unions, so he said, provision should be made to instruct the members in the Church's social teachings. Trade unions were exhorted to work for conciliatory methods in disputes, to set up common funds for the relief of their needy members, and to seek for the continuous employment of their members.

LEO XIII: ANTI-SLAVERY ADVOCATE

In addition to his programme for labour-capital relations Leo XIII concerned himself with Negro slavery. Here he and other Roman Catholics did not play as important a role as did Protestants. We have already seen something of the latter and are to see still more in later volumes. But while his was not the leading part, Leo was emphatically on the side of emancipation and of those who were fighting the African slave trade. On May 5, 1888, after Negro slavery had been ended in most of the New World, in the encyclical *In plurimis* Leo took the occasion of the abolition of slavery in Brazil to set forth the historic position of the Church on slavery and the treatment of slaves. He congratulated the Brazilian bishops on the action of their Government. He declared that the system of slavery was "wholly opposed to that which was originally ordained by God and by nature." He deplored the continuation of the slave trade internally in Africa. On November 20, 1890, he made a further pronouncement on slavery. He encouraged Lavigerie and others in their campaign against slavery in Africa.[266]

LEO XIII: ATTEMPTS TO GUIDE THE INTELLECTUAL REVOLUTION

Leo XIII was deeply concerned with the intellectual revolution which was in progress. In the encyclical *Immortale Dei* he declared that the Church would welcome whatever would spread the range of knowledge. He recognized that it was particularly important that Christians should face the issues posed to theology by the contemporary currents of thought, both in philosophy and in the natural sciences. Here he did not content himself with pointing out what he deemed errors, as had his immediate predecessors. He endeavoured to give positive guidance. Early in his pontificate, in his encyclical *Æterni Patris,* or *De philosophia Cristiana ad mentem Sancti Thomas Aquinatis Doctoris Angelici in scholis catholicis instauranda* (August 4, 1879), he urged the study and teaching of Thomas Aquinas as the guide and basis of theology.[267] In this, as in his extolling the medieval guilds in *Rerum novarum* and in his preparing a massive mausoleum in St. John Lateran for the remains of the great medieval Pope Innocent III, he was viewing the Middle Ages as having attained a height of Christian thought, life, and organization which was in contrast with what he regarded as the deterioration wrought by the revolution in which Christendom now found itself. Turning away from the current efforts of devout Roman Catholics to state the faith in the current patterns of philosophy, Leo went back to the outstanding school man who in the thirteenth century endeavoured to do what many nineteenth-century theologians were attempting, namely, to formulate theology in a sound and convincing fashion to meet the challenges of the contemporary climate of opinion. The revival of scholasticism had begun some years earlier. Leo had been convinced by it. While Bishop of Perugia he

[266] Leo XIII and Husslein, *Social Wellsprings,* pp. 91–112; Soderini, *Il Pontificato di Leone XIII,* Vol. I, pp. 303–307.

[267] Soderini, *op. cit.,* Vol. I, pp. 280 ff.; Leo XIII and Husslein, *op. cit.,* pp. 247–264.

had utilized it in the training of priests in his diocese. He was now essaying its spread to the entire Church. In doing so he gave an emphasis which was to govern much of the study by Roman Catholics of philosophy and theology in the remainder of the nineteenth century and in the twentieth century.

In reverting to the Middle Ages for guidance through the nineteenth-century revolution Leo was following a method which was in striking contrast with what was happening in Protestantism. As we have hinted and as we are to see more at length in a later volume, the Protestant theologians who were exerting the widest influence were seeking to blaze new trails in finding their way through the new world of the day. They were not abandoning the Christian faith or ignoring what theologians had said and written in earlier centuries. But they were attempting to examine the Gospel afresh and to state it in a fashion consistent with whatever fresh light the revolutionary age had brought. Some rejected these efforts and sought a secure foundation in the theological formulations by Protestants in the sixteenth and seventeenth centuries, but they were not the ones who commanded the widest hearing. Whether wisely or unwisely, in his attempt to give positive and constructive guidance through the bewildering maze of revolution, Leo XIII was joining his predecessors in setting the Roman Catholic Church more in opposition to it than were Protestants.

LEO XIII: HIS ENCOURAGEMENT TO THE RELIGIOUS LIFE

Statesman and scholar though he was and deeply concerned with the Church's involvement in political, social, and intellectual issues, Leo XIII was by no means oblivious to the religious practices of his fellow believers. Even here, however, some of his pronouncements had social goals. Thus in the encyclical *Laetitiae sanctae* (September 8, 1892) he commended the use of the rosary and declared that if devoutly used it was "bound to benefit not only the individual but society at large." [268] Near the end of his pontificate by what he deemed the greatest act of his pontificate Leo consecrated all mankind to the Sacred Heart of Jesus. This was through the encyclical *Annum sacrum* (May 25, 1899). Devotion to the Sacred Heart had been mounting since the seventeenth century and its spread was one of the features of the nineteenth-century revival in the Roman Catholic Church. To Leo the Sacred Heart symbolized not only the sufferings of Christ for the redemption of mankind but also the right of Christ to reign over all. The consecration of mankind to the Sacred Heart, therefore, had in it the implication of the world-wide spread of the Christian faith and the acceptance by all of Christ's rule through the Church.[269] Moreover, in his emphasis on prayer to Joseph, Leo was thinking of him as the head and protector of the

268 Leo XIII and Husslein, *op. cit.*, pp. 207–215.
269 *Ibid.*, pp. 219–226.

Holy Family and as the Patron of the Church. He saw in Joseph one to encourage true family life and to hearten labourers by his example.[270]

Yet it would distort the facts to leave the impression that Leo's interests were solely political, intellectual, and social. His repeated encyclicals and letters encouraging the faithful to the daily use of the rosary and to prayer to Mary, as *Supremi apostolatus* (September 1, 1883), *Salutaris ille* (December 24, 1883), *Superiore anno* (August 30, 1884), *Octobri mense* (September 22, 1891), *Magna Dei Matris* (September 8, 1892), *Jucunda semper* (September 8, 1894), *Adiutricem populi* (September 5, 1895), *Fidentem piumque Augustissimae Virginis* (September 12, 1897), and *Diuturni temporis* (September 5, 1898), were proof of a deep personal piety and devotion to the Virgin.

LEO XIII: IN RETROSPECT

In the twenty-five years of his pontificate Leo XIII had witnessed what on the whole were remarkable advances in the Roman Catholic Church in rising to the challenge of the world in revolution. Reverses there had been, but the gains had more than offset the losses. For this achievement Leo was by no means entirely responsible. Mounting tides of life to which we are to call attention in later chapters were the chief factors. But to them Leo gave able leadership. Although he was of sterling moral character and sincerely devout, his contribution was more that of the clear-headed statesman and theologian than of the saint. Firmly grounded in the history and completely committed to the teachings of his church, again and again he sought to remind the world, and especially the peoples who by heredity were of its family, of that history and of those teachings. He did not hesitate to condemn what in the revolutionary world was counter to them. Yet he also strove to conciliate where that could be done without compromise of essentials and to suggest positive programmes for meeting the needs of the new age.

PIUS X (1903–1914): PREVIOUS HISTORY AND ACCESSION

Leo XIII was followed by a Pontiff of quite different background and temperament. In contrast with Leo and his other predecessors of the nineteenth century, he was from humble and not from aristocratic stock: he was the "peasant Pope." A man of simple and sincere piety, within a generation after his death his saintly character was officially recognized by canonization, the first Pope to be so honoured since another Pius, the fifth to choose that title, who had reigned from 1566 to 1572.

Giuseppe Melchior Sarto (1835–1914) was the son of the postmaster of the village of Riesc on the Venetian plains. A lively, merry child, intelligent, charm-

[270] Doheny and Kelly, compilers, *Papal Documents on Mary*, pp. 45–51.

ing, and naturally a leader, as an acolyte in the village church he was early devout and devoted to the Virgin. With the aid of two local priests he was given a rudimentary education and through them obtained a scholarship which enabled him to go to a seminary in Padua. There he made a brilliant record. Graduating at twenty-three, by a Papal dispensation he was ordained priest a year before the canonical age of twenty-four. For eight years he served as curate in a rural parish. He continued to study, out of his pittance was generous to the poor, conducted schools for the parishioners, and began to win more than local fame as a preacher. Appointed rector of a larger parish, he continued to live with almost ascetic simplicity, giving to the poor and never sparing himself to serve his flock. At forty he was made chancellor and residential canon in the cathedral of Treviso and was appointed spiritual director of the seminary. In 1884 he became Bishop of Mantua. Always a prodigious worker, cutting his sleep to a few hours each night, he gave himself to his diocese with exemplary zeal. He established friendly relations with the local civil authorities, which was something of an achievement in the chronic tension between Church and state. He set himself to make good the shortage of priests, insisted that the children be given catechetical instruction, initiated the first Italian Social Congress, and had a mission preached to the boys and young men.

In 1893 Sarto was appointed by Leo XIII Patriarch of Venice and created Cardinal. The Italian Government, claiming the right to appoint, delayed its *exequatur* for sixteen months. He came to his post at a time when anti-clericalism was rampant, when the Government seemed intent on forbidding religious teaching in the schools, on expropriating the goods of religious confraternities and charitable societies, and on naming the bishops. In Venice he found a strongly anti-clerical element, but he rallied the Catholic forces. By his energy and his combination of charm and dignity he won a wide following. He lived simply: his two sisters and his niece kept house for him and without servants. He mixed with the populace in friendly fashion, sought to raise the quality of the priesthood, insisted on religious instruction for adults as well as children, carried through systematic diocesan visitation, and gave sacrificially to the poor.

On his way to Rome for the conclave to elect the successor to Leo XIII, Sarto bought a round-trip ticket. For a time it looked as though Rampolla would be the next Pope, and that in spite of the opposition of Austria: the French foreign minister asked the French Cardinals to vote for him. However, on the fourth day of the voting, to his dismay, Sarto was chosen. He accepted the unanticipated and undesired burden as the will of God and was to carry it for eleven eventful years.[271]

[271] Forbes, *Life of Pius X*, pp. 1–71; Ledré, *Pie X*, pp. 25 ff.; Merry del Val, *Memories of Pope Pius X*, pp. 1–3; F. Engel-Janosi, *l'Autriche au Conclave de 1903*, in *Revue Belge de Philologie et d'Histoire*, Vol. XXIX, pp. 1119–1141. For an admiring account of Sarto's career from his birth

PIUS X: CHARACTER

The only Pope for many generations to have had experience as a secular priest as a pastor in local parishes, Sarto brought to his high office not only the training of a bishop but also that of the intimate care of souls in the day-by-day ministry in village and town. It was characteristic of him that in his first encyclical he dealt only with spiritual matters and defined his aim as *instaurare omnia in Christo* ("to restore all things in Christ"). He also was a seasoned and able administrator, hard-working, practical, and punctual. In contrast with Leo XIII, who was cold, a stickler for etiquette, an aristocrat who valued ceremonial, Pius X was genial and kindly, disliked ceremonial, and so far as possible dispensed with guards and chamberlains. It was complained that he was a bishop rather than a statesman. But he had native shrewdness and tenacity of purpose, and his easy ways and directness of speech won the hearts of many.[272]

PIUS X: EARLY ACTS

As his Secretary of State Pius X appointed Raphael Merry del Val, a Spaniard and a seasoned ecclesiastical diplomat who had been a favourite of Leo XIII. His mother was English and he had had much of his education in England. He therefore possessed from heredity and training cosmopolitan contacts. Educated in part by the Jesuits, wealthy, pious, he was extremely conservative and orthodox.[273]

One of the earliest acts of Sarto as Pope was to issue a *motu proprio* on church music. While not excluding the use of modern music, providing it was not from the theatre or the opera, he recommended the Gregorian chant. To further the Gregorian chant he founded the Academy of Sacred Music in which clergy from various lands could study it and carry it back to their dioceses and monasteries.[274]

Pius X followed the precedent of his predecessor in concerning himself with social action. In a *motu proprio* in the initial year of his pontificate he summarized and reaffirmed the encyclicals of Leo XIII on this subject and more than once recurred to it. In a letter in December, 1905, he encouraged the Italian bishops to seek "to reinstate Jesus Christ in the family, the school, and society, to reëstablish the principle that human authority represents that of God, to take

---

through his election see *Life of His Holiness Pope Pius X. Together with a Sketch of the Life of his Venerable Predecessor . . . Pope Leo XIII . . . with a Preface by . . . Cardinal Gibbons* (New York, Benziger Brothers, 1904, pp. 401), pp. 131 ff.

[272] Merry del Val, *op. cit.*, pp. 12–14, 23–42, 62–69.

[273] On his choice, see *ibid.*, pp. 15–18.

[274] Forbes, *op. cit.*, pp. 74–77; Olf, *Their Name is Pius*, pp. 495–497; Merry del Val, *op. cit.*, pp. 50–53.

intimately to heart the interests of the people, especially those of the working and agricultural classes." [275]

PIUS X: RELATIONS WITH GOVERNMENTS

One of the first set of crises which Pius X was compelled to face was in France. In 1904 a law was passed which ordered all teaching congregations suppressed and all schools taught by them closed. A ten-year interval was permitted to allow adjustment, partly because at least half of the enrolment in secondary education was in these institutions. The property of the congregations was liquidated.[276] That same year France broke off diplomatic relations with the Holy See. The immediate causes were the protest of Pius against the official visit of the President of France to the King of Italy and the act of the French Government in forbidding two French bishops to heed a summons to go to Rome for an enquiry into their conduct.[277] The following year (1905) legislation was enacted which annulled the Concordat of 1801 and effected the separation of Church and state. With some exceptions, including provision for pensions for clergy, all subventions for the Church and public worship were discontinued. While religious liberty was guaranteed and the Church might exercise its own discipline, most of the church fabrics, together with the seminaries and the residences of the clergy, were declared to be the property of the state.[278] Pius denounced the law as "contrary to the constitution of the Church as founded by Jesus Christ" (February 11, 1906) and a few months later (August 20, 1906) reaffirmed his condemnation of the associations through which the Government would authorize the use of the buildings for the services of the Church. He also forbade compliance with a compromise which the state devised.[279] Pius did not relax his attitude and throughout his reign the embarrassing impasse continued.

In Portugal the pontificate of Pius X saw a similar collision. In 1910 a revolution ended the monarchy and inaugurated a republic. Anti-clericalism prevailed. In 1910 the religious orders were expelled and their properties were confiscated. The teaching of religion in the primary schools was forbidden. The marriage of priests was permitted. The bishops protested and at least one was expelled. In 1911 the separation of Church and state was decreed. In 1913 relations with the Holy See were broken off. Pius welcomed the exiled clergy and religious to Rome and on May 24, 1911, in his encyclical *Jamdudum,* condemned the

[275] Forbes, *op. cit.,* pp. 78, 79.
[276] Phillips, *The Church in France, 1848–1907,* pp. 273–275.
[277] *Ibid.,* pp. 275–277.
[278] *Ibid.,* pp. 279, 280.
[279] *Ibid.,* pp. 285–298.

anti-clerical legislation. Not until after his death were diplomatic relations resumed.[280]

Strain in Italy continued but was reduced. In effect the attitude embodied in *non expedit* was somewhat relaxed and in 1909 the faithful were permitted to vote. This was partly to relieve what Pius deemed the threat posed by the Christian Democracy Movement, which was acting independently of ecclesiastical direction. Also the better to deal with the situation, by an encyclical (June 11, 1905), Pius dissolved the *Opera dei Congressi* (Catholic Congresses) and founded the *Azione Cattolica* (Catholic Action).[281]

PIUS X: ATTITUDE TOWARDS INTELLECTUAL CURRENTS

On the issue of the adjustment of the faith to modern thought and of the application of the current methods of historical study to the Church's dogma and the Scriptures Pius X was adamant. Again and again he pointed out what seemed to him to be the danger of the new theological methods.[282] The conflict with the contemporary trends was especially marked in what was known as Modernism. Of this we are to hear more in a later chapter, but since it loomed large in the pontificate and actions of Pius we must here say something about it. Its leaders were mostly devout. Some of them had come to the faith out of severe struggle or, reared in the faith, after wrestling with the questions propounded by the scholarship of the day believed that they could honestly remain in the Roman Catholic Church. They were in several countries, but Loisy in France and Tyrrell in England were especially prominent. They maintained that the dogma and organization of the Church were a development influenced by the environment and needs of successive ages. They applied the current methods of historical criticism to the Bible and welcomed the contemporary comparative study of religion and of the history of religion. Their views spread among the clergy, especially in France, Italy, and Germany.

The Modernists believed that the Roman Catholic Church had the answer to the wistful questing and the despairs of the day, but that because of its use of archaic approaches and formulas it was failing to communicate the truth of which it was the custodian. They held that if the truth was to be effective, those who presented it must take account of the current environment. This they believed the Catholic Church had done in the past, and that here was a reason for its vitality and periodic renewal. They longed for it to repeat that achievement in the new and revolutionary age of the nineteenth century. As, in the early Christian centuries, culminating in Augustine, a synthesis had been per-

---

[280] *Encyclopædia Britannica*, 14th ed., Vol. XVIII, p. 282; Olf, *op. cit.*, p. 282; Forbes, *op. cit.*, pp. 153–155.
[281] *Enciclopedia Cattolica*, Vol. IX, p. 1527; Olf, *op. cit.*, pp. 287, 288.
[282] *The Catholic Encyclopedia*, Vol. XII, pp. 137–139.

fected of the Gospel and Platonism and Neo-Platonism, and in the thirteenth century, notably by Aquinas, with Aristotelianism, so they laboured for one with the intellectual challenges of their day.[283]

Both Leo XIII and Pius X saw in Modernism a threat to the faith and took action against it. In this they were following the precedents set by their predecessors against somewhat similar movements, notably those symbolized by Lamennais and Hermes. On November 18, 1893, Leo XIII in the encyclical *Providentissimus Deus* condemned forms of Biblical study which were gaining currency, especially in France. In it he declared that "all those books, and those books in their entirety, which the Church regards as sacred and canonical were written with all their parts under the inspiration of the Holy Spirit. Now, far from admitting the co-existence of error, Divine inspiration by itself excludes all error, and that also of necessity, since God, the Supreme Truth, must be incapable of teaching error." [284] In July, 1907, in the decree *Lamentabili* Pius X condemned sixty-five propositions which he considered to be errors. While it did not obtain the public notice which was given to the Syllabus of Errors of Pius IX, *Lamentabili* plainly showed the direction in which his mind was moving.[285] On September 8, 1907, in the encyclical *Pascendi* Pius came out with a thoroughgoing condemnation of Modernism. He described it as having agnosticism as the basis of its philosophy, as lifting conscience to the same level as revelation, and as placing science above faith. He believed its source to lie in uncontrolled curiosity, pride, and an ignorance of the scholastic method. To root out Modernism he enjoined the bishops to enforce the study of scholastic philosophy in the seminaries and universities, to exercise a ceaseless vigilance in the censorship of books in their dioceses, and to require an oath of all clergy and professors in universities to bind themselves to reject the errors denounced in *Lamentabili* and *Pascendi*.[286]

PIUS X: POSITIVE EFFORTS TO STRENGTHEN FAITH AND IMPROVE MORALE

Pius X was not content with negative measures to protect the Church from error. He put forth positive efforts to strengthen the faith of the Church's children. He established in Rome the Biblical Institute as a centre to which young ecclesiastics could come after their course in philosophy and theology for special

---

[283] On Modernism, see the following accounts, all sympathetic with the movement and tending to be either moderately or strongly critical of ecclesiastical authority, including the Popes: Fawkes, *Studies on Modernism;* Houtin, *Histoire du Modernisme Catholique;* Lilley, *Modernism, a Record and Review.* For an account, very fair and comprehensive, reflecting the official attitude of the Church, see *Dictionnaire de Théologie Catholique,* Vol. X, pp. 2010–2047.

[284] Lilley, *op. cit.,* p. 203.

[285] *The Catholic Encyclopedia,* Vol. XII, pp. 137–139; Forbes, *op. cit.,* p. 114; Ledré, *Pie X,* pp. 157, 158.

[286] Forbes, *op. cit.,* pp. 144 ff.; Ledré, *op. cit.,* pp. 158–160.

study of the Scriptures.[287] He projected a revision of the Vulgate and entrusted it to the Benedictines.[288] He paid special attention to the priesthood. "In order that Christ may be formed in the faithful," he said, "he must first be formed in the priest." He concerned himself particularly with the seminaries in Italy. He suppressed small ones, notably in the South, where several dioceses were too poor adequately singly to support a good one, and had two or more bishops combine their efforts in a joint institution. Uniform rules of study, of discipline, and of curriculum were prescribed and provision was made for periodic inspection. Bishops were urged to be careful in their selection of candidates for the priesthood, to have high standards in the examinations before ordination, and to be diligent in the supervision of priests in the initial years of their ministry. On August 4, 1908, on the fiftieth anniversary of his ordination to the priesthood, Pius issued an exhortation to priests the world over (*Exhortatio ad clerum catholicum*). He set before them his conception of the perfect parish priest, "the man of God." The priest was to take care to be "the salt of the earth and the light of the world," to be fervent and assiduous in prayer, in daily meditation, in the reading of good books, especially the Scriptures, and to subject himself to frequent examination of conscience. The priest was to remember that he was not only the servant but also the friend of Christ and must seek to conform himself to the mind of the Master. In his preaching he was to avoid flowery rhetoric and was to set forth plain and simple Gospel truths. He was to instruct both children and adults in Gospel doctrine.[289]

Pius revised with his own hands the catechism in use in North Italy, prescribed it for the dioceses in the Province of Rome, and recommended it for general use. A lover of the breviary, he had it reworked to make it more useful and to ensure the recitation of the whole Psalter once a week.[290] For the faithful in general Pius recommended frequent, even daily, communion. Indeed, he was sometimes called "The Pontiff of the Eucharist." He said that children need not wait until they were fourteen or fifteen to take communion but commanded that they be admitted to the sacrament as soon as they understood the simple doctrines of the Church.[291] He stressed Christian marriage and family life. In the decree *Ne temere* he simplified the regulations for matrimony.[292] In 1904, on the semi-centennial of the proclamation of the immaculate conception, he issued an encyclical enjoining devotion to Mary.[293]

[287] *Enciclopedia Cattolica*, Vol. IX, p. 1527; Forbes, *op. cit.*, pp. 126, 127.

[288] *Enciclopedia Cattolica*, Vol. IX, p. 1527.

[289] Forbes, *op. cit.*, pp. 133, 134; *Enciclopedia Cattolica*, Vol. IX, p. 1527; *The Catholic Encyclopedia*, Vol. XII, pp. 137–139; Premoli, *Contemporary Church History*, pp. 79, 80.

[290] Forbes, *op. cit.*, pp. 136–138; *Enciclopedia Cattolica*, Vol. IX, p. 1527; Premoli, *op. cit.*, p. 81.

[291] *Enciclopedia Cattolica*, Vol. IX, p. 1527; Olf, *Their Name is Pius*, pp. 291, 292.

[292] *Enciclopedia Cattolica*, Vol. IX, p. 1529.

[293] *The Catholic Encyclopedia*, Vol. XII, p. 137.

Pius X: His Care for Organization and Law

In addition to his care to fulfil his duties as the pastor and teacher of all Christians, Pius X gave attention to the governmental machinery of the Church. Although some in that elaborate bureaucracy held him in disdain for his lowly birth and his lack of previous experience in the central administration, he set about the reorganization of the curia to make it more efficient. He also ordered the codification of the canon law. A mammoth enterprise, it was continued during the reign of Pius and was promulgated in 1918, after his death.[294]

Pius X: Later Years and Death

As the years passed, the reverence for Pius X among the faithful mounted. Criticism there inevitably was, but it was chiefly from those outside the Roman Catholic Church or on its fringes. The Papal pronouncements on the issues which arose out of the separation of Church and state in France and on Modernism were so emphatic and uncompromising that they could not but be met with sharp and even bitter retorts. Pius was not a man to mince words and when to his mind the faith and the honour of the Church were at stake he was forthright and unyielding. He was accused of being intransigent, of failing to understand the world and the revolution in the midst of which his times had been set, and of being too much under the influence of Merry del Val. His Secretary of State was said to be an arch conservative and his evil genius. Yet among a widening circle of those loyal to the Roman Catholic Church increasingly Pius was regarded as a saint. Reports of miracles of healing through his prayers and his blessing were ardently believed. Sometimes the cures were said to have followed immediately upon his laying his hands on the afflicted: sometimes they were effected upon sufferers at a distance in response to letters asking for his intercession.[295] Whatever the judgement of the sceptical upon the validity of these miracles, there can be no doubt of the pastoral solicitude of Pius both for individuals and for multitudes in distress. Turkish massacres of Christians in Armenia and Macedonia evoked his commiseration. An earthquake in South Italy in 1908 which brought death to thousands and suffering to the survivors called forth his prompt efforts for tangible and immediate relief. Reports of atrocities on Indians in South America led him to exhort the bishops of that region to redress the wrong. He showed concern for individuals who came to him for spiritual counsel. Cruelty to children and the weak aroused his indignation.[296]

It speaks both for his character and for the estimate of the Roman Catholic

[294] *Ibid.*, pp. 137–139; *Enciclopedia Cattolica*, Vol. X, p. 1529; Olf, *op. cit.*, pp. 293–295.
[295] Forbes, *op. cit.*, pp. 148–162.
[296] *Ibid.*, pp. 141–147.

Church of what constitutes the ideal Christian that within less than half a century after his death Pius X was formally canonized. The essence of canonization, it will be recalled, is that the Church through the Pope declares the one so singled out to have been correct in doctrine, to have practised Christian virtues to an heroic degree, and through his or her intercession to have been the means of miracles, and commands the public veneration of the individual by the entire Church. That Pius X was so early placed in that category is a commentary on what the Roman Catholic Church of the twentieth century esteemed to be Christian sanctity.

Then came the shooting at Sarajevo which dramatically ushered in World War I. In the heart of the historic Christendom the forces of the revolution, in spite of the traditional faith of its people, had precipitated a holocaust which quickly assumed dimensions, geographical and in the numbers of peoples involved, far vaster than any which mankind had thus far experienced. A combination of many factors, among them the nationalism and the mechanical appliances which were phases of the revolution, within the short space of a few weeks proved illusory the complacent optimism of the nineteenth century with its soothing confidence in the ability of man to perfect himself and human society through his own reason and effort.

To Pius X the onset of the war brought deep agony of soul. Asked by a representative of the Emperor Francis Joseph, an octogenarian only a few years older than himself, to bless the Austro-Hungarian armies, Pius sternly replied: "I bless peace, not war." He exhorted Catholics the world over, led by their clergy, to turn to prayer that the war might soon be ended. Not himself primarily a statesman, in face of the failure of the most experienced statesmen of the day Pius explored possibilities of bringing peace. On August 20, 1914, less than a month after the first declaration of war, death claimed him. Presumably the burden of the world's suffering which he believed that he must bear as the Vicar of Christ had crushed him.[297]

THE NINETEENTH-CENTURY PAPACY: SUMMARY REFLECTIONS

The career and death of Pius X high-lighted and epitomized the course of the Papacy in the nineteenth century and the situation of the Roman Catholic Church in that revolutionary era. In the judgement of his church Pius was the noblest of the Pontiffs of that century, and, indeed, of those who had worn the tiara for 350 years the one most to be revered. All of his predecessors of the nineteenth century had been hard-working men of high purpose. They were not weak, as had been some of those who had gone before them in the tenth century. None was morally corrupt, as had been several who sat on the throne of

[297] *Ibid.*, pp. 162–168; Ledré, *Pie X*, pp. 275 ff.; Merry del Val, *op. cit.*, pp. 19–22, 70–76.

Peter in the time of the Renaissance and the Reformation. None had been guilty of the nepotism which had marred the record even of some of the Pontiffs of the seventeenth and eighteenth centuries, when reform had purged the Holy See of its worst abuses. Both of the two bearing the name of Pius whose reigns had spanned the violent outburst of the revolution which had racked Europe from 1789 to 1815 had suffered for the faith and might be said to have taken their place with the confessors and martyrs of the early Christian centuries. Under those who came after them the Roman Catholic Church had closed its ranks and was more and more presenting a united front against the hostile world which was emerging from the quondam Christendom. The trends towards the disintegration of the Roman Catholic Church into national bodies controlled by aristocratic bishops or dominated by "enlightened" monarchs had been arrested. That church was more closely integrated under the Popes than it had ever been, even under such great Pontiffs as Gregory I, Gregory VII, and Innocent III. The Pope was now officially and explicitly declared to have full and supreme power of jurisdiction over the universal Church and to be infallible when as pastor and doctor of all Christians he defined a doctrine regarding faith and morals to be held by the universal Church. The improved means of communication which were one of the aspects of the revolution made more possible than at any previous time the effective exercise of these prerogatives. To this all the bishops had submitted. Only small minorities of priests and laity had sufficiently dissented to withdraw from the Roman Catholic Church.

The Roman Catholic Church, more nearly united than ever under the Popes, led by them was firmly set against many of the currents of the revolution. Pope after Pope had rejected and censured attempts of some of its sons to re-think and re-state its dogmas and re-study the Scriptures in terms of the prevailing patterns of thought. The Popes had denounced the Socialism which was widely popular in revolutionary circles and some of the political theories which, esteemed by many as progressive and liberal, were shaping the governments of Europe. They placed themselves adamantly against the efforts of increasingly secularized states to take from the Church the education of youth and the control of marriage. Leo XIII, the Pontiff who most concerned himself with the economic and social problems presented by the Industrial Revolution, came out against the *laissez faire* which dominated much of the economic theory and legislation of the century. In their resistance to many features of the revolution the Popes could not have carried their church with them had they not been the spokesmen for the convictions of the majority of the bishops, the clergy, and the faithful laity. Here and there individuals and minorities either opposed the Papal actions and pronouncements or doubted their timeliness. But, with few exceptions, when once the Pope had spoken they concurred.

Millions of its nominal children were not in accord with the attitude which the Roman Catholic Church, led by the Popes, was taking towards the revolution. Some had so far separated themselves from the church of their fathers that they did not bring their offspring to the clergy for baptism. Many were indifferent. Others regarded the Church as the enemy of the advance on which they believed the Western world had embarked. De-Christianization was proceeding, either actively through open opposition or passively through neglect.

Yet the Popes and the faithful who rallied about them were not capitulating. Within the Vatican they maintained a court which in its pomp equalled that of secular monarchs, and diplomatic relations were kept up with various governments. The Popes again and again declared that through the neglect or hostility to the Church which had cradled and nurtured Western civilization tragic evils were arising to threaten the very existence of Western civilization. They sought to recall those whom they considered their erring children to the loyalty in which, to their minds, lay the only hope. The Popes were making active attempts not only to save Occidental society but also to win all mankind to the faith. They were endeavouring to attract those whom they now often designated, with less hostility than formerly, as the separated brethren, Protestants and the members of the Eastern Churches. Yet in doing so they did not relax what they deemed their divinely ordained authority. Numerical gains were being made among the traditionally non-Christian peoples of Asia, Africa, and the Pacific. Except for small minorities which included some notable individuals who were coming from the Catholic wing of the Church of England and from Protestant churches on the Continent and the United States, no headway was being made against Protestantism. More was being accomplished by the growth of Uniate bodies from the Eastern Churchces. Yet, through political manipulation, chiefly by the Russians, thousands of Uniates were being lost.

It was this Roman Catholic Church, consolidated under the Popes and resistant to the main forces of the revolution, which was ushered by World War I into a century in which the storm of revolution was vastly augmented, both in intensity and in geographic extent.

CHAPTER VIII

The Roman Catholic Church Is Reinforced by the Revival of Old Religious Orders and Congregations and the Emergence of New Ones, of Societies and Associations for Worship and Service, and of Movements Which Seek to Meet the Challenge of the New Day

A CHARACTERISTIC of the life of the Roman Catholic Church had long been monasticism in one or another of its forms. Enlisting those who in theory and at the heights of religious devotion in practice had given themselves fully to the Christian life, monasticism had provided a gauge to measure the vitality in that church. When the tides of life ran high, new houses of old orders and congregations appeared, existing orders and congregations were revived and reformed, and new orders and congregations emerged. Parallel with them were organizations of those who had not undertaken the religious life through the characteristic vows of poverty, chastity, and obedience, but who, still living in the world, associated themselves in prayer and service. When the tides of life ran low, existing orders and congregations became havens of ease and even centres of moral corruption, numbers declined, few or no new orders and congregations appeared, and associations for prayer and philanthropy languished. Harbingers of a turn in the tide were efforts to bring back lax foundations to their pristine devotion and the appearance of new bodies of "religious."

A feature of the course of Christianity in the nineteenth century was the revival of the Society of Jesus, the quickening of several of the old orders, the multiplication of new congregations, and the strengthening or creation of almost numberless societies and associations for the enlistment of the faithful in worship and service. While comprehensive figures are lacking, it seems probable that more new congregations, societies, and associations emerged than in any previous century in the history of the Roman Catholic Church, or, indeed, of any church.

The revival and birth of monasteries, congregations, societies, and associations proceeded in spite of recurring adverse government action. Not only on the eve of the French Revolution and during the Revolution and the Napoleonic Wars were monasteries, religious orders, and congregations suppressed. Again and again in the nineteenth century in more than one state anti-clericalism brought about the abolishment of religious houses, the secularization of their property, and the expulsion of orders and congregations. Significantly this was chiefly in France, Germany, Switzerland, Italy, Spain, and Portugal—the territorial strongholds of the Roman Catholic Church.

Here was evidence of amazing vitality. In the face of the widespread antagonism to Christianity which was a feature of the revolution through which Western Europe was passing, the Roman Catholic Church was making an astounding recovery from what some observers hailed as its impending demise. Through it thousands, probably more that at any previous time, were seeking to commit themselves completely to Christ. In doing so large numbers followed the road hallowed by long precedent and became members of a monastic order or congregation. Others remained at their work-a-day occupations but joined one or more organizations for nourishing and expressing the Christian life. In the face of more openly hostile movements than Western Europe had known since the mass conversion of the invading barbarians and the Moslem conquests centuries earlier, thousands were rallying to the Roman Catholic Church. For effective action they were gathering into a great variety of organizations. These were more and more under centralized control, that of the bishops, or, in the case of monastic orders and congregations, of their various superiors, and all, ultimately, of the Pope.

Moreover, more than in any earlier period these organizations, whether in the monastic tradition or outside it, were seeking to win the world. They were not merely endeavouring to counter the hostile aspects of the revolution, to hold to the faith the historic Christendom, and to permeate it with the faith. They were also striving to reach all mankind. A large proportion of the new congregations gave themselves to teaching youth, to nursing, to service among the underprivileged, to efforts to win Protestants and the Eastern Churches, and to missions among non-Christians. The orders and congregations which withdrew from the world sought by intercession to further the efforts of the more active bodies which were seeking to serve the world.

It seems probable that of those who took vows as "religious" a larger proportion were women than in the earlier centuries. Why this was so is not clear. One reason seems to have been that in missions outside Christendom less of physical peril was entailed and that it was more nearly possible than earlier for women to endure the kind of sacrifices and hardships which were involved.

Even to enumerate all the developments in existing orders and congregations and to give a complete list of the new ones between 1815 and 1914 would lengthen this chapter unduly. We must restrict ourselves to a few of the more outstanding bodies and movements. We will first speak of what was taking place in the orders and congregations which ante-dated the century, then of the congregations which arose in the nineteenth century. Finally we will give examples of the societies and organizations whose members did not bind themselves with the traditional obligations of the "religious."

REVIVAL IN THE OLDER ORDERS

In the eighteenth century the oldest of the orders, the Benedictines, had suffered a decline in numbers and morale. During the French Revolution and the wars of Napoleon many of its houses had been suppressed. In the nineteenth century the Benedictines experienced a marked revival. Even before 1815 they were renewed in Hungary. After that year several abbeys in Bavaria were restored. In France the main stimulus for the renewal was from Prosper Louis Pasqual Guéranger (1805–1875). In 1833 Guéranger became the reorganizer of the monastery of St. Peter in Solesmes, not far from Cambrai, and in 1837 Gregory XVI appointed him Abbot of Solesmes and Prefect of a new Gallican Congregation. Several daughter houses arose. The law of 1880 closed the Benedictine monasteries in France. After a resurgence, in 1901 the state again banned them. Some of the Benedictines banished from France in 1901 sought refuge in England and transported their Solesmes library to a house on the Isle of Wight. Others found asylum in Belgium.[1]

In Germany the leader of the Benedictine revival was Maurus Wolter (1825–1890). Aided by Princess Katharina von Hohenzollern, in 1862 he took possession of an ancient foundation of Augustinian Canons at Beuron which had been secularized in 1802. Lost in 1875 through the May Laws of the *Kulturkampf,* it was restored in 1885. Beuron became the mother house of several monasteries in Germany and other countries. Among them was Maria Laach near Andernach on the Rhine. An ancient Benedictine foundation which had been dissolved during the period of the French Revolution and Napoleon, in 1863 Maria Laach was acquired by the Jesuits but was lost to them through the *Kulturkampf.* The Benedictines obtained it in 1892. In 1884 Leo XIII approved the constitution of the Beuron Congregation and named Wolter Archabbot. By 1914 the Beuron Congregation comprised houses not only in Germany but also in Italy, Brazil, Portugal, England, Bohemia, and Jerusalem.[2] A German Benedictine house which gave itself primarily to missions was founded in 1884 by a Beuron monk and in 1887 was moved to St. Ottilien. In 1896 it became

---

[1] Ambroise Ledru, *Dom Guéranger, Abbé de Solesmes, et Mgr. Bouvier, Évèque du Mans* (Paris, Honoré Champion, 1911, pp. vii, 383); Heimbucher, *Die Orden und Congregationen der katholischen Kirche,* Vol. I, pp. 331–333; *The Catholic Encyclopedia,* Vol. II, pp. 450, 451.

[2] Heimbucher, *op. cit.,* Vol. I, pp. 334–339; *The Catholic Encyclopedia,* Vol. II, p. 451; *Enciclopedia Cattolica,* Vol. VIII, p. 138.

an independent priory and in 1902 an abbey. Through priests, lay brothers, and sisters, it inaugurated missions in Africa and Brazil.[3]

Italy was also the scene of a Benedictine revival. This took the form of the Cassinese Congregation of the Primitive Observance. Initiated in Genoa in 1851 by Casaretto, Abbot of Subiaco, it was recognized in 1872 by Pius IX as a distinct congregation and formed its houses into a loose federation. The name Cassinese was obviously from Monte Cassino, famous for its association with the founder of the Benedictines, and Subiaco was the place where Benedict began the monastic life. The Cassinese Congregation of the Primitive Observance spread not only in Italy but also in Belgium, France, England, Spain, and Jerusalem.[4] In Austria a congregation suppressed in 1803 was restored in 1809 and 1816.[5] In the violent anti-clerical movements in Spain, in 1835, sixty-six Benedictine monasteries were dissolved, but in a pro-Catholic reaction several were renewed.[6] In England and Scotland, in addition to the monasteries sprung from the Benedictine congregations on the Continent, such as Downside, made an abbey in 1899, and that at Fort Augustus in the Highlands, one arose in the Church of England which in 1913 submitted to the Roman Catholic Church. In 1929 it affiliated with the Cassinese Congregation.[7] Also through several congregations the Benedictines were planted in the United States.[8]

A Benedictine tradition was the self-government of each monastery. Originally no closely knit structure had existed such as that developed by the Franciscans, Dominicans, Jesuits, and other orders. Across the centuries modifications had developed and affiliations had arisen, latterly called congregations, which for the purposes of discipline grouped together several monasteries. To this the decrees of the Council of Trent gave a marked impetus. However, no comprehensive structure had been created to embrace all the Benedictine family. In 1893, in an attempt to bring this about Leo XIII appointed an Abbot Primate with residence at Rome. While much of the independence of each congregation was preserved, here was an expression of the nineteenth-century trend in the Roman Catholic Church towards centralization under the direction of the Pope.[9]

In the nineteenth century the Benedictines continued their characteristic contributions in liturgy, art, education, and historical studies.

While a majority of the Benedictines were men, for centuries houses of

[3] Heimbucher, *op. cit.*, Vol. I, pp. 340, 341.
[4] *Ibid.*, pp. 342, 343.
[5] *The Catholic Encyclopedia*, Vol. II, p. 450.
[6] *Ibid.*, p. 449.
[7] Peter F. Anson, *The Benedictines of Caldey* (London, Burns, Oates & Washbourne, 1940, pp. xxx, 205), *passim; The Catholic Encyclopedia*, Vol. II, p. 447.
[8] Heimbucher, *op. cit.*, Vol. I, p. 343.
[9] *The Catholic Encyclopedia*, Vol. II, p. 459.

women had followed the rule of St. Benedict. The nineteenth-century revival effected the creation of a number of new convents in several different countries.[10]

Under the French Revolution and Napoleon the Cistercians, once flourishing but then in decline, were dealt severe blows. In 1791 the mother house, Citeaux, was expropriated and its great church was razed. The following year Clairvaux, made famous by Bernard, met a similar fate. Even the graves were violated and the bones of Bernard scattered. The nineteenth century did not see a complete restoration, but something of a revival occurred and by the end of the century there were about twenty-five monasteries, nearly half of them in Austria-Hungary.[11]

The Trappists, from a reform of the Cistercians late in the seventeenth century, in the nineteenth century displayed more vigour than did the older branch of their order. The strictness of their discipline appealed to youths who were eager to give themselves without reservation to the religious life. Driven from France by the Revolution and Napoleon, Trappists found refuge in several countries, among them England. After the downfall of Napoleon the mother house, La Trappe, was restored and new foundations were made, including some in France. By the end of the century the Trappists were in several European countries, notably in France, and had planted monasteries in countries outside Europe, among them Palestine, China, Japan, Algeria, Brazil, Natal, German East Africa, Canada, and the United States. In 1898 they recovered Citeaux. Giving themselves to worship and to the cultivation of the soil, they kept largely apart from the world, but they felt the pressure for centralization which characterized the nineteenth-century Roman Catholic Church. In the 1890's Leo XIII approved a new constitution for the order which brought together three congregations and an Abbot General was appointed, independent of the General of the Cistercians and with his residence in Rome. In 1902 a Papal decree recognized Citeaux as the mother house. Trappist nuns, or Trappestines, were not as numerous as Trappist monks, but in the nineteenth century they had several houses.[12]

The Carthusians, like the Cistercians, of eleventh-century origin, had dwindled by the eighteenth century. Yet some of their "Charterhouses" survived. As with the other orders, the storm of the French Revolution swept out some of their foundations. The Grand Chartreuse, the mother house, was suppressed in 1793. In 1816 it was regained.[13] By 1900 there were eleven monasteries in France and nine in other parts of Europe. Financial support came largely from

---

[10] Heimbucher, *op. cit.*, Vol. I, pp. 389–401.

[11] *Ibid.*, pp. 435–437.

[12] *Ibid.*, pp. 460 ff. *La Trappe in England, Chronicles of an Unknown Monastery*, by a Religious of Holy Cross Abbey, Stapehill, Dorset (London, Burns, Oates & Washbourne, 1937, pp. xii, 224), gives a brief comprehensive history as well as an account of a modern English abbey.

[13] Cottineau, *Repertoire Topo-Bibliographique des Abbeyes et Prieurés*, Vol. I, p. 717.

the sale of a liqueur, the formula for whose manufacture was invented in the nineteenth century and was a closely guarded secret. By 1907 the order had been driven out of France but houses had been opened elsewhere.[14]

The Premonstratensians, another order of the Middle Ages, had suffered severe losses from the Protestant Reformation and then from the secularization of most of its houses late in the eighteenth century. A few new houses were founded in the ninetenth century and in 1883 the order was organized afresh.[15]

It was to be expected that the orders which had arisen from the great religious awakenings of early centuries, such as the Benedictines, and of the early Middle Ages, such as the Cistercians, Carthusians, and Premonstratensians, would not make a full recovery: their heyday had passed. The devotion aroused by later awakenings would be more inclined to seek outlet through younger orders and congregations.

So it would probably be with the orders of friars which came out of the mounting currents of life of the thirteenth century. The Franciscans and Dominicans had carried most of the missionary burden of the Roman Catholic Church of the thirteenth and fourteenth centuries. They and to a lesser extent the Augustinians had been prominent in the amazing missionary surge of the sixteenth, seventeenth, and eighteenth centuries. But they were now old. They had been dealt heavy blows by Josephism, the French Revolution, and the spread of the Revolution through Napoleon. While they revived after the downfall of the Corsican, the secularizations of the nineteenth century, notably in Italy, France, Spain, and Portugal, coming on the heels of that partial recovery, were particularly disheartening. Yet all three orders survived and spread into new areas.

In their earlier course the Franciscans had developed several bodies—from a congenital vigour which was ill content with compromises of the primitive ideals and discipline. In the nineteenth century no new major divisions were seen. On the contrary, four branches of what were known as the Observants were brought together: the Observants, the Reformed, the Recollects, and the Discalced or Alcaterines. In 1895 preliminary steps towards coöperation were taken. Two years later, at Papal behest, an overall structure was adopted. They were given a General and a central office in Rome.[16] The Conventuals, who represented an early relaxed adherence to the original rule of the order, persisted. So did the Capuchins, who had been born early in the sixteenth century from the urge to return to an exact observance of that rule. Like the other branches of the Franciscans, the Capuchins lost heavily in houses and members from the secularization of the late eighteenth and the early nineteenth century.

[14] *The Catholic Encyclopedia,* Vol. III, p. 390.
[15] Heimbucher, *op. cit.,* Vol. II, pp. 58, 59.
[16] *Ibid.,* p. 386; Holzapfel, *Handbuch der Geschichte des Franziskanerordens,* pp. 377–379.

Then, following a partial recovery after 1815, fresh secularizations, especially in Italy, brought further reverses. In 1908 the numbers of houses and members was somewhat less than in 1847 and less than half of what it had been in 1712.[17] Yet the Franciscans had spread to other countries, notably the United States, and were active in missions outside the Occident.

The Order of Preachers shared with other orders the reverses brought by the Emperor Joseph II, the French Revolution, Napoleon, and the anti-clerical storms of the nineteenth century. In Spain alone in a single year, 1835, more than half their houses were closed.[18] The number of Dominicans at any one time seems never to have sunk below 3,500. Undaunted, faithful members refounded old houses or founded new ones. In 1910 Dominicans are said to have totalled about 4,472 in nearly 400 convents or secondary establishments in 28 provinces and 5 congregations.[19]

The renewal of the Dominicans in France was by Jean Baptiste Henri Lacordaire (1802–1861). A lawyer who had already begun the practice of his profession, he was inspired to study for the priesthood by Lamennais's Essai sur l'Indifférence en Matière de Religion. Ordained priest in 1828, he began a remarkable career of which we are to hear more in a later chapter. A great orator and preacher, he won a wide hearing. He dreamed of bringing France back to the Catholic faith through a revival of the Order of Preachers. To this end he went to Rome and there in 1839 or 1840 donned the habit of the Preaching Friars. By 1850 he had so far made progress towards his purpose that the French province of the Dominicans was canonically erected. It flourished and later was subdivided.[20]

Outstanding among those whom Lacordaire induced to come into the order was Jean Joseph Alexander Jandel (1810–1872). A native of Lorraine, Jandel had been ordained a secular priest (1834) and was about to become a Jesuit when Lacordaire shared with him his vision of what the Order of Preachers could do to reverse the trend towards de-Christianization. In 1843 he became superior of a newly founded house in Nancy and later was moved to other posts, including one in Paris. In 1850, Pius IX appointed him General of the Dominicans. He sought to bring the order back to the ideals of its founder and to the full observance of its constitutions. In this he met opposition, notably in Italy. In France, since a fresh beginning was being made, the resistance was not great.[21] In England the order had experienced heavy going since the death of Queen Mary, but it persisted and in the nineteenth century grew and ex-

---

[17] Holzapfel, op. cit., pp. 621, 622.
[18] Heimbucher, op. cit., Vol. II, p. 125.
[19] The Catholic Encyclopedia, Vol. XII, pp. 368H, 369.
[20] Devas, The Dominican Revival in the Nineteenth Century, p. 3; The Catholic Encyclopedia, pp. 368H, 369.
[21] Devas, op. cit., pp. 20–55.

tended its activities to the West Indies.[22] Jandel travelled extensively in Europe, enforcing discipline and restoring the order in more than one country. The appointment of a General of the Dominicans by a Pope was unprecedented: the post had always been filled by election by a general chapter of the order. The act was one more instance of the trend which was rapidly centralizing the control of the Roman Catholic Church in the hands of the Supreme Pontiff. However, the wisdom of the choice and the success of the reforms were demonstrated by the continuation of Jandel for a third term as General, this time (1862) by an overwhelming vote of a general chapter. By the time of his death Jandel had the satisfaction of seeing the Dominicans reformed, reunited, equipped with revised constitutions, and with expanding missionary activities outside Europe.[23]

True to their traditions, in the nineteenth century the Dominicans gave themselves not only to preaching but also to scholarship. In a later chapter we shall have occasion to note their contributions in theology. They addressed themselves to the study of the Scriptures: their *Revue Biblique* became notable.[24]

The nineteenth century witnessed a revival and extension of the Third Order of the Dominicans. In 1895 it had about 55 congregations, with approximately 800 establishments and 20,000 members. It devoted itself largely to teaching and to works of charity.[25]

The Augustinians were further than the Franciscans and Dominicans from making a full recovery. By 1910 they could count only about a tenth as many monasteries as at the height of the order. However, in 1908 they still had twenty-three provinces in several different countries under an elected Prior General with headquarters in Rome. There were, in addition, the Discalced Augustinians.[26]

THE REVIVED SOCIETY OF JESUS

We have repeatedly seen the vigour and the stormy history of the Society of Jesus. After their restoration the Jesuits still faced enmity—within the Roman Catholic Church and even more among anti-clericals in traditionally Roman Catholic lands. In the nineteenth century they were expelled from country after country.[27] Yet they persisted, flourished, and renewed their extensive missionary programme and their activities in education and literature.

The revived Society was fortunate in its leadership. In January, 1820, only six years after the full restoration of the Society, the General, Brzozowski, and the

22 Bede Jarrett, *The English Dominicans* (London, Burns, Oates & Washbourne, 1937, pp. xi, 200), pp. 166.
23 Devas, *op. cit.*, pp. 56 ff.; Heimbucher, *op. cit.*, Vol. II, pp. 125–130.
24 *The Catholic Encyclopedia*, Vol. XII, pp. 368H, 369.
25 *Ibid*.
26 *Ibid.*, Vol. VII, pp. 281, 282.
27 Campbell, *The Jesuits 1534–1921*, pp. 734–764; Becher, *Die Jesuiten*, p. 343.

other members were expelled from Russia where after its suppression in 1773 the Society had had its chief haven. A few weeks later Brzozowski died. Under the next General, Aloysius Fortis, some new houses were erected, but he died in 1829, after less than a decade in office. He was followed by John Philip Roothaan (1785–1853). During his nearly quarter of a century in office (July 9, 1829–May 8, 1853) the Society spread so widely that Roothaan has been called its rebuilder.[28] A native of Holland, in his teens Roothaan decided to join the Jesuits and went to Russia to enter the novitiate. There he completed his theological studies, was ordained, and was fully admitted to the Society. Driven from Russia, he found refuge in Switzerland. Then he was entrusted with the difficult assignment of head of a college in Turin, a centre of liberalism. Soon, after a few weeks as Vice-Provincial with residence in Rome, he was elected the twenty-first General. Under him the Society increased in numbers: by the time of his death it had 5,209 members. Largely through his initiative its foreign missions were resumed: under him enterprises were begun in India, China, Algeria, Madagascar, Egypt, Australia, and Brazil. To his letter, in 1833, calling for volunteers over half of the approximately 2,000 members of that time responded with the offer of service. He had much to do with planting the Society in the United States and helped lay the foundations for the growth which in the next century enrolled in that country a fourth of the entire membership. Taking office, as he did, so soon after the restoration of the Society, Roothaan had much to do with shaping its programme. He was intensely loyal to the founder, Ignatius Loyola. He prepared an edition of the famous *Spiritual Exercises* and placed them at the centre of the spiritual life of the Society. He supervised a revision of the *Ratio Studiorum* under which the Jesuits had once been the schoolmasters of much of Europe. Nearly half a century before Leo XIII urged on the bishops of the entire Church Aquinas as the basis of theological instruction, under Roothaan Thomism had been made an integral part of the Jesuit curriculum. This was done in a modified form and at the outset not without the opposition of those in the Society who regarded Thomism as unsuited to the intellectual climate of the day. Roothaan also came out firmly against Lamennais, Hermes, and others who in their efforts to state the Christian faith in the thought patterns of the nineteenth century seemed to him to be endangering the faith. He sought to promote friendly relations with other orders: although in the past severe tensions had existed between them and the Jesuits, he aided the restoration of the Dominicans in France.

Roothaan was followed as General by a Belgian, Pierre Jean Beckx (1795–

---

[28] See an appreciative biography by a fellow Jesuit, Robert G. North, *The General Who Rebuilt the Jesuits* (Milwaukee, The Bruce Publishing Co., 1944, pp. xii, 292). See also Becher, *op. cit.*, pp. 362–366.

1887).[29] Under Beckx the Society continued its growth. On his accession its members totalled 5,209, and in 1883 they were 12,070 (another figure given is 11,480). This was in spite of expulsion from Spain for several years, banishment from parts of Italy, and proscription in Germany during the *Kulturkampf*. More provinces were created, more colleges were founded, and retreats and parish missions were conducted.

Beckx was succeeded by Anton Maria Anderley (1819-1892). Swiss by birth, Anderley had entered the Society when the expulsion of the Jesuits from his native land caused him to be sent to the United States to complete his studies. After a brief pastorate in Wisconsin he was assigned to Germany and in 1859 became head of the province in that country. In 1870 he was elected Assistant General and in 1883 became Vicar General with the right of succession. On the death of Beckx he became General.[30]

Luis Martin, General from 1892 to 1906, stimulated a new series of histories on the Society by a number of authors.[31]

Francis Xavier Wernz (1842-1914) was the next General. A scholar and administrator, from 1882 to 1906 he had been rector of the Gregorian University in Rome. While head of the Society (1906-1914) he vigorously supported Pius X in the campaign against Modernism. He had an important share in the renewal of the mission in Japan which had been interrupted by the persecutions of the sixteenth and seventeenth centuries. At his death the Society had 16,894 members.[32]

Throughout the nineteenth century the Jesuits were staunch supporters of ultramontanism. They also did much to promote the practice of mental prayer according to the method of Loyola as interpreted by Roothaan, and contributed to the spread of devotion to the Sacred Heart of Jesus.[33] They became famous not only in education but also in science, particularly for their contributions in meteorology and astronomy.[34]

THE REVIVAL AND GROWTH OF NEWER PRE-NINETEENTH-CENTURY CONGREGATIONS

The Society of Jesus was only one of several bodies of religious which arose in the sixteenth and seventeenth centuries and the fore part of the eighteenth century. Under the stress of the French Revolution some of them seemed to die. However, in the nineteenth century a number were revived.

The Oratorians, associated with the name of Philip Neri, had spread widely.

29 *The Catholic Encyclopedia*, Vol. II, p. 382; *Enciclopedia Cattolica*, Vol. II, pp. 1131, 1132; Aubert, *Le Pontificat de Pie IX*, p. 458; Becher, *op. cit.*, pp. 366-370.
30 *The Catholic Encyclopedia*, Vol. I, p. 466.
31 *Ibid.*, Vol. XIV, p. 100; Becher, *op. cit.*, p. 372.
32 *Enciclopedia Cattolica*, Vol. XII, p. 1670; Becher, *op. cit.*, p. 374.
33 Aubert, *op. cit.*, p. 458.
34 Campbell, *op. cit.*, pp. 825 ff.

A congregation of secular priests, they placed much emphasis on preaching. Strong in France and Italy, they were dealt serious blows by the Revolution and Napoleon. In the nineteenth century they came back. They were made memorable by the membership of John Henry Newman, distinguished convert from the Church of England and Cardinal.[35]

Before the French Revolution the Congregation of Priests of the Mission, better known as the Lazarists or Vincentians, founded in 1625 by Vincent de Paul, had displayed a striking growth and had spread into several countries. Since they were of French origin and with headquarters in Paris, the Revolution was particularly disturbing. They survived. Indeed, in 1804 Napoleon reinstated them. However, until 1827 they had only a provisional organization. In that year the Pope gave them a Superior General. By the end of the nineteenth century they had houses in all five continents and the islands of the Pacific and counted more than three thousand members.[36]

The Society of Saint Sulpice had been founded in 1642 in France by Olier for training recruits for the priesthood by teaching in theological seminaries. Since its main strength was in France, the Revolution was especially hard on it. It was restored in 1816. In 1903 in addition to the one in Paris it had seminaries in philosophy and theology in twenty-four bishoprics in France. Soon thereafter adverse legislation crippled its labours in the land of its origin, although only for a time. It throve in Canada and the United States.[37]

The Eudists (the Society of Jesus and Mary) were also from the seventeenth century. The foundation date was 1643, only a year after that of the Sulpicians. Similarly of French birth, like the latter they had as their purpose the preparation of priests. In addition they conducted missions to raise the level of Christian life in local parishes and engaged in secondary education. During the French Revolution one of their number was confessor to Louis XVI and several were killed. In 1826 the Eudists were refounded, but it was not until the second half of the century that they really prospered. When, soon after 1900, many of them were expelled from France, they established themselves in Canada, the United States, the Antilles, and in Central and South America. Some persevered in France and there continued to hold missions.[38]

Roughly contemporary in origin with the Sulpicians and the Eudists, but of German birth, were the Bartholomites, officially the *Institutum Clericorum Saecularium in Communi Viventium*. Begun by Bartholomew Holzhauser near the end of the Thirty Years' War, the Institute had as its purpose the improve-

[35] Heimbucher, *Die Orden und Congregationen der katholischen Kirche*, Vol. III, pp. 418–424; *The Catholic Encyclopedia*, Vol. XI, p. 273.

[36] Heimbucher, *op. cit.*, Vol. III, pp. 434–442; *The Catholic Encyclopedia*, Vol. X, pp. 362–367.

[37] Heimbucher, *op. cit.*, Vol. III, pp. 446–448; *The Catholic Encyclopedia*, Vol. XIII, pp. 378–380.

[38] Heimbucher, *op. cit.*, Vol. III, pp. 449–452; *The Catholic Encyclopedia*, Vol. V, pp. 596, 597.

ment of the quality of the secular clergy in Germany, impaired by that long conflict. This the Institute sought to accomplish through seminaries. At the time when, under the stress of the Napoleonic era, it was dissolved, it had 1,595 members. In 1866 Pius IX gave his approval to a restoration of congregations of secular priests on the pattern of the Bartholomites. They arose in France, Belgium, Spain, Italy, and America.[39]

Another organization of seculars was the Society of Foreign Missions of Paris. Founded in 1663, its objective was to send as missionaries priests who would help in the work of conversion and raise up an indigenous secular clergy through whom the Church would be firmly planted. Its enterprises were in East and South-east Asia and Canada. In spite of difficulties brought by the French Revolution, it managed to survive. In the nineteenth century it expanded the territories in which it operated.[40]

The Institute of the Brothers of Christian Schools, of men not in holy orders, was founded by Jean Baptiste de La Salle in 1680. As its name suggests, its members devoted themselves to teaching. Suppressed in 1792, it was restored in 1802 under Napoleon. After 1810 it grew rapidly. Its headquarters were in Paris, but it spread into several countries both in and outside Europe. By 1874 it had 1,149 houses, 10,235 brothers, and 388,000 pupils in its schools. Through the legislation of 1904 its schools were closed in France, but it continued to operate in Latin America, the United States, and Canada.[41]

The Passionists were founded in Italy in the first quarter of the eighteenth century by Francis Danei, better known as Paul of the Cross. The statutes of the congregation, drafted in 1720, outlined the objectives as the propagation of the Gospel, the preaching of repentance through word and example, and especially the promotion of reverence for the sufferings of Christ. Before the outbreak of the French Revolution the Passionists had spread to other countries. They survived that storm and by 1914 had about one hundred houses. They were chiefly in Italy but were also in Belgium, Spain, the United States, Mexico, Argentina, the British Isles, Rumania (Wallachia), Bulgaria, Australia, and the Antilles. They combined the contemplative life of the Carthusians with the active missionary life of the Jesuits.[42]

The Congregation of the Most Holy Redeemer, popularly designated as the Redemptorists, was begun in Italy, near Amalfi, in 1732. The Redemptorists had as their primary purpose the deepening of the Christian life of the nominally Catholic population: their initial growth was chiefly in the Kingdom of Naples. By the end of the century they had spread north of the Alps. The

[39] Heimbucher, *op. cit.*, Vol. III, pp. 454–456.
[40] The fullest account is Adrien Launay, *Histoire Générale de la Société des Missions Étrangères* (Paris, Pierre Tequi, 3 vols., 1894).
[41] Heimbucher, *op. cit.*, Vol. III, pp. 298–309; *The Catholic Encyclopedia*, Vol. VIII, pp. 56–61.
[42] Heimbucher, *op. cit.*, Vol. III, pp. 309–313; *The Catholic Encyclopedia*, Vol. XI, pp. 522–524.

founder had been dead only a few years when the storm of the French Revolution broke. Yet in 1803 a house was planted in Germany. In 1808 Napoleon closed the house in Warsaw, but its head, Clemens Maria Hofbauer, took refuge in Vienna. By the time Hofbauer died, in 1820, the Redemptorists, largely through him, were active in Austria, Poland, Bulgaria, and Switzerland. Before many years they were also in France, Belgium, more than one German state, the British Isles, Luxemburg, and the United States. By 1914 they had spread as well into Spain, Canada, South America, Australia, Central America, the West Indies, and Denmark. They persisted in Italy, chiefly in the South and Sicily.[43]

NINETEENTH-CENTURY CONGREGATIONS, SOCIETIES, AND MOVEMENTS

Taken alone, the revival of pre-nineteenth-century orders and congregations might be regarded as an example of social lag. Conceivably they were the sunset after-glow, the dying reflections of a great day in man's religious pilgrimage. Doubt on this interpretation was cast by the fact that many of them grew as the century progressed. Few attained the numerical dimensions that had once been theirs, but in spite of recurring spasms of anti-clericalism which dealt successive blows in traditionally Roman Catholic countries, by 1914 all that we have mentioned had attained larger dimensions than were theirs in 1815.

Further cause for questioning the valetudinarian diagnosis was the large number of new congregations, societies, and movements which emerged in the nineteenth century. Most of the fresh bodies were efforts to meet the challenge of the revolution by penetrating society and by capturing the processes and institutions which characterized the revolution. They were prevailingly missionary, for the purpose of holding to the faith those threatened by de-Christianization, winning back the de-Christianized, and spreading the faith among non-Christians the world over. Some were substantially new in their structure, novel attempts to seize the opportunities presented by the new day. Moreover, most of them arose in those parts of the Occident which had long been Roman Catholic. Here the Roman Catholic Church was embattled against de-Christianizing forces. Yet it was not content to be on the defensive. More effectively mobilized than ever under a centralized administration, it was seeking to demonstrate that what it regarded as the cohorts of evil were the besieged, that the Church of Christ was the besieger, and that, true to the promise which had been given to Peter, the gates of the beleaguered fortress would ultimately give way. That confidence was reinforced by the appearance of several of the new organizations on the geographic frontiers of the Church. Presumably here was proof that when planted in fresh territories and environments the Roman Catholic Church had sufficient vigour to put forth new shoots.

[43] Heimbucher, *op. cit.*, Vol. III, pp. 313–325; *The Catholic Encyclopedia*, Vol. XII, pp. 683, 684.

We will first say something of the new congregations which were reminiscent of the familiar monastic heritage: some were made up of regulars; others were societies of seculars. We will then speak of organizations and movements which took substantially original forms.

We have noted that even before the downfall of Napoleon, in France, the centre of the revolutionary storm, new congregations were being born. Thus in 1800 the Society of the Sacred Heart came into being, followed by the Picpus Fathers.

Not far from the fall of Napoleon more than one congregation sprang up. In 1808 Jean Baptiste Rauzan (1757–1847) inaugurated a missionary movement in Lyons which sought to save the soul of France, badly de-Christianized by eighteenth-century rationalism and the Revolution. When Napoleon broke with Pius VII the movement was suppressed. In 1814 it was revived as the Missionaries of France, a congregation of priests. It was dispersed by the upheaval of 1830. In 1834, encouraged by Gregory XVI, it was refounded, but as the Fathers of Mercy. Driven out of France by adverse legislation, in 1905 the congregation moved its headquarters to Belgium. It expanded to the United States.[44] Rauzan also founded the Association of the Ladies of Providence to aid pastors in France and the Congregation of the Sisters of St. Clotilde for the education of girls.[45]

In 1816 Charles Joseph Eugene Mazenod (1782–1861) founded the Oblates of Mary Immaculate, officially the *Congregatio Missionariorum Oblatorum Sanctissimae et Immaculatae Virginis Mariae*. Mazenod was from an old aristocratic family which to escape the Revolution took refuge in Italy. Returning to France when Napoleon had made peace with the Church, he received his theological training in Paris. Seeing a sad fruit of the Revolution in the religious destitution of the population in his native Provence, he began to assemble priests in an attempt to counter it. In 1826 the rules framed by Mazenod obtained Papal approval. The announced goals of the congregation were "to preach the Gospel to the poor," leadership in seminaries for the training of priests, the religious rearing of youth, spiritual care of prisoners, and, later, foreign missions. The congregation spread into several European countries, the United States, Canada, Mexico, Australia, Ceylon, and South Africa. Driven out of France by adverse legislation, it continued to expand its services in other lands.[46]

The year 1816 also saw the beginning, in Lyons in France, of the Society of Mary (*Societas Mariae*). Its founder was Jean Claude Colin (1790–1875). A self-effacing parish priest, he was distressed by the religious destitution in rural districts, where the de-Christianization of the Revolution and the lack of clergy

---

44 Heimbucher, *op. cit.*, Vol. III, p. 522; *The Catholic Encyclopedia*, Vol. V, pp. 794, 795.
45 *The Catholic Encyclopedia*, Vol. V, p. 794.
46 Heimbucher, *op. cit.*, Vol. III, pp. 333–339; *The Catholic Encyclopedia*, Vol. XI, pp. 184–186.

had left deep marks. He and a few other priests associated themselves in efforts to remedy the situation. In 1836 Gregory XVI, in need of missionaries in the Pacific, gave it formal recognition and committed to it Oceania. There it extended its activities to many islands, including New Zealand. Until the adverse Associations Act of 1901 it continued in France, partly in education. It also spread to the British Isles and the United States. The motto, *ignoti et quasi occulti in hoc mundo,* was characteristic of the founder: he stressed humility and the hidden life.[47]

Almost coincident with the Society of Mary and in its name easily confused with it was another Society of Mary. Its members were usually called the Marianists to distinguish them from the Marists, a designation reserved for the slightly older body. This second Society of Mary was founded in 1817 in Bordeaux by Guillaume Joseph Chaminade (1761–1850). Chaminade was a priest who in spite of the perils brought by the Revolution had succeeded in carrying on his ministry in France until 1797. Then, forced to flee, for three years he was a refugee in Spain. While there he gave much thought and prayer to means of reviving the faith in France. Returning to Bordeaux in 1800, with that purpose he organized sodalities of men and women. In 1816 he gave them more permanent form in the Daughters of Mary and in 1817 in the Society of Mary. The Society of Mary was composed of priests and brothers. It devoted itself primarily to nourishing youth in the faith through schools, orphanages, and associations of youth. Not confined to France, it extended its labours to other countries in Europe and to Africa, China, Japan, Hawaii, Canada, Mexico, and the United States. When in 1903 numbers were expelled from France they went chiefly to Japan and America.[48]

The Congregation of the Holy Cross, made up of priests and brothers, had as its purpose preaching, especially in country places and in foreign missions, and the instruction of youth. Rome combined in it the Brothers of St. Joseph, founded in 1820, and the Auxiliary Priests of Le Mans, established in 1835. The first Superior was Basile Antoine Moreau, professor in Le Mans diocesan seminary. In the early years the priests were called Salvatorists and the brothers Josephites, but after 1872 the designation was simply the Fathers and Brothers of the Holy Cross. Expelled from France by a law of 1901, the members went to Canada, Bengal, and the United States. In 1914 the largest province was in the United States: there the congregation had a number of educational institutions, notably Notre Dame in Indiana.[49]

A congregation with an extraordinary history was that of the Holy Ghost and the Immaculate Heart of Mary. It was in 1707 that the Society of the Holy Ghost was begun in Paris by a Breton of noble birth, a brilliant lawyer recently

[47] Heimbucher, *op. cit.,* Vol. III, pp. 339–342; *The Catholic Encyclopedia,* Vol. IX, pp. 750–752.
[48] Heimbucher, *op. cit.,* Vol. III, pp. 357, 358; *The Catholic Encyclopedia,* Vol. IX, p. 752.
[49] *The Catholic Encyclopedia,* Vol. VII, pp. 403–405.

become priest. The founder wished to serve poverty-stricken students and to recruit them for the priesthood. His purpose was missions among the most abandoned souls in Christian and pagan countries. In time the Society had missions in the French colonies, India, and China. Then came the French Revolution and from it the Society emerged with only one survivor. In the revival of faith which followed the Revolution a young Jew, after his conversion known as Francis Maria Paul Libermann, the son of a rabbi, was baptized. He had been brought to that step while trying to win back to Judaism a brother who had become a Christian. In spite of the handicap of epilepsy he prepared for the priesthood and was ordained. He was gripped by the dream of undertaking missions to the Negroes, both in the New World and in Africa, and from it grew the Congregation of the Immaculate Heart of Mary. At the instance of the Holy See the new congregation was grafted onto the older one (1848) and Libermann became the first Superior General. The united congregation centred its efforts on the older French colonies and Africa. It also had establishments in the West Indies and South America and conducted seminaries in Europe and the United States. The death toll in tropical Africa was heavy: by 1914 about seven hundred of the members had succumbed to disease in their inclement fields.[50]

What was officially the Pious Society of Missions (*Pia Societas Missionum*) was founded in 1835 in Rome by Vincenzo Maria Pallotti (1795–1850). Its members were, accordingly, often known as the Pallottini Fathers. Pallotti, an Italian of noble birth, a secular priest, had the prospect of becoming a distinguished theologian. Instead of pursuing an academic and scholarly career, he gave himself to the work of a pastor—preaching, hearing confessions, and devoting himself in a highly sacrificial manner to the personal service of the poor. It was natural that he should seek to expand and perpetuate his mission through a congregation. The Pallottini were made up of priests, lay brothers, and sisters. Associated with them were clergy and laity who assisted by their prayers and labours. Their purpose was to preserve the faith among Catholics, especially emigrants, and to propagate the faith among Protestants and non-Christians. To this end they sought to cultivate their own holiness of life, to preach, to administer the sacraments, to instruct youth in the catechism, to conduct missions, and to hold retreats. Their initial field was Italy, where they endeavoured to counteract de-Christianizing forces. They spread to other countries in Europe and to Africa, North and South America, and Australia.[51]

[50] Heimbucher, *op. cit.*, Vol. III, pp. 477–484; *The Catholic Encyclopedia*, Vol. III, pp. 416, 417; Heinrich Döring, *Vom Juden zum Ordenstifter. Der ehrw. P. Libermann und die Gründung der afrikanischen Mission in 19 Jahrhundert* (Neuss, Missionshaus Knechtsteden, 2nd ed., 1930, pp. xv, 343), *passim.*

[51] Heimbucher, *op. cit.*, Vol. III, pp. 484–487; *The Catholic Encyclopedia*, Vol. XI, p. 429, Vol. XII, p. 107.

The Assumptionists, of the Congregation of the Augustinians of the Assumption (namely, of the Virgin Mary), were begun in Southern France, in Nimes, in 1844, and received Papal approval twenty years later. They had schools, organized pilgrimages, and emphasized especially the preparation and distribution of literature. They spread to Bulgaria, Greece, Constantinople, Asia Minor, and Jerusalem.[52]

The Missionaries of the Sacred Heart of Jesus were founded in 1854 in Issoudun in the Archdiocese of Bourges in France by a priest, Jules Chevalier. They were designed to perpetuate the devotion to the Heart of Jesus: the immediate impetus was the proclamation of the immaculate conception. The members were secular priests and were to further the objective of the congregation by the education of the young and by missions among Christians and non-Christians. They spread to several European countries, North and South America, and Australia, and were especially noted for their achievements in Micronesia and Melanesia.[53]

One of the most remarkable chapters in the history of the Roman Catholic Church in the nineteenth century was the rise and spectacular spread of the Society of St. Francis de Sales, or, as they were appropriately known, the Salesians of Don Bosco. John Bosco (Giovanni Melchior Bosco, 1815–1888) was born in very humble circumstances in North Italy. Left fatherless at the age of two, he knew extreme poverty. Aided by an indomitable mother and a discerning priest, he began an education which carried him through the seminary. Ordained priest, he gave himself to the street waifs in the ancient city of Turin, then burgeoning under the Industrial Revolution into a leading manufacturing centre and a centre of anti-clericalism. He gathered them about him, taught them the catechism, played with them, and heard their confessions in the open air in "festive oratories." To him lads were to be made over into worthy men, not through harsh punishments, but by love and trust. He developed methods of education for his boys, trained older pupils to instruct the younger, and recruited some of the abler for the priesthood. To give wider extension to his methods, in 1859 he began the Society of St. Francis de Sales, based on rules first framed in 1857 and named for the famous Bishop of Geneva of the sixteenth and seventeenth centuries who had sought to awaken and develop in others love for God and men. Here was a striking instance in which within the Roman Catholic Church the Christian faith was inspiring men and women (for there was an associated organization of sisters, the Congregation of Daughters of Mary Help of Christians) to rise to the challenge brought by the industrial and social aspects of the revolution.

The Society of St. Francis de Sales was not the only one of its kind. In their

[52] Heimbucher, *op. cit.*, Vol. III, pp. 343–345.
[53] *Ibid.*, pp. 488–491; *The Catholic Encyclopedia*, Vol. XIII, p. 306.

appropriate places we will note others by Roman Catholics. We shall see, too, the fashion in which Protestants were responding to the challenge. Bosco was an older contemporary of William Booth, who was creating the Salvation Army, and of George Williams, founder of the Young Men's Christian Association, and a younger contemporary of John Frederick Denison Maurice, who, like Booth and Williams, was labouring indefatigably in London to help those upon whom the Industrial Revolution and its attendant social changes bore heavily. So, too, a slightly older contemporary, Johann Hinrich Wichern, out of a Pietist background, was instituting the Inner Mission in Germany, at the outset to aid the underprivileged and delinquent children who were the victims of the rapidly growing commercial city of Hamburg.

The Salesians of Don Bosco expanded rapidly. Bosco lived to see about 250 houses of the Society serving approximately 130,000 children. From the schools which were maintained nearly 6,000 priests had gone forth. Of them some 1,200 had remained in the Society. Giuseppe Allamano (1851–1926), trained personally by Bosco, founded in 1901 a congregation, the Missionaries of the Consolation, and in 1910 the Missionary Sisters of the Consolation. After the death of Bosco the Society continued to grow. By the year 1914 it had establishments in all five continents. It conducted Sunday Schools, elementary schools, evening schools, hospices, orphanages, agricultural schools, schools in the handicrafts, normal schools to prepare teachers, and theological seminaries.[54]

Typical of the response of Roman Catholics to the geographic expansion of the Occident which was a phase of the revolution was the Congregation of the Immaculate Heart of Mary. It was begun in 1863 in Belgium, prospering under independence and rapidly growing industrialization. Its founder was Theophile Verbist. Since its headquarters were at Scheutveld, a suburb of Brussels, it often went by the name of Scheut. The Congregation's first field was Inner Mongolia, a region recently made accessible by the treaties of 1858 between the Western powers and China. Verbist himself went with the initial contingent: before the enterprise was firmly established death had taken him. But the Congregation continued and eventually had missions not only in Inner Mongolia but also in the Belgian Congo, the Philippines, and Celebes.[55]

In 1866 Herbert Vaughan, later head of the English hierarchy and Cardinal, founded a missionary college. Before many years the institution was placed at Mill Hill, on the outskirts of London. Recruits were chiefly from Holland. By

[54] François Veuillot, *Saint Jean Bosco et les Salésiens* (Paris, Éditions "Alsatia," 1943, pp. 227); Heimbucher, *op. cit.,* Vol. III, pp. 491–498; *The Catholic Encyclopedia,* Vol. II, pp. 689–691, Vol. XIII, pp. 398, 399. On Allamano see Lorenzo Sales, *La Dottrina Spirituale del Servo di Dio Can. Giuseppe Allamano, Fondatore dei Missionari e delle Missionarie della Consolata* (Turin, Missioni Consolato, 2 vols., 1949), especially Vol. I, pp. v–vii.

[55] Joseph Rutten, *Les Missionnaires de Scheut et leur Fondateur* (Louvain, Éditions de l'Aucam, 1930, pp. 228), *passim.*

1914 missions had been undertaken in India, New Zealand, Borneo, Africa, and the Philippines.[56]

We have already met Charles Martial Allemand Lavigerie. Primate of the renewed Roman Catholic Church in North Africa, he dreamed of making that foothold a coign of advantage for the evangelization of all the vast continent. Accordingly, in 1868 he founded the Society of the Missionaries of Our Lady of the Missions of Africa (*Societas Missionariorum ab Africa*). Because of their garb, an adaptation of the Arab costume of North Africa, its members were known as the White Fathers. They were active not only in North Africa, but also in more than one section of Africa south of the Sahara.[57]

In spite of the storm of the *Kulturkampf*, then acute, in 1875 the Society of the Divine Word was begun by Arnold Janssen. Its purpose was to provide a distinctly German organization for participation in the missions of the Roman Catholic Church. Because of the untoward conditions in Germany, headquarters were placed in Holland, at Steyl, not far from the border. The first mission was in China, but the Society expanded to other countries.[58]

The Salvatorians, the usual designation of members of the Society of the Divine Saviour, were founded in Rome in 1881 by John Baptist Jordan. They were early assigned territory in Assam and spread to several European countries, the United States, Brazil, and Colombia.[59]

It is tempting to continue with the listing of congregations of nineteenth-century origin which were composed primarily of priests, some technically seculars and others regulars. But the limitations of space forbid. Most of them had their beginnings in France and Italy. The larger proportion were of French birth.[60]

Many organizations of brothers arose. Most of them had teaching as their purpose.[61] More of them came into being in France than in any other country. From them we will merely single out a few, and those almost at random.

In 1817 Joseph Benedict Marcellin Champagnat, one of the earliest members of that Society of Mary which had been founded by Colin the previous year, began the Little Brothers of Mary, or the Marist School Brothers. The mother house was near Lyons, in France. Champagnat set the example by devoting himself to the elementary education of children. When in 1903 anti-clerical legislation closed their institutions in France, the Brothers had about 60,000

56 Heimbucher, *op. cit.*, Vol. III, pp. 502–504.
57 S. Bouniol, editor, *The White Fathers and Their Missions* (London, Sands and Co., 1929, pp. 334), *passim*.
58 H. Fischer, *Arnold Janssen, Gründer des Steyler Missionswerke, ein Lebensbild* (Steyl, Missionsdruckerei, 1919, pp. v, 493), *passim;* Herm. auf der Heide, *Die Missionsgenossenschaft von Steyl. Ein Bilde der ersten 25 Jahre ihres Bestehens* (Steyl, Missionsdruckerei, 1900, pp. 607), *passim*.
59 Heimbucher, *op. cit.*, Vol. III, pp. 516–518; *The Catholic Encyclopedia*, Vol. V, p. 53.
60 See a partial list in Heimbucher, *op. cit.*, Vol. III, pp. 348–356.
61 *Ibid.*, pp. 356–364, gives a list of twenty-seven.

pupils in over 500 schools. They also had four orphanages. The adversities in France did not end the Little Brothers of Mary. By 1914 they were operating schools in several European countries, Africa, the islands of the Pacific, China, Syria, Ceylon, Arabia, Canada, the United States, and seven Latin American lands. They conducted primary schools, boarding schools, academies, orphanages, and homes for working boys.[62]

Like the Little Brothers of Mary, the Brothers of the Sacred Heart began in the region of Lyons and had as their purpose Christian education. The date of founding was 1821. Although inaugurated by a priest, André Coindre, their members were laymen who took life vows and eventually had a brother as their head. When suppressed in France by the law of 1901, they numbered 1,100 members and conducted about 150 schools with approximately 25,000 pupils. They branched out into Spain, Belgium, and Canada.[63]

In 1824 a priest, Jean Marie Robert de Lamennais, brother of the more famous Lamennais whom we have again and again met, founded the Brothers of Christian Instruction, also called the Little Brothers, the School Brothers of Ploermel, and the School Brothers of Brittany. As early as 1817 Lamennais had begun gathering youths in a centre in Brittany to help pastors in their schools. A year earlier another priest had been assembling a few teachers in a pilgrimage centre. In 1819 the two groups merged. In 1824 a novitiate was opened in a former Ursuline monastery at Ploermel. The Brothers multiplied rapidly in France and when legislation ended their work in that country they had 2,550 members teaching in 352 schools. After their expulsion from France they established headquarters in England.[64]

The Brothers of Christian Instruction, founded in 1845 with its mother house in Alsace, confined its activities chiefly to that region. The Brothers of St. Vincent de Paul were started in the same year in Paris. The latter congregation had in it both priests and laity. It spread through France and to Belgium, England, and America. It conducted orphanages, homes for boys, and schools and hostels for young workingmen and journeymen.[65]

Congregations of women especially multiplied. Here, too, we must take the space to mention only a few of the more prominent.

Even during the Napoleonic era, before 1815 and after the most destructive wave of the Revolution had passed, numbers of congregations of women came into being. Among them were the Ladies of the Sacred Heart, founded in Paris in 1800 by Madeleine Sophia Barat (1779–1865), which, in spite of hostile measures which later in the nineteenth century drove them out of France and

[62] *Ibid.*, p. 342; *The Catholic Encyclopedia*, Vol. IX, p. 749.
[63] *The Catholic Encyclopedia*, Vol. XIII, p. 305.
[64] Heimbucher, *op. cit.*, Vol. III, p. 359.
[65] *Ibid.*, pp. 362, 363.

Germany, spread to numbers of countries in Europe and the Americas and to Egypt and Australia. The rules of the congregation were based on those of the Society of Jesus.[66] In 1802 the Sisters of Mercy of the Christian Schools were begun in Cherbourg.[67] The Sisters of Notre Dame of Namur were inaugurated in 1803 in the diocese of Amiens by Julie Billiart, a devout woman who had been cured through prayer from a long invalidism. The headquarters were eventually moved to Namur. The purpose of the congregation was the salvation of poor children and the education of the underprivileged.[68] Associated with the name of Cluny, famous in monastic annals, were the Sisters of Joseph of Cluny, begun in 1807 to give spiritual and physical aid to members of the lower classes who had suffered from the Revolution.[69] That same year saw the inauguration in Rome of the Sisters of the Perpetual Adoration. "Enclosed" nuns, they devoted themselves to unceasing prayer before the Blessed Sacrament. Interrupted by the French occupation of Rome in 1808, they were renewed in 1814 and later spread to several cities in Italy and to other countries.[70] The year 1807 witnessed the founding of the Sisters of the Childhood of Jesus and Mary in Metz. Their chief occupation was teaching, in both elementary and higher schools.[71] At least three other congregations of women arose between 1807 and 1815. One of them was for the care of children made orphans by the Revolution.[72]

After the downfall of Napoleon the number of women's congregations mounted. Thus in 1828 the Sisters of Our Lady of Charity of the Good Shepherd were refounded. French, they dated from 1692, and had been victims of the Revolution. Renewed, they multiplied very rapidly. By 1906 they had 248 houses, of which 116 were in Europe. They gave themselves especially to the reclamation of fallen women and the care of delinquent girls and abandoned infants. In non-Christian lands they also conducted elementary schools.[73] The Little Sisters of the Poor, begun in Brittany, had as their objective the care of the aged indigent. They spread widely in Europe, Asia, Africa, Australia, the United States, and South America.[74] The Grey Sisters of St. Elizabeth had their mother house in Breslau, founded in 1842. Their purpose was ministry to the sick, but they also conducted orphanages, homes for girls and the poor,

[66] Baunard, *Histoire de Madame Barat, Fondatrice de la Société du Sacre Cœur de Jésus* (Paris, Librairie Poussielgue Frères, 2 vols., 1826), *passim;* Heimbucher, *op. cit.,* Vol. III, pp. 375–377.

[67] Heimbucher, *op. cit.,* Vol. III, p. 379.

[68] Frances De Chantal, *Julie Billiart and Her Institute* (London, Longmans, Green & Co., 1938, pp. x, 280), *passim; The Catholic Encyclopedia,* Vol. VIII, p. 559.

[69] Heimbucher, *op. cit.,* Vol. III, p. 382.

[70] *Ibid.,* pp. 380, 381.

[71] *Ibid.,* pp. 381, 382.

[72] *Ibid.,* pp. 383, 384.

[73] *Ibid.,* pp. 384–386.

[74] Baunard, *Ernest Leliévre et les Foundations des Petites Sœurs des Pauvres, 1826–1889* (Paris, Librairie Vᵛᵉ Ch. Poussielgue, 2nd ed., 1905, pp. xv, 496), *passim;* Heimbucher, *op. cit.,* Vol. III, pp. 388, 389.

hospices for labourers, schools in industrial arts and domestic science, and elementary schools, and in war time nursed sick and wounded soldiers.[75] In 1843 two converts from Judaism, Maria Theodore and Maria Alphonse Ratisbonne, began the Sisters of Our Lady of Zion. In Jerusalem the Sisters worked and prayed for the conversion of Jews and in other lands had orphanages, schools, and pensions. They also concerned themselves with seeking conversions from Islam and the Eastern Churches.[76] Out of the Religieuses de Marie Réparatrice, founded in 1855 in Paris, came the largest community of missionary sisters, the Franciscan Missionaries of Mary. They were initiated by Helene Marie Philippine de Chappotin, better known as Mary of the Passion. Going to India under the older body, she broke with it and founded a new congregation.[77] The year 1855 was also that of the beginning, likewise in France, of the Institute of the Sisters of the Holy Humility of Mary. The purpose was the education of youth in rural districts and small towns and the care of the sick and orphans. When for conscience' sake its founder, John Joseph Begel, a priest, opposed the position which Napoleon III was taking towards the Church, the Institute was refused permission to open schools. It thereupon discovered a field in the United States.[78] The Missionary Sisters of the Sacred Heart of Jesus, who dated their beginning from 1880, sought to spread devotion to the Sacred Heart of Jesus and to visit prisoners, conduct orphanages, and care for the sick and aged. They spread in Europe and America.[79]

It was in England in 1877 that the Sisters of the Little Company of Mary came into being. Designed to honour the maternal heart of Mary, especially in the mystery of Calvary, they regarded as their special assignment care for the sick and dying and engaged in continuous prayer for the latter. With them was affiliated an assocation of women who, while living in their own homes, shared in the prayers and good work of the Sisters. The Sisters extended their service to Ireland, Italy, Malta, the United States, Australia, and South Africa.[80] These are examples of what a fuller coverage would disclose of the character and purpose of the many congregations of women which arose in Europe in the nineteenth century.

As we are to see, Protestantism also displayed multiplying women's organizations. They did not exactly parallel in purpose or programme those in the Roman Catholic Church. But through deaconesses they were performing some of the functions which engaged Catholic sisters.

[75] Heimbucher, *op. cit.*, Vol. III, pp. 389–391.
[76] Élie Marie, *Histoire des Instituts Religieux et Missionnaires* (Paris, Lethielleux, 1930, pp. xii, 343), pp. 309–313.
[77] Dominic Davas, *Mother Mary of the Passion, Foundress of the Franciscan Missionaries of Mary (1839–1904)* (London, Longmans, Green & Co., pp. 102), *passim.*
[78] *The Catholic Encyclopedia*, Vol. VII, p. 418.
[79] *Ibid.*, Vol. XIII, p. 305.
[80] *Ibid.*, Vol. XIV, p. 29.

Within the Roman Catholic Church were many other kinds of organizations. Several were of patterns which ante-dated the nineteenth century. But in the nineteenth century within these patterns new organizations multiplied.

One pattern was what was technically known as Pious Associations, sometimes also as Pious Works, Pious Unions, Pious Leagues, and Pious Societies. Instituted for works of piety and charity and approved by ecclesiastical authority, they had simple rules and were without elaborate rituals. Outstanding examples of nineteenth-century origin were the Society of St. Vincent de Paul, the Society for the Propagation of the Faith, the Association of the Holy Childhood, and the Apostleship of Prayer.[81] The Pious Association of Germany, founded in 1848 by a canon of the Cathedral of Mainz, sought to organize the Catholics of the country in defence of their religious freedom and civil rights. In Germany Pious Associations to nourish the religious life of students were greatly stimulated by the *Kulturkampf*. The Pious Association of Switzerland, founded in 1855 by a member of the nobility, endeavoured to develop and centralize Catholic life in that country. In 1899 its name was changed to the Swiss Catholic Association. In Austria a Pious Association promoted the Catholic press.[82]

The Society of St. Vincent de Paul was founded in Paris in May, 1833, by Antoine Frédéric Ozanam (1813–1853). Lawyer, author, professor in the Sorbonne, Ozanam wished to refute the assertions of social radicals of the day that Christianity was too nearly moribund to give rise to such efforts to relieve and remedy human suffering as those which it had fathered in earlier centuries. Named for the great Frenchman of the seventeenth century who had been noted for his varied ministry to the unfortunate, the Society enlisted laymen for personal service to the poor, the sick, and the unemployed without distinction of race or creed. Although members of the clergy were not normally members, they were welcomed. Laymen in all walks of life were enrolled, some as active members and others as subscribing and honorary members. Organized by groups or "conferences" by parishes and dioceses, they served without financial remuneration. Among their many undertakings were convalescent homes, day nurseries, the care of homeless boys, the custody of paroled prisoners, the maintenance of chaplains in public institutions, a ministry to immigrants, and fresh air camps. They spread widely in and outside Europe.[83]

The Society for the Propagation of the Faith was without exact precedent and was an example of a vitality within the nineteenth-century Roman Catholic Church which stimulated the emergence of fresh kinds of organizations. Here-

[81] *Ibid.*, Vol. II, p. 5.

[82] *Ibid.*, Vol. XII, p. 139.

[83] Albert Paul Schimberg, *The Great Friend Frederick Ozanam* (Milwaukee, The Bruce Publishing Co., 1916, pp. 344), *passim;* Duroselle, *Les Débuts du Catholicisme Social en France (1822–1870)*, pp. 154 ff.

tofore Roman Catholic foreign missions had depended chiefly either upon subventions from governments or on the resources of individual orders and congregations. Here was an attempt to enlist every Catholic in the active undergirding of the world-wide effort to win all non-Christians.

The Society for the Propagation of the Faith was begun in 1822 in Lyons, one of the major industrial centres of France. Its chief creator was Pauline-Marie Jaricot (1799–1862). From a well-to-do family, Mlle. Jaricot seems to have owed her conversion to contact with Colin, founder of the Marists. She devoted herself to the poor in the industrial population. The Society was designed to be of such a nature that those with the lowest incomes as well as the prosperous could share. Its members were to pray daily for missions and to contribute one centime a week for missions. The Society was not itself to send out missionaries, but the sums which it raised were to be distributed among organizations which were doing so. Although for several decades more than half the money raised was from France, the organization spread to other lands and in 1922 its headquarters were moved to Rome.[84]

The Association of the Holy Childhood, also of French origin and long with French leadership, seems to have sprung partly from contact with Mlle. Jaricot. Its purpose was to enlist the gifts of Christian children on behalf of non-Christian children outside Christendom. Its first council was held in 1843.[85]

The Leopoldinen-Stiftung, organized in 1829 and appealing chiefly to an Austrian constituency,[86] and the Ludwig-Missionsverein, with a preliminary organization in 1829 and formally founded in 1838, to stimulate giving in Bavaria, had purposes similar to those of the Society for the Propagation of the Faith.[87]

The organizations which sought to enlist the rank and file of Roman Catholics in the support of foreign missions were akin to ones which were emerging in Protestantism. Both branches of Christianity were displaying a mounting conviction and loyalty among the masses of their adherents which, in the face of threats posed by the revolutionary age, were rising to the opportunities in other parts of the world opened by that expansion of Europe which was a phase of the revolution.

[84] Pourrat, *La Spiritualité Chrétienne*, Vol. IV, p. 592; Edward John Hickey, *The Society for the Propagation of the Faith. Its Foundation, Organization and Success* (Washington, The Catholic University of America, 1922, pp. x, 196); M. J. Maurin, *Vie Nouvelle de Pauline-Marie Jaricot, Fondatrice de la Propagation de la Foi et du Rosaire-Vivant* (Brussels and Paris, Alfred Vromant et Cie, 1892, pp. xxii, 568); Burton, *Difficult Star. The Life of Pauline Jaricot, passim;* Theodore Roemer, *Ten Decades of Alms* (St. Louis, B. Herder Book Co., 1942, pp. vii, 322), pp. 15 ff.

[85] Friedrich Schwager, *Die katholische Heidenmission der grossen Vergangenheit* (Steyl, Missionsdruckerei, 1907, pp. 446), p. 37; Paul Lesourd, editor, *L'Année Missionaire 1931* (Paris, Desclée de Brouwer et Cie, pp. 667), pp. 305–309.

[86] Hickey, *op. cit.*, pp. 40–42; Roemer, *op. cit.*, pp. 32 ff.

[87] Roemer, *op. cit.*, pp. 47 ff.; Roemer, *The Ludwig-Missionsverein and the Church in the United States (1838–1918)* (Washington, The Catholic University of America, 1933, pp. xii, 161), pp. 42, 43.

The Apostleship of Prayer, or a League of Prayer in Union with the Heart of Jesus, was founded in Vale, France, in 1844, by Francis X. Gautrelet and owed its widespread popularity to a Jesuit, Henri Ramière, who in 1861 adapted it to parishes and various Catholic institutions and made it known through his book, *The Apostleship of Prayer,* translated into many languages. Statutes were given it by Pius IX in 1879 and, in a revised form, in 1896 by Leo XIII. Its object was to promote the practice of prayer for the mutual intentions of its members in union with the intercession of Christ in heaven. Its members were to make a daily offering of prayers, good works, and sufferings, daily to recite a decade of beads for the special intentions recommended each month by the Pope, and to receive Communion monthly or weekly on assigned days with the motive of reparation. The Moderator General of the Apostleship was the General of the Society of Jesus, who usually acted through a deputy. About 1910 the Apostleship was said to have about 62,500 centres in many countries and about 25,000,000 members.[88]

Another pattern of organizations was confraternities or sodalities, voluntary associations of Catholics established and guided by ecclesiastical authority for the promotion of works of charity or piety. They were of early origin and after the sixteenth century their numbers rapidly multiplied.[89]

ADAPTATIONS TO THE REVOLUTIONARY AGE

Not as strictly in the religious realm as the orders, congregations, and other organizations which we have thus far named were Catholic labour unions. Like the guilds of the Middle Ages, they had religious features and were evidence of adaptability in the Roman Catholic Church to the changing economic scene. They were more under ecclesiastical control than the guilds had been.[90] In this they were another indication of the tightening of the administrative structure of the Roman Catholic Church. Mention of a few will give some indication of their character.

In the 1840's a priest, Adolph Kolping (1813–1865), who had struggled up through dire poverty to obtain the education requisite for ordination, began organizing the *Gesellenverein.* The first unit was at Elberfeld, in a centre of rapidly mounting industrialization. He later established his headquarters in Cologne, as a convenient point to reach the major industrial districts of Germany. From there he travelled extensively through Germany, Austria, Hungary, and Switzerland, forming other units. By 1901 they totalled about 1,086

---

[88] *The Catholic Encyclopedia,* Vol. I, p. 633.

[89] *Ibid.,* Vol. IV, p. 223.

[90] For examples, see *ibid.,* pp. 243, 248; Gaston de Marcieu, *Les Syndicats Catholiques du Commerce et de l'Industrie* (Paris, La Vie Universitaire, c. 1922, pp. 160); Paul Ardoin, *Le Syndicalisme Ouvrier Chrétien en Provence 1884–1935* (Marseille, La Société du "Petit Marseille," 1936, pp. 175).

with a membership of approximately 600,000. They were made up of young journeymen and master workmen. They stressed the moral, mental, and physical improvement of their members. The discussion of political issues was forbidden. Each unit or union was under the direction of a priest appointed by a bishop. By 1901 about 360 of the unions had their own houses.[91]

Also in the 1840's, in the midst of the social and political ferment which led to the explosion of 1848, a national assembly of Roman Catholics, the *Katholikentag,* arose in Germany as an outgrowth of the Pious Associations. Its first meeting was in Mainz in 1848, the year which witnessed the effort of the liberals to unite Germany through the Frankfurt Assembly. The *Katholikentag.* met regularly, eventually annually. It concerned itself not only with the Pious Associations but also with all other German Catholic societies. In time it became a general assembly of German Catholics. More and more it gave attention to social questions.[92] Similar assemblies were convened for Swiss Catholics and for Belgian Catholics.[93]

The emphasis of the German assemblies upon social questions was stimulated by the formation, not far from 1890, of the People's Union (*Volksverein*) of Catholic Germany. In connexion with its meetings gatherings of Catholic workmen were held. By the year 1914 from 25,000 to 40,000 workmen were said to be in attendance, a larger number, it was claimed, than at any other gathering of labourers in Europe. The aims were limited to social work of a practical character.[94]

Germany also had Christian Trade Unions and Christian Farmers' Unions.[95] The majority of Catholic labourers were in unions whose members were not all of one religious affiliation. Efforts were made to draw Catholic workmen into distinctly Catholic unions, and a United Catholic Workingmen's Union was organized with headquarters in Berlin. In 1899 a Catholic Teachers' Union was founded in Germany.[96]

A leader in furthering organizations of German workmen and legislation on behalf of labour was Wilhelm Emmanuel von Ketteler, Bishop of Mainz. Leo XIII declared that he was his predecessor in the policy outlined in *Rerum novarum.*[97] We are to hear more of him.

Of a somewhat different character, but also for the purpose of meeting the challenge of the age, was the Society of St. Charles Borromeo. Founded in

[91] Schnabel, *Deutsche Geschichte in neunzehnten Jahrhundert,* Vol. IV, pp. 208, 209; Vigener, *Ketteler,* p. 420; *The Catholic Encyclopedia,* Vol. VIII, p. 630.

[92] Vigener, *op. cit.,* pp. 101 ff., 436, 475, 734.

[93] *The Catholic Encyclopedia,* Vol. IV, p. 242.

[94] *Ibid.,* p. 244.

[95] *Ibid.*

[96] *Ibid.,* p. 248.

[97] Vigener, *op. cit.,* pp. 417 ff.; Aubert, *Le Pontificat de Pie IX,* p. 491.

1845, it had as its objective the provision and circulation of literature which would offset sceptical and heretical writings. It enrolled tens of thousands of members in scores of societies and hundreds of branches. To each member it sent one or more books a year. It maintained free reading rooms, supported libraries, and aided workingmen's libraries.[98]

As was to be expected from the number of new congregations which emerged in that country, many fresh movements arose in France to meet the· situation brought by the revolutionary age.

In 1844 Ledreuille, a priest, organized an agency to obtain employment for members of various occupations and professions.[99]

In 1871 Comte Albert de Mun, a noted orator, began the *Cercles Catholiques d'Ouvriers*. Through them he sought to counteract the secularizing trends of the day by organizing the working classes on strictly Catholic patterns. He dreamed of reviving the guild system of the Middle Ages. *Cercles* were formed in many parts of France and an elaborate national structure was set up. In taking this step, the founder had been stimulated by contacts with Ketteler. The way had been prepared under the Second Empire by a priest, Maurice Maignen, who had organized a labour union. The example of Kolping was important. Mun was aided by another member of the old nobility, the Marquis René de La Tour du Pin, who provided much of the theory, and Leon Harmel, a man of action from a family of manufacturers who had come to feel a responsibility for his employees. Since they were under lay direction, the *Cercles* were distrusted by many of the clergy. They were also held suspect by numbers of labourers as controlled by conservatives. Yet through their leaders important legislation was enacted to better the lot of the workers.[100]

Both Mun and La Tour du Pin were influenced by Pierre Guillaume Frédéric Le Play (1806–1882). Learned, widely travelled, Le Play studied working families. Although not fully appreciative of the Church, he believed profoundly in God and Christ and rejected as false the basic assumption of eighteenth-century rationalism and of much of nineteenth-century humanism—the original goodness of man.[101]

Many other organizations and movements emerged in France from Catholic initiative for bettering the lot of the workers. Thus, at the instance of Harmel

[98] Wilhelm Spael, *Das Buch im Geisteskampf. 100 Jahre Borromäusverein* (Bonn, Verlag des Borromäus-Vereins, 1950, pp. 403), *passim*.

[99] Duroselle, *Les Débuts du Catholicisme Social en France*, pp. 272–277.

[100] Moon, *The Labour Problem and the Social Catholic Movement in France*, pp. 177 ff.; Aubert, *op. cit.*, pp. 494, 495; Danzette, *Histoire Religieuse de la France Contemporaine*, Vol. II, pp. 185 ff.; Brugerette, *Le Prêtre Français et la Société Contemporaine*, Vol. II, pp. 15–19, 390, Vol. III, p. 109; Duroselle, *op. cit.*, pp. 586 ff.; Rollet, *l'Action Sociale des Catholiques en France (1871–1901)*, pp. 13 ff., 223 ff.; Miriam Lynch, *The Organized Social Apostolate of Albert de Mun* (Washington, The Catholic University of America Press, 1952, pp. lx, 234), *passim*.

[101] *The Catholic Encyclopedia*, Vol. XII, pp. 162–164.

and with the approval of Leo XIII, a number of study groups arose which, correlated through a federation, held their first national congress in Rheims in 1893. They sought to make widely known and apply the principles of *Rerum novarum*.[102] A priest, Boyreau, organized an association of labourers to co-operate in production. It had a school of apprentices in which technical instruction was combined with instruction in religion.[103] In connexion with many parishes rural banks were formed which through farmers' unions aided in the purchase of needed implements and machinery.[104] About 1892, inspired by the example of the *Volksverein* of Germany, a kind of peripatetic university was developed in the form of Social Weeks (*Semaines Sociales*) which in village after village held annual conferences on social problems. After the separation of Church and state they were given special impetus as a means of offsetting the secularization of the nation.[105]

It was characteristic of the new age that French Catholics utilized the press to discuss and spread their convictions. Numbers of periodicals were created for that purpose.[106]

As time passed, still other organizations were brought into being in France to counter de-Christianization. Thus in 1886 the indefatigable Albert de Mun founded the Association of French Catholic Youth (*l'Association Catholique de la Jeunesse Française*). It sought to strengthen French Catholic youth in the faith and to reorganize French society on a Christian basis. Eventually it enrolled several scores of thousands and held national conventions.[107] About 1894 a movement called Sillon was born, largely on the initiative of Marc Sangnier. Begun as a strictly religious, even mystical fellowship, more and more it moved into the realm of action. Through its journal and study circles it endeavoured to offset the secularist education which the enemies of the Church were spreading. It attacked conservatives as the enemies of Catholicism. Predominantly a lay movement, it was accused by many of the clergy of being tainted with Modernism. Yet some bishops endorsed it. Rejecting collectivism, it supported political measures for the improvement of the conditions of labour and won the respect of many of the working class.[108] In 1910 Pius X addressed a letter to the French bishops in which he criticized Sillon for being inter-confessional and not under ecclesiastical direction. He ordered the Sillonist groups to take the name of Catholic and diocese by diocese to put themselves under the super-

---

[102] Dansette, *op. cit.*, Vol. II, p. 206; Brugerette, *op. cit.*, Vol. II, pp. 387 ff.
[103] Brugerette, *op. cit.*, Vol. III, pp. 406, 407.
[104] *Ibid.*, p. 112.
[105] *Ibid.*, pp. 98, 99.
[106] *Ibid.*, Vol. II, pp. 377 ff.
[107] *Ibid.*, Vol. III, p. 721.
[108] *Ibid.*, pp. 224–235; Dansette, *op. cit.*, Vol. II, pp. 407 ff.; Barbier, *Histoire du Catholicisme Libéral et du Catholicisme Social en France du Concile du Vatican à l'Avènement de SS. Benoît XV*, Vol. IV, pp. 371 ff.

vision of the bishops. This spelled death for the movement. Sangnier unequivocally submitted.[109]

In 1912 what was called the League of the Young Republic (*Ligue de la Jeune République*) was founded by Marc Sangnier. Through it he would defend the Christian faith, act in the field of politics and economics, and, in contrast with those Catholics who still hoped for the restoration of the Monarchy, stand for democracy and the Republic. It enlisted the enthusiastic support of the Sillonists and many young priests.[110]

Numbers of other organizations were created in France to meet various social needs. Among them was a Catholic league for the protection of young girls. We hear of several movements in which Catholics and Protestants collaborated—among them consumers' coöperatives.[111]

Partly in response to the urging of Leo XIII and Pius X and to present a common solid front to the peril brought by the separation of Church and state, in the last few years before 1914 a number of Catholic Unions were formed in France. They sought to draw together all Catholics, diocese by diocese. They owed their origin to the initiative of the bishops. However, in only about a fourth of the dioceses did the bishop succeed in creating them, and even there they did not obtain the unanimous support of all Catholics.[112]

Earlier, from 1872 to 1892, in an effort to bring into collaboration all forms of Catholic associations, annual congresses were held to which they were encouraged to send representatives.[113]

Movements such as those in Germany and France arose in other countries in Europe to meet the revolutionary age. In Austria Baron Charles von Vogelsang, from Mecklenburg, inspired by the example of Ketteler, opposed the capitalistic upper bourgeoisie and advocated organizing the professions, not in a fashion advocated by many Socialists, but after the manner of the medieval guilds.[114] Switzerland had a similar movement. In highly industrialized Belgium Charles Perin, professor of economics in Louvain, in a book which was translated into several European languages, bewailed the exploitation of the labouring classes and sought the solution in the progress of morality and the Christian spirit among both employers and employed.[115] In 1867 at Malines a federation of Catholic labour unions was formed. By 1875 over 50,000 workmen were connected with it.[116] In Italy in 1868 the *Gioventù Cattolica Italiana* was inaugurated in Bologna to band youth together for the defence of the Church under

[109] Dansette, *op. cit.*, Vol. II, pp. 426–428; Barbier, *op. cit.*, Vol. V, p. 178.
[110] Brugerette, *op. cit.*, Vol. III, p. 299.
[111] *Ibid.*, pp. 120, 121; *The Catholic Encyclopedia*, Vol. IV, p. 245.
[112] Brugerette, *op. cit.*, Vol. III, pp. 75 ff.
[113] *The Catholic Encyclopedia*, Vol. IV, p. 243.
[114] Aubert, *op. cit.*, pp. 491, 492.
[115] *Ibid.*, p. 495.
[116] *Ibid.*, p. 496; *The Catholic Encyclopedia*, Vol. IV, p. 283.

the motto "Prayer, action, sacrifice": beginning in 1876 annual national congresses were held. The Society of Catholic Interests was founded in 1870. The year 1872 saw the organization of the Society to Promote Good Works. Before long, with the approval of Pius IX, the *Federazione Piana* emerged, a national congress of Catholics for the coördination of their activities somewhat akin to what was developing in Germany and Belgium.[117]

These many efforts by Roman Catholics to meet the challenge of the Industrial Revolution and the altered economic situation were paralleled, as we are to see, by similar ones by Protestants. Nothing comparable came from the Eastern Churches.

SUMMARY

From the developments sketched so rapidly and in abbreviated form, several general characteristics and thought-provoking facts emerge.

The revival of old orders and congregations, the creation of new congregations, and the multiplication of fresh organizations, some of them of a quite novel kind, were evidence of prodigious vitality. The Roman Catholic Church, considered by many observers to be moribund, had recovered from the lassitude from which it had suffered in the latter part of the eighteenth century and was experiencing a marked renewal.

The prominence given by the new congregations to the Sacred Heart of Jesus and the immaculate conception of the Virgin Mary was an indication of major trends in the worship and devotion of Roman Catholics—trends of which we are to hear more in the next chapter.

Notable, too, was the activist emphasis of many of the new congregations. To be sure, the Trappists were renewed and some of the women's congregations were of "enclosed" nuns who gave themselves primarily to prayer. However, a majority of the new congregations, while not neglecting prayer, devoted their major energies to education and to various forms of service to the aged, the sick, the underprivileged, and the poor. They were seeking through reaching the on-coming generations to mould revolutionary Europe on Christian patterns and to exemplify Christian love among those who were most subject to the stresses of that Europe. They were also endeavouring to extend the Catholic faith throughout the world.

Characteristic was the large part played by the laity. No figures are obtainable to make possible exact comparisons with earlier periods. But a striking feature of the nineteenth-century Roman Catholic Church was the active participation of lay folk, both women and men. That was not only in the organizations of laity of which we have given examples, in lay brothers in orders and congregations, and in sisters who took the vows of the religious life, but

[117] Aubert, *op. cit.*, pp. 371, 372.

also in the third orders: their members lived in the world and not in community and pursued secular occupations. In the dedicated bodies of laity was another evidence of the trend towards a growing distinction between nominal and practising Catholics and towards the drawing of sharper lines between the partially or completely de-Christianized and the faithful. Through Catholic Action, a movement of varied expressions which in the next century assumed mounting dimensions, "the participation of the laity in the apostolate of the hierarchy" was greatly enhanced.

Here, too, were parallels in Protestantism. Much of Protestantism was intensely activistic. Because of the emphasis on the priesthood of all believers the laity had an even larger part than in the Roman Catholic Church.

One of the most arresting set of facts was in the French scene. More of the new congregations and movements were born in France than in any other country. From France more missionaries went to extend the frontiers of the faith outside Europe than from any other land. In France the Society for the Propagation of the Faith was founded, an organization which eventually collected more funds for missions than any other one Roman Catholic agency. Here sprang up the Society of St. Vincent de Paul, which enlisted in active service more laymen throughout the world than any other movement developed up to that time by the Roman Catholic Church. Yet France was the country in which the forces of the revolution seemed to bring the most marked de-Christianization.

What did this mean? Did it prove the failure of the efforts of an awakened Roman Catholic Church to win the new Europe which was being created by the revolution? Or was there something deeper? Would it find parallels in other branches of Christianity? Was it a vivid example of an antagonism between Christianity and the world? Did the Roman Catholic Church and at least some other forms of Christianity possess such vitality that attacks on them would stimulate fresh movements not only in defence but also in counter-attacks? Would the fresh movements in turn provoke more virulent attacks? Can we discern in the record the fashion in which the Gospel operates?

Whatever our answer to these questions, at least we can say that in France on the one hand obvious departure from Christianity proceeded further than in any other country in Western Europe. The large majority were still baptized and were nominally Roman Catholic, but for many the rite was merely an inherited social convention. On the other hand in no other land did the Roman Catholic Church have a loyal constituency which was so active in seeking to serve and mould the changing society, so faithful and zealous in its observance of the sacraments and in the devotional life, so creative in thought, and so earnest in seeking to perpetuate the faith and to spread it throughout the globe.

CHAPTER IX

Worship and the Devotional Life of Roman Catholics in Europe in the Nineteenth Century

How did Roman Catholics respond in worship and devotional life to the conditions brought by the revolutionary age? In the nineteenth century, vigour in activity there undoubtedly was. Was it also in worship and in the interior life? Certain generalizations seem to fit in with the picture which has been emerging in the last two chapters.

First we notice a contrast—as in other aspects of the life of the time. On the one hand were thousands who paid only a minimum attention to the sacraments and who neglected individual private devotions. They were baptized, but chiefly as a social convention; seldom if ever did they go to mass or confession or take communion; they gave little or no time to private prayer. A minority which seemed larger because it was vocal and politically aggressive was militantly anti-clerical. On the other hand were thousands who were faithful in their observance of the sacraments and in their religious duties. They were probably more numerous than in the eighteenth century. Frequent communion became more common and beginnings were seen of the Liturgical Movement, with its increased intelligent participation of the laity. The line was becoming more distinct between non-practising Catholics and practising Catholics. It had long been there—from the time when the faith had spread widely in the Roman Empire. In what were sometimes called "the ages of faith" in the high Middle Ages of Western Europe possibly as large a proportion of the population were no more genuinely committed to the Christian faith than in the nineteenth century: yet outwardly they conformed more nearly than did those of similar temper in that century. Probably the average level of intelligent faith and of morality was higher in the nineteenth-century clergy, particularly in Germany and France, where the struggle with the revolutionary forces making for de-Christianization was especially acute, even than in the thirteenth century. It was certainly higher than in the fifteenth and the fore part of the sixteenth century. As we shall see in the next volume, the contrast was paralleled in Protestant and Orthodox lands in Europe.

Next we remark what might also have been gathered from the record in the two preceding chapters: in popular piety, both among the clergy and the rank and file, devotion to the Sacred Heart of Jesus and to the Virgin Mary was mounting. It was reflected in Papal encyclicals and in the names of some of the new congregations.

As a third generalization we do well to observe that devotional classics had a wide circulation, indication that private prayer and meditation were widespread. Some of the classics were inherited from earlier days: others were fresh creations.

IMPROVEMENT IN THE CHARACTER OF THE CLERGY

Indispensable in the growth of the devotional life of the rank and file was a body of clergy who could give adequate leadership. Improvement in the character of the clergy was one of the features of the nineteenth century. It was most marked in the lands in which the revolutionary forces centred, chiefly in France, Belgium, and Germany. It was less marked in lands in Central and Southern Europe, particularly in Poland, Hungary, Spain, Portugal, and Southern Italy—areas shaken by the revolution but in which the old social, economic, and political order more nearly persisted than in the North-west. In France, Belgium, and Germany the political phases of the revolution worked greater changes in inherited ecclesiastical patterns, industrialization and its attendant alterations in the economic and social structure were more pronounced, and the innovations in thought and knowledge and in the programmes for the reorganization of mankind were more extensively developed. Under these conditions the vitality inherent in the Roman Catholic Church was released to produce a more devoted and less worldly clergy than on the eve of the French Revolution. Frequent retreats nurtured the devotional life. Here and there the clergy were organized into associations for spiritual fellowship and stimulus.[1] Yet in retrospect the criticism was made that, marked as was the increase in moral quality, spiritual earnestness and discipline, and faithfulness to parish duties among the Roman Catholic clergy in lands most affected by the revolution, the training of the clergy was not such as to enable them to meet the problems presented by the social, economic, and intellectual changes.[2]

INCREASED EMPHASIS ON THE EUCHARIST

The increased emphasis on the sacraments among the devout was especially seen in the Eucharist. The encouragement given by Pius X to frequent communion gave additional impetus to a movement which was already under way. In the second half of the century in more than one country and by many priests

---

[1] Aubert, *Le Pontificat de Pie IX,* pp. 451–454.
[2] *Ibid.,* pp. 454–456.

the faithful were being stimulated to weekly and even daily communion. For example, John Bosco urged that children be admitted to their first communion as soon as they could be taught to distinguish between common bread and Eucharistic bread—perhaps as early as seven or eight years. Pius IX recommended the perpetual adoration of the Blessed Sacrament.[3] As early as the sixteenth and seventeenth centuries congregations had been founded with perpetual adoration as their purpose. Now, in 1857 in Belgium a congregation known as the Religious of Perpetual Adoration was begun.[4] Since the fifteenth century confraternities of the Most Holy Sacrament had been known:[5] in the nineteenth century they multiplied. In the 1850's and 1860's several were created in France. Their members attended additional masses to expiate the wrath of God for those who failed to be present at mass on Sundays and holy days. We also read of a sodality, the Perpetual Adoration of Catholic Nations, founded in Rome in 1883 and conducted by the Redemptorists, and of another, the Perpetual Adoration of the Blessed Sacrament under the Protection of St. Benedict, begun in 1877.[6]

A phenomenon of the nineteenth century which took on increased proportions in the twentieth century was a series of Eucharistic Congresses, to celebrate and glorify the Eucharist. Consonant with what we have found to be true of the rise of congregations and other Roman Catholic organizations in the nineteenth century, the origin and much of the early development were in France. The first Eucharistic Congress, purely local, seems to have been in Lille in 1881. While it took place with the blessing and the leadership of the bishop, a prime mover appears to have been a layman, Philibert Vrau, a manufacturer who, reared a Catholic, after several years of scepticism in his youth was converted and, with a brother-in-law and lifelong friend, Camille Féron-Vrau, was seeking to make Lille Christian and was organizing benevolent societies and building model villages among the employees in the industries of the city.[7] The next two were in Avignon, France, in 1882, and Liège, Belgium, in 1883. The fourth, in Fribourg, Switzerland, in 1885, took on large dimensions. The fifth and sixth were in France—in Toulouse, in 1886, and Paris, in 1888. The seventh was in Antwerp, in 1890. The eighth, in Jerusalem, in 1893, had as an incidental object winning the allegiance to Rome of members of the Eastern Churches. That in London, in 1908, was a foreshadowing of the ones of mammoth dimensions after World War I. As time passed the Eucharistic Congresses helped to stimulate local Eucharistic leagues.[8]

[3] *Ibid.*, pp. 463, 464; Cayré, *Patrologie et Histoire de la Théologie*, Vol. III, p. 302.
[4] *The Catholic Encyclopedia*, Vol. XI, pp. 697, 698.
[5] *Ibid.*, Vol. XIV, p. 121.
[6] *Ibid.*, p. 122.
[7] *Ibid.*, Vol. XV, p. 515.
[8] *Ibid.*, Vol. V, pp. 592–594.

BEGINNINGS OF THE LITURGICAL MOVEMENT

The nineteenth century witnessed the inception of the Liturgical Movement which in the following century was to swell to major proportions and was to enlist an increasing proportion of the rank and file of the laity in a more intelligent participation in the central rite of the Church. For years not much study had been given to the liturgy: more attention had been paid to private prayer. The Jansenists had clamoured for the vernacular in the Eucharist, the distribution of missals among the laity, and simplicity, even austerity, in the service and its accoutrements. Somewhat similar efforts came out of Febronianism and the *Aufklärung*. Romanticism may have given stimulus.[9] The quickened interest which issued in the Liturgical Movement is usually said to have begun with Prosper Louis Pasqual Guéranger (1805–1875), whom we have already met as Abbot at Solesmes. In his *l'Année Liturgique* and his *Institutions Liturgiques* he aroused some in the Church in France to an appreciation of liturgical prayer. He also inaugurated the scholarly study of Gregorian music. However, he was not attempting, as was the later Liturgical Movement, to bring the liturgy to the masses.[10] By his *motu proprio* in 1903 in which he stressed the singing of the Gregorian chant by the congregation, Pius X added impetus to a trend. At the Benedictine monastery at Maria Laach research was done on the liturgy and in 1914 a liturgical week for laymen was held there. Earlier, in 1911, a similar week was conducted at Louvain, in Belgium.[11]

Guéranger aided substantially in the spread of the Roman liturgy in France. Under the influence of Gallicanism, varieties of the liturgy had flourished. As part of the trend towards the centralization of the Roman Catholic Church under the Papacy, they were suppressed: the Roman rite prevailed.[12] Whether this aided or hampered the Liturgical Movement could be debated.

MUSIC AND PUBLIC WORSHIP

Associated with the liturgy and public worship was music. It was not only Guéranger and Pius X who were responsible for the increasing use of the Gregorian. Not far from the middle of the century it was revived here and there in France, Belgium, and Germany. Pius IX recommended an edition, prepared at the direction of the Congregation of Rites and issued in the 1870's, the wide use of which was later said to have delayed the determination of texts which historically were more nearly correct. Under Pius X better texts were

---

[9] Koenker, *The Liturgical Renaissance in the Roman Catholic Church*, pp. 22–31.

[10] *Ibid.*, pp. 10, 11; Aubert, *op. cit.*, pp. 472, 473; Cayré, *op. cit.*, Vol. III, p. 311; Jungmann, *Missarum Sollemnia*, Vol. I, p. 210; Prosper Guéranger, *Institutions Liturgiques* (Paris, Société Générale de Librairie Catholique, 4 vols., 1878–1885); Ambroise Ledru, *Dom Guéranger, Abbé de Solesmes, et Mgr. Bouvier, Évèque du Mans* (Paris, Honoré Champion, 1911, pp. vii, 383).

[11] Koenker, *op. cit.*, pp. 12, 13, 154; Jungmann, *op. cit.*, Vol. I, pp. 211–213.

[12] Koenker, *op. cit.*, p. 205; Aubert, *op. cit.*, pp. 473, 474; Cayré, *op. cit.*, Vol. III, p. 321.

issued.[13] Not much new in music was produced which seemed to the experts to be more than mediocre. Palestrina enjoyed local revivals, Bach was utilized, and Gounod (1818–1893), César Franck (1822–1890), and a few others rose above the uninspired level, but some of the compositions which attained popularity were highly emotional and resembled the love songs of the day. One, indeed, incorporated the theme of a drinking song.[14] The spread of the Gregorian was an additional phase of centralization under Rome.

Devotion to the Sacred Heart of Jesus

. As can be gathered from the names given several of the congregations and other organizations which had their inception in the nineteenth century as well as from Papal pronouncements to which we have called attention, devotion to the Sacred Heart of Jesus was increasingly stressed.

The emphasis had several sources. It was partly a continuation and revival of practices of long standing. Some of it was a reaction against the austerity of Jansenism and the cold rationalism of the Enlightenment. Much of it emanated from Italy: the growth of ultramontanism contributed to the spread of Italian practices. To some degree it was fostered by romanticism. Phases of it were promoted by the Jesuits.

Devotion to the Sacred Heart was a phase of the current concentration on Jesus—his humility in the incarnation and his sufferings on Calvary. In this the nineteenth continued what had been common among the devout in the Middle Ages and especially in the seventeenth century. Now even more compelling than in the earlier development of the cult of the Sacred Heart was the motive of making reparation for indignity done by sinners to the victim on the cross through the widespread defection and hostility among the traditionally Catholic populations of Europe. In it, too, was the aspiration to join with Paul in completing what was lacking in the sufferings of Christ and to share in the responsibility for the salvation of the world.[15]

The nineteenth century has been called the "century of the Sacred Heart." In France those who wished the restoration of the Bourbon monarchy remembered that before his execution Louis XVI had undertaken to consecrate France to the Sacred Heart. Pius IX and Leo XIII gave impetus to the trend. The latter, as we have seen, said that the supreme act of his pontificate had been the consecration of all mankind to the Sacred Heart. The former had declared "blessed" Marguerite Marie Alacoque (1647–1690), the young woman whose visions of Christ (the chief in 1675) had given great stimulus to devotion to the Sacred Heart. At the request of the French bishops Pius IX extended the

[13] Aubert, *op. cit.*, pp. 475, 476; Aigrain, *La Musique Religieuse*, pp. 81–84.

[14] Koenker, *op. cit.*, p. 154; Aubert, *op. cit.*, pp. 474, 475; Aigrain, *op. cit.*, pp. 202 ff.

[15] Aubert, *op. cit.*, pp. 464, 465; Cayré, *op. cit.*, Vol. III, p. 305.

feast of the Sacred Heart to the universal Church. Individuals, families, religious congregations, and dioceses were consecrated to the Sacred Heart. On the eve of the Vatican Council a Belgian prelate dedicated his country to the Sacred Heart. Since the vision of 1675 of Mlle. Alacoque had made much of the universal sovereignty of the Sacred Heart and the duty to labour for its recognition, not far from 1870 a French motet was composed: *Christus vincit, Christus regnat, Christus imperat*. The movement reinforced the trend towards ultramontanism and the authority of the Universal Pontiff as the vice-gerent of Christ. A French archbishop took the initiative in circulating a petition, ultimately signed by all the bishops and heads of orders of the Roman Catholic Church and more than a million of the faithful, asking Pius IX to dedicate the entire universe to the Sacred Heart. Pius IX responded by approving, in 1875 on the bi-centennial of the vision, a public recitation of a formula of consecration.[16]

DEVOTION TO THE VIRGIN MARY

Paralleling devotion to the Sacred Heart were honours to the Virgin Mary. As we have seen, the proclamation of the dogma of the immaculate conception by Pius IX in 1854 came as a climax to a rising tide of practice and demand. Both before and after that event congregations bearing the name of Mary were formed. Pilgrimages to places connected with Mary mounted.[17]

New centres of pilgrimage developed in spots associated with what were devoutly believed to be appearances of the Virgin. Some of the most famous were in France. In them as in many other aspects of Roman Catholic life in the nineteenth century the contrast was marked between widespread scepticism and anti-clericalism on the one hand and intense religious fervour on the other. Two appearances of the Virgin were reported in Paris, in 1830 and 1836. In 1846 two young Savoyard shepherds on the plateau of La Salette declared that a "beautiful lady" had been seen by them and had charged them to convey to "all her people" her concern about keeping Sunday holy, respect for the name of God, and abstinence. When miracles began to be reported on the scene of the apparition, the Bishop of Grenoble adjudged them (1851) and the appearance to have been authentic. In 1854, in spite of the doubts of the Archbishop of Lyons and some others of the clergy, his successor reaffirmed that opinion. The fame of the "holy mountain of La Salette" spread widely in the Roman Catholic world.[18] The Missionaries of La Salette, a congregation which had

---

[16] Aubert, *op. cit.*, pp. 465, 466.

[17] *Ibid.*, p. 466. On the cult of Mary, chiefly in the seventeenth and eighteenth centuries, see Clement Dillenschreiber, *La Mariologie de S. Alphonse de Liguori* (Freiburg, Studia Friburgensis, 2 vols., 1931–1934).

[18] Aubert, *op. cit.*, p. 467.

its beginnings in 1852 to care for the pilgrims who flocked to the shrine, extended their labours to several parts of the United States and Canada.[19]

Most famous of all the appearances were eighteen which were believed to have come over several months in 1858 to Bernadette Soubirous, a peasant girl of fourteen years, in a grotto near Lourdes, an ancient fortress town in the Pyrenees in the south of France. Bernadette declared that on the next to the last appearance in response to her enquiry of the Lady for her name the reply had come: "I am the immaculate conception!" Reports of the appearances created great excitement. Throngs gathered. At first both ecclesiastical and civil authorities were sceptical and the latter attempted to break up what they regarded as superstitious hysteria. Miracles of healing were reported from bathing in the stream which issued from the grotto. In 1862 the bishop, after careful investigation, authorized the faithful to believe the appearances to be authentic. Bernadette spent most of her adult life in the Institute of the Sisters of Charity of Nevers, became a full member of the congregation, and died in 1879 at the age of thirty-five. In 1933, on the Feast of the Immaculate Conception, she was formally canonized. Before her death two special churches had been erected at Lourdes. At the consecration of the second a Cardinal, five bishops, three thousand priests, and a hundred thousand of the faithful were said to have been present. Lourdes continued to be a place of pilgrimage and hundreds of cures were reported.[20] The thousands who thronged to Lourdes, some out of curiosity, many out of wistful longing for healing, and the ultimate endorsement of the highest ecclesiastical authorities gave insight into an important phase of the Roman Catholic faith of the nineteenth century. In contrast with the rampant unbelief which attended the revolution, they were evidence of a continuing kind of vitality. It was seen not only in France. Congregations of religious named for Our Lady of Lourdes sprang up, at least two of them in a country as distant from Lourdes as the United States.

OTHER EXPRESSIONS OF POPULAR DEVOTION

In something of the same category was Marie Françoise Thérèse Martin (1873-1897), better known as Sister Thérèse of the Child Jesus of the Holy Face, Thérèse of Lisieux, or the Little Flower. She was born to a father who in youth had wished to become a monk and to a mother who had desired the life of a nun. The parents were faithful in their religious observances, devoted to the care of the needy, and dedicated their children to God. Of their nine

---

[19] *The Catholic Encyclopedia,* Vol. IX, p. 9.

[20] Margaret Gray Blanton, *Bernadette of Lourdes* (London, Longmans, Green & Co., 1939, pp. xi, 265), *passim;* Don Sharkey, *After Bernadette: The Story of Modern Lourdes* (Milwaukee, The Bruce Publishing Co., 1945, pp. 166), *passim;* Franz Werfel, *The Song of Bernadette,* translated by Ludwig Lewisohn (New York, The Viking Press, 1942, pp. 575), *passim;* Michel de Saint-Pierre, *Bernadette and Lourdes,* translated from the French by Edward Fitzgerald (New York, Farrar, Straus & Young, 1954, pp. 267), *passim.* All these are in the nature of hagiographies.

children four died in infancy and the five survivors, daughters, became nuns. Thérèse, the youngest, at an early age wished to follow her older sisters, but her petition to be allowed to do so before she had reached the required years was denied by her bishop, the congregation, and Leo XIII himself, to whom she appealed in a moving audience. But when she was fifteen she gained her wish and entered a convent of the Carmelites, an order of enclosed nuns who gave themselves to prayer. This was at Lisieux, in Normandy, where her home had been. There she spent the rest of her days, dying of tuberculosis before she was twenty-five. In her autobiography, letters, and poems she expressed her love for the Child Jesus and her complete committal to the love of God. In her last illness she was said to have declared that she had never given God anything but love, and that He would so repay with love that from heaven she would do good on earth and "would let fall a shower of roses." After her death there were those in various places who were convinced that she had appeared to them. Her autobiography, translated into many languages, had an enormous circulation. Her "shower of roses" was the miracles believed to have been wrought through her and her intercession. They were of many kinds—of healing, of conversions of non-believers, of gifts of money to worthy causes, of a great draught of fishes, and of the raising of a sunken vessel. The Little Flower was also known as the Little Mother, from a playful name given her by her father in her childhood. Shrines were erected to her. High and low revered her. Cardinal Mercier of Belgium, outstanding scholar and churchman, famous for his heroism in World War I, died with her picture and her relic by his side. So widespread was her cult and so numerous the miracles attributed to her that in 1925, less than three decades after her death, she was canonized.[21]

Another nineteenth-century French Catholic who was early canonized was Jean Baptiste Marie Vianney (1786–1859), the Curé of Ars. Of rural parentage and reared to gruelling labour in the fields, he knew from early experience the hard lot of the peasant. He was religious from childhood, and that in spite of the surrounding godlessness which came with the Revolution. He early felt a vocation to the priesthood, but he had no aptitude for learning, found it almost impossible to acquire the necessary Latin, failed to pass the prerequisite examinations, and only through the leniency of his superiors in the shortage of clergy was given ordination. For a time he was curate to a priest. Then, on the death of the latter, he was transferred to Ars, a village about twenty-five miles north of Lyons. There he discovered that through the recent turmoil and anti-

[21] Thomas N. Taylor, *Saint Thérèse of Lisieux, The Little Flower of Jesus: A Revised Translation of the Definitive Carmelite Edition of Her Autobiography & Letters, together with the Story of Her Canonization, and an Account of Her Heavenly Roses* (New York, P. J. Kenedy & Sons, 1927, pp. viii, 456), *passim;* Lucie Delarue-Mardus, *Saint Therese of Lisieux,* translated by Helen Younger Chase (London, Longmans, Green & Co., 1929, pp. 134), *passim;* August Pierre Laveille, *Life of the Little Flower, St. Therese of Lisieux,* translated by M. Fitzsimmons (New York, McMullen Books, 1952, pp. xiv, 376), *passim.*

Christian measures his parishioners had lapsed into near-paganism and the young had grown up illiterate and without religious instruction. Alcoholism, blasphemy, and a kind of dancing which induced immorality were the bane of the community. He set himself by prolonged prayer accompanied by weeping, personal asceticism, short hours of sleep, fasting, self-inflicted floggings, humble service to the poor, love, and stern preaching to winning the souls of his flock. In the face of bitter persecution and calumnies he freed the village from the cabarets which sold the drink and from the corrupting dances, drew people to church—although as a preacher he was not eloquent and vigorously denounced the sins which he was convinced were condemning his hearers to hell. He suffered torments from what he believed to be personal attacks of the Devil. Gradually he prevailed. He saw to it that education was improved, both in the catechism and in the simple rudiments of secular learning. He drew orphans into an establishment which he called *The Providence,* the food for which was from the prayer of faith. The parish was transformed. The fame of the achievement spread and visitors began to stream to the village. Many came to make their confessions and to obtain spiritual counsel. There were months when he spent from sixteen to eighteen hours out of the twenty-four in the confessional. He had an uncanny capacity for discerning the inmost soul and a homely, direct wisdom in counsel. High and low, bishops, priests, and laity sought him. From 1826 to 1859 the pilgrimages continued. Again and again Vianney wished to retire to a life of solitude and prayer, but his bishop forbade it: he remained in Ars until his death. In his lifetime the most famous priest in France, he remained unspoiled by adulation. His was a simple piety which prized relics, knew no intellectual difficulties, and gave itself unstintedly to the poor and to the love of God. In 1925 he was canonized.[22]

One is reminded by both similarity and contrast of an older contemporary, the Protestant Pastor John Frederick Oberlin (1771–1824), whose parish, also in France, was in the Vosges Mountains less than three hundred miles to the north. Both wrought a spiritual and moral transformation in what at the outset was a backward, poverty-stricken, and degraded community. Both were deeply and sincerely devout and completely committed to God in selfless service to those about them. Yet Oberlin brought a material as well as a religious transformation, and his piety did not show itself in weeping, maceration, self-inflicted scourgings, and prolonged prayers, or in the veneration of relics as did that of Vianney. Nor did he give his spiritual counsel through long hours in the confessional.[23]

[22] Francis Trochu, *The Curé d'Ars: St. Jean-Marie Vianney (1786–1859),* translated by Ernest Graf (Westminster, Md., The Newman Press, 1950, pp. xxiii, 586), *passim;* John Oxenham, *A Saint in the Making: From the Valley of the Singing Blackbird to St. Peter's, Rome (The Story of the Curé d'Ars)* (London, Longmans, Green & Co., 1931, pp. xi, 208), *passim.*
[23] Beard, *The Story of John Frederic Oberlin, passim.*

The Curé of Ars was a friend of Pauline Jaricot, the foundress of the Society for the Propagation of the Faith in the neighbouring Lyons. Mlle. Jaricot had not confined her efforts to bringing that society into being. She shared in the devotion which centred in the Sacred Heart and the Virgin and sought to promote it. Even before the beginning of the movement for which she was best remembered, distressed by the trend away from Christianity, she gathered an informal circle of women, largely among the workers in the silk mills of the city, and called them *Réparatrices du Cœur de Jésus.*[24] Late in 1826 or early in 1827 she began the Association of the Living Rosary. Its purpose was to enlist prayer for the revival of faith and to distribute literature and undertake other works with this objective. The idea caught fire: by the end of 1827 scores of groups sprang up in France and before long similar ones were reported in many countries on both sides of the Atlantic and in Asia. Mlle. Jaricot was criticized in clerical circles for acting without hierarchical authorization and for assuming the direction of souls. However, she obtained Papal approval. Through the Association the use of the rosary was revived, stations of the cross were placed in many churches, and holy pictures, litanies, and pious books were distributed. Mlle. Jaricot furthered the process which led to the canonization of Philomena, a young Roman girl believed to have been martyred in the early days of the faith. In 1802 remains of Philomena had been found in a catacomb in Rome and devotion to her had been spreading in Italy. Mlle. Jaricot obtained a relic, shared a fragment of it with the Curé of Ars, and through what was held to be the intercession of Philomena in a journey to Italy made an astonishing recovery from what looked like mortal illness. In a chapel on the outskirts of Lyons she sought to institute perpetual adoration of the Blessed Sacrament. Distressed by the living conditions of the labourers in Lyons and by insurrections among them in the troubled 1830's, she endeavoured to have constructed a model village for the workmen. This, however, brought her into financial difficulties: her vision was greater than her administrative ability.[25]

Although France was a major source of movements and outstanding examples of the devotional life, other countries were not without them. Notable was Anne Catherine Emmerich (1774–1824). Of Westphalia, a region where, as we have seen, Protestant Pietism flourished in the seventeenth and eighteenth centuries, she was devoutly Roman Catholic. In the face of the vigorous opposition of her parents, she fulfilled a deep sense of vocation by entering an Augustinian convent. From childhood sensitive and profoundly religious, she early believed that she saw the Child Jesus. Repeatedly across the years she had visions and ecstasies in some of which she was convinced that she was given

[24] Burton, *Difficult Star,* pp. 57, 58.
[25] *Ibid.,* pp. 86 ff.

supernatural knowledge of events in the Old Testament and in the life of Christ and of the Virgin. Many of them came during a prolonged invalidism which followed the dissolution of her convent by Napoleon. They were written down by another and corrected by her. Translated into numbers of languages, they had an enormous circulation. She developed the stigmata, not only of the nails but also of the crown of thorns. The news spread widely, aroused controversy, and they were investigated by both ecclesiastical and civil authorities.[26]

What seems to have been another authenticated instance of the stigmata appeared in Malta in 1886. A young novice in the Society of Jesus bore not only the five wounds of Christ but also the marks on his back of the scourgings. He had previously been instantaneously cured of almost complete blindness.[27]

MORE INTELLECTUAL AND LESS SPECTACULAR DEVOTION AND MYSTICISM

To some Roman Catholics much of the devotion and the eager acceptance of the miraculous which we have described seemed over-sentimental and credulous and even to verge on superstition.[28] Among Roman Catholics there was a substantial core of less spectacular devotional life undergirded by solid thought.

In Germany a contemporary of Catherine Emmerich, Johann Joseph Görres (1776–1848), wrote as his major work *Christliche Mystik*. Born in the Catholic faith, as a journalist Görres was early caught up in the rationalism of the day. Converted in his late youth, in 1827 he became professor of ecclesiastical history at the University of Munich. An ardent and eloquent apologist, the better to confirm faith in the supernatural he delved deeply into mysticism. He defined mysticism as that through which man comes in touch with the occult forces of nature and has communication with God, the angels, or demons. He sought to disclose physical and psychological forces which might explain phenomena hitherto ascribed to the supernatural. He endeavoured to trace the line which separates the supernatural and divine from the lower and infernal. Learned in several fields, particularly in history and the natural sciences, he exerted a wide and continuing influence. Many years after his death, in 1876, the Görres Society (*Görres Gesellschaft*) was organized by Catholic scholars to continue through publications his apologetic mission.[29]

The nineteenth century witnessed a marked interest in Roman Catholic

[26] Pourrat, *Spiritualité Chrétienne*, Vol. IV, pp. 520–526; *The Catholic Encyclopedia*, Vol. V, p. 407.

[27] Herbert Thurston, *The Physical Phenomena of Mysticism* (Chicago, Henry Regnery Co., 1952, pp. viii, 419), pp. 97, 98.

[28] Aubert, *Le Pontificat de Pie IX*, p. 469; Cayré, *Patrologie et Histoire de la Théologie*, Vol. III, p. 304.

[29] Pourrat, *op. cit.*, Vol. IV, pp. 516–520; *Dictionnaire de Théologie Catholique*, Vol. VI, pp. 1473–1476.

circles in the great Christian mystics of the past, an extensive use of manuals of meditation and prayer, and a large output of fresh devotional literature. That interest stimulated the publication of the writings, some of them voluminous, of acknowledged experts in the way of the mystic. To pick out only a few, almost at random, in mid-century the works of Fénelon were issued.[30] Germany experienced a revival of the study of the mystics who had flourished in that country in the fourteenth century.[31] Contributions to an acquaintance with the devotional life of the past came from the renewal of the project of the Bollandists, begun in the seventeenth century and interrupted by the French invasion of 1792, the monumental *Acta Sanctorum*.[32] A renewal was seen of attention to Pascal, both to his religious pilgrimage and philosophy and to his mysticism.[33] Editions of the outstanding Spanish mystics of the sixteenth century appeared—Teresa of Avila and John of the Cross.[34] They were especially popular in Spain but were not confined to that country. An edition was issued early in the century [35] and the interest persisted and appears to have increased. The writings of Tauler were brought out.[36]

Not only were the texts of the great mystics of the past published: mysticism was the subject of fresh study. Sometimes it was directed to an individual mystic, and from that example general principles were deduced. Not a particularly profound book, designed more for edification and an apologetic, was on a thirteenth-century Franciscan Tertiary hermit, Angela of Foligno. Converted from a dissolute life, she had visions which were much of the kind that we have seen in nineteenth-century Catholic mystics.[37] More solid was a great work on French religious life, chiefly on mysticism, by Henri Bremond, a history embracing mostly the seventeenth and eighteenth centuries.[38] Baron von

---

[30] *Œuvres de Fénelon, Archevêque de Cambrai Precédées d'Études sur sa vie par Aimé-Martin* (Paris, Didot Frères, Fils et Cie, 3 vols., 1856).

[31] Pourrat, *op. cit.*, Vol. IV, p. 527.

[32] *Ibid.*, pp. 533–535.

[33] Dorothy Margaret Eastwood, *The Revival of Pascal: A Study of His Relation to Modern French Thought* (Oxford, The Clarendon Press, 1936, pp. xii, 212), *passim*.

[34] *Storia di Santa Teresa Ricavata dai Ballandisti, da Diverse Biografie e dalle sue "Opere Complete"* (Milan, Tipografia Santa Lega Eucaristica, 2 vols., 1909), approved by various Italian, French, and English bishops; *Vie et Œuvres Spirituelles de l'Admirable Docteur Mystique le Bienheureux Père Saint Jean de la Croix . . . Traduction Nouvelle . . . Publiée par les Soins des Carmélites de Paris*, preface by Chocarne, Provincial of the Dominicans (Paris, H. Oudin, 5th ed., 4 vols., 1910); *The Life of Saint Teresa, Taken from the French of "A Carmelite Nun" by Alice Lady Lovat with a Preface by Mgr. Robert Hugh Benson* (London, Herbert & Daniel, no date, pp. xxi, 629).

[35] *Œuvres Tres- Complètes de Saint Thérèse, de S. Pierre d'Alcantara, de S. Jean de la Croix, du Bienheureux Jean d'Avila*, by various editors (Paris, Migne, 4 vols., 1840–1845).

[36] E. Pierre Noel, O.P., *Œuvres Complètes de Jean Tauler* (Paris, A. Tralin, 8 vols., 1911–1912).

[37] Algar Thorold, *An Essay in Aid of the Better Appreciation of Catholic Mysticism Illustrated from the Writings of Blessed Angela of Foligno* (London, Kegan Paul, Trench, Trubner & Co., 1900, pp. 186).

[38] Henri Bremond, *l'Histoire Litteraire du Sentiment Religieux en France depuis la Fin des Guerres de Religion jusqu'à nos Jours* (Paris, Bloud & Gay, 11 vols., 1916–1933).

Hügel (1852–1925), a devout and learned layman who spent a large part of his life in England, devoted much time, thought, and personal practice to mysticism and used as a central subject and example the fifteenth- and sixteenth-century Catherine of Genoa. But he ranged far beyond her for illustrations and dealt with the entire problem.[39]

Manuals on the devotional life were numerous. Some were for the guidance of spiritual directors. They embraced what was technically known as mystical theology, described as "the extension of the love of God by the desire of love," or as "a science and experience that increases, extends, and perfects" the love of God.[40] The fact that some were issued in edition after edition and in more than one language was evidence of the large and continuing numbers of those who engaged in the practices with which they dealt.[41] After *Christliche Mystik* by Görres, and concentrating more on distinctly Christian mysticism than did that book, the outstanding work, one which supplanted all its predecessors, was by the Jesuit Auguste Poulain (1836–1919), *Des Grâces d'Oraison.*[42]

Several schools flourished for the guidance of souls in prayer and meditation either by personal counselling or by books. Some were continuations of pre-nineteenth-century trends developed by outstanding individuals or in particular orders and congregations. Others were of nineteenth-century origin. Augustine was prized, with his emphasis upon the manner in which God speaks to the soul through the conscience. Out of the revival of the Order of St. Benedict came men and women who were notable in their aid to the life of the spirit. In addition to Guéranger, whose chief contribution was in liturgical prayer and the Gregorian music, Cécile Bruyère (1845–1909), from a distinguished French family, and as abbess of a convent a leader in the renewal of the women's branch of the Benedictines, was the author of *La Vie Spirituelle* ("The Spiritual Life"), first issued privately in 1886, then published in 1899, and translated into English and German.[43] The English Benedictine William Ullathorne (1806–

[39] Baron Friedrich von Hügel, *The Mystical Element in Religion as Studied in Saint Catherine of Genoa and Her Friends* (London, J. M. Dent & Sons, 2 vols., 2nd ed., 1923. The first edition was in 1908).

[40] Arthur Devine, *A Manual of Mystical Theology or The Extraordinary Graces of the Supernatural Life Explained* (London, R. & T. Washbourne, 1903, pp. xv, 664), p. xi.

[41] Examples, each with ecclesiastical approval, are E. Lamballe, *Mystical Contemplation or the Principles of Mystical Theology* (London, R. & T. Washbourne, 1913, pp. xi, 202); P. Lejeune, *An Introduction to the Mystical Life,* translated from the French by Basil Levett (London, R. & T. Washbourne, 1915, pp. vii, 314).

[42] Cayré, *Patrologie et Histoire de la Théologie,* Vol. III, p. 422; A. Poulain, *The Graces of Interior Prayer (Des Grâces d'Oraison). A Treatise on Mystical Theology,* the first edition in 1904; the fifth edition in 1907, with the approbation of Pius X, the first English edition in 1910 translated from the sixth French edition by Leonora L. Yorke Smith and corrected to accord with the tenth French edition with an introduction by J. V. Bainvel (St. Louis, B. Herder Book Co., 1950, pp. 665). The bibliography in the 1950 edition of Poulain is mostly of works published after 1914 but contains several issued between 1900 and 1914.

[43] Cayré, *op. cit.,* Vol. III, pp. 313, 325, 326.

1889) had at least three books which dealt with the life of the spirit.[44] An anonymous Carthusian wrote a book on the interior life which was meant not for beginners but for the more advanced, and was also the author of a brochure on the contemplative life which was intended to show to the modern world with its emphasis on action the greater usefulness of that kind of sacrifice.[45] Two Trappist abbots, Lehodey and Chautard, composed books on prayer which became well known—the one, published in 1908, on mental prayer, and the other, in 1912, with the thesis that the life of prayer is essential to effective Christian work, and giving practical advice for its pursuit. The latter, fitting as it did into an activist age, had a wide circulation.[46] Franciscans were prominent, more as preachers and spiritual directors than as authors. Thus Bernardin de Portogruaro (1822–1895), named Minister General of the order in 1869, in addition to the pulpit and the confessional carried on a voluminous correspondence and stressed the love which is conjoined with sacrifice.[47] Ludovic de Besse (1831–1910), a Capuchin, spent most of his life in Paris as preacher and spiritual director. In his *La Science de la Prière* ("the Science of Prayer"), published in 1903, he made primary the prayer of faith.[48] From the Dominicans came *Traité de la Vie Intérieure* ("Treatise of the Interior Life") (1885) by André-Marie Meynard (1824–1904), which sought to unite ascetic theology with mystical theology, and *l'Évolution Mystique* ("Mystical Development") (1908) and *Cuestiónes Misticas* ("Questions Regarding Mysticism") (1920) by Juan Arintero (1860–1928), professor of theology and apologetics at Salamanca.[49] The Society of Jesus produced many writers on the religious life. Among them were Jean Nicholas Grou (1731–1803). Although he died before 1815, a refugee in England, his writings were widely circulated in the nineteenth and even the twentieth century. Grou's *Caractères de la Vraie Dévotion* ("Characteristics of True Devotion"), first published in 1788, had appeared in more than thirty editions before 1862, in addition to translations into other languages. His *l'École de Jésus Christ* ("The School of Jesus Christ") did not come out in print until 1885 and the first complete English translation was published in 1932.[50] The writings of Francis de Sales were circulated widely by several groups.[51]

Several Anglican clergymen who entered the Roman Catholic Church in the nineteenth century made marked contributions to the devotional life. Among

[44] *Ibid.*, pp. 327, 328.
[45] *Ibid.*, pp. 331, 332.
[46] *Ibid.*, pp. 332–334.
[47] *Ibid.*, pp. 338, 339.
[48] *Ibid.*, p. 341.
[49] *Ibid.*, pp. 347–351.
[50] Jean Nicolas Grou, *The School of Jesus Christ*, translated by Mrs. Rodolph Stawell (London, Burns, Oates & Washbourne, 1932, pp. xxiii, 458), pp. x–xvi and *passim*.
[51] Cayré, *op. cit.*, Vol. III, pp. 312.

them were John Henry Newman (1801-1890) and Frederick William Faber (1814-1863). Although an intellectual, in his approach to the spiritual life Newman was not speculative or abstract. He viewed the Christian mysteries as a source of divine power to the soul.[52] While at his death he had barely entered middle age, through his pen Faber was a major force in furthering the devotional life. His conversion to the Roman Catholic Church occurred in 1845. Year after year from 1853 to 1860 there came from him a succession of books, among them *All for Jesus* (1853), *The Creator and the Creature* (1856), and *The Foot of the Cross* (1858), and a series of hymns. Some of his books circulated not only in English but also in other languages.[53] Among others he helped to shape was the Frenchman Charles Gay (1815-1892). Returning at the age of twenty-one to the faith which he had lost in his earlier student days, Gay prepared for the priesthood. Although he had the soul of an artist and was a great lover of music, he gave up the latter to devote himself to his priestly vocation and became noted for his profound inner life. His first books did not appear until after he had entered his sixties and showed a depth of devotional and theological insight born of maturity. For him the mystery of Christ was above all one of harmony, love, and union.[54]

The above list of writers, preachers, and counsellors who ministered to the devotional life of their age on a high intellectual and deep spiritual level is far from complete. Although so condensed as to seem little more than an arid catalogue, leaving out or passing lightly over the inner struggles through which faith and insight had been reached, it has omitted many who should have a place on it. Yet as it stands it may give some hint of the richness and the distinctive features of prayer, meditation, and contemplation in a church set in the midst of a revolution which challenged its basic convictions.

The Influence of Roman Catholic Devotional Life upon Other Branches of Christianity

A striking aspect of the devotional life of the Roman Catholic Church was the repercussions upon Christians who were not of that communion. They were especially potent among Protestants. Some influences flowed from Protestantism into Roman Catholic devotional life, but most of them came indirectly and were relatively slight. Among Protestants, as among Roman Catholics, a warm devotional life eagerly welcomed reinforcement from earlier eras. In addition to what came from their own predecessors, Protestants made use of Roman Catholic devotional classics. Some were from the centuries before Protestants had broken with the Roman Catholic Church—such as Augustine's

---

[52] Pourrat, *La Spiritualité Chrétienne*, Vol. IV, p. 554.
[53] *Ibid.*, pp. 563–579; Cayré, *op. cit.*, Vol. III, pp. 397–400.
[54] Cayré, *op. cit.*, Vol. III, pp. 401–404.

Confessions and the *Imitation of Christ*. Francis of Assisi was highly prized.[55] Others were after the breach: the great Spanish mystics and Francis de Sales, Pascal, Madame Guyon, and Fénelon, to mention only a few, were known and cherished. Many Roman Catholic hymns found their way into Protestant hymnals.

The repercussions on the Eastern Churches were chiefly through the Uniate bodies, but, as we are to see in the next volume, the Russian Orthodox Church also felt them.

SUMMARY

Placed in a revolution which centred in a part of the globe where was its historic stronghold and which increasingly was sweeping away from it much of its traditional constituency, in its public worship and individual and group devotion the Roman Catholic Church experienced a mounting revival as the nineteenth century wore towards its close. That worship and devotion took many forms. Some were in emphasis on the Eucharist and its attendant liturgy. Others were in a growing stress on the Sacred Heart of Jesus and the Virgin Mary. Many of the faithful were impressed by the visions and apparitions which came to a few highly sensitive souls. Others cultivated the less spectacular forms of prayer. Evidence of the appeal of the Roman Catholic faith to different levels of culture and intelligence, they issued from continuing vigour.

---

[55] For example, the French Protestant Paul Sabatier wrote a sympathetic *Life of St. Francis of Assisi* (translated by Louise Seymour Houghton, New York, Charles Scribner's Sons, 1909, pp. xxxv, 448) which became a classic.

CHAPTER X

The Intellectual Response of Roman Catholics in Europe to the Revolution in the Nineteenth Century

WHAT was the response of the Roman Catholics of Europe to the intellectual phases of the nineteenth-century stage of the revolution? This question naturally divides itself into three others. What was taking place in the formulations of theology? What were the attitudes and achievements in Biblical studies? What, if any, contributions were made to intellectual life and science outside the field of religion?

As in so many other sections of our story, even an extensive summary would take us far beyond the proper limits of this volume. We must content ourselves with a few generalizations and some outstanding figures, trends, and events. Our major concern must be to see in what manner Roman Catholics and especially the Roman Catholic Church responded to the intellectual currents of the revolutionary age. We can do this the more quickly in view of the fact that some of the chief figures and events have been given a place in the chapter on the Papacy and here can be dismissed with the barest mention. We will first enumerate the generalizations. Then we will develop them rapidly, with concrete illustrations of men, movements, and ecclesiastical actions.

The generalizations in which the theological and other intellectual developments of the nineteenth century can be embraced are as follows. First, as in other phases of the Church's life, and in face of hostile aspects of the revolution, the century witnessed a remarkable renewal of theological activity. Second, that renewal stemmed in part from attempts to meet the challenge of the intellectual currents of the day and was most marked in France and Germany, lands where the challenge was especially strident, but was not confined to them. Third, the increasing authority of the Papacy was accompanied by curbs on what Rome deemed departures from the faith, positive measures in the affirmation of important dogmas, and the revival of the scholastic approach. Fourth, within the limits set by Rome theological ferment was pronounced and was seen in the discussion of issues on which as yet no Papal pronouncements had been made. Fifth, because of the nature of Protestantism and the absence of a central ecclesiastical authority, adventuring in theological thought and Biblical studies was much more marked and the range much wider in that branch of Christianity than in the Roman Catholic Church. Sixth, devout Roman Catholics made striking contributions to the achievements of the century in natural sciences. Seventh, Roman Catholics did not lead in the intellectual life of Europe as they had in the Middle Ages, nor did they produce works in theology comparable in their sweep and power with those of the school men or of the great thinkers of the sixteenth and seventeenth centuries.

THE RENEWAL OF THEOLOGICAL ACTIVITY

The nineteenth century early witnessed a revival of theological activity which paralleled the rising tide in other phases of the life of the Roman Catholic Church.

In the Roman Catholic Church the latter part of the eighteenth century and the period of the French Revolution and Napoleon were theologically sterile. No figures emerged comparable with Kant or Schleiermacher in Protestantism. The nearest approach was Chateaubriand, but the tremendous effect of his *Génie du Christianisme* was more because of literary charm than of intellectual depth.[1] The decline was more marked in France and Germany than in Spain or Italy, for the one was less affected by the disintegrating currents and the other had the Papacy as a centre of strength.[2] But in no place was there much fresh thought. The revival had its first stirrings before 1815, but not until later was it fully under way.

THE VARIED ATTEMPTS TO MEET THE CHALLENGE OF THE NEW DAY WERE CHIEFLY BUT NOT ENTIRELY IN FRANCE AND GERMANY

As in other aspects of its response to the challenge of the age, in theological thought the Roman Catholic Church displayed most vigour in lands where the revolution had its rise and its most provocative expressions. That was mainly in France and Germany, but it was also in Italy, England, and Belgium. Whether this was because of a surging vitality in these lands which expressed itself both in challenge to Christianity and in constructive response in Christianity we need not attempt to determine. The intellectual activity was ample evidence that the Roman Catholic Church was far from moribund.

The intellectual ferment was sufficiently potent to have varied expressions. Some were attempts to meet the attacks on the faith made by those who relied on reason by utilizing the methods of rationalism to support the faith and to restate the basic Christian convictions in terms which could be defended by

---

[1] Bellamy, *La Théologie Catholique au XIXe Siècle*, pp. 1–10; Hocedez, *Histoire de la Théologie au XIXe Siècle*, Vol. I, pp. 13–21.

[2] Hocedez, *op. cit.*, Vol. I, pp. 38–66.

reason. Others were by those who, reacting against the emphasis upon reason and seeing the weaknesses of rational processes, despaired of reaching a knowledge of God in that fashion, held that such knowledge could come only through the act of God in revelation, and maintained that the sole proper response of man must be faith. Increasingly the trend was towards the historic Roman Catholic position, most notably set forth by Thomas Aquinas, that knowledge of God comes through both reason and faith.

ATTEMPTS TO MEET THE CHALLENGE THROUGH REASON

As might have been expected, those who stressed reason were especially prominent in Germany, for here the *Aufklärung* had borne fruit in particularly turbulent and creative debate which centred around the place of the intellect. Kant, Schelling, Fichte, Herder, and later Hegel were potent. Before and after 1815 in several universities Catholics with a rationalistic approach held chairs of philosophy and theology.[3] Two men, Georg Hermes (1775–1831) and Anton Günther (1783–1871), were outstanding. In connexion with the condemnation of his views by Gregory XVI we have already met Hermes.[4] For some years after his death those influenced by him occupied important university posts and through them disseminated his philosophy and theology.

In contrast with Hermes, Günther, although he was offered several, did not have a professorship. Reared and educated a Catholic, in his young manhood he came under the influence of Kant, Fichte, and Schelling and for a time his faith was weakened. Later it was restored, and he studied theology and in his mid-thirties was ordained priest (1820). For two years he was in the Jesuit novitiate. Although he did not go on to full membership in the Society, he remained earnestly Christian. As Hermes had sought to answer the scepticism of Kant, Günther was disturbed by the pantheistic aspects of the then popular Hegelian philosophy and strove to refute them. While regarding revelation as necessary, he believed that he could establish through reason the fundamental tenets of Christianity, including the Trinity. Some of his followers were in university chairs of Catholic philosophy and he had the support of at least two Cardinals. After prolonged examination, in 1857, when he was in his seventies, Rome placed his books on the Index. He submitted, published no more, and retained his devotion to the Church and his ardent piety. Later some of his adherents joined the Old Catholic movement.[5]

[3] *Ibid.*, pp. 168 ff.
[4] For brief treatments of Hermes see *ibid.*, pp. 177–203 (with a bibliography); *The Catholic Encyclopedia*, Vol. VII, pp. 276–278; *Dictionnaire de Théologie Catholique*, Vol. VI, pp. 282 ff., 2288–2303; Brück, *Geschichte der katholischen Kirche in Deutschland*, Vol. II, pp. 485 ff. For a major work of Hermes see his *Einleitung in die christkatholische Theologie, passim.*
[5] *The Catholic Encyclopedia*, Vol. VII, pp. 85–88; *Dictionnaire de Théologie Catholique*, Vol. VI, pp. 1992, 1993; Brück, *op. cit.*, Vol. II, pp. 460–463; Hocedez, *op. cit.*, Vol. II, pp. 40–58; Aubert, *Le Pontificat de Pie IX*, pp. 200–202.

Traditionalism and Fideism: Attempts to Meet the Challenge by Minimizing or Rejecting Reason and Stressing Faith

In contrast with those who through the tools of rationalism sought to meet the attacks on Christianity were those who discredited reason as a way of arriving at a knowledge of God and maintained the priority of faith. Their positions were known as traditionalism and fideism. The two were not identical but were closely related. They were not new. In one form or another they had existed for centuries and in their extreme manifestations had again and again been officially condemned by Popes and councils.[6]

In their nineteenth-century forms traditionalism and fideism were developed chiefly in France. To no small degree they were reactions against the confidence in reason which was a feature of the Revolution. They were also a protest against the rampant individualism which was a corollary of reliance on reason.

Traditionalism held that human reason of itself is unable to know any truth with certainty—or at least fundamental truths of metaphysics and of the religious and moral order. Hence our first step towards attaining knowledge must be an act of faith based upon revelation: through revelation religious truth is given directly to mankind and must be accepted antecedently to any act of reason. Hints of traditionalism were seen in Joseph de Maistre (1754-1821), whom we have already met as an early herald of the revival of the Roman Catholic faith in France. He and Viscount Louis de Bonald (1754-1840) were in substantial agreement. Bonald maintained that the history of the past four centuries had demonstrated that atheism and anarchy were the inevitable fruits of the confidence in the use of reason by the individual which had been proclaimed by Luther. He found his sole refuge in adherence to the traditional Christian faith based upon the authority of the Catholic Church.[7]

Maistre and Bonald warmly defended Félicité de Lamennais (1784-1854), who, in the brilliant apologetic through which he strove to renew the Roman Catholic faith, sought to show the basic weakness of reason and asserted that the only hope of attaining certitude was through an authority superior to reason. This Lamennais found as a firm rock in the Church and its dogmas. He held that this authority was confirmed, with other aspects of religious and political certainty, by the general consensus of mankind.[8] His approach met with Papal condemnation in the encyclical *Singulari nos* (1834).[9]

---

[6] See a long survey of fideism, including the nineteenth century, in *Dictionnaire de Théologie Catholique*, Vol. VI, pp. 55 ff. On traditionalism see *The Catholic Encyclopedia*, Vol. XV, pp. 13, 14.

[7] Hocedez, *op. cit.*, Vol. I, pp. 80-83, 107-111; Horton, *The Philosophy of the Abbé Bautain*, pp. 7-16.

[8] Horton, *op. cit.*, pp. 17-23; Hocedez, *op. cit.*, Vol. I, pp. 83-87; Vidler, *Prophecy and Papacy*, pp. 85 ff.

[9] Vidler, *op. cit.*, pp. 251, 254.

Fideism had relations with romanticism. Romanticism became popular in Germany and France. A reaction against classicism and rationalism, it viewed with enthusiasm the Christian art and architecture of the Middle Ages and the beauty and richness of Catholic ceremonies. Moved by it, many became Roman Catholics. But in doing so they did not always have a solid intellectual foundation in Roman Catholic dogma.[10] At Munich, for example, Franz Xavier von Baader (1765–1841), a mystic and philosopher whose favourite authors were Meister Eckhart and Jakob Böhme, a Catholic by rearing and in his death, was intensely critical of ultramontanism. Under his influence Schelling in later years approached a semi-Catholic position.[11] With its emphasis on feeling and intuition romanticism encouraged the direct apprehension of God and the discounting of reason.

An outstanding exponent of fideism was Louis Eugène Marie Bautain (1796–1867). A native of Paris, brilliant, precocious, in his student days he had departed from the simple Catholic faith in which he had been reared, partly through the influence of the eclectic and popular philosopher Victor Cousin (who was influenced by Scottish thinking) and of the German idealists. In his mid-twenties, after a severe nervous collapse he was converted and restored to health through the devotion of a woman, Mlle. Humann, of rare intelligence and profound piety. She brought him in touch with the writings of some of the great mystics, among them Jakob Böhme. He became familiar with Baader. He believed that the path of reason leads to neither the proof nor the disproof of the existence of God: knowledge of God is to be reached, not through the rational processes, which he had tried and which had brought him only to impotence, but through self-mortification, faith, and immediate insight. To him Protestantism was too rationalistic. Suspicion of the authorities for his newly formulated philosophy led to his suspension from the University of Strasbourg, where he had been lecturing with striking success. But in that city he gathered about him a group of young men, some of whom he won to the Catholic faith. Convinced that in that faith was the key to satisfying the spiritual cravings and healing the moral ills of the day, and seeking to reshape the teaching of philosphy in the Roman Catholic Church to make it more germane to the temper of the times, Bautain was ordained to the priesthood. In the 1830's his writings brought him international renown. Holding in contempt the scholastic arguments for Christianity, the eclecticism of Victor Cousin, and the "general consensus" philosophy of Lamennais, he precipitated controversy. As required by ecclesiastical authority, he obediently recanted (1840) what were regarded as his errors. If disappointed in his effort to remake Catholic philosophy, he was not unhappy. An obedient son of the Church, for more than a quarter of a

10 Horton, *op. cit.*, pp. 30, 31, 38–46.
11 *Ibid.*, pp. 50–54.

century longer he lectured, wrote, preached, and was spiritual adviser, especially to intellectuals.[12]

Not all who showed an anti-intellectual trend and discounted reason went as far as Maistre, Bonald, Lamennais, and Bautain. Yet in Belgium, notably at Louvain, and in France many moved in that direction. Partly through the writings of Lamennais repercussions were heard in Poland, Spain, and Italy.[13]

Rome not only condemned what it deemed the exaggerated reliance on rational processes and the misuse of reason by Hermes and Günther. It also ruled out the dismissal or deprecation of reason by those who affirmed the traditional dogmas of the Church. Thus in 1855 the Congregation of the Holy Office insisted that faith is subordinate to reason, that since both are from God no contradiction can exist between them, that the existence of God, the spirituality of the soul, and the freedom of man can be proved by reason, that the use of reason precedes faith and with the help of revelation and grace leads to it, and that, if followed, the methods of Thomas Aquinas, Bonaventura, and other school men would avoid the pitfalls of contemporary rationalism and pantheism.[14]

The Vatican Council condemned fideism and taught as dogma that "one true God and Lord can be known with certainty by the natural light of human reason by means of the things which are made." [15]

THE ONTOLOGIST ATTEMPT TO MEET THE CHALLENGE

Another attempt by Roman Catholic thinkers to meet the intellectual challenge of the times was by what was known as ontologism. Like traditionalism and fideism, ontologism was not new. In general it maintained that God and divine ideas are the first object of our intelligence, that we have an immediate perception of God, and that our intuition of God is the initial step in our intellectual knowledge. Ontologism had roots in Platonism, in Clement and Origen, in Augustine, and in Bonaventura.[16] It had been developed and given a particular form by Malebranche (1638–1715). Devout and of a simple and austere life, Malebranche had worked out a system which was optimistic and repudiated pantheism, but which had been attacked by Bossuet and censured by Rome.[17]

In the nineteenth century the term "ontologism" was adopted by Vincenzo Gioberti (1801–1852) to oppose the Cartesian philosophy. Priest and statesman involved in the tangle of Italian politics, Gioberti had a philosophy which was

---

[12] *Ibid., passim*, especially pp. 56–101; Hocedez, *op. cit.*, Vol. II, pp. 69–82; *The Catholic Encyclopedia*, Vol. II, p. 253, Vol. VII, pp. 68, 69.

[13] Hocedez, *op. cit.*, Vol. II, pp. 83–112; *The Catholic Encyclopedia*, Vol. VI, pp. 68, 69; Aubert, *op. cit.*, pp. 189, 190.

[14] Hocedez, *op. cit.*, Vol. II, pp. 95, 96.

[15] *The Catholic Encyclopedia*, Vol. VI, p. 69.

[16] Aubert, *op. cit.*, pp. 190, 191.

[17] *The Catholic Encyclopedia*, Vol. IX, pp. 568, 569.

a mixture of Platonism and traditionalism with what were accused of being pantheistic implications.[18]

Gioberti's theology and philosophy were much influenced by Antonio Rosmini-Serbati (1797–1855). Born in the Italian Tyrol and educated in Italy, Rosmini, a priest, encouraged by Pius VII, undertook a reform of philosophy. To that end he gave himself for some years to the study of the school men, especially Aquinas. He reacted strongly against the French Revolution, but he refused to be content with the views of those Catholics who regarded the world as too wrong ever to be set right, who took towards the Revolution the attitude of passive pessimism, who believed that nothing that the contemporary age had to say was worth heeding, and who shut themselves up in the past. For himself he adopted two principles: first, to give priority to the amendment of his faults rather than to service to his neighbour, since of himself he was powerless to do any one service, and, second, not to turn aside from works of charity when divine providence presented them to him. As he saw it, the love of God is primary and extends to all intelligent creatures made in God's image. In quiet confidence in God's love, even in a revolutionary world, Rosmini would, therefore, devote himself to prayer, labour, and study to be prepared to respond to any call for service when it came. To him the most important service was the cure of souls. In the 1820's he founded an Institute of Charity designed to embody these principles. Its constitutions obtained Papal approval in 1838. Rosmini became its Provost-General. Houses were early established in Italy and England and eventually the Institute spread to other countries. The Rosminians, as the members were usually called, did not wear a special garb and were permitted on occasion to have individual possessions.[19]

In one form or another ontologism had exponents in Italy, France, Belgium, Switzerland, and the United States. With its emphasis upon the immediate knowledge of God and its contemplation of eternal ideas, it attracted many, especially those with inclinations towards mysticism.[20]

Ontologism was not without severe critics. The future Leo XIII wished the Vatican Council to condemn what he regarded as one of its tenets—that man naturally has immediate and direct knowledge of God.[21]

Those showing ontologist proclivities were not all of one mind. Rosmini was

[18] *Ibid.*, Vol. VI, pp. 562, 563.
[19] *The Philosophical System of Antonio Rosmini-Serbati, Translated, with a Sketch of the Author's Life, Bibliography, Introduction and Notes,* by Thomas Davidson (London, Kegan Paul, Trench & Co., 1882, pp. cxvi, 396); *The Ruling Principle of Method Applied to Education,* translated by Mrs. William Grey (Boston, D. C. Heath and Co., 1889, pp. xxv, 363); H. C. Sheldon, *The Teachings of Antonio Rosmini and the Censures Passed on them by Ecclesiastical Authority,* in *Papers of the American Society of Church History,* Vol. VIII, pp. 41–46; *The Catholic Encyclopedia,* Vol. XIII, pp. 194–201.
[20] Hocedez, *op. cit.,* Vol. II, pp. 126 ff.
[21] *Ibid.,* p. 137.

unhappy over the direction which Gioberti was giving to the spiritual revival in Italy.[22] Indeed, again and again he denied that he was an ontogolist and argued against the ontologism of Malebranche. He and Gioberti entered into vigorous and not always amicable controversy. Gioberti accused Rosmini of taking a position which could lead only to scepticism or subjective pantheism. Rosmini defended himself against the charge.[23] In France were Jesuits who were classed as ontologists, but they were silenced by their General, Roothaan.[24]

For decades the battle was waged within the Roman Catholic Church between ontologists of various stripes and their opponents. The revival of the study of Aquinas accentuated the conflict and hastened the eclipse of ontologism: the idealism in the latter could scarcely survive in the face of an orthodoxy in which the *doctor angelicus* was the acknowledged master. Annoyed by the debate, Gregory XVI enjoined silence on the disputants. Pius IX ordered a full investigation. In 1854 in reviewing the report he declared that nothing in it implied disparagement of Rosmini or of the Institute of Charity, and again ordered that debate cease.[25] In 1861 and 1862 the Holy Office condemned some of the propositions ascribed to ontologism. Leo XIII permitted a resumption of the discussion and in 1887 and 1888 the Holy Office came out against forty propositions taken from the works of Rosmini which smacked of ontologism. The Pope confirmed the decree. In the meantime Rosmini had died (1855) in full communion with the Church. His successor as head of the Institute at once submitted.[26]

Casimir Ubaghs (1800–1875) of Louvain was accused of a combination of traditionalism and ontologism and in the 1860's his writings came under censure from Rome.[27]

ATTEMPTS THROUGH HISTORY TO MEET THE CHALLENGE: THOSE REGARDED AS ORTHODOX

As we have seen, one phase of the intellectual revolution through which Western Europe was passing was in the study of history. The documents which are the sources on which historians depend were being examined critically to determine their authors, dates, and reliability and were being edited and published in large quantities. Fresh studies were being made—some detailed monographs on particular subjects, others covering a broad range of time and geography. Philosophies of history were being developed. The current historical method and approach constituted a challenge to Roman Catholic scholars. A religion so intertwined with history as Christianity and a church with so long a past as the

---

[22] *Ibid.,* p. 120.
[23] *Ibid.,* pp. 144, 145; La Piana, *Recent Tendencies in Roman Catholic Theology,* p. 237.
[24] Hocedez, *op. cit.,* Vol. II, p. 128.
[25] *The Catholic Encyclopedia,* Vol. XIII, p. 195.
[26] *Ibid.,* Vol. XI, p. 258; Hocedez, *op. cit.,* Vol. II, pp. 153, 154.
[27] Aubert, *op. cit.,* pp. 192, 193; *The Catholic Encyclopedia,* Vol. XV, p. 114.

Roman communion obviously called for historical treatment. Much of the vast literature which issued from the pens of Roman Catholics on the history of their faith won ecclesiastical approval. Some of it, particularly near the end of the century, labeled as "Modernism," fell under ecclesiastical censure.

An early centre of historical studies which contributed to the support of the faith was in Tübingen. There, in Württemberg, was a university with a Protestant theological faculty which made notable contributions to theological, historical, and Biblical scholarship. In 1817 a Catholic university founded in 1812 at Ellwangen by the King of Württemberg was transferred to Tübingen to become the Catholic faculty. Believing that theology had a historical foundation, members of that faculty adopted the historical approach. The founder of the Catholic Tübingen school was Johann Sebastian Drey (1777–1853). Influenced by current German philosophy, and particularly by Schelling and the romantic movement, he proposed to reform and revive the study of theology through the conception of the continuity of history. He believed Christianity to be in an eternal divine plan and to have had an organic development. With his colleagues he founded a periodical, *Theologische Quartalschrift,* to be a vehicle for that approach.[28]

The chief glory of the Tübingen school was Johann Adam Möhler (1796–1838). Esteemed an ideal priest, devout, modest, disliking controversy and seeking peace between warring creeds and convictions, Möhler first attracted attention by a book, *Die Einheit in der Kirche* ("The Unity in the Church"). His most notable studies were in the creeds, or symbolics. In his *Symbolik oder Darstellung der dogmatischen Gegensätze der Katholiken und Protestanten nach ihren öffentlichen Bekenntnisschriften* ("Symbolic, or the Presentation of the Contrasts in Dogma between Catholics and Protestants in their Published Confessional Writings"), he endeavoured to set forth the differences between the two branches of Christianity, but not in an extremely polemic manner. He insisted that Christ had founded a visible society, the Church, and that this corresponded to the needs and aspirations of man. As did all the Catholic Tübingen school, he regarded tradition as dynamic and organic, as "the word of God living eternally in the body of the faithful." He held that the Church must have a head, the successor of Peter, instituted by Christ, or it would break into fragments. That primacy had both "accidental" powers, which varied with the times and might become anachronisms, and "essential" rights, which were unchanging. The book had a wide reading, confirming the faith of Catholics and working some conversions among Protestants.

Inevitably Möhler had his critics, among both Catholics and Protestants. Hermes blocked his call to a professorship at Bonn, and some Catholics deemed

---

[28] Hocedez, *op. cit.,* Vol. I, pp. 213, 214; Bellamy, *La Théologie Catholique au XIXe Siècle,* pp. 39, 40.

him to err on the side of being at least semi-rationalistic. An attack by the Protestant Baur of the Tübingen faculty contributed to Möhler's decision to accept a position at Munich.[29]

The Tübingen school did not die out with its first creative figures. It was continued, although not solely in that university, by men who had been trained by them. Thus Franz Anton Staudenmaier (1800–1856), who did much of his teaching and writing at Giessen and at Freiburg im Breisgau, was an opponent of ultramontanism and of the revival of scholasticism, applied the Hegelian method to Catholic thought, and believed that by doing so he was upholding the historic Catholic faith against what he deemed the errors of the *Aufklärung,* Hegel, Schleiermacher, Fichte, Catholic traditionalism, and the semi-rationalism of Hermes and Günther. To counter the *Leben Jesu* of Strauss, he wrote *Das Leben Jesu wissenschaftlichen bearbeitet,* as a scientific life of Jesus. Although while it was under debate an opponent of Papal infallibility, as a loyal son of the Church he submitted to the decrees of the Vatican Council.[30]

To the Tübingen school also belonged Karl Joseph Hefele (1809–1893). Teaching in Tübingen from 1836 to 1869, he closely followed the method of Möhler. Hundreds of students from Germany and Switzerland flocked to his lectures. Like Möhler, while the issue was being discussed he refused to endorse Papal infallibility, but after the decision was reached, he conformed. His major literary contribution, long standard in its field, was his *Conciliengeschichte*. It brought the history of the Councils down to the fifteenth century [31] and was continued to the Council of Trent by a younger contemporary, Joseph Hergenrother (1824–1890). Hergenrother was a staunch defender of Papal infallibility, a vigorous opponent of Döllinger, and in his last years a Cardinal. His most widely used contribution to historical studies was his *Handbuch der allgemeine Kirchengeschichte* ("Handbook of General Church History"), which went into many editions and was long standard.[32]

ATTEMPTS THROUGH HISTORY TO MEET THE CHALLENGE; THOSE WHOSE ORTHODOXY WAS QUESTIONED OR WHOSE VIEWS CAME UNDER OFFICIAL CONDEMNATION; "MODERNISM"

As the century wore on the pursuit of the historical method raised many problems, partly in the history of the Church and of dogma and partly in Biblical studies. As within Protestantism, debate waxed warm. Some scholars came under ecclesiastical suspicion but were never actually condemned, others held views condemned by Rome but remained in communion with Rome, and still

---

[29] Hocedez, *op. cit.*, Vol. I, pp. 231 ff.; Brück, *op. cit.*, Vol. II, pp. 70–72; *The Catholic Encyclopedia*, Vol. X, pp. 430–432; *Dictionnaire de Théologie Catholique*, Vol. X, pp. 2048–2063.
[30] Hocedez, *op. cit.*, Vol. II, pp. 299 ff.; *The Catholic Encyclopedia*, Vol. XIV, p. 282.
[31] *The Catholic Encyclopedia*, Vol. VII, pp. 191, 192.
[32] *Ibid.*, pp. 262–264.

others, their views condemned, refused to submit, and their ties with Rome were severed.

Early outstanding in this last category was one whom we have already met, Johann Joseph Ignaz von Döllinger (1799–1890). The leading authority in mid-century Germany on the history of the Church, he rejected Papal infallibility and was excommunicated. He took his stand on what he believed to be the evidence of history.

One who had studied with Döllinger at Munich, John Emerich Edward Dalberg, Baron Acton (1834–1902), was, as we have also seen, a vigorous critic of both the Syllabus of Errors and Papal infallibility. He stood for freedom of scientific enquiry and deeply distrusted the Roman curia. While wishing to be loyal to the Catholic Church and escaping excommunication, he declared that he belonged to its soul rather than its body.[33]

For a time and in some quarters John Henry Newman, eminent convert from the Church of England, was accused of being a "liberal." It was true that he sympathized with Montalembert and Lacordaire, who were under a cloud, especially for their political "liberalism." While holding to Papal infallibility as defined by the Vatican Council, he would not, as did some extreme ultramontanists, include under it all Papal utterances.[34] He also believed that, while the original deposit of faith entrusted to the Church was unchanged, there had been developments in doctrine, explications by uninspired thinkers of what had been given through inspired teachers.[35] Some were scandalized by the thought of such development.[36] However, he denounced such "liberal" tenets as the statements that Christianity is necessarily modified by the growth of civilization and the exigencies of the times and that there is no positive proof in religion but that one creed is as good as another. Moreover, he denied the right of private judgement.[37] Although the conservative Pius IX distrusted him, one of the early acts of Leo XIII was to raise him to the Cardinalate and, in contrast with the custom which required all Cardinals not having diocesan duties to reside in Rome, to permit him to continue to live in England.[38]

In an earlier chapter we have seen a little of "Modernism" and of the manner in which it was met by Leo XIII and Pius X. We must now enter into a slightly longer but still highly condensed account. "Modernism" was especially connected with historical studies, but with it were associated movements to "lib-

[33] *The Dictionary of National Biography, Second Supplement, 1901–1911*, pp. 8–12.
[34] Ward, *The Life of John Henry Cardinal Newman*, Vol. II, p. 213.
[35] John Henry Cardinal Newman, *An Essay on the Development of Christian Doctrine* (London, Longmans, Green & Co., 11th impression, 1900, pp. xvi, 445), *passim*, especially pp. 29, 30.
[36] Hocedez, *op. cit.*, Vol. III, pp. 161 ff.
[37] Ward, *op. cit.*, Vol. I, pp. 458 ff.; Newman, *Apologia pro Vita Sua*, pp. 295 ff.; *The Dictionary of National Biography*, Vol. XIV, pp. 340–351; Newman, *History of My Religious Opinions*, pp. 285 ff., especially pp. 294–296.
[38] Ward, *op. cit.*, Vol. II, p. 438.

eralize" the attitude of the Roman Catholic Church on political and social issues. It was also an attempt to reconcile faith and modern science.[39]

Some who employed the methods of historical criticism remained, somewhat precariously, within the bounds set by ecclesiastical authority and continued in communion with Rome. In France Roman Catholic scholarship was given great impetus by the erection, by authorization of a law of 1875, of five Catholic Institutes with theological faculties.[40] In the application of current critical processes some of their members made notable contributions to scholarship but in doing so appeared to the more conservative to be taking highly questionable positions. Thus Louis Marie Olivier Duchesne (1843–1922), a priest, professor on the theological faculty of Paris, wrote extensively and in distinguished fashion on the early history of the Church. In dealing with the history of doctrine he held that its transmission and development were determined by the factors which shaped other phases of thought and seemed to some of the clergy to ignore the work of the Holy Spirit. The Superior General of Saint Sulpice forbade the seminarists to attend his lectures, the disquiet was conveyed to Rome, and his *History of the Early Church* was condemned. But Duchesne had a horror of "Modernism," submitted, and taught that the doctrines of the Church were unimpeachable and immutable.[41]

In France the most severe storm arose around Alfred Firmin Loisy (1857–1940).[42] Loisy was a native of Champagne, of peasant parentage. A frail child and obviously unfitted to till the soil, Loisy was sent to school. At the age of sixteen, at a retreat conducted by the Jesuits, he felt a vocation to the priesthood. He was devout, for a time ardently so, and would have offered himself to the Dominicans had not bodily frailty debarred him from the exacting physical demands of that order. At the seminary he was introduced to theology, but his four years of the study of doctrine were to him an excruciating experience: he was tortured by doubts. Yet the instruction was strictly orthodox and his questionings were from within and not from the currents abroad in the revolutionary world. On his own initiative he studied scholastic philosophy, in-

[39] For a general study of Modernism from a Roman Catholic standpoint see Lucio da Veiga Continho, *Tradition et Histoire dans la Controverse Moderniste* (Rome, 1954). See also Rivière, *Le Modernisme dans l'Église, passim.*

[40] Hocedez, *Histoire de la Théologie au XIXe Siècle*, Vol. III, p. 39.

[41] *Ibid.*, pp. 57, 149; Loisy, *My Duel with the Vatican*, pp. 116, 119, 120; Barbier, *Histoire du Catholicisme Libéral et du Catholicisme Social en France du Concile du Vatican à l'Avènement de S.S. Benoît XV*, Vol. IV, pp. 208 ff., Vol. V, pp. 259 ff.

[42] The biographical material is from Alfred Loisy, *Choses Passées* (Paris, Émile Nourry, 1913, pp. x, 399), in its English form *My Duel with the Vatican, the Autobiography of a Catholic Modernist*, authorized translation by Richard Wilson Boynton (New York, E. P. Dutton & Co., 1924, pp. xvii, 357); the highly sympathetic Friedrich Heiler, *Der Vater des katholischen Modernismus, Alfred Loisy (1857–1940)* (Munich, Erasmus-Verlag, 1947, pp. 252); a sympathetically objective appraisal by a friend, M. D. Petre, *Alfred Loisy, His Religious Significance* (Cambridge University Press, 1944, pp. xi, 129); Rivière, *op. cit.*, pp. 154–191, 224 ff., 298 ff., 381 ff.; and Barbier, *op. cit.*, Vol. III, pp. 346 ff.

cluding the *Summa Theologica* of Aquinas. Aquinas did not resolve his uncertainties: to Loisy the Catholic theological structure was imposing and, once the basic premises were granted, irrefragable, but the premises seemed to him shaky. When he was slightly over twenty-two years of age he was ordained priest and was assigned successively to two parishes. Here he continued his studies and contemplated a large work which would demonstrate from history and philosophy the truth of Catholicism.

At his request Loisy was permitted to resume an enrolment in the Catholic Institute in Paris which had been interrupted by ill health before his parish experience. There he became a favourite pupil of Duchesne. Through a study of the Gospel texts he came to perceive what he deemed discrepancies and contradictions which led him to believe that they were not reliable as history. Inwardly he gave up his belief in the historicity of the Virgin birth and the resurrection of Christ. With the approval of his confessor, for three years he attended the lectures of Renan on Hebrew and the Bible in the Collège de France. He hoped to defend the Catholic faith against Renan and to employ against him the latter's own principles of criticism. So far as he could later judge, without direct influence from either Duchesne or Renan, but through his own mental processes, he arrived at the conclusion that the pronouncements of councils and Popes were subject to the same relativity as the Scriptures and so were not infallible. He was slowly coming to "the absolute negation of any supernatural character for religion whatsoever." The religious feelings which he had cherished evaporated. Yet he remained determined to serve the Church as "an essential institution and the most divine upon earth," the educator of the human race and the guarantor of "the happiness of the family and the peace of society." In his purpose to serve the Church, Loisy gave courses in the Catholic Institute in Paris in the Bible, Hebrew, and Assyrian. In the Institute he obtained his Doctorate in Theology.

Partly through his lectures in the Institute, but chiefly through his publications, Loisy began to meet with criticism from within the Roman Catholic Church. Among the issues were the historical reliability of the first chapters of Genesis, the authorship of the Pentateuch and of Daniel, and whether the Prophets were primarily preachers or foretellers of events. The students of Saint Sulpice were told not to attend his lectures. In the Institute Loisy was no longer permitted to give courses on the Bible but was continued as a teacher of the ancient languages. In time he was completely removed from the Institute and made chaplain to a convent of Dominican nuns. It was to counter views which had come indirectly from him that in 1893 Leo XIII issued his encyclical *Providentissimus Deus*. Loisy wrote the Pope making his submission, but in a somewhat equivocal fashion. After about six years a severe illness led him to resign the chaplaincy and he was permitted to live quietly, saying his daily mass in his own room. He still wrote, sometimes under a pseudonym, and one of his articles evoked an official condemnation from the Cardinal Archbishop of Paris. In November, 1902, *The Gospel and the Church* was published and soon created a sensation.[43] Loisy had intended it as an answer to *Das Wesen des Christentums* ("What Is Christianity?"), by the eminent Protestant German church historian Adolph von Harnack. It was an attempt to show that "liberal" Protestantism did not give the essence of Christianity. Rather, so Loisy said, Christianity was a growth from an original seed, changing as it developed, but still essentially the same, and the resulting plant was the Catholic Church: true Christianity was not to be discerned, as Harnack appeared to say, by seeking to go back to the original seed and regarding all later growth as a corruption. In setting forth his argument Loisy took positions on the Gospels and on the development of the organization, dogma, and worship of the Church which scandalized many of the hierarchy. Late in 1903 Rome placed five of his books on the Index. In 1908, since he had refused to submit to the anti-Modernist Papal measures, he was formally excommunicated.

Expelled from the Roman Catholic Church, Loisy was soon elected to the chair in the Collège de France once filled by Renan. He continued to lecture and to write. For a time he seemed to formulate a religion of humanity (humanity not as an object of worship, but through which the true object of worship is apprehended), but in his later years he held to a religion of the spirit more nearly akin to historic Christianity. Retiring because of age, he lived on, honoured by students of religion, and died in 1940 as German troops were approaching Paris.

A tortured soul, Loisy seems never to have found inward peace. A scholar, something of a recluse, sensitive, quite lacking in humour, unworldly, basically religious, an individualist, impatient of contradiction and resentful of criticism, he longed to be at home in the Roman Catholic Church, found Protestantism inadequate, yet could not, without violating his conscience, submit to ecclesiastical authority on issues where he believed truth was at stake.[44]

The other outstanding figure in the Modernist movement was George Tyrrell (1861–1909).[45] Tyrrell was born in Dublin, was reared in the (Anglican) Church of Ireland and by a devout mother to whom he was deeply attached, and in his teens became absorbed in religion. For a time a high-churchman,

---

[43] Alfred Loisy, *The Gospel and the Church*, translated by Christopher Home, new edition, with an introduction by Newman Smythe (New York, Charles Scribner's Sons, 1909, pp. xxxii, 276).

[44] See a thoughtful appraisal by a friend in Petre, *op. cit.*, especially pp. 110, 111.

[45] Aside from his writings, the chief sources are *Autobiography and Life of George Tyrrell . . . Arranged, with Supplements, by M. D. Petre* (London, Edward Arnold, 2 vols., 1912) and *George Tyrrell's Letters*, selected and edited by M. D. Petre (New York, E. P. Dutton and Co., 1920, pp. xviii, 301). See also J. Lewis May, *Father Tyrrell and the Modernist Movement* (London, Eyre & Spottiswoode, 1932, pp. 288). On Tyrrell's later days see Raoul Gout, *l'Affaire Tyrrell* (Paris, Émile Nourry, 1910, pp. 323). See also Fawkes, *Studies in Modernism*, pp. 1 ff.; Rivière, *op. cit.*, pp. 192–223, 265 ff., 302 ff.

when he was eighteen he became a Roman Catholic. From his conversion he made it his aim to work for religion in the world at large. He believed that he could do this best by joining the Society of Jesus. In 1891 he was ordained priest.

Life for Tyrrell was never easy. Intense, suffering much of the time from severe headaches aggravated by over-work and over-strain, craving friendship, but with a frankness which sometimes deeply wounded those who loved him, highly sensitive, possessed of a keen and at times devastating humour, able to work at high speed and under pressure, with the inevitable reaction of periods of depression, lassitude, and doubt, ruthlessly honest, with a hunger for God and much of the temperament of a mystic, he could scarcely escape a tempestuous career.

After a year, 1893–1894, in a mission in industrial Lancashire, Tyrrell was assigned to a chair of philosophy in the Jesuit institution at Stonyhurst. There he applied himself to the study and teaching of Aquinas and believed that that great master could be applied to modern religious needs. But his interpretations differed so sharply from those of his colleagues in philosophy that he was relieved of his post.

It was in his writings that Tyrrell made his chief contribution. They attracted wide notice, first in the Society of Jesus and then in a larger public. The first of his books, *Nova et Vetera*,[46] issued in 1897, was made up of brief meditations and was an attempt "to give a new edge to truth and truisms blunted by use" in unaccustomed expression which would make the reader "stop and listen." A second, *Hard Sayings*,[47] came out in 1898 and had as its purpose "to illustrate . . . in various ways a few of the deepest and most wide-reaching principles of Catholic Christianity." Like its predecessor, it bore episcopal imprimatur and was obviously the outpouring of a devout soul who wished to present constructively some of the great affirmations of the Church.

It was not until 1900 that Tyrrell began to have serious trouble. His first major difficulty arose from an article in which he challenged some of the popular conceptions of hell and seemed to question eternal punishment. More and more he came to believe in the necessity and "the right of each age to adjust the historico-philosophical expression of Christianity to contemporary certainties, and thus to put an end to this utterly needless conflict between faith and science which is a mere theological bogey."[48] He held that Catholicism as an on-going life could survive, but that the conflict between traditional Catholic theology

---

[46] George Tyrrell, *Nova et Vetera: Informal Meditations* (London, Longmans, Green & Co., 4th ed., 1902, pp. viii, 415).

[47] George Tyrrell, *Hard Sayings: A Selection of Meditations and Studies* (London, Longmans, Green & Co., 7th impression, 1910, pp. xix, 469).

[48] Tyrrell to A. L. Lilley, Sept. 21, 1904, in Petre, *Autobiography and Life of George Tyrrell*, Vol. II, p. 185.

and modern thought was such that neither could "yield to the other without suicide." [49]

In 1905 Tyrrell sought to withdraw from the Society of Jesus as a way to save both it and himself from embarrassment. In 1906 the General acceded and formally dismissed him. In 1907 he was suspended from receiving the sacraments. He considered returning to the Anglican communion but did not do so. Death came in July,. 1909, after a brief illness. In his last hours Tyrrell was given extreme unction and conditional absolution. But he was denied burial in Roman Catholic ground and was interred in an Anglican cemetery.

Loisy and Tyrrell were merely the most outstanding figures in the Modernist movement. In it or related to it were many others. Their views varied. Some remained with the Church but did not disavow their convictions. Others submitted. Still others were cut off by excommunication. We can take the space only for the barest mention of a few. The layman Baron Friedrich von Hügel was a warm friend of both Loisy and Tyrrell—but the relation with Loisy cooled.[50] Devout and scholarly, he had a profound influence among Roman Catholics and Protestants, although directly upon a limited number of similar tastes.[51] Wilfrid Philip Ward (1856–1916), a layman, famous for his studies of Newman, was a liberal without coming under ecclesiastical censure and sought to be a mediator between various schools of thought.[52] Henri Bremond (1865–1933), for a time a Jesuit, who continued to be a priest after severing his connexion with the Society, was a close friend of Tyrrell, gave him conditional absolution on his death-bed, and for a while was suspended by Rome from saying mass because he officiated in a simple cassock at the latter's funeral. But he submitted and his right to celebrate mass was restored.[53] In France were Marcel Hébert, priest and professor at the École Fénelon, who left the Church,[54] Albert Houtin, some of whose works were placed on the Index and who eventually gave up the priesthood, and a pious layman, Édouard LeRoy, professor of mathematics, a defender of Loisy.[55] Classed by some as Modernists were

[49] Tyrrell to Wilfrid Ward, Dec. 11, 1903, in Petre, Autobiography and Life of George Tyrrell, Vol. II, pp. 215–219.

[50] Petre, Alfred Loisy, pp. 30 ff.; Petre, Autobiography and Life of George Tyrrell, Vol. II, pp. 85 ff.; Michael de la Bedoyere, The Life of Baron von Hügel (London, J. M. Dent & Sons, 1951, pp. xviii, 366), pp. 65–235.

[51] Baron Friedrich von Hügel, Selected Letters 1896–1924, Edited with a Memoir, by Bernard Holland (London, J. M. Dent & Sons, 1928, pp. v, 396).

[52] Dictionary of National Biography, 1912–1921, pp. 552, 553.

[53] Henry Hogarth, Henri Bremond (London, S.P.C.K., 1950, pp. xv, 180), pp. xiii, 14–16; Alfred Loisy, George Tyrrell et Henri Bremond (Paris, Émile Nourry, 1936, pp. viii, 205), pp. 1–46.

[54] Holland, Baron Friedrich von Hügel, p. 19; Houtin, Histoire du Modernisme Catholique, pp. 4–7, 67–70.

[55] Lilley, Modernism, pp. 149 ff.; Houtin, op. cit., pp. vi, 131–134; Holland, op. cit., p. 19. See also a historical survey, Albert Houtin, La Question Biblique chez les Catholiques de France au XIXe Siècle (Paris, Alphonse Picard et Fils, 2nd ed., 1902, pp. iv, 378), and Édouard LeRoy, Dogme et Critique (Paris, Bloud et Cie, 1907, pp. xvii, 387).

Maurice Blondel (1861–1949), professor of theology in the University of Aix, whose *l'Action*, first published in 1893,[56] attracted wide attention, and his friend and pupil Lucien Laberthonnière (1860–1932). Blondel differed profoundly from neo-Thomism and was, accordingly, regarded with suspicion by its exponents, but the Pope held him to be orthodox and a valuable apologist for the faith.[57] Writings of Laberthonnière, priest, Oratorian, and specialist on the philosophy of religion, were condemned by the Holy Office.[58] Outstanding in the movement in Italy were a priest, Romolo Murri, who brought into being the *Lega Democratica Nazionale* (the Democratic National League), which aimed not so much at intellectual as at political, moral, and religious renovation, and Antonio Fogazzaro, a layman, centre of a group in Milan who published a review, *Rinnovamento*. Numbers of other periodicals appeared in Italy, among them *Nova et Vetera*, written chiefly by priests, and *Studi Religiosi*, mainly on Biblical criticism, initiated in 1901 by Salvatore Minocchi.[59] In his book *Il Santo* ("The Saint"), published in 1905, Fogazzaro urged on the Pope a reform of the Church that would attack four evils which he believed rampant—falsehood, clerical domination, avarice, and immobility.[60] In Germany Franz-Xavier Kraus of Freiburg and Hermann Schell (1850–1906) of Würzburg were prominent. In 1897 a book by the latter was published, *Der Katholizismus als Prinzip des Fortschritte* ("Catholicism as Principle of Progress"), the title of which was an indication of the contents. It created an enormous stir, especially in Germany. Eventually his apologetic works were placed on the Index. A little later he came out with *Die neue Zeit und der alte Glaube* ("The New Age and the Old Faith"), with much the same general theme. In *Christus* (1902) he sought to take advantage of the critical studies of the New Testament to trace a picture of Jesus.[61] In the University of Strasbourg two professors, Martin Spahn and Albert Ehrhard, a priest, were promulgating Modernist views. Two periodicals in Bavaria, founded by priests, were advocating religious reform.[62] Modernism also had advocates among the clergy in Belgium, Holland, and Poland.[63]

Modernism, then, was a movement for adjusting the Roman Catholic Church

---

[56] Maurice Blondel, *l'Action* (Paris, Félix Alcan, 2 vols., 1937).

[57] Houtin, *Histoire du Modernisme Catholique*, pp. 12, 13, 28, 29, 51; Blaise Remeyer, *La Philosophie Religieuse de Maurice Blondel, Origine, Évolution, Maturité et Achèvement* (Aubier, Éditions Montaigne, 1943, pp. 348); Katherine Gilbert, *Maurice Blondel's Philosophy of Action* (Chapel Hill, Department of Philosophy, University of North Carolina, 1924, pp. 94).

[58] *Enciclopedia Cattolica*, Vol. VII, pp. 775–777; Houtin, *op. cit.*, pp. 98, 146.

[59] Sabatier, *Modernism*, pp. 118–128; Buonaiuti, *Il Modernismo Cattolico*, pp. 133–173; Perrotta, *The Modernist Movement in Italy*, pp. 37 ff.; Rivière, *op. cit.*, pp. 265 ff.

[60] Houtin, *Histoire du Modernisme Catholique*, pp. 135, 136; Lilley, *op. cit.*, pp. 129 ff.

[61] Buonaiuti, *op. cit.*, pp. 225–240; Hocedez, *Histoire de la Théologie au XIXe Siècle*, Vol. III, pp. 172–179; Rivière, *op. cit.*, pp. 274 ff.

[62] Houtin, *Histoire du Modernisme Catholique*, pp. 105, 106.

[63] *Ibid.*, pp. 112, 113.

intellectually to the currents of the revolutionary age more widespread, especially among the clergy, than any earlier one of the century. It was akin to contemporary movements in Protestantism which were attempting so to reshape theology and attitudes towards the Bible as to take account of recent findings and theories in natural science and of the critical historical approach to the Scriptures.[64] It aroused much interest among Protestants, especially Protestant liberals. In France the Protestant pastor and scholar Paul Sabatier was actively and sympathetically concerned and hoped for a fresh reform within the Roman Catholic Church.[65]

As we have seen, Rome took vigorous action which nipped the Modernist movement in the bud. In 1893 Leo XIII, in *Providentissimus Deus,* came out against forms of Biblical study which were a feature of Modernism. However, it was the more conservative Pius X who in 1907 in the decree *Lamentabili* and the encyclical *Pascendi* took the decisive steps to purge the Church of Modernism.[66] The requirement of an anti-Modernist oath from the clergy, set forth in a *motu proprio* of September, 1910, specifically applied to those about to be promoted to major orders, parish priests, priests who preached or heard confessions, canons, officials in the bishop's curia, ecclesiastical tribunals, congregations and tribunals in Rome, superiors of religious communities, and teachers. The oath included the firm acceptance of the belief that God can be known by natural reason, external proofs of revelation, including miracles and prophecies, and the divine institution of the Church by Christ while on earth, founded upon Peter and his successors forever. It also demanded the rejection of the suggestion of the evolution of dogmas in such fashion that they pass to a sense different from that first held by the Church, the condemnation of the use of textual criticism as the one and supreme rule in interpreting Scripture, the disavowing of the position that there is nothing divine in sacred tradition and that those who deal with history and theology must strip themselves of the preconceived opinion of the supernatural origin of Catholic tradition and of the divine assistance promised for the perpetual preservation of each revealed truth. The oath also entailed the abjuration of believing the unchanging truth otherwise than as "it was preached by the Apostles from the beginning." [67]

The effect of the firm action of Pius X was the nearly complete termination of the Modernist movement in the Roman Catholic Church. Some who had espoused it submitted. A few were excommunicated or left the Church. Journals which smacked of Modernism were suppressed. A few men were dis-

---

[64] Petre, *Modernism,* pp. 101–112.

[65] See, for example, Sabatier, *op. cit., passim.*

[66] See an English translation of *Pascendi* in George Tyrrell, *The Programme of Modernism* (New York, G. P. Putnam's Sons, 1908, pp. xvii, 245), pp. 149 ff.

[67] Petre, *Modernism,* pp. 241–246.

missed from teaching posts.[68] Some continuation there was, but such clergy as espoused it were ultimately expelled from the Church. Thus the learned and deeply religious priest and professor Ernesto Buonaiuti (1881–1946), a native and long resident of Rome, ordained priest in 1903, and with a prodigious literary and scholarly output, was sometimes called the last of the Modernists. He was excommunicated in 1921, reconciled, and finally excommunicated in 1924.[69] In Spain a layman, Miguel de Unamuno y Jugo (1864–1936), a university professor, not usually classed as a Modernist, was beginning to write in a vein which from the standpoint of the Roman Catholic Church was far from orthodox, and his books spread far beyond the borders of the country. After 1914 much more was to come from his pen.[70]

ATTEMPTS TO MEET THE CHALLENGE: POSITIVE OFFICIAL MEASURES THROUGH THE PROMOTION OF THE STUDY OF THOMAS AQUINAS

The ecclesiastical authorities were not content with censuring the several attempts to meet the challenge of the revolutionary age which seemed to them to endanger the faith. We have seen that beginning with Leo XIII Rome vigorously supported the study of scholastic philosophy and theology, especially that of Thomas Aquinas. We have also noted that the revival of scholasticism and Thomism had begun before Leo gave it his blessing. It had precursors in Italy, in France, in Germany, where Mainz was a centre, and in Spain.[71] In the Syllabus of Errors Pius IX had accorded the movement support by condemning the assertion that the principles employed by the school men were not in accord with the needs of the times and the progress of science. But it was Leo XIII in the encyclical *Æterni Patris,* issued in 1879, near the beginning of his pontificate, who gave the revival its greatest impetus. Leo did not content himself with that pronouncement. He knew that in some quarters it was greeted more with astonishment than with praise. He followed it by appointments of Thomist scholars to chairs in institutions in Rome, including the Roman College, the College of the Propaganda, the Minerva, and the Gregorian University, and pressed on Catholic universities in other centres and countries the importance of similar action. In 1880 he decreed Thomas Aquinas patron of all Catholic schools. Later he inscribed the name of Aquinas in the martyrology and inserted lessons from him in the Roman breviary. He commanded the preparation of a new complete edition of the works of Aquinas and entrusted it to the Dominicans. To promote the study of Thomistic theology he en-

[68] Houtin, *Histoire du Modernisme Catholique,* pp. 204 ff.

[69] Marcella Rava, *Bibliografia Degli Scritti di Ernesto Buonaiuti* (Florence, Nuova Italia, 1951, pp. xxvi, 226), pp. vii–xxi.

[70] See, for example, Miguel de Unamuno, *Esayos* (Madrid, Publiciones de Residencia de Estudiantes, 7 vols., 1916–1918).

[71] Hocedez, *op. cit.,* Vol. III, p. 45; Bellamy, *La Théologie Catholique au XIXe Siècle,* pp. 146, 147.

couraged the formation of philosophical academies and himself founded the Academia Romana di San Tommaso.[72]

With such active patronage from the Pope, Thomistic studies became popular in Roman Catholic circles. The Gregorian University in Rome became a noted centre. There the outstanding authority was the Jesuit Louis Billot (1846–1931), who for a quarter of a century held the chair of dogmatics and in 1911 was created Cardinal.[73]

Variant interpretations of Aquinas arose. Thus some of the Dominicans declared that Billot was reading into Aquinas his own theories. Since the *doctor angelicus* was of their order, they felt a proprietary interest in him.[74]

A distinct school of scholastic studies was developed at Louvain under the leadership of Désiré Joseph Mercier (1851–1926). During student days at Louvain Mercier had given himself to the study of Aquinas. When on the continued insistence of Leo XIII in his efforts to promote Thomistic studies a post in them was created at Louvain, in 1882 Mercier, still young, was appointed to it. There he sought to achieve a synthesis of the experimental sciences with Thomistic philosophy. To do this he made himself familiar with the natural sciences, especially psychology. His lectures attracted an increasing number of students and in 1888 with the hearty approval and financial aid of Leo he launched the Higher Institute of Philosophy. Through it he sought to encourage Catholics in the study of "science for its own sake" who by their attainments would "win the right to speak to the scientific world and compel attention" and to do this in a fellowship in which the integration with Thomistic philosophy would be accomplished. Although in 1906 Mercier was transferred to Malines as Archbishop, the Institute continued.[75]

Criticism of Mercier's enterprise came from two sides. On the one hand were the traditional Thomists who could see in modern thought only errors.[76] In the main Mercier and Maurice de Wulf, who supported him, sought to disarm this opposition, by insisting that the Institute avoided theological issues, concerned itself only with philosophy, and regarded that discipline as neutral: its students would not deal with physics, chemistry, biology, history, and economics with the purpose of finding in them confirmation of their religious beliefs.[77] On the other hand, some Modernists regard the Institute as hopelessly medieval. When

[72] Hocedez, *op. cit.*, Vol. III, pp. 47, 48; Bellamy, *op. cit.*, pp. 148, 149.

[73] La Piana, *Recent Tendencies in Roman Catholic Theology*, pp. 242, 243, 257–267; *Enciclopedia Cattolica*, Vol. II, pp. 1637, 1638.

[74] La Piana, *op. cit.*, p. 243.

[75] A. Laveille, *A Life of Cardinal Mercier*, translated by A. Livingstone (New York, The Century Co., 1928, pp. 251), pp. 1–127; L. de Raeymaeker, *Le Cardinal Mercier et l'Institut Supérieur de Philosophie de Louvain* (Louvain, Publications Universitaires de Louvain, 1952, pp. 275), *passim*.

[76] Hocedez, *op. cit.*, Vol. III, p. 51.

[77] La Piana, *op. cit.*, pp. 249–256.

in supporting Pius X in the condemnation of Modernism Mercier mentioned Tyrrell as of that school, the latter replied with a vigorous defence which was also an attack.[78]

THE CONTINUATION OF THEOLOGICAL DEBATE
WITHIN THE LIMITS SET BY THE CHURCH

While the Roman Catholic Church was narrowing the scope of theological discussion inside its ranks, within the limits which it set theological activity and debate continued. In ruling out Hermes, Günther, traditionalism, fideism, ontologism, and Modernism, and in affirming the immaculate conception and Papal infallibility, the Church restricted the boundaries of its theology. However, issues remained on which it had not officially spoken. Within its family, interest in them was keen and writing extensive. Many of its sons were occupied in setting forth its teachings in systematic form for the instruction of its clergy and laity and in defending them against its critics. Because of the deepening gulf between the Roman Catholic Church and the revolutionary world, beyond the walls of that body most of this intellectual activity attracted little attention. Yet in any survey of that branch of Christianity it must be at least summarized.

One of the issues was the relation of grace to free will. Here the debate continued which had raged between "Molinism," taking its name from the Jesuit Louis de Molina (1535–1600), and those who followed the Dominican Dominic Bañez (1528–1604), an ardent Thomist, confessor and faithful friend of Teresa of Avila. The Council of Trent had declared to be dogmas of the Church both the supremacy of God's grace in effecting salvation, as against Pelagianism and semi-Pelagianism, and the unimpaired consent of the will, as against some forms of Protestantism. Obviously such related questions were involved as the foreknowledge and providence of God and predestination to eternal life or damnation. Molina had attempted to resolve the dilemma by what he called the Divine *scientia media*. In general the Jesuits adhered, with modifications, to his position, which emphasized the unrestrained freedom of the will but sought to do so without detracting from the efficacy and priority of grace, while the Dominicans, with Bañez as their early spokesman, interpreted Aquinas as stressing the infallibility of grace without denying the necessity of the free cooperation of the will. The controversy had died down with the suppression of the Society of Jesus. After the Society was restored it was renewed. It continued through the nineteenth century and in its course many books and articles were written.[79]

---

[78] George Tyrrell, *Medievalism: a Reply to Cardinal Mercier* (London, Longmans, Green & Co., 1909, pp. viii, 214), *passim*.

[79] Hocedez, *op. cit.*, Vol. III, pp. 236–244.

Questions related to the problem of grace and free will are the fate of un-baptized infants and of non-Christians who have not had sufficient opportunity to hear of Christ to accept the salvation provided through him. In the seven-teenth and eighteenth centuries the prevailing opinion among Roman Catholic theologians held out little or no hope for the majority of mankind. In the nine-teenth century the trend was towards a less grim view. Numbers of theologians believed that unbaptized infants who died at birth or before reaching the age of responsibility had natural happiness and some even maintained that they might enjoy heaven. Several taught that if a non-Christian did not oppose the grace of God, God would not fail him but would accord him justification. Some Thomists argued that every man on attaining the age of full reason is given the alternative of directing his life towards the supernatural goal or of falling into mortal sin. Salvation would, then, be possible for one who had never heard of Christ or who through invincible ignorance had not accepted the Catholic faith.[80]

A similar discussion was being carried on in some Protestant groups. As in the Roman Catholic Church, the trend was towards hope for those who had died outside the faith. Here may have been a phase of the optimism which characterized much of the nineteenth-century Occident.

Another subject which engaged the attention of Roman Catholic theologians was whether sanctification, the partaking of the divine nature, is through uncreated or created grace. If through uncreated grace, it is through the presence in the soul of the Holy Spirit and the union of the soul with the Trinity. This was said to have been the view of the Greek Fathers. The school men, in contrast, believed that the partaking of the divine nature was through created grace and that this is through infused grace by which the image of God emerges by a supernatural assimilation with God of him who is sanctified. In the nineteenth century at least one theologian argued for a combination of both views. Another held that the two forms of grace are inseparable. The question was also debated whether the Scriptures present an ambiguity: they seem to teach that all three Persons of the Trinity dwell in the soul of the justified and yet some passages and the Greek Fathers appear to affirm a special relation between the justified soul and the Holy Spirit.[81]

Still another problem was an analysis of the act of faith. The Vatican Council declared that the ground of faith is the authority of the divine revelation. It also affirmed that faith should be consonant with reason. How are the two to be reconciled? The specialists were not fully agreed.[82]

The sacraments were the subject of much discussion. Had they, as the

[80] *Ibid.*, pp. 245–253.
[81] *Ibid.*, pp. 154–160.
[82] *Ibid.*, pp. 260–272.

Modernists declared, developed gradually, or, as had been held by theologians from the sixteenth century, had they from their institution by Christ been seven in number? Since the Council of Trent theologians had been divided over whether the sacraments had been endowed by God, as the source of all grace, with immediate and instrumental efficacy, or whether their effect was that of mediating grace and dependent upon prayer and other means. The one was called the "perfective," the other the "dispositive" view. In the nineteenth century each had its advocates. Some sought to combine them.[83]

What is the essence of the Eucharist? Is it an oblation, a sacrificial rite which embodies the sovereignty of God over life and death, not only commemorating the passion and death of the Saviour, truly present on the altar, but with the victim actually sacrificed? This view had nineteenth-century advocates. Another view defended in the nineteenth century held that since the risen Christ does not suffer, he is not sacrificed, but that in the change in the bread and wine on the altar, their substance destroyed to produce Christ, there is the necessary essence of sacrifice. Another opinion, learnedly supported in the nineteenth century, was that the humanity of Christ has two modes of being: one in heaven, where he enjoys all the prerogatives of his glory and is not the victim, and in the mass in the transubstantiation of the bread and wine, where he has a state equivalent to death and is delivered to the will of men who are able to dispose of the sacramental elements as they please. Another position, set forth by Billot, was that the death of Jesus on the cross cannot be repeated and that therefore Christians cannot in the mass put their Saviour to death as an offering to the Father, but that to perpetuate the sacrifice on Calvary Christ instituted a rite in which under the appearance of bread and wine his body and blood are present. There were other problems connected with transubstantiation to which solutions were offered. Some of the solutions were condemned by Rome.[84]

The official decree proclaiming the immaculate conception as dogma gave marked impetus to the already popular mariology. The demand arose and was pressed on the Vatican Council to pronounce the assumption of the Virgin as dogma, but it was not until the next century that the request was granted. Many wished Mary proclaimed the mother of men, the coöperatrix, the core-demptrix, and the mediatrix of the graces. Mercier was outstanding in pressing for this definition. His efforts were so far successful that the feast was instituted of Mary mediatrix of all the graces. Theologians devoted attention to these aspects of the Virgin and some came out plump for them.[85] Concurrently the rising devotion to the spouse of Mary reinforced by Pius IX, who proclaimed Joseph patron of the universal Church, and by Leo XIII, who in an encyclical

[83] *Ibid.*, pp. 272–280.
[84] *Ibid.*, pp. 280–305.
[85] *Ibid.*, pp. 314–316; Bellamy, *La Théologie Catholique*, pp. 268 ff.

in 1889 gave reasons for supporting this step, encouraged the development of a theology of Saint Joseph.[86]

In the face of the hostility of a revolutionary world towards the Church and in view of the need of defining the relations of the Church with that world and of the increasingly closely knit character of the Roman Catholic Church, much attention was paid to ecclesiology.[87] Here was a major contribution of Leo XIII to theology. To him both the denial that the Church is a visible institution and the view that it is a human institution without contact with the divine life were errors to be denounced. He regarded the Church as the mystical body of Christ composed of two elements, the one human and visible, and the other divine. He declared it to be one and a perfect society.[88]

Moral theology had its students, and especially the relation of Christianity to the society in which it is placed. The resurgence of the life of prayer and devotion also brought increased concern for mystical theology.[89]

The renewal of the great historic orders, especially the Dominicans, Franciscans, and Jesuits, promoted interest in theology, for all three had traditionally been engaged in its study. Current attacks on the faith stimulated the development of apologetics. A flood of handbooks in theology furthered the preparation of the clergy.[90]

It seems almost invidious to single out for mention any of the many orthodox theologians of the century. Some we have already noted. Two others may be named as among the more prominent. One was Johann Baptist Franzelin (1816–1886). A Jesuit who spent most of his life in Rome, in spite of chronic ill health he wrote prodigiously. He was skilled in Hebrew, Arabic, Syriac, and Chaldean, but it was for his writings in theology that he was chiefly noted. They had an extensive circulation and formed the basis of the preaching of many of the clergy. In 1876, against his vigorous protests, he was created Cardinal. He continued to live abstemiously and distributed his income among the poor, foreign missions, and convents impoverished by the expropriations by the Italian Government.[91] A younger contemporary, Matthias Joseph Scheeben (1835–1888), whose works on theology were widely read and quoted, was trained in the Gregorian University and was committed to neo-scholasticism. For more than a quarter of a century (1860–1888) he taught in the major seminary in Cologne and thus helped to shape many priests.[92]

[86] Hocedez, *op. cit.*, Vol. III, p. 317.

[87] *Ibid.*, pp. 319–321; Bellamy, *op. cit.*, pp. 226 ff.

[88] Hocedez, *op. cit.*, Vol. III, pp. 387–394.

[89] *Ibid.*, pp. 323–349; Cayré, *Patrologie et Histoire de la Théologie*, Vol. III, pp. 420 ff.

[90] Hocedez, *op. cit.*, Vol. III, pp. 357 ff.; Cayré, *op. cit.*, Vol. III, pp. 457 ff.

[91] *The Catholic Encyclopedia*, Vol. VI, p. 242.

[92] Matthias Joseph Scheeben, *Gesammelte Schriften* (Freiburg, Herder, 4 vols., 1949–1951); *Dictionnaire de Théologie Catholique*, Vol. XIV, pp. 1270–1274.

GROWING ATTENTION TO BIBLICAL STUDIES AND ARCHEOLOGY

Roman Catholics were not content to leave Biblical questions to those who from the standpoint of the Church were employing the modern critical methods in a manner dangerous to faith. An increasing number were devoting themselves to the scholarly study of the Scriptures.

The Vatican Council condemned what it believed to be a false conception of the inspiration of the Scriptures and held that they should be interpreted according to the tradition of the Church.[93]

Far from being quieted by the pronouncement of the Vatican Council, debate and discussion mounted. The temper in intellectual circles and in Protestantism was such that the problems disclosed by critical scholarship became more rather than less prominent. The positions of the disputants ranged all the way from those who refused to yield any point to modern criticism, through those who, though conservative, would take account of the new criticism, to those who saw in the Bible a book whose values were purely religious and which was not designed to teach either the natural sciences or "profane" history. The range within the last group was wide and included such men as Loisy. Controversy became explosive when Maurice le Sage d'Hauteroche de Hulst (1841–1896), rector of the Catholic Institute in Paris, came out with an article, *La Question Biblique* ("The Biblical Question"), which he meant to be a defence of Loisy, then a member of his faculty. It was this which precipitated the issue by Leo XIII of the encyclical *Providentissimus Deus* (1893) which we have already noted.[94] Later, in 1901–1902, Leo inaugurated in Rome the Biblical Commission (*Commissio Pontifica de re Biblica*) which among other objects was intended to maintain the observance of the encyclical, to decide on Biblical questions debated among Catholic scholars, to publish studies on the Bible, and to see that the Vatican Library was properly equipped with the appropriate tools. Among its early pronouncements were endorsements of the Mosaic authorship of the Pentateuch and the composition of the Fourth Gospel by the Apostle John.[95]

Shortly before the storm aroused by *La Question Biblique,* a centre of Biblical studies was begun in Jerusalem which was to have a long and distinguished history. The founder was Albert Lagrange (1855–1938), a Dominican, the date was 1890, and the place was the traditional site of the martyrdom of Stephen. In connexion with that centre, beginning in 1892 a periodical, *Revue Biblique Internationale,* was published. From the pen of Lagrange an amazing number of books, articles, and book reviews flowed which showed an

---

[93] Hocedez, *op. cit.,* Vol. III, p. 124.
[94] *Ibid.,* pp. 124–130; Bellamy, *op. cit.,* p. 78; Lecanuet, *La Vie de l'Église sous Leo XIII,* pp. 353 ff.; Lilley, *Modernism,* pp. 45 ff.
[95] *The Catholic Encyclopedia,* Vol. II, pp. 557, 578.

acquaintance with the more significant current literature in the field, both Roman Catholic and Protestant. Lagrange was attacked by conservatives on the right and extremists on the left, but he sought to remain within the bounds set by Papal encyclicals and decrees and had the confidence of Leo XIII. For a time under the next pontificate he was viewed with suspicion in high quarters, but he made a full submission to Pius X, and the latter declared himself completely satisfied. Temporarily removed by his superiors from his post in Jerusalem, in Paris he continued to write and before long was reinstated. With Papal approval the *Revue Biblique* was continued under his editorship.[96]

The nature and method of the inspiration of the Scriptures were debated. In what way was the phrase *Deus est auctor,* confirmed by the Vatican Council, to be understood? Franzelin put forward a view which was long held by the Jesuits, that God so controlled the choice of words as to prevent any error. From this the Dominicans dissented, and yet did not reach agreement among themselves: Lagrange criticized Franzelin's position, but by no means all in the Order of Preachers followed him.[97]

Roman Catholic scholars were not blind to the importance of archeology. Throughout the Western world interest in it was mounting. Its achievements shed light on the Bible. In Rome archeologists were unearthing much of the city's past: Roman Catholic savants were particularly concerned with what investigation could disclose about the course of Christianity. The catacombs, as the burial places of the early Christians and scenes of Christian worship, were excavated and explored: about the middle of the century Giovanni Battista de Rossi was a distinguished pioneer, continuing the work of Marchi. Under pressure from the enthusiasts and somewhat reluctantly, Pius IX created the Commission on Sacred Archeology. Through it the excavations and the study of epigraphy were pursued and amplified.[98]

ACHIEVEMENTS IN SCIENCE

Roman Catholics aided in the advances in the natural sciences which were a striking feature of the revolution. Their part was not as great as those of Protestant heritage or of some who had abandoned the Christian faith. It was far less than had been that of their Catholic predecessors at the dawn of science in the Middle Ages. Yet some, among them both clergy and devout laity, made notable contributions. We have suggested the achievements of the Jesuits. They were particularly marked in meteorology and in geology, including the observations of earthquakes. As we have suggested, the Mendelian theory of inheritance which had a major role in biology was based upon prolonged experiments

[96] F. M. Braun, *l'Œuvre du Père Lagrange, Étude et Bibliographie* (Freiburg, St. Paul, 1943, pp. xv, 343), *passim;* Lecanuet, *op. cit.,* pp. 332–334.

[97] Hocedez, *op. cit.,* Vol. III, pp. 135–140.

[98] Aubert, *Le Pontificat de Pie IX,* p. 186; *The Catholic Encyclopedia,* Vol. I, p. 690.

in the hybridizing of plants made in the garden of an Augustinian monastery in Moravia by the Abbot, Johann Gregor Mendel (1822–1884).[99] Louis Pasteur (1822–1895), a French layman of sincere and simple Catholic faith, achieved distinction by his discoveries of micro-organisms which led to antiseptic surgery and, through his initiative, curbed a disease of silkworms then decimating the silk industry, and were followed by vaccinations to control anthrax, hydrophobia, and rabies.[100] To Branley, a French Catholic, was attributed a share in the invention of wireless.[101] De Hulst organized International Scientific Congresses of Catholics.[102]

SUMMARY REFLECTIONS

The brief survey contained in this chapter of the response of Roman Catholics of Europe to the intellectual aspects of nineteenth-century revolutionary movements has already been partly summarized in the generalizations with which it was introduced. They need not be repeated. However, to them may be added two reflections supported by the preceding pages.

First, in theological thought and Biblical scholarship is further evidence of what was seen in other aspects of the life of the Roman Catholic Church, the rapid centralization of the total life of the Church under the Pope and the Roman curia, with frank opposition to many of the trends in the revolution in the midst of which the Church was set. Rome watched carefully the several attempts by earnest intellectuals to think through afresh the Catholic faith with loyalty to it, but with regard to the thought patterns of the day. When it judged them to be departing from the faith of which it believed the Pope to be the divinely appointed custodian, it condemned them. No prudential considerations entered: even when it was clear that adverse action would bring the accusation that the Papacy was holding to an outmoded past and that defections would follow, no compromise was tolerated. Rome was willing to face the hypotheses and conclusions of contemporary scholarship, but it was firm that they must be examined in the light of the historic deposit of faith and if contrary to it be rejected.

Second, in marked contrast with the sixteenth century, no great religious revolution issued from the Roman Catholic Church. As we have seen, that church displayed a marked revival after the low ebb in the latter part of the eighteenth century. Yet from none who differed from Rome sufficiently to be condemned by it or to secede from it did there arise a religious movement comparable in dimensions to Protestantism. The Old Catholics were a small minority. Such men as Hermes, Günther, Loisy, and Tyrrell did not head

[99] *The Encyclopædia Britannica,* 14th ed., Vol. XV, pp. 241, 242.
[100] *Ibid.,* Vol. XVII, pp. 358–360.
[101] Moody, *Church and Society,* p. 157.
[102] *The Catholic Encyclopedia,* Vol. VII, p. 538.

awakenings which affected millions and led to new churches as did Luther, Calvin, and the other Protestant reformers. Nor did they move over into Protestantism.

Why this contrast? The answer must in part be conjectural. Negatively it can be said with assurance that it was not from any lack of vigour in Protestantism. As we are to see in the next two volumes, never before had Protestantism showed more life and never had it spread as widely as in the nineteenth century. It may have been that no new movements comparable to Protestantism emerged from the Roman Catholic Church because Protestantism had preempted the field. Certainly it had long carried with it the large majority of the populations of non-Latin Western Europe. The fact that even in the first wave of the Protestant movement only small minorities of Latin culture joined it may help to account for the unwillingness of most of those who revolted from the Roman Catholic Church in the nineteenth century to become Protestants. Indeed, it may be significant that the largest defection, that of the Old Catholics, was chiefly in Southern Germany, on the border of the Latin world, and that a majority of those condemned by Rome for doctrinal aberrations were from the northern fringes of what had once been within the limes of the Roman Empire—outstanding among them Hermes, Günther, Döllinger, Loisy, and Tyrrell. The Roman Catholic Church had long had its chief strength among peoples fully assimilated to Latin culture. From them had arisen most of its monastic orders and congregations, its leading theologies, and its major revivals. It was no accident that its official language was Latin and its ecclesiastical capital the former capital of the Roman Empire. So far as the Latin world was Christian, it felt more at home in the Roman Catholic Church. In spite of the progress of de-Christianization, through baptism the vast majority in Latin Europe were still nominally in the Roman Catholic fold.

CHAPTER XI

The Country-by-Country Course of the Roman Catholic Church in Nineteenth-Century Europe

W E ARE now to sketch country by country the course of the Roman Catholic Church in Europe in the nineteenth century. Because of the limitations of space it must be done briefly. Moreover, in tracing the history of the Papacy and of the main phases of life of that church in Europe which transcended national boundaries we have already dealt with much which otherwise would be covered as we pass from land to land. In this chapter we will confine ourselves chiefly to the relations of Roman Catholics with political and social movements, mention a selection of the outstanding personalities whom we have thus far not met, and here and there say a little about major figures and trends in the literature which was shaping the attitudes of a large portion of the reading public. Because it was there that the Roman Catholic Church had its historic centre and reflected its genius, we will begin with Latin Europe and then will pass on to other sections. Since it was not only the country from which the political and much of the intellectual revolution spread but at the outset of the century had also been the dominant power on the Continent, France will first engage our attention. As the seat of the Papacy, Italy must follow. Then will come other Latin lands and later the countries outside Latin Europe.

FRANCE: THE COMPLEX SCENE

From the standpoint of Christianity in the nineteenth century France presented a scene which was apparently kaleidoscopic—an aftermath of the revolutionary storm that had rocked the country and Europe from 1789 to 1815. The factions and forces which had contested for mastery continued: the Bourbons and the old aristocracy who resisted change; the republicans of various hues with their slogan of liberty, fraternity, equality; the Bonapartists who rallied around Napoleon and his family; loyal Roman Catholics, some liberal, some Gallican, some ultramontane; and the religiously sceptical, many actively hostile. These forces fought for mastery with the result that in the hundred years from 1815 to 1914 France had successively five forms of government—the restored Bourbons, the July Monarchy, the Second Republic, the Second Empire, and the Third Republic.

The scene was increasingly complex. Socially it was compounded of the old aristocracy, now generally loyal to the Roman Catholic Church, the *bourgeoisie,* among whom were many indifferent or antagonistic to the Church, the peasants, a large proportion of them conservative and holding to the traditional faith, and the labourers in the growing industries drifting from the Church or at times violently hostile. Philosophers, in the first half of the century including Victor Cousin (1792–1867), who was much influenced by Scottish thinkers and by Schelling and Hegel, tended to be religiously unorthodox. Most of the great literary figures who helped to shape the reading public did not conform to Christian morals or faith—among them Flaubert, Balzac, George Sand, and the Dumas, father and son, especially the father. For a time Sainte-Beuve was a devoted Catholic and a disciple of Lamennais. Victor Hugo had a Catholic phase. Protestants were a small but at times influential minority. Roman Catholics were deeply divided.

FRANCE: UNDER THE RESTORED BOURBONS TO 1830

When, in 1815, the great coalition overthrew the Napoleonic empire and safely exiled the Corsican to remote St. Helena, the Bourbons were restored to the throne of France. Many of the returning *emigrés* would have liked to renew the *ancien régime* in its entirety. But the clock could not be put back. France had been changed. The ground had been prepared for the continuation of the conflict between the Roman Catholic Church and the forces arrayed against it which was to characterize the ensuing century. On the one hand was the inheritance of the age of Voltaire and of the anti-Christian features of the Revolution. Many of the *bourgeoisie* and of the masses were either unbelieving or lukewarm. The character of the older clergy reinstated by the restoration did not lessen the indifference and hostility: for the most part the priests were sober, pious, and conscientious, but they were out of touch with the currents of the new age and were unsympathetic towards them. On the other hand was the revival of the Roman Catholic faith of which Chateaubriand was a pioneer and Maistre, Bonald, and Lamennais were apostles. In their years of exile numbers of the returning aristocracy had repudiated the scepticism which had been fashionable in their circles on the eve of the Revolution and were ardent supporters of the union of throne and altar. Zealous *missionnaires* traversed the countryside and the towns and by highly emotional methods sought to win back the de-Christianized. The scene was further confused by the ecclesiastical arrangements under the Concordat of 1801 negotiated by Napoleon, the Organic Articles by which he had sought to govern the Church, the return of bishops and clergy of the *Petite Église* who had refused to subscribe to that settlement, reinvigorated remnants of Gallicanism, the militant ultramontanism which had Lamennais as its leading prophet, the reëntrance of the Jesuits, the survival of the enmity which in the last century had driven the Society out of the realm, and the issue of the support of the clergy and of the possible return of the properties of the Church which had been confiscated during the Revolution.

For a time Louis XVIII sought to mediate between the voices raised in strident discord. Privately sceptical but publicly conforming to his expected role of "his most Christian Majesty," not wishing to go again on his travels, he promised to rule as a constitutional monarch with a parliament and ministry and consented to the retention of some of the features of the ousted regime. Among them were the Napoleonic code and the state educational system headed by the *Université*. In 1817 a concordat was negotiated with Rome to displace that of 1801, but violent opposition in France prevented its ratification and led to compromise arrangements under the earlier document.

Beginning with 1820 conservative pro-clericals gained control of the Government and with variations retained it for ten years. Louis XVIII died in 1824 and was succeeded by his brother, Charles X. Charles had had a profligate youth but had reformed, had become staunchly religious, and was an ardent supporter of the Church. Drastic legislation was passed which was intended to buttress the Catholic faith. *Petits séminaires* taught by Jesuits, ostensibly for the preparation of the clergy, enrolled many sons of the aristocracy who had no intention of entering the priesthood but whose parents wished them to have a strongly Catholic education. Independent of the state system, their existence provoked intense criticism from anti-clericals. On the other hand, the Gallican tendencies of the regime were subjected to the blasts of Lamennais: that fiery ultramontane stigmatized the Government and even the bishops as "schismatics."

In July, 1830, an uprising in Paris sparked by the liberals and strongly anti-clerical unseated the unpopular Charles X and brought in a liberal monarchy under Louis Philippe, Duke of Orleans, of a branch of the Bourbons which had a record of sympathy with the Revolution.[1]

FRANCE: THE CHURCH UNDER THE JULY MONARCHY, 1830–1848

The July or Orleans Monarchy, as the regime of Louis Philippe was called,

[1] On the years 1815–1830 see Dansette, *Histoire Religieuse de la France Contemporaine*, Vol. I, pp. 233–284; Brugerette, *Le Prêtre Français et la Société Contemporaine*, Vol. I, pp. 1–63; Phillips, *The Church in France, 1789–1848*, pp. 151–229, 262, 263; Leflon, *La Crise Révolutionnaire, 1789–1846*, pp. 328–335, 393–400, 417–421; Debidour, *Histoire des Rapports de l'Église et de l'État en France*, Vol. I, pp. 325–412; Vicomte de Guichen, *La France Morale et Religieuse au Début de la Restauration* (Paris, Émile Paul, 1911, pp. 311); Geoffrey de Grandmaison, *La Congregation (1801–1830)* (Paris, Plon, 1889, pp. xxiv, 409).

lasted for eighteen years. Its head was known as the Citizen King, officially King of the French rather than King of France. The Government was largely in the hands of the *bourgeoisie.*

The Government took a middle course as far as the Church was concerned. For the most part its leaders were not hostile, but many of them were sceptical. Prominent in it was the historian and statesman François Pierre Guillaume Guizot (1787–1874), a man of high integrity and a firm believer in divine revelation, by heredity and conviction an unwavering Protestant. Louis Philippe himself was at best lukewarm, and while his queen and sister were deeply religious, he could not be expected to give the Church the zealous endorsement accorded it by his predecessor. At the outset some of the clergy, including the Archbishop of Paris, were unreconciled to the new regime. However, Pius VIII urged the bishops to coöperate and conferred on Louis Philippe the designation "his most Christian Majesty." [2] In general the policy of the Government was to employ the Church as a useful adjunct of the state and to recommend to the Pope as bishops men of strong Gallican principles.

This Erastianism met with vehement opposition. The Catholic revival was not halted by the anti-clericalism which had contributed to the uprising of 1830. Moreover, under the leadership of Lamennais a group of young men insisted that the Church be not subject to the state but under the full control of Rome: the Church was to be liberated from domination by the state; it was not to be dependent on the state for financial support and the state was not as heretofore to name the bishops. Only thus, they held, could the Church fulfil its function of saving individual souls and society. Prominent among those who in their youthful ardour rallied around Lamennais were Jean Baptiste Henri Lacordaire (1802–1861), inspiring orator and, as we have seen, the reviver of the Dominicans in France, Charles Forbes René de Montalembert (1810–1870), born in London to a distinguished emigré, Guéranger, whom we have met as a leader of the renewed Benedictines,[3] and Alphonse Marie Louis de Lamartine (1790–1869), poet, statesman, man of letters, a precursor of the romantic movement in France. Victor Hugo (1802–1885), earlier a Voltairian sceptic, drawn to the faith by reading Chateaubriand and Lamennais, made his first confession to the latter and for several years had him as his spiritual director. In his Catholic stage Sainte-Beuve (1804–1869) was one of Lamennais's disciples.[4]

To give his ideas wider circulation, in October, 1830, Lamennais began in Paris a daily newspaper, *Avenir,* with the significant motto *Dieu et la liberté* ("God and liberty"). It advocated complete religious liberty, separation of Church and state, freedom of schools and colleges, freedom of the press, liberty

[2] Leflon, *op. cit.,* pp. 420, 421; Vidler, *Prophecy and Papacy,* pp. 153–157.

[3] George Goyau et P. de Lallemand, *Lettres de Montalembert à La Mennais* (Paris, Desclée de Brouwer et Cie, 1932, pp. xxvii, 321), *passim.*

[4] Phillips, *op. cit.,* pp. 234–237; Vidler, *op. cit.,* pp. 146–149.

of association, universal suffrage, and decentralization.[5] In the venture Lacordaire and Montalembert actively shared. To promote the policies set forth in *Avenir* Lamennais organized the *Agence générale pour la défense de la liberté religieuse*. *Avenir* quickly won an international hearing, partly because of its literary quality and even more because many welcomed its views. Numbers of the students for the priesthood and of the younger clergy warmly agreed with it.

Vehement opposition to *Avenir* promptly developed. The Government was hostile. Many of the bishops were outspoken critics, and some forbade their clergy to read the sheet. The Holy See, now occupied by the newly elected conservative Gregory XVI rather than Pius VIII, who had been friendly to Lamennais, was critical. In November, 1831, after a little more than a year from its inception, Lamennais discontinued *Avenir*. As we have seen, he, Lacordaire, and Montalembert went to Rome to lay their case before the Pope: Gregory was unconvinced and the following August issued an encyclical, *Mirari vos*, which condemned some of the principles for which *Avenir* stood. All three submitted.[6] While never formally excommunicated, in 1834 Lamennais broke with the Church. Lacordaire and Montalembert did not follow him and their friendship with him ended.[7]

The discontinuance of *Avenir* and the waning of Lamennais's star did not seriously check the return to religion. The years covered by the July Monarchy were marked by a resurgence of life in France in both the Catholic and the Protestant Church and by striking revivals in other countries in the Roman Catholic Church and in Protestantism.

The rising tide in French Roman Catholicism had many expressions. Men thronged Notre Dame to listen to the eloquence with which Lacordaire, preaching from its pulpit, was presenting the Christian faith. Gustave Xavier Lacroix de Ravignan (1795–1858), a Jesuit, attracted only slightly smaller audiences. In his later days even Talleyrand, the former bishop and Voltairian sceptic who chameleon-like had served the state in every regime since before the first Revolution and who died in 1838 at the age of eighty-four, was reconciled to the Church. The Dominicans and Franciscans reëntered the country, various congregations, especially of women, were formed, the Society of St. Vincent de Paul, founded by Ozanam in 1833, swelled to major proportions, devotions to the Sacred Heart multiplied, and pilgrims flocked to the Curé of Ars.

Many Roman Catholics were politically and socially more or less liberal. A addition to those we have mentioned, Armand de Melun had begun his social

---

[5] Vidler, *op. cit.*, pp. 162–165; Mourret, *Le Mouvement Catholique en France de 1830 à 1850*, pp. 75–108.

[6] Vidler, *op. cit.*, pp. 187 ff.; Mourret, *op. cit.*, pp. 109–141; Leroy-Beaulieu, *Les Catholiques Liberaux: l'Église et la Liberalisme de 1830 à nos Jours*, pp. 78 ff.; J. A. Ryan in *The Catholic Historical Review*, Vol. XXIII, pp. 31–37.

[7] Vidler, *op. cit.*, pp. 218 ff.; Phillips, *op. cit.*, pp. 254 ff.

activity, and in the same camp, among others, were an economist, Villeneuve-Bargemont, Gerbet, a bishop, Buchez, returned to the Catholic faith from being a *Carbonaro* and a Saint-Simonian Socialist, and Charles de Coux, a professor.[8]

Notable though the Catholic revival was, after 1830 the number of ordinations to the priesthood declined sharply and did not increase until 1847. Of the clergy still serving in 1848 nearly half had been ordained before 1830 and tended to favour the senior Bourbon branch.[9]

FRANCE: THE CHEQUERED COURSE OF THE CHURCH UNDER THE SECOND REPUBLIC AND NAPOLEON III, 1848–1870

The explosion of 1848 releasing the rising pressures of Western European liberalism was set off by a blast in Paris which sent the prudent Louis Philippe to quiet refuge in England and gave France the Second Republic.

In 1848 the attitude towards the Church of those who inaugurated the Second Republic was almost the reverse of that of the public in 1830. In 1830 the Church had been regarded as the bulwark of the hated Charles X. In 1848 the leaders of the Revolution hailed Christ as the friend of democracy and viewed the Church with respect. Pius IX, still in his liberal stage, felicitated the people of Paris. The bishops welcomed the new Government. Priests endorsed the trees of liberty which symbolized the Republic. The change was due at least in part to Lamennais and the men, like Lacordaire, who had once hailed him as a prophet.[10] Ozanam and early efforts on behalf of workmen in the new industries contributed to it.[11] The labours and examples of devoted priests and religious, men and women, most of them obscure, had widespread fruit. New congregations, some of which we have noted, were coming into being. Others which we have not had the space so much as to name were springing from the faith and heroism of those who placed Christ above all earthly rewards.[12]

[8] Phillips, *op. cit.*, pp. 259–285; Spencer, *Politics of Belief in Nineteenth-Century France*, pp. 61–103; Collins, *Catholicism and the Second French Republic*, pp. 34, 35; Leroy-Beaulieu, *op. cit.*, pp. 105 ff.; Moon, *The Labor Problem and the Social Catholic Movement in France*, pp. 16–25; Weill, *Histoire du Catholicisme Libéral en France, 1828–1908*, pp. 51 ff.

[9] Phillips, *op. cit.*, pp. 286–304; Spencer, *op. cit.*, pp. 104–115; Debidour, *op. cit.*, Vol. I, pp. 444–480; Collins, *op. cit.*, pp. 37–46; Mourret, *op. cit.*, pp. 188–232; Paul Thureau-Dangin, *l'Église et l'État sous la Monarchie de Juillet* (Paris, E. Plon et Cie, 1880, pp. viii, 497), pp. 123 ff.; Leflon, *l'Église de France et la Révolution de 1848*, p. 25.

[10] Phillips, *The Church in France, 1848–1907*, pp. 22–25; Brugerette, *Le Prêtre Français et la Société Contemporaine*, Vol. I, pp. 123–131; Debidour, *Histoire des Rapports de l'Église et de l'État en France*, Vol. I, pp. 482–484; Collins, *op. cit.*, pp. 54 ff.; Leflon, *l'Église de France et la Révolution de 1848*, pp. 14 ff., 31 ff.

[11] Duroselle, *Les Débuts du Catholicisme Social en France*, pp. 198 ff.; Horton, *The Philosophy of the Abbé Bautain*, pp. 28, 29.

[12] See an account of one of these and of the beginning in 1848 out of years of sacrifice of the founder, Pierre Jean Gailhac, of the Religious of the Sacred Heart of Mary, in Helene Magaret, *Gailhac of Beziers* (New York, Longmans, Green & Co., 1946, pp. 262).

At the outset the Government was well disposed towards the Church. A majority of those elected to the new Assembly were either convinced Catholics or friendly. Catholic votes contributed to the election of Louis Napoleon to the presidency of the Republic. That adventurer, who was swept into power through the fame of his uncle, Napoleon I, conveniently declared himself for freedom of religion and education and the temporal sovereignty of the Pope, three objectives of Catholics.[13]

Early results of the alliance of the Catholics with the new regime were the reinstatement of Pius IX in Rome by French arms and the passage of the Falloux Laws. Catholics maintained that the educational system instituted by Napoleon I and controlled by the *Université* was in the hands of irreligious men and was de-Christianizing the youth. Under the July Monarchy they had attempted to have it altered but had failed. Now (1850) they succeeded. The legislation took its name from Frédéric Alfred Pierre, Comte de Falloux (1811–1886), a Catholic, minister of public instruction and religion. A compromise, it satisfied neither the anti-clericals nor the more extreme among the Catholics. There were still to be "public" schools under the state and for their supervision a national board and regional or departmental bodies were set up on which Catholics, Protestants, Jews, and the *Université* were represented. In addition *libres* ("voluntary") schools were to be conducted by associations or individuals. While no mention was made of religious orders and congregations, it was understood that they might maintain schools if their teachers met certain professional qualifications.[14]

The issue of education was to plague Church-state relations for the rest of the century. It was not confined to France but was present in many other countries. In Western Europe since the collapse of the Roman Empire schools had traditionally been a function of the Church. In the nineteenth century secular-minded nationalists insisted that to ensure the loyalty of the on-coming generations all education must be maintained and directed by the state. The Roman Catholic authorities and many Protestants and Orthodox declared that if youth were not to be de-Christianized the Church must at least have a voice in education and urged that a place for instruction in religion be made in the curriculum.

It was debatable whether the monopoly of education by the Church would prevent departure from Christianity. Most of those who before the nineteenth century led in the movement away from the faith had had their formal educa-

[13] Phillips, *op. cit.*, pp. 25–32; Collins, *op. cit.*, pp. 71 ff.; Debidour, *op. cit.*, Vol. I, pp. 485–487; Brugerette, *op. cit.*, Vol. I, pp. 137–148; Leflon, *l'Église de France et la Révolution de 1848*, pp. 78 ff.; Weill, *op. cit.*, pp. 91 ff.

[14] Phillips, *op. cit.*, pp. 35–38; Debidour, *op. cit.*, Vol. I, pp. 501 ff.; Brugerette, *op. cit.*, Vol. I, pp. 149–163; Mourret, *op. cit.*, pp. 233–270; Collins, *op. cit.*, pp. 266 ff.; Weill, *op. cit.*, pp. 99 ff.

tion in schools supported by one of the orders and congregations or by one or another of the churches. In the nineteenth and twentieth centuries church schools and instruction in Christianity in state schools did not prevent millions who had had their formal education in them from becoming indifferent or even antagonistic to the faith. That was true whether the form of Christianity was Roman Catholic, Protestant, or Orthodox.

FRANCE: THE SECOND EMPIRE

In 1852 Louis Napoleon had himself proclaimed Emperor of the French with the title Napoleon III and thus restored the Napoleonic empire.

Under the Second Republic and the Second Empire new Roman Catholic leadership came to the fore. Lamennais still had friends and admirers and was a member of the Assembly, but he had broken with the Church. He died in 1854. Lacordaire welcomed the Republic and as a member of the Assembly sat on the left. He was openly critical of Napoleon III and, retiring from politics, gave himself chiefly to his duties as the Provincial of the Dominicans and to a school of which he became the head.[15] He died in 1861. Montalembert lived until 1870. However, he was unhappy over the trend away from the liberalism and the high hopes of the early days of the Second Republic. A new star was arising in the person of Louis Veuillot (1813–1883). Of humble parentage and having had a long early struggle with poverty, at the outset Veuillot was not friendly to the Church. However, a trip to Rome made him an ardent Catholic. A journalist, wielding a fearless and mordant pen, before 1848 he had gained fame as a writer for *l'Univers,* a Catholic journal run by laymen. As a poet, pamphleteer, and novelist he also attracted attention. Vehement in whatever he espoused or attacked, he was emphatically ultramontane, was anti-liberal in politics, and denounced free-thinking.[16] Often opposed to Veuillot was Félix Antoine Philibert Dupanloup (1802–1878). Of prodigious energy, a fiery pulpit orator, a skilled director of souls, Dupanloup had a prominent and stormy career. As the head of a preparatory seminary he acquired fame as an educator. He won notable converts and was credited with bringing Talleyrand back to the faith. In 1849 he was appointed Bishop of Orleans and remained in that see until his death. He developed the life of his diocese in many ways but also found time to be an outstanding figure in Paris, the nation, and Rome. He had a large share in shaping the Falloux Laws, stood for preserving the Papal States, and opposed the affirmation of Papal infallibility, but acquiesced when that dogma was promulgated.[17] From these representative men it can be seen

[15] Spencer, *op. cit.,* pp. 143, 144.
[16] W. Gurian in *The Catholic Historical Review,* Vol. XXXVI, pp. 385–414; Spencer, *op. cit.,* pp. 108 ff.; *The Catholic Encyclopedia,* Vol. XV, pp. 394–396; Weill, *op. cit.,* pp. 117 ff.
[17] R. Aubert, *Monseigneur Dupanloup et le Syllabus* in *Revue d'Histoire Ecclésiastique,* Vol. LI,

that during the Second Empire French Roman Catholics were badly divided between liberals, Gallicans, and ultramontanes.[18]

The relations between the Second Empire and the Roman Catholic Church were chequered. At first Napoleon III had the Church as an ally,[19] but as the years passed relations became strained. To be sure, some of the bishops appointed by the emperor remained loyal to him. However, through his coöperation with Cavour in the war with Austria and the ensuing absorption of the larger part of the Papal States by the Kingdom of Italy Napoleon incurred the enmity of both liberals and conservatives among the Catholics. The Government suppressed *l'Univers* for its attacks. Louis Édouard Désiré Pie (1815–1880), Cardinal and Bishop of Poitiers, educated by the Jesuits and Benedictines, staunchly orthodox, advocate of the restoration of the Bourbons, was a thorn in the flesh. Catholic schools were producing graduates who were against the emperor and his ministers.[20] From 1860 onward the Government tightened restrictions on religious congregations and church schools. Victor Duruy, a pronounced anti-clerical, was for a time minister of instruction.[21]

While the Church made some gains, opposition to it and to the Christian faith was rising. Although the Government removed Renan from his professorship in the Collège de France, his *Vie de Jésus* had a wide reading. Stories derogatory to the morals of the clergy were blazoned in newspapers and books and what were declared to be clerical superstitions were derided. The affirmation of the immaculate conception was greeted with scepticism. The endorsement by the Bishop of Grenoble of the appearances of the Virgin at La Salette was met with hoots. The Syllabus of Errors aroused a storm of criticism. Among writers who dominated the world of literature and social and philosophic thought the picture was mixed. Some were Protestant, others were loyally Catholic, others, with a Catholic heritage, were deeply religious but were groping for faith, and still others were sceptical, some sorrowfully, some belligerently. Victor Hugo passed out of his Catholic stage but retained his belief in immortality and God.[22]

pp. 79–142, 471–512, 837–915; Spencer, *op. cit.*, pp. 148–150; *The Catholic Encyclopedia*, Vol. V, pp. 202, 203.

[18] Maurain, *La Politique Ecclésiastique du Second Empire de 1852 à 1869*, pp. 31 ff.

[19] John Plamenatz, *The Revolutionary Movement in France, 1815–1871* (New York, Longmans, Green & Co., 1952, pp. xiv, 184), p. 107; Maurain, *op. cit.*, pp. 40, 41.

[20] Spencer, *op. cit.*, pp. 167–172; *The Catholic Encyclopedia*, Vol. XII, p. 76; Brugerette, *op. cit.*, Vol. I, pp. 166–176; Maurain, *op. cit.*, pp. 325 ff.

[21] Phillips, *op. cit.*, pp. 103–109, 130, 131; Maurain, *op. cit.*, pp. 567 ff., 580 ff., 676 ff., 748 ff.

[22] Phillips, *op. cit.*, p. 130; Spencer, *op. cit.*, pp. 206, 207; Maurain, *op. cit.*, pp. 164, 165. On various trends in literature and thought see Albert Leon Guérard, *French Prophets of Yesterday: a Study of Religious Thought under the Second Empire* (London, T. Fisher Unwin, 1913, pp. 288), *passim*.

FRANCE: THE THIRD REPUBLIC AND MOUNTING ANTI-CLERICALISM

The Franco-Prussian War with its crushing defeat and the fall of Napoleon III precipitated a complex struggle in which the majority of practising French Roman Catholics were arrayed against the Government. We have already seen something of the role played by the Popes. We must now rapidly sketch the story in the French setting.

The defeat and capture of Napoleon III by the Germans was quickly followed by the proclamation of a Republic. However, it was not at all clear that this, the third government since 1789 to bear that designation, would prove more viable than its two predecessors. In its early days it was challenged by the radical Commune which took possession of Paris and was suppressed in a blood bath in which both sides showed no mercy and the Archbishop, Georges Darboy (1813–1871), was slain by the insurgents. The Republic might not have endured had its opponents been able to unite. Those who wished the restoration of the monarchy were divided between the "Legitimists," who, intensely conservative, supported the grandson of Charles X, and the "Orleanists," who, "Liberal Loyalists," wished a constitutional monarchy like that in Great Britain and presided over by a grandson of Louis Philippe. The "Imperialists," supporters of the Bonaparte family, discredited by the recent fiasco, had little strength. In contrast with their welcome to the Second Republic, most of the bishops and clergy were set against the Third Republic and advocated the restoration of the monarchy.

At the outset the Church and the Government were reciprocally friendly. In the newly elected National Assembly conservatives were in the large majority. They succeeded in obtaining legislation favourable to the Church, including an increase in the appropriations for the support of public worship and the founding of five theological faculties on a par with the state universities.[23] In the first few years of the Republic the Government was inclined to seek the counsel of Rome in nominating bishops: increasingly, in contrast with the earlier decades after 1815, the episcopate was not from the aristocracy and Gallican in conviction, but was from outside the aristocracy and was ultramontane.[24] This circumstance contributed to friendly relations with the Vatican, and that in spite of the well-known antipathy of Pius IX to democracies.

However, in France the tide of secularism was mounting. Bishops bewailed the lack of students in the seminaries.[25] For those who enrolled, the training was more designed to produce saints, in the sense accepted in the Church, than

---

[23] Phillips, *op. cit.*, pp. 165–168, 182; Debidour, *l'Église Catholique et l'État sous la Troisième Republique (1870–1906)*, Vol. I, pp. 9–15, 25–28; Brugerette, *Le Prêtre Français et la Société Contemporaine*, Vol. II, pp. 66 ff.

[24] Brugerette, *op. cit.*, Vol. II, pp. 26 ff.

[25] *Ibid.*, p. 43.

to meet the intellectual, political, and social currents of the age.[26] Freemasons, while numbering only a few tens of thousands, were influential in state and society and in general were anti-clerical.[27] In 1877 Gambetta, a Freemason, starred in an election campaign with the battle-cry, coined before 1870, *Le cléricalisme, voilà l'ennemi*, which helped to bring the republican forces into power. The anti-clericals were the more venomous because of their intense nationalism. They were trying to rebuild and unify a France weakened by defeat and inner divisions. To them the Roman Catholic Church seemed the major obstacle to that goal. They wished to strengthen the state and to subordinate the Church to it. To this end they strove for a secular education in which all schools would be those of the state.[28]

In facing these threats the Catholic cause was handicapped by dissensions among its supporters. Some Catholics were "Legitimists," some "Orleanists," others, at first a minority but later more numerous, *"Ralliés,"* who supported the Republic but in turn were divided over the policies to be pursued, and still others "Christian Democrats." Pie was followed at Poitiers by Henri Bellot des Minieres, bishop from 1881 to 1888, who, a nominee of the Government, in striking contrast with his predecessor was emphatically for the Republic and was under attack from most of his clergy.[29] Veuillot and Dupanloup were often verbally at swords' points, the former intransigent and the latter more conciliatory towards the Republic.[30] A large proportion of the parish clergy were swayed by *l'Univers*, with its pro-Royalist polemics. The majority of the bishops believed it too extreme, and with most of the laity it counted for little.[31]

The Roman Catholic Church was losing ground in the cities. The time had passed when laymen thronged Notre Dame, as they had to hear Lacordaire. Even when not hostile, many were indifferent and left religion to their wives and daughters. The labourers in the industries were increasingly moving away from the Church: thousands either ignored the efforts to win them and redress their wrongs which were made in the name of the faith by such men as Albert de Mun, La Tour du Pin, and Harmel (Chapter VIII) or viewed them with jaundiced eyes as too paternalistic and aristocratic.[32]

If the Catholics did not present a solid front, neither did their opponents. Bitter personal rivalries sometimes paralyzed their efforts. Nor did they pursue

---

[26] *Ibid.*, pp. 47 ff.; Phillips, *op. cit.*, pp. 187, 188.

[27] Spencer, *Politics of Belief in Nineteenth-Century France*, pp. 252, 253; Phillips, *op. cit.*, pp. 185, 186; Lecanuet, *Les Dernières Années du Pontificat de Pie IX*, pp. 482 ff.; Acomb, *The French Laic Laws (1879–1889)*, pp. 113 ff.

[28] Phillips, *op. cit.*, pp. 189, 190; Lecanuet, *op. cit.*, pp. 492 ff.; Acomb, *op. cit.*, pp. 94 ff.

[29] Corrigan, *The Church in the Nineteenth Century*, p. 220; J. B. Woodall, *Henri Bellot des Minieres, Republican Bishop of Poitiers 1881–1888*, in *The Catholic Historical Review*, Vol. XXXVIII, pp. 257 ff.

[30] Phillips, *op. cit.*, pp. 173, 174.

[31] Lecanuet, *op. cit.*, p. 338.

[32] Lecanuet, *Les Premières Années du Pontificat de Léon XIII*, p. 427.

a consistent policy of hostility. In its extension of the French colonial empire the Government found it advantageous to support French missionaries. The formation by Bismarck in 1882 of the Triple Alliance of Germany, Austria-Hungary, and Italy left France in dangerous isolation, and its statesmen found it wise to avoid antagonizing Leo XIII, who was proving an adroit diplomat.[33]

We have already (Chapter VII) summarized most of the main stages in the struggle between the Church and its enemies. We need here do no more than briefly review them and slightly amplify them. In 1880 the laws bearing the name of Jules Ferry, anti-clerical minister of public instruction, were enacted after debates which stirred the country. These eliminated the clergy from the national and local bodies which controlled the schools and reduced the privileges of the theological faculties so recently authorized.[34] Also in 1880 decrees were issued which commanded the Jesuits, as a congregation unauthorized by law, to disband within three months and required all other unauthorized congregations to apply for recognition within that time. In spite of protests from the Pope and the French bishops and the resignation of scores of civil officials the Jesuits were expelled. The other unauthorized congregations refused to apply for authorization. On pressure from Rome most sought a compromise, but some refused. The unauthorized congregations were suppressed, in several instances by armed force.[35] The anti-clericals now focussed their enmity on the authorized congregations. In 1884 a special death tax was enacted which was to be collected on the demise of each of their members. Some congregations paid it; others evaded it.[36] In 1880 fees for primary education in state schools and teacher training schools were abolished, to the disadvantage of Church schools, and provision was made for state secondary schools for girls, a form of education in which the Church had had a monopoly. In 1882 religious instruction in the state schools was abolished: to meet the challenge numbers of new Catholic schools were set up.[37]   .

The advance of secularization took place not only in education. Civil funerals became common, more and more charities once a responsibility of the Church were taken over by civil authorities, and in 1884 divorce was legally sanctioned.[38]

FRANCE: ATTEMPTED RECONCILIATION WITH THE THIRD REPUBLIC

As the years passed and the Republic seemed firmly established, more Roman Catholics became convinced that, however much they disliked its policies, they

---

[33] Debidour, *l'Église Catholique et l'État*, Vol. I, pp. 315 ff.; Phillips, *op. cit.*, pp. 212, 213.

[34] Phillips, *op. cit.*, pp. 195–198; Debidour, *l'Église Catholique et l'État*, Vol. I, pp. 208 ff.; Acomb, *op. cit.*, pp. 136 ff.

[35] Brugerette, *op. cit.*, Vol. II, pp. 166 ff.; Debidour, *l'Église Catholique et l'État*, Vol. I, pp. 240 ff.

[36] Brugerette, *op. cit.*, Vol. II, pp. 187, 188.

[37] Phillips, *op. cit.*, pp. 204–207.

[38] Acomb, *op. cit.*, pp. 193 ff.

must accept it: they had the support of Leo XIII. What was called *ralliement* followed. By the encyclical *Immortale Dei* (November 19, 1885) in which he approved the general principle of participation of the people in government, although not specifically mentioning France, Leo encouraged the faithful to coöperate with the Republic. In 1881 in the encyclical *Libertas praestantissimum bonum* Leo reinforced *Immortale Dei*.[39] Many Catholics, among them staunch royalists and Mun, supported Boulanger in the latter's ill-starred campaign in 1888–1889 to revise the constitution and set up a dictatorship.[40] The defeat of Boulangism was followed by progress in *ralliement*. The Boulangist scare persuaded many supporters of the Republic that they must conciliate the Catholics. Moreover, some of their leaders feared that the abrogation of the concordat which had long been desired by the radicals would deprive the state of the control which it now exercised over the Church through the nomination of bishops and the payment of the salaries of the clergy. Many of the officers in the army and navy had been educated under Jesuit influence and were friendly to the Church. In international and colonial affairs the Government needed the goodwill of the Papacy. On their side, the Catholics had been shaken by the Boulangist fiasco. Among the younger priests were some who believed that if the de-Christianization of the country, particularly of the cities and the workingmen, was to be halted, the Church must make common cause with democracy and the Republic: they led the "Christian Democrats." [41] The Assumptionists, ardent ultramontanes, had those who sought recognition of the Republic as a means of reshaping it in the interests of the Church.[42]

Ralliement, with its attempt to bring Catholics to the support of the Republic and to induce the Government to take a less unfriendly attitude towards the Church, was beset with difficulties but for several years seemed to make progress. By his encyclical *Sapientiae Christianae* (January 10, 1890) Leo gave it impetus. The tempest aroused by the open endorsement by Lavigerie (November 12, 1890), prominent in the French hierarchy, of the full coöperation of the Church and the Republic, a position taken with the approval of the Pope, temporarily clouded the fair prospect.[43] Most of the French bishops were far from assenting but could scarcely come out openly against the Holy See. Cardinal Richard, Archbishop of Paris, from intensely royalist stock, publicly interpreted Leo XIII as wishing the faithful to rise above partisan political disputes and refrain both from condemning any form of government and from participating in any. With this the majority of the bishops agreed and in April, 1891,

---

[39] Phillips, *op. cit.,* p. 215; Lecanuet, *Les Premières Années du Pontificat de Léon XIII*, pp. 304 ff., 350, 351; Moon, *The Labor Problem and the Social Catholic Movement in France*, pp. 207, 208.
[40] Lecanuet, *Les Premières Années du Pontificat de Léon XIII*, pp. 358–378.
[41] Phillips, *op. cit.,* pp. 220–228; R. F. Bynes in *The Catholic Historical Review*, Vol. XXXVI, pp. 286–306.
[42] Lecanuet, *La Vie de l'Église sous Léon XIII*, pp. 220 ff.
[43] Lecanuet, *Les Premières Années du Pontificat de Léon XIII*, pp. 377 ff.

the *Union Chrétienne de la France* was organized with a programme of political neutrality.[44] In January, 1892, five of the six French Cardinals came out with a declaration, promptly adhered to by seventy-five other bishops, which denounced the sins of the Republic against the Church but exhorted the faithful while resisting the encroachments of the secular on the spiritual domain to a "frank and loyal acceptance of political institutions." [45] With this the Pope seems not to have been satisfied, for the next month he issued the encyclical *Inter innumeras sollicitudines* in which he tactfully but firmly declared it the obligation of Catholics to take their part in the Republic, "for the civil power is of God and always of God," and from within to work for the rectification of wrongs done to the Church.[46] The ultra-royalists were angered by the encyclical and did not hesitate to speak their minds.[47] Yet a large number of Catholics agreed with the Pope. Those then in power in the Government were eager to accept the olive branch and a spokesman pronounced himself for the "new spirit, the spirit which tends to reconcile all Frenchmen round the ideas of good sense, justice, and charity." [48]

The reconciliation of French Catholics with the revolutionary age appeared to be gaining in meeting the problems brought by industrialization and the attitudes of youth. We have already noted (Chapter VIII) that as early as the 1870's Comte Albert de Mun was founding *Cercles Catholiques d'Ouvriers,* that in the 1890's, encouraged by *Rerum novarum,* Harmel was organizing study groups, that in the 1880's Mun began *l'Association Catholique de la Jeunesse Française,* and that in the 1890's Sillon came into being.[49] In 1899 *Action Libérale Populaire* (the Popular Liberal Party) was formed by Jacques Piou, a Catholic, under the full endorsement of Mun, with an emphasis on social action and a programme of economic and political reform.[50]

France: The Third Republic; The Final Rupture

In a France badly splintered politically and with the Catholics no more united than their opponents, the "new spirit" could not last. Anti-clericals were resolute and vocal. In the Dreyfus scandal which rocked the nation during the 1890's not all Catholics were against that scapegoat of anti-semitism and the army, and the Pope came out frankly for the victim, but enough Catholics sided with his enemies to reinforce the enmity against the Church.[51]

[44] *Ibid.,* pp. 408 ff.
[45] *Ibid.,* pp. 472–495.
[46] Soderini, *Leo XIII, Italy and France,* pp. 203–222. The French text is in Debidour, *l'Église Catholique et l'État,* Vol. II, pp. 524–534.
[47] Lecanuet, *Les Premières Années du Pontificat de Léon XIII,* pp. 515 ff.
[48] Phillips, *The Church in France 1848–1907,* p. 236.
[49] On a phase of Sillon see Charles Maurras, *La Démocratie Religieuse* (Paris, Nouvelle Librairie Nationale, 1921, pp. 560), pp. 3–175.
[50] Moon, *op. cit.,* pp. 227 ff.; Rollet, *l'Action Sociale des Catholiques en France, passim.*
[51] Phillips, *The Church in France 1848–1907,* pp. 250 ff.; Debidour, *l'Église Catholique et*

In 1901 the foes of the Church succeeded in pushing through the Associations Act. That law was directed chiefly against religious orders and congregations. For authorization each congregation must have a special legislative act. No one could teach in an educational establishment who was a member of an unauthorized congregation. Existing unauthorized congregations were given three months to comply: failure to do so meant dissolution. As we have seen, as a feature of the Catholic revival congregations had been multiplying, particularly in France, and had long been a target of anti-clericals. In 1876 authorized congregations for men numbered 32 with 22,843 members, and for women 903 with 113,750 members. In that year the men in unauthorized congregations totalled 7,444 and the women 14,003.[52] The congregations had not helped their cause by the chronic refusal of the majority to pay taxes levied by what they deemed unjust legislation. The large majority of the congregations decided to seek authorization, but a substantial minority refused. The enforcement of the law fell to the Premier, Combes, once a teacher in a seminary and a fervent ultramontane, but now as fiercely anti-clerical. Thousands of schools were closed. More than fifty congregations who made application were refused and were suppressed. Many of the members who were priests continued as seculars. A few congregations obtained authorization.[53]

Further measures against the Church followed. Late in 1893 nuns were expelled from the naval hospitals. The following April the crucifix was ordered removed from the law courts. Soldiers were forbidden to attend Catholic social clubs and restrictions were placed on collections in churches for the poor. In 1904 teaching of any kind except to novitiates for service abroad was forbidden to congregations, and all schools conducted by congregations were to be closed within ten years, and within ten years all teaching congregations were to be suppressed and no new members were to be admitted.[54]

Rupture of relations with the Papacy was not long delayed. As we have recorded, at French initiative diplomatic ties were severed in 1904, and in 1905 the step was taken which the more radical anti-clericals had long desired and some Catholics favoured: by legislative act the Concordat of 1801 under which Church and state had operated since the days of the first Napoleon was annulled.[55] By the law of separation, which applied to Protestants and Jews as

---

l'État, Vol. II, pp. 168 ff.; Nichols, *History of Christianity, 1650–1950*, p. 229; Moon, *op. cit.*, pp. 208–211; Brugerette, *Le Prêtre Français et la Société Contemporaine*, Vol. II, pp. 415 ff.

[52] Acomb, *op. cit.*, pp. 17, 18.

[53] Phillips, *The Church in France 1848–1907*, pp. 259 ff.; Debidour, *l'Église Catholique et l'État*, Vol. II, pp. 288–359; Lecanuet, *Les Signes Avant-Coureurs de la Séparation: les Dernières Années de Léon XIII et l'Avènement de Pie X*, pp. 255 ff.

[54] Phillips, *The Church in France 1848–1907*, pp. 273–275; Lecanuet, *Les Signes Avant-Coureurs de la Séparation*, pp. 548 ff.; Debidour, *l'Église Catholique et l'État*, Vol. II, pp. 545 ff.

[55] Of the extensive bibliography on the separation of Church and state, see Eug. Reveillaud, *La Separation des Églises et de l'État. Précis Historique Discours et Documents* (Paris, Fischbacher, 1907, pp. xii, 615), *passim;* Paul Sabatier, *Disestablishment in France* (New York, Charles Scrib-

well as to Roman Catholics, most of the church edifices, including the residences of the clergy, were declared to belong to the state. The buildings could be used rent free by voluntary associations of the faithful, but these must bear the expenses of the public exercise of religion. The voluntary support of the churches was the prevailing practice in the United States and the new commonwealths which were arising in the British Empire. In the next century it became general through much of Europe. However, in 1905 it was contrary to what had long been customary in most of Europe. Pope Pius X denounced the law of separation and condemned the associations authorized by that act.

FRANCE: AFTER THE RUPTURE

How serious would the rupture of relations with Rome and the separation of Church and state prove to be? At first sight to some it appeared disastrous, the more so because it followed closely on the heels of the dissolution of many of the congregations, the closing of thousands of Catholic schools, and the secularizing of other aspects of life. Moreover, these were the years when Modernism was mounting and when the Pope by his drastic measures against it was placing the Church athwart some of the most potent non-political features of the revolution. Was "the eldest daughter of the Church" on the way to being thoroughly de-Christianized?

The adjustment was difficult and at times painful, but the Roman Catholic Church survived. To be sure, many of the clergy were badly inconvenienced. The aged Cardinal Richard, Archbishop of Paris, was forced to move from his palace into another house and left under the sympathetic acclaims of members of his flock.[56] Some priests asked to be relieved of their clerical duties that they might make a living. Many continued their functions as pastors while working at other occupations to support themselves. The number of young men entering the priesthood sharply declined: within two years after disestablishment the enrolment in the seminaries fell off by about 50 per cent. No longer was the priest the chief man in the rural village. Now that state education prevailed, the teacher, trained in the secular attitude, competed with him and in places overshadowed him.[57] The control of the Vatican over the episcopate was heightened. The Pope need no longer be guided by nominations from the state or even confine his choice to a list provided by the bishops of the ecclesiastical

---

ner's Sons, 1906, pp. 173), *passim;* Brugerette, *op. cit.,* Vol. II, pp. 530 ff.; Debidour, *l'Église Catholique et l'État,* Vol. II, pp. 339 ff., 548 ff.; Phillips, *The Church in France 1848–1907,* pp. 275 ff.; Premoli, *Contemporary Church History,* pp. 111–114. Some of the expelled members of congregations hoped that the abrogation of the Concordat would facilitate their reëntry to the country: J. H. Moynihan, *The Life of Archbishop John Ireland* (New York, Harper & Brothers, 1953, pp. xii, 441), pp. 275 ff.

[56] Yvonne de la Vergne, *Good Cardinal Richard Archbishop of Paris,* translated by Newton Thompson (St. Louis, B. Herder Book Co., 1942, pp. 235), pp. 216 ff.

[57] Brugerette, *op. cit.,* Vol. III, pp. 22–33.

province in which the vacancy was found. The Pope early filled the fourteen sees left vacant by recent controversies with the Government and himself consecrated the new appointees, and in St. Peter's.[58] Bishops and their clergy were now liberated from control by the civil authorities. The Church could arrange as it saw fit the boundaries of its dioceses. The clergy were no longer subject to penalties for displeasing the state, such as the suspension of their salaries. Traces of Gallicanism survived, but on the whole ultramontanism had conquered. Working arrangements were devised, made possible by a law passed in January, 1907, by which the church buildings could continue to be used for worship. Parish committees laboured to maintain public worship, and private gifts came to the rescue of Catholic charities.[59]

The difficulties of the Roman Catholic Church in France after the separation from the state were heightened by the anti-Modernists, who were self-appointed vigilantes to detect and expose what they deemed departures from orthodoxy. They were not new: they had been active decades before the pronouncements of Pius X. Yet by their excesses they disturbed not only Pius X but even the ultra-conservative secretary of state, Merry del Val. Their efforts, sometimes akin to espionage, to detect heresy and to bring charges against the suspected, created a widespread spirit of fear among the clergy which lowered the morale of a body of men already suffering from the acts of the civil authorities.[60]

ITALY: GENERAL CONSIDERATIONS

As we move from France to Italy we must condense our account even more drastically because we have already seen most of its main outlines. In Italy the Papacy and the state were so closely interlocked that in our coverage of the one we have dealt with its relations with the other.

In approaching Italy we must remember that at the outset of the nineteenth century it was divided politically into many states, large and small. Geographically and to a certain degree culturally Italy was a unit. Yet cultural differences existed, especially between the North and the South. The achievement of political unity did not erase cultural and social diversity. Indeed, the Industrial Revolution accentuated the contrast between the North, increasingly given to manufactures and commerce, and the South, predominantly agricultural.

In as brief a sketch as this must be we can only hint at some of the religious manifestations of the hereditary differences. The new currents set up and released by the French Revolution had their chief leadership from the North: witness Mazzini and Garibaldi, the less extreme but more effective Cavour, the essentially pagan Giosué Carducci (1836–1907), outstanding in the literary

58 *Ibid.*, p. 11; Premoli, *op. cit.*, p. 115.
59 Brugerette, *op. cit.*, Vol. III, pp. 3–16; Premoli, *op. cit.*, pp. 115, 116.
60 Brugerette, *op. cit.*, Vol. III, pp. 303 ff.

revolt against the faith, and the sickly, physically deformed and pessimistic poet, Giacomo Leopardi (1798–1837). It was also from the area north of Rome that most of those came who, either as ecclesiastics or as laymen, led in the support of the Christian faith. All the Popes of the century except Leo XIII were born there and Leo was a native of a region only slightly south of Rome. Most of the new congregations had their rise in the North. The same was true of the chief figures in the Catholic intellectual revival. Among the latter was Alessandro Francesco Tommaso Manzoni (1785–1873). A native of Milan, in his young manhood he had lived in Paris in liberal, anti-clerical circles. Converted in his mid-twenties, he was profoundly Catholic and his poems, hymns, plays, and novels combined a high faith with a strong nationalism and a sympathy with the labouring classes.[61] However, one of the greatest and most original minds of the century, Benedetto Croce, was a Neapolitan.

Italy: The Progress of the Struggle Between De-Christianization and the Church

In Italy as in France the scene was complex, but in general there were two streams. Almost all the population were baptized in the Roman Catholic Church: Protestants were a much smaller minority than in France and until late in the century were mostly in the mountain valleys in the North to which persecution had confined them. But on the one hand were those, nominally Catholic, who were indifferent, sceptical, or openly critical and anti-clerical. Especially after the erasure of the Papal States and the Papal prohibition of participation in the government, a boycott more severe than that of the Third Republic by the Catholics of France, the governing classes were alienated. Few of the devout were on the faculties of the state universities. As a result a gulf existed between the clergy, trained in ecclesiastical institutions, and the lay intelligentsia. In the growing industrial and commercial cities, with notable exceptions the middle classes were too intent on making money to give more than formal attention to their religious duties. As elsewhere in much of Europe, the labourers in the factories were drifting away from the Church or were antagonistic. On the other hand, after 1815 the Roman Catholic faith had a decided revival. Not subjected in the latter part of the century to a series of blows such as those progressively dealt it in France by the Third Republic, the Church achieved some gains.[62]

---

[61] Hughes, *The Catholic Revival in Italy, 1815–1915*, pp. 3 ff.; Pietra, *Storia del Movimento Cattolico Liberale*, pp. 63, 66, 127 ff.

[62] As a partial bibliography of the relations between Church and state see Tomaso Chiusa, *La Chiesa in Piemonte dal 1797 ai Giorni Nostri* (Turin, Giulio Speirani e Figli, 4 vols., 1887–1892); Soderini, *Leo XIII, Italy and France*, pp. 2–122; Pierre de Montesquieu-Fezensac, *Rapports de la Papauté avec le Royaume d'Italie depuis 1870* (Paris, Recueil Sirey, 1936, pp. 158); Arturo Carlo Jemolo, *Chiesa e Stato in Italia negli ultimi cento anni* (Giulio Einaudi, 3rd ed., 1952, pp. 752), pp. 1–562. See also Halperin, *Italy and the Vatican at War, passim,* for its useful footnotes.

While it was not until 1929 that peace was formally declared and a working arrangement officially entered into, as time passed the sharp disjunction between the Church and the state was lessened. To be sure, the Roman question, as the issue of Papal sovereignty was known, remained an irritant, and in the 1880's, although educated in a seminary and a professing Catholic, Francesco Crispi (1819–1901), as Prime Minister, had annoying legislation passed. There were other disturbing incidents and measures.[63] Yet more and more Catholics participated in Italian politics, at first chiefly on the local and then on a national level. The rupture of diplomatic relations with France (1904) cancelled the long-cherished hope of the intervention of that government in behalf of Papal sovereignty and made for a less intransigent attitude towards the entrance of Catholics into Italian political life. Here was one reason for the creation in 1905 of the *Unione Popolare* (Chapter VII). The *Unione Popolare* was articulated with two other organizations, the *Unione Economico-social* and the *Unione Elettorale*.[64]

As a means of sharing in national life, although not confined to the political sphere, beginning in 1874 a National Congress of Catholics convened. It arose out of a youth movement, *Gioventù Cattolica Italiana,* which had as its motto "Prayer, action, sacrifice," sought to stem the wave of de-Christianization, and, with Papal approval, opened clubs for young men, mostly in the North. Out of the National Congress, as a permanent committee to coördinate what came to be called Catholic Action, *Opera dei Congressi* was begun. Its chief creator and its president until 1902 was Giovanni Battista Paganuzzi (1841–1923). A lay organization under the guidance of the clergy, it had self-sacrifice as a guiding motive. It was in conscious opposition to the Catholic liberalism which wished reconciliation with the Kingdom of Italy. In 1897 it counted 188 diocesan committees, 3,982 parochial committees, 708 boys' clubs, and 12 clubs for university students. In 1905, as we have seen, Pius X dissolved it and substituted for it the *Unione Popolare*.[65]

No such extensive social Catholic movement arose to deal with the problems brought by the Industrial Revolution as in France, Germany, Switzerland, Austria, and Belgium. The *Opera dei Congressi* and the *Unione Popolare* had more inclusive objectives. But Giuseppe Toniolo (1845–1918) was a Catholic economist who deserves to be ranked with such men as Ketteler, Mun, La Tour du Pin, and Perin. A native of Venice, for a generation he was a professor in the University of Pisa. In opposition on the one hand to *laissez-faire* individualistic economics and on the other to state Socialism, he was a warm advocate of a Christian school of social science as the one way of saving civilization from

[63] Soderini, *op. cit.,* pp. 49 ff.; Fonzi, *I Cattolici e la Società Italiana dopo l'Unità,* pp. 75 ff.
[64] Fonzi, *op. cit.,* pp. 89 ff.; Premoli, *op. cit.,* p. 79.
[65] Hughes, *op. cit.,* pp. 97 ff.; Premoli, *Contemporary Church History,* pp. 74, 75; *Enciclopedia Cattolica,* Vol. XII, pp. 305–308; Fonzi, *op. cit.,* pp. 59 ff.

disaster. Before promulgating the encyclical *Rerum novarum* Leo XIII more than once brought him into consultation. He was the first president of the *Unione Popolare* and sought to make of that movement a counterpart of the *Volksverein* of Germany.[66]

We have already seen (Chapter VIII) the amazing developments which came out of John Bosco's efforts to care for the youth in industrialized Turin. Bosco was trained in a seminary founded by the priest Pio Brunone Lanteri (1759–1830). Before the outbreak of the French Revolution Lanteri had been the moving spirit in the *Amicizia Cristiana,* an organization which sought to make "Christ reign as king over every heart" and which had many branches in Northern Italy and in adjacent countries. After that storm passed, he promoted the *Amicizia Cattolica* and the *Amicizia Sacerdotale* for the defence and restoration of the Christian faith and was the friend of such leaders of the revival as Maistre and Lamennais. He assisted in the founding of Catholic newspapers and of a new congregation, the Oblates of Mary.[67]

In addition to those which we have noted, other movements arose to meet specific challenges of the revolutionary age. Out of the *Gioventù Cattolica Italiana* eventually developed the *Federazione Universitaria Cattolica Italiana* for Catholic students in the state universities, with Giovanni Domenico Pini (1871–1930) as their creative chaplain.[68] In 1908, partly to take advantage of the increasing participation of women in public and professional life, the Italian Catholic Women's League was formed (*Unione fra le donne Cattoliche d'Italia*). It arose to oppose the discontinuation of religious instruction in government schools which was recommended by the National Council of Italian Women held in that year.[69]

Clergy emerged who gave outstanding leadership in meeting the challenge of the revolutionary century. Thus in 1897 the Barnabite Giovanni Semeria (1867–1931) by his preaching in Rome began attracting large congregations.[70] To the historic see of Milan, made doubly important by the centrality of that city in the industrialized North, there came as Archbishop in 1894 Andrea Carlo Ferrari (1850–1921). In that centre, threatened with de-Christianization, for more than a quarter of a century Ferrari revived seminaries, improved the quality of the clergy, promoted religious instruction, defended Catholic principles in family, school, and public affairs, furthered social reform, and favoured the participation of Catholics in the political life of the country.[71] Roughly contemporary with Ferrari was Pietro Maffi (1858–1931), in 1903

[66] Hughes, *op. cit.,* pp. 67–80, 102; *Enciclopedia Cattolica,* Vol. XII, pp. 305–308; Premoli, *op. cit.,* pp. 77, 78.

[67] Hughes, *op. cit.,* pp. 122 ff.; *Enciclopedia Cattolica,* Vol. VII, p. 898.

[68] Hughes, *op. cit.,* p. 103; *Enciclopedia Cattolica,* Vol. IX, p. 1486.

[69] Hughes, *op. cit.,* pp. 103, 104.

[70] *Ibid.,* pp. 110–114; *Enciclopedia Cattolica,* Vol. XI, pp. 275–277.

[71] Hughes, *op. cit.,* pp. 120, 121; *Enciclopedia Cattolica,* Vol. V, pp. 1190, 1191.

appointed Archbishop of Pisa, a university centre. A man of learning, he insisted on the solid education of the clergy. Adding to his duties as archbishop those of the director of the Vatican Observatory, he made that institution notable in the scientific world in the field of astronomy and meteorology.[72]

In Italy the nineteenth century ended, as it had begun, with the overwhelming majority of the population professedly Catholic. The headquarters of the Catholic Church were still in Rome, and that in spite of the fact that the Pope considered himself a "prisoner"; not since the sixteenth century had there been a non-Italian Pope. In its central administration the Roman Catholic Church remained predominantly Italian. In spite of the indifference and even the hostility of a large proportion of the population, the Church retained the loyal support of millions, and the decades after 1815 had witnessed a resurgence from the low ebb in the decades immediately before that year.

THE REVOLUTION IN SPAIN

The revolutionary forces which swept across Europe were not indigenous to Spain, but their effects on that country were profound and at times shattering. Spain had had her great day in the sixteenth and seventeenth centuries. By the nineteenth century she was in decline and had ceased to be the source of fresh movements in religion, thought, or art: the century witnessed the loss of most of her colonial empire and devastating internal convulsions.

Spanish Catholicism could not escape involvement. Since the conquest of the Moors and the expulsion of the Jews and Moriscos Spain had been solidly Catholic. The Protestant Reformation had touched only a small minority. The Inquisition had eliminated dissent or had driven it underground. Administratively the Church tended to be independent of Rome, but it was sturdily, even fanatically orthodox. Under these circumstances the political tempests of the century inevitably impinged on the Church. Complicated as they were by revolutionary liberal ideas from abroad, they had anti-clerical aspects.

The Napoleonic invasion brought with it a flood of the ideas and measures of the French Revolution, among them the suppression of the Inquisition and of many monasteries and the confiscation of much Church property. In 1812 anti-French patriots, but with liberal purposes largely from the French, drafted a constitution which, while preserving the monarchy, introduced an elected parliament and individual liberty and equality. Although declaring that the religion of the Spanish people was and always would be that of the Apostolic Church of Rome, it decreed the secularization of Church property and continued the annulment of the Inquisition.[73]

The expulsion of the French was followed by the return of the Bourbons

[72] Hughes, *op. cit.*, pp. 114–120; *Enciclopedia Cattolica*, Vol. VII, pp. 1813, 1814.
[73] Gams, *Die Kirchengeschichte von Spanien*, Vol. III, Part 2, p. 429; Peers, *Spain, the Church and the Orders*, p. 62.

with Ferdinand VII as king. Having learned nothing and forgotten nothing, Ferdinand and his entourage attempted to revive the pre-Napoleonic regime. But liberalism would not be quenched. In 1820 an insurrection compelled Ferdinand to adopt the constitution of 1812. Within a few months the liberal government forced the dissolution of nearly half the monasteries, tithes for the support of the clergy were halved and then completely cancelled, and many priests sought refuge in France.[74] But in 1823, by agreement of Austria, Prussia, and Russia, France, then ruled by ultra-conservatives, sent in an army which enabled the king to crush the liberals and the monasteries were restored.[75]

The death of Ferdinand VII in 1833 was followed by long years of civil strife in which the Church was involved. Ferdinand died without male issue. Before his demise he set aside the Salic Law which, followed by the Bourbons, forbade the throne to a woman, and named his infant daughter as his successor. Her claim, as Isabella II, was disputed by Ferdinand's brother Charles (Don Carlos). In general the conservatives sided with Don Carlos and the liberals with the cause of Isabella II. The liberals were divided between the extremists, *Exaltados,* and the moderates, *Moderados.* For some years during the minority of Isabella the *Exaltados* were in the saddle. The regime set up in her name forbade monasteries to receive additional novices, expelled the Jesuits, abolished the Inquisition, and dissolved the smaller monastic houses. Numbers of monks and priests were killed by mobs. Before long all monastic property was sequestered by the state, several bishops were exiled, an effort was made to separate the Spanish church from the Pope, tithes were abolished, and the possessions of the secular clergy were nationalized.[76] The regent, the Queen Mother Christina, sought to return to a conservative policy and was driven into exile in France (1841). The general in control pursued anti-clerical measures with a renewed attempt to sever the tie with Rome.[77] In 1843 Isabella, although only thirteen, was declared of age. Another general, Narvaez, came to power and, with a brief interruption, until 1854 was practically a dictator. A more moderate policy towards the Church was adopted, but the state was still far from friendly. Largely because of the long-continued restrictions and friction, on June 1, 1846, out of fifty-nine bishoprics thirty-eight, or more than half, were vacant.[78] The Church in Spain was in a sad plight.

Conditions slowly improved. In 1851 a concordat was reached with Rome. By it the existing archbishoprics were confirmed and a new one was created. Some bishoprics were suppressed and others, including Madrid, were erected. With the concordat the Spanish church began to revive. No attempt was made

[74] Gams, *op. cit.,* Vol. III, Part 2, pp. 431, 432; Peers, *op. cit.,* pp. 64–67.
[75] Gams, *op. cit.,* Vol. III, Part 2, p. 433.
[76] *Ibid.,* pp. 44–451; Peers, *op. cit.,* pp. 68 ff.
[77] Gams, *op. cit.,* Vol. III, Part 2, pp. 451–460.
[78] *Ibid.,* pp. 461–467.

to restore church lands which had been sold, but the state undertook to return those still in its hands, to provide stipends for the clergy, to promote the teaching of the Catholic faith in its schools, and to aid in the suppression of heresy. New seminaries were begun.[79]

The political situation was kaleidoscopic. Although attached to the Church, Isabella II proved to be incompetent as ruler, untrustworthy, extravagant, and notoriously immoral. Chief ministers had brief tenures. In 1868 Isabella was forced to leave the country and her rule was permanently at an end. The general who took over the Government convened a National Assembly which voted for a constitutional monarchy and looked around for a king. After several princes had declined the dubious honour, Amadeo, second son of Victor Emmanuel II of Italy, accepted. He landed in 1870 but faced the opposition of the clergy, who disliked him as a member of the royal family which had despoiled the Pope of his States. Many of them backed the Carlists. The country seemed hopelessly divided and in 1873, in disgust, Amadeo abdicated and left. A brief effort at a republic followed. The Carlists made a bid for power. Anarchy threatened. With something approaching mingled despair and relief the country acquiesced in the restoration of the Bourbon monarchy (December, 1874, and January, 1875) under Alfonso XII, the sixteen-year-old son of Isabella II.

Under Alfonso XII many of the better elements rallied and brought peace to the distracted country. After his death (1885) a posthumous son, Alfonso XIII, came to the throne under the regency of the queen-mother, an Austrian princess. Her tact, dignified order of life, and political wisdom encouraged stability. Her son attained his majority in 1902 and in 1906 married a granddaughter of Queen Victoria. As we have suggested (Chapter VII), for more than two decades internal tensions, while still present, did not break out into such acute civil strife as in the earlier portions of the century. The monarchy operated under a constitution with a cabinet responsible to the Cortes, or Parliament. Neither of the two parties which alternated in power was extreme. Until after World War I Alfonso XIII remained on the throne.

For more than two decades after the Bourbons were given a new lease of life anti-clericalism, while present, was unable to impel the Government to such extreme measures as earlier in the century. Relations between Church and state were regulated by the Concordat of 1851. The constitution of 1876 came out for religious toleration but declared the Catholic religion to be that of the state. Public instruction was under the inspection of the bishops and other diocesan authorities. The state maintained the church buildings, fixed the remuneration of the bishops, accorded legal status to Catholic marriages, and confirmed the Church in its supervision of cemeteries. Partly to compensate for the confisca-

[79] *Ibid.*, pp. 468, 469; *The Cambridge Modern History*, Vol. XI, p. 558; Peers, *op. cit.*, pp. 80 ff.

tion of earlier foundations, benevolent institutions multiplied, some supported by the state, but many by private beneficence, and were extensively staffed by members of religious communities.[80]

Under these circumstances the Roman Catholic Church re-couped many of its losses. Although irreligion was spreading and loyalty to the Church varied from section to section, the practice of daily communion grew and pious confraternities flourished among the laity. Many congregations grew: the law of 1887 which required all to register their members and all but three to apply for authorization was flouted. Although theological faculties no longer had a place in the state universities, by 1910 four Catholic institutions of university grade existed and priests were trained in diocesan seminaries. In addition to the primary and secondary state schools were many conducted by the Church and the congregations. The Fathers of Pious Schools had colleges for the training of teachers. In spite of their recurring expulsion, the Jesuits maintained similar colleges.[81]

Soon after 1900 anti-clericalism again became insistent. Spanish Roman Catholics did not present a united front: they were badly divided on several issues. In 1901, under a decree signed by the queen-regent, the religious congregations were ordered to comply with the law of 1887.[82] In 1910–1911 fresh efforts were made to enforce the law. In an attempt to halt the entrance of additional congregations, relations with the Vatican were broken off. The coming of refugees fleeing from Portuguese measures against religious congregations further complicated the situation.[83] The assassination of the anti-clerical prime minister in 1912 momentarily eased the measures against the Church and was followed by the resumption of diplomatic relations with the Papacy. But the growth of Syndicalism, Anarchism, and Marxist Socialism and the sharpened cleavage between them and the conservatives boded ill for the future.

In the struggle for the minds of men the record of Spanish literature and scholarship in the nineteenth century is ambiguous. On the one hand, very critical of the existing order were Benito Pérez Galdós (1845–1920) and Vincente Blasco Ibañez (1867–1938), the latter a pronounced assailant of the Church. Neither was of outstanding literary merit, but their books, written for popular consumption, had a wide circulation. On the other hand, Marcelino Menéndez y Pelayo (1856–1912), historian and critic, called the dominant figure in nineteenth-century Spanish literature, was a militant champion of Roman Catholic orthodoxy.[84] Juan Donoso Cortés, Marques de Valdegamas (1809–

[80] *The Catholic Encyclopedia*, Vol. XIV, pp. 187, 191; Peers, *op. cit.*, pp. 90 ff.
[81] *The Catholic Encyclopedia*, Vol. XIV, pp. 175, 191.
[82] Schmidlin, *Papstgeschichte der neuesten Zeit*, p. 446.
[83] *The Encyclopædia Britannica*, 14th ed., Vol. XXI, p. 142.
[84] *The Cambridge Modern History*, Vol. XII, pp. 268, 269.

1853), a descendant of the Conquistador Hernando Cortés, warmly admired by Louis Veuillot and influenced by the writings of Maistre and Bonald, was deeply interested in the philosophy of history and, especially in his later years, interpreted it from the standpoint of a warm believer. He held that man was not making progress towards perfection and maintained that history disclosed "the natural triumph of evil over good and the supernatural triumph of God over evil by means of direct, personal, sovereign action." He viewed the Protestant "revolt" with its "resultant rationalism" as a major stage in the triumph of evil, took a pessimistic view of the future of European civilization, and looked for a general collapse of European society. He saw as the only hope a return to the Catholic faith and the reform of society by reforming the individuals who compose it. He believed that in time Russia would walk, armed and unopposed, across Western Europe.[85] A contemporary of Cortés, Jaime Luciano Balmes (1810–1848), a priest, was the most eminent Spanish philosopher of the century. He did not rank with the greatest in Europe, but he had a wide familiarity with both ancient and modern philosophers and, like Cousin in France, was much influenced by Scottish thought. He was a prolific writer,[86] edited periodicals, and engaged in politics. He was a staunch defender of the Roman Catholic faith and his reply to Guizot's *Histoire de la Civilisation en Europe* as a Catholic apologetic went into many editions and was translated into more than one language.[87] He defended the liberal policy which Pius IX espoused in the early days of his pontificate. His early death was attributed to his prodigious labours.[88]

Disturbed though Spain had been and was, by 1914 it had not yet felt the full force of the revolutionary age. Modern industries had begun to appear, especially in the North-east, but the country was still predominantly agricultural. Many of the intelligentsia were subject to the intellectual tides which were coursing through Western Europe, but the masses were only dimly aware of them. In spite of the shocks dealt it, the Roman Catholic Church remained firm and was anchored to the past. Modernism was much less a problem than in Italy and north of the Pyrenees. The Church continued to draw strength from the great traditions of its sixteenth-century mystics, especially Teresa of Avila.

[85] Thomas P. Neill, in *The Catholic Historical Review*, Vol. XL, pp. 385–410; Juan Donoso Cortés, *Ensayo sobre el Catolicismo, el Liberalismo y el Socialismo, Considerados en sus Principios Fundamentales* (Madrid, La Publicidad, 1851, pp. 414), *passim; The Catholic Encyclopedia*, Vol. V, p. 132.

[86] See his collected works in Jaime Luciano Balmes, *Obras Completas* (Madrid, La Editorial Catolica, 8 vols., 1948–1950).

[87] See, for example, Jacques Balmes, *Le Protestantisme Comparé au Catholicisme dans ses Rapports avec la Civilisation Européenne* (Paris, Vaton Frères, 8th ed., 3 vols., 1870), and J. Balmes, *Protestantism and Catholicity Compared in their Effects on the Civilization of Europe* (Baltimore, J. Murphy & Co., 1851).

[88] *The Catholic Encyclopedia*, Vol. II, pp. 224–226.

STORMS IN PORTUGAL

The nineteenth-century story in Portugal had striking similarities to that in France, Italy, and Spain. There, too, liberal and radical political movements had anti-clerical expressions. There, also, they were directed against the orders and congregations and succeeded in reducing their influence. As in France, after efforts to bring the Church in subjection to the state, the tie between the two was severed. However, the Church was much more nearly moribund than in any of the other three countries and no fresh movements issued from it as in France and Italy. As in its larger Iberian neighbour, the revolution was not indigenous but came by contagion from the North. Like Spain, Portugal had passed its apex. But its Church did not have as great a past to inspire it as did that of Spain.

In 1807 the inept House of Braganza sought refuge in Brazil from the French invasion. After the expulsion of the French, King John VI, who had taken that title in 1816 on the death of the insane queen, remained in Brazil. In 1820 a cortes, meeting in Portugal and dominated by liberal sentiments, drew up a constitution and abolished the Inquisition. In 1821 the king returned to Portugal and left his son, Dom Pedro, as regent in Brazil. The following year Brazil declared its independence with Dom Pedro as emperor.

For many years Portugal suffered from a near approach to anarchy. Civil strife was prolonged between the adherents of Dom Miguel, a brother of Dom Pedro, who had himself proclaimed king, and the supporters of a minor, Dona Maria da Gloria, daughter of Dom Pedro. Miguel was backed by the conservatives, Maria by the liberals. After an exhausting war and with English aid the forces of Maria, led by her father, prevailed (1833). The victors abolished tithes, closed numbers of monasteries and convènts, and nationalized their properties. Dom Pedro died in the hour of victory. At the time his daughter, Queen Maria II, was in her teens and her prince consort was not much older. A reign followed marked by internal conflict which was ended by foreign intervention and left the country exhausted.[89]

During the years of disorder the Church suffered severely. The defeat of the Miguelists made for the suppression of the orders and congregations of men and for the extinction of congregations of women by a prohibition on accepting new members. The secular clergy were unable to give adequate care to their flocks and bishops and clergy were bound hand and foot to the state. Yet, as we have suggested (Chapter VII), in an attempt to maintain its position in its colonial possessions, the Government insisted on continuing the *padroado* with its control of all Catholic missions in India, and in doing so had friction with the Pope.[90]

[89] *The Cambridge Modern History*, Vol. X, pp. 310–339.
[90] *The Catholic Encyclopedia*, Vol. XII, p. 304.

From about 1851 until 1910 Portugal escaped serious internal strife and foreign wars. She greatly expanded her colonial empire in Africa. But she was far from prosperous: industries developed even more slowly than in Spain and in the early 1890's the Government was bankrupt.

In the latter half of the century restrictions on the Church were somewhat eased. The Concordat of 1886 brought agreement with the Papacy on several disputed issues. Under it the bishops were nominated by the Government, appointed by the Pope, and paid by the state, a government license was required for the ordination of priests, pastors were assigned to parishes by the minister of justice after the bishops had certified to their fitness, a certain number of seminaries for training the clergy were authorized, and members of the clergy were exempted from military and jury duty. A decree issued in 1896 permitted religious orders under certain conditions. The Jesuits returned and opened colleges. In 1901 religious congregations were allowed if they were dedicated exclusively to teaching or good works or to spreading Christianity and civilization in the colonies. Even when anti-clerical, officials in charge of the colonies were willing to have Portuguese missionaries, for they furthered Portuguese rule and culture and without them missionaries of other nationalities might weaken Portuguese control.[91] After the encyclicals of Leo XIII on Christian democracy and labour, circles for workingmen, mutual aid societies, and associations of Catholic youth were organized.[92]

Shortly after 1900 the Church was confronted by a fresh wave of anti-clericalism. The coming of the French queen of Dom Carlos, who became king in 1899, was followed by an influx of members of French orders and congregations. They met mounting criticism.[93] In 1901 a number of religious congregations were suppressed. The assassination of the king and crown prince in 1908 was followed by a revolution (1910), the perpetual banishment of the House of Braganza, and the setting up of a republic. In 1911 a law was passed which resembled the slightly earlier one in France. It separated Church and state. Freedom to every religious belief was granted, each religious confession was required to provide for the maintenance of its worship, and its accounts were subject to government inspection. Churches and other ecclesiastical buildings were declared to be the property of the state but were permitted to be used free of charge through associations similar to those in France. Only priests who had had their education in Portugal could officiate. Priests were permitted to marry. The teaching of the catechism in government schools, previously the custom, was forbidden. The bishops protested against these actions, but in vain. Yet diplomatic relations with the Vatican were not severed until 1913.[94]

---

[91] *Ibid.*, p. 305.
[92] *Ibid.*, p. 307.
[93] *The Cambridge Modern History*, Vol. XII, p. 271.
[94] *The Catholic Encyclopedia*, Vol. XII, p. 305; *The Encyclopædia Britannica*, 14th ed., Vol., XVIII, p. 282; Premoli, *Contemporary Church History*, pp. 178–181.

In spite of the many anti-clerical measures, the overwhelming majority of the population in Portugal, as in Italy and Spain, remained nominally Catholic. The average quality of the secular clergy was low and the restrictions on the orders and congregations prevented the improvement in the instruction and spiritual care of the masses which the regulars might have brought. In Portugal the Roman Catholic Church entered the twentieth century in a much poorer condition than in France or Italy and probably than in Spain.

THE RECORD IN BELGIUM

In Belgium the Roman Catholic Church showed much more vigour in meeting the challenge of the revolutionary age than it did in either Spain or Portugal.

We have already noted the independence of Belgium after the revolutionary year of 1830, the coolness of Gregory XVI towards the constitution of 1831 with its approach to "a free Church in a free state," the ensuing opposition of the Liberals to ultramontanism, and the notable educational project at Louvain headed by Mercier.

The achievement of the independence of Belgium was by a union of Liberals and Catholics. The attempt by the victorious powers to establish a strong buffer in the North-west against a possibly resurgent France by merging Holland and what had been the Austrian Netherlands was ill starred. The two areas had been separated politically since late in the sixteenth century. The South was overwhelmingly Catholic; in the North, while Catholics constituted a large minority, Protestants predominated and were the rulers. Although with basic differences, the Liberals, perpetuating some of the ideas of the French Revolution, and the Catholics joined in opposing the regime. In 1828 they came together in the Union to advocate liberty of worship, instruction, and the press. In their opposition to the Austrian rule under the Emperor Joseph II and to the attempt after the French conquest to extend to Belgium the ecclesiastical measures of the Revolution, the Catholics had become ultramontane and had sought to free their church from domination by the civil power. They were therefore prepared to welcome the ideas of Lamennais, with their ultramontanism and "a free Church in a free state." But they were critical of the French Revolution with its rationalism: their union with the Liberals was a marriage of convenience which could not last.[95] At the outset, however, in spite of the fact that it was a lay movement, the bulk of the clergy, both lower and higher, favoured the Union as an instrument of resistance.[96] The writings of Lamennais both reinforced and modified the attitude and programme of the Catholics who entered into the Union.[97]

[95] Haag, *Les Origines du Catholicisme Libéral en Belgique (1789–1839)*, pp. 43–110.
[96] *Ibid.*, pp. 110–119.
[97] *Ibid.*, pp. 127–138.

For a few years the Union continued, although not without internal strains. The king chosen to head the new state, the Prince of Saxe-Coburg-Gotha, under the title Leopold I, proved an able ruler and, although a Protestant, sympathetic with the Catholic Church.[98] The constitution under which he governed, a product of the Union, provided for freedom of worship, of education, of association, and of the press. Marriage by civil law was obligatory and was accorded priority over the religious ceremony. Catholicism was declared to be the dominant religion of the state.[99] However, some of the clergy were dissatisfied and wished the complete union of Church and state.[100] In general, the Catholics who collaborated with the Union were in accord with *Avenir*. When *Avenir* suspended publication, a new journal, *Union*, was begun in Brussels which partly continued its policies.[101] The encyclical *Mirari vos* with its condemnation of liberty of conscience and of the separation of Church and state brought consternation to the Catholics in the Union.[102] Engelbert Sterckx (1792–1867), Archbishop of Malines and Primate of Belgium from 1832 to 1867, Cardinal, who had been influential in the gaining of Belgian independence, did not go along with Rome. He supported the Union, had had an important share in framing the constitution, was for religious liberty, and endorsed Montalembert. He approved the publication of *Union*. Nor would he publish the encyclical *Singulari nos*, which condemned Lamennais's *Paroles d'un Croyant*.[103] Leopold I was checked but not entirely defeated in his effort at a strong central government which would tighten the bond between Church and state with the subordination of the ecclesiastical to the civil power.[104]

The final major achievement of the Union was the educational legislation of 1842, legislation which remained the guiding standard for thirty-seven years. It made obligatory the maintenance at public expense of at least one primary school in each commune, in which religion would be taught, but made it possible for those who objected to have their children excused from the courses in religion. The clergy coöperated and allowed over two thousand private schools to close.[105]

In the mid-1840's the last remnant of the Union broke down. In 1846 the Liberals, led by Freemasons, called a congress which organized and consolidated their party and drew up a programme of reform. In a general election in 1847

---

[98] S. Simon, *La Politique Religieuse de Léopold Ier. Documents Inédits* (Brussels, Goemaere, 1953, pp. 183), *passim*.
[99] *The Catholic Encyclopedia*, Vol. II, p. 399; Haag, *op. cit.*, pp. 151 ff.
[100] Haag, *op. cit.*, pp. 145, 147.
[101] *Ibid.*, pp. 163 ff.
[102] *Ibid.*, pp. 73 ff.
[103] *Enciclopedia Cattolica*, Vol. XI, p. 1323; Haag, *op. cit.*, pp. 114, 152, 155, 159–162, 166, 176, 216, 217.
[104] Haag, *op. cit.*, pp. 197 ff.
[105] *The Catholic Encyclopedia*, Vol. II, p. 399; *The Cambridge Modern History*, Vol. XI, pp. 669, 670; Simon, *l'Église Catholique et les Débuts de la Belgique Indépendante*, pp. 101 ff.

they were swept into power by a large majority. They did not touch the primary education law of 1842, but in 1849 they regulated higher education and in 1850 secondary education in a way that aroused the opposition of the bishops and Rome.[106] They also sought to have all charitable endowments turned over to state bureaux. The nation was divided into two camps, Catholics, conservative on the whole, and Liberals, with an anti-clerical bent.[107]

After a brief interlude, 1855–1857, in which the Catholics were in power, the Liberals came into office and retained control until 1870. In the latter year the Catholic vote overthrew the Liberal Government. The Liberals were strong in the large cities, especially in the Walloon South, where French influence was potent; the Catholic vote was chiefly in the rural districts and in the Flemish-speaking North, where resentment against Walloon domination was vocal. The Catholics held the Government until 1878, but did not repeal the anti-Catholic laws of the Liberals.[108] In 1878 the Liberals were once more in the saddle. Owing to the strict property qualification for the franchise, they were largely men of means, urban, free-thinking, and anti-clerical. In 1879 they carried through legislation which upset the educational system of the bill of 1842. It placed all communal schools under strict state supervision, banished from them the teaching of religion, and barred as teachers all graduates of religious normal schools. Since under the constitution freedom of education was guaranteed, the Catholics quickly erected thousands of schools which soon enrolled more than half the children receiving primary education. The Government recalled its ambassador to the Holy See. The Catholics organized a Union for the Redress of Grievances. They won the election of 1884, promptly repealed the school law of 1879, but left to each commune the decision as to whether religious instruction should be given in its schools. In many communes the clergy were in full charge of education.[109] The structure thus set up remained in force until after 1914.

In the meantime the rapid progress of the Industrial Revolution was bringing into being a large number of workingmen. Stirred by Socialist agitation of the Marxist kind, they were becoming class conscious and were demanding the franchise. In 1886 the Socialist Party was formed, chiefly of workingmen.

In successive elections the Catholics were returned to power and held it until 1914. Under pressure from the Socialists and Catholic leaders the franchise was made universal (1893), for some years limited by proportional representation, and many democratic measures were passed. Old-age pensions were inaugu-

[106] Simon, *l'Église Catholique*, pp. 110 ff.; *The Catholic Encyclopedia*, Vol. II, p. 400.

[107] *The Catholic Encyclopedia*, Vol. II, p. 400.

[108] *The Cambridge Modern History*, Vol. XI, pp. 673, 674; *The Catholic Encyclopedia*, Vol. II, p. 401.

[109] *The Cambridge Modern History*, Vol. XII, pp. 251, 252; *The Catholic Encyclopedia*, Vol. II, p. 402.

rated, and subsidies encouraged mutual aid societies, savings banks, building societies, and technical education. In 1886, 1887, and 1890 Catholics held congresses on social work. With the encouragement of the bishops a Democratic Christian League was organized. Among the secular priests a new organization, the Almoners of Labour, came into being. Legislation was passed regulating wages and the labour of women and children. Councils of industry and labour were formed. In 1895 the Social Department of Labour was created.[110]

Not all Catholics were agreed on the steps towards democracy and social legislation. The bishops had difficulty in holding the two wings together and in places an open rupture occurred.[111]

Moreover, in spite of the prolonged Catholic control of the Government, religious instruction was not enforced in all the schools. While Protestants were a very small minority and the overwhelming majority of the population were baptized in the Roman Catholic faith, secularism and free-thinking were said to be on the increase.[112]

Yet in Belgium in the latter part of the century, prosperous from mounting industry and commerce, to a greater extent than in any other country Catholics were putting through measures, some by private initiative and more by government action, which were seeking to remedy the evils brought by the Industrial Revolution and to use it for the benefit of the growing bodies of labourers. That policy was not radical or Socialist. It followed much of the moderate economic philosophy propounded not far from the middle of the century by Charles Périn. Périn opposed unrestrained economic individualism on the one hand and on the other hand Socialism and the political and social ideas of the French Revolution. He advocated social legislation and the formation of voluntary Christian guilds and the education of employers in Christian ideals.[113]

THE ROMAN CATHOLIC CHURCH IN HOLLAND

What happened to those Roman Catholics in the Netherlands who were not in the territory which went with Belgium? At the separation about a million were in the area remaining with the House of Orange. Of these about two-thirds were in the South and about a third in the predominantly Protestant North.[114]

Under the rule of Louis Bonaparte, whom Napoleon made King of Holland, something approaching tolerance had been adopted towards the Catholics. Sev-

[110] *The Catholic Encyclopedia,* Vol. II, pp. 403, 404; *The Cambridge Modern History,* Vol. XII, pp. 251–255.
[111] *The Catholic Encyclopedia,* Vol. II, p. 404.
[112] *Ibid.,* p. 405.
[113] Moon, *The Labor Movement and the Social Catholic Movement in France,* pp. 134, 135.
[114] *The Catholic Encyclopedia,* Vol. VII, p. 390. This is the figure for 1841. Other sets of figures give a total of about 600,000 in 1814, 890,000 in 1843, and 1,171,910 in 1847. Nippold, *Die Römisch-katholische Kirche im Königreich der Niederlande,* pp. 138, 169.

eral Catholics had been placed in positions of honour, some large church buildings, earlier lost to Protestants, had been returned to the Catholics, new church buildings had been erected, and the clergy, as were those of the Protestants, had been paid by the state.[115]

The return to power of the House of Orange was followed by some restrictions. Decrees on education issued in 1825 were regarded by Catholics as directed against them. But the Concordat of 1827, while leaving Holland under the Propaganda, provided for two bishoprics. By 1847 there were five bishops.[116] The revision of the constitution which came out of the revolutionary year of 1848 assured all religious denominations liberty of worship and provided for the payment of the clergy by the state. While public primary education was placed under the control of the state, full freedom was given to private education, and thus church schools were possible. Moreover, the new constitution abolished the *placet,* the consent of the state for the publication of Papal decrees. In obtaining these measures Catholics and Liberals joined forces. But although religious orders were represented, the erection of new houses was not permitted.[117] As we have seen (Chapter VII), in 1853 Pius IX restored the hierarchy in Holland. In bringing this about the laity had been active. Some of the higher clergy at first resented the lay initiative but later concurred. Negotiations between the Government and the Vatican had led to an agreement (October 16, 1852) on the terms. As was to have been expected, the step, like the one in England three years earlier, aroused criticism among Protestants. It was the more vigorous because in making the announcement the Pope stressed the importance of counteracting what he declared to be the errors of Calvin—and in Dutch Protestantism Calvin was influential. As a result the ministry which had carried on the negotiations with Rome fell and a church associations law was passed forbidding any foreigner to assume ecclesiastical office without royal consent and prohibiting the wearing of religious garb outside closed buildings.[118] This arose from a fear which we have repeatedly met in other countries and will meet again, that the Catholic Church, led by Rome, would subvert national independence.[119]

As in many other lands, among both Catholics and Protestants the control of education became a burning issue. In 1857 a law was passed which made every state school "mixed" or neutral religiously, with instruction only in the simple

---

[115] Nippold, *op. cit.,* p. 140.

[116] *Ibid.,* pp. 149, 169; *The Catholic Encyclopedia,* Vol. VII, p. 390. On an early stage in the Catholic revival and emancipation, see G. Gorris, *J. H. LeSage ten Broek en de Eerste Faze van de Emancipatie der Katholieken* (Amsterdam, Urbi et Orbi, 2 vols., 1947), *passim.*

[117] Nippold, *op. cit.,* pp. 208, 209.

[118] *Ibid.,* pp. 210 ff.; *The Catholic Encyclopedia,* Vol. VII, p. 391; *The Cambridge Modern History,* Vol. XI, p, 665.

[119] On the entire period after 1853 see L. J. Rogier and N. de Rooy, *In Vrijheid Herborn. Katholiek Nederland 1853–1953* (The Hague, N. V. Uitgeversmij Pax, 3 vols., 1953).

truths common to all forms of religion. To this Catholics and the more conservative Protestants strenuously objected. Both organized schools of their own. In 1868 the bishops forbade parents to send children to a neutral school where a Catholic school was available. Catholic schools multiplied. The education law of 1878, while preserving the principle of liberty of teaching, by discriminatory subsidies for the state schools placed the private schools at a financial disadvantage. It was on the school issue that the coalition between Catholics and Liberals foundered, a coalition which under the leadership of Jan Rudolf Thorbecke (1798–1872), scholar and orator, had done much to win greater freedom for Catholics. Most Catholics now allied themselves with what was known as the Anti-Revolutionary Party, a party supported by religiously conservative Protestant elements. The alliance of Catholics and Anti-Revolutionaries obtained legislation which granted state subsidies to private schools.[120]

As the century wore on, the Roman Catholic Church in Holland continued to flourish. Not only were Catholic schools built, but churches were restored or erected and many monasteries, seminaries, and colleges were constructed. Catholic social action prospered: a Catholic People's Union was formed, and every diocese had a union of workingmen's societies. In the mounting population of the country Catholics increased in numbers. Yet because of unfavourable economic conditions in their stronghold, the southern provinces, the proportion of Catholics in the entire nation declined from 38.99 per cent in 1839 to 35 per cent in 1909.[121]

The Roman Catholic Church in Switzerland

On the eve of the French Revolution Switzerland was a loose confederation of cantons which were essentially sovereign states and had widely varying internal structures. The region was divided racially among Germans, French, Italians, and Romansch and religiously between Protestants and Roman Catholics. The Protestants were in the majority and possessed most of the main cities. The Roman Catholics, a large minority, were dominant in the "forest cantons," the heart of the old Switzerland, rural and pastoral, and in a few of the cities.

The French Revolution profoundly shook the old order. In the Helvetic Republic, into which Switzerland was reorganized in 1798, many of the existing patterns were abolished and liberty of belief and of the press was ordained. Under Napoleon two political parties arose, the Federalists, having their main support among the Catholics in the forest cantons and wishing to return to the

---

[120] *The Catholic Encyclopedia*, Vol. VII, p. 392; *The Cambridge Modern History*, Vol. XI, pp. 665, 666, Vol. XII, pp. 245, 246; Premoli, *Contemporary Church History*, pp. 194, 195.

[121] *The Catholic Encyclopedia*, Vol. VII, p. 392; K. du Bois de Vroijlande, *Volksverheffing in der R. K. Standsorganisatie der Werklieden in Nederland* (Louvain, Vlaamsche Boekenhalle, 1924, pp. 295).

pre-Revolutionary structure, and the Unitary, which held to the liberal ideals of the Revolution. In 1803 Napoleon through his Act of Mediation restored the independence of the cantons within a confederation whose central authority had the power to make war and conclude treaties and which maintained the equality of all men before the law.

After the fall of Napoleon a Federal Pact was concluded which further weakened the central government. In it, as in the Act of Mediation, nothing was said of liberty of belief. But monasteries were given a federal guarantee. In some cantons religious tolerance ceased and in the Catholic cantons the Jesuits reappeared. The revolutionary years of 1830 and 1831 brought new cantonal constitutions in the direction of democracy: the majority called for freedom of belief.[122]

Religious differences were the source of many disputes and at times of violence. In 1834 several of the cantons sought to give the state control of the Church and in such fashion that the Pope condemned the plan.[123] In the canton of Aargau in 1841 the legislature attempted to suppress the monasteries. Since this was contrary to the Federal Pact, the Catholic cantons protested. In another canton the radicals overthrew a clerical government by force and in still another the Catholics put down the liberals by a civil war. In several cantons feeling against the Jesuits mounted. In 1845 seven Roman Catholic cantons entered into a defensive covenant against the rest of Switzerland. They formed the *Sonderbund,* an armed league with a council of war to oppose liberalism, maintain the Jesuits, and reëstablish the monasteries in Aargau. In 1847 the Federal Diet ordered the dissolution of the *Sonderbund* and the expulsion of the Jesuits. The *Sonderbund,* comprising only about a fifth of the population of the country, mobilized their forces. The Federal Diet applied force, and by the end of 1847, with slight loss of life, the *Sonderbund* was broken.[124]

The dissolution of the *Sonderbund* combined with the tide of European revolution in 1848 to bring about the revision of the Federal Pact of 1815. Among other provisions the new constitution gave freedom of belief to all Swiss citizens who were members of any Christian denomination, liberty of press and of public assembly, and freedom of residence. Thus Catholics might move into any predominantly Protestant canton and practise their faith, and Protestants had the same right in Catholic cantons. The Jesuits were excluded from the country.[125] As an aftermath of the Vatican Council the Old Catholic

---

[122] *The Cambridge Modern History,* Vol. XI, pp. 234–241; MacCaffrey, *History of the Catholic Church in the Nineteenth Century,* Vol. I, pp. 130–133.

[123] See texts in Lambert, *Kirche und Staat in der Schweiz,* Vol. III, pp. 103 ff.

[124] MacCaffrey, *op. cit.,* Vol. I, pp. 131–137; *The Cambridge Modern History,* Vol. XI, pp. 246–252; *The Catholic Encyclopedia,* Vol. XIV, p. 360.

[125] MacCaffrey, *op. cit.,* Vol. I, pp. 137, 138; *The Cambridge Modern History,* Vol. XI, pp. 253, 254; Lambert, *op. cit.,* Vol. III, p. 141.

movement was strong in Switzerland. It gave rise to the Christian Catholic National Church, a body which was officially recognized by the Federal Government and several cantons and which obtained from them some church buildings. Controversy led to an amendment to the federal constitution (1874) which declared that no new episcopal sees could be erected without the permission of the Federal Government, that no new monasteries could be built, and that civil ceremonies were obligatory for marriages.[126]

In spite of restrictions, the Roman Catholic Church in Switzerland was very much alive. In 1910 Catholics were about 43 per cent of the population. Proportionately they were growing more rapidly than Protestants, chiefly by immigration. A Catholic People's Union coördinated organizations for charity, social work, and education. Financial aid was given by Catholics to their cause outside the Catholic cantons. An association was formed of Catholic students.[127] Swiss Catholics were active in furthering labour legislation. As early as 1868 Bishop Gaspard Mermillod (1824–1892), later Cardinal, declared the social question the great problem of the age and championed the cause of the workingman. He was closely in touch with Mun's movement and La Tour du Pin. He was reinforced by Gaspard Decurtins. Through the coöperation of Radicals, Socialists, and Catholics, laws were passed for accident compensation, the limitation of the hours of the working day, and the protection of women and children. Decurtins advocated the establishment of a minimum wage and compulsory insurance against sickness and accidents and an international code of labour legislation.[128] Nor must we forget an earlier figure, Jean Baptiste Girard (1765–1850), a Franciscan, who as an educator sought to stimulate the minds of children rather than to cram them with rules and facts. But neither must we fail to recall that he was opposed by the Jesuits.

GERMANY: THE POLITICAL AND CULTURAL SETTING

As in other lands, the course of the Roman Catholic Church in Germany was profoundly modified by the political and cultural setting. When in 1815 it emerged from the Napoleonic Wars, Germany was divided into thirty-eight different states, large and small: before the blows to the old order given by the Corsican the number had been much larger. They were associated in a loose German Confederation with a Diet over which Austria presided. The two most powerful states were Prussia and Austria, the one Protestant and the other Catholic. The rising tide of nationalism made for the unification of the country. The revolutionary years of 1830 and 1848 had marked repercussions. In 1848 a German National Assembly dominated by liberals convened in Frankfurt and

---

[126] *The Cambridge Modern History*, Vol. XI, p. 258; *The Catholic Encyclopedia*, Vol. XIV, p. 364.

[127] *The Catholic Encyclopedia*, Vol. XIV, p. 364.

[128] Premoli, *op. cit.*, pp. 199–202; Moon, *The Labor Problem and the Social Catholic Movement in France*, pp. 132, 133.

sought to effect union. The liberal effort failed.[120] Union finally came through Prussia led by its chief minister, Otto von Bismarck. In 1867, after the Seven Weeks' War in which Russia defeated Austria and lesser German states, the North German Confederation was formed with the King of Prussia as hereditary president. Early in 1871, as a consequence of the Franco-Prussian War, the North German Confederation was enlarged by the accession of the South German States and became the German Empire with the King of Prussia as emperor. Austria remained outside.

Religiously the complexion of Germany was determined by the rulers of the several states. By the principle of *cuius regio, eius religio* every prince decided which form of Christianity would prevail in his domains. Some states were Catholic, some Lutheran, and some Reformed. Throughout the nineteenth century each state had its established church and sought to control ecclesiastical affairs within its borders. These *Landeskirchen* persisted into the twentieth century. In the empire Roman Catholics were a minority. At the close of the century they constituted about 36 per cent of the population. The North was fairly solidly Protestant. The Catholic Church was strongest in the South.

Culturally Germany was in ferment. Here lived, wrote, and taught most of the outstanding European philosophers of the century. Here were theologians and Biblical scholars, the majority of them Protestants, who branched out in fresh ways and who challenged the thinking of Christians. Here, too, great literature and great music were composed. Outstanding scientists appeared. The Industrial Revolution entered and began to work major economic and social changes.

It was in this Germany, profoundly moved by the revolutionary forces of the age, that the Roman Catholic Church was immersed. Could it recover from the debilitating effects of the *Aufklärung?* Could it preserve its independence against the rising power of the state? Would the authority of the Pope prevail against the intense nationalism with its resentment of foreign interference? What would be the effect of the intellectual currents of the day? Could the Church make itself felt effectively in the new society which was issuing from the Industrial Revolution?

In previous chapters we have seen some of the answers. We have noted how Napoleon by his drastic measures with the ecclesiastical states gave a body blow to Febronianism. We have recounted some of the struggles with individual states, notably Prussia, when they attempted to extend their authority over ranges of life, such as marriage, the family, and education, which had been functions of the Church and to ensure that the clergy would not give their primary al-

---

[129] For a survey of the treatment of the revolution of 1848 by German historians see T. S. Hamerow, *History and the German Revolution of 1848*, in *The American Historical Review*, Vol. LX, pp. 27–44.

legiance to the Pope, whom they regarded as a foreign potentate. We have covered at some length the *Kulturkampf* with Bismarck-led Prussia and the resulting consolidation of Catholic political action through the Centre Party. We have sketched the intellectual ferment in Roman Catholic circles, much of it stimulated by the *Aufklärung,* in the effort to meet the challenge of the age. We have recorded how some of it, that which found expression through Hermes and Günther, was thrust outside the pale by Rome as detrimental to the faith, but how some of it was accepted. We have spoken of several of the movements to solve the problems brought by industrialization. We need not here rehearse what we have said about these events, persons, and movements. It is aspects of the story which have thus far been omitted that here demand our attention.

GERMANY: THE *Coup de Grâce* IS GIVEN TO FEBRONIANISM AND JOSEPHISM

Napoleon's measures did not immediately kill Febronianism and Josephism. Indeed, as we have seen (Chapter IV) for a time they seemed to encourage them in another form. Napoleon made Dalberg Prince Primate of the Confederation of the Rhine. Although Dalberg died in 1817, the dream of a German Catholic Church only loosely tied to Rome cherished by him was continued by his junior, Ignaz Heinrich von Wessenberg (1774–1860). Dalberg had appointed Wessenberg Vicar General and Administrator of the Diocese of Constance. The Pope ordered Wessenberg deposed but the canons of Constance elected him Vicar of the chapter. Pius VII declared the election invalid. Wessenberg went to Rome but refused to subscribe to the complete submission to Papal authority which Pius VII demanded. Reared in a Josephist family, he proposed that the Church conform to patterns which were in accord with eighteenth-century rationalism. He wished mass said in German, encouraged weekly sermons and semi-weekly instruction of the children by the pastors, dispensed his clergy from reading the breviary, and longed to weaken the barriers which separated Catholicism from Protestantism. Wessenberg had sought to induce the Congress of Vienna to endorse the project of a national church, but had failed. He laid his plan before the Diet of the German Confederation at Frankfurt, but Prussia feared that the church which he proposed would become a satellite of Austria. Others of the German higher clergy were out of accord with him. The Pope suppressed the Diocese of Constance. In 1827, Wessenberg retired to private life. He continued to expound his views, but his particular project of a German national church was dead.[130]

More nails were driven into the coffin of a German national church as conceived by Dalberg and Wessenberg by the concordats which, as we have seen,

---

[130] Goyau, *l'Allemagne Religieuse: le Catholicisme,* Vol. I, pp. 119–139; Brück, *Gechichte der katholischen Kirche in Deutschland im neunzehnten Jahrhundert,* Vol. I, pp. 145–153, 294–331.

were negotiated by Consalvi with individual German states. The separate arrangements precluded the possibility of a German Catholic Church united on Febronian or Josephist principles.[131]

GERMANY: ABORTIVE EFFORTS AT A GERMAN CATHOLICISM

However, movements within the Catholic Church sought to bring about a distinctive German Catholicism with a married clergy and a German liturgy.[132]

In the 1840's a project was developed for a new kind of German Catholic Church. It had as an early leading figure a priest, Johannes Ronge (1813–1887), who had recently been suspended because of his criticism of Rome and who in 1844 in an open letter to Bishop Arnoldi of Treves protested against the latter's action in reviving the exhibition of what was declared to be the seamless robe of Christ—an exhibition which was attracting thousands of pilgrims. Ronge denounced the "idolatrous celebration" and urged the German people "to check the tyrannical power of the Roman hierarchy." For this contumacy he was excommunicated and degraded. But he travelled through Germany and Switzerland organizing congregations. He was joined by another priest, Johann Czerski (1813–1893), who had begun (1845) a similar "Christian Catholic Church." In the rising tide of liberalism national conventions were held in 1845 and 1847. Wessenberg indignantly refused an invitation to associate himself with the movement. The German Catholic Church repudiated the compulsory celibacy of the priesthood, auricular confession, and the primacy of the Pope. It departed further and further from historic Christian convictions, such as the divinity of Christ, and in 1850 merged with a liberal Protestant movement, self-styled the *Lichtfreunde* ("Friends of Light"). It was never large numerically.[133]

GERMANY: SUCCESS IN EFFORTS AT THE NATIONAL COÖRDINATION OF ROMAN CATHOLICS IN FULL ALLEGIANCE AND SUBORDINATION TO THE HOLY SEE

Although the dream of Dalberg and Wessenberg of a German Catholic Church in communion with Rome but administratively only loosely tied to it was not realized and that of a German Catholic Church independent of Rome attracted only a small following, German Roman Catholics achieved a kind of national solidarity which was in marked contrast with the badly divided state of their brethren in France. To be sure, in Germany as in France differences existed between liberals and conservatives. On the one hand were those who listened sympathetically to Lamennais and Montalembert and who wished cordial acceptance of democratic procedures in government. On the other were

---

131 Goyau, *op. cit.*, Vol. I, pp. 140 ff.; Brück, *op. cit.*, Vol. II, pp. 12–267.
132 Goyau, *op. cit.*, Vol. II, pp. 285–293.
133 *Ibid.*, pp. 295–309; Brück, *op. cit.*, Vol. II, pp. 512 ff.; *The New Schaff-Herzog Encyclopedia of Religious Knowledge,* Vol. IV, pp. 466–468.

those to whom these measures were anathema.[134] In the revolutionary year 1848 at a conference of German bishops in Würtzburg Johannes von Geissel (1796–1864), the powerful Cardinal Archbishop of Cologne, supported a project for a Reich church constitution under a German Primate. This would have made possible corporate action by the German episcopate. To Rome it smacked too much of Febronianism and before the end of the year it was vetoed.[135] But also in 1848 a Catholic Assembly was held at Mainz presided over by Ritter von Buss (1803–1878), who had been prominent in private welfare work. It coincided with the famous Frankfurt National Assembly and was the precursor of the *Katholikentag,* the semi-annual and then annual national Catholic gathering.[136] In a pastoral letter (April 20, 1848) Geissel exhorted Catholics to be active in politics. This was the more imperative for those who, like him, were in the domains of Prussia, a predominantly Protestant state: the Catholic minority needed to come together to make its weight effective. A few weeks later the Cologne Catholic Democratic Party was founded to elect to the Prussian Diet those who would protect Catholic rights and privileges. In 1852 what was called the Catholic Fraction drew together the Catholics in that body. In 1854 it became the Centre, the beginning of the Centre Party—between the Conservatives on the Right and the Liberals on the Left—whose notable role in the *Kulturkampf* we have already remarked. Its early leaders were the Reichensberger brothers, whose outlook was indicated by their self-designation, the "Rhenish liberals." A cleavage developed between the group with that slant and the Conservatives of South Germany.[137]

THE ROMAN CATHOLIC CHURCH IN GERMANY: REVIVAL, SPIRITUAL AND INTELLECTUAL

We have noted (Chapters IX and X) the revival of the Roman Catholic Church in Germany which had begun before 1815 and continued after that year. At the outset it centred in Münster around the remarkable Princess Amalie Gallitzin. We have met such men as Fürstenberg, Overburg, and Stolberg. We have mentioned the parts played by Hofbauer, Schlegel, and Sailer. We have seen that as the century wore on other figures appeared—Hermes and Günther, who, seeking to defend the faith, were adjudged by Rome to be distorting it; the Tübingen school, who were regarded as sound advocates; and Görres, who won the respect of many, both within and outside the Catholic

[134] Schnabel, *Deutsche Geschichte im neunzehnten Jahrhundert,* Vol. IV, pp. 164–202; E. Alexander in Moody, *Church and Society,* pp. 366 ff., 435 ff.

[135] Alexander in Moody, *op. cit.,* p. 443; *The Catholic Encyclopedia,* Vol. XI, p. 405.

[136] Alexander in Moody, *op. cit.,* p. 443; Brück, *op. cit.,* Vol. III, pp. 551 ff.; Windell, *The Catholics and German Unity, 1866–1871,* p. 9.

[137] Alexander in Moody, *op. cit.,* pp. 444–446. On documents largely concerned with the Centre Party see Bergsträsser, *Der politische katholizismus: Dokumente seiner Entwicklung II (1871 bis 1914), passim.*

Church. To these should be added, if there were time, the names of others. The list would certainly include him who is called the last champion of Catholic romanticism, Joseph von Eichendorff (1788–1851). In his student days he had succumbed to the charm of Görres. Some of his poems sang themselves into the hearts of thousands of his fellow countrymen.[138] Franz Xavier von Baader (1765–1841), whom we have already met, may be described as the philosophical genius and social conscience of Catholic romanticism. For a brief time he was in conflict with Rome, but he died in full peace with the Church.[139] We have called attention to the rootage gained by the Liturgical Movement through Maria Laach. Although the Catholics of Germany did not give birth to as many as did those of France, several new congregations and societies sprang from their devotion. We have remarked that the Old Catholic movement, although chiefly with German leadership and constituency, carried with it only a small minority of the Church's children. In this it was in sharp contrast with the revolt led by Luther three centuries earlier. The movement for a German Catholic Church on a national basis had even less success. In spite of the pressures of the revolutionary age the vast majority of German Roman Catholics kept at least a formal adherence to the church of their fathers. From them, too, sprang quite new organizations to meet the challenge of the day—the *Gesellenverein* of Kolping, the *Katholikentag,* the *Volksverein,* the Centre Party, a variety of unions of farmers and industrial labourers, and the Society of St. Charles Borromeo for the preparation and circulation of literature pertinent to the needs of the day.

THE ROMAN CATHOLIC CHURCH IN GERMANY: CONFLICTS WITH THE SEVERAL STATES

Inevitably the revival in the Roman Catholic Church was accompanied by conflicts with several of the states which made up that country. We have recounted the chief struggles—the ones with Prussia over the marriage question, Hermes, and the control of theological education in the Rhineland, and the *Kulturkampf.* In a summary as brief as ours must be we can do no more than call attention in a most general way to the others. A chronic conflict was over the share of the state in the choice of bishops.[140] As in the Prussian domains, the control of education and of marriage was a source of recurring friction. Baden, Hesse-Darmstadt, and Saxony each had its *Kulturkampf.* Even Catholic Bavaria sought to dominate the Church in the interest of the state.[141] Some

---

138 Alexander in Moody, *op. cit.,* pp. 386–388; *The Catholic Encyclopedia,* Vol. V, p. 363.

139 Alexander in Moody, *op. cit.,* pp. 393–406.

140 For some of the documents down to 1870 see Emil Friedberg, *Der Staat und die Bischofswahlen in Deutschland* (Leipzig, Duncker & Humbolt, 1874, pp. viii, 488), *passim.*

141 On some of these conflicts see Brück, *op. cit.,* Vol. III, pp. 261–320, 462–484; Corrigan, *The Church in the Nineteenth Century,* p. 216; Geffcken, *Church and State,* Vol. II, pp. 224–227, 260–267.

conflicts were accentuated by the fact that soon after 1815 Rome made provision for the episcopal supervision of Catholic minorities. This was either by assigning them to dioceses or by placing them under the jurisdiction of vicars apostolic.[142]

GERMANY: THE AGE OF KETTELER

The outstanding German bishop of the second half of the nineteenth century and one who had a prominent part in the Church-state conflicts of his day was Wilhelm Emmanuel von Ketteler (1811–1877).[143] We have met him briefly as a friend of labour. Indeed, it is for his championship of labour and his constructive programme for meeting the challenges of modern industry that he was chiefly remembered. Ketteler was born in Westphalia of an ancient family and inherited the title of baron. Although reared a Catholic, in his youth he was not particularly zealous for the faith: on graduating from the university he entered the service of the state. But in 1837 he was so outraged by the arrest of Archbishop Droste-Vischering of Cologne (Chapter VII) that he resigned his post and studied for the priesthood. Ordained in 1844, he was a pastor when in 1848 he was elected to the Frankfurt National Assembly. There he rose to prominence through his fearless oratory. Later in the year in six sermons in the Cathedral of Mainz on *The Great Social Questions of the Day* he attracted · wide attention by his forceful statements on the right of private property, the liberty of man, man's destiny, marriage and family life, and the authority of the Church. In 1850, when he was not yet forty, he was created Bishop of the ancient and important see of Mainz. In his more than a quarter of a century in that post he made his weight profoundly felt not only in his diocese but also in all Catholic Germany. He improved the quality of his clergy by founding a seminary and equipping it with an able teaching staff. He brought in religious orders and congregations, conducted missions in the parishes, was diligent in hearing confessions and in administering confirmation, and founded charitable institutions. He furthered the organization of the *Gesellenverein* of Kolping, began a society for the erection of inexpensive and sanitary dwellings for workers in industrial districts, and formulated (1864) what he deemed the Christian position on the labour question and programmes for social reform. He stood for higher wages and shorter hours of labour and opposed child

---

[142] Brück, *op. cit.*, Vol. II, pp. 135–139; Windell, *op. cit.*, pp. 86–90.

[143] Fritz Vigener, *Ketteler, ein deutsches Bischofsleben des 19. Jahrhunderts* (Munich and Berlin, R. Oldenbourg, 1924, pp. 750), is a standard life, with an extensive bibliography. On Ketteler's attitudes and achievements in the problems brought by industrialization see E. de Girard, *Ketteler et la Question Ouvrière avec une Introduction Historique sur le Mouvement Social Catholique* (Berne, K.-J. Wyss, 1896, pp. 354), and George Metlake, *Christian Social Reform. Program Outlined by Its Pioneer, William Emmanuel Baron von Ketteler, Bishop of Mainz* (Philadelphia, The Dolphin Press, 1923, pp. iv, 246).

labour in factories and the labour of young girls and women.[144] He initiated (1867) the national conferences of German bishops which were to become almost annual. At the first of them he proposed the founding of a German Catholic University and for the second (1869) formulated for the episcopate a pronouncement on the Church and the social question. He stood by the Prussian bishops in their resistance to Bismarck in the *Kulturkampf.*

GERMANY: THE CATHOLIC CHURCH IN THE CLOSING YEARS OF THE CENTURY

For the Roman Catholic Church in Germany the last decades of the century were ones of comparative peace and prosperity. In the *Kulturkampf* the great Bismarck had been defeated. The Centre Party was powerful in politics. No major heresies and no fresh secessions vexed the Church. Ultramontanism had won and the Church was united under the direction of Rome. Modernism had gained a much slighter foothold than in France and Italy.[145]

German Roman Catholics built on the precedent set by Ketteler for dealing with the problems brought by industrialism. Outstanding were two priests, Christopher Moufang and Franz Hitze. A protégé of Ketteler, Moufang went beyond his master in the advocacy of labour legislation. He served as a member of the upper house of the Hessian Landtag and then in the Reichstag as a representative of the Centre Party.[146] When, in 1886, Moufang retired from public life, he was succeeded as the leader of the Catholic social movement by Franz Hitze (1851–1921). Serving in highly industrialized Westphalia, Hitze had devoted himself to workingmen. He organized the Catholic labour movement, trained it in social politics, and won for it an important place in the German Christian labour movement. The latter was interconfessional, in 1899 adopted a programme, and in 1901 formed a Federation of Christian Trade Unions (*Gesamtverband der Christlichen Gewerkschaften*). In coöperation with Windthorst and Brandts Hitze founded the *Volksverein für das katholische Deutschland* ("Popular Union for Catholic Germany"), for the education of Catholics for social and political activity. As a long-time member of both the Prussian Diet and the Reichstag he strove unobtrusively and successfully for social legislation.[147] In addition to Moufang and Hitze many German Catholics devoted themselves to the social and labour problems which sprang from industrialization. Some periodicals concentrated on them. Catholic employers organized a Society for the Welfare of the Labourer.[148]

As we have seen (Chapter VII), in the *Kulturkampf* the German Catholics

144 In addition to the bibliography in note 143; on Ketteler's social measures see Nitti, *Catholic Socialism,* pp. 116 ff., and Windell, *op. cit.,* pp. 24, 25, 29, 30, 38, 39–278.

145 Premoli, *Contemporary Church History,* p. 158. For some of the documents on the political aspects of Catholic activity in these years see Bergsträsser, *op. cit.,* Vol. II, pp. 149 ff.

146 Moon, *The Labor Problem and the Social Catholic Movement in France,* pp. 125–127.

147 Alexander in Moody, *Church and Society,* pp. 422–430.

148 Moon, *op. cit.,* pp. 128, 129.

found an organ for united political action in the Centre Party, with the redoubtable Ludwig Windthorst (1812–1891) as its first outstanding leader. A diminutive figure physically, with a huge head and bandy legs, Windthorst had a rapier-like mind and was a consummate parliamentary tactician and an able debater. After the *Kulturkampf* the Centre Party persisted as a potent, solid bloc in both the Prussian Diet and the imperial Reichstag. Through it Catholics played a more important and constructive part in representative parliamentary government in Germany than, in their opposition to the Third Republic, they were able to do in France.[149]

Even though politically strong, Roman Catholics continued to feel aggrieved over what they believed to be discriminatory measures in several of the predominantly Protestant German states. Protestants united in the Evangelical League to oppose the relaxation of restraints on Catholics. Although through the Society of St. Boniface (*Bonifatiusverein*) by 1902 Catholics had established several hundred parishes for those of their faith in Protestant territories, that organization declared that in Prussia the majority of the children of mixed marriages were reared as Protestants and that mixed marriages were increasing. In Protestant regions, moreover, in spite of the efforts of the *Bonifatiusverein* to erect Catholic schools, thousands of Catholic children were educated in Protestant schools.[150]

On the whole, however, in 1914 the Roman Catholic Church in Germany was more prosperous and presented a more nearly united front to the country than it had at mid-century. It was in a much more wholesome condition than on the eve of the French Revolution or in 1815.

Contrasts were striking and important between German Protestantism and German Catholicism in the nineteenth century. Both branches of the faith displayed abounding vigour. However, on the one hand in Protestantism, as we are to see more at length in the next volume, wide and rich variety existed. In the freshness and daring of its theological thought and Biblical scholarship German Protestantism led the world. At the same time a fresh surge of devotion flowed through the many and diverse Pietist channels and from them issued movements such as ones for foreign missions and the Inner Mission to serve German society. In state after state the two main wings of German Protestantism, Lutheran and Reformed, were united. Strict Lutheran confessionalism experienced a revival, in opposition both to the union and to the newer trends in theology and Biblical study. In German Catholicism, on the other hand, such fresh thinking waned as had earlier been represented by Hermes and Günther, theology was channeled through the revived Thomism, Rome

[149] Alexander in Moody, *op. cit.*, pp. 462, 463; Bergsträsser, *op. cit.*, Vol. II, *passim; The Catholic Encyclopedia*, Vol. XV, pp. 655, 656.

[150] Premoli, *op. cit.*, pp. 151–164.

was more and more in control, and a common front was achieved for effective action within the state. In the Reich as a whole Catholics were a minority on the aggressive defensive. German Catholicism was giving rise to many new organizations and was beginning to take part in the world-wide extension of the faith.

AUSTRIA

Although deliberately excluded from the Bismarck-created empire, Austria was historically a part of Germany. For centuries its rulers, the Hapsburgs, had been the ranking princes in that realm. Since its population was overwhelmingly of its faith, the Catholic Church did not there face the severe competition of Protestantism which confronted it in the Prussian domains and the new Reich. At the outset of the century Josephism was still strong, with its tradition of the control of the Church by the state: its effect on the Church was enervating.

Josephism passed, but slowly. By 1815 the independence of education from the Church which had been a feature of the policy of Joseph II was beginning to weaken and the bishops were having a larger voice in the schools.[151] As chancellor, Metternich favoured a greater freedom of the Church from the domination of the state: the Emperor Francis I was not completely averse to the change, but he was handicapped by the opposition of those who inherited the Josephist tradition. For years the bishops were controlled by the civil officials, even in their communications with their own clergy.[152] As a result of the revolutionary year of 1848 the bishops claimed and were granted more independence of the state and freedom of communication with the Holy See. In 1855, after many decades of failure to reach such an agreement a concordat was entered into with the Pope. It abolished the state's *placet,* gave the bishops more freedom in administering discipline, provided for instruction in the Catholic religion in both private and public schools and placed it under the supervision of the bishops, gave the latter the right to forbid the circulation of books on religion and morals which seemed to them obnoxious, declared the sole competence of Church courts in matrimonial questions, but still gave the emperor a voice in the naming of the bishops. The document was chiefly notable because, in contrast with the Josephist system by which the state acted unilaterally in ecclesiastical affairs, it was entered into jointly by the state and the Holy See. Much of what the ultramontane advocates desired was granted. Yet not a little of the Josephist tradition remained. The clergy were well paid but were regarded as state employees. Disputes with Rome continued. The dogma of Papal

---

[151] Brück, *Geschichte der katholischen Kirche in Deutschland im neunzehnten Jahrhundert,* Vol. I, pp. 422–424.
[152] *Ibid.,* Vol. II, pp. 139 ff.

infallibility was denounced by the state as changing the nature of the Church. On one occasion the emperor threatened to establish a national church.[153]

In spite of the weakening of Josephism, the latter part of the century saw little vigour in the Catholic Church in Austria. Freemasonry was influential, and both nobility and clergy were described as being apathetic and somnolent, the schools religiously neutral, and the press in the hands of anti-clericals. Jews were prominent in university faculties.[154] Leo XIII was deeply concerned and endeavoured to rouse the Austrian church from its apathy and to stir the heads of monasteries to the reform of their congregations.[155]

Austrian Catholics could not fully escape the interest in social issues which was mounting among their German brethren. The chief leaders were the aristocratic Prince Aloysius von Lichtenstein and especially Baron Karl von Vogelsang, a convert from a Protestant North German family of Mecklenburg. Members of the Austrian landed nobility were especially stirred to action by the spectacle of the domination of capital and industry by wealthy Jews. They demanded that the state come to the defence of the industrial proletariat.[156]

The Christian Socialist Party, founded in the 1880's, had as its organizer Karl Lueger (1844–1910), a lawyer of peasant stock and a friend of Vogelsang. A zealous Catholic, in the mid-nineties he became Burgomaster of Vienna and in that office sought to exclude from the administration Jews, Social Democrats, and pan-Germans, and to capture the university for the Church. He made Vienna an exemplar of municipal reform and ownership. Through the Christian Socialist Party legislation in behalf of workmen was enacted—regulating mines and factories, forbidding Sunday labour, and limiting employment of women and children in industry.[157]

Shortly before 1900 a *Los von Rom* ("Away from Rome") movement broke out. It was essentially political and pan-German and had as its object the union of Austria with Germany. It attacked the Catholic Church as an enemy of that union. Within a few years several scores of thousands left the Catholic Church. Of these somewhat fewer than half became Protestants and about a fourth joined the Old Catholics.[158]

Before 1914 Catholic Congresses were being held to encourage unity in a badly divided constituency. In them Germans constituted the majority, but the other races in the polyglot Hapsburg empire were represented and the Catholic

[153] *Ibid.*, Vol. III, pp. 21 ff.; Premoli, *op. cit.*, p. 142; Geffcken, *Church and State*, Vol. II, pp. 246 ff.
[154] Schmidlin, *Papstgeschichte der neuesten Zeit*, Vol. II, pp. 474–476; Premoli, *op. cit.*, p. 139.
[155] Schmidlin, *op. cit.*, Vol. II, pp. 477, 478.
[156] Alexander in Moody, *op. cit.*, pp. 417–422; Moon, *op. cit.*, pp. 129–131; Fuchs, *Geistige Strömungen in Österreich*, pp. 49 ff.
[157] Alexander in Moody, *op. cit.*, pp. 477, 478; Moon, *op. cit.*, pp. 131, 132; Fuchs, *op. cit.*, p. 53.
[158] Hermelink, *Das Christentum in der Menschheitsgeschichte von der französischen Revolution bis zur Gegenwart*, Vol. III, pp. 88, 89; Premoli, *op. cit.*, pp. 135, 136; Fuchs, *op. cit.*, pp. 165 ff.

faith was declared to be the cement which held the realm together. An international Marian Congress in Salzburg in 1910 and an International Eucharistic Congress in Vienna in 1912 helped Catholic morale. Soon after 1900 other Catholic organizations sprang up, evidence of vitality.[159]

HUNGARY

In Hungary, joined with Austria by the personal tie of a common sovereign (after 1867 through the Dual Monarchy) the situation in the Catholic Church had some likenesses to that in the latter country. However, racially and economically the two countries were contrasts. Austria was overwhelmingly German and was being rapidly industrialized, while in Hungry the Magyar element prevailed and modern industry was making little headway in a predominantly agricultural population. Moreover, Protestantism was much stronger than in Austria, and there were Orthodox enclaves. Throughout the nineteenth century the Josephist tradition was potent. The state controlled the Church and directed the education of the clergy. Something of a gulf existed between the bishops and the priests who served the peasants. In the fore part of the century especially the state permitted little direct access to Rome. The monarch appointed the bishops without consulting the Holy See. Religious orders were forbidden to keep in touch with their superiors in Rome. The members of the nobility, still showing the aftermath of eighteenth-century rationalism, seldom went to mass. It was chiefly among the *bourgeoisie* that the Catholic faith flourished.

The revolutionary year of 1848 had repercussions in Hungary which for a time threatened to shatter the old order. Catholic romanticism united with liberalism to abolish serfdom, and the clergy surrendered the tithes which were associated with it. Yet the great landholdings of bishops, cathedral chapters, and religious orders remained intact and under the new constitution the state retained control of the Church. In the ensuing fighting many of the lower clergy sided with Kossuth and the liberals, while the higher clergy tended to support the Hapsburgs. After the triumph of the Hapsburgs, many a priest fell victim to the terror which suppressed the republic. The stresses of the conflict cost the reason of the devotedly Catholic István Széchenyi (1791–1860), who had earlier laboured to further the Magyar tongue and literature and the economic improvement of the country. It was another Catholic, Ferencz Déak (1803–1876), who by his wisdom, disinterested integrity, and tact led the moderates in obtaining the compromise settlement, or *Ausgleich,* in 1867, under which the Dual Monarchy operated until the defeat of World War I.

In the decades which followed the *Ausgleich* Catholicism ceased to be the

159 Hermelink, *op. cit.,* Vol. III, p. 89; Premoli, *op. cit.,* pp. 137, 138.

religion of the state, but the Government continued to select the bishops and other higher clergy: it wished them to be loyal to the state rather than "pro-Roman." Jozsef Eötvös (1813–1871), a loyal and liberal Catholic, a friend and disciple of Montalembert, a highly cultured statesman and author who modernized the Magyar novel, as minister of education in the cabinet which came into power in 1867 gave Hungarian national education the structure under which it long operated. He also advocated the independence of the Church from the state.

As time passed, developments made for a more earnest religious life. Some of them came through growing relations with Rome. Buttressed by large land-holdings, the great monastic orders, Benedictines, Cistercians, Premonstratensians, Piarists, and especially the Jesuits, maintained schools. The priesthood was one of the few channels through which the son of a peasant could mount socially. The mendicant orders were prominent and life in them combined physical comfort with some contact with the humble. Not long before 1914 efforts were made at monastic reform. A new kind of prelate began to emerge, seeking closer contacts with the lower clergy.

Here and there in the Catholic Church of Hungary were those who championed the cause of the poor. Thus in the latter part of the century the priest Ottokar Prohaszka, who had drunk deeply at the spring of Francis of Assisi, as writer and preacher befriended the weak and had many followers among the parish priests. Another priest, Sándor Giesswein, was in accord with the principles of Prohaszka and formulated a social programme which went beyond that of the Social Democrats.[160]

In the multi-racial society of Hungary the Magyars attempted to maintain their supremacy and to crush or assimilate to their language and culture the minority nationalities. In the growing restlessness of the latter the Catholic clergy drawn from their ranks were leaders in the movements for greater autonomy. This was true among the Croats and the Slovaks.[161] Thus Joseph George Strossmayer (1815–1905), consecrated in 1850 Bishop of Diakovár (Djakovo) for Bosnia, Slavonia, and Sirmium, fostered nationalism among the South Slavs. Of immigrant German peasant stock, he had early shown intellectual brilliance and had been court chaplain in Vienna. He embarrassed Vienna by advocating the federal principle as a means of the peaceful coexistence of the many nationalities in the Hapsburg empire and was the central figure in the movement for the autonomy of the South Slavs. He employed the vast revenues of his see to foster education among them. He reorganized the entire educational system in Dalmatia and Croatia-Slavonia and founded

[160] Moody, *Church and Society*, pp. 659 ff.
[161] *Ibid.*, p. 674.

primary schools, an academy of Jugoslavic arts and sciences, a theological seminary, and a university.[162]

BOHEMIA AND MORAVIA

In Bohemia the aftermath of the Thirty Years' War (1618–1648) had reduced the once flourishing Protestant communities to small and persecuted minorities. Under the triumphant Hapsburgs Roman Catholicism prevailed. The Hapsburgs set about the Germanization of the country and the Czech language became merely a peasant tongue.

Under the "enlightened despotism" of Maria Theresa and Joseph II, while German was employed in the higher schools, economic burdens were somewhat lightened, personal liberty was granted to the peasants (1781), religious liberty for the Protestants was decreed (1781), the land became more prosperous, population mounted, and a Czech renaissance began.

The leader in the revival of Slavonic studies and the pioneer in the renewal of Czech as a literary language was a Catholic priest, Josef Dobrovsky (1753–1829). In his teens he had joined the Society of Jesus and on its dissolution continued his theological studies. He was influenced by the *Aufklärung* and Freemasonry and was chiefly remembered for his grammar and dictionary, the basis of the revived Czech philology and speech. It was through him that the way was paved in the Augustinian monastery of Brno in Moravia for the remarkable scientific achievements of Mendel.[163]

For several decades after 1815 the Enlightenment was potent in Bohemia. Until 1848 most of the bishops adhered to it. It was given a wide vogue among the clergy by Bernard Bolzano (1781–1848). A priest, from 1805 to 1820 Bolzano taught at the University of Prague. He made use of Leibnitz, Wolff, and Kant and educated a whole generation of priests. He faced criticism within the Church, but, protected by Archbishop Salm-Salm of Prague, he continued to lecture until 1820. Then he was dismissed and was suspended from priestly functions. However, a theological seminary was founded in his honour and Michael Fesl and a bishop initiated the Federation of Christian Friendship, which was a rallying centre of his adherents. One of Bolzano's followers edited a magazine for priests.[164]

The revival of Czech nationalism, with its rebirth of Czech literature, stimulated by priests, came to a head in the revolutionary year of 1848. Yet, partly because the Vienna Government insisted on filling bishoprics with non-Czechs and sought to use the Church to support Hapsburg authority, the currents of

---

[162] *Dictionnaire de Théologie Catholique*, Vol. XIV, pp. 2630–2635; *The Catholic Encyclopedia*, Vol. XIV, p. 316.

[163] Nemec, *Church and State in Czechoslovakia*, pp. 96 ff.

[164] *Ibid.*; *The New Schaff-Herzog Encyclopedia of Religious Knowledge*, Vol. II, p. 219; *The Catholic Encyclopedia*, Vol. II, pp. 643, 644.

liberalism were largely anti-clerical. After 1855 concordats gave the Roman Catholic Church extensive jurisdiction in education. But in the course of a few years the state took measures which Catholics complained were a violation of these agreements. Freedom of the press and of religion, civil marriage, and the provision that in mixed marriages the sons should be reared in the faith of their father and the girls in that of their mother provoked the condemnation of Pius IX in an allocution of January 22, 1868.[165] Disregarding this opposition, an Austrian constitution of 1875 permitted each denomination to govern its internal affairs, "subject to state law." [166]

Support for Czech nationalism came from Leo XIII. In 1890 he encouraged the founding of a Czech college in Rome and endowed it. In 1901 he endorsed the use of the Czech language. Earlier (1860) the Jesuits and the Archbishop of Olomouc had aided the birth of the Association of Saint Cyril and Saint Methodius which had as its object the unity of all Slavic nations.[167]

In spite of the active sympathy for Czech nationalism shown by Leo XIII and the fact that the overwhelming majority of the people were baptized in the Catholic faith, in the closing decades of the nineteenth century the tide was running against the Roman Catholic Church. The intelligentsia were influenced by philosophic rationalism. Although reared a Catholic, T. G. Masaryk, who was outstanding in scholarly and political circles and after World War I became the first President of Czechoslovakia, rebelled against the church of his birth and for a time aligned himself with the Orthodox and then with Protestantism. Many of the workingmen fell under the spell of Marxist Socialism with its description of religion as the opiate of the people.[168]

The challenge of disaffection and of the new forces of the age roused Catholics to constructive action which was evidence of creative vigour. In the 1890's, stirred by a book by a priest, Matej Prochazka of Brno, on the problems of the workers, Czech and Moravian Catholics organized a Christian Social Party. An association of Czech Catholic intellectuals was formed to educate Czechs for participation in public life.[169]

POLAND

Throughout the nineteenth century the Roman Catholic Church in Poland had always to face the political division of its constituency and the alien rule of Prussia, Austria, and Russia. Russia had the major section of the country. We have seen (Chapter VII) how Gregory XVI opposed the revolutionary effort of the early 1830's to throw off the Russian yoke but was distressed by the

[165] Nemec, *op. cit.*, pp. 96 ff.
[166] *Ibid.*, p. 105.
[167] *Ibid.*, pp. 108, 117.
[168] *Ibid.*, p. 108; Moody, *op. cit.*, p. 639.
[169] Nemec, *op. cit.*, p. 116.

high-handed fashion in which the tsar sought to dominate the hierarchy and to constrain the Uniates to return to the Russian Orthodox fold. We have also called attention to the way in which the continued measures to Russify the Uniates troubled both Pius IX and Leo XIII. The Polish revolts of 1830 and 1863 led to the tightening of Russian control. In Posen and East Prussia German rule was also harsh. In Galicia Austrian administration was somewhat milder, especially in the latter part of the century.

Ecclesiastically Poland was divided. The Poles were overwhelmingly Roman Catholics of the Latin rite. However, a minority numbering several millions, Ruthenians, Ukrainians or "Little Russians," formerly Orthodox, by the Union of Brest (1595) had submitted to Rome and had been permitted to retain their old rite. The union had been achieved more by political, social, and cultural forces than from strictly religious motives.[170]

It was natural that when the area came under the tsar the latter would seek to bring the Uniates again into the Orthodox fold by amalgamation with the Russian church. Early in the nineteenth century Buhusz, Archbishop of Mohilev and Metropolitan of the Latin bishoprics in the Russian zone, headed an Ecclesiastical Commission appointed by the tsar which was created to supervise both the Latin and the Uniate dioceses without reference to Rome. He openly endorsed a Bible Society which arose through British Protestant initiative. In 1816 he was rebuked by Pius VII, especially for his attitude towards the Bible Society.[171] Tsar Nicholas I, who reigned from 1825 to 1855, incorporated the Ecclesiastical Commission into the Holy Synod which governed the Russian Orthodox Church. Men were appointed as bishops of the Uniate body who favoured integration with the Russian Orthodox Church, many priests who resisted were exiled to Siberia, and in 1839 the consummation of the union was proclaimed. Numbers of Ruthenians who did not conform were expelled from the country or sent to Siberia.[172]

Attempts were not lacking to strengthen those Poles who, under the Latin rite, retained their connexion with Rome. A visit of Nicholas to Rome in 1845 was followed in 1847 by a concordat which dealt with the number and boundaries of bishoprics and the method of electing bishops and appointing parish priests, and which provided for episcopal jurisdiction in ecclesiastical affairs, especially in the education of prospective priests. Yet Pius IX held that he was unreconciled to the restrictions on direct communication of Polish Catholics with Rome, Russian laws on mixed marriages and divorce, the ease of conversion to the Russian Orthodox Church, and the measures against the Ruthenian Uniates.[173] In 1842 a religious congregation known as the Resurrectionists was

[170] Attwater, *The Christian Churches of the East*, Vol. I, pp. 69, 70.
[171] MacCaffrey, *History of the Catholic Church in the Nineteenth Century*, Vol. I, p. 189.
[172] *Ibid.*, pp. 193, 194.
[173] *Ibid.*, pp. 194, 195.

formed among Polish refugees. In 1846 a Jesuit, Charles Antoniewicz, went on a preaching tour with remarkable results in districts in Galicia disturbed by peasant uprisings.[174]

The president of the provisional government set up by the Poles in 1830 was Count Adam George Czartoryski (1770–1861), who had been a close friend of Tsar Alexander I and for a time in control of Russian diplomacy. In his youth affected by the Enlightenment, in middle age he had become convinced that religion was indispensable if the nation was to survive. In his last years he declared: "Catholicism should not be founded on the love of country, but patriotism on the love of God." [175]

The efforts of the Poles in 1863 to throw off the Russian yoke were followed by the suppression of all self-government and the enforcement of the Russian language in schools, courts, and official proceedings. The Russians viewed the Roman Catholic Church as a support of Polish nationalism. Some bishops were deported, many of the clergy were sent to Siberia, several churches were closed, the seminaries were placed under the civil authorities and were required to teach Russian, and numbers of monasteries were suppressed and their schools closed or turned over to Russian lay teachers. Priests were put under police surveillance. They could give religious instruction in the schools, but only in the presence of a Russian official whose duty it was to see that no sedition was taught. The Russians accused the Pope of fomenting the rebellion and in 1866 broke off diplomatic relations with the Vatican and abrogated all conventions with the Holy See. The seminaries in Poland and Russia were removed from the control of the bishops and placed under Orthodox officials, and scores of Uniate parishes were annexed to the Russian Orthodox Church.[176]

Under Leo XIII relations with the Holy See improved and some of the measures against the Roman Catholic Church in Poland and Russia were relaxed. By an agreement between the Pope and Tsar Alexander III in 1882 vacant sees were filled and the seminaries were partly restored to the control of the bishops, but with the continuation of instruction in the Russian language and literature. Contrary to the wish of the Russian Government, Leo XIII, like Pius IX, supported the use of Polish in non-liturgical services and religious instruction. In 1898 Tsar Nicholas II agreed to recognize the Uniates as Roman Catholics, but only on condition that they adopt the Latin rite. But Leo XIII discouraged efforts to force the Uniates to employ that rite.[177] In the meantime, with the progress of industrialization and the rise of an urban proletariat, the Russian Social Democratic movement with its anti-Christian trend gained followers.

[174] Moody, *op. cit.*, p. 589.
[175] *Ibid.*, pp. 594, 595.
[176] MacCaffrey, *op. cit.*, Vol. I, pp. 399–402; Moody, *op. cit.*, p. 595.
[177] MacCaffrey, *op. cit.*, Vol. I, pp. 402–404.

The defeat of Russia by Japan in 1905 and the consequent outbreak of domestic disorders were followed by liberalizing measures. Among them was the proclamation of religious freedom. As a result, several scores of thousands of former Uniates left the Russian Orthodox Church and resumed their connexion with Rome.[178]

In the Prussian-governed portion of Poland the Roman Catholic Church was less restricted than in the Russian sector. A Catholic group introduced new methods of agriculture and began a popular press and vocational education for small farmers. After 1848 more than one Polish Catholic priest served in the Prussian Diet. As in other Prussian territories, the *Kulturkampf* brought difficulties to the Catholic Church in the Polish districts.[179]

In Galicia, in the Austrian zone, Poles were in the majority and sought to dominate the Ruthenians and to block Ruthenian nationalism. In 1867, after the Hungarian *Ausgleich,* the Poles enjoyed a large degree of home rule. Leaders in a conservative party, some of them professors in the University of Cracow, stressed Catholicism as a contributor to Poland's greatness and as a safeguard against anarchy. A Jesuit, later provincial of his Society, encouraged Catholic workers' organizations.[180]

The Austrians gave the Ruthenians full religious liberty. The abolishment of serfdom in 1848 and 1860 favoured the Ruthenians, who were almost entirely peasants. The children of the married clergy of the Uniate Church constituted an important element in a rising cultural middle class.[181]

SCANDINAVIA

In Denmark, Iceland, Norway, and Sweden, where dissent, either Protestant or Catholic, from the state churches, Lutheran, was long under strong legal disabilities, and in Finland, where the Lutheran Church was established, at the outset of the nineteenth century the very few Roman Catholics were almost entirely foreigners. About the mid-century restrictions on dissent began to be relaxed. Availing themselves of the lowering of the barriers, Catholic missionaries entered, converts were made, churches were erected, schools and charitable institutions were begun, and the faithful were organized into confraternities. By their care of the sick, Catholic sisterhoods won favour among many of the populace. Prefectures apostolic and vicariates apostolic were erected. Converts were most numerous in Denmark but even there in 1914 numbered less than twenty thousand.[182]

[178] *Ibid.,* p. 404.
[179] Moody, *op. cit.,* pp. 593–595.
[180] *Ibid.,* pp. 596, 597.
[181] Attwater, *op. cit.,* pp. 72, 73.
[182] MacCaffrey, *op. cit.,* Vol. I, pp. 410–417; Premoli, *Contemporary Church History,* pp. 204–212, 231; Arne Palqvist, *Die Römisch-katholische Kirche in Schweden nach 1781. I. Das apostolische*

IRELAND

Ireland had an important place in the Roman Catholic Church in the nineteenth and twentieth centuries, but not so much because of what happened within the island itself. The large majority of the Irish Catholics were poverty-stricken and from them came few new congregations and no major contributions to Roman Catholic thought or devotional life. Rather, Irish emigration played a large part in the growth and character of the Roman Catholic Church in England, Scotland, the United States, Canada, Australia, New Zealand, and South Africa. We will defer until later volumes our account of the Irish share in the Roman Catholic Church in the United States and the British dominions. Here we must say something of developments in Ireland itself and then go on to what they meant in Great Britain.

For centuries the history of Ireland was one of tragedy. Ireland had once been known as the isle of the saints. Spared the impact of the invasions which had wrecked much of the Continent and Great Britain, in the sixth, seventh, and eighth centuries its monastic life had flourished and from it missionaries had gone who had shared in the conversion of the barbarians. Then, beginning in 795 and for three hundred years or more, successive raids and settlements of the Northmen brought destruction. In the twelfth century the Anglo-Normans introduced English rule, but for generations much of the island was practically independent under local rulers of Irish or Anglo-Norman descent. Henry VIII imposed on the Irish church separation from Rome and under Edward VI and Elizabeth the official Church of Ireland became Protestant. Protestant settlers came, chiefly to Ulster, from England and Scotland. The established church was in communion with that of England, but the majority of the Irish remained true to Rome. The Roman Catholic faith became a symbol and bond of Irish nationalism, all the more so since Roman Catholics were under legal disabilities.

In the latter part of the eighteenth century the restrictions on Roman Catholics began to be lightened. A few Catholics were acquiring wealth and education. In the 1770's and 1780's concessions were made to them.[183] Population was increasing—from about 1,250,000 in 1700 to about 4,500,000 in 1800. Of the latter, a little over two-thirds were Roman Catholics, about a tenth belonged to the established Church of Ireland, and about a fifth were Presbyterian Scotch-Irish. In 1795, with government funds, the National St. Patrick's College was founded at Maynooth, near Dublin. It became a notable centre for the training

---

Vikariat 1783–1820 (Uppsala and Stockholm, Almqvist & Wiksells Boktryckeri, 1954, pp. 508), *passim.*

[183] MacCaffrey, *op. cit.*, Vol. II, pp. 98 ff.; Reynolds, *The Catholic Emancipation Crisis in Ireland,* pp. 7, 8; Philip Hughes, *The Catholic Question 1688–1829: A Study in Political History* (New York, Benziger Brothers, 1929, pp. 334), pp. 172 ff.

of the clergy. In 1800 the Irish parliament was discontinued and the Union effected in which the Irish were represented in the Parliament in Westminster. The Union weakened one of the obstacles to Catholic emancipation, namely, the right to vote for members of Parliament, for in an Irish Parliament the extension of the franchise to the Catholic majority might mean a Catholic legislature. Of that there was no danger in the Parliament in Westminster.

In 1829 what was known as Catholic emancipation removed most of the legal discrimination under which members of that faith had laboured. Catholics not only in Ireland but also throughout the United Kingdom were allowed to sit in the House of Commons and the House of Lords, to become members of corporations, and with a few exceptions to hold civil office. In the long discussions which preceded the passage of the act proposals had been made for state support of the Catholic clergy and a royal veto in the choice of bishops. These, however, were not adopted.[184]

Early in the nineteenth century many Irish Roman Catholics became Protestants. Through Bible societies, the Scripture Readers' Society (organized in 1822), schools, itinerant preachers, and public disputations, supported by bishops of the (Anglican) Church of Ireland, something of a movement towards Protestantism was seen. Numbers of Roman Catholics sprang to the vigorous defence of their faith. From 1849 to 1861 efforts at conversion to Protestantism were renewed, but without much substantial success.[185]

Roman Catholic leaders agitated against the tithes which were levied for the support of the Church of Ireland. Not only communicants but also non-communicants of that church, both Roman Catholic and Protestant, were required to pay them. A leader in the campaign against the tithes was Daniel O'Connell (1775-1847). He also urged the termination of the Union. He headed the Catholic Association which, with the support of the priests, eventually enrolled the large majority of the Catholics. From time to time some relief was granted but it was not until 1869 that the Church of Ireland was disestablished.[186]

In the meantime Ireland suffered from severe famine which brought intense suffering. The cause was a blight which ruined the island's chief food crop, the potato. The years 1846 and 1847 were the worst. Relief was given by the Government and by private agencies, many of them Protestant, and especially from the United States. The death rate was heightened by an epidemic of cholera in 1849. Distress was augmented by an increase of population in the earlier decades of the century which the land was unable to sustain except in extreme poverty. The situation was further aggravated by the repeal in 1846 of the corn laws which had protected native agriculture. Hundreds of thousands, usually of the

[184] MacCaffrey, *op. cit.,* Vol. II, pp. 142–173; Reynolds, *op. cit.,* pp. 14 ff.; Hughes, *op. cit.,* pp. 191 ff.
[185] MacCaffrey, *op. cit.,* Vol. II, pp. 173–175, 210, 211.
[186] *Ibid.,* pp. 176 ff.

more energetic youth, left the island for Great Britain, Canada, Australia, and New Zealand, but chiefly the United States. In 1901 the population was less than half what it had been in 1841. Since the economic level of Catholics was lower than that of Protestants, the percentage of loss was somewhat higher among them than among the latter. The Roman Catholic clergy were active in famine relief. John MacHale (1791–1881), Archbishop of Tuam, was especially prominent. Educated in Maynooth, he championed the cause of Ireland, was a friend of Daniel O'Connell, and had stood with him for the repeal of the Union.[187]

By the year 1914 conditions had improved. A series of legislative measures eased the lot of the tenants, predominantly Catholic. Acts were passed by Parliament which enlarged educational opportunities for Catholics. In 1831 a system of national schools was inaugurated. They were for both Catholics and Protestants and Catholics as well as Protestants were on the board which supervised them. On one or two days of each week they were to be open for religious instruction by representatives of the several denominations. At least one of the Catholic bishops condemned the schools as not positive enough religiously. In 1841 Rome left it to each bishop to decide whether he would permit them.[188] In time only the minority of the children were in the mixed schools and an increasing majority were in schools which in fact if not in name were denominational. Rather than have their teachers prepared in normal schools which were neutral religiously, as were those maintained by the state, Catholics organized and financed their own teacher-training institutions.[189] Through various religious orders and congregations Catholics conducted secondary schools and in 1878 an act was passed which aided secondary education of whatever denomination. The Catholic bishops denounced what were known as the Queen's Colleges, authorized by the Government in 1846 for higher education, as religiously unsatisfactory and in this were supported by Rome. In 1851 Catholics inaugurated a Catholic University with funds raised in Ireland, the United States, Canada, and Great Britain. In 1908 the Irish Universities Act, although seeming to Catholics to be far short of placing them on an equality with Protestants, was regarded by them as a step in the right direction.[190]

For the training of clergy, Maynooth received subsidies from the Government. In 1869, on the disestablishment of the Church of Ireland, Maynooth was also cut adrift from the state, but with a substantial terminal grant. The Irish bishops administered the school and in 1876 it became a college of the Catholic University. The Holy See authorized it to confer degrees in theology,

---

[187] *The Catholic Encyclopedia*, Vol. VIII, p. 114, Vol. IX, pp. 496–501.
[188] MacCaffrey, *op. cit.*, Vol. II, pp. 223, 224.
[189] *Ibid.*, pp. 226–230.
[190] *Ibid.*, pp. 230–252.

canon law, and philosophy. In 1842 All Hallows College was founded in Dublin to train priests for the Irish who had emigrated to other lands. In 1826 the Irish College in Rome was reëstablished. Paul Cullen (1803–1878), the first Irishman to be appointed Cardinal (1867), from 1832 to 1850 was rector of the college. In 1849 he was created Archbishop of Armagh and in 1850 was made Archbishop of Dublin. In the latter post he was the guiding spirit of the Roman Catholic Church in Ireland in the third quarter of the century. A strong advocate of Papal infallibility, he drafted the formula of the declaration of that dogma.[191]

From the Roman Catholic Church in Ireland came Theobald Mathew (1790–1856). A scion of the Catholic gentry, he was a Capuchin and from 1822 was the Provincial of his order in Ireland. He had already served fearlessly the victims of cholera when in 1838 he joined a total-abstinence society. As we are to see in later volumes, in the nineteenth century a widespread agitation stemmed from Protestants against alcoholic beverages. In Ireland in the fore part of the century the drinking of liquors with heavy alcoholic content had mounted alarmingly. Protestants had agitated for moderation and then for complete abstention. Mathew quickly became the most prominent figure in the movement and by his eloquence persuaded thousands to take the pledge of total abstinence. Bishops and priests endorsed him. He reached Protestants as well as Catholics and extended his labours to England, Scotland, and America. During the worst years of the Irish famine he paused in his campaign to administer relief. When he died, worn out by his intense exertions, he was the most widely and favourably known of the Irish clergy.[192]

ENGLAND

The restoration of the hierarchy in England by Pius IX in 1850 came as a culmination of a striking revival of the Roman Catholic Church in that country and gave impetus and direction to further growth.

When the step was taken the Roman Catholic constituency in England was composed of three elements. First were the descendants of the small minority who had held to the faith in the centuries when to do so meant political disabilities and social obloquy. On the eve of the nineteenth century they may have numbered 50,000 and were served by 4 vicars apostolic and about 350 priests.[193] The public attitude towards them was eased by the sympathy felt for Catholic refugees from the French Revolution, many of them clergy.[194] The position of the minority was still further aided by the Catholic Emancipation Act

[191] *Ibid.*, pp. 262–266; *The Catholic Encyclopedia*, Vol. IV, pp. 564–566.
[192] Patrick Rogers, *Father Theobald Mathew, Apostle of Temperance* (Dublin, Browne & Nolan, 1944, pp. xxiii, 166), *passim.*
[193] MacCaffrey, *op. cit.*, Vol. II, p. 1; Beck, *The English Catholics, 1850–1950*, pp. 223 ff.
[194] MacCaffrey, *op. cit.*, Vol. II, pp. 11–13.

of 1829.[195] The old English Catholic families had lived quietly, shunning publicity. But from them came some of the outstanding leaders in the revival. Among them was the rugged William Bernard Ullathorne (1806–1889), a Benedictine. After helping to lay the foundations of his church in Australia he long had a prominent place in the English hierarchy successively as Vicar Apostolic, Bishop of Birmingham, and on retirement because of age as honorary Archbishop of Cabasa.[196] Also from that stock was Herbert Alfred Vaughan (1832–1903), an Oblate of St. Charles, who became the third Archbishop of Westminster and Cardinal.[197]

To the native English of long Catholic ancestry were added immigrants from Ireland. They soon constituted by far the largest proportion of the Roman Catholic body. At the outset poverty-stricken and unskilled labourers, they gathered chiefly in the main cities. In 1841, on the eve of the Irish famine 224,128 Irish-born were said to be in England. In 1851 the total was said to be 419,256.[198] From the Irish, although not all from this immigration, sprang notable bishops. Born in Spain of an Irish merchant family and educated in Rome, Nicholas Wiseman (1802–1865) was the first Archbishop of Westminster and a Cardinal.[199] The fourth Archbishop of Westminster, Francis Bourne (1861–1935), also a Cardinal, was a native Londoner, the son of an English father and an Irish mother.[200]

Prominent in the revival of the Roman Catholic Church were a small minority from the Church of England. Although conversions had begun earlier, a number came from a renewal of the Catholic tradition in that church through what was usually known as the Oxford or Tractarian movement, which began in 1833. Of it we are to hear more in the next volume. One of its outstanding leaders, John Henry Newman (1801–1890), whom we have repeatedly met, submitted to Rome in 1845.[201] Others followed, although it was not until 1851

---

[195] On the steps leading to that act and including it, see Bernard Ward, *The Eve of Catholic Emancipation. Being the History of the English Catholics during the First Thirty Years of the Nineteenth Century* (London, Longmans, Green & Co., 3 vols., 1911, 1912).

[196] William Bernard Ullathorne, *From Cabin-boy to Archbishop: the Autobiography of Archbishop Ullathorne* (London, Burns, Oates & Washbourne, 1941, pp. xxvi, 310); Cuthbert Butler, *The Life and Times of Bishop Ullathorne 1806–1889* (London, Burns, Oates & Washbourne, 2 vols., 1926).

[197] J. G. Snead-Cox, *The Life of Cardinal Vaughan* (London, Herbert & Daniel, 2 vols., 1910).

[198] Mathew, *Catholicism in England 1535–1935*, pp. 182, 183. But see a figure of 679,067 for 1851 in Beck, *op. cit.*, p. 45.

[199] Wilfrid Ward, *The Life and Times of Cardinal Wiseman* (London, Longmans, Green & Co., 2 vols., 2nd ed., 1897); Denis Gwynn, *Cardinal Wiseman* (Dublin, Browne & Nolan, 1950, pp. x, 197).

[200] Ernest Oldmeadow, *Francis Cardinal Bourne* (London, Burns, Oates & Washbourne, 2 vols., 1940).

[201] Of the enormous bibliography by and about Newman see especially John Henry Newman, *Apologia pro Vita Sua, Being a History of His Religious Opinions*, first written in 1865 and later appearing in many revisions, printings, and impressions (see an edition, London, Longmans, Green & Co., 1908, pp. 398, and an earlier one under the title *History of My Religious Opinions*, London,

that Henry Edward Manning (1807–1892), who had risen to be an archdeacon in the Church of England, took the decisive step. He succeeded Wiseman as Archbishop of Westminster.[202] Two others were Frederick William Faber (1814–1863) and William George Ward (1812–1882). Faber was the son of a priest of the Church of England, at Oxford came under the influence of Newman, and after his conversion joined the Oratory.[203] Like Faber, Ward was from Balliol College, Oxford. He took the decisive step to Rome before Newman.[204] After the Oxford conversions the trickle into the Roman Catholic Church was largely from the professions and the aristocracy, and especially from the wives and daughters of the nobility. By the late 1860's it had begun to subside, but it persisted through the century.[205] Now and again it attracted men of letters. Among them were Robert Hugh Benson (1871–1914), a son of an Archbishop of Canterbury and a clergyman in the Church of England, the poet and critic Coventry Kersey Dighton Patmore (1823–1896), and Gilbert K. Chesterton (1874–1936), humorist, journalist, and publicist, whose trenchant pen won him a wide reading.[206]

In spite of conversions and immigration from Ireland, Roman Catholics remained a small minority. In 1914 they were probably a little less than one-tenth of the population.[207] Immigration from Italy added to the total, but not as significantly as that from Ireland.

Although in England Roman Catholics continued to be numerically a small proportion of the population, the legal and social disabilities under which they had laboured were progressively lightened, they displayed marked religious vigour, and among them were men prominent in public life and in the literary and scholarly world.

In education the Roman Catholics were increasingly on an equal basis with Protestants. By 1914 they were enrolled in Oxford and Cambridge and in the new city universities.[208] In 1847 they obtained a share in the government funds assigned to elementary education. The Forster Education Act of 1870 which set up state-subsidized national or board schools provided for undenominational religious instruction and observances in them.[209] Many Catholics viewed the

---

Longmans, Green, Reader, & Dyer, 1869, pp. xxiv, 388); the standard biography, Wilfrid Ward, *The Life of John Henry Cardinal Newman, Based on His Private Journals and Correspondence* (London, Longmans, Green & Co., 2 vols., 1912); and Beck,-*op. cit.,* pp. 243 ff.

[202] Purcell, *Life of Cardinal Manning, passim.*

[203] Mathew, *op. cit.,* pp. 203, 204.

[204] Wilfrid Ward, *William George Ward and the Oxford Movement* (London, Macmillan & Co., 1889, pp. xxix, 462); Wilfrid Ward, *William George Ward and the Catholic Revival* (London, Macmillan & Co., 1893, pp. xlvi, 468).

[205] Mathew, *op. cit.,* pp. 209–221; Beck, *op. cit.,* pp. 232–238.

[206] *The Autobiography of G. K. Chesterton* (New York, Sheed & Ward, 1936, pp. vii, 360).

[207] That was the figure for 1926. *Catholic Emancipation,* p. 261.

[208] Purcell, *op. cit.,* Vol. II, p. 810; *Catholic Emancipation,* p. 48; Beck, *op. cit.,* pp. 291 ff.

[209] Nichols, *History of Christianity,* pp. 258, 259; Beck, *op. cit.,* pp. 365 ff.

new schools as "godless" and supported the growing number of their own elementary schools, even though that was under a financial handicap.[210] In 1902 another Education Act was passed which, in spite of the opposition of Protestant Nonconformists, gave grants from school taxes to denominatinal schools, chiefly Anglican and Roman Catholic.[211] In this educational advance the Catholic Poor School Committee, begun in 1847 and followed in 1904 by the Catholic Education Council, was of great help.[212]

Religiously the Roman Catholic community was very vigorous. In the restored hierarchy the Archbishop of Westminster was the head and in Catholic eyes was in the succession of the Archbishops of Canterbury interrupted by the separation of the Church of England from Rome. In Westminster an imposing cathedral arose, in modified romanesque style. Churches and chapels multiplied, in both cities and rural districts. Religious orders and congregations of men and women flourished.[213] Seculars mounted in numbers: Manning favoured them and looked askance at regulars, notably the Jesuits.[214]

Increasingly Roman Catholics were prominent in government, in literature, and in scholarship. By the end of the century they were beginning to be represented in the civil service, in law, and in medicine.[215] In literature, in addition to the converts whom we have mentioned, were men of Catholic parentage and rearing, among them the poet Francis Thompson (1859–1907), with his tragic life, and Hilaire Belloc. The Catholic community numbered outstanding scholars in the field of religion, some converts, such as Newman and Tyrrell, and others reared in that faith, among them Lord Acton and Baron Friedrich von Hügel (1852–1925).[216] The latter two were as much Continental as English.

English Roman Catholics could scarcely avoid being concerned with the social issues of the day. In a land seething with unrest among the toilers and where Protestants were engaged in social legislation and other remedial measures, many among the Roman Catholic clergy and laity were active in efforts to minister to sufferers from the ills of the time and to remove or at least to alleviate the injustices of the social order. Manning particularly was outstanding in helping to settle strikes, in support of the anti-slavery movement, in advocacy of temperance, and in efforts to improve the lot of labourers, whether in agriculture or industry.[217]

[210] Purcell, *op. cit.*, Vol. II, pp. 494, 495; *Catholic Emancipation*, pp. 54–56.
[211] Nichols, *op. cit.*, p. 259; *Catholic Emancipation*, pp. 59 ff.
[212] *Catholic Emancipation*, pp. 74, 75.
[213] Mathew, *op. cit.*, pp. 213 ff.; *Catholic Emancipation*, pp. 177 ff.; Beck, *op. cit.*, pp. 337 ff., 442 ff.
[214] Purcell, *op. cit.*, Vol. II, pp. 756 .
[215] Mathew, *op. cit.*, p. 234.
[216] Michael de la Bedoyere, *The Life of Baron von Hügel* (London, J. M. Dent & Sons, 1951, pp. xviii, 366).
[217] Purcell, *op. cit.*, Vol. II, pp. 587 ff.; Nitti, *Catholic Socialism*, pp. 311 ff.; Georgiana Putnam

WALES

In Wales as in England were families which from pre-Reformation times had held tenaciously to the Roman Catholic faith. With the first half of the nineteenth century came the immigration of Irish labourers. Most of them were in a desperate economic plight and were eyed with hostility by the Welsh as "cheap labour" and "Papists." They were served by heroic priests. In 1840 Wales was grouped with Herefordshire in a new vicariate. With the restoration of the hierarchy in 1850 Wales was divided between two dioceses which included adjacent parts of England. Progress was slow. In 1895 most of Wales was included in a new vicariate. Twenty-one years later, in 1916, it was constituted an ecclesiastical province with two dioceses. In spite of some conversions, Wales remained overwhelmingly Protestant.[218]

SCOTLAND

At the dawn of the nineteenth century the Scottish Roman Catholics were almost entirely in the Highlands. They were served by two vicariates and by priests educated on the Continent. In the fore part of the century Catholics multiplied in the Lowlands—by migration from the Highlands and immigration from Ireland. The famine in Ireland brought a great influx from that island. Glasgow, the largest city in the country, became the chief Irish and Catholic centre, for it was here that the refugees most readily found employment as unskilled labourers. In 1878 Leo XIII restored the hierarchy. Soon after 1900 Roman Catholics numbered about half a million.[219]

SUMMARY

As we look back across the nineteenth-century record which we have rapidly sketched of the Roman Catholic Church in the countries of Europe, features emerge which were common to them all. In all the Holy See exercised an increasing control over the Church. Such attempts at national or regional administrative autonomy as Gallicanism, Febronianism, and Josephism were progressively curbed. Rome also succeeded in eliminating all deviations from doctrines and policies which it regarded as orthodox, even when they were entered upon in honest efforts to enable the Church to meet the challenge of the revolutionary age. Again and again the state and the Church clashed. Repeatedly the state sought to name the bishops and to determine whether a Papal decree should be published within its borders. In the main Rome more

---

McEntee, *The Social Catholic Movement in Great Britain* (New York, The Macmillan Co., 1927, pp. x, 312), *passim*.

[218] Donald Attwater, *The Catholic Church in Modern Wales: A record of the Past Century* (London, Burns, Oates & Washbourne, 1935, pp. ix, 235).

[219] MacCaffrey, *History of the Catholic Church in the Nineteenth Century*, Vol, II, pp. 86–97.

and more had its way. Often the contest was over education and marriage. Traditionally they had been functions of the Church. Now the state insisted upon shaping youth for its purposes and upon regulating marriage and determining in the unions between Catholics and non-Catholics the religion in which the children should be reared. Here and there, as in the *Kulturkampf*, the state yielded. In many instances state and Church compromised. In general, however, the tide was running against the Church. The secularization of the processes by which the oncoming generations were born and reared was gaining. Associated with the secularizing of education and marriage were the efforts of the state to rid the country of monastic orders and congregations. That was in part from opposition to the participation of the orders and congregations in the education of youth. Moreover, the temper of the age viewed as an anachronism the monastic way of life and objected to the vast endowments, chiefly in lands, which previous pious generations had given to maintain it. Here, too, the Church was losing. Yet a large proportion of its children were loyal and were being knit ever more tightly into a structure controlled and directed by the Pope.

CHAPTER XII

The World Outreach of the Roman Catholic Church: The European Phase

T HE Roman Catholic Church, apparently on a retreating defensive in its historic stronghold, Western Europe, against revolutionary forces which could be in part traced to it, was not willing to accept defeat. It was, rather, intent on victory. Not only was it valiantly resisting, often to its seeming loss, elements in the revolution which it believed hostile to the faith of which it was the custodian. It was also seeking to hold to its faith its children who were migrating to other continents and to win that larger world which was outside the Occident and upon which the Occident was impinging. In this, except in the United States of America and those British colonies which were on the way to becoming autonomous nations—Canada, Australia, New Zealand, and South Africa—it had little help from the emigrants. Even from the Catholics in these countries not until after 1914 did much assistance come in planting the faith among non-Occidental peoples. During the nineteenth century from the embattled Roman Catholic Church of Western Europe thousands of missionaries went in a mounting stream to revive and nourish the faith among peoples where in the closing decades of the eighteenth century it had been waning and to plant it where it had never been represented. As we have suggested, the largest number of missionaries from any one country were from France, the land in which the de-Christianizing movements were the most militant. Likewise, as we have seen, to aid in the support of the missionaries new kinds of organizations arose.

In our third volume we are to give in brief summary the accomplishments of these missions outside Europe. Here we must say something about what was achieved within Europe. In Europe the main efforts were directed towards bringing into the Roman Catholic fold Christians who did not acknowledge the Pope as the head of the Church. That was because, aside from the Jews, Roman Catholic missionaries could gain little access to the traditionally non-Christian peoples: the Moslem minorities were mostly in lands where the Orthodox Churches were the chief representatives of Christianity and the pagans were in the eastern portions of Russia from which the tsar's Government excluded the Roman Catholic Church. A few Jews were won, but not much effort was directed towards their conversion. As we have noted, only a few thousand Protestants became Roman Catholics: except for the migrations of the Irish into Great Britain the geographic boundaries between the two branches of the faith which had been established in the seventeenth century remained substantially intact. In Europe the Christians who were neither Roman Catholic nor Protestant were almost entirely in one or another of the Orthodox Churches. Rome endeavoured to win them not so much by inducing them to conform to the Latin rite as by strengthening the Uniate bodies. In these bodies many of the customs of the Orthodox, such as a married parish clergy, were maintained, and the liturgies were in the languages and the forms inherited from the Orthodox past. What was required was acknowledgement of the primacy of the Holy See and conformity to the faith as defined by the Church of Rome. In the existence of the Uniate bodies Roman Catholics saw tangible evidence to support the claim of their church to a universality embracing in its broad bosom all who held to the Christian Gospel in its purity.

We can take the space merely to enumerate such of the Uniate Churches as existed in Europe and to say a little of their record in the nineteenth century. In a later volume we will note those that were in Asia and Africa.[1] One of the Uniate Churches was made up of Italo-Greeks. From the early Christian centuries there were Christians in Southern Italy and Sicily who, from the strong Greek elements in these regions, had Greek as their liturgical language and followed their own rites. Before the schism between Rome and Constantinople they were in communion with Rome. In the course of time the Greek rite all but died out. By 1914 it survived in only a few villages in Calabria and Sicily and among the descendants of Greek refugees in Corsica and Leghorn.[2] We have already seen (Chapter XI) something of the record of the Ruthenian Uniates. We have noted that under political pressures from Russia many of those within the tsar's domains resumed the Orthodox connexion which had been severed in 1595.[3] The Ruthenians in Galicia, under Austrian rule, retained their Uniate status. Their secular clergy were trained in a seminary at Lwow (Lemberg) founded in 1783 after the acquisition of the area by Austria (1772), at the Ruthenian College in Rome erected by Leo XIII in 1897, in Vienna, and in Innsbruck. They had their own monastic congregations—the Basilians, organized early in the seventeenth century and in the latter part of the nineteenth century revived and reformed by the Jesuits under instructions by Leo

---

[1] For a comprehensive summary description of the Uniates see Fortescue, *The Uniate Eastern Churches*, pp. 1–44.

[2] *Ibid.*, pp. 47–184; Attwater, *The Christian Churches of the East. Volume I: Churches in Communion with Rome*, pp. 59–66.

[3] Attwater, *op. cit.*, pp. 68–72.

XIII given in 1882, and the Studites, who were begun about 1900 and who sought to follow the Byzantine monastic pattern. In 1914 the Ruthenian Uniates in Galicia numbered more than two million.[4] South of the Carpathians, in what was later called Ruthenia, or Podcarpathia, were Ruthenian Uniates who dated their submission to Rome from the seventeenth century. In the nineteenth century the Hungarian Government sought to assimilate them to the Magyars and the Latin rite. Unrest followed and shortly before 1914 numbers moved back into Orthodoxy.[5] In Croatia, which was long tied to Hungary, were Uniates, some of them Serbs, refugees from Turkish rule, and some of them immigrants from Galicia and Podcarpathia.[6] The Rumanian Uniates, of the Byzantine rite, dated from a union which was formally accomplished in 1701 and which brought about 200,000 into the fold of Rome. A generation or so later about half of them returned to Orthodoxy, but the remainder held true to their connexion with the Holy See.[7] In the nineteenth century, owing to missionary activity, a few hundred Greek Orthodox in Constantinople became Uniates. In that century several thousand Bulgars submitted to Rome, retaining their Byzantine rite.[8] After the revolution of 1905 brought a degree of religious liberty in Russia, a few groups of Uniates, some of them from the Old Believers, were gathered in the tsar's realms who kept their traditional rite.[9] In Constantinople were Armenian Uniates, but their main strength was in Asia Minor.[10]

[4] *Ibid.*, pp. 72–81, 225–227.
[5] *Ibid.*, pp. 80–84, 88–90.
[6] *Ibid.*, p. 95.
[7] *Ibid.*, pp. 99, 100.
[8] *Ibid.*, pp. 116, 117, 121, 122.
[9] *Ibid.*, p. 125.
[10] *Ibid.*, pp. 183, 184.

CHAPTER XIII

A Pause for Perspective

I N THE century which was ushered in by the final defeat and exile of Napoleon the Roman Catholic Church was confronted by handicaps but in spite of them displayed amazing life. The handicaps were many.

On the eve of the violent outbreak of revolution in 1789 the Roman Catholic Church was suffering from serious decline. It was tied hand and foot to political, economic, and social structures which were being challenged and were soon to be shattered. In France, Spain, Portugal, and much of Italy it was controlled by princely houses which in the next hundred years were to be swept into the discard. Its bishops were largely of the aristocracy, and luxurious living separated them as by a vast gulf from the rank and file of the parish clergy who ministered to the humble folk making up the majority of the Church's flock. In Germany, particularly in the Rhine Valley, the bishops were as much secular princes as Christian pastors—usually, indeed, more so. The Popes, while not morally corrupt as had been their predecessors of the fifteenth and the fore part of the sixteenth century, were not especially strong either in force of character or in sanctity, and their power to lead in reforms, even had they desired them, was curbed by the claims of monarchs over the Church and by the aspirations of bishops to autonomy. The main intellectual currents, potent in the popular rationalism, undercut the Church's faith. The widespread confidence in the perfectibility of man and of human society ran counter to basic Christian convictions of the corruption of man's nature by sin. In the dissolution of the Society of Jesus, forced on the Pope by secular princes, the Roman Catholic Church lost one of its most zealous missionary and educational agencies.

From 1789 to 1815 the storm of revolution and war dealt further blows to the weakened Church. In France the extremists wished to be rid of the Christian faith, and the more moderate revolutionaries sought to subordinate the Church to their purposes. The mighty Napoleon endeavoured to make the Church and the Pope subserve his ends and dealt cavalierly with both. In Germany Kant formulated a philosophy which, while challenging the eighteenth-century rationalism, seemed to render the Roman Catholic faith anachronistic.

The downfall of Napoleon did not end the revolution. To be sure, attempts were made to restore the old order, but they were never completely successful. Recurring political explosions, notably in 1830 and 1848, blew off the lid by which Metternich and his kind attempted to contain the revolutionary ferment. The Industrial Revolution with its accompanying economic and social changes mounted. Nationalism, at times allied with political liberalism, was increasingly clamant. New theories for the reorganization of society, among them Socialism of various kinds, increasingly that formulated by Marx, were becoming popular and many of them ruled out the Christian faith. Philosophy, historical scholarship, and the advancing natural sciences undermined for many the foundations on which the Roman Catholic Church was erected. The direction of psychology was towards a denial of the conception of man inculcated by the Church. Much of the most widely read fiction, poetry, and drama made light of Christian morality. Governments more and more sought to wrest from the Roman Catholic Church its long-standing control of the education of youth and of marriage and its historic monopoly of the care of the sick, the aged, and the poor. Monastic properties were confiscated. The new Kingdom of Italy annexed the Papal States, and the Pope, vainly protesting, became the "prisoner of the Vatican."

Yet in the face of these handicaps and adversaries the Roman Catholic Church displayed abounding vigour which issued in an amazing revival. On paper its numerical losses were slight. In the territories which historically had yielded it allegiance the overwhelming majority of the population were still baptized into its fold: even most anti-clericals were technically Catholics. Some advances were made in traditionally Protestant lands—Holland, Great Britain, several German states, and Scandinavia. That was more by migration and a high birth rate than by conversions, but there were some of the latter.

The loyal core of practising Catholics numbered tens of millions. The large majority were humble folk: the disaffection was chiefly among the *bourgeoisie,* the intellectuals, and, latterly, among the urban proletariat. But numbers of the old aristocracy returned to the faith which they or their fathers had scorned in the days of the Enlightenment, and among the intellectuals were not wanting many who were convinced and devout believers.

This loyal core was increasingly under the direction of the Papacy. As the century wore on, the quality of the Popes mounted. Not since the Middle Ages had the See of Peter had as great a statesman and diplomat as Leo XIII. All the nineteenth-century Pontiffs were men of high personal character who shunned as they would the plague a chronic besetting sin of even some of the best of their predecessors, nepotism. The last to fill the Chair of Peter before 1914, Pius X, was so obviously a saint that before a generation had passed he was officially recognized as such. The Popes were now formally acknowledged to be the infallible spokesmen of the Church in faith and morals and to possess supreme and absolute administrative authority.

The loyal Roman Catholics and the Papacy were reinforced by a striking growth in orders and congregations of those committed to the religious life. The Society of Jesus was reconstituted by the Pope. In many quarters it was still viewed with suspicion and it was excluded from some countries, but it grew in numbers and spread. Some of the older orders recovered from the lethargy of the eighteenth century and the expropriations of the revolutionary years and displayed new life. Numbers of congregations of men and women sprang into being. Indeed, more new ones were created than in any other century in Christian history. Most of them were activist—for missions to the de-Christianized in Europe and the non-Christians outside of Europe, for education, and for service to the sick, the poor, and the aged—but some were contemplative, primarily for prayer. Societies were organized to enlist for missions the support of the laity in finances and prayer. Fresh kinds of movements arose to grapple with the problems presented by industrialization and to unite Catholics in the defence of their faith.

The devotional life of the rank and file of practising Roman Catholics was markedly enhanced. Frequent communion was encouraged. Eucharistic Congresses attracted attention and aroused enthusiasm for the central rite of the Church. Devotion to the Sacred Heart of Jesus increased. The proclamation as dogma of the immaculate conception of Mary gave an impetus to the veneration of the Virgin. What were believed by the devout to be appearances of the Virgin added centres of pilgrimage. The Curé of Ars attracted thousands. Some women and men of the century were adjudged to be saints. The revival of the Gregorian music and the beginnings of the Liturgical Movement strengthened public worship. Many works of devotion were produced.

By what superficially seemed a striking paradox but what may have been an indication of the fashion in which Christianity evokes response, most of the newer congregations and societies and the revival in devotion were in the regions where the challenge of the revolution was the most pronounced, notably in France.

Intellectually the reaction of Roman Catholics to the revolution was ambiguous. On the one hand were keen minds who, wishing to be loyal to the truth, often at the price of severe inner struggle fought their way through to formulations of the faith which seemed to them at once to be consistent with whatever was valid in the thought and scholarship of the age and to be in accord with the Catholic heritage. Some, like Lamennais, endeavoured to maintain allegiance to the Pope with the adoption of much of liberal democracy. Others, prominent among them Hermes and Günther, employed the processes of rationalism to sustain Catholic dogma. Bautain was outstanding among those who, despairing of reason, looked for the answer in faith. Others adopted the ontologist approach. Tyrrell and Loisy were the most prominent of the "Modernists," men who applied to the Scriptures and the record of the Church the methods of historical study by which scholars were attempting to ascertain what had transpired in the past. All these approaches in their extreme forms were condemned by Rome as imperilling souls. But many acute and fearless minds remained within the bounds of orthodoxy as defined by Rome. Rome held up as the norm Thomas Aquinas, who in a similar age of intellectual transition had so taken account of the prevailing currents of thought that he had stated the Catholic faith in compelling form.

In its revival the Roman Catholic Church was holding true to its heritage, even when that meant rejection by those who were committed to the revolution. Its stress on the authority of the Pope was but a clarification of what the majority of the faithful believed had been implicit from the first century. Many of the new organizations followed, sometimes exactly, sometimes with modifications, the traditional patterns of the "religious." The forms of devotion were a reëmphasis upon what had long been the practice of the Church. The leaders of the Church were aware, sometimes painfully so, that they were running counter to the currents of the age. Yet they believed that these currents were sweeping Western civilization towards destruction and that the only salvation lay in a return to the Church in which, they maintained, that civilization had been cradled. They were prepared to suffer persecution for the truth, even though all Europe went against them.

Marked as was the revival in the Roman Catholic Church, no figures emerged from it which in stature were equal to the greatest of the earlier centuries. No Pope made his will felt in Europe as effectively as had Gregory the Great and Innocent III. No theologians appeared with intellectual and spiritual power comparable to that of Augustine, Anselm, or Thomas Aquinas. No mystics were of the high quality of Ruysbroeck, Teresa of Avila, John of the Cross, or Francis de Sales. No founder of a monastic order or congregation could rank with Benedict of Nursia, Bernard of Clairvaux, Francis of Assisi, or Ignatius Loyola.

Moreover, as we are to see more at length in the next volumes, striking as was the fresh surge of life in the Roman Catholic Church, that in Protestantism was much more so. Proportionately Protestantism had a more extensive geographic spread. From it issued far more novel movements for the amelioration of mankind. Among them were the Red Cross, the abolition of the African slave trade and Negro slavery, an achievement in which Roman Catholics had only a minor share,[1] the extensive social legislation pushed through the British

---

[1] On the Roman Catholic share see Gaston-Martin, *l'Abolition de l'Esclavage* (Paris, Presses Universitaires de France, 1948, pp. 64).

Parliament by the Evangelicals, and the temperance campaigns. Protestants dealt more daringly with theology and with Biblical questions propounded by historical scholarship. From within regions where Protestantism was the prevailing form of the faith emerged on the one hand more drastic and ruthless intellectual denials of Christianity and proposed negative or positive alternatives than in Catholic countries and on the other hand more fresh formulations of the Christian faith, more positive new interpretations of the Bible, and more movements of a novel kind for reaching the de-Christianized and for planting the faith outside traditionally Christian lands.

As we conclude our survey of the course of the Roman Catholic Church in nineteenth-century Europe we must be painfully aware that we may have missed or only hinted at what may be the most significant parts of the story. Only here and there have we caught glimpses of what the faith meant in the millions of inconspicuous lives which made up the rank and file of the Church. We have called attention to individuals and organizations which loomed large in the public eye and for which, accordingly, written records survive. Occasionally we have hinted at the homes in which they were nurtured and from which they came.

Yet perhaps this is not as serious an omission as might at first appear. Although the individuals and movements which attracted wide notice were in part the fruits of families, persons, and parishes otherwise obscure, they in turn helped to shape thousands and in many cases millions. It is not by the mere accident of fuller documentation that we have directed our chief attention to them.

Inevitably the question arises as to whether the parts of Europe where the Roman Catholic Church was the dominant form of Christianity were being de-Christianized. On first thought the answer would seem to be a very positive affirmative. In spite of the undoubted revival in the Church and the fact that the vast majority of the population in its traditional territories were baptized, the grim fact remains that the Church was being ushered out of education, the control of the family, and an acknowledged place in the state. That the symbols of the Christian faith were being removed from the law courts of France was symptomatic of what looked like secularization. The pronounced anti-clericalism was serious enough, for it bespoke antagonism. But it was evidence that the Church was still strong enough to awaken hostility. More serious was the apathy which betokened an indifference that dismissed the Church and its faith as irrelevant and looked upon baptism as a social convention to be observed but not to be taken too seriously. It was clear that Christianity as represented by the Roman Catholic Church was less prominent in the political, economic, intellectual, and, in general, cultural life of Europe than it had been in the thirteenth or even in the fore part of the eighteenth century.

Yet this sombre picture is an over-simplification. We must remember that at the height of "the age of faith" when the Roman Catholic Church was generally accepted throughout Western Europe and was profoundly influencing every aspect of life, much resistance was presented to its claims and in practice its standards were widely flouted. In the universities students, most of them preparing for one or another form of service in the Church, were openly immoral and parodied the most sacred mysteries. Even at the peak of religious fervour, many ecclesiastics, often in prominent posts, were self-seeking, secular-minded, drew the income from more than one benefice and were resident in none of them, and paid only formal deference to the rule of chastity. In training and morals the average of the clergy in the latter part of the nineteenth century was probably higher than even in the thirteenth century, that climax of vigour in the medieval Church. In the "age of faith," crusades, waged in the name of the cross, were marked by extreme cruelty; on the south and east shores of the Baltic conversion was accomplished by force and in large sections the agents, the Teutonic Knights, a monastic order ostensibly committed to the single-hearted following of Christ, exploited the peasantry whom they ruled; among a large proportion, perhaps the majority of the laity, theoretically Christian though they were, the violation of Christian ethical standards was so marked that a serious acceptance of the faith was called conversion. Although statistical data are unobtainable, it may well be that in 1914 a larger proportion of the population in Latin Europe were closer to an approximation to Christian standards as defined by the Roman Catholic Church than at the crest of medieval devotion.

As we have more than once suggested and as we will have occasion to remark again and again, in the record not only of the Roman Catholic Church but also of the other branches of Christianity we are here face to face with profound issues which permit of no simple or easy explanations. On the deepest and the highest levels they have to do with the interpretation of history and, to the Christian, the fashion in which God operates in history.

BIBLIOGRAPHY

T HE bibliography which follows is by no means exhaustive. In it are listed only those works which have been cited more than once in the footnotes. For those cited only once the necessary bibliographical data are given with the citation. They number fully as many as those which have been included in the appended list. Moreover, while the author has endeavoured to consult all the more important works, he is painfully aware that there are hundreds which would have proved useful to which he has not had access or which the inexorable pressure of time has denied opportunity to seek out and to read. He hopes that with all its defects the bibliography included below will be of use to those who seek a comprehensive selection as an introduction to further study.

Abbey, Charles J., *The English Church and Its Bishops 1700–1800* (London, Longmans, Green & Co., 2 vols., 1887). Largely biographies of bishops. Based upon fairly extensive research. Tends towards sympathy with the Church and praise for ＼ it and the bishops.

Abbey, Charles J., and Overton, John H., *The English Church in the Eighteenth Century* (London, Longmans, Green & Co., revised and abridged, 1906, pp. xvi, 495). By Anglicans, based on extensive research, well balanced and comprehensive.

Abetti, Giorgio, *The History of Astronomy*. Translated from the Italian by Betty Burr Abetti (New York, Henry Schuman, 1952, pp. 338). A competent survey.

Acomb, Evelyn M., *The French Laic Laws (1879–1889). The First Anti-Clerical Campaign of the Third French Republic* (New York, Columbia University Press, 1941, pp. 282). Well documented, carefully done.

Acton, John Emerich Edward Dalberg-Acton, *Essays on Freedom and Power*. Selected, with an introduction by Gertrude Himmelfarb (Boston, The Beacon Press, 1948, pp. xlvi, 452). By a famous historian, a liberal Roman Catholic.

Adeney, W. F., *The Greek and Eastern Churches* (New York, Charles Scribner's Sons, 1908, pp. xiv, 634). A useful summary.

Aigrain, René, *La Musique Religieuse* (Paris, Bloud & Gay, 1929, pp. 240). A standard Roman Catholic survey. There is an English translation by C. Mulcahy, with a further section on English and Irish religious music (London, Sands & Co., no date, pp. 292).

Alexander, A., editor, *Biographical Sketches of the Founder and Principal Alumni of the Log College, together with an Account of the Revivals of Religion under*

Their Ministry (Princeton, J. T. Robinson, 1845, pp. 369). Sympathetic, based upon careful research.

Allen, W. O. B., and McClure, Edmund, *Two Hundred Years: the History of The Society for Promoting Christian Knowledge 1698–1898* (London, Society for Promoting Christian Knowledge, 1898, pp. vi, 547). An official history, well documented and carefully done.

Allies, Mary H., *The Life of Pope Pius the Seventh* (London, Burns & Oates, 1875, pp. xvi, 374). A laudatory biography, based upon good sources.

Attwater, Donald, *The Christian Churches of the East. Volume I: Churches in Communion with Rome* (Milwaukee, The Bruce Publishing Co., revised ed., 1947, pp. xiv, 248). From a Roman Catholic viewpoint.

Aubert, R., *Le Pontificat de Pie IX (1846–1878)* (Paris, Bloud & Gay, 1952, pp. 510). Extremely well done by a highly competent Roman Catholic scholar.

Aulard, A., *Christianity and the French Revolution.* Translated by Lady Frazer (London, Ernest Benn, 1927, pp. 164). By an expert, based upon primary sources and secondary works.

Ballerini, Raffaele, *Le Prime Pagine del Pontificato di Papa Pio IX* (Rome, Civilta Cattolica, 1909, pp. 232). Posthumous, by a Jesuit.

Barbier, Emmanuel, *Histoire du Catholicisme Libéral et du Catholicisme Social en France du Concile du Vatican à l'avènement de S. S. Benoît XV (1870–1914)* (Bordeaux, Y. Cadoret, 6 vols., 1924). Well documented. A standard account. Objective. Sees the weaknesses of the movement.

Barclay, Wade Crawford, *History of Methodist Missions. Part One. Early American Methodism 1769–1844* (New York, The Board of Missions and Church Extension of the Methodist Church, 2 vols., 1949, 1950). An official history, based upon extensive research.

Beard, Augustus Field, *The Story of John Frederic Oberlin* (Boston, The Pilgrim Press, 1909, pp. xiii, 196). A semi-popular, admiring biography.

Bebb, E. D., *Nonconformity and Social and Economic Life 1660–1800. Some Problems of the Present as they appeared in the Past* (London, The Epworth Press, 1935, pp. 198). Based upon careful research.

Becher, Hubert, *Die Jesuiten. Gestalt und Geschichte des Ordens* (Munich, Kösel, 1951, pp. 438). Semi-popular, friendly.

Beck, George Andrew, editor, *The English Catholics 1850–1950. Essays to Commemorate the Centenary of the Restoration of the Hierarchy in England and Wales* (London, Burns, Oates, 1950, pp. xix, 640).

Béhaine, Édouard Lefebvre de, *Léon XIII et le Prince de Bismarck. Fragments d'Histoire Diplomatique avec Pièces Justificatives (Munich 1872–1879–Rome 1882–1887).* Long introduction by Georges Goyau (Paris, P. Lethielleux, 1898, pp. lxxxviii, 480). Especially valuable for its documents and for the first-hand knowledge of one who as a member of the French diplomatic service had unusual opportunity to watch the progress of events both before and after the accession of Leo XIII.

Bellamy, J., *La Théologie Catholique au XIXe Siècle* (Paris, Gabriel Beauchesne & Cie, 1904, pp. lvi, 290). A competent survey by a French priest.

Bergsträsser, Ludwig, *Der politische Katholizismus. Dokumente seiner Entwicklung II (1871 bis 1914)* (Munich, Drei Masken Verlag, 1923, pp. 396). A valuable selection of documents.

Berkeley, G. F. H. and J., *Italy in the Making January 1st 1848 to November 16th 1848* (Cambridge University Press, 1940, pp. xxvii, 489). A standard work.

Bolshakoff, Serge, *Russian Nonconformity* (Philadelphia, The Westminster Press, 1950, pp. 192). An historical, comprehensive survey, by a Russian Orthodox expert.

Boutard, Charles, *Lamennais, sa Vie et ses Doctrines* (Paris, Perrin et Cie, 3 vols., 1913). By a priest. The first volume with episcopal imprimatur. The first two volumes with the recognition of the French Academy.

Bready, J. Wesley, *England: Before and After Wesley. The Evangelical Revival and Social Reform* (London, Hodder & Stoughton, pp. 463). Colourful; based upon careful research.

Brilioth, Yngve, *Svensk Kyrkokunskap* (Stockholm, Svenska Kyrkans Diakonistyrelses Bokförlag, revised ed., 1946, pp. 479). By an Archbishop of Uppsala.

Brück, Heinrich, *Geschichte der katholischen Kirche in Deutschland im neunzehnten Jahrhundert* (Mainz, Franz Kirchheim, 4 vols., 1887–1901). By a Catholic, with official imprimatur. Well documented. Includes Austria. Brings the story down into the 1870's.

Brugerette, J., *Le Prêtre Français et la Société Contemporaine* (Paris, P. Lethielleux, 3 vols., 1933–1938). A standard work, well documented, sympathetic with the Roman Catholic Church.

Buonaiuti, Ernesto, *Il Modernismo Cattolico* (Modena, Guanda, 1943, pp. 337). By a distinguished Italian Modernist; written after his excommunication.

Burton, Katherine, *Difficult Star: The Life of Pauline Jaricot* (London, Longmans, Green & Co., 1947, pp. x, 239). Well written, in popular style.

Bury, J. B., *History of the Papacy in the 19th Century (1864–1878)* (London, Macmillan & Co., 1930, pp. lx, 175). By a distinguished historian, dealing with the Syllabus of Errors and the Vatican Council. Very critical of Pius IX.

Butler, Cuthbert, *The Vatican Council. The Story Told from Inside in Bishop Ullathorne's Letters* (New York, Longmans, Green & Co., 2 vols., 1930). Carefully done. It includes much more than Ullathorne's letters.

The Cambridge Modern History (Cambridge University Press, 13 vols., 1934).

Campbell, Thomas J., *The Jesuits 1534–1921. A History of the Society of Jesus from Its Foundation to the Present Time* (London, The Encyclopedia Press, 1921, pp. xvi, 937). By a Jesuit, strongly biased.

Catholic Emancipation 1829 to 1929. Essays by various writers with an introduction by Cardinal Bourne (London, Longmans, Green & Co., 1929, pp. ix, 281).

The Catholic Encyclopedia (New York, Robert Appleton Co. and The Encyclopedia Press, 16 vols., 1907–1914).

The Catholic Historical Review (Washington, The Catholic University of America Press, 1905 ff.). The official organ of the American Catholic Historical Association.

Cayré, F., *Patrologie et Histoire de la Théologie* (Paris, Desclée & Cⁱᵉ, 3 vols., 1944–1947). A standard work.

Cesare, R. de, *The Last Days of Papal Rome 1850–1870.* Abridged and translated by Helen Zimmern with an introductory chapter by G. M. Trevelyan (London, Archibald Constable & Co., 1909, pp. xxiii, 488). Carefully done, well-written, sympathetic with Italian nationalism, but in the main objective.

Church History. Organ of the American Society of Church History, 1932 ff.

Clark, G. Kitson, *The English Inheritance. An Historical Essay* (London, S. C. M. Press, 1950, pp. 184). By an Anglican, a Conservative. Attempts to appraise the place of Christianity in the formation of the life of England, especially in the 18th and 19th centuries. Fair, thoughtful, based on wide reading.

Clerici, Edoardo, *Pio IX, Vita e Pontificato* (Milan, Federazione Giovanile Diocesana Milanese, 1928, pp. 479). With ecclesiastical approval.

Collins, Ross William, *Catholicism and the Second French Republic, 1848–1852* (New York, Columbia University, 1923, pp. 360). Based on careful research.

Consalvi, *Mémoires du Cardinal Consalvi Secretaire d'État du Pape Pie VII.* Introduction and notes by J. Crétineau-Joly (Paris, Henri Plon, 2 vols., 1864).

Corrigan, Raymond, *The Church and the Nineteenth Century* (Milwaukee, The Bruce Publishing Co., 1938, pp. xviii, 326). By a Jesuit scholar. Semi-popular, for a Catholic constituency.

Cottineau, L. H., *Repertoire Topo-Bibliographique des Abbayes et Prieurés* (Macon, Protat Frères, 2 vols., 1939). A standard work by a Benedictine.

Cunningham, John, *The Church History of Scotland from the Commencement of the Christian Era to the Present Time* (Edinburgh, James Thin, 2nd ed., 2 vols., 1882). A useful survey, friendly to the Free Church of Scotland.

Dale, R. W., compiled and edited by A. W. W. Dale, *History of English Congregationalism* (London, Hodder & Stoughton, 2nd ed., 1907, pp. xii, 787). By a distinguished Congregational clergyman.

Dampier, William, *A History of Science and Its Relations with Philosophy and Religion* (Cambridge University Press, 1932, pp. xxi, 514). By a distinguished scientist.

Dansette, Adrien, *Histoire Religieuse de la France Sous la IIIème République* (Paris, Flammerion, revised ed., 2 vols., 1948, 1951). Lacking in footnotes, but with bibliographies for each chapter.

Debidour, A., *l'Église Catholique et l'État sous la Troisième République (1870–1906)* (Paris, Félix Alcan, 2 vols., 1906, 1909). Based on extensive research, believing in the separation of Church and state.

Debidour, A., *Histoire des Rapports de l'Église et de l'État en France de 1789 à 1870* (Paris, Félix Alcan, 2nd ed., 1911, pp. ii, 740). Carefully done, from the conviction that neither Church nor state ought to seek to impose its will on the other.

Devas, Raymond, *The Dominican Revival in the Nineteenth Century. Being Some*

Account of the Restoration of the Order of Preachers Throughout the World under Fr. Jandel, the Seventy-Third Master-General (London, Longmans, Green & Co., 1913, pp. xiii, 147). By a Dominican.

Dictionary of American Biography, edited by Allen Johnson and Dumas Malone (New York, Charles Scribner's Sons, 20 vols., 1928–1937). Supplementary Volume XXI, edited by Harold E. Starr, 1944.

Dictionary of National Biography, edited by Leslie Stephen and Sidney Lee (London, Smith, Elder & Co., 22 vols., 1908–1909). Five supplementary volumes covering 1901–1940.

Dictionnaire de Théologie Catholique (Paris, Librairie Letouzey et Ané, 15 vols., 1930–1950).

Dietz, Frederick C., *An Economic History of England* (New York, Henry Holt & Co., 1942, pp. xii, 616). A competent survey.

Doheny, William J., and Kelly, Joseph P., compilers, *Papal Documents on Mary* (Milwaukee, The Bruce Publishing Co., 1954, pp. x, 270). Encyclicals and letters of Pius IX, Leo XIII, Pius X, Benedict XV, Pius XI, and Pius XII.

Duroselle, Jean-Baptiste, *Les Débuts du Catholicisme Social en France (1822–1870)* (Paris, Presses Universitaires de France, 1951, pp. xii, 787). Objective, based on careful research.

Edwards, Alfred George, *Landmarks in the History of the Welsh Church* (London, John Murray, 1912, pp. vi, 317). By a Bishop of St. Asaph.

Edwards, Maldwyn, *After Wesley. A Study of the Social and Political Influence of Methodism in the Middle Period (1791–1849)* (London, The Epworth Press, 1935, pp. 190). An objective, critical appraisal.

Ehler, Sidney Z., and Morrall, John B., *Church and State Through the Centuries. A Collection of Historic Documents with Commentaries* (Westminster, Md., The Newman Press, 1954, pp. xiv, 625). Translations of documents from the beginning to the present, more than half on the nineteenth and twentieth centuries.

Elliott-Binns, L. E., *The Early Evangelicals: A Religious and Social Study* (London, Lutterworth Press, 1953, pp. 464). Competent.

Enciclopedia Cattolica (Vatican City, Enciclopedia Cattolica e per Libro Cattolico, 12 vols., 1948–1954). An official publication.

Fawkes, Alfred, *Studies in Modernism* (London, Smith, Elder & Co., 1913, pp. x, 468). Well informed, sympathetic with Modernism, critical of the Vatican and the Papacy.

Fedetov, G. P., compiler and editor, *A Treasury of Russian Spirituality* (New York, Sheed & Ward, 1948, pp. xvi, 501). By an expert. Largely a translation of writings of saints and mystics, with introductory biographical sketches.

Fischer, Engelbert Lorenz, *Cardinal Consalvi, Lebens und Charakterbild des Grossen Ministers Papst Pius VII* (Mainz, Franz Kirchheim, 1899, pp. xv, 350). Under ecclesiastical imprimatur.

Foerster, Erich, *Adalbert Falk. Sein Leben und Wirken als Preussischer Kultusminister dargestellt auf Grund des Nachlasses unter Beihelfe des Generals d. J. Adalbert von Falk* (Gotha, Leopold Klotz, 1927, pp. xvi, 712).

Fonzi, Fausto, *I Cattolici e la Società Italiana dopo l'Unità* (Rome, Editrice Studium, no date, pp. 121). A competent survey.

Forbes, F. A., *Life of Pius X* (London, R. & T. Washbourne, 1918, pp. ix, 177). Uncritical and admiring, but giving much of the essential data.

Fortescue, Adrian, *The Uniate Eastern Churches: the Byzantine Rite in Italy, Sicily, Syria and Egypt,* edited by George D. Smith (London, Burns, Oates & Washbourne, 1923, pp. xxi, 244). A competent study by an English Roman Catholic.

Frelinghuysen, Peter H. B., *Theodorus Jacobus Frelinghuysen* (Princeton, privately printed, 1938, pp. vii, 89). Based on careful research.

Frere, W. H., *Some Links in the Chain of Russian Church History* (London, Faith Press, 1918, pp. xvi, 200). By a distinguished Anglican scholar.

Fuchs, Albert, *Geistige Strömungen in Osterreich 1867–1918* (Vienna, Gobus-Verlag, 1949, pp. xxxv, 320).

Fülop-Miller, René, *Leo XIII and Our Times. Might of the Church-Power in the World.* Translated by Conrad M. R. Bonacina (New York, Longmans, Green & Co., 1937, pp. 202). Favourable to Leo XIII.

Gams, Pius Bonifacius, *Die Kirchengeschichte von Spanien* (Regensburg, Georg Joseph Manz, 3 vols., 1862–1879). By a Benedictine. The story is brought down to 1879.

Gazier, Augustin, *Histoire Générale du Mouvement Janséniste depuis ses Origines jusqu'à nos Jours* (Paris, Librairie Ancienne Honoré Champion, 2 vols., 1923, 1924). Friendly to the Jansenists.

Geffcken, Heinrich, *Church and State: Their Relations Historically Developed.* Translated and edited, with the assistance of the author, by Edward Fairfax Taylor (London, Longmans, Green & Co., 2 vols., 1877). A standard survey, about half on the nineteenth century. Critical of the Roman Catholic Church.

Geikie, Archibald, *The Founders of Geology* (London, Macmillan & Co., 2nd ed., 1905, pp. xi, 486). By a distinguished geologist.

Gewehr, Wesley M., *The Great Awakening in Virginia, 1740–1790* (Durham, N.C., Duke University Press, 1930, pp. viii, 292). A first-class piece of research.

Good, James I., *History of the Reformed Church of Germany 1620–1890* (Reading, Pa., Daniel Miller, 1894, pp. 646). Sympathetic, especially with Pietism.

Goyau, Georges, *l'Allemagne Religieuse: le Catholicisme 1800–1870* (Paris, Perrin et Cie, 4 vols., various editions 1905–1910. Preface, 1905). Well documented.

Granderath, Theodor, *Geschichte des Vatikanischen Konzils von seiner ersten Ankündigung bis zu seiner Vertagung* (Freiburg, Herdersche Verlagshandlung, 3 vols., 1903–1906). By a Jesuit, based upon the Vatican archives.

Gregorio XVI. Miscellanea Historicae Pontificiae edita a Facultate Historiae Ecclesiasticae, in Pontificia Universitate Gregoriana Vol. XIV. Collectionis n. 37–47 (Rome, Pontificia Universita Gregoriana, 2 vols., 1948). Various aspects of Gregory XVI and his pontificate by a number of authors, mostly in Italian, but also in English and German. Some of the articles are laudatory of Gregory.

Gurian, Waldemar, *Die politischen und sozialen Ideen des französischen Kath-*

olizismus 1789/1914 (Volksvereins-Verlag GmbH., M. Gladbach, 1928, pp. xv, 418). Well documented, objective.

Haag, Henri, *Les Origines du Catholicisme Libéral en Belgique (1789–1839)* (Louvain, Bibliothèque de l'Université, 1950, pp. 300). Based upon extensive research in the archives and in the literature. Excellent.

Haldane, Alexander, *Memoirs of the Lives of Robert Haldane of Airthrey, and of His Brother, James Alexander Haldane* (New York, Robert Carter & Brothers, 1853, pp. 604). Sympathetic, incorporating many letters and other documents.

Hales, E. E. Y., *Pio Nono. A Study in European Politics and Religion in the Nineteenth Century* (London, Eyre & Spottiswoode, 1954, pp. xiii, 352). An important, careful study, favourable to Pius IX.

Halperin, S. William, *Italy and the Vatican at War. A Study of Their Relations from the Outbreak of the Franco-Prussian War to the Death of Pius IX* (The University of Chicago Press, 1939, pp. xvii, 483). Based on careful research.

Hammond, J. L. and Barbara, *The Rise of Modern Industry* (London, Methuen & Co., 1925, pp. xi, 280). By outstanding experts.

Hammond, J. L. and Barbara, *The Village Labourer 1760–1832. A Study in the Government of England before the Reform Bill* (London, Longmans, Green & Co., 1912, pp. x, 418). By distinguished specialists.

Hanus, Francis, *Church and State in Silesia under Frederick II (1740–1786)* (Washington, The Catholic University of America Press, 1944, pp. x, 432). A doctoral dissertation.

Hayes, Carlton J. H., *Contemporary Europe Since 1870* (New York, The Macmillan Co., 1953, pp. xiii, 785).

Hayes, Carlton J. H., *Modern Europe to 1870* (New York, The Macmillan Co., 1953, pp. xii, 837). A useful summary by an outstanding expert.

Hayward, Fernand, *Léon XIII* (Paris, Bernard Grasset, 1937, pp. 333). A useful summary, but lacking documentation.

Hazard, Paul, *European Thought in the Eighteenth Century from Montesquieu to Lessing* (New Haven, Yale University Press, 1954, pp. xx, 477). An admirable survey and critique.

Heimbucher, Max, *Die Orden und Kongregationen der Katholischen Kirche* (revised ed., Paderborn, Ferdinand Schöningh, 3 vols., 1907). A third revised edition was issued in 2 volumes through the same publisher in 1933–1934. The references in the footnotes are to the second edition. The third edition is valuable chiefly for additions to its bibliography and for congregations organized after 1907. A standard work.

Hermelink, Heinrich, *Das Christentum in der Menschheitsgeschichte von der französischen Revolution bis zur Gegenwart* (Tübingen, J. B. Metzler und R. Wunderlich, 3 vols., 1951–1955). A good survey, centering on Germany and strongest on Protestantism.

Hermelink, Heinrich, *Geschichte der evangelischen Kirche in Württemberg von der Reformation bis zur Gegenwart* (Stuttgart und Tübingen, Hermann Leins, 1949, pp. xx, 528). By an expert, but lacking adequate footnotes and bibliographies.

Hermes, Georg, *Einleitung in die christkatholische Theologie* (Münster, in der Coppenratschen Buch- und Kunsthandlung, 2nd ed., 2 vols., 1831).

Hetherington, W. M., *History of the Church of Scotland from the Introduction of Christianity to the Period of the Disruption in 1843* (New York, Robert Carter & Brothers, 1870, pp. 500). In the form of annals.

Heussi, Karl, *Kompendium der Kirchengeschichte* (New York, American Commission of Aid of the World Council of Churches, 5th ed., Preface 1922, pp. xxxi, 481). A handbook especially useful for Germany.

Hocedez, Edgar, *Histoire de la Théologie au XIXe Siècle* (Paris, Desclée de Brouwer, 3 vols., 1947–1952). Standard.

Höffding, Harald, *Geschichte der neueren Philosophie. Eine Darstellung der Geschichte der Philosophie von dem Ende der Renaissance bis zu unseren Tagen.* Translated from the Danish by F. Bendixen (Leipzig, O. R. Reislund, 1895, 1896). A standard survey.

Holland, Bernard, *Baron Friedrich von Hügel. Selected Letters 1896–1924. Edited with a Memoir* (London, J. M. Dent & Sons, 1928, pp. 396).

Holmquist, Hjalmar, *Handbook i Svensk Kyrkohistoria* (Stockholm, Svenska Kyrkans Diakonistyrelses Bokförlag, 3 vols., 1952, 1953). By an outstanding authority.

Holzapfel, Heribert, *Handbuch der Geschichte des Franziskanerordens* (Freiburg im Breisgau, Herder, 1909, pp. xxi, 732). Carefully done, by a Franciscan.

Horton, Walter Marshall, *The Philosophy of the Abbé Bautain* (New York University Press, 1926, pp. xii, 327). Carefully done, objective, by a Protestant theologian.

Houtin, *Histoire du Modernisme Catholique* (Paris, by the author, 1913, pp. vii, 458). Seeks to be impartial. By a Modernist.

Hubben, William, *Four Prophets of Our Destiny. Kierkegaard, Dostoevsky, Nietzsche, Kafka* (New York, The Macmillan Co., 1952, pp. viii, 170). Thoughtful, penetrating.

Hughes, H. L., *The Catholic Revival in Italy, 1815–1915* (London, Burns, Oates & Washbourne, 1935, pp. xii, 177). Semi-popular, by a Roman Catholic.

Hughes, Philip, *The Popes' New Order. A Systematic Summary of the Social Encyclicals and Addresses from Leo XIII to Pius XII* (London, Burns, Oates & Washbourne, 1943, pp. viii, 232). A useful summary and commentary from a Roman Catholic viewpoint.

Jarry, E., *l'Église Contemporaine* (Paris, Bloud & Gay, 2 vols., 1935). A useful survey by a French Catholic.

Jemolo, Arturo Carlo, *Chiesa e Stato in Italia negli ultimi cento anni* (Turin, Giulio Einaudi, 3rd ed., 1952, pp. 752). By a Roman Catholic layman. Scholarly, well documented.

Jervis, W. Henley, *The Gallican Church and the Revolution* (London, Kegan Paul, Trench & Co., 1882, pp. xxiii, 524). By an Anglican clergyman.

The Journal of Ecclesiastical History (London, Faber & Faber, 1950 ff.). Scholarly.

Jüngst-Stettin, J., *Pietisten* (Tübingen, J. C. B. Mohr, 1906, pp. 80). A semi-popular sketch of leading Pietists.

Jungmann, Josef Andreas, *Missarum Sollemnia. Eine genetische Erklärung der römischen Messe* (Vienna, Herder, 3rd ed., 2 vols., 1952). A standard work.

Keller, Charles Roy, *The Second Great Awakening in Connecticut* (New Haven, Yale University Press, 1942, pp. ix, 275). Well done. Based on careful research.

Knowles, L. C. A., *The Industrial and Commercial Revolutions in Great Britain during the Nineteenth Century* (London, George Routledge & Sons, 1921, pp. xii, 412). An excellent survey, with important sections on the eighteenth century.

Koch, G. Adolf, *Republican Religion: The American Revolution and the Cult of Reason* (New York, Henry Holt & Co., 1933, pp. xvi, 334). Based upon extensive research.

Koch, Hal, *Danmarks Kirke gennem Tiderne* (Copenhagen, Gyldendal, 1949, pp. 250). A semi-popular survey by a brilliant expert.

Koch, Hal, and Kornerup, Bjorn, editors, *Den Danske Kirkes Historie,* Vol. V, 1699–1799 (Copenhagen, Gyldendalske Boghandel Nordisk Forlag, 1951, pp. 505). Vol. VI, 1800–1848 by Hal Koch (Copenhagen, Gyldendalske Boghandel Nordisk Forlag, 1954, pp. 365). A standard work.

Koenker, Ernest Benjamin, *The Liturgical Renaissance in the Roman Catholic Church* (University of Chicago Press, 1954, pp. xi, 272). Carefully done, sympathetic; by a Protestant.

La Gorge, Pierre de, *Histoire Religieuse de la Révolution Française* (Paris, Librairie Plon, 5 vols., 1912–1923). Based in part on primary sources.

Laidler, Harry W., *Social-Economic Movements. An Historical and Comparative Survey of Socialism, Communism, Co-operation, Utopianism, and Other Systems of Reform and Reconstruction* (New York, Thomas Y. Crowell Co., 1944, pp. xx, 828). A competent, objective survey.

Oeuvres Complètes de F. de La Mennais (Paris, various publishers, 18 vols., 1836–1856).

Lampert, U., *Kirche und Staat in der Schweiz* (Freiburg and Leipzig, Universitäts-buchhandlung, 3 vols., 1939). Volume III is made up of nineteenth-century documents.

La Piana, George, *Recent Tendencies in Roman Catholic Theology (The Harvard Theological Review,* Vol. XV [1922], pp. 233–292). By a former Roman Catholic priest, a theologian and historian.

Latourette, Kenneth Scott, *A History of the Expansion of Christianity* (New York, Harper & Brothers, 7 vols., 1937–1945).

Latreille, André, *l'Église Catholique et la Révolution Française* (Paris, Librairie Hachette, 2 vols., 1946, 1950). A summary account based on monographs and sources.

Lea, Henry Charles, *Chapters from the Religious History of Spain Connected with the Inquisition* (Philadelphia, Lea Brothers & Co., 1890, pp. 522). By the scholarly and hostile expert on the Inquisition.

Lecanuet, *l'Église de France sous la Troisième République.* Four volumes under the titles:

1. *Les Dernières Années du Pontificat de Pie IX (1870–1878).*

2. *Les Premières Années du Pontificat de Léon XIII (1878–1894).*

3. *Les Signes avant-coureurs de la Séparation: Les Dernières Années de Léon XIII et l'Avènement de Pie X (1894–1910).*

4. *La Vie de l'Église sous Léon XIII.*

(Paris, Félix Alcan, 1930, 1931). Carefully documented, sympathetic with the Church.

Ledré, Charles, *l'Église de France sous la Révolution* (Paris, Robert Laffont, 1949, pp. 321). A competent survey.

Ledré, Charles, *Pie X* (Paris, Spes, 1952, pp. 293). Admiring, for popular consumption, only slightly documented.

Leflon, Jean, *La Crise Révolutionnaire 1789–1846*. Vol. 20 in *Histoire de l'Église,* edited by Augustin Fliche and Victor Martin (Paris, Bloud & Gay, 1949, pp. 524). Based upon extensive use of monographs. Deals chiefly with France.

Leflon, Jean, *l'Église de France et la Révolution de 1848* (Paris, Bloud & Gay, 1948, pp. 134). A competent sketch, by a Roman Catholic scholar.

Leo XIII, Pope; Husslein, Joseph, editor, *Social Wellsprings. Fourteen Epochal Documents* (Milwaukee, Bruce Publishing Co., 1940, pp. xiii, 284). Translations of encyclicals.

Leroy-Beaulieu, Anatole, *Le Catholiques Libéraux: l'Église et la Libéralisme de 1830 à nos Jours* (Paris, E. Plon, Nourrit et Cie, 1885, pp. xx, 298).

Lexikon für Theologie und Kirche (Herder & Co., 2nd ed., 10 vols., 1930–1938). An official Roman Catholic publication.

Lilley, A. Leslie, *Modernism, a Record and Review* (London, Sir Isaac Pitman & Sons, 1908, pp. xv, 277). By an Anglican. Made up in part of his articles in various journals; sympathetic with the Modernist movement.

Loane, Marcus L., *Cambridge and the Evangelical Succession* (London, Lutterworth Press, 1952, pp. 276). Sympathetic; based upon extensive reading in the pertinent material.

Loisy, Alfred, *Mémoires pour Servir à l'Histoire Religieuse de Notre Temps* (Paris, Émile Nourry, 3 vols., 1930, 1931). Fuller than *Choses Passées.*

Loisy, Alfred, *My Duel with the Vatican. The Autobiography of a Catholic Modernist.* Authorized translation (of *Choses Passés*) by Richard Wilson Boynton (New York, E. P. Dutton & Co., 1924, pp. xiii, 356).

MacCaffrey, James, *History of the Catholic Church in the Nineteenth Century (1789–1908)* (Dublin, M. H. Gill & Son, 2 vols., 1909). By a Roman Catholic historian.

Macinnes, John, *The Evangelical Movement in the Highlands of Scotland 1688–1800* (Aberdeen, The University Press, 1951, pp. xii, 299). Based upon careful research in the sources.

Mackay, John, *The Church in the Highlands, or the Progress of Evangelical Religion in Gaelic Scotland, 563–1843* (London, Hodder & Stoughton, 1914, pp. 280). A useful survey.

McNeill, John T., *Modern Christian Movements* (Philadelphia, The Westminster Press, 1954, pp. 197). Brief summaries, by a mature expert, of English Puritanism,

German Pietism, the Evangelical Movement, Tractarianism and Anglo-Catholicism, the Ecumenical Movement, and Modern Roman Catholicism.

McSorley, Joseph, *An Outline History of the Church by Centuries (From St. Peter to Pius XII)* (St. Louis, B. Herder Book Co., 1944, pp. xxviii, 1084). A useful, comprehensive compendium of the history of the Roman Catholic Church, by a Paulist.

Mallott, Floyd E., *Studies in Brethren History* (Elgin, Ill., Brethren Publishing House, 1954, pp. 382). Carefully done.

Manning, Bernard L., *The Hymns of Wesley and Watts. Five Informal Papers* (London, The Epworth Press, 1942, pp. 143). Lectures by an expert.

Mathew, David, *Catholicism in England 1535–1935. Portrait of a Minority: Its Culture and Tradition* (London, Longmans, Green & Co., 1936, pp. xii, 304). A sympathetic, scholarly account by a Roman Catholic.

Mathieson, William Law, *Church and Reform in Scotland. A History from 1797 to 1843* (Glasgow, James MacLehose & Sons, 1916, pp. xii, 378). Rather supercilious towards the Evangelicals.

Maurain, Jean, *La Politique Ecclésiastique du Second Empire de 1852 à 1869* (Paris, Félix Alcan, 1930, pp. li, 989). A well-documented doctoral thesis of the University of Paris.

Maurras, Charles, *Le Bienheureux Pie X, Sauveur de la France* (Paris, Librairie Plon, 1953, pp. xxvii, 222). An admiring sketch.

Merry del Val, Cardinal, *Memories of Pope Pius X* (London, Burns, Oates & Washbourne, 1939, pp. xiii, 81). By one who worked intimately with him and who writes admiringly.

Meulemeester, Maurede, *Bibliographie Générale des Écrivains Rédemptoristes* (Louvain, Imprimerie S. Alphonse, 3 vols., 1933–1939).

Autobiography of John Stuart Mill (New York, Columbia University Press, 1924, pp. vii, 221). Published for the first time without alterations or omissions from the original manuscript.

Miller, Perry, *Jonathan Edwards* (New York, William Sloane Associates, 1949, pp. xv, 348). By an eminent specialist, not always sympathetic.

Moody, Joseph N., editor, *Church and Society. Catholic Social and Political Thought and Movements, 1789–1950* (New York, Arts Inc., 1953, pp. 914). By several authors.

Moon, Parker Thomas, *The Labor Problem and the Social Catholic Movement in France. A Study in the History of Social Politics* (New York, The Macmillan Co., 1921, pp. xiv, 472). Very well done, by a Catholic convert.

Moorman, John R. H., *A History of the Church in England* (London, Adam & Charles Black, 1953, pp. xx, 460). An admirable survey, confined in post-Reformation times to the Church of England.

Morais, Herbert M., *Deism in Eighteenth Century America* (New York, Columbia University Press, 1934, pp. 203). A competent doctoral dissertation.

Moss, C. B., *The Old Catholic Movement, Its Origins and History* (London, S.P.C.K., 1948, pp. viii, 360). Carefully done, by an Anglican.

Mourret, Fernand, *Le Mouvement Catholique en France de 1830 à 1850* (Paris, Bloud & Gay, 1917, pp. 272). By a professor in the seminary of Saint-Sulpice.

[Mullinger, James Bass], *The New Reformation. A Narrative of the Old Catholic Movement from 1870 to the Present Time with a Historical Introduction by Theodorus* (London, Longmans, Green & Co., 1875, pp. xiv, 293). Highly critical of the Vatican Council and warmly sympathetic with the Old Catholics. Contains much valuable first-hand information.

Nemec, Ludvik, *Church and State in Czechoslovakia, Historically, Juridically, and Theologically Documented* (New York, Vantage Press, 1955, pp. xi, 577). From a strongly Roman Catholic standpoint, chiefly on the post-World War II period.

Newman, John Henry, *Apologia Pro Vita Sua. Being a Reply to a Pamphlet Entitled "What, Then, Does Dr. Newman Mean?"* (London, Longmans, Green & Co., 1887, pp. xxviii, 395) (written 1864).

Newman, John Henry, *History of My Religious Opinions* (London, Longmans, Green, Reader, & Dyer, 1869, pp. xxiv, 388). Written after his conversion to the Roman Catholic Church.

Nichols, James Hastings, *Democracy and the Churches* (Philadelphia, The Westminster Press, 1951, pp. 298). A careful study by a Protestant church historian.

Nichols, James Hastings, *History of Christianity 1650–1950: Secularization of the West* (New York, The Ronald Press, 1956, pp. vi, 493). A competent survey with an excellent bibliography.

Nielsen, Fredrik, *The History of the Papacy in the Nineteenth Century*. Translated under the direction of A. J. Mason, from the second edition (London, John Murray, 2 vols., 1906). By a Protestant.

Nippold, Friedrich, *Einleitung in die Kirchengeschichte des neunzehnten Jahrhunderts* (Berlin, Wiegandt & Schotte, 5 vols., 1889–1906). Standard, by a liberal Protestant. The chief attention is to Germany, but much more is covered. Very critical of the Papacy.

Nippold, Friedrich, *The Papacy in the 19th Century*. Translated by Laurance Henry Schwab (New York, G. P. Putnam's Sons, 1900, pp. iv, 372). A part of Nippold's *Manual of the Latest Church History,* partly condensed. The book is highly critical of the Papacy and its anti-liberal actions.

Nippold, Friedrich, *Die Römisch-katholische Kirche in Königreich der Niederlande. Ihre Geschichtliche Entwickelung seit der Reformation und ihr gegenwärtiger Zustand* (Utrecht, Kemink & Zoon, 1877, pp. xxxi, 536). A competent survey, from a decidedly Protestant angle.

Nitti, Francesco S., *Catholic Socialism*. Translated from the second Italian edition by Mary Mackintosh (London, Swan Sonnenschein & Co., 1895, pp. xx, 432). Embodying careful research.

Olf, Lillian Browne, *Their Name is Pius. Portraits of Five Great Modern Popes* (Milwaukee, The Bruce Publishing Co., 1941, pp. xv, 382). Popular, laudatory accounts of Pius VI, VII, IX, X, XI.

O'Reilly, Bernard, *A Life of Pius IX down to the Episcopal Jubilee of 1877* (New York, P. F. Collier, 6th ed., 1877, pp. xvi, 506). Laudatory.

Orr, James, *English Deism, Its Roots and Its Fruits* (Grand Rapids, Wm. B. Eerdmans Publishing Co., 1934, pp. 289). An excellent survey.

Papadopoullos, Theodore H., *Studies and Documents Relating to the History of the Greek Church and People under Turkish Domination* (Brussels, 1952, pp. xxiv, 507). A useful study with important documents.

Pastor, Ludwig Freiherr von, *The History of the Popes from the Close of the Middle Ages.* Translated from the German. Vols. XXXIII–XL cover the 18th century (London, Kegan Paul, Trench, Trubner & Co., and Routledge & Kegan Paul, 1941–1953). The standard official history.

Peers, E. Allison, *The Church in Spain 1737–1937* (London, Burns, Oates & Washbourne, 1938, pp. 41). By an expert on the Spanish mystics.

Peers, E. Allison, *Spain, the Church and the Orders* (London, Eyre & Spottiswoode, 1939, pp. xi, 219). A semi-popular survey, sympathetic, largely since 1700, by an expert on the Spanish mystics.

Perrotta, Antonio, *The Modernist Movement in Italy and Its Relation to the Spread of Protestant Christianity* (Boston, The Gorham Press, 1929, pp. 116). Warmly sympathetic.

Petre, M. D., *Alfred Loisy: His Religious Significance* (Cambridge University Press, 1944, pp. xi, 129). An interpretation by a friend.

Petre, M. D., *Modernism: Its Failure and Its Fruits* (London, T. C. & E. C. Jack, 1918, pp. xvi, 249). Sympathetically objective, by a specialist in the subject.

Phillips, C. S., *The Church in France 1789–1848: A Study in Revival* (London, A. R. Mowbray & Co., 1929, pp. viii, 315). Friendly to the Church, without footnotes, but an excellent survey.

Phillips, C. S., *The Church in France, 1848–1907* (London, Society for Promoting Christian Knowledge, 1936, pp. 341). Competently and carefully done.

Phillips, Walter Alison, editor, *History of the Church of Ireland from the Earliest Times to the Present Day. Volume III. The Modern Church* (Oxford University Press, 1933, pp. 499). Standard.

Pietra, Angela, *Storia del Movimento Cattolico Liberale* (Milan, Dottor, Franceso Villardi, 1948, pp. xi, 220). An account of the Italian liberal Catholic movement.

Pinchbeck, Ivy, *Women Workers and the Industrial Revolution 1750–1850* (London, George Routledge & Sons, 1930, pp. x, 342). Well documented.

Pirri, Pietro, *Pio IX e Vittorio Emanuele II dal loro carteggio privato. La Laicizzazione dello stato Sardo 1848–1856* (Rome, Pontificia Universitá Gregoriana, 1944, pp. 253) in *Miscellanea Historiae Pontificiae,* Vol. VIII, *Collectionis* n. 17. Largely documents.

Pirri, Pietro, *Pio IX e Vittorio Emanuele II dal loro carteggio privato, La Questione Romana* (Rome, Pontificia Universitá Gregoriana, 2 vols., 1951) in *Miscellanea Historiae Pontificiae,* Vol. XVII, *Collectionis* n. 49. The first volume is text, the second is documents.

Pistolesi Erasmo, *Vita del Sommo Pontefice Pio VII* (Rome, Francesco Bourlie, 4 vols., 1824). An admiring biography produced soon after the death of Pius VII.

Chiefly valuable for texts of some important documents either in the original or in translation.

Pleijel, Hilding, *Karolinsk Kyrofromhet Pietism och Herrnhutism 1680–1772*. Vol. V in *Svenska Kyrkans Historia*, edited by Hjalmar Holmquist and Hilding Pleijel (Stockholm, Svenska Kyrkans Diakonistyrelses Bokförlag, 1935, pp. 637). By an outstanding authority.

Poulet, Charles, *A History of the Catholic Church. For the Use of Colleges, Seminaries, and Universities.* Translated and adapted from the fourth French edition by S. A. Raemers (St. Louis, B. Herder Book Co., 2 vols., 1848). A Roman Catholic handbook.

Pourrat, P., *la Spiritualité Chrétienne* (Paris, Librairie Lecoffre, Vol. IV, Part 2, 1947, pp. xii, 680). A standard survey of Roman Catholic prayer and devotion, with special attention to France.

Pouthas, Charles, *l'Église Catholique de l'Avènement de Pie VII à l'Avènement de Pie IX* (Paris, Centre de Documentation Universitaire, Tournier & Constans, no date, mimeographed, pp. 315, iii). An excellent, judicious summary.

Premoli, Orazio M., *Contemporary Church History (1900–1925)* (London, Burns, Oates & Washbourne, 1932, pp. xvi, 407). By a Barnabite, strongly pro-Catholic; useful for its many details and comprehensive coverage.

The Presbyterian Historical Society, *Journal of the Department of History (The Presbyterian Historical Society)* (Philadelphia, Department and Society, 1919 ff.). The *Journal* has various titles, among them *Journal of the Presbyterian Historical Society.*

Purcell, Edmund Sheridan, *Life of Cardinal Manning Archbishop of Westminster* (New York, The Macmillan Co., 2 vols., 1896). Based upon the sources, friendly, but objective and at times critical.

Ranke, Leopold von, *Die Römische Päpste in den letzen vier Jahrhunderten* (Stuttgart, K. F. Koehler, 1953, pp. xxxix, 584, 876). A standard work. Closes with the end of the reign of Pius VII.

Reynolds, James A., *The Catholic Emancipation Crisis in Ireland, 1823–1829* (New Haven, Yale University Press, 1954, pp. viii, 204). Very well done.

Ritschl, Albrecht, *Geschichte des Pietismus* (Bonn, Adolph Warens, 3 vols., 1880–1886). The first volume is on Pietism in the Reformed Churches, the second and third volumes on Pietism in the Lutheran Churches in the seventeenth and eighteenth centuries. Based on extensive research.

Rivière, Jean, *Le Modernisme dans l'Église, Étude d'Histoire Religieuse Contemporaine* (Paris, Letouzey et Ané, 1929, pp. xxix, 589). Carefully documented, with ecclesiastical imprimatur.

Robertson, J M., *A History of Freethought in the Nineteenth Century* (New York, G. P. Putnam's Sons, 2 vols., 1930). Sympathetic, based on extensive research.

Rollet, Henri, *l'Action Sociale des Catholiques en France (1871–1901)* (Paris, Boivin & Cie, no date, pp. 725). Objective, based on careful research.

Ross, James, *A History of Congregational Independency in Scotland* (Glasgow,

James MacLehose & Sons, 1900, pp. xv, 282). By a minister of a Scottish Congregational church.

Rouse, Ruth, and Neill, Stephen Charles, editors, *A History of the Ecumenical Movement 1517-1948* (London, Society for Promoting Christian Knowledge, 1954, pp. xxiv, 822). The standard account, in which several authors joined.

Ruhenstroth-Bauer, Renato, *Bismarck und Folk im Kulturkampf* (Heidelberg, Carl Winter, 1944, pp. viii, 104). Based on careful research.

Sabatier, Paul, *Modernism. The Jowett Lectures, 1908.* Translated by C. A. Miles (New York, Charles Scribner's Sons, 1909, pp. 351). By a Protestant, warmly sympathetic with Modernism.

Schaff, Philip, *Bibliotheca Symbolica Ecclesiæ Universalis. The Creeds of Christendom with a History and Critical Notes. Vol. II. The Greek and Latin Creeds, with Translations* (New York, Harper & Brothers, revised ed., Preface 1889, pp. vii, 607). A standard work.

The New Schaff-Herzog Encyclopedia of Religious Knowledge, edited by Samuel Macauley Jackson (New York, Funk and Wagnalls Co., 13 vols., 1908-1914). Especially valuable for its competent summary articles appended by excellent bibliographies.

Schmid, Heinrich, *Geschichte des Pietismus* (Nördlingen, C. H. Beck-schen Buchhandlung, 1863, pp. vi, 507). Good on the early history, but not as comprehensive as the one by Ritschl.

Schmidlin, Josef, *Papstgeschichte der neuesten Zeit* (Munich, Josef Kösel & Friedrich Pustet, 3 vols., 3rd ed., 1933-1936). A standard work by an eminent Roman Catholic scholar. The years covered are 1800-1922.

Schnabel, Franz, *Deutsche Geschichte im neunzehnten Jahrhundert,* Vol. 4. *Die religiösen Kräfte* (Freiburg, Herder, 2nd ed., 1951, pp. xii, 617). Thoroughly competent, by a Roman Catholic.

Schuster, Hermann, *Das Werden der Kirche. Eine Geschichte der Kirche auf deutschen Boden. Mit Beiträgen von Hans Frh. von Campenhausen und Hermann Dörries* (Berlin, Alfred Töpelmann, 2nd ed., 1950, pp. xix, 569). An excellent summary with suggestive interpretations and comments.

Shafer, Robert, *Christianity and Naturalism* (New Haven, Yale University Press, 1926, pp. viii, 307).

Siegmund-Schultze, editor, *Ekklesia.*

   I. *Die Britischen Länder.*
     1. *Die Kirche von England,* 1934, pp. 123.
   II. *Die Skandinavischen Länder.*
     Die Kirche in Schweden, 1935, pp. 179.
     Die Kirche von Norwegen, 1936, pp. 207.
     Die Kirche in Dänemark, pp. 195   ⎫
     Die Kirche in Island, pp. 35   ⎬ 1937.
                                       ⎭
     Die Kirche in Finnland, 1938, pp. 203.
   III. *Die Mitteleuropäischen Länder.*
     Die Altkatholische Kirche, 1935, pp. 15.

Die Evangelischen Kirchen der Niederlande, 1934, pp. 175.

Die Evangelischen Kirchen der Schweitz, 1935, pp. 253.

IV. *Deutschsprachige Länder.*

Die Evangelische Kirche in Österreich, 1935, pp. 168. (Gotha and Leipzig, Leopold Klotzverlag). By various authors; uneven in quality.

Simon, A., *l'Église Catholique et les Débuts de la Belgique Indépendante* (Wetteren, Scaldis, 1949, pp. 147). Carefully done.

Simpson, W. J. Sparrow, *Roman Catholic Opposition to Papal Infallibility* (London, John Murray, 1909, pp. xv, 374). By an Anglican, critical of ultramontanism, using Roman Catholic source material.

Soderini, Eduardo, *Il Pontificato di Leone XIII* (Milan, A. Montadori, 3 vols., no date. An official biography, based upon extensive use of archives.

Soderini, Eduardo, *Leo XIII Italy and France.* Translated by Barbara Barclay Carter (London, Burns, Oates & Washbourne, 1935). Strongly sympathetic with Leo XIII, but utilizing first-hand documents.

Spencer, Philip, *Politics of Belief in Nineteenth-Century France: Lacordaire, Michon, Veuillot* (London, Faber & Faber, 1954, pp. 284). Well written, based on extensive research, objective.

Stephen, Leslie, *History of English Thought in the Eighteenth Century* (New York, G. P. Putnam's Sons, 2 vols., 1876). A standard older survey.

Stock, Eugene, *The History of the Church Missionary Society* (London, The Church Missionary Society, 4 vols., 1899–1916). An official history, by a secretary of the Society. Very well done.

Stokes, Anson Phelps, *Church and State in the United States* (New York, Harper & Brothers, 3 vols., 1950). The standard work.

Stromberg, Roland N., *Religious Liberalism in Eighteenth-Century England* (Oxford University Press, 1954, pp. xi, 192). Chiefly on Deism.

Stumpf, Samuel Enoch, *A Democratic Manifesto. The Impact of Dynamic Christianity upon Public Life and Government* (Nashville, Vanderbilt University Press, 1954, pp. viii, 168). By a philosophic expert on jurisprudence.

Sweet, William Warren, *Religion in Colonial America* (New York, Charles Scribner's Sons, 1942, pp. xiii, 367). A useful summary with an excellent bibliography.

Sweet, William Warren, *Religion in the Development of American Culture 1765–1840* (New York, Charles Scribner's Sons, 1952, pp. xiv, 338). By an outstanding authority.

Sykes, Norman, *Church and State in England in the XVIIIth Century* (Cambridge University Press, 1934, pp. xi, 455). Based on careful research. Seeks to correct prevalent views of the degeneracy and decay of the Church of England in the eighteenth century.

Theiner, Augustin, *Documents Inédits relatifs aux Affaires Religieuses de la France 1790 à 1800. Extraits des Archives Secrètes du Vatican* (Paris, Firmin Didot Frères, Fils et Cie, 2 vols., 1857).

Thornton, Mary Crescentia, *The Church and Freemasonry in Brazil, 1872–1875. A*

Study in Regalism (Washington, The Catholic University of America Press, 1948, pp. viii, 287). Based on careful research.

Torbet, Robert G., *A History of the Baptists* (Philadelphia, The Judson Press, 1950, pp. 538). A competent survey.

Townsend, W. J., Workman, H. B., and Eayrs, George, editors, *A New History of Methodism* (London, Hodder & Stoughton, 2 vols., 1919). A standard work, by several writers, embodying fresh research.

Trollope, T. Adolphus, *The Story of the Life of Pius the Ninth* (London, Richard Bentley & Son, 2 vols., 1877). Seeks to be fair, but is critical.

Usher, Abbott Payson, *An Introduction to the Industrial History of England* (Boston, Houghton Mifflin Co., 1920, pp. xxi, 529, xxxiv). A competent handbook.

Vercesi, Ernesto, *Pio IX* (Milano, Corbaccio, 1930, pp. 260). Written in a lively style.

Vidler, Alec, *Prophecy and Papacy: A Study of Lamennais, the Church, and the Revolution* (New York, Charles Scribner's Sons, 1954, pp. 300). Carefully done.

Vigener, Fritz, *Ketteler, Ein deutsches Bischofsleben des 19. Jahrhunderts* (Munich and Berlin, R. Oldenbourg, 1924, pp. xv, 750). A standard biography, with much on general developments in the Roman Catholic Church in Germany.

Wallace, Lillian Parker, *The Papacy and European Diplomacy 1869–1878* (Chapel Hill, The University of North Carolina Press, 1948, pp. ix, 349). By a Protestant, objective. Based chiefly on primary sources.

Walters, Thomas B., *Robert Raikes, Founder of Sunday Schools* (London, The Epworth Press, 1930, pp. 128). Semi-popular, based upon extensive reading in the pertinent secondary materials.

Ward, Wilfrid, *The Life of John Henry Cardinal Newman, Based on His Private Journals and Correspondence* (London, Longmans, Green & Co., 2 vols., 1912). Sympathetic, standard.

Ward, Wilfrid, *William George Ward and the Catholic Revival* (London, Macmillan & Co., 1893, pp. xlvi, 468). An important study, carefully documented, not only of an outstanding convert to the Roman Catholic Church but also of Roman Catholic theological trends in the mid-nineteenth century, especially in England.

Weigle, Luther A., *American Idealism* (New Haven, Yale University Press, 1928, pp. 356). A competent summary of the history of religion in the United States.

Weill, Georges, *Histoire du Catholicisme Libéral en France 1828–1908* (Paris, Félix Alcan, 1909, pp. 312). By a professor in the University of Caen.

Welle, Ivar, *Norges Kirkehistorie: Kirkens Historie III* (Oslo, Lutherstiftelsens Forlag, 1948, pp. 393). A semi-popular, competent survey.

Wesley, John, *The Journal of the Rev. John Wesley,* edited by Nehemiah Curnock (London, The Epworth Press, 8 vols., 1938).

White, L. W., *Industrial and Social Revolution 1750–1937* (London, Longmans, Green & Co., 1938, pp. vii, 308). An excellent survey.

Whitley, W. T., *A History of British Baptists* (London, The Kingsgate Press, 2nd ed., 1932, pp. xii, 384).

Wilberforce, Robert Isaac and Samuel, *The Life of William Wilberforce* (London,

John Murray, 5 vols., 1838). By two sons. Valuable for extensive extracts from their father's journals and letters.

Windell, George G., *The Catholics and German Unity 1866–1871* (Minneapolis, University of Minnesota Press, 1954, pp. xi, 312). Carefully done and objective.

Wiseman, Cardinal, *Recollections of the Last Four Popes and of Rome in Their Times* (London, Hurst & Blackett, no date, pp. xiii, 336. "New and revised edition"). Covers Pius VII, Leo XII, Pius VIII, Gregory XVI.

Wright, William Kelley, *A History of Modern Philosophy* (New York, The Macmillan Co., 1941, pp. xvi, 633). A competent survey.

Zenkovsky, V. V., *A History of Russian Philosophy*. Translated from the Russian by George L. Kline (London, Routledge & Kegan Paul, 2 vols., 1953). A standard survey.

Zittel, Karl Alfred von, *Geschichte der Geologie und Paläontologie bis Ende des 19. Jahrhunderts* (Munich, R. Oldenbourg, 1899, pp. xi, 868). Scholarly, exhaustive.

INDEX